W9-BNA-458

SPARTAN FOOTBALL

100 SEASONS OF GRIDIRON GLORY

KEN HOFFMAN
with
LARRY BIELAT

SAGAMORE PUBLISHING
CHAMPAIGN, IL 61820

Interior design: Michelle R. Dressen
Production Manager: Susan M. McKinney
Dustjacket design: Jack W. Davis, Michelle R. Dressen
Proofreader: Phyllis L. Bannon

Library of Congress Catalog Card Number: 96-70014
ISBN: 1-57167-040-8

Printed in the United States.

To my family: wife Brenda, daughters Natalie and Lauren, and son Lucas.

For all their love and support during the production of this book; for all the nights and weekends when I wasn't there to kiss them "goodnight." For understanding that this was the right thing do at the right time in MSU's football history.

A special dedication to my loving mother, Gertrude, and to my late father, Louis, who remain instrumental in my life.

And finally, to all Spartans everywhere. Go Green!

—Ken Hoffman

To my wife, Lois of Laurium,
to all Spartan players, coaches, trainers and managers,
to all cheerleaders, band members, and students,
to all groundskeepers, ticket takers and ushers,
and of course to all loyal Spartan fans everywhere. Go White!

—Larry Bielat

THANK YOU

to the following sponsors for their generous support.

GREEN AND WHITE SPONSORS

Meijer
Sears Roebuck and Company
Student Book Store

CENTENNIAL SPONSOR

Ralph Young Fund

SPARTAN SPIRIT SPONSOR

Michigan State University Alumni Association

LOYALTY SPONSORS

Citizens Bank
Downtown Coaches Club
Finley's American Restaurants
Michigan State University Federal Credit Union

CONTENTS

ACKNOWLEDGMENTS

Any author, particularly one writing his first book, will tell you that it's nearly impossible to thank everyone who has offered a helping hand along the way. From the people who actually assisted in my research of the 100 years of Spartan gridiron history, to those who simply offered insight or encouragement, please accept my undying gratitude. My only regret is that I could not have included all of the stories I wanted to, but space limitations prevented me from doing so.

To the terrific Spartan coaching staffs with whom I have served, a heartfelt thank you. People such as George Perles, Doug Weaver, Hank Bullough, Nick Saban and others have demonstrated what it means to be a Spartan.

I've been blessed with a wonderful Sports Information staff as well. The list of people includes John Farina, Lori Schulze, Rob Kaminski, Paulette Martis, Brenda McGuire and many talented interns and student assistants. Thanks in part to their efforts, MSU's athletic program has enjoyed tremendous visibility throughout Michigan and across the country.

The three men who have preceded me as MSU's Sports Information Director played as big a role as any in assembling the treasure chest of information for this book: the late Nick Kerbawy, the school's first full-time SID; the legendary Fred Stabley, Sr., who defined the profession as we know it; and Nick Vista, who joined Stabley to form the top PR tandem in college sports.

Also, thanks to Mike Pearson, the former SID at MSU and currently Director of Acquisitions and Development at Sagamore Publishing who added his ample insight to the book, and Susan McKinney, also at Sagamore Publishing, for her yeoman effort.

To the multitude of athletes who I have served during my nine years at State, please accept my humble gratitude. I've enjoyed watching your special talents from the sidelines.

If pictures are indeed worth a thousand words, then a great deal of the praise must go to the photographic genius contained within these pages. In particular, MSU photographers Bruce Fox and (retired photographer) Bill Mitchum and Sports Information intern Kevin Fowler.

Finally, thanks to Jack Seibold for sharing his Spartan knowledge and background and to Dr. Todd Harburn and Gerald Harburn for their historical accounts of the early MIAA years.

Ken Hoffman

It is impossible to thank everyone who offered a helping hand in putting together *Spartan Football: 100 Seasons of Gridiron Glory*. But especially we wish to acknowledge all the wonderful people at MSU Archives; the MSU Museum and Library; Bob Bao, Dave Giordan and Sara Stid with the *MSU Alumni Magazine*; Bev VandenBerg and Kim Cornelisse for research assistance; and Jim Adams and Hank Bullough for historical memories.

Larry Bielat

Years of Glory

This is the 50th year of my love affair with Michigan State — as professor, administrator, and sports enthusiast. I arrived in 1947, with a Yale Ph.D. and, like most parochial Easterners, not quite certain where East Lansing was in that wilderness we knew as the Midwest. I came, in part, because I knew that Biggie Munn, Duffy Daugherty, and Forrest Evashevsky had accepted the challenge of reviving Michigan State's football fortunes. I never regretted my decision.

Biggie's first outing was against Michigan in Ann Arbor. He absorbed a merciless, 55-0 trouncing that he never forgot. Patiently, he built his team and, starting in 1950, he never lost to the Wolverines again. During his coaching career, he amassed a spectacular record of 54 wins, 9 losses, and 2 ties. His triumphs included a national championship (1953), a 28-game winning streak, a Big Ten co-championship, and a victory over UCLA in the 1954 Rose Bowl. As All-American end Don Dohoney put it, Biggie had the singular talent to instill a "winning philosophy" in his players and his staff. He made Michigan State a national football power.

Duffy carried on the tradition. In his first 13 seasons as head coach, his record against Notre Dame was an impressive 9-2-1, and against Michigan an equally impressive 8-3-2. Two of his teams were undefeated Big Ten champions (1965 and 1966). He beat UCLA on his first Rose Bowl outing (1956), but lost a heartbreaker to the Bruins in the 1966 Rose Bowl. Win or lose, however, Duffy's good natured humor and wisecracks were accorded national attention—not only in sports publications, but also in *The New York Times* and the *Wall Street Journal*. He, too, put Spartan football on the national map.

The Munn/Daugherty era was marked not only by stellar success on the gridiron, but also by a transformation of Michigan State from what its detractors called a "cow college", with an enrollment of roughly 10,000, into a world-class, 40,000-student university. Yet critics, both within and outside the university raised the perennial question about the compatibility of athletics and academics.

It was not a novel concern. Some 75 years earlier, the distinguished botanist W.G. Beall (at what was then Michigan Agricultural College) had argued that "success in sports advertises the college by drawing an increasing percent of athletes, instead of brainy young persons for success in the classroom and laboratory....The exercise is too violent, not infrequently dangerous....Strenuous efforts are often made to win games by unfair means—by cheating if necessary to win....Athletes are unduly stimulated by their associates and the newspapers to overestimate their enormous importance." A young college, Beall warned, should avoid an overemphasis on athletics.

Walter Adams

Notwithstanding these concerns, President John A. Hannah, who masterminded MSU's fabulous growth after World War II, believed in strong athletic programs. He understood that, at times, overenthusiastic and overzealous coaches, boosters, and players would transgress the bounds of integrity, and thus bring embarassment and opprobrium to the institution. Yet he was convinced that a flourishing football program—under proper supervision and firm institutional control—was a vital bond uniting the diverse constituencies of a megaversity: students and staff, alumni and the community. Often, he would wryly observe that football preeminence was not a blemish on the academic reputation of Harvard, Yale, and Chicago in those halcyon days when their teams were the scourge of the gridiron.

It is remarkable that novels authored by MSU graduates in the post-World War II era typically contain some reference to a football Saturday. Regardless of their basic theme, these novels would describe—with some nostalgia—the hoopla surrounding the event, the excitement of the crowd, the electricity generated by the band, the spectacle of the game itself. To the authors, bigtime football was obviously an indelible part of their college experience.

Perhaps, I am an eternal sophomore. At home games, I follow a routine of long standing. I accompany the inimitable Spartan Marching Band on its parade from Landon Field to the stadium. I offer words of encouragement to the team as it returns from its pregame warmups. I wait for the team at the northend goalposts when the game is over. Win or lose, I applaud the boys for their efforts. After all, they are wearing the green-and-white which I have loved for 50 years.

Walter Adams
13th President
Michigan State University

In the Beginning...

In 1850, the State Agricultural Society petitioned the State Legislature of Michigan for an agricultural college. While the State Legislature could not finance such a plan, it in turn, petitioned the Congress of the United States for a grant of 350,000 acres to foster agriculture education in Michigan. They reasoned that the establishment of an agricultural college would provide a pattern for a national educational revolution and therefore deserved assistance from the federal government.

After the legal establishment of the college in February, 1855, the State Board of Education was directed to take over the implementation of the law (Morrill Act). Their first act was to acquire 677 acres of almost virgin forest. A hilltop was cleared, clay was dug, bricks were made by hand and baked on the ground, and three buildings were erected. Thus, the campus came into being.

Michigan Agricultural College formally opened with dedication services held in the chapel of College Hall on May 13, 1857. The following day classes began with an enrollment of 63 students— a very large number at the time for a new college.

Though its first official season wasn't until 1896, records of the sport of football date back to 1884 at Michigan Agricultural College, just 15 years after the first collegiate contest had been played between Rutgers and Princeton. That year, football took its infantile steps at MAC. The sport was on such tenuous footing—frowned upon by the administration, haphazardly scheduled and amateurishly, if at all, coached—that it was 1896 before it became established enough to be considered a regular sport.

The 1884 team played no games for some reason lost in time, but did have this picture taken. The coach was Prof. Rolla Carpenter, instructor in mathematics and civil engineering.

The 1884 MAC football team, lt. to rt.: R.J. Coryell, '84; C.P. Gillett, '84; E.A. Bartmess, '85; W.C. Sanson, '87; D.J. Stryker, '85; J. D. Towar, '85; (G. Morrice, '85; front with ball); J.Y. Clark, '85; W.I. Power, '85; E.C. Bank, '84; R. Edling; '86; C.C. Lillie, '84; Coach, Prof. Rolla Carpenter.

Identification key for front cover illustration

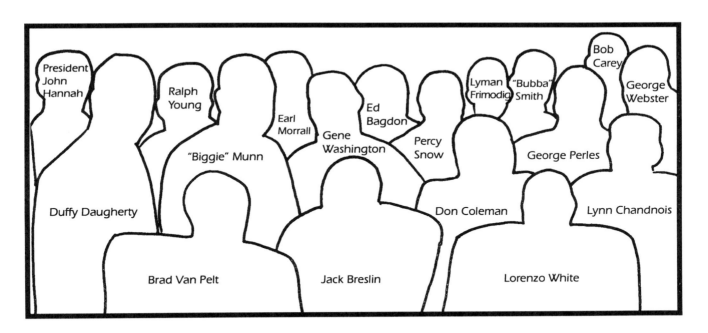

1896-1899

MICHIGAN STATE UNIVERSITY

SPARTAN
FOOTBALL

100 Seasons

MAC - MSC - MSU

THE TEAM

1896 Aggie football team. See pages 309-321 for player identifications.

THE SCORES

10	Lansing H.S.*	0
0	Kalamazoo	24
0	Alma*	0
16	Alma	18

1-2-1
(* = home game)

Aggie Moment

Game action from the second contest against Alma on November 14, 1896. After a scoreless tie the first time around, this one, played at Alma after a week's postponement due to inclement weather, resulted in an 18-16 MAC defeat.

AGGIE ITEM

This is a picture of the map of the original campus of 1857 showing the Indian grounds, south of the Red Cedar River, where the current stadium is located. These were hunting and fishing grounds for the local tribesmen.

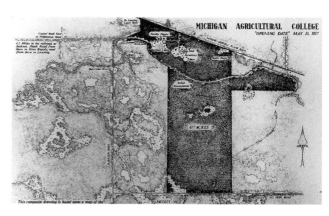

GREEN & WHITE HIGHLIGHTS

- Football made its official debut with a schedule of four games. Credit was due, in part, to a revised academic schedule which switched the traditional long vacation period to the summer. Previously, this break had come in late fall through the winter to permit MAC students to teach in country schools.

- MAC played its games at Elton Park in Lansing. GEORGE WELLS (Ithaca) scored MAC's first points as he tallied all 10 in the win over Lansing High.

- An interesting note is that "touchdowns" only counted four points while the point-after-touchdown —known as a "goal" —counted two points.

4

1897

THE SCORES

28	Lansing H.S.*	0
26	Olivet*	6
0	Kalamazoo*	28
18	Olivet	18
30	Alma	16
38	Alma*	4
6	Notre Dame	34

4-2-1

THE STAFF

HENRY KEEP held the distinction of being Michigan State's first head football coach. Not much is known about Keep, other than he was an engineering student from Detroit who also trained the track team. He led MAC to two winning seasons and a combined record of 8-5-1. The 1897 team produced a 4-2-1 mark.

THE TEAM

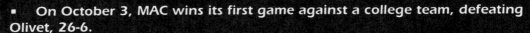

No photo of 1897 team available. These are star performers from various MAC athletic teams circa 1897.

AGGIE ITEM

In the early days, MAC was located three miles east of the village of Lansing upon a 700-acre farm that was purchased for $15 an acre. There was a lack of transportation because the college was started in the woods nearly 30 miles from a railroad, with terrible wagon roads making getting to class very difficult. Students in Lansing either walked the three miles or stayed at home. The "half-way stone"—the resting place— was near where Frandor Shopping Center is located. With the installation of electricity, transportation facilities were greatly enhanced, and finally a street car was run right onto campus.

GREEN & WHITE HIGHLIGHTS

- On October 3, MAC wins its first game against a college team, defeating Olivet, 26-6.
- MAC paid back the 1896 loss to Alma with two resounding victories, 30-16 and 38-4.
- The Aggies also played Notre Dame for the first time, falling 34-6. MAC was only the second team to score on Notre Dame that year—Chicago was the other.
- Practice used to be 45 minutes long, followed by a mile run and, finally, a rubdown.

THE TEAM

1898 Aggie football team. See pages 309-321 for player identification.

THE SCORES

11	Ypsilanti	6
0	Michigan	39
0	Notre Dame	53
62	Albion*	6
45	Olivet	0
24	Ypsilanti*	6
0	Kalamazoo	17

4-3-0

Aggie Moment

The hero of the season-opening Ypsilanti game was WILLIAM E. RUSSELL who scored all of MAC's points (two touchdowns and an extra point) in the 11-6 upset win. The second TD was a 40-yard run.

AGGIE SALUTE

ELLIS W. RANNEY (Belding) is considered the first football hero of MAC's earliest days competing in the sport. He was noted for his aggressive play. He quarterbacked the grid team to four successful seasons and also played second base for the baseball team. Ranney was captain of both teams in his final year.

GREEN & WHITE HIGHLIGHTS

- The MAC Record account of the season-opening game at Ypsilanti indicates that the game had to be stopped on numerous occasions as the MAC alumni and fans poured onto the field to help the team celebrate successful plays.
- After lopsided losses to Michigan (39-0) and Notre Dame (53-0), played on a Wednesday and Saturday of the same week, MAC won three straight one-sided games over Albion (62-6), Olivet (45-0) and Ypsilanti (24-6).
- Former Ivy League players KNIGHT (Princetown) and (Ed) FITCH (Cornell) were part-time volunteer coaches who helped the team.
- The scoring system for college football was changed to: touchdown = 5 pts.; safety = 2 pts.; goal from field (drop kick field goal) = 5 pts.; goal from touchdown (P.A.T.) = 1 pt.

1899

THE SCORES

0	Notre Dame	40
6	Detroit A.C.	16
6	Kalamazoo*	10
11	Alma	11
18	Ypsilanti	0
7	Olivet	18
23	DePauw*	6

2-4-1

THE STAFF

CHARLES O. BEMIES took over as MAC's second coach. An ordained Presbyterian minister, Bemies was named head coach by MAC President Jonathan Snyder in 1899. Bemies not only coached football, but also directed Aggie basketball, baseball and track teams. He served for two seasons in that capacity.

THE TEAM

1899 Aggie football team. See pages 309-321 for player identification.

AGGIE ITEM

ATHLETICS

A campus cartoonist created this pen-and-ink drawing, which appeared on the cover of the Wolverine yearbook. It was intended to depict the student excitement and drama of the early football contests at Michigan Agricultural College.

GREEN & WHITE HIGHLIGHTS

- MAC closed the season with wins over Michigan State Normal College (Ypsilanti) and DePauw sandwiched around a one-point loss to Olivet. After the Kalamazoo game, Coach Bemies and the team complained that they couldn't present a respectable team because they had to work in the fields, so the school officials juggled the schedule so they could work in the morning and still have practice time in the afternoon.
- The season finale was played on Thanksgiving Day at the old baseball park two blocks from the Capitol Building. Admission was 25 cents. The game was scheduled to kick off precisely at noon as the clock on the old City Hall struck 12. MAC won the game, 23-6, over DePauw.

1900-1909

MICHIGAN STATE UNIVERSITY
SPARTAN
FOOTBALL
100 Seasons
MAC - MSC - MSU

THE SCORES

0	Albion*	23
45	Adrian*	0
6	Detroit A.C.	21
0	Alma*	23

1-3-0

Aggie Moment

In 1900, L. Whitney Watkins, a young alumnus and member of the State Board of Agriculture, proposed that the Board purchase for athletic purposes the 13 acres of land south of the Red Cedar River, now known as Old College Field. The facilities on the land were developed with a $5,000 donation from a Mr. Lawrence and a Mr. Van Buren.

THE TEAM

1900 Aggie football team. See pages 309-321 for player identification.

AGGIE ITEM

The man who received the most credit for getting Aggie athletics started was President Jonathon L. Snyder, who took office in 1896. He had been an outstanding college athlete at Westminster College in Pennsylvania and remained an avid fan. He made his position quite clear when he declared to associates: "If we must have football, I want the kind that wins."

GREEN & WHITE HIGHLIGHTS

- A Mr. Close was hired for two weeks to assist professor/coach Bemies to "get the football team in shape."
- A dressing room and bathroom in the basement of Abbott Hall were turned over to football so the players would not have to continue to dress in their rooms.
- The playing field was 110 yards (330 ft.) long by 53.33 yards (160 ft.) wide.
- The Adrian game (45-0 victory) was stopped at 3:45 p.m. to allow the Adrian team time to catch a train. MCINTYRE posted 65-, and 75-yard runs for TDs and scored three times in the game.

1901

THE SCORES

5	Alma	6
22	Hillsdale	0
11	Albion	0
0	Detroit A.C.	33
42	Kalamazoo*	0
17	Albion*	17
5	Kalamazoo	15
18	Olivet*	23

3-4-1

THE STAFF

GEORGE DENMAN (1901-02) was the school's third football coach. His Aggie teams won seven of 17 games. Denman was a much more successful basketball coach, having led MAC to a perfect two-year 11-0 record in that sport. Career Record: 7-9-1.

THE TEAM

1901 Aggie football team. See pages 309-321 for player identification.

AGGIE ITEM

MAC MEMBERS OF THE 1901 All-MIAA TEAM:

- ARTHUR PETERS, Left tackle, who became MAC's best end in 1902.

- DON CHILDS, right halfback, who became the best quarterback in the MIAA and a fine tackler as a back on defense in 1902. He hailed from Lansing High.

- MATT CROSBY, left end.

- WARD SHEDD, center.

GREEN & WHITE HIGHLIGHTS

- MAC earned its first victory over Kalamazoo (42-0) after four unsuccessful attempts. The game was called on account of darkness with 13 minutes to play in the second half (fairly common occurrence). CHILDS, BRAINERD and CROSBY each scored two touchdowns.
- MAC closed the season versus Olivet on Thanksgiving Day at the state grounds on Walnut St. in Lansing.
- The team practiced from about 4:15 to 5:00 each day, at which time the military drill began.
- CROSBY gained at least 103 yards and scored two TDs on runs of 65 and 20 yards in a 17-17 tie with Albion.

1902

THE SCORES

0	Notre Dame	32
11	Detroit*	0
0	Michigan	119
35	Hillsdale*	0
2	Michigan Fresh.*	0
12	DePauw*	17
6	Olivet	11
22	Albion	11
5	Alma*	16

4-5-0

THE TEAM

1902 Aggie football team. See pages 309-321 for player identification.

Aggie Moment

Right halfback HAROLD CHILDS tallied three touchdowns in the 35-0 win over Hillsdale. The game was shortened in the second half to allow the visitors to catch their train.

AGGIE ITEM

Old College Field was made available for use by athletic teams. The 13 acres was purchased by the school in 1900. It became the main outdoor athletic area with running track, football and baseball facilities. A 14-foot-wide by 85-foot-long bridge was completed across the Red Cedar at a cost of $525, to serve as the approach to the field. The bridge rested on six bents of piles sunk 15 feet below the river bottom. This picture was taken from behind what is now the right-field fence of the baseball facility (Kobs Field).

GREEN & WHITE HIGHLIGHTS

- The All-Michigan College Team included five MAC players: left end ARTHUR PETERS (Springport); right guard HARRY MEEK (Manton); right tackle FRANK KRATZ (Albion); quarterback DON CHILDS (Lansing); and fullback HAROLD CHILDS (Lansing); who was also the best punter in the Michigan Intercollegiate Athletic Association.
- Helmets were not part of the Aggie uniform, but leather noseguards were. The noseguards tied behind the head and were simply hung from the neck when not in use.

CHESTER BREWER
(1903-10, 1917, 1919)

This Owosso native revolutionized MAC's football program during his first of three stints as Aggie coach. Chester Brewer was a four-sport star at Wisconsin, earning All-Western honors in football. A defensive genius, Aggie teams posted shutouts in 49 of the 88 games Brewer directed. His greatest efforts included a 0-0 tie against Fielding Yost's 1908 Michigan team and a 17-0 shutout over Notre Dame in 1910. Brewer, who later coached at Missouri, died in 1953 at the age of 77.

Career Record: 58-23-7

1903

THE SCORES

0	Notre Dame	12
11	Alma	0
45	Olivet*	0
11	Michigan Frosh *	0
11	Kalamazoo*	0
43	Hillsdale	0
51	Detroit YMCA*	6
6	Albion*	6

6-1-1

THE STAFF

Owosso native CHESTER BREWER revolutionized MAC's football program during his first of three stints as Aggie coach. Brewer was a four-sport star at Wisconsin, earning All-Western honors in football. A defensive genius, Aggie teams posted shutouts in 49 of the 88 games Brewer directed. His greatest efforts included a 0-0 tie against Fielding Yost's 1908 Michigan team and a 17-0 shutout over Notre Dame in 1910. Brewer, who later coached at Missouri, died in 1953 at the age of 77. CAREER RECORD: 58-23-7.

THE TEAM

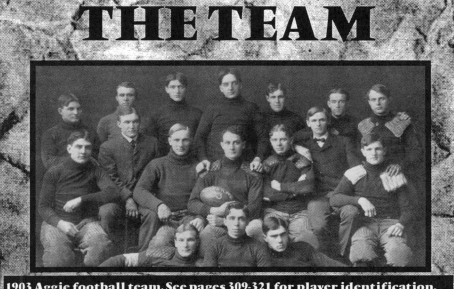

1903 Aggie football team. See pages 309-321 for player identification.

AGGIE SALUTE

CHESTER BREWER was a four-sport star at Wisconsin, earning All-Western honors in football and baseball, and competing as well in track and crew. For two years after graduation, he served the UW athletic department. In the summers of those two years, he played second base for the Chicago White Sox. From Wisconsin, he went to Albion College as football coach and director of athletics. His amazing record during his first stint at MAC (eight of his 10 years) from 1903-10 was 54-10-6! Brewer was also appointed director of athletics. It is possible that this marked the first time for a coach to be honored with a faculty rank anywhere in the U.S. A man of the highest integrity, character, and a staunch supporter of charitable organizations, Forest Akers established in 1951 the Chester Brewer Award in his honor, given annually to a graduating senior for distinguished performance in athletics and scholarship and for possessing a high degree of character, leadership and personality which forecast a successful career.

GREEN & WHITE HIGHLIGHTS

- MAC tied Albion, 6-6, in the season finale, to win the MIAA championship. One of the truly unusual incidents in the history of college football occurred. Touchdowns counted five points then. Albion scored first and converted for a 6-0 lead; ED MCKENNA then scored for MAC. But the validity of McKenna's subsequent kick for the tying extra point was contested by Albion. The debate centered on the complicated conversion rules of those days. After a heated post-game meeting with referee Walter Fishleigh, both MAC coach BREWER and Albion coach Jim Nufer agreed to abide by the decision of two neutral observers — Fielding Yost and Keene Fitzpatrick of the U of M. A few days later, Yost and Fitzpatrick ruled that the MAC kick was legal, and MAC and Albion were named co-champions.
- The season's only loss was to Notre Dame, 12-0. MAC posted five consecutive shutouts and outscored its opponents, 178-24 overall; 116-6 in the MIAA.
- Brewer was also athletic director at MAC. MAC first used green and white as uniform colors when Brewer became A.D. and coached the school's four sports—football, basketball, baseball and track.

1904

THE SCORES

47	Mich. Deaf Sch.*	0
28	Ohio Northern *	6
29	Port Huron YMCA*	0
0	Albion	4
104	Hillsdale*	0
39	Michigan Fresh.*	0
35	Olivet	6
40	Alma	0
58	Kalamazoo*	0
	8-1-0	

Aggie Moment

In the Hillsdale massacre, MAC scored the second-highest point total in the school's history (104). The previous MIAA record was 66 points in one game. The halftime score was 58-0. Halfback "BABE" KRATZ scored five of MAC's touchdowns and at least eight different players tallied scores for the Aggies.

THE TEAM

1904 Aggie football team. See pages 309-321 for player identification.

AGGIE ITEM

The school's highest scoring team ever! MAC posted an 8-1 record, outscoring its opponents by an astounding total of 380-16, including six shutouts. The most points scored against MAC was six, by Ohio Northern (28-6) and Olivet (35-6). The loss came at the hands of Albion, 4-0 (field goals counted four points; touchdowns counted five), on a field described as a "sea of mud." MAC whipped Hillsdale, 104-0, in an MIAA game in which MAC tallied 18 touchdowns (MIAA record), 12 "goals" and a safety.

GREEN & WHITE HIGHLIGHTS

- This MAC team was considered the strongest team ever developed by any of the Michigan colleges to that point in time.

- Members of the All-MIAA Team: BELL, tackle; HOLDSWORTH, end; MCKENNA, halfback; SMALL, quarterback.

- For at least selected games, the west bleachers were reserved for "ladies and gentlemen accompanied by ladies."

1905 Aggie football team. See pages 309-321 for player identification.

THE SCORES

42	Mich. Deaf Sch.*	0
0	Notre Dame	28
43	Port Huron YMCA*	0
24	Michigan Frosh.*	0
30	Olivet*	0
18	Hillsdale*	0
18	Armour Inst.*	0
30	Kalamazoo	0
46	Albion*	10
11	Northwestern	37
18	Alma	0
	9-2-0	

Aggie Moment

MAC unseated Albion, 46-10, to complete a 5-0 league season and capture another MIAA title. Albion scored the first touchdown of the game. ED MCKENNA scored three times for MAC who built a 23-5 lead at halftime. The highlight of the second half came after the visitors worked the ball to within a few feet of the MAC goal. Albion fumbled, and the ball was scooped up by JESSE BOYLE who ran the length of the field for a MAC touchdown.

AGGIE SALUTE

WALTER SMALL was a standout performer in both football and track & field. He earned five football letters from 1903-1907 and four track monograms through 1908, thus making him one of only nine athletes ever in MSU history to earn nine (or 10) letters.

GREEN & WHITE HIGHLIGHTS

- MAC compiled a 9-2 record, the most wins ever in a single season at MAC. Brewer's charges shut out eight opponents, including six consecutively. MAC's only losses were to Notre Dame (28-0) and Western Conference (Big Ten) member Northwestern (37-11).

THE TEAM

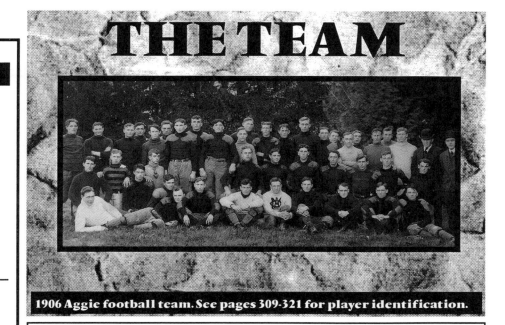

1906 Aggie football team. See pages 309-321 for player identification.

THE SCORES

23	Olivet*	0
37	Albion*	0
0	Alma	0
38	Kalamazoo*	0
33	DePauw*	0
0	Notre Dame	5
5	Albion	0
12	Alma*	0
35	Hillsdale	9
6	Olivet	8
6	Detroit A.C.	6
	7-2-2	

Aggie Item

In spite of MAC's season-opening 23-0 victory over Olivet, the squad finished second in the MIAA because that game did not count toward the MIAA standings. The second game between the schools—the next to last game of the season—was the match which was designated as a league contest, and Olivet scored an 8-6 triumph. Therefore, Olivet had a 4-0-1 MIAA mark to MAC's 4-1-0 record.

AGGIE SALUTE

ED McKENNA was a rare four-sport man for MAC, competing as a halfback in football, forward in basketball, outfielder in baseball and hurdler in track. He starred in all four, but was especially recognized throughout the West as a sensational running back. He was captain of the '05 team and chosen for the All-MIAA squad in his senior season of '06.

GREEN & WHITE HIGHLIGHTS

- MAC enjoyed another sterling defensive season while compiling a record of 7-2-2 overall, 4-1 (2nd) in its final season in the MIAA. The Aggies blanked seven of the 11 opponents, and the most points scored against them was nine, in a 35-9 thrashing of Hillsdale. MAC outscored its 11 opponents by a total of 195-28.
- Members of the All-MIAA Team selected by Olivet Coach Bert Kennedy: SHEDD, end; PARKER, guard; MOORE, center; CAMPBELL, guard; EXELBY, tackle; CORTRIGHT, end; VAUGHN, halfback; and E. MCKENNA, halfback.
- The MAC athletic association voted to drop out of the MIAA, as MAC was quickly outgrowing the conference. MAC was officially 13-2 over the last three years of football competition in the MIAA.
- In two decades of MIAA action, MAC won 15 titles in track, two in football, five in baseball and one in tennis.

1907

THE TEAM

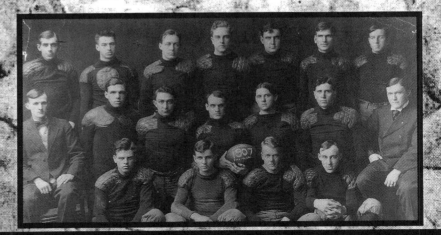

1907 Aggie football team. See pages 309-321 for player identification.

THE SCORES

17	Detroit*	0
40	Mich. Deaf Sch.*	0
0	Michigan	46
15	Wabash*	6
55	Olivet*	4
0	Alma	0
0	Detroit A.C.	4

4-2-1

THE STAFF

The 1907 Coaching staff, lt. to rt.: Manager Clyde Merwin, Captain Walter Small, Coach Chester Brewer.

AGGIE ITEM

President Theodore Roosevelt gladly accepted MAC's request to deliver the Commencement address on the occasion of the school's semi-centennial because he said that he had a message he wished to deliver to the American farmer and could think of no better place to deliver that message than at Michigan Agricultural College.

GREEN & WHITE HIGHLIGHTS

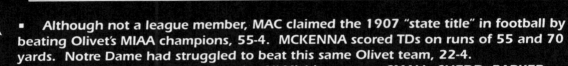

- Although not a league member, MAC claimed the 1907 "state title" in football by beating Olivet's MIAA champions, 55-4. MCKENNA scored TDs on runs of 55 and 70 yards. Notre Dame had struggled to beat this same Olivet team, 22-4.
- Nine players were selected to the All-Michigan team: SMALL, SHEDD, PARKER, MOORE, CAMPBELL, FRAZER, MCKENNA, VAUGHN and CORTRIGHT.
- In what was considered the biggest game of the season, MAC defeated Wabash—considered one of the fastest teams in the west—15-6. Following the game, the students ran onto the field and carried coach Brewer and all the players from the field.
- "Close Beside the Winding Cedar" was the alma mater, adopted in 1907, and in use until 1948.

1908

THE SCORES

0	Michigan*	0
35	Kalamazoo*	0
51	Mich. Deaf Sch.*	0
0	DePaul	0
6	Wabash*	0
46	Olivet	2
30	Saginaw Nav. Br.*	6
37	Detroit A.C.	14

6-0-2

THE TEAM

M.A.C. Rah-Rah-Rah.

1908 Aggie football team. See pages 309-321 for player identification.

Aggie Moment

MAC's first undefeated season and another defensive gem. The Aggies win six and tie two, opening the season with a great effort during a 0-0 tie against Fielding Yost's UM squad. It marked the first time in four meetings that MAC played on even terms with Michigan and kept alive MAC's streak of having never been beaten on the home field.

AGGIE SALUTE

WILLIAM FRAZER was the first athlete in Michigan State history to compete in the Olympic Games. He was a football letterwinner from 1906-08. Frazer gained immortality in Spartan lore as a member of the U.S. Olympic Pistol Team in 1924. An Army major from Ft. Monroe, Virginia, he did not win a medal in Paris, but tied for ninth place out of 66 competitors, scoring 17 of a possible 18 points.

GREEN & WHITE HIGHLIGHTS

- The Aggies shut out their first five opponents, winning three and tying two (Michigan and DePaul). They won the last three games by a combined score of 113-22.

- MAC did not have its goal line crossed until the seventh game of the season, when the Saginaw Naval Brigade scored a touchdown on a long triple forward pass.

- The first halftime entertainment was performed for the Wabash game —a push ball contest between Wells and Williams Halls.

THE SCORES

27	Detroit*	0
34	Alma*	0
28	Wabash*	0
0	Notre Dame	17
29	Culver	0
51	DePaul*	0
10	Marquette*	0
20	Olivet*	0
34	Detroit A.C.	0
	8-1-0	

THE STAFF

Coach Brewer's standards of athletic performance and conduct were exemplified in a speech at the student mass meeting prior to the Notre Dame game in South Bend: "Boys, we're going to show them that we have a great team. That team of ours is going in to fight to the last ditch. We may lose, but win or lose, let's show them that MAC has the cleanest, finest, and most gentlemanly bunch of sportsmen that they have ever played against."

THE TEAM

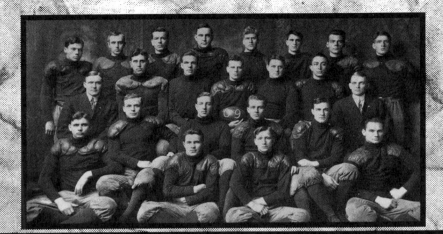

1909 Aggie football team. See pages 309-321 for player identification.

AGGIE SALUTE

PARNELL MCKENNA competed in two sports and earned a total of nine letters, making him one of only nine athletes in MSU history to earn nine (or 10) monograms. McKenna earned his fourth football letter and fifth basketball letter in 1909-10.

GREEN & WHITE HIGHLIGHTS

- MAC posted a record of 8-1 in the most remarkable defensive season in the school's early history. The Aggies could not be scored upon in eight of the nine games, with MAC rolling up an unbelievable advantage of 233-0 in those games! The team's only loss came against powerful Notre Dame, 17-0.
- The 10-0 win over powerhouse Marquette came in front of what was called the largest and most enthusiastic crowd ever at Old College Field.
- EXELBY tallied three TDs in the 27-0 season-opening win over Detroit.
- BREWER's last two squads had now compiled a ledger of 14-1-2 (.882) with 13 shutouts on defense.

1910-1919

MICHIGAN STATE UNIVERSITY

SPARTAN

FOOTBALL

100 Seasons

MAC - MSC - MSU

THE SCORES

35	Detroit A.C.*	0
12	Alma*	0
3	Michigan	6
37	Lake Forest*	0
17	Notre Dame*	0
3	Marquette	2
62	Olivet*	0

6-1-0

Aggie Moment

In an historical feat, MAC (soundly) defeated Notre Dame for the first time (17-0) after eight earlier unsuccessful attempts (MAC had only scored six points vs ND prior to this game; those coming in 1897). Notre Dame had been undefeated in '09 and "undisputed champions of the west."

THE TEAM

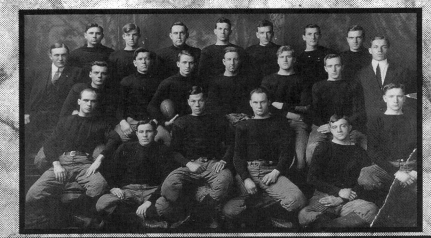

1910 Aggie football team. See pages 309-321 for player identification.

AGGIE SALUTE

LEON C. EXELBY was a four-year standout fullback for MAC from 1907-10. He earned a spot on Eckersall's All-Western first team in 1910 and was mentioned by many for All-America. MAC was 26-4 during his playing years, and lost only two games in which Exelby played. The 17-0 victory over Notre Dame in 1910 was credited, in part, to his fine defensive play. The 1913 yearbook states in the 1912 football review that "he is probably the most consistent offensive and defensive player MAC has ever had."

GREEN & WHITE HIGHLIGHTS

- Another fine year with BREWER's last team going 6-1. The defense added five more shutouts to its total and the only loss was 6-3 to Michigan, after LEON HILL returned a punt about 70 yards for a score but was nullified by a phantom holding call. MAC dominated its opponents in 1910 by a 168-8 count!
- For the first time, members of the team were given recognition by Walter H. Eckersall, who selected the All-Western football squad, generally from the much larger universities: LEON EXELBY, second team All-Western fullback; ERNEST BALDWIN (Midland) second team All-Western guard; L.W. CAMPBELL (tackle); and LEON HILL (Benton Harbor; halfback); honorable mention All-Western.
- BREWER's last three teams combined for a record of 20-2-2 (.875). His overall record was 54-10-6 and MAC had still never lost a home game (44 in a row under Brewer)! Brewer left MAC to become athletic director at Missouri (1910-17) where the Chester A. Brewer Fieldhouse was later named in his honor.

JOHN F. MACKLIN
(1911-15)

An outstanding athlete at Pennsylvania, John Macklin succeeded Chester Brewer as Aggie coach. He was said to have stood about 6-foot-5 and weighed around 250 pounds. Macklin won more than 85 percent of his games at MAC, compiling 29 victories in 34 contests. Among his greatest accomplishments were a 35-20 win over Ohio State in 1912, the first achieved by MAC over a Big Ten team; the school's first victory over Michigan, 12-7, in 1913; a 6-3 upset win against Penn State in 1914; and a 24-0 shutout of Michigan in 1915. Macklin died in 1949 at the age of 65.

Career Record: 29-5-0

1911

THE SCORES

12	Alma*	0
3	Michigan*	15
29	Olivet*	3
6	DePauw	0
26	Mt. Union*	6
17	Wabash*	6

5-1-0

Aggie Item

DEORMAND "TUSS" McLAUGHRY lettered as a tackle for MAC in 1911 before tranferring to Westminster College. His greatest fame came as a coach, spending five seasons at Westminster (1916-21), four years at Amherst (1922-25), 15 seasons at Brown (1926-40) and his final 12 years at Dartmouth (1941-54). He was inducted into the National Football Hall of Fame in 1962.

THE TEAM

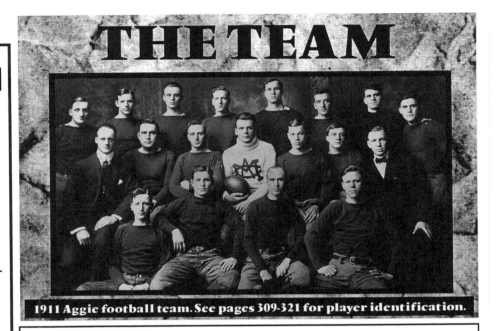

1911 Aggie football team. See pages 309-321 for player identification.

AGGIE SALUTE

JOHN MACKLIN succeeded Brewer as MAC football coach, and picked up right where Brewer had left off. Macklin— approximately 6-5 and 250 pounds—had been an outstanding athlete at Pennsylvania. He won better than 85 percent of his games at MAC, compiling an awesome slate of 29-5. Among his greatest accomplishments were a 35-20 win over Ohio State in 1912, the first achieved by MAC over a Big Ten team; the school's first victory over Michigan, 12-7 in 1913; a 6-3 upset of Penn State in 1914, and a 24-0 shutout of Michigan in 1915. Macklin died in 1949 at the age of 65.

GREEN & WHITE HIGHLIGHTS

- Macklin's first unit won five of six games, losing only to Michigan, 15-3. That game was called the greatest game ever played on College Field. MAC held the Maize and Blue scoreless for the first half. In the third quarter, pandemonium broke loose when MAC scored a field goal to take the lead. The score was 3-3 after three quarters, before Michigan prevailed.
- The Ohio Northern game was originally scheduled to be played on Saturday, November 18, but was rescheduled for Friday, November 17, to allow the players to see the Michigan-Pennsylvania game on Saturday. As it turned out, the Ohio Northern game had to be cancelled when a downpour turned the home field into a miniature lake.
- Season tickets cost $2.00. All seats were reserved for the Michigan, Wabash and Ohio Northern games.

1912

THE SCORES

14	Alma*	3
7	Michigan	55
52	Olivet*	0
58	DePauw*	0
46	Ohio Wesleyan*	0
61	Mt. Union*	20
24	Wabash*	0
35	Ohio State	20

7-1-0

THE STAFF

1912 Coaching staff: John Macklin (above), head coach; Ion Courtright, asst., R.C. Houston, asst.

THE TEAM

1912 Aggie football team. See pages 309-321 for player identification.

AGGIE ITEM

Following the season-ending 35-20 upset victory over Ohio State, the team, the band and the MAC students gathered in front of the Capitol. The Aggie contingent arrived at the Lansing train station and walked to the Capitol on the way back to campus. The students filled the steps as well as the second- and third-story balconies.

GREEN & WHITE HIGHLIGHTS

- MAC won seven of eight games, including the Aggies' first win over a Big Ten team —at 6-2 Ohio State on Thanksgiving Day—by a score of 35-20. MAC trailed OSU at halftime, 20-14, when Macklin's halftime speech inspired one of the most dramatic and incredible comebacks in MAC history! The Aggies scored 21 points in the second half while holding the Big Ten power scoreless! (1912 was OSU's first year as a member in the Big Ten).
- The team's only loss was, again, to Michigan, 55-7. BLAKE MILLER scored the only TD for MAC—the first touchdown against a Michigan team in seven contests. After that game (the second of the season) Macklin moved GAUTHIER to quarterback and RIBLET to halfback as MAC rolled to six more victories in impressive style.
- Macklin's second squad registered four shutouts. In the seven victories, MAC rolled up an impressive 290 points to 43 for the opponents (average score: 41.4 -6.1).

1913

THE TEAM

1913 Aggie football team. See pages 309-321 for player identification.

THE SCORES

26	Olivet*	7
57	Alma*	0
12	Michigan	7
12	Wisconsin	7
41	Akron*	0
13	Mt. Union*	7
19	South Dakota*	7

7-0-0

Aggie Moment

BLAKE MILLER carries the ball 10 yards around end for MAC's first touchdown during the big 12-7 road win over the University of Wisconsin. The picture shows CARP JULIAN at the extreme right, then Miller, then a Wisconsin tackler ready to dive. Next, to the left, is HUGH BLACKLOCK, then GIDEON SMITH.

AGGIE ITEM

CARP JULIAN plunges in from the three-yard line for the first score of the Michigan game. The arrow points out Julian in the endzone. MAC scored again when HEWITT MILLER alertly scooped up a UM fumble early in the second half and raced untouched 46 yards to give the Aggies a 12-0 lead. MAC went on to win the game, 12-7. Hewitt had replaced his brother, Blake, who had been injured when Michigan QB Tommy Hughitt jumped on Blake's neck with both knees. Blake, unconscious for three hours at the nearby hospital, returned to the team the following Tuesday and went on to gain recognition on Collier's All-Western team.

GREEN & WHITE HIGHLIGHTS

- MAC produced its first victory over Michigan, 12-7, in a bone-breaking, crunching battle—the Wolverines' only loss of the season. It was the school's first undefeated and untied team (7-0-0) and clearly one of the greatest in school history.
- MAC defeated Wisconsin, the defending Big Ten champion, by the same 12-7 score. This team garnered MAC the recognition as a national grid power.
- "CARP" JULIAN was named on Collier's All-Western second team and Walter Eckersall's All-America squad after scoring 10 TDs. CHESTER GIFFORD was also accorded second-team laurels along with end RALPH HENNING and tackle GIDEON SMITH. "DUTCH" LENARDSON was mentioned in Grantland Rice's All-America selections as well as All-Western.

1914

THE SCORES

36	Olivet*	7
60	Alma*	0
0	Michigan*	3
0	Nebraska	24
75	Akron*	6
21	Mt. Union*	14
6	Penn State	3

5-2-0

Aggie Moment

MAC—UM game action with the final score, 3-0, on a fourth-quarter Michigan field goal. MAC used only the 11 starters for the entire game.

THE TEAM

1914 Aggie football team. See pages 309-321 for player identification.

AGGIE SALUTE

When "CARP" JULIAN finished his career in 1914, he was considered one of the greatest players—and the greatest fullback—to have played for MAC. The MAC yearbook ran this photo with the inscription "To 'Carp' Julian—Michigan Aggies' greatest gridder—we dedicate the Athletic Section." Several writers listed Julian on their All-Western teams—Eckersall named him captain of the All-Western team—and some mentioned him for All-American honors. Wisconsin coach W.J. Juneau called Julian "the greatest fullback I have ever seen." He was an organizer and charter member of the Varsity "S" Club. Later, he was president of the Downtown Coaches Association for several years and of the MSU Alumni Association (1938-40).

GREEN & WHITE HIGHLIGHTS

- The Aggies build a 5-2 record, including a tough 6-3 win in the season finale at Penn State.

- The school's first homecoming was held on October 17th. In accordance with the resolutions adopted by the alumni, the Michigan game was designated as the "Alumni Game," with an informal reunion of "old grads." The MAC Record reported that a crowd of over 10,000 spectators attended the game.

- BLAKE MILLER was again accorded All-Western honors.

1915

THE SCORES

34	Olivet*	0
77	Alma*	12
56	Carroll*	0
24	Michigan	0
0	Oregon State*	20
68	Marquette*	6

5-1-0

THE STAFF

1915 Coaching staff: John Macklin (center) head coach; George Gauthier (left) ass't.; Oscar Miller (right) ends; Chester Gifford, line; J.E. McWilliams, freshmen.

THE TEAM

1915 Aggie football team. See pages 309-321 for player identification.

AGGIE SALUTE

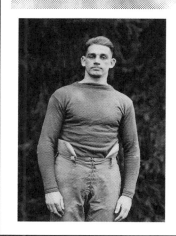

In 1915, BLAKE MILLER, one of the greatest gridders of his day, gained 115 yards in the 24-0 romp over Michigan. His effort was so inspiring, UM coach Fielding Yost personally gave the game ball to Miller. Blake was one of only eight men to earn nine varsity letters. He won four monograms in football, three in baseball (as a star pitcher) and two in basketball. Miller was named to MSU's all-time Old-Timers Team in 1969 as an end. He passed away January 9, 1987, at the age of 97. Miller and DAPRATO were named as MAC's first All-Americans.

GREEN & WHITE HIGHLIGHTS

- MAC completed COACH MACKLIN's five years as head man with a 5-1 record, destroying each opponent with the sole exception of Oregon State. Other than that loss, the closest any team could come to MAC was 24 points (Michigan). The Aggies shut out three opponents and outscored their six foes, 259-38.
- The 24-0 victory over Michigan was the most overwhelming MAC victory over the Wolverines until 1951 (25-0). DAPRATO totaled 153 yards rushing and receiving, scored all three of MAC's TDs and drop-kicked a 23-yard field goal. Defensively, Smith was credited with over half the tackles.
- Player jerseys were numbered for the first time at MAC, and the football programs were printed with the players' names opposite their numbers to help the fans identify the players. The idea came from the East, when MAC played at Penn State in '14.

1916

THE SCORES

40	Olivet*	0
20	Carroll*	0
33	Alma	0
0	Michigan	9
30	N. Dakota State*	0
3	South Dakota	3
0	Notre Dame*	14

4-2-1

THE STAFF

1916 Coaching staff: Frank Sommer, head coach (above); George Gauthier, ass't.; Chester Gifford, line; Howard Beatty, freshmen; R.C. Huston, reserve.

THE TEAM

1916 Aggie football team. See pages 309-321 for player identification.

AGGIE SALUTE

Cheerleader Francis Irving Lankey wrote the school's original version of the "fight song." Lankey lost his life as an airplane pilot in World War I. The original verse:

"On the banks of the Red Cedar,
There's a college known to all;
Their specialty is farming,
But the farmers play football.
chorus:
Smash right thru that line of blue,
Watch that score keep growing,
Aggie teams are sure to win,
They're fighting with a vim.
Rah! Rah! Rah!
Michigan is weakening, we're going
to win this game;
Fight! Fight! Rah, team, fight—
Victory for MAC."

GREEN & WHITE HIGHLIGHTS

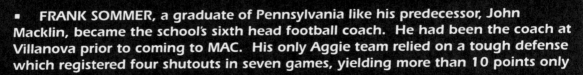

- FRANK SOMMER, a graduate of Pennsylvania like his predecessor, John Macklin, became the school's sixth head football coach. He had been the coach at Villanova prior to coming to MAC. His only Aggie team relied on a tough defense which registered four shutouts in seven games, yielding more than 10 points only once.
- MAC carved a record of 4-2-1, losing only to Michigan and Notre Dame, while scoring 126 points and holding the opposition to only three touchdowns and a total of 26 points.
- The 9-0 loss to Michigan in Ann Arbor was witnessed by some 22,000 fans, the largest crowd to see a Michigan—MAC game to date.

THE SCORES

7	Alma*	14
3	Kalamazoo*	7
0	Michigan	27
0	Detroit*	14
0	Western State*	14
6	Northwestern	39
0	Notre Dame	23
7	Syracuse*	21
0	Camp MacArthur*	20

0-9-0

THE STAFF

1917 Coaching staff, lt. to rt: Chester Gifford, line; George "Carp" Julian, backfield; Chester Brewer, head coach; George Gauthier, ass't.

THE TEAM

1917 Aggie football team. See pages 309-321 for player identification.

AGGIE SALUTE

Two years earlier, in 1915, MAC's former star tackle GIDEON SMITH (top) played professionally for the Canton Bulldogs with Jim Thorpe (bottom). Smith was one of the first—if not the first—African-American to play pro football. Another ex-Aggie—"CARP" JULIAN—played on that pro team.

GREEN & WHITE HIGHLIGHTS

- CHESTER BREWER returned to coach the gridders, but the depleted ranks could not muster a victory in nine games. MAC's football veterans were to be found in training camps, in the navy and in France. Only a handful of under-classmen had previous varsity experience.

- The loss to Michigan came after a valiant effort by MAC, trailing only 6-0 at halftime.

- LYMAN FRIMODIG became State's first athlete to win 10 varsity letters. He won four each in basketball and baseball and two in football. He turned down a Notre Dame baseball offer to come to MAC.

1918

THE SCORES

21	Albion*	6
66	Hillsdale*	6
16	Western State*	7
6	Purdue*	14
13	Notre Dame*	7
6	Michigan	21
6	Wisconsin	7

4-3-0

THE STAFF

1918 Coaching staff: George Gauthier, head coach (above); Ion J. Cortright, asst.

THE TEAM

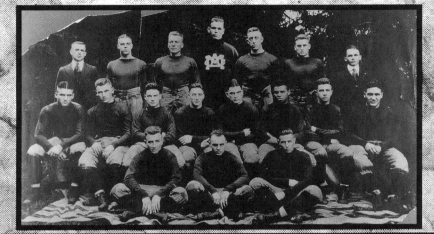

1918 Aggie football team. See pages 309-321 for player identification.

AGGIE SALUTE

JACK HEPPINSTALL begins his fifth year after coming to MAC in 1914. Here he carries his familiar black bag that he carried for all 45 years. From 1913, when he left his native Durham County, England, until 1959 when he retired, Heppinstall served as the school's first athletic trainer. He served under 12 different coaches from Chester Brewer through Duffy Daugherty. A former professional soccer player in England, he came to Lansing and read in the paper that the college needed a trainer. Jack came on a temporary basis, which eventually spanned five decades.

GREEN & WHITE HIGHLIGHTS

- COACH BREWER was one of the Aggies who answered his country's call to service. Consequently, coach GEORGE GAUTHIER was named interim head coach. From humble beginnings, due to the ravages of the war—Coach Gauthier started practice with only four lettermen from the 0-9 1917 team—a formidable team was developed which produced a 4-3 record.
- A three-week flu epidemic knocked the Aggies out of action and all activity before returning to beat Western State Normal (now Western Michigan), 16-7.
- MAC pulled off a huge upset over Notre Dame (Nov. 16), 13-7, in the mud at Old College Field. The Irish came to town with a first-year head coach named Knute Rockne. After a Graves-to-Young 20-yard pass play for a TD and a 6-0 lead, Notre Dame came back to take a 7-6 lead at halftime. The Aggies scored in the first five minutes of the third quarter and held on for the upset. It was ND's only loss of the year and Rockne's only defeat over the three-year period from 1918 through 1920!

THE SCORES

14	Albion*	13
46	Alma*	6
18	Western State*	21
0	Michigan	26
27	DePauw*	0
7	Purdue	13
13	South Dakota*	0
0	Notre Dame	13
7	Wabash*	7

4-4-1

THE STAFF

1919 Coaching staff, lt. to rt.: George Gauthier; Chester Brewer, head coach; Lyman Frimodig; Blake Miller.

THE TEAM

1919 Aggie football team. See pages 309-321 for player identification.

AGGIE SALUTE

MAC once had five captains on the same team, and they were not co-captains! It was 1919, the result of World War I drafts which called up players for active military duty at various times, and sent them all home again for the 1919 season. The captains were (lt. to rt.): "IRISH" RAMSEY, captain-elect in 1918; ADELBERT "DEL" VANDERVOORT, captain-elect in 1917; HARRY "SIWASH" FRANSON, the 1919 captain; LARRY ARCHER, the 1918 captain; and SHERMAN CORYELL, the 1917 captain.

GREEN & WHITE HIGHLIGHTS

- BREWER's last MAC team ended the season with a 4-4-1 mark.

- Fullback JOHN HAMMES was named by Walter Eckersall to the All-Western team.

- For the first time, the Detroit MAC Club and the U of M Club joined on the Friday night before the Michigan game to hear coaches Brewer and Yost speak about the game.

- F.I. Lankey's fight song was formally introduced as the school's cheer song.

- Enrollment for 1919 was 1,341, including an all-time high number of women—327.

1920-1929

MICHIGAN STATE UNIVERSITY

SPARTAN FOOTBALL

100 Seasons

MAC - MSC - MSU

Jenison Fieldhouse, c. 1940

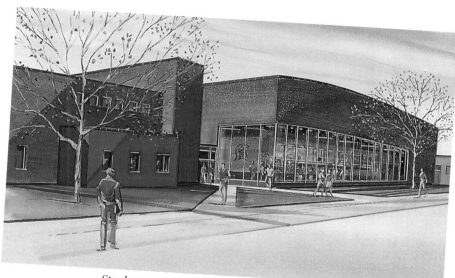

Student-Athlete Academic Center, c. 1997

Throughout its history, gifts from alumni and friends have helped create a tradition of excellence at Michigan State University. One such gift was made by Frederick Cowles Jenison, who studied engineering at Michigan State and went on to build a successful career in real estate and insurance. His gift to the university built the facility that bears his name: Jenison Fieldhouse, the home of Spartan athletics.

Over the past 33 years, the Ralph Young Fund – named for MSU's longtime athletic director and former football coach – has raised more than $40 million in private gifts that have provided scholarships and other support for thousands of student-athletes. Now, as the Spartan football team begins its second century of achievement on the field, a new era of excellence is beginning off the field with construction of the Student-Athlete Academic Center. The facility will house expanded educational resources and a more comprehensive academic support program for all student-athletes, and further strengthen Michigan State's commitment to providing the best possible education to all students – for when they are successful, that truly is a victory for MSU.

Victory for MSU: The Campaign for the Student-Athlete Academic Center

The Ralph Young Fund, 4700 South Hagadorn Road, Suite 220, East Lansing, MI 48823 • 517- 355- 8257

1920

THE SCORES

2	Kalamazoo*	21
16	Albion*	0
48	Alma*	0
0	Wisconsin	27
0	Michigan	35
7	Marietta*	23
109	Olivet*	0
81	Chicago YMCA*	0
7	Nebraska	35
0	Notre Dame*	25
	4-6-0	

THE STAFF

Head coach GEORGE "POTSY" CLARK coached the 1920 team to a 4-6 record after coming to MAC just over two weeks prior to the start of the season. One of his four wins was a record 109-0 rout of Olivet. An All-America quarterback for the legendary Bob Zuppke at Illinois, Clark is probably best known as head coach of the Detroit Lions, who won the 1935 NFL title. He passed away in 1972 at the age of 78. The rest of the 1920 Coaching Staff included "Swede" Rundquist, line; Chester Brewer, coach; and Lyman Frimodig, freshmen.

THE TEAM

1920 Aggie football team. See pages 309-321 for player identification.

AGGIE SALUTE

"BIG JOHN" HAMMES, a powerful fullback, was even more widely known for his defensive prowess, compared to Leon Exelby in that area. He lettered in 1917, 1919, and 1920. Hammes was given a berth on Eckersall's All-Western second team and on the first team by many writers. He also lettered as a valuable guard on the basketball team and first baseman for baseball.

GREEN & WHITE HIGHLIGHTS

- The schedule included Notre Dame, probably the top team in the country; Wisconsin, runner-up in the Big Ten; Michigan and Nebraska.
- MAC played in Madison against the Badgers, who, early in the season, were thought to be the the top team in the Big Ten. Wisconsin eventually finished second to Ohio State. In MAC's game vs. UW, the Aggies frustrated the bigger Badgers by limiting them to a 6-0 lead after three quarters before falling, 27-0.
- For the first time, newspaper accounts report two complete eleven-man units being used in several games —not offense and defense, but rather first team and second team.

1921

THE STAFF

1921 Coaching staff: Albert Barron, head coach (above); Chester Brewer, coach; Dick Rauch, line.

THE TEAM

1921 Aggie football team. See pages 309-321 for player identification.

AGGIE ITEM

This 1921 photo shows the grandstand at Old College Field, located approximately where the third base line is at Kobs Field. On the left side, behind the bleachers, you can see Women's Gymnasium in the background, which was built four years earlier in 1917.

GREEN & WHITE HIGHLIGHTS

- ALBERT BARRON was chosen to replace "Potsy" Clark. A deal with Notre Dame's Knute Rockne fell through, so Barron became MAC's ninth man to coach an Aggie football team. He had lettered at Penn State in 1910, '13 and '14.
- Interestingly, Rockne's three-year deal with MAC called for the Irish coach to receive $4,500 the first season with a $500 increase each of the next two years. After Notre Dame offered Rockne a contract, he asked to be let out of the MAC agreement and went on to fame as coach of the Irish, compiling a record of 105 victories, 12 losses and five ties. During his tenure, Notre Dame won six national championships and produced 20 first-team All-Americans. Rockne died in a plane crash on March 31, 1931.

1922

THE SCORES

33	Alma*	0
7	Albion*	7
0	Wabash	26
7	South Dakota*	0
6	Indiana	14
0	Michigan	63
6	Ohio Wesleyan*	9
0	Creighton	9
45	Mass. State*	0
7	St. Louis	7
	3-5-2	

THE STAFF

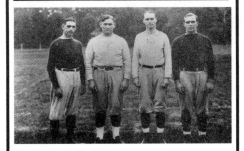

1922 Coaching staff, lt. to rt.: Blake Miller, ass't.; Fred Walker, ass't./ freshman; Albert Barron, head coach; Dick Rauch, line.

THE TEAM

1922 Aggie football team. See pages 309-321 for player identification.

AGGIE SALUTE

LYMAN FRIMODIG was promoted to Business Office Manager. In 1917, Frimodig became State's first athlete to win 10 varsity letters. He won four each in basketball and baseball and two in football, and he turned down a Notre Dame baseball offer to come to MAC. Frimodig died in 1972—he was inducted into the Michigan Sports Hall of Fame in 1976 and was a member of the Charter Class of MSU's Athletics Hall of Fame in 1992.

GREEN & WHITE HIGHLIGHTS

- BARRON's second and final team compiled a 3-5-2 record.

- BLAKE MILLER served as an assistant coach while also playing professional football.

- The band started the tradition of raising the American flag and playing the National Anthem as part of the pre-game ceremony.

RALPH YOUNG
(1923-27)

An outstanding player for both Fielding Yost at Michigan and Amos Alonzo Stagg at Chicago, the roly-poly Ralph Young coached MAC and MSC with only moderate success. However, he brought stability to a program that badly needed it, laying the foundation on which the school's athletic structure grew. The only time MAC nearly surprised powerful Michigan was in its stadium dedication game of 1924, losing 7-0. Young, who also was a fine track and field coach, is best known for his success as State's athletic director, 1923-54. He died in 1962 at the age of 72.

Career Record: 18-22-1

1923

THE TEAM

1923 Aggie football team. See pages 309-321 for player identification.

THE SCORES

0	Chicago	34
21	Lake Forest*	6
0	Wisconsin	21
13	Albion*	0
0	Michigan	37
14	Ohio Wesleyan*	19
7	Creighton*	27
2	Detroit	0

3-5-0

Aggie Moment

Game action from MAC's season-opening contest at the powerful University of Chicago which turned in a 7-1 record, 5-1 in the Western Conference (Big Ten). (MAC tackles UC's Zorn.)

AGGIE ITEM

Football moved from Old College Field to the new football stadium with a capacity of 14,000. MAC defeated Lake Forest (IL), 21-6, in the first game in the new stadium before a crowd estimated at nearly 7,000. The new stadium was built at a cost of $160,000. Temporary bleachers behind each end zone could raise the capacity to over 20,000. This drawing shows the track that originally encircled the football field. It also shows the fencing that surrounded the stadium and the two ticket booths at the gate entrance on the north end of the stadium where today's tunnel is located.

GENERAL INFORMATION

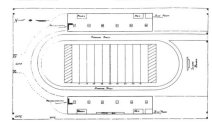

EACH spectator is requested to hold his own ticket when approaching and entering gate and portal.

Men's and women's rest rooms are located underneath the stands.

Spectators are requested to keep off the playing field after the game. Exit from the stadium can be made more quickly from the gates at the front and side.

Concession booths are located at the north entrance of each stand.

GREEN & WHITE HIGHLIGHTS

- MAC battled competitively for three quarters a Michigan team that would go undefeated (8-0).
- Former MAC coach GEORGE GAUTHIER was head coach at Ohio Wesleyan, which beat MAC, 19-14.
- 16 mm. movies of the MAC -Michigan game were taken by EVERETT N. HUBY. This is the first movie made of intercollegiate football in the U.S. as far as it is known.
- WKAR's radio broadcast of that same game from the stadium also is believed to be the first on-site broadcast of an intercollegiate football contest in the U.S.

1924

THE SCORES

59	North Central*	0
54	Olivet*	3
0	Michigan*	7
34	Chicago YMCA*	3
9	Northwestern	13
42	Lake Forest*	13
3	St. Louis	9
9	South Dakota State*	0

5-3-0

Aggie Moment

MAC's ROBINSON gains 21 yards on a pass play from BECKLEY in the Michigan game.

THE TEAM

1924 Aggie football team. See pages 309-321 for player identification.

AGGIE ITEM

MAC's new stadium is viewed from this 1924 aerial photo of the dedication game versus defending Big Ten (Western Conference) co-champion Michigan, which came to East Lansing for the first time in ten years. The photo shows the sellout crowd of some 22,000 in attendance, including those in temporary bleachers used for the game. In a tremendous struggle, the score was 0-0 at halftime and was still scoreless after three quarters. With less than three minutes to go, Michigan scored on a 47-yard pass play to its captain, Herb Steger, to win, 7-0. Between 1924 and 1935, the field was referred to as "College Field" and "College Stadium" and, after 1926, "Spartan Stadium." It would be officially named Macklin Field in 1935.

GREEN & WHITE HIGHLIGHTS

- COACH YOUNG'S second team was his most successful one, shaping a 5-3 campaign on the strength of a staunch defense which allowed an average of only six points per game. The only losses were close games with St. Louis and Big Ten schools Michigan and Northwestern.
- Macklin Field was first dedicated. Its seating capacity was 14,000.
- ELTON NELLER, playing in his final game, not only gained more than 200 yards from scrimmage, but also intercepted two passes and drop-kicked a 53-yard field goal in a 9-0 win over previously undefeated Northern Conference champion North Dakota State.
- Halfback VERN SCHMYSER scored four touchdowns in the season-opening 59-0 romp over North Central College.

1925

THE SCORES

16	Adrian*	0
0	Michigan	39
0	Lake Forest*	6
15	Centre*	13
6	Penn State	13
0	Colgate*	14
58	Toledo*	0
10	Wisconsin	21

3-5-0

THE STAFF

1925 Coaching staff: Ralph Young, head coach; John Taylor, ass't.

THE TEAM

1925 Aggie football team. See pages 309-321 for player identification.

AGGIE ITEM

Sophomore halfback PAUL SMITH (far right) kicked a 48-yard field goal with three minutes to play to give State a 15-13 victory over Centre, the 1924 champions of the South.

GREEN & WHITE HIGHLIGHTS

- MAC was renamed "Michigan State College."

- In MSC's season opener with Adrian, the Aggies won 16-0, and outgained Adrian in total offense, 379 yards to 49.

- In most games, the heaviest player on the field was 200-210 pounds.

- MSC came the closest of any Michigan opponent to scoring a touchdown during the 1925 season. QB LES FOUTS ran 78 yards to the Michigan 4-yard line only to be tackled by All-America end Bennie Oosterbann.

THE TEAM

1926 Spartan football team. See pages 309-321 for player identification.

THE SCORES

16	Adrian*	0
9	Kalamazoo*	0
3	Michigan	55
14	Cornell University	24
0	Lake Forest*	0
6	Colgate	38
42	Centre*	14
7	Haskell Inst.*	40

3-4-1

THE STAFF

1926 Coaching staff, lt. to rt.: Miles Casteel; Ralph Young, head coach; Bernard Traynor.

SPARTAN ITEM

On April 2, MSC athletic teams were given the name of Spartans by GEORGE S. ALDERTON, sports editor of the *Lansing State Journal*. The college had sponsored a contest to select a nickname to replace "Aggies" and had picked "The Michigan Staters." Alderton decided the name was too cumbersome for newspaper writing. After sorting through the entries that still remained from the contest, he selected the entry of "Spartans." Then, rewriting game accounts from the baseball team's first southern training trip (supplied by gridder Perry Fremont, a catcher on the squad), Alderton first used the name sparingly and then ventured into the headlines with it. As Mr. Alderton explained: "Happily for the experiment, the name took. It began appearing in other newspapers and when the student publication used it, that clinched it."

GREEN & WHITE HIGHLIGHTS

- Captain MARTIN RUMMEL was injured in an automobile accident in the summer of 1926 and lost to the team for the entire season. "RUDY" BOEHRINGER was chosen as "Acting Captain" to replace Rummel, who did not miss a single practice during the season.

- State's 28-point triumph over Centre was, at the time, the largest margin of defeat suffered by a Centre team in that school's history.

- MSC closed the season versus Haskell Indian Institute (Lawrence, Kansas), a nationally renowned team, comprised of many players with professional experience.

1927

M.S.C.

THE SCORES

12	Kalamazoo*	6
27	Ohio University*	0
0	Michigan	21
13	Cornell, Iowa	19
7	Detroit*	24
7	Indiana	33
20	Albion*	6
25	Butler*	0
0	North Carolina State	19

4-5-0

THE STAFF

1927 Coaching staff, lt. to rt.: Ralph Young, head coach; Ralph Henning; Leon Exelby; Bernard Traynor, ass't. coach; Herb Straight; Miles Casteel, ass't. coach. Several times during the season, former star players were invited back by coach Young. For several days prior to the Homecoming game with the University of Detroit, Herb Straight, Leon Exelby and Ralph Henning—all stars of a decade or so earlier—aided in preparing the team for the game.

THE TEAM

1927 Spartan football team. See pages 309-321 for player identification.

SPARTAN ITEM

MSC had one of the first radio broadcasts in college history. In an effort to bring the action of the games to the fans, MSC nailed a phone booth on the top of the stadium press box, brought a phone line to the booth and broadcast the games over the telephone. The information was called back to the radio station

where the phone was held up to the microphone to go out over the air to the listeners. Many of the home games were broadcast this way on WKAR with JIM HASSELMAN on the press box end of the telephone.

GREEN & WHITE HIGHLIGHTS

- RALPH YOUNG's fifth and final Spartan squad started out 2-0 before finishing with a 4-5 mark.
- The Michigan game was played before a crowd of 37,000 in new Michigan Stadium.
- MSC won its final home game of the season, a 25-0 upset over favored Butler, which was coached by former Aggie mentor "Potsy" Clark.
- BERNARD P. TRAYNOR, football line coach, wrote "MSC Shadows". It officially became the alma mater in 1949.

THE SCORES

103	Kalamazoo*	0
0	Albion*	2
37	Chicago YMCA*	0
0	Colgate*	16
6	Mississippi St.	6
0	Detroit	39
0	Michigan	3
7	North Carolina State*	0

3-4-1

THE STAFF

1928 Coaching staff, lt. to rt.: Miles Casteel, ass't.; Harry Kipke, head coach; Hugh Wilson, ass't.; Ed Vandervoort, ass't. This four-man varsity staff was the largest varsity staff in school history.

THE TEAM

1928 Spartan football team. See pages 309-321 for player identification.

SPARTAN ITEM

Athletic Director Young hired HARRY KIPKE, the great Michigan All-American, in what was hailed as a brilliant move for MSC. Perhaps it would have been, but after just one season (3-4-1), his alma mater hired him as coach of the Wolverines. A Lansing High School Grad, Kipke began his college coaching career with a near-record 103-0 victory over Kalamazoo College. He nearly directed State to an upset of Michigan, which probably enticed U of M to hire him away from MSC. After his coaching career, Kipke was inducted into the National Football Foundation Hall of Fame.

GREEN & WHITE HIGHLIGHTS

- In the rout of Kalamazoo, reserve halfback MAX CRALL scored four touchdowns and kicked five extra points. One of his TDs was an 85-yard dash, the Spartans' longest run of the season.
- In the season finale, MSC defeated North Carolina State, 7-0, on a fourth quarter, 14-yard TD run by fullback FRED DANZIGER.
- At the end of the season, something original occurred in the annals of State gridiron history. VERNE DICKESON and FRED DANZIGER were jointly elected to lead the '29 team (State's first co-captains).

JIM CROWLEY
(1929-32)

Jim Crowley, one of Notre Dame's immortal Four Horsemen, joined Michigan State's staff as its head coach in 1929. His arrival became the catalyst that transformed a mediocre program into a nationally respected major power for the first time since the coaching era of John Macklin. "Sleepy Jim" produced four straight winning seasons for the Spartans. A pair of 0-0 ties against Michigan in 1930 and '31 broke State's 14-game losing streak to the Wolverines, a span which saw UM outscore MSC by a cumulative total 392-9. A night-game loss at Georgetown spoiled the Spartans' otherwise undefeated season in 1930. He was named head coach at Fordham in 1933, becoming the architect of the "Seven Blocks of Granite." Crowley died in 1986 at the age of 83.

Career Record: 22-8-3

1929

M.S.C.

THE SCORES

59	Alma*	6
0	Michigan	17
0	Colgate	31
74	Adrian*	0
40	North Carolina State*	6
38	Case*	0
33	Mississippi State	19
0	Detroit*	25

5-3-0

THE STAFF

1929 Coaching staff, lt. to rt.: Miles "Mike" Casteel, backfield; Jim "Sleepy" Crowley, head coach; Glenn "Judge" Carberry, line & ends. Not pictured: Hugh Wilson, ass't. line

THE TEAM

1929 Spartan football team. See pages 309-321 for player identification.

SPARTAN SALUTE

JIM CROWLEY, one of Notre Dame's immortal Four Horsemen, became head coach in 1929. His arrival was the catalyst that transformed a mediocre program into a nationally respected major power for the first time since the coaching era of John Macklin. "Sleepy Jim" produced four-straight winning seasons for the Spartans, including two campaigns that combined for a record of 12-2-2. A loss to Georgetown spoiled the Spartans' otherwise un-defeated season in 1930, and a loss to Michigan kept MSC from an undefeated year in '32. A pair of 0-0 ties with Michigan in 1930 and '31 broke State's 14-game losing streak to the Wolverines. His MSC career record was a sterling 22-8-3. He passed away in 1986 at the age of 83. This picture of Crowley in his retirement years, shows him with his "Four Horsemen" and Knute Rockne photo on the wall.

GREEN & WHITE HIGHLIGHTS

- State compiled a 5-3 record in CROWLEY's first year, after four consecutive losing seasons.

- The Spartans accumulated 436 yards of offense in a 40-6 Homecoming win over North Carolina State. MAX CRALL raced 71 yards around right end for a touchdown.

- Captain VERN DICKESON scored three TDs in a 33-19 victory at Mississippi State—MSC's first road win in six years.

1930-1939

MICHIGAN STATE UNIVERSITY

SPARTAN FOOTBALL

100 Seasons

MAC - MSC - MSU

1930

THE SCORES

28	Alma*	0
0	Michigan	0
32	Cincinnati*	0
14	Colgate*	7
45	Case*	0
13	Georgetown U.	14
19	North Dakota State*	11
0	Detroit*	0

5-1-2

THE STAFF

1930 Coaching staff: Jim Crowley, head coach; Glenn Carberry, line and ends; Miles Casteel, backfield.

THE TEAM

1930 Spartan football team. See pages 309-321 for player identification.

SPARTAN ITEM

ABE ELIOWITZ, sophomore fullback, plunged onto the scene in a big way with one outstanding game after another. In the 32-0 conquest of Cincinnati, he reeled off the longest run of the day with a 55-yard TD jaunt off tackle. Abe was later enshrined in the Canadian Football Hall of Fame after all-star seasons playing for the Ottawa Roughriders and the Montreal Alouettes.

GREEN & WHITE HIGHLIGHTS

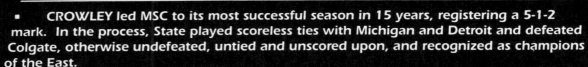

- CROWLEY led MSC to its most successful season in 15 years, registering a 5-1-2 mark. In the process, State played scoreless ties with Michigan and Detroit and defeated Colgate, otherwise undefeated, untied and unscored upon, and recognized as champions of the East.
- A superb defense spun five shutouts in eight games. In all, MSC outscored its opponents, 151 to 32. The 4.0 points allowed per game is the lowest scoring defense per game average in Spartan annals. (The record book does not reflect the results prior to World War II. The teams also played fewer games in the early days.)
- The Spartans overpowered Case, 45-0, in a game that witnessed six long TD runs that averaged 57 yards in length.

Spartan Moments

It was just minutes before kickoff of the Michigan game. State had lost its center (and captain-elect for 1930), HAROLD SMEAD, a strapping all-stater from Sturgis, through a tragic motorcycle accident during the summer. One leg had to be amputated. Into the State dressing room came Smead in a wheelchair. His attendant moved him among the squad as the players shook his hand. Emotions soared. The Spartans fought the highly favored Wolverines to a scoreless tie.

Spartan List

MSU's All-Time Old-Timers Team
(selected in 1969-70 Homecoming game program, Alumni Magazine and MSU State News voting)

Ends	Ed Klewicki	1934
	Blake Miller	1915
Linemen	Sid Wagner	1935
	Hugh Blacklock	1916
	Frank Butler	1933
	Gideon Smith	1915
	Lyle Rockenbach	1939
Backs	John Pingel	1938
	Bob Monnett	1932
	Carp Julian	1914
	Neno	
	Jerry DaPrato	1915

SPARTAN SALUTE

BOB MONNETT, sophomore halfback, stepped into the spotlight in the final two minutes of the Colgate game. With the score tied, 7-7, he carried to the left and picked his way through a hole in Colgate's right side, and dodged his way 62 yards for the winning touchdown. It was the first time State had defeated one of the nation's prominent teams since beating Notre Dame 12 years earlier. The next week, against Case, he scored on runs of 41 and 55 yards. In the 19-11 North Dakota State win, Monnett was the outstanding player of the game. He intercepted three NDS passes and returned one 65 yards for a touchdown that regained the lead for MSC, 12-11. Monnett would later be honorable mention All-America as the second highest scorer in the nation in his junior and senior seasons. He would play for Green Bay from 1933-38 and be inducted into the NFL Packers' Hall of Fame in 1973.

★ MSC ALL-STARS ★

Roger Grove

Cecil Fogg

THE TEAM

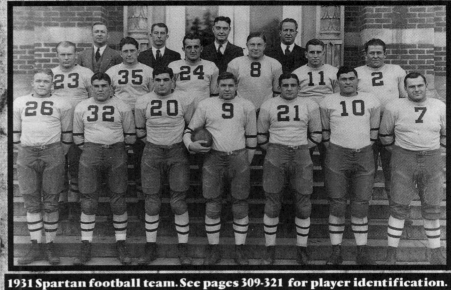

1931 Spartan football team. See pages 309-321 for player identification.

THE SCORES

74	Alma*	0
47	Cornell, Iowa*	0
7	Army	20
34	Illinois Wesleyan*	6
6	Georgetown U.*	0
10	Syracuse*	15
100	Ripon*	0
0	Michigan	0
13	Detroit	20

5-3-1

Spartan Moment

Game action from State's 74-0 season-opening warmup over Alma. Later in the season, the Spartans would score nearly at will in a near-record 100-0 domination of Ripon College.

SPARTAN ITEM

The new "wig-wag" system of official hand signals was introduced in 1931 to help the fans to follow the game more intelligibly and enjoy it more fully by understanding the penalty calls made on the field.

GREEN & WHITE HIGHLIGHTS

- State turned in a 5-3-1 slate, including five more defensive shutouts —a total of ten in the last two seasons! The Spartans outscored their nine opponents, 291-61.
- State played Michigan to a scoreless tie for the second straight year.
- In the Cornell College (Iowa) romp, MVP ELIOWITZ was credited with a 103-yard TD run (kick return).
- MSC lost at Army, a team that had never been defeated at Michie Field. BOB MONNETT carried 63 yards for a TD that brought the Spartans to within 13-7 in the third quarter before finally dropping a 20-7 decision.

THE SCORES

93	Alma*	0
0	Michigan	26
27	Grinnell*	6
27	Illinois Wesleyan*	0
19	Fordham	13
27	Syracuse	13
20	South Dakota*	6
7	Detroit*	0

7-1-0

THE STAFF

1932 Coaching staff, lt. to rt.: Miles Casteel, ass't.; Jim Crowley, head coach; Glenn Carberry, ass't.; Frank Leahy, ass't.

THE TEAM

1932 Spartan football team. See pages 309-321 for player identification.

SPARTAN SALUTE

In 1930 when State lost at Georgetown, Crowley was so impressed by a young Georgetown assistant, he later persuaded him to come to East Lansing as one of Crowley's assistants. That is how FRANK LEAHY came to State. Leahy, of course, would go on to Notre Dame and become one of its legendary coaches. Leahy won 85% of his games, including six undefeated seasons and five national championships, plus an unbeaten streak of 39 games in the late 1940s. His record was 87-11-9 in 11 seasons.

GREEN & WHITE HIGHLIGHTS

- CROWLEY led State to one of the school's greatest seasons, which resulted in a widespread reputation of the Michigan State program —particularly in the influential eastern part of the country. Included in the 7-1 record were consecutive road wins at Fordham and Syracuse.
- In the 93-0 season-opening massacre of Alma, center/linebacker FRANK BUTLER intercepted an Alma pass and returned it for a touchdown. According to RALPH YOUNG, this was the first time at MSC that a linebacker had returned an interception for a score.
- Halfback BOB MONNETT ran 80 yards for a TD on the first play of the Fordham game as State upset Fordham, 19-13. MCNUTT added a 63-yard run vs. Fordham. State solidified the victory by intercepting five of the Rams' 18 pass attempts!
- State rolled up 504 yards of total offense in the 20-6 Homecoming win over South Dakota.
- State's first win since 1923 (four losses and a tie in the previous five games)over the strong Detroit team and first victory over a Detroit squad since Gus Dorais had been the Titans' head coach. Some 10,000 spectators attended the game at MSC.

CHARLES BACHMAN
(1933-46)

Charlie Bachman, another Notre Dame alumnus, succeeded Jim Crowley as head football coach at Michigan State, coming to East Lansing after a successful stint at Florida. A teammate of Knute Rockne, Bachman employed the Notre Dame system and forged 10 winning seasons in 13 years. During his second season with the Spartans in 1934, he led State to an 8-1 record, which included a 16-0 victory over Michigan, the school's first since 1915. That marked the first of four straight wins over UM. MSC posted another 8-1 regular-season record in 1937 and received the school's first bid to a postseason bowl game, the 1938 Orange Bowl. Among Bachman's greatest Spartan players were guard Sid Wagner, State's first All-American since 1915, halfback John Pingel and fullback Jack Breslin. Bachman died in 1985 at the age of 93.

Career Record: 70-34-10

THE SCORES

14	Grinnell*	0
6	Michigan	20
20	Illinois Wesleyan*	12
6	Marquette	0
27	Syracuse*	3
0	Kansas State*	0
0	Carnegie Tech*	0
0	Detroit	14

4-2-2

THE STAFF

1933 Coaching staff, lt. to rt.: Tom King, ass't.; Charlie Bachman, head coach; Miles Casteel, ass't.

THE TEAM

1933 Spartan football team. See pages 309-321 for player identification.

SPARTAN ITEM

RUSSELL LAY, a letterman in 1932 and 1933, was the first of many Spartans to play for the Detroit Lions. He performed on the Lions' first squad in 1934. Some other noteworthy names to have played for the Lions include ED KLEWICKI (1935-38), SID WAGNER (1936-38), JOHN PINGEL (1939), DORNE DIBBLE (1951 & 1953-57), EARL MORRALL (1958-64), JIM NINOWSKI (1960-61), SAM WILLIAMS (1960-65) and JERRY RUSH (1965-71).

GREEN & WHITE HIGHLIGHTS

- BACHMAN'S first team went 4-2-2 against one of the most difficult schedules to date, including highly touted Syracuse, eventual Big Ten and national champion Michigan, rugged Marquette, and powerful Kansas State and Carnegie Tech. The home opener with Grinnell College was witnessed by a record crowd of some 12,000.
- State lost to Michigan, 20-6, but scored its first TD vs. a Wolverine team since 1918. A MUTH-to-WARMBEIN pass culminated an 86-yard drive in the second half.
- A large share of the success was due to four sophomores: halfback KURT WARMBEIN, tackle SID WAGNER, halfback DICK COLINA and fullback CHUCK BROWN.
- WARMBEIN's 70-yard TD run vs. Syracuse was the Spartans' longest run of the season. He averaged 21 yards in six carries against the Orangemen.

S

Spartan Moments

State lost to Michigan, 20-6, but scored its first TD vs. a Wolverine team since 1918. A CHUCK MUTH-to-KURT WARMBEIN pass culminated an 86-yard drive in the second half. Muth, a versatile and talented athlete, later became a top professional bowler in Kalamazoo, Michigan.

Spartan List

State's 10 Scoreless Ties

1. 1896 vs. Alma
2. 1906 vs. Alma
3. 1907 vs. Alma
4. 1908 vs. Michigan
5. 1908 vs. DePaul
6. 1926 vs. Lake Forest
7. 1933 vs. Kansas State
8. 1933 vs. Carnegie Tech
9. 1940 vs. Santa Clara
10. 1941 vs. Purdue

SPARTAN SALUTE

CHARLES BACHMAN, another Notre Dame alumnus, succeeded Jim Crowley as head football coach, coming to East Lansing after a successful stint at the University of Florida. Bachman had been an All-Western guard in 1914 and 1916, and an all-service center on the Great Lakes National championship football team in 1918. He was a six-letter man in football and track and held the world record in discus throwing in his last year in college. A teammate of Knute Rockne, Bachman employed the Notre Dame system and forged 10 winning seasons in 13 years. Jim Crowley had put MSC on the road to big time football and started the program moving down that road —Bachman's teams rode into higher country! His Michigan State career record was 70-34-10. He beat Michigan four times in succession and took the school to its first bowl game—the 1938 Orange Bowl. Bachman died in 1985 at the age of 93.

★ MSC ALL-STARS ★

BERNARD MCNUTT, '33 captain and three-year backfield performer, was a crowd favorite.

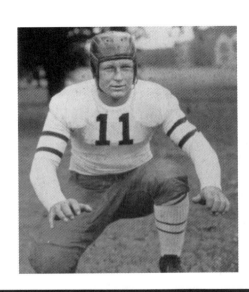

ART BUSS, MVP tackle, then divided four years between the NFL Chicago Bears and the Philadelphia Eagles. He became the first Spartan to block a Michigan punt.

1934

THE SCORES

33	Grinnell*	20
16	Michigan	0
13	Carnegie Tech*	0
39	Manhattan	0
13	Marquette*	7
0	Syracuse	10
7	Detroit*	6
6	Kansas	0
26	Texas A&M	13

8-1-0

THE STAFF

1934 Coaching staff, lt. to rt.: Miles Casteel, backfield; Henry Johnson, ass't. coach; Charlie Bachman, head coach; Tom King, line and ends.

THE TEAM

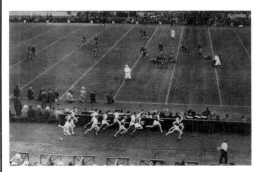

1934 Spartan football team. See pages 309-321 for player identification.

SPARTAN ITEM

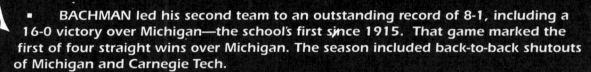

MSC held a cross country meet on November 3, 1934, which started and ended on the track at the stadium. The meet was supposed to end at halftime of the MSC-Marquette football game, but when the first half lasted a bit longer than expected, the runners entered the stadium and completed the race during the first-half action.

GREEN & WHITE HIGHLIGHTS

- BACHMAN led his second team to an outstanding record of 8-1, including a 16-0 victory over Michigan—the school's first since 1915. That game marked the first of four straight wins over Michigan. The season included back-to-back shutouts of Michigan and Carnegie Tech.

- The '34 team ended the season at Texas A&M (26-13 victory). The train trip was two days each way and the itinerary covered Wednesday, December 5 through Tuesday morning, December 12.

S Spartan Moments

Junior halfback DICK COLINA (40) totes the ball during the 13-0 win over Carnegie Tech.

Action from the 16-0 upset of Michigan in 1934. ED KLEWICKI (23) carries for a gain of 25 yards after receiving a pass from halfback KURT WARMBEIN. Notice the uniforms: Bachman changed to black and gold and for the Michigan game, had white tape sewn onto the State jerseys on the shoulders and around the mid-section.

Spartan List

State's Top Total Letterwinners Who Played Football

1.	Lyman Frimodig	10	1924-17
2.	Bob Carey	9	1949-52
	Ion Cortright	9	1907-11
	Parnell McKenna	9	1906-10
	Wilson Millar	9	1902-04
	Blake Miller	9	1912-15
	Walter Small	9	1903-08
	Fred Ziegel	9	1933-36
9.	Arthur Campbell	8	1906-10
	John Hammes	8	1917-20
	Irving Snider	8	1917-20

SPARTAN SALUTE

ED KLEWICKI was a star end for State from 1932 through '34. He was the team MVP in 1934 when he caught 25 passes, including several in the 16-0 win over Michigan. The Hamtramck native was called by then-coach Charlie Bachman "the greatest all-around end I ever coached." Klewicki played with the Detriot Lions for four seasons and was a member of the 1935 World Championship team.

★MSC ALL-STARS★

All-Star fullback Richard Colina.

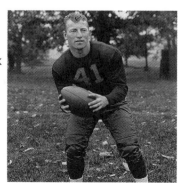

All-Star halfback Steve Sebo.

1935

M.S.C.

THE SCORES

41	Grinnell*	0
25	Michigan	6
42	Kansas*	0
6	Boston College	18
47	Wash. (St. L.)*	13
12	Temple	7
7	Marquette*	13
27	Loyola (Cal.)	0

6-2-0

THE TEAM

1935 Spartan football team. See pages 309-321 for player identification.

THE STAFF

1935 Coaching staff, l. to r.: Henry Johnson, Miles Kasteel, head coach Charlie Bachman, Tom King, and Bob Terlaak.

SPARTAN ITEM

State's offensive line: lt. to rt., left end LOU ZARZA, left tackle HOWARD ZINDEL, left guard GORDON DAHLGREN, center JOE BUZOLITS, right guard SID WAGNER, right tackle JULIUS SLEDER, right end BOB ALLMAN.

GREEN & WHITE HIGHLIGHTS

- Big plays were the key for State in the second straight win over Michigan, 25-6. DICK COLINA—who also scored on a pass from WARMBEIN — returned a punt 60 yards for a score, and AL AGETT registered a 46-yard TD jaunt.
- The football stadium was officially dedicated as Macklin Field in honor of JOHN FARRELL MACKLIN, Philadelphia industrialist who for five years (1911-15) coached MAC to an outstanding combined record of 29-5.
- *Chicago Tribune* Sports Editor Arch Ward promoted the annual All-Star game in Chicago. Through nationwide balloting, Bachman was chosen as the #1 assistant to Frank Thomas of Alabama who had just won the Rose Bowl. State's ED KLEWICKI and RUSS REYNOLDS played for the college all-stars, who lost to the Chicago Bears, 5-0.

S
Spartan Moments

Halfback AL AGETT gains yardage in State's 42-0 conquest of Kansas. Other identifiable Spartans are quarterback FRED ZIEGEL (42) and end FRANK GAINES (28).

Spartan List

Top Ten Tackles in a Single Game

1. Dan Bass	Ohio State, 1979	32
2. Don Law	Ohio State, 1969	28
3. Dan Bass	Notre Dame, 1979	24
4. Percy Snow	Illinois, 1989	23
Sid Wagner	Boston Col., 1935	23
6. Ty Hallock	Minnesota, 1992	21
Shane Bullough	Indiana, 1985	21
Brad VanPelt	Notre Dame, 1971	21
Doug Barr	Ohio State, 1969	21
Don Law	Indiana, 1967	21

SPARTAN SALUTE

The Macklin Stadium dedication honored JOHN MACKLIN, MAC's coach from 1911-15, compiling a remarkable record of 29 wins versus just 5 losses. MSC President R.S. Shaw stated that Macklin "achieved football victories over...noted competitors and focused the attention of the nation on M.A.C. ...He brought to us an answer to the defeatist who said, 'It cannot be done.' I believe the name 'Macklin Field' will be an inspiration which will help State teams in all future games."

★MSC ALL-STARS★

SID WAGNER, MVP, became State's first All-American since 1915. He was a superb blocker and a sure tackler. In the 16-6 loss to Boston College, Wagner was credited with 23 tackles by the United Press. He was selected All-America guard by United Press, Associated Press, *New York Sun* and *Liberty Magazine*.

1936

M.S.C.

THE SCORES

27	Wayne State*	0
21	Michigan	7
7	Carnegie Tech	0
13	Missouri*	0
7	Marquette*	13
13	Boston College	13
7	Temple	7
41	Kansas	0
7	Arizona*	0

6-1-2

THE TEAM

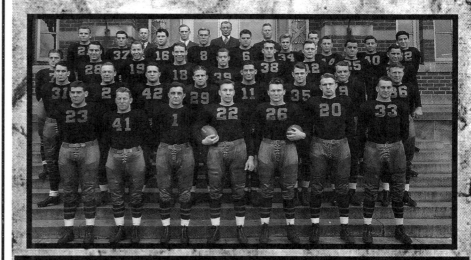

1936 Spartan football team. See pages 309-321 for player identification.

THE STAFF

1936 Coaching staff: Charlie Bachman (top left), Tom King (top right), Miles Casteel (bottom left), and Bob Terlaak.

SPARTAN ITEM

FRED ZIEGEL is the only man in Michigan State history to letter for three seasons in football, baseball and swimming. George Alderton, the late Lansing State Journal Sports Editor, called Zeigel, a graduate of Detroit Northwestern High, "the most versatile athlete ever for the Spartans." He earned a total of nine letters during 1934-35-36.

GREEN & WHITE HIGHLIGHTS

- State recorded a 6-1-2 mark, defeating Michigan for the third straight year and losing only to Marquette and tying Boston College and Temple. The Spartans shut out five opponents.

- In the 21-7 defeat of Michigan, AL AGETT notched an 82-yard touchdown run near the end of the third quarter to add to a 14-7 lead.

- The stadium capacity was increased to 26,000 by lowering the field level and adding 12 rows of seats all the way around the field on what had been the running track.

S Spartan Moments

State defeated Michigan for the third straight year. This time the Spartans knocked off the Wolverines, 21-7, in Ann Arbor. Here, Steve Sebo carries in the triumph over U of M in the second game of the season.

Spartan List

Top 10 Moments in Spartan Gridiron History

1. '74 Levi Jackson's 88-yard TD run—OSU
2. '55 Dave Kaiser's '56 Rose Bowl-winning field goal vs. UCLA
3. '54 Rose Bowl Ellis Duckett's blocked punt and TD
4. '51 Dick Panin's 88-yard TD run on the game's second play —ND
5. '51 Transcontinental pass from Tom Yewcic to Al Dorow to beat Ohio State
6. '32 Bob Monnett's 80-yard TD run on the first play in upset of Fordham
7. '84 Bobby Morse's punt return for TD vs. Michigan
8. '36 Al Agett's 82-yard TD run to clinch Michigan win
9. '49 Lynn Chandnois' 90-yard TD run vs. Arizona —still the record
10. '87 John Langeloh's game-winning '88 Rose Bowl-winning field goal vs USC.

SPARTAN SALUTE

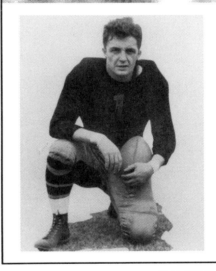

The Spartans' MVP was "iron man" SAMMY KETCHMAN (1, Battle Creek Central) who played 328 minutes as one of the few players to star on both the varsity and junior varsity teams. Ketchman later coached at Wayne State and Ferris.

★ MSC ALL-STARS ★

ART BRANDSTATTER (right) (Sr., Ecorse) was named All-America at his fullback position. He was a bruising runner on the 1934-36 teams which compiled a won-lost-tied record of 20-4-2 and beat Michigan every time. Among his awards since graduation are the Jack Breslin Lifetime Achievement Award and induction into MSU's Athletic Hall of Fame.

"AGONY" AL AGETT (below) (Kingsport, Tenn.) was MSC's triple-threat halfback of the day. He played a major role in the College All-Stars' 6-0 upset of the 1937 Green Bay Packers. Agett ran with the ball as an offensive back, punted well and intercepted a pass against Curly Lambeau's World Champions.

OTHER AWARD WINNERS

SAM KETCHMAN, MVP

1937

M.S.C.

THE SCORES

19	Wayne State*	0
19	Michigan	14
0	Manhattan	3
2	Missouri	0
21	Marquette*	7
16	Kansas*	0
13	Temple	6
13	Carnegie Tech*	6
14	San Francisco	0
	Orange Bowl	
0	Auburn	6
	8-2-0	

THE STAFF

1937 Coaching staff, lt. to rt.: Al Agett, Miles Casteel, Tom King, Charlie Bachman, Henry Johnson, Bob Terlaak.

THE TEAM

1937 Spartan football team. See pages 309-321 for player identification.

Spartan Moments

The Spartans return from San Francisco after the regular season finale—a 14-0 victory. Pictured is the crowd that assembled at the Lansing train station to greet the team upon its arrival.

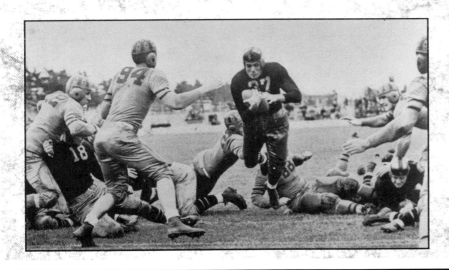

Here JOHN PINGEL shows his stuff during the 1937 season, when he was named second-team All-America and led MSC to its first bowl game—the 1938 Orange Bowl.

GREEN & WHITE HIGHLIGHTS

- MSC posted another 8-1 regular season record and received the school's first bid to a post-season bowl game, the 1938 Orange Bowl (lost, 6-0, to Auburn).
- State beat Michigan for the fourth straight year and, in week #7, handed Temple its first loss of the season, 13-6. State blanked four opponents and only Michigan reached double figures in scoring during the Spartans' 19-14 victory in front of an opening-day crowd of 71,800 in Ann Arbor. That win marked the first time Michigan had lost four in a row to any opponent since the turn of the century!
- OLE NELSON ranked 8th in national pass receiving stats provided by the American Football Statistical Bureau. MSC was rated #2 in total team performance behind only Pitt.
- Sensational junior JOHN PINGEL (Mt. Clemens) earned All-Midwest laurels and second team All-America laurels, and was singled out as the country's best punter!
- Through BACHMAN's first five years, State posted a record of 32-8-4 (.772).

63

1937 All-Stars (clockwise from top left): Senior tackle HOWARD SWARTZ, senior guard WALT LUECK, junior halfback STEVE SZASZ, senior end FRANK GAINES, and junior halfback GENE CIOLEK.

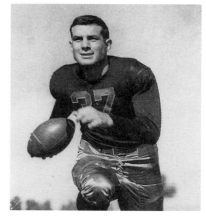

Junior standout JOHN PINGEL had many memorable games. In the 1937 regular season finale at San Francisco, he accounted for both of the game's TDs in a 14-0 victory. Pingel scored on TD scampers of 75 and 66 yards.

OTHER AWARD WINNERS

HARRY SPEELMAN, tackle, MVP

Spartan List

Top 10 Career Punting Average

Greg Montgomery,
1985-86-87 .... 45.2

Ralf Mojsiejenko,
1981-82-83-84 .... 43.8

Ray Stachowicz,
1977-78-79-80 .... 43.3

John Pingel, 1937-38 ...... 42.1

Josh Butland, 1988-89-90-91 ...... 40.7

Bill Simpson, 1971-72-73 .... 39.8

Earl Morrall, 1953-54-55 .... 39.2

Lou Bobich, 1962-63-64 .... 39.0

Tom Yewcic, 1951-52-53 .... 38.7

Tom Birney, 1974-75-76 .... 37.8

SPARTAN SALUTE

HARRY SPEELMAN, Lansing senior, earned the distinction of a "triple honor" in 1937. He was the team captain, the president of the Varsity Club and was awarded the Most Valuable Player award. Speelman anchored a Michigan State defensive unit which allowed Auburn only six points in the 1938 Orange Bowl. Captain Speelman and his teammates were brilliant throughout the '37 campaign, allowing an average of only four points per game en route to an 8-1 regular season.

1938 Orange Bowl (January 1, Miami, FL): Leading 6-0, Auburn back George Kenmore tries to advance against the Michigan State defense in the third quarter. His progress is stopped by (lt to rt.) tackler HELGE PEARSON (22), guard NORM OLMAN (16), and a diving FRED SCHROEDER (12, tackle).

Key starters in the 1938 Orange Bowl, lt.to. rt.: Usif Haney, John Pingel, Al Diebold, Dave Diehl, and Steve Szasz.

THE SCORES

34	Wayne State*	6
0	Michigan	14
18	Illinois Wesleyan*	0
26	West Virginia	0
19	Syracuse*	12
6	Santa Clara*	7
0	Missouri	6
20	Marquette	14
10	Temple*	0

6-3-0

THE STAFF

1938 Coaching staff, lt. to rt.: Myron Vandermere, ass't.; Tom King, ends; Richard Colina, reserves; Miles Casteel, backs. Not pictured: Gordon Dahlgren, line.

THE TEAM

1938 Spartan football team. See pages 309-321 for player identification.

SPARTAN ITEM

ED PEARCE lettered for State from 1937-39. The 5-foot-7, 167-pound halfback from Flint Northern was considered State's best defensive back. He seemed to always play in the shadow of a teammate. As a prep, he yielded stardom to Fred Trosko, who went on to star at Michigan. At MSC, he played beside All-American Johnny Pingel. During his three years, the Spartans compiled a record of 18-9-1.

GREEN & WHITE HIGHLIGHTS

- State fought to a 6-3 season record, including a 20-14 Homecoming victory over Marquette in front of a crowd of 10,000.

- BACHMAN started the second team versus Illinois Wesleyan.

- State's black and gold jerseys were the reason the team was referred to as the "Black Knights of the Red Cedar."

- Halfback and punter JOHN PINGEL became State's fourth All-American.

S
Spartan Moments

Santa Clara captains came to MSC sideline to shake the hand of GENE CIOLEK (Michigan City, IN) who was in a wheelchair after fracturing a vertebra in the West Virginia game.

Spartan List

Top 10 Single-Season Leaders in Total Punts

John Pingel, 1938	99
Ralf Mojsiejenko, 1982	77
Ralf Mojsiejenko, 1984	76
Greg Montgomery, 1985	75
Ralf Mojsiejenko, 1983	74
Josh Butland, 1991	73
Bill Simpson, 1972	73
Ray Stachowicz, 1980	71
Greg Montgomery, 1987	70
Bill Simpson, 1973	67

SPARTAN SALUTE

Junior guard LYLE ROCKENBACH (5-9, 184) was to become the captain and team MVP in 1939. "Rocky" played his high school ball for Crystal Lake (Illinois). At the suggestion of Jim Van Zylen, a former Spartan star, he entered State in 1936 and became a guard because of his speed and aggressiveness. The Associated Press accorded him honorable mention All-America honors.

★ MSC ALL-STARS ★

State's fourth All-American, MVP JOHN PINGEL did it all: he completed 54 of 101 passes for 571 yards and seven TDs, rushed the ball 110 times for 556 yards and five more TDs (5.0 avg.); and punted 99 times for a 41.8 yard average. Pingel's 1938 season is one of State's all-around great performances. In the 20-14 victory over Marquette, Pingel threw three TD passes to HANEY, KINEK and AMON to win the game.

1939

THE TEAM

1939 Spartan football team. See pages 309-321 for player identification.

THE SCORES

16	Wayne State*	0
13	Michigan	26
14	Marquette*	17
7	Purdue	20
13	Illinois Wesleyan*	6
14	Syracuse	3
0	Santa Clara	6
7	Indiana*	7
18	Temple*	7

4-4-1

THE STAFF

1939 Coaching staff, front, lt. to rt.: Joe Holsinger, backfield; Charlie Bachman, head coach; Tom King, line; Back row, Gordon Dahlgren, ass't. line, Al Agett, ass't.

SPARTAN SALUTE

The senior captain of the Syracuse team that the Spartans played in 1939 was a guard by the name of HUGH DUFFY DAUGHERTY. In spite of Duffy's efforts, the Spartans won a 14-3 battle on the way to a 4-4-1 season. Daugherty, of course, would come to State as an assistant to coach to "Biggie" Munn and eventually would be the long-time, successful head coach with the most wins ever in Spartan gridiron history.

GREEN & WHITE HIGHLIGHTS

- State turned in a 4-4-1 season, including wins over Syracuse and Temple.
- The colorful Spartans had four different sets of jerseys to wear: green, white, black and red. And the freshmen wore blue.
- State lost the Michigan game, 26-13 in Ann Arbor, as two high profile Wolverines did most of the damage. Tom Harmon scored one TD and threw two perfect TD passes to Forest Evashevski for two more scores.
- In the season finale versus Temple, MIKE SCHELB rushed for 180 yards, the most of any Spartan back in 1939.

1940-1949

MICHIGAN STATE UNIVERSITY
SPARTAN FOOTBALL
100 Seasons
MAC - MSC - MSU

1940

THE SCORES

14	Michigan	21
20	Purdue*	7
19	Temple	21
0	Santa Clara*	0
32	Kansas State*	0
0	Indiana	20
6	Marquette	7
17	West Virginia*	0

3-4-1

THE STAFF

1940 Coaching staff, lt. to rt.: Gordon Dahlgren, ass't. line; J. Budinski; Al Kircher, ass't. line; Charlie Bachman, head coach; Tom King, ends; Don Rossi, ass't. backfield; Joe Holsinger, backfield.

THE TEAM

1940 Spartan football team. See pages 309-321 for player identification.

SPARTAN ITEM

The Spartans battled Michigan in the season opener, but lost to the Wolverines, 21-14, as All-American Tom Harmon (98) scored all three TDs for UM. WY DAVIS (54) closes in for MSC.

GREEN & WHITE HIGHLIGHTS

- MSC struggled to a 3-4-1 mark, the school's first losing season since 1928 and BACHMAN's only such blemish on his MSC coaching tenure. State still managed victories over Purdue, Kansas State and West Virginia, and played Santa Clara to a scoreless tie.

- In the 7-6 loss to Marquette, WY DAVIS scored on a 79-yard dash and had a 78-yard TD run called back.

M.S.C.

THE SCORES

7	Michigan	19
13	Marquette*	7
0	Santa Clara	7
39	Wayne State*	6
0	Missouri	19
0	Purdue	0
46	Temple*	0
31	Ohio Wesleyan*	7
14	West Virginia	12

5-3-1

THE STAFF

1941 Coaching staff, lt. to rt.: J. H. Kobs, G.A. Dahlgren, E.F. Pogor, J.F. Holsinger, C.W. Bachman, A.P. Kawal, D.D. Diehl.

THE TEAM

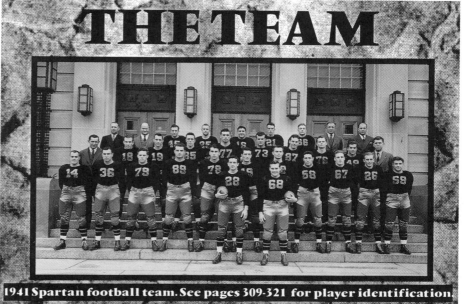

1941 Spartan football team. See pages 309-321 for player identification.

SPARTAN SALUTE

Senior center TONY ARENA (Detroit Northwestern), was State's MVP in '41. For three years, Arena was a two-way star. "Tackled by Arena" became the most familiar phrase to come through the Macklin Field public address system. In its final huddle of the season, the varsity voted to give Arena the "Croix de Guerre," presented by Michigan's Governor Van Wagoner at the December football bust.

GREEN & WHITE HIGHLIGHTS

- State responded with a 5-3-1 effort in '41, including conquests of Marquette, Temple and West Virginia.

- Temple brought a 6-1 record into East Lansing, but MSC conquered the Owls, 46-0. It was the worst defeat in Temple's history.

- DICK KIEPPE booted an 87-yard punt in the rain (on a grass field) versus Missouri.

1942

 M.S.C.

THE SCORES

0	Michigan	20
46	Wayne State*	6
7	Marquette*	28
14	Great Lakes*	0
7	Temple	7
13	Washington State	25
19	Purdue*	6
7	West Virginia*	0
7	Oregon State*	7

4-3-2

THE STAFF

1942 Coaching staff, lt. to rt.: Joe Holsinger, backfield; Charlie Bachman, head coach; Al Kawal, line; Karl Schlademan, ass't.

THE TEAM

1942 Spartan football team. See page 309-321 for player identification.

SPARTAN ITEM

REFRESHMENTS

For the convenience of spectators who do not care to leave the stands during the game or the halves, salesmen are circulating through the stands offering refreshments for sale at the following prices:

Sandwiches - - -	10c
Peanuts - - - -	10c
Hot Dogs - - -	10c
Coffee - - - -	10c
Candy Bars -	5c and 10c
Chewing Gum - - -	5c
Pop - - - -	10c
Cigarettes - - -	15c
Cigars - - -	10c

This service is sponsored by the Athletic Association of Michigan State College and is operated entirely by student help.

Almost all "refreshments" cost either a nickel or a dime in this era of Spartan football. Notice that the "hawkers" in the stands were referred to as "salesmen." Tobacco products were commonly advertised and sold at the stadium. Cigarettes were the highest priced items at 15 cents.

GREEN & WHITE HIGHLIGHTS

- The Spartans earned a 4-3-2 slate, including a stunning 14-0 shutout of the Great Lakes team which was loaded with pro and college stars. Bachman had laughingly proposed that if State won that game, he would wade across the Red Cedar River Sunday morning (in November weather). And he fulfilled that icy promise with thousands of students and townspeople cheering him on.

1943

Due to World War II, varsity football was suspended on campus and no intercollegiate games were played. However, a campus league formed, consisting of five teams. Several members of future Spartan teams gained experience from the intra-campus league. The league reflected administration forethought and played a major role in keeping football alive on campus. Here the teams are pictured in formation prior to the military parade on Nov. 6, 1943. Out in front is company commander Glenn Deibert. Team identifications can be found on page 312.

■ ON CAMPUS ENGINEERS FOOTBALL TEAM

■ VETERINARIANS FOOTBALL TEAM

■ R.O.T.C. FOOTBALL TEAM

■ OFF CAMPUS ENGINEERING FOOTBALL TEAM

■ CIVILIAN FOOTBALL TEAM

1944

M.S.C.

THE TEAM

1944 Spartan football team. See pages 309-321 for player identification.

THE SCORES

40	Scranton*	12
2	Kentucky	0
45	Kansas State*	6
8	Maryland	0
32	Wayne State	0
7	Missouri	13
33	Maryland*	0

6-1-0

THE STAFF

1944 Coaching staff: Charlie Bachman, head coach; Joe Holsinger, backfield; John Kobs, line; Karl Schlademan, ends and tackles; Gordon Dahlgren, guards and centers.

SPARTAN ITEM

This is an aerial view of the post-war athletic facilities in 1944—over 50 years ago. Notice #10, the lighted football practice field, and #11, the secret football practice field.

GREEN & WHITE HIGHLIGHTS

- MSC entered the post-war era with a 375-game record of 220 wins, 128 losses and 27 ties.
- The post-war Spartans charged to a 6-1 campaign, including four defensive shutouts. The only loss came at the hands of Missouri, 13-7.
- The football team continued to wear black & gold jerseys.
- MSC games (except two night contests) were broadcast on WKAR by Larry Frymire and C.L. Cole.
- In a scheduling oddity, MSC played Maryland twice. The Spartans blanked the Terrapins both times, 8-0 in mid-season, and 33-0 in the season finale.

Spartan Moments

After the war, coach BACHMAN rebuilt the squad, starting with just seven lettermen in the spring of 1944. Only two of them participated in spring practice: center BRADY SULLIVAN — honorary captain of the MSC team — and halfback FRED ARONSON. The other five letterwinners (JACK BRESLIN, TOM MITZELFELD, BOB GODFREY, MIKE PRASHAW and RICH MINEWEASER) were involved in other spring sports.

Spartan List

Top 10 Homecoming Victories

1.	Maryland	1944	33-0
2.	Penn State	1949	24-0
3.	Penn State	1952	34-7
4.	Notre Dame	1918	13-7
5.	Iowa	1970	37-0
6.	Wisconsin	1972	31-0
7.	Purdue	1974	31-7
8.	Indiana	1956	53-6
9.	Arizona	1948	61-7
10.	No. Carolina St.	1929	40-6

Spartan Salute

NICK KERBAWY became MSC's sports publicist in 1944. He took over as General Manager of the Detroit Lions in May of 1948. Kerbawy, who would later establish the Michigan Sports Hall of Fame in downtown Detroit, was MSC's first "full-time" SID. Prior to Kerbawy, George Alderton (1930-44) covered MSC sports while the sports editor at the *Lansing State Journal* and Jim Hasselman (1917-24) publicized sports while serving as the one-man band for all information and news at the school.

★ MSC ALL-STARS ★

Fullback JACK BRESLIN (Battle Creek Lakeview) officially started a brilliant Spartan career — both on and off the gridiron — as State's MVP in 1944. Among his various skills, Breslin ranked as the third best punter in the nation in '44.

1945

THE SCORES

0	Michigan	40
7	Kentucky*	6
12	Pittsburgh	7
27	Wayne State*	7
13	Marquette*	13
14	Missouri*	7
7	Great Lakes*	27
33	Penn State*	0
7	Miami (Fla.)	21

5-3-1

THE STAFF

1945 Coaching staff, lt. to rt.: Joe Holsinger, backfield; Karl Schlademan, ends; John Kobs, line; Charlie Bachman, head coach; Gordon Dahlgren, ass't. line; (not pictured, John Pingel, ass't. backfield).

THE TEAM

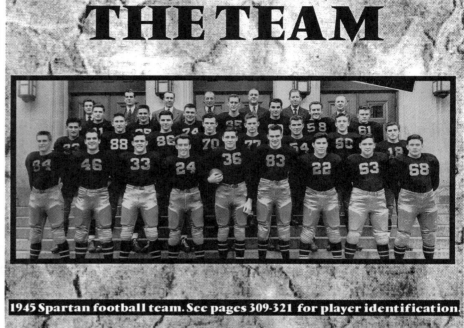

1945 Spartan football team. See pages 309-321 for player identification.

SPARTAN ITEM

MSC's offensive unit. Kneeling, lt. to rt., end WARREN HUEY, tackle KENT ESBAUGH, guard BOB LAMSSIES, center BILL PAGEL, guard DON BLACK, tackle WALT VEZMAR, end NICK ZIEGLER. Standing, lt. to rt., halfback STEVE CONTOS, fullback JACK BRESLIN, halfback RUSS READER, quarterback GLENN JOHNSON.

GREEN & WHITE HIGHLIGHTS

- State compiled a 5-3-1 record for BACHMAN's 10th winning season (and one .500 season) out of 12 at the helm.

- Halfback STEVE CONTOS (Toledo, Ohio) was State's MVP.

S
Spartan Moments

In a big game versus Pitt, JACK BRESLIN gains six yards around left end in the fourth quarter. Breslin went on to score the winning touchdown in a 12-7 victory.

Spartan List

Top 10 Single Season Kickoff Return Yardage Leaders

Derrick Mason, 1994 (36 ret.)	966
Derrick Mason, 1995 (35 ret.)	947
Eric Allen, 1969 (20 ret.)	598
Eric Allen, 1970 (24 ret.)	549
Courtney Hawkins, 1991 (21 ret.)	548
Larry Jackson, 1984 (20 ret.)	522
Larry Jackson, 1983 (23 ret.)	500
Derek Hughes, 1979 (16 ret.)	497
Tyrone Willingham, 1976 (23 ret.	454
Courtney Hawkins, 1989 (18 ret.)	454

SPARTAN SALUTE

The Spartan statue was unveiled and dedicated on June 9, 1945. MSC's athletic team symbol, "SPARTY" was designed and produced by Leonard D. Jungwirth of the College Art Department. More than two years were required to complete its construction. The Spartan stands 10-feet, 6-inches, mounted on a brick and concrete base, 5-feet, 5-inches high. It weighs three tons and is one of the largest free-standing ceramic figures in the world. Figures representing the 12 sports then included in the varsity intercollegiate athletic program are incised on the base of the statue.

★MSC ALL-STARS★

JACK BRESLIN would win two letters each in football and baseball. In football, he would win the MVP award in '44 and would be captain of the '45 squad. His awards are too numerous to mention, but include having the Jack S. Breslin Student Events Center named to his honor. In 1989, the most prestigious honor MSU awards annually to selected support staff members was renamed the Jack Breslin Distinguished Staff Awards.

Breslin is revered as one of the men who guided MSC through its remarkable growth in the years following World War II. He served MSU in administrative capacities for over 30 years and became known as "Mr. MSU." He was responsible for making the presentations to the appropriate legislative committees that resulted in the construction of many of the buildings on campus.

1946

THE SCORES

42	Wayne State*	0
20	Boston College*	34
0	Mississippi State*	6
19	Penn State	16
7	Cincinnati*	18
14	Kentucky	39
7	Michigan	55
20	Marquette*	0
26	Maryland*	14
26	Washington State*	20

5-5-0

THE STAFF

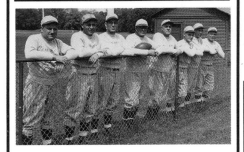

1946 Coaching staff, lt. to rt.: Lou Zarza, ends; Al Kawal, line; John Pingel, backfield; Charlie Bachman, head coach; John Kobs, j.v.; Al Kircher, j.v.; Gordon "Jake" Dahlgren, j.v.; Ed Pogor, j.v..

THE TEAM

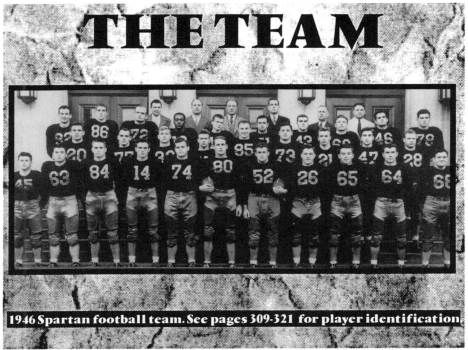

1946 Spartan football team. See pages 309-321 for player identification.

SPARTAN ITEM

Sophomore halfback GEORGE GUERRE receives the MVP award (watch) from Dean Lloyd C. Emmons, chairman of the MSC athletic council. The football banquet was held in the Union Building on Fri., December 6, 1946. Charles Bachman resigned as MSC's head coach on the same evening.

GREEN & WHITE HIGHLIGHTS

- MSC completed a 5-5 season in Bachman's 13th and final season as head coach. The Spartans defeated Penn State, 19-16, and won the final three games of Bachman's tenure, notching victories over Marquette, Maryland and Washington State.
- Halfback GEORGE GUERRE (Flint Central) was State's MVP as a sophomore. He went on to become one of the all-time greats in Spartan annals.
- A talented freshman class included the following names which would soon become extremely familiar to Spartan fans: ED BAGDON, LYNN CHANDNOIS, PETE FUSI, GENE GLICK, JOHN POLONCHEK and FRANK "MUDDY" WATERS.

S
Spartan Moments

In Michigan game action, State's #23 readies to make the tackle as MSC's "BUCK" MCCURRY (52) closes in.

Spartan List

Top 10 Kickoff Returns

Derrick Mason, LSU '95 (TD)	100
Derrick Mason, Penn State '94 (TD)	100
Derek Hughes, Oregon '79 (TD)	100
Derek Hughes, Wisconsin, '79 (TD)	94
Russ Reader, Wayne State '46 (TD)	98
Mike Holt, UCLA '73 (TD)	85
Dwight Lee, Northwestern '67 (TD)	95
Larry Jackson, Ohio State '84 (TD)	93
Blake Ezor, Indiana '87	90
Derrick Mason, Indiana '95 (TD)	87

SPARTAN SALUTE

HARRY WISMER, State grad and once the radio voice of Michigan State (WKAR), appeared at a State pep rally in '46. Standing next to Wismer in this picture is Van Patrick, longtime and immensely popular announcer of the Detroit Lions, Detroit Tigers and University of Notre Dame. Wismer also worked at WJR and WXYZ in Detroit in the early '30s. Wismer became the No. 1 football announcer in the country for four consecutive years according to *The Sporting News*. He became sports director of ABC in 1942. Among his many awards and honors, he won the Sportscaster of the Year Award in 1944 in a poll of more than 1,000 sportscasters.

★ MSC ALL-STARS ★

This 1946 quartet (left) was touted as the biggest and fastest backfield in State history. They averaged 192 pounds. Lt. to rt., quarterback RUSS GILPIN, halfback (and future All-American) LYNN CHANDNOIS, fullback STEVE SIERADZKI and halfback RUSS READER.

The '46 captains, lt. to rt., end WARREN HUEY, center BOB "BUCK" McCURRY and tackle JOHN PLETZ.

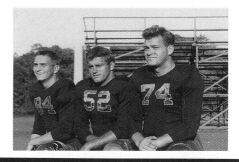

1947

THE SCORES

0	Michigan	55
7	Mississippi State*	0
21	Washington State	7
20	Iowa State*	0
6	Kentucky State	7
13	Marquette*	7
28	Santa Clara*	0
14	Temple	6
58	Hawaii	19

7-2-0

THE STAFF

1947 Coaching staff, left to right: Hugh Duffy Daugherty, line; Forest Evashevski, backfield; Clarence "Biggie" Munn, head coach; Leverne "Kip" Taylor, ends

THE TEAM

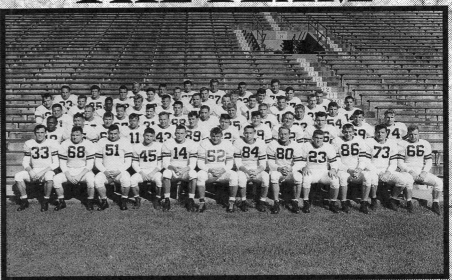

1947 Spartan football team. See pages 309-321 for player identification.

SPARTAN ITEM

The 1947 team ended the season with a game in Hawaii, which the Spartans won handily, 58-19. Here the team members are pictured in front of the plane as they begin the first leg of the trip.

GREEN & WHITE HIGHLIGHTS

- Munn's first MSC unit preserved three shutouts (Mississippi State, Iowa State and Santa Clara) during a seven-game stretch in which the most points scored by an opponent in a game was seven. Munn's first-year effort resulted in a fine 7-2 record.

- The season finale—a 58-19 romp—was played in Hawaii. MSC took 36 players and 16 coaches and administrators on the seven-day excursion. The plane trip took two days with an overnight stay in Los Angeles each direction. Thirty players became airsick over Denver on the way there.

S
Spartan Moments

COACH MUNN pictured with 1947 award winners: from left, Biggie Munn, Oil Can Award winner (humorist) PETE FUSI (Flint Northern), team MVP WARREN HUEY (Punxsutawney, Pennsylvania) and captain-elect ROBERT "BUCK" MCCURRY (Lewistown, Pennsylvania). McCurry went on to become the school's — and perhaps the nation's — only three-time captain.

Spartan List

Top Single Season Pass Interception Leaders (six or more)

Todd Krumm, 1987	9
Kurt Larson, 1988	8
John Miller, 1987	8
Jesse Thomas, 1950	8
Demetrice Martin, 1994	7
Lynn Chandnois, 1949	7
Phil Parker, 1983	7
Jim Ellis, 1951	6
Mark Anderson, 1977	6
Paul Hayner, 1972	6
Bill Simpson, 1973	6
Lynn Chandnois, 1947	6
Brad VanPelt, 1970	6

SPARTAN SALUTE

HORACE SMITH won seven letters in football and track at Michigan State from 1946-50. As a gridder, Smith played behind such backfield stars as Lynn Chandnois, George Guerre and Sonny Grandelius, but still managed to score seven career touchdowns and average 16 yards per punt return, the second-best career figure at that time.

★ MSC ALL-STARS ★

GEORGE GUERRE led MSC with 354 yards rushing in just 47 carries (7.5 avg.)!

LYNN CHANDNOIS (14) in action during the 21-7 win over Washington State. The sophomore halfback from Flint Central was soon to become a Spartan All-American and the school's all-time leading pass interceptor. From 1946-49 he intercepted 20 opponent passes for 384 yards in returns.

1948

M.S.C.

THE SCORES

7	Michigan*	13
68	Hawaii*	21
7	Notre Dame	26
61	Arizona*	7
14	Penn State	14
46	Oregon State	21
47	Marquette*	0
48	Iowa State	7
40	Washington State*	0
21	Santa Clara	21

6-2-2

Spartan Moment

I n December of 1948, MSC officially was voted into the Big Ten Conference. Competition began in 1950 for all sports except football, which, due to advance scheduling, started league play in the 1953 season.

THE TEAM

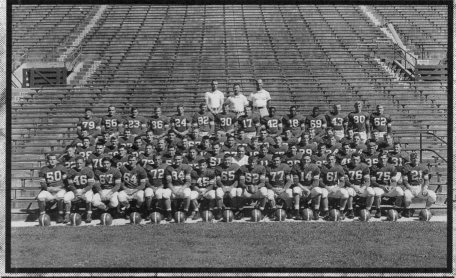

1948 Spartan football team. See pages 309-321 for player identification.

SPARTAN ITEM

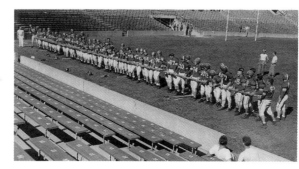

Moving the flagpole into position for MSC's new Macklin Field Stadium was a job that called for plenty of brawn. So, the varsity football team, in practice nearby, was called into service.

GREEN & WHITE HIGHLIGHTS

- One of the highest scoring teams in Spartan gridiron history, the '48 squad racked up 359 points while compiling a 6-2-2 record. MSC averaged 35.9 points per game while allowing just 13 per game.
- Halfback LYNN CHANDNOIS (Flint Central), State's standout triple threat performer, threw the first Spartan touchdown pass in "new" Macklin Field Stadium in '48.
- This team still holds the school record for rushing yardage per game (304.1).
- Macklin Field was enlarged and the capacity was increased to 51,000 in preparation for Big Ten membership.
- "Shadows" becomes official alma mater. A campus-wide lyrics contest was won by assistant football coach BARNEY TRAYNOR.

Spartan Moments

Halfback GEORGE GUERRE (Flint Central) draws a crowd of Wolverines as he looks downfield to throw.

September 25, 1948, Michigan vs. Michigan State, Macklin Field Stadium Dedication Game. President Hannah, introducing honored guests in new Macklin Stadium. Shown in background, lt. to rt., Ralph Young, MSC Director of Athletics; Fritz Crisler, Michigan Director of Athletics; John Macklin, former MSC coach, Clark Brody, chairman, State Board of Agriculture; and President Ruthven of the University of Michigan.

Spartan List

Top 10 Single-Season Rushing Averages

Lynn Chandnois, 1948	7.48
George Guerre, 1946	7.03
Lynn Chandnois, 1949	6.86
Steve Smith, 1978	6.71
Sherman Lewis, 1963	6.41
Sonny Grandelius, 1950	6.27
George Guerre, 1948	6.22
Levi Jackson, 1974	6.16
Jim Earley, 1977	6.12
Dick Gordon, 1964	6.02

SPARTAN SALUTE

FRED STABLEY (Dallastown, Pennsylvania) came to East Lansing, where he served as Sports Information Director from 1948-80. Fred was one of the pioneers of the Sports Information profession and became known as one of the true "greats" in the sports publicity world. If there had been an All-Time Greatest S.I.D. Team, Stabley would be on it, if not the captain! He was a member of the charter classes of the CoSIDA (College Sports Information Director's of America) Hall of Fame and MSU's Intercollegiate Athletics Hall of Fame. He mentored dozens and dozens of students who entered the field of collegiate or professional sports publicity. The Stabley family now boasts three generations of SID work, with son, Fred, Jr., at Central Michigan and granddaughter, Amy, at Texas.

★ MSC ALL-STARS ★

MSC's backfield: Left to right, HORACE SMITH, JIM BLENKHORN (Saginaw High), GENE GLICK (Saginaw Arthur Hill), JOHN POLONCHEK (East Chicago, Indiana).

OTHER AWARD WINNERS

LYNN CHANDNOIS, halfback MVP

THE SCORES

3	Michigan	7
48	Marquette*	7
14	Maryland*	7
42	William & Mary*	13
24	Penn State*	0
62	Temple*	14
21	Notre Dame*	34
20	Oregon State	25
75	Arizona	0

6-3-0

THE STAFF

1949 Coaching Staff: lt. to rt.: Robert Flora, freshmen; Duffy Daugherty, line; Clarence "Biggie" Munn, head coach; Forest Evachevski, backfield; Earle Edwards, ends. Also (not pictured) Warren Huey assisted with the freshmen team; baseball coach John Kobs assisted part-time with the line; and new basketball coach Al Kircher was utilized on Saturdays to scout the opposition.

THE TEAM

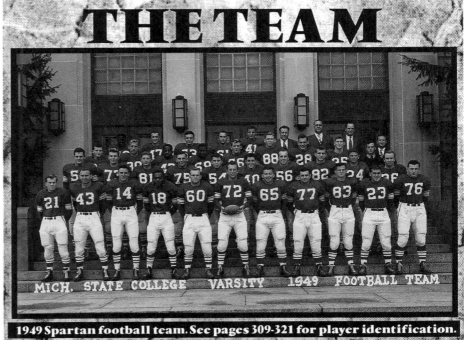

MICH. STATE COLLEGE VARSITY 1949 FOOTBALL TEAM

1949 Spartan football team. See pages 309-321 for player identification.

SPARTAN ITEM

Left halfback LYNN CHANDNOIS, center RALPH WENGER (Saginaw Arthur Hill), end JOHN GILMAN (Clinton High) and right halfback BUD CRANE (Highland Park) receive a lesson from an unidentified cowboy prior to the '49 game at Arizona.

GREEN & WHITE HIGHLIGHTS

- The Spartans crush Penn State, 24-0, and Temple, 62-14, in consecutive weeks during a five-game win streak.
- MSC concluded a 6-3 season with a 75-0 blowout at Arizona — the most points scored in one game since 1932, when State beat Alma, 93-0. In that game, LYNN CHANDNOIS ran 90 yards for a TD, still the longest rushing play in Spartan gridiron annals.
- LYNN CHANDNOIS, DON MASON and ED BAGDON are named All-Americans and Bagdon wins the prestigious Outland Trophy as the nation's top lineman. Mason and Bagdon formed the outstanding tandem at guard, unmatched anywhere in the country.
- State officially becomes a member of the Big Ten on May 20, 1949. Spartans are to begin competition in all sports with the 1950-51 school year, with the exception of football which will begin in 1953.

S

Spartan Moments

All-America halfback LYNN CHANDNOIS, pictured here during the '49 Michigan game, amassed 885 yards rushing and 10 touchdowns in 129 carries for an average gain of 6.86 yards! And, remember, the Spartans played only nine games!

Spartan sideline shot including classic Biggie Munn pose. Notice that some players sat on chairs, others on the ground and still others in the first several rows of the stands. Players and coaches would never stand during the game, allowing the fans a clear view.

Spartan List

100-Yard-Plus Rushing Games by Spartan Players

23	Lorenzo White
16	Blake Ezor
16	Tico Duckett
13	Eric Allen
10	Levi Jackson
9	Steve Smith
9	Rich Baes
7	Duane Goulbourne
7	Craig Thomas
7	Sonny Grandelius

SPARTAN ITEM

The Notre Dame Club of Detroit initiated the Megaphone Trophy, to be awarded annually to the winner of the Michigan State vs. Notre Dame football game. The Spartans won 13 of the first 16 games. The trophy is sponsored jointly by the Michigan State and Notre Dame Alumni Clubs of Detroit. The large megaphone is half blue with a gold ND monogram, and half white with a green MSC. All the scores of the games between the schools are inscribed on it.

★MSC ALL-STARS★

DON MASON and ED BAGDON — the top guard tandem in college football in '49 and perhaps one of the greatest combinations of all-time.

All-America halfback LYNN CHANDNOIS.

OTHER AWARD WINNERS

EUGENE GLICK, QB - Most Valuable Player; JOHN POLONCHEK, HB—F. Ward "Potsy" Ross Award for Scholar-Athlete; PETE FUSI, tackle - Oil Can (Humorist) Award.

CLARENCE "BIGGIE" MUNN
(1947-53)

The most successful Spartan coach of all-time in terms of winning percentage was former Minnesota All-American Clarence "Biggie" Munn. He came to MSC directly from Syracuse where he served for only one season. Despite an inauspicious 55-0 drubbing from Michigan in his Spartan debut, Munn turned things around quickly, ending that 1947 campaign with a 7-2 record. Workman-like progress continued the next two seasons, but then the Spartans exploded onto the national scene in 1950 with an 8-1 mark, a record that included victories over excellent Notre Dame and Michigan clubs. That year's eighth-place national ranking was improved to second in 1951, a year that saw State go 9-0, its first unbeaten-untied record since 1913. MSC reached the pinnacle in 1952, claiming the mythical national championship with a second straight 9-0 record. For that performance, Munn was named college football's "Coach of the Year." Success continued in 1953, the Spartans' first campaign as a member of the Big Ten Conference, running their winning streak to 28 in a row, before falling, 6-0, at Purdue. State went on to post five more victories after that, including a win over UCLA in the 1954 Rose Bowl. During Munn's seven seasons at MSC, he produced 17 different All-America players, headlined by the great two-way tackle Don Coleman. Biggie was voted into the College Football Hall of Fame in 1959. About a week after State's Rose Bowl victory, Munn stepped down from coaching to assume duties as MSC's athletic director. He served in that capacity for 18 years, building the Spartans into a nationally prominent program. A stroke in 1971 forced him to retire from Michigan State. Munn died four years later in 1975 at the age of 66.

Career Record: 54-9-2

1950

THE SCORES

38	Oregon State*	13
14	Michigan	7
7	Maryland*	34
33	William & Mary*	14
34	Marquette*	6
36	Notre Dame	33
35	Indiana*	0
27	Minnesota*	0
19	Pittsburgh	0

8-1-0

THE STAFF

1950 Coaching staff, lt. to rt.: Lowell "Red" Dawson, backfield; Duffy Daugherty, line; "Biggie" Munn, head coach; Earle Edwards, ends; (not pictured: John Kobs, ass't. line; Steve Sebo, freshmen; Harold Vogler, ass't. freshmen; Dan Devine, ass't. freshmen).

THE TEAM

1950 Spartan football team. See pages 309-321 for player identification.

Spartan Moments

SONNY GRANDELIUS follows his blockers during the 35-0 rout of Indiana. He became one of the first backs in college football to gain 1,000 yards on the ground — 1,023 in 163 rushes (6.3).

State's only blemish in 1950 came in week #3, losing to powerful Maryland, 34-7. The following week, prior to the William & Mary game, the coaches used the blackboard to remind the team of the Maryland loss. After the 33-14 triumph, one Spartan wrote back to the coaches! Identifiable Spartans, lt. to rt., are RICHARD KUH (75), DICK TAMBURO, DORNE DIBBLE (82) and DON MCAULIFFE (40) (Biggie's hat and jacket can be seen in the middle of the players).

Halfback VINCE PISANO (New Kensington, Pa.) outruns the opposition as BOB CAREY (88, Charlevoix High) and FRANK KAPRAL (58, Courtdale, Pa.) look on. Pisano added 485 yards rushing to State's offense.

GREEN & WHITE HIGHLIGHTS

- The Spartans exploded onto the national scene in 1950 with an 8-1 mark, a record which included victories over excellent Notre Dame and Michigan (ranked #3) teams. The team was ranked 8th in the nation (final AP poll) — a harbinger of things to come.
- The only loss of the season was a 34-7 defeat at the hands of Maryland in game #3. MSC then began the school's longest winning streak — 28 straight games — which extended through the fourth game of the 1953 season (lost, 6-0, to Purdue in game #5).
- Munn's defensive units registered five consecutive shutouts, including the final three games of 1950 (Indiana, Minnesota and Pittsburgh) and the first two games in '51 (Oregon State and Michigan)!
- Halfback EVERETT "SONNY" GRANDELIUS (Muskegon Heights) and end DORNE DIBBLE (Adrian) earned All-America honors.

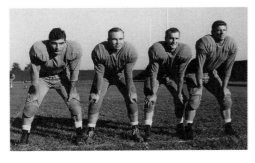

1950 Backfield: Left to right, right halfback VINCE PISANO, fullback LEROY CRANE, quarterback AL DOROW (Imlay City High) and left halfback "SONNY" GRANDELIUS. Crane added 534 rushing yards as State nearly tripled the opposition on the ground: 2,424 to 874 over nine games.

End BOB CAREY

Safety JESSE THOMAS

Def. end DORNE DIBBLE

OTHER AWARD WINNERS

JOHN YOCCA, Guard, F. Ward "Potsy" Ross Scholar-Athlete Award;
JACK MORGAN, tackle - Oil Can (Humorist) Award

Spartan List

Pass Interception Leaders in a Single Game

John Miller, Michigan, 1987 4
Jim Ellis, Oregon State, 1950 3
Jesse Thomas, Indiana, 1950 3
Jesse Thomas, Michigan, 1950 3
John Polonchek,
   William & Mary, 1949 3
Brad VanPelt,
   Washington State, 1970 3
Mark Anderson,
   Notre Dame, 1977 3

Spartan Item

BIGGIE'S CREED — "Spartan sportsmanship throughout our lives...knowing that the difference between good and great is a little extra effort."

SPARTAN MOMENTS

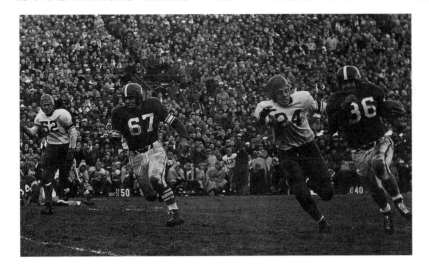

Senior fullback and captain LEROY CRANE seems to be enjoying this run in the Minnesota game. Guard JOHN YOCCA runs interference as State wallops the Gophers, 27-0.

VINCE PISANO scores from 15 yards out to tie Notre Dame at 6-6. The sophomore halfback accounted for 124 yards and two scores in 19 carries as MSU went on to win, 36-33.

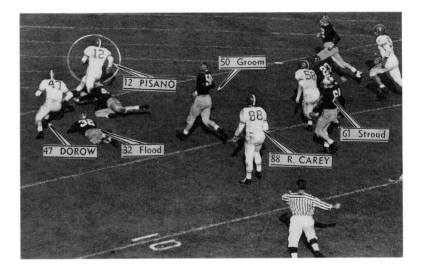

SONNY GRANDELIUS shows his determination during the Spartans' 14-7 victory over Michigan.

1951

M.S.C.

THE SCORES

6	Oregon State*	0
25	Michigan	0
24	Ohio State	20
20	Marquette*	14
32	Penn State	21
53	Pittsburgh*	26
35	Notre Dame*	0
30	Indiana	26
45	Colorado*	7

9-0-0

Ranking
AP: 2nd
UPI: 2nd

THE STAFF

1951 Coaching staff, l. to r.: Earle Edwards, ends; John Kobs, ass't. line; "Biggie" Munn, head coach; Lowell "Red" Dawson, backfield; Duffy Daugherty, line; and Steve Sebo, ass't. (not pictured: Harold Vogler, ass't., and Dan Devine, j.v. coach)

THE TEAM

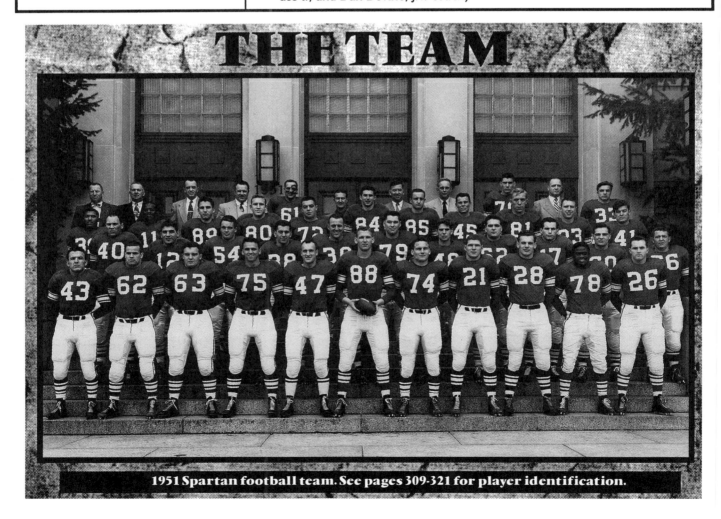

1951 Spartan football team. See pages 309-321 for player identification.

Spartan Moments

In the season opener, MSC butted heads with rugged Oregon State in Macklin Field Stadium. Triple-threat DON McAULIFFE (Chicago, Ill.) replaced SONNY GRANDELIUS at halfback. Here, McAuliffe sweeps right end for the only touchdown of the game in MSC's 6-0 victory. What do you think is going through the mind of the official who is obviously caught out of position!?!

Two weeks later, Ohio State hosted the Spartans. Quarterback AL DOROW (47) catches a "trans-continental" pass from sophomore TOM YEWCIC in the closing moments of the game to give MSC a come-from-behind 24-20 win over the Buckeyes. It marked Yewcic's first-ever pass attempt at MSU.

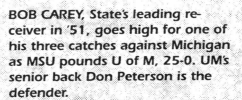

BOB CAREY, State's leading receiver in '51, goes high for one of his three catches against Michigan as MSU pounds U of M, 25-0. UM's senior back Don Peterson is the defender.

GREEN & WHITE HIGHLIGHTS

- This squad turned in the first unbeaten-untied season in the post-war era. The perfect 9-0 mark vaulted MSC to #2 in the national polls. However, State was not yet eligible to compete for the Big Ten title and, thus, could not go to the Rose Bowl.

- Four Spartans earned All-America recognition: end BOB CAREY, tackle DON COLEMAN, quarterback AL DOROW, halfback JAMES ELLIS (Saginaw High).

- The season included lopsided victories over Michigan, 25-0, and Notre Dame, 35-0.

Ten players were drafted by the professional ranks: tackle DON COLEMAN, ends BOB and BILL CAREY, qb AL DOROW, linebacker BILL HUGHES (defensive captain, Lewiston, Pa.), tackle MARV MCFADDEN (Lansing Eastern), guard FRANK KAPRAL, center JIM CREAMER (Flint), guard DICK KUH (Chicago, Ill.) and end ORLANDO MAZZA (Niagara Falls, N.Y.).

BILL (left) and BOB CAREY

DON COLEMAN

BOB CAREY was a nine-letter winner at State — three each in football, basketball and track. In '51, he was a football All-American, the center on the basketball team, and a track All-American!

OTHER AWARD WINNERS

DON COLEMAN, tackle, Most Valuable PLayer; FRANK KAPRAL, guard, F. Ward "Potsy" Ross Scholar-Athlete Award; DOUG WEAVER, center, Oil Can (Humorist) Award

Spartan List

Top 10 Single-Season Leaders in Punt Return Yardage

Jesse Thomas, 1950 (18 rets.)	358
Todd Krumm, 1987 (36 rets.)	322
Jim Ellis, 1951 (24 rets.)	305
Bill Simpson, 1972 (21 rets.)	286
Frank Waters Jr., 1967 (24 rets.)	264
Allen Brenner, 1966 (22 rets.)	256
George Guerre, 1946 (16 rets.)	253
Steve Smith, 1978 (22 rets.)	224
Bobby Morse, 1984 (20 rets.)	218
Todd Krumm, 1986 (22 rets.)	211

SPARTAN ITEM

So great was Michigan State's 1951 football squad that the Michigan Legislature adopted a resolution recognizing the Spartans as the outstanding team in the nation. The 1951 team recorded a 9-0 record, as did the 1952 squad, compiling a 28-game winning streak that spanned four seasons.

SPARTAN MOMENTS

One of only two players (and President Hannah's 46 for his 46 years of service to MSU) to have his number retired, senior tackle DON COLEMAN (78) was a consensus All-American in '51. He has been called the finest lineman ever to play for State. Here he leads the way for MSC's top rusher in '51, DON MCAULIFFE (40) vs. Michigan

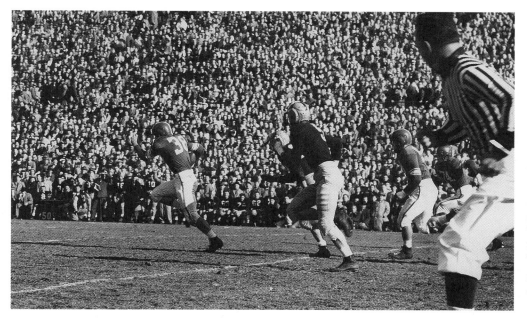

One of the classic shots in Spartan football history. State's DICK PANIN (38, Detroit Denby) shows his heels to a pair of unidentified Notre Dame defenders en route to an 88-yard touchdown run on the second play of the '51 game. The Spartans won, 35-0, on the way to a perfect 9-0 season. This play and this victory came to be regarded as pivotal in Michigan State history. They vaulted the Spartans into the "big time" of college football.

PAUL DEKKER (Muskegon High), junior end, hauls in this reception against Pitt. Dekker caught four aerials for 52 yards and a touchdown as State prevailed, 53-26. Dekker's 17 receptions for 226 yards and three TDs was second only to Bob Carey's 20 catches for 283 yards and three scores.

1952

National Champions!

THE SCORES

27	Michigan	13
17	Oregon State	14
48	Texas A & M*	6
48	Syracuse*	7
34	Penn State*	7
14	Purdue	7
41	Indiana	14
21	Notre Dame*	3
62	Marquette*	13

9-0-0

Ranking
AP: 1st
UPI: 1st

THE STAFF

MICHIGAN STATE STAFF

1952 national championship staff, top center: Clarence "Biggie" Munn, head coach; Top right, Duffy Daugherty, line and Earle Edwards, ends. Top left, Ralph Young, Director of Athletics and Steve Sebo, backfield. Lower half, top row from lt.: Don Mason, ass't. freshmen; John Kobs, ass't; Lloyd Emmons, Faculty Rep.; Dan Devine, freshmen; Fred Stabley, sports information. Lower half, bottom row, from lt.: Lyman Frimodig, Business Manager; Dr. Charles Holland, team physician; Jack Heppinstall, trainer; William Smith, student manager; Erwin Kapp, equipment manager.

THE TEAM

1952 Spartan football team. See pages 309-321 for player identification.

Spartan Moments

In game #2, EUGENE LEKENTA (Grand Rapids Union), an unsung and unused fullback, came off the MSC bench in the last eight seconds of the Oregon State game and kicked a 24-yard field goal to give the Spartans a thrilling 17-14 victory over the hosts. Lekenta actually missed the field goal from 29 yards, but Oregon State was called for an offsides penalty, moving the ball five yards closer. Lekenta's kick was good with two seconds left on the clock. It was only Gene's second field goal of his high school and college career.

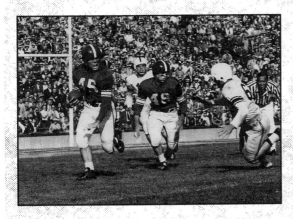

JOHN WILSON (45, Lapeer High) (left) intercepts a Texas A & M pass and returns it 16 yards to help the Spartans cruise to a 48-6 thumping of the visitors in the third game of the season.

BILLY WELLS (14) (right) is the recipient of great blocks from GORDIE SERR (left, Corunna) and EVAN SLONAC (right, St. Michael, Pa.) in the Indiana game. State won, 41-14, as the junior halfback carried 24 times for 135 yards and two TDs.

GREEN & WHITE HIGHLIGHTS

- MSC reached the pinnacle in 1952, claiming the national championship with a second straight 9-0 record. State was the recipient of the O'Donnell Trophy, symbolic of the national football championship. The Spartans could smell the roses, but still had to wait one more year to officially compete for the Big Ten crown.
- Coach MUNN was named college football's "Coach of the Year."
- No opponent scored more than 14 points in a game and the Spartans yielded an average of just 9.3 points per game. On offense, MSC never scored fewer than 14 points and averaged 34.6 points per game.
- In the Notre Dame game, DICK TAMBURO recovered three Irish fumbles in leading State to the 21-3 victory.
- Six players were selected to All-America status: guard FRANK KUSH (Windber, Pa.), halfback DON McAULIFFE, center DICK TAMBURO (New Kensington, Pennsylvania), end ELLIS DUCKETT, Jr. (Grand Rapids High), quarterback TOM YEWCIC (Conemaugh, Pa.) and halfback JIM ELLIS (Saginaw).

DON McAULIFFE (8th in the voting for the Heisman Trophy)

DICK TAMBURO

FRANK KUSH

TOM YEWCIC

"DIAMOND JIM" ELLIS

OTHER AWARD WINNERS

JOHN WILSON, Halfback, State's first Academic All-American, also "Potsy" Ross Award
DICK TAMBURO, center, Most Valuable Player; GORDON SERR and DOUG WEAVER - Oil Can (Humorist) Award

Spartan List

Top 10 Single-Season Point-After-Touchdown Kicks (PATs)

Morten Andersen, 1978	52/54
John Langeloh, 1989	42/44
George Smith, 1948	39/50
John Langeloh, 1990	38/38
George Smith, 1949	38/41
Evan Slonac, 1952	37/43
Bill Stoyanovich, 1993	32/34
Chris Caudell, 1986	31/36
Chris Gardner, 1994	30/30
Dick Kenney, 1966	30/35

SPARTAN ITEM

Planned by coach BIGGIE MUNN and band director Leonard Falcone, the State band changed from military uniform to marching band uniform for the Michigan game, and the Spartans won 27-13. Here, coach Munn inspects the new uniform of the band major.

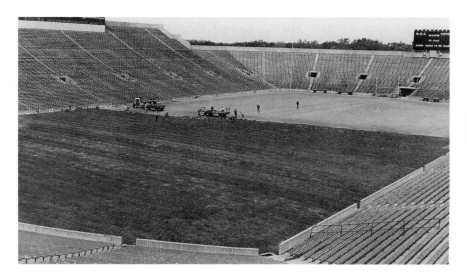

Macklin Field gets new sod for the season.

State was selected the No. 1 college football team of 1952 in the Associated Press annual pre-season poll, edging out Maryland in what amounted to a two-team race for the top spot. MSC's backfield runs a handoff play for the cameras on Sept. 2nd: left to right, halfback VINCE PISANO, fullback EVAN SLONAC, halfback and captain DON McAULIFFE and quarterback TOM YEWCIC.

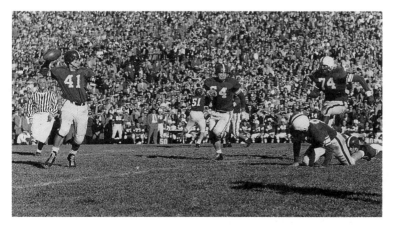

All-America QB TOM YEWCIC (41) threw for nearly 1,000 yards (941) with 10 TD passes to lead the 1952 national championship squad. His total offensive production was 1,007 yards — and in just nine games! Yewcic also punted 44 times for an average of 39.5 yards.

1953

M.S.C.

THE SCORES

21	Iowa	7
21	Minnesota	0
26	Texas Christian*	19
47	Indiana*	18
0	Purdue	6
34	Oregon State*	6
28	Ohio State	13
14	Michigan*	6
21	Marquette*	15

Rose Bowl
28	UCLA	20

9-1-0
Big Ten: 5-1-0, T-1st

THE STANDINGS

	W	L	T
Michigan State	5	1	0
Illinois	5	1	0
Wisconsin	4	1	1
Ohio State	4	3	0
Minnesota	3	3	1
Iowa	3	3	0
Michigan	3	3	0
Purdue	2	4	0
Indiana	1	5	0
Northwestern	0	6	0

Ranking
AP: 3rd
UPI: 3rd

THE STAFF

1953 Coaching staff: Steve Sebo, backfield; Duffy Daugherty, line; DeWayne King, ass't freshmen; "Biggie" Munn, head coach (pictured), Dan Devine, freshmen; John Kobs, ass't.; Don Mason, ass't.; Bob Devaney, ass't.; and Earle Edwards, ends. This staff was later recognized (1986) by the *Chicago Tribune* as the No. 6 collegiate coaching staff of all time. State's '54 staff was tabbed the #1 staff in college football history.

THE TEAM

1953 Spartan football team. See pages 309-321 for player identification.

Spartan Moments

ELLIS DUCKETT (32) comes up to make the tackle in the Purdue game — MSC's only loss (6-0) in the 1953 season, snapping a 28-game win streak.

Michigan State's famous "Pony Backfield," left to right, right halfback BILLY WELLS, fullback EVAN SLONAC, left halfback LEROY BOLDEN and quarterback TOM YEWCIC.

GREEN & WHITE HIGHLIGHTS

- Biggie's final season as head coach was MSC's first year playing for the Big Ten Conference title. State won the championship (tied with Illinois) in its first campaign as a full member running its winning streak to 28 in a row before falling, 6-0 at Purdue. State went on to post five more victories after the loss, including a win over UCLA in the 1954 Rose Bowl—the Spartans' first Rose Bowl trip.

- The "Pony Backfield" became famous as State gained national acclaim.

- In six Big Ten games, State outscored its opponents, 131-50 (21.8 - 8.3). The five victories were by an average margin of 15.4 points per game.

- MSC scored an average of 24 points per game while allowing opponents an average of 11 ppg.

LEROY BOLDEN scores from the one-yard line to cap a 78-yard, 14-play drive, to tie the score at 14 in the third quarter. Bolden followed LARRY FOWLER (70, Lansing Eastern) to paydirt. On the trip home, teammates elected Bolden and DON KAUTH (Paducah, Kentucky) co-captains for 1954.

SPARTAN ALL-AMERICANS:

End DON DOHONEY

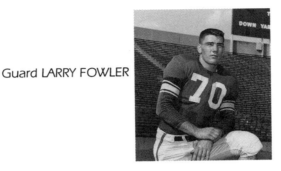

Guard LARRY FOWLER

Halfback LEROY BOLDEN

OTHER AWARD WINNERS

All-Big Ten honorees, first team: DONALD C. DOHONEY, end; LEROY BOLDEN, back; second team: FERRIS E. HALLMARK, guard; THOMAS YEWCIC, quarterback; honorable mention: ELLIS DUCKETT, end; HENRY C. BULLOUGH, guard; JAMES E. NEAL, center; EVAN J. SLONAC, fullback; WILLIAM P. WELLS, back. CARL DIENER, end, Academic All-America; LEROY BOLDEN, halfback, MVP; JIM NEAL, center, "Potsy" Ross Scholar-Athlete; LARRY FOWLER, tackle Oil Can (Humorist) Award.

Spartan List

Top 10 Career Rushing-Passing Yardage

Ed Smith, 1976-77-78 5,556

Dave Yarema, 1982-83-84-85-86 5,269

Lorenzo White, 1984-85-86-87 4,887

Jim Miller, 1990-91-92-93 4,748

Dan Enos, 1987-88-89-90 4,301

Tico Duckett, 1989-90-91-92 4,212

John Leister, 1979-80-81-82 4,073

Charlie Baggett, 1973-74-75 4,041

Bobby McAllister, 1985-86-87-88 ... 3,871

Blake Ezor, 1986-87-88-89 3,749

SPARTAN ITEM

Governor G. Mennen Williams initiates the Paul Bunyan Trophy, to be awarded to the winner of the Michigan State vs. Michigan football game. The trophy is a four-foot, hand-carved, wooden statue of the legendary figure of the north woods astride an axe, mounted on a majestic five-foot stand. The Spartans took the trophy home 12 of the first 15 years.

BOWL Highlights

BILLY WELLS and movie star Debbie Reynolds on stage together at pre-Rose Bowl Big Ten Alumni banquet in Los Angeles. Reynolds was Wells' "dream girl" movie star.

On December 28, 1953, the Spartans visited Warner Brothers Studio. Pictured are, left to right, BILLY WELLS, DON DOHONEY, film actress Doris Day, actor Phil Silvers, LARRY FOWLER and LEROY BOLDEN.

In this Warner Brothers Studio picture, actress Hedda Hopper is joined by linemen (kneeling, left to right) BILL QUINLAN, LARRY FOWLER, FERRIS HALLMARK, FRED RODY, JIM JEBB and ELLIS DUCKETT. Standing are backfield mates (left to right) BILLY WELLS, JERRY PLANUTIS, EARL MORRALL and JIM ELLIS.

BILLY WELLS was another hero of the day, gaining a game-high 80 yards in 14 carries, and returning a Cameron punt 92 yards for the clinching score at 10:09 of the fourth quarter.

One of State's famous historical photos. In the second quarter, ELLIS DUCKETT blocks a Paul Cameron punt, scoops up the ball and runs it in for the touchdown from the 16-yard line. The blocked punt/TD brought State to within seven points of the Bruins, 14-7.

HUGH "DUFFY" DAUGHERTY
(1954-72)

One of the most popular coaches in the history of college football was Michigan State's personable Duffy Daugherty. An undergraduate star for Syracuse, he was a member of Biggie Munn's staff there in 1946 when State hired Munn. Daugherty served initially as line coach at MSU, tutoring such Spartan standouts as Don Coleman and Frank Kush. Then, following State's 1954 Rose Bowl victory over UCLA, Munn stepped in as athletic director and named Duffy as head coach. He suffered through a losing campaign in 1954, but soon returned Michigan State to national prominence. Daugherty's '55 club went 8-1 and received the Big Ten's Rose Bowl bid, defeating UCLA, 17-14. His greatest teams, though, came in 1965 and '66 when those two star-studded squads posted a cumulative record of 19-1-1 and two Big Ten championships. The only loss was a 14-12 defeat at the hands of UCLA in the 1966 Rose Bowl and the lone tie was the monumental 10-10 "Game of the Century" vs. Notre Dame in '66. Duffy's 1965 Spartans were a defensive juggernaut and won the No. 1 ranking in the final UPI poll. During Duffy's 19 seasons at MSU, 29 different players earned first-team All-America honors. The list included such stars as Earl Morrall, Sherman Lewis, George Webster, Clinton Jones, Gene Washington, Bubba Smith, Brad VanPelt, and Billy Joe DuPree. Daugherty's individual honors included national "Coach of the Year" laurels in both 1955 and '65, and induction into the College Football Hall of Fame in 1984. Duffy died in 1987 at the age of 72, in Santa Barbara, California.

Career Record: 109-69-5

Duffy (right) with former MSU coach, Biggie Munn.

1954

THE SCORES

10	Iowa	14
0	Wisconsin*	6
21	Indiana	14
19	Notre Dame	20
13	Purdue*	27
13	Minnesota	19
54	Washington State*	6
7	Michigan	33
40	Marquette*	10

3-6-0
Big Ten: 1-5-0, T-8th

THE STANDINGS

	W	L	T
Ohio State	7	0	0
Wisconsin	5	2	0
Michigan	5	2	0
Minnesota	4	2	0
Iowa	4	3	0
Purdue	3	3	0
Indiana	2	4	0
Michigan State	1	5	0
Northwestern	1	5	0
Illinois	0	6	0

THE STAFF

1954 Coaching staff: Duffy Daugherty's first coaching staff at State was later tabbed by the Chicago Tribune as the greatest coaching staff in collegiate football history: Seated, l. to r., John Kobs, Head Coach Duffy Daugherty, Bob Devaney, Dan Devine. Second row, lt. to rt., Everett "Sonny" Grandelius, Burt Smith, Don Mason, Bill Yeoman.

THE TEAM

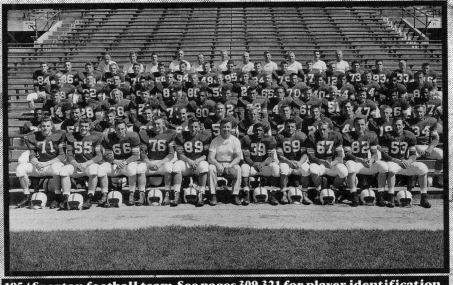

1954 Spartan football team. See pages 309-321 for player identification.

SPARTAN ITEM

In 1954, JIM ADAMS became the assistant sports editor at WKAR-TV and radio. A 1952 graduate of MSC, Adams held that post through 1957. He then held jobs in Kalamazoo, Michigan and Waterloo, Iowa, before returning to East Lansing in 1963 as sports director at WKAR. Adams broadcast over 1,600 Michigan State athletic events during his career before his retirement in 1993.

GREEN & WHITE HIGHLIGHTS

- After the 1953 season and '54 Rose Bowl, "BIGGIE" MUNN took over for RALPH YOUNG as Director of Athletics. DUFFY DAUGHERTY becomes head football coach.

- Halfback JOHN MATSOCK was voted the team's Most Valuable Player. And why not! He was the third-leading rusher on the team with 268 yards in a team-high 70 carries; he completed 10-of-20 passes for 121 yards; he caught two passes for 19 yards; he intercepted a pass for 14 yards; he returned seven punts for a team-high 129 yard (18.4 avg.!); he returned 11 kickoffs for 265 yards (24.1 avg.); and he scored three TDs!

Spartan Moments

Two pairs of hands reach for this pass intended for Notre Dame's Jim Morse (17, who would later send son, Bobby, to star for the Green & White in the '80's), but State's CLARENCE PEAKS (26, Flint Central) flips it from Morse, catching it on the rebound at the Spartans' four-yard line. Peaks returned the interception to State's 25, but a holding penalty moved it back to MSC's 10.

Spartan List

Top 10 Career Rushing Touchdowns Leaders

Lorenzo White, 1984-85-86-87	43
Blake Ezor, 1986-87-88-89	34
Lynn Chandnois, 1946-47-48-49	29
Eric Allen, 1969-70-71	28
Eric Allen, 1969-70-71	28
Tico Duckett, 1989-90-91-92	26
Craig Thomas, 1990-91-92-93	25
Leroy Bolden, 1951-52-53-54	23
Steve Smith, 1977-78-79-80	21
Charlie Baggett, 1973-74-75	21
Clinton Jones, 1964-65-66	20

Spartan Salute

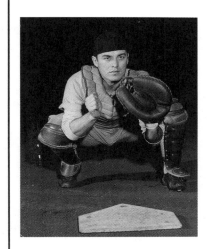

All-America quarterback TOM YEWCIC leads the football team to the Rose Bowl victory. Then, just a few months later, All-America catcher Tom Yewcic leads the baseball team to the semi-finals of the NCAA College Baseball World Series. Yewcic was State's first first-team All-American in baseball. He went on to play professional baseball with the Detroit Tigers and pro football with the Boston Patriots.

★ MSC ALL-STARS ★

The Spartans' backfield (left) prepares for the Notre Dame game: lt. to rt., right halfback CLARENCE PEAKS, quarterback EARL MORRALL (Muskegon High), fullback VIC POSTULA (Marshall High), left halfback JOHN MATSOCK (Detroit Pershing).

Four of State's receivers, including three of the top four in reception statistics (above), lt to rt.: Junior JOHN LEWIS (10 for 338 yds.), co-captain and senior end DON KAUTH (8 for 102 yds.), senior end ELLIS DUCKETT, Jr. (6 for 81 yds.), and junior CARL DIENER.

OTHER AWARD WINNERS

All-Big Ten honorees, honorable mention: RANDALL P. SCHRECENGOST, tackle; HENRY C. BULLOUGH, gaurd; JOHN J. MATSOCK, back; LeROY BOLDEN, back; DON KAUTH, end, Academic All-Big Ten; "Potsy" Ross Student-Athlete; and JOHN MATSOCK, halfback, MVP; HENRY BULLOUGH, guard, Oil Can (Humorist); AL FRACASSA, quarterback, Frederick W. Danziger Award (Detroit area).

1955

THE SCORES

20	Indiana	13
7	Michigan	14
38	Stanford*	14
21	Notre Dame*	7
21	Illinois*	7
27	Wisconsin	0
27	Purdue	0
42	Minnesota*	14
33	Marquette*	0

Rose Bowl
17	UCLA	14

9-1-0
Big Ten: 5-1-0, 2nd

THE STANDINGS

	W	L	T
Ohio State	6	0	0
Michigan State	5	1	0
Michigan	5	2	0
Purdue	4	2	1
Illinois	3	3	1
Wisconsin	3	4	0
Iowa	2	3	1
Minnesota	2	5	0
Indiana	1	5	0
Northwestern	0	6	1

Ranking
AP: 2nd
UPI: 2nd

THE STAFF

1955 Coaching staff, front, lt. to rt.: Don Mason, freshmen; Burt Smith, off. line; Duffy Daugherty, head coach; "Sonny" Grandelius, backfield; Bob Devaney, ends; back row, lt. to rt., Bill Yeoman, ass't.; Lou Agase, def. line.

THE TEAM

1955 Spartan football team. See pages 309-321 for player identification.

Spartan
Moments

Senior QB EARL MORRALL threw for nearly 1,000 yards (941) and five touchdowns. On defense, he returned two interceptions for 109 yards!

The 1955 assemblage of quarterback talent (lt. to rt.): soph. JIM NINOWSKI (Detroit Pershing); soph. MIKE PANITCH (Chicago); sr. EARL MORRALL; jr. PAT WILSON; soph. BOBBY POPP (Conemaugh, Pennsylvania).

GREEN & WHITE HIGHLIGHTS

- Duffy's first outstanding team, which went 8-1, and received the Big Ten's bid to the Rose Bowl, defeating UCLA, 17-14.

- Beat #4 Notre Dame, 21-7. State's defense never surrendered more than 14 points in a game, allowing an average of 8.3 points per game. The offense averaged 25.3 ppg.

- Four Spartans earned All-America laurels: QB EARL MORRALL, tackle NORM MASTERS, guard CARL "BUCK" NYSTROM (Marquette Graveraet), and fullback GERRY PLANUTIS (W. Hazelton, Pennsylvania).

- MSC became MSU.

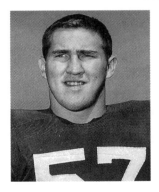

All-America tackle
NORM MASTERS

All-America quarterback
EARL MORRALL

All-America fullback
GERRY PLANUTIS

All-America guard
CARL "BUCK"
NYSTROM.

OTHER AWARD WINNERS

All-Big Ten honorees, first team: NORMAN D. MASTERS, tackle; EARL E. MORRALL, quarterback; second team: CARL W. NYSTROM, guard; GERALD R. PLANUTIS, fullback; honorable mention: DAVID KAISER, end; JOHN R. LEWIS, end; PATRICK F. BURKE, tackle; JOSEPH H. BADACZEWSKI, center; WALTER J. KOWALCZYK, back; CLARENCE E. PEAKS, back; CARL "BUCK" NYSTROM, guard, MVP, Academic All-Big Ten, Academic All-America, "Potsy" Ross Scholar-Athlete; DUFFY DAUGHERTY, AFCA and FWAA Coach of the Year; EARL MORRALL, QB, 4th in balloting for Heisman; EMBRY ROBINSON, guard, Oil Can (Humorist); NORM MASTERS, tackle, Frederick W. Danziger (Detroit area).

Spartan List

Top 10 Upset Wins over Ranked Opponents

1. 16-13 over #1 Ohio State, 1974, MSU unranked.
2. 28-27 over #1 Michigan, 1990, MSU unranked.
3. 17-7 over #2 Southern Cal, 1964, MSU unranked.
4. 28-23 over #4 Notre Dame, 1983, MSU unranked.
5. 24-15 over #5 Michigan, 1978, MSU unranked.
6. 19-12 over #5 Ohio State, 1972, MSU unranked.
7. 14-7 over #3 Michigan, 1950, MSC #19
8. 21-17 over #5 Notre Dame, 1968, MSU unranked.
9. 21-7 over #4 Notre Dame, 1955, MSU #13.
10. 30-13 over #8 Wisconsin, 1963, MSU unranked.

SPARTAN ITEM

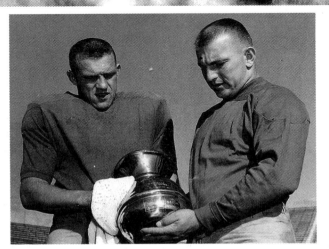

DON GILBERT (DuBois, Pennsylvania) and JOHN MATSOCK polish the Old Brass Spittoon prior to the '55 game with Indiana. State won the battle for the first eight years and 13 of the first 14. The spittoon came from the old Ackley Place, one of Michigan's earliest trading posts, and was believed to be more than 100 years old in 1950.

BOWL
Highlights

One of the greatest moments in Spartan football history. DAVE KAISER's (Alpena High) 41-yard field goal splits the uprights as a mesmerized crowd looks on. Kaiser's kick, with seven seconds left in the game, gave MSU a 17-14 victory.

Panoramic view of the sellout crowd (100,809) inside the Rose Bowl.

Senior end JOHN LEWIS (87, Fremont, Ohio), (above) moments before making the biggest catch of his career, as he hauled in a halfback pass from CLARENCE PEAKS at the 50 and outraced the UCLA defense to the endzone. The play covered 67 yards, giving MSU a 14-7 lead, 49 seconds into the fourth quarter.

In the postgame locker room, DAVE KAISER kisses the football used in his game-winning FG. Incredibly, it was Kaiser's only field goal of the season. He had only attempted two other field goals, missing both—one against Indiana and the other against Notre Dame. As State's "long-range" kicker, this was only the third time his number had been called—and he made it count when it counted the most!

1956

MSU

THE TEAM

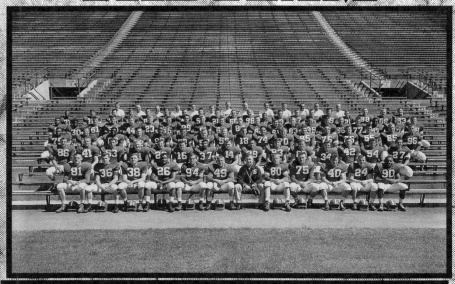

1956 Spartan football team. See pages 309-321 for player identification.

THE SCORES

21	Stanford	7
9	Michigan	0
53	Indiana*	6
47	Notre Dame	14
13	Illinois	20
33	Wisconsin*	0
12	Purdue*	9
13	Minnesota	14
38	Kansas State*	17

7-2-0
Big Ten: 4-2-0, T-4th

THE STANDINGS

	W	L	T
Iowa	5	1	0
Michigan	5	2	0
Minnesota	4	1	2
Michigan State	4	2	0
Ohio State	4	2	0
Northwestern	3	3	1
Purdue	1	4	2
Illinois	1	4	2
Wisconsin	0	4	3
Indiana	1	5	0

THE STAFF

1956 Coaching staff, kneeling, lt. to rt.: Bob Devaney, ends; Duffy Daugherty, head coach; "Sonny" Grandelius, backs. Standing, lt. to rt., Doug Weaver, freshmen; Burt Smith, off. line; Bill Yeoman, ass't.; Lou Agase, def. line; John Polonchek, ass't.

SPARTAN ITEM

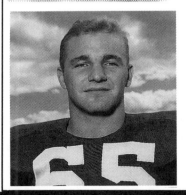

JOE CARRUTHERS (Detroit Western) lettered as a tackle for MSU from 1955-57. He played three seasons of Canadian professional football for Hamilton, then joined George Perles' staff in 1963 at Detroit St. Ambrose. Carruthers later earned "Coach of the Year" honors at St. Ambrose before moving to Grosse Pointe North High in 1968. He was a member of the MSU coaching staff from 1969-72.

GREEN & WHITE HIGHLIGHTS

- The '56 team was eight points away from an undefeated season, finishing with a 7-2 mark, 4-2 in the Big Ten, tied for fourth.

- Macklin Field was again enlarged and the capacity increased to 60,000.

- Indicative of his tremendous success on the field and personal media appeal off the field, Duffy Daugherty appeared on the cover of the October 8, 1956 issue of Time magazine.

Spartan Moments

CLARENCE PEAKS (26) (left) takes advantage of the blocking provided by fullback DON GILBERT (42) and halfback WALT KOWALCZYK (14, Westfield, Massachusetts) in the Michigan game.

Spartan List

Jim Adams' Top 10 Games

1. 1956 17-14 Rose Bowl win over UCLA; Kaiser's kick.
2. 1990 28-27 over Michigan; Wolves ranked #1.
3. 1974 16-13 over Ohio State; Jackson's run; Buckeyes #1
4. 1966 10-10 tie with Notre Dame; suspense to the end; #1 vs. #2
5. 1942 14-0 over Great Lakes; sailors loaded with pro and college stars.
6. 1951 24-20 over Ohio State; transcontinental pass; State #1
7. 1913 12-7 over Michigan; first win over UM; Wolves' only loss of year.
8. 1918 13-7 over Notre Dame; huge upset over Rockne & Co.
9. 1954 28-20 over UCLA; Rose Bowl heroics by Duckett and Wells
10. 1951 35-0 over Notre Dame; Panin run; worst loss by a Leahy team.

Spartan Salute

DUFFY DAUGHERTY worked two years in coal mines (starting at age 18) to pave the way for his college education. He played three seasons at Syracuse as a lineman and captained the team as a senior in '39. He served four years in the Army during World War II, and rose from private to major. Daugherty was named "Coach of the Year" in 1955 after the Spartans won the Rose Bowl game and finished second in the national rankings.

★ MSU ALL-STARS ★

Senior DENNIS MENDYK led the team in rushing with 495 yards in 85 carries (5.8 per carry) and also led the Spartans with seven TDs for 42 points.

Senior end JIM HINESLY (Detroit Country Day) was State's top receiver with nine receptions (131 yds.)

OTHER AWARD WINNERS

All-Big Ten honorees, second team: JOEL JONES, end; DANIEL G. CURRIE, guard, JOHN MATSKO, centr; honorable mention: ANTHONY M. KOLODZIEJ, end; PATRICK F. BURKE, tackle; DENNIS A. MENDYK, back; WALTER J. KOWALCZYK, back; DONALD D. GILBERT, fulback; JIM HINESLY, end, MVP; and Frederick W. Danziger (Detroit area); PAT WILSON, qb, "Potsy" Ross Scholar-Athlete; JOE CARRUTHERS, tackle, Oil Can (Humorist).

1957

THE SCORES

54	Indiana*	0
19	California	0
35	Michigan	6
13	Purdue*	20
19	Illinois*	14
21	Wisconsin	7
34	Notre Dame*	6
42	Minnesota*	13
27	Kansas State*	9

8-1-0
Big Ten: 5-1-0, 2nd

THE STANDINGS

	W	L	T
Ohio State	7	0	0
Michigan State	5	1	0
Iowa	4	1	1
Purdue	4	3	0
Wisconsin	4	3	0
Michigan	3	3	1
Illinois	3	4	0
Minnesota	3	5	0
Indiana	0	6	0
Northwestern	0	7	0

Ranking, AP: 3rd, UPI: 3rd

THE STAFF

1957 Coaching staff, lt. to rt.: Gordie Serr, ass't.; Doug Weaver, ass't.; John Polonchek, freshmen; Burt Smith, off. line; Duffy Daugherty, head coach; Lou Agase, def. line; "Sonny" Grandelius, off. backs; Bill Yeoman, def. backs.

THE TEAM

1957 Spartan football team. See pages 309-321 for player identification.

SPARTAN ITEM

The upper decks were constructed in Spartan Stadium (name changed from Macklin Field) and the capacity increased to 76,000.

GREEN & WHITE HIGHLIGHTS

- Spartans' only loss in an 8-1 campaign (5-1 in Big Ten) was by seven points to Purdue. State's high-powered offense averaged 29.3 points per game while the defense held nine opponents to 75 points — an average of 8.3 per game.
- Senior halfback WALT KOWALCZYK — the MVP of the '56 Rose Bowl — was named an All-American along with senior center DAN CURRIE.
- MSU received the Touchdown Club Trophy for the Outstanding College Team of the Year, by a slim margin over Ohio State and Auburn.

Spartan Moments

WALT KOWALCZYK (14) — "the sprinting blacksmith" — led the team with 545 yards in 101 rushes (5.4 per carry). In his three-year career, he averaged 5.5 yards per rush and scored 17 touchdowns.

Spartan List

Top 10 Heisman Trophy Vote-Getters

1. Walt Kowalczyk, hb   1957, 3rd
   (John David Crow-Texas A & M)
   Sherman Lewis, HB   1963, 3rd
   (Roger Staubach-Navy)
3. Earl Morrall, qb   1955, 4th
   (Howard Cassady-Ohio State)
   Lorenzo White, tb   1985, 4th
   (Bo Jackson-Auburn)
   Lorenzo White, tb   1987, 4th
   (Tim Brown-Notre Dame)
6. Dean Look, qb   1959, 6th
   (Billy Cannon-Louisiana State)
   Steve Juday, qb   1965, 6th
   (Mike Garrett-Southern Cal)
   Clint Jones, hb   1966, 6th
   (Steve Spurrier-Florida)
   Tony Mandarich, ot   1988, 6th
   (Barry Sanders-Okla. State)
10. George Saimes, fb   1962, 7th
    (Terry Baker-Oregon State)

SPARTAN SALUTE

JIM NINOWSKI (Detroit Pershing) had his best passing day as a Spartan on October 19, 1957, but State lost to Purdue, 20-13. The senior quarterback threw for 151 yards, but it wasn't enough as the Boilermakers upset the top-ranked Spartans before 64,950 fans. At the same time, it was the largest crowd in Spartan Stadium history. Ninowski completed 8-of-14 passes, including a 30-yard scoring strike to Sam Williams in the fourth quarter. He ended the year with 718 yards passing and six TDs on 45-of-79 (.570) aerial attempts.

★ MSU ALL-STARS ★

Senior halfback WALT KOWALCZYK (rt.) and senior center DAN CURRIE with their Associated Press All-America certificates.

OTHER AWARD WINNERS

All-Big Ten honorees, first team: SAMUEL F. WILLIAMS, end; PATRICK F. BURKE, tackle; ELLISON L. KELLY, guard; DANIEL G. CURRIE, center; JAMES NINOWSKI, quarterback; WALTER J. KOWALCZYK, back; second team: DAVID KAISER, end; third team: FRANCIS J. O'BRIEN, gaurd; BLANCHE MARTIN, fullback; honorable mention, JOHN L. MIDDLETON, guard; DONALD D. GILBERT, fullback; BOB JEWETT, end, Academic All-Big Ten and Academic All-America 2nd team; BLANCHE MARTIN, back, Academic All-Big Ten and Academic All-America 1st team; WALT KOWALCZYK, back, 3rd in balloting for Heisman; DAN CURRIE, center, 8th in balloting for Heisman and MVP; DON ZYSK, back, "Potsy" Ross Scholar-Athlete; BOBBY POPP, qb, Oil Can (Humorist); JIM NINOWSKI, qb, Frederick W. Danziger (Detroit area).

1958

THE SCORES

32	California*	12
12	Michigan*	12
22	Pittsburgh*	8
6	Purdue	14
0	Illinois	16
7	Wisconsin*	9
0	Indiana	6
12	Minnesota	39
26	Kansas State*	7

3-5-1
Big Ten: 0-5-1, 10th

THE STANDINGS

	W	L	T
Iowa	5	1	0
Wisconsin	5	1	1
Ohio State	4	1	2
Purdue	3	1	2
Indiana	3	2	1
Illinois	4	3	0
Northwestern	3	4	0
Michigan	1	5	1
Minnesota	1	6	0
Michigan State	0	5	1

THE STAFF

1958 Coaching staff, standing, lt. to rt.: Gordie Serr, freshmen; Carl "Buck" Nystrom, ass't.; Bill Yeoman, def. backs; "Sonny" Grandelius, off. backs; John Polonchek, ass't.; kneeling, lt. to rt., Burt Smith, off. line; Duffy Daugherty, head coach; Lou Agase, def. line.

THE TEAM

1958 Spartan football team. See pages 309-321 for player identification.

SPARTAN ITEM

Senior captain SAM WILLIAMS led the team in receptions with 15 for 242 yards while also playing brilliantly at left defensive end to earn first-team All-America honors in 1958. Prior to earning three varsity letters at State, Williams played service ball in the Navy, which enabled him to be drafted by the Los Angeles Rams.

GREEN & WHITE HIGHLIGHTS

- State started 2-0-1 with wins over California and #10 Pittsburgh, sandwiched around a 12-12 tie with Michigan. But the Spartans would only win one other game in a 3-5-1 season.
- Senior end SAM WILLIAMS earned All-America laurels.
- Lost to eventual Big Ten runner-up Wisconsin by the narrow margin of 9-7. Reserve QB MIKE PANITCH hit SAM WILLIAMS with a seven-yard pass in the end zone on the last play of the third quarter to narrow the 9-0 Badger lead to 9-7. Panitch led State on a 13-play drive that covered 87 yards.

Spartan Moments

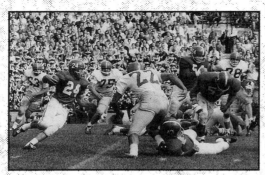

MSU halfback DEAN LOOK (24, Lansing Everett) follows ELLISON KELLY (57, Sandusky, Ohio) and DON WRIGHT (54, Dearborn High) for a first down against California in the season-opening victory. Fullback BOB BERCICH (Summit, Illinois) partially blocks Cal qb/db Joe Kapp (22) who moves in to make the tackle.

MSU halfback HERB ADDERLEY (26, Philadelphia) brings down Pitt halfback Fred Riddle after a short gain during State's 22-8 victory.

Spartan List

Awards for Varsity-Alumni Spring Games

1957	Old Timers	Jerry Planutis
1957	Varsity	Jim Ninowski
1958	Old Timers	Bob Jewett
1958	Varsity	Blanche Martin
1959	Old Timers	Jim Ninowski
1959	Varsity	Tommy Wilson
1960	Old Timers	Tom Yewcic
1960	Varsity	Herb Adderley
1961	Old Timers	Clarence Peaks
1961	Varsity	Sherman Lewis

SPARTAN SALUTE

NICK VISTA served as Sports Information Director from 1980-87. But he gained his reputation as the long-time assistant to Fred Stabley (1955-79). Vista and Stabley formed one of the top sports publicity tandems of all-time at any level of sports. Vista, who served MSU for 33 years, still owns the distinction of being the only person ever to be inducted into the CoSIDA (College Sports Information Directors of America) Hall of Fame when he was an Assistant S.I.D.

★ MSU ALL-STARS ★

Senior end and captain SAM WILLIAMS.

OTHER AWARD WINNERS

All-Big Ten honorees, first team: SAMUEL F. WILLIAMS, end; ELLISON L. KELLY, guard; second team: DEAN Z. LOOK, back; DICK BARKER, end, Academic All-Big Ten and Academic All-America; ELLISON KELLY, guard, Academic All-Big Ten and Academic All-America; BLANCHE MARTIN, back, Academic All-America (honorary); SAM WILLIAMS, end, MVP; JOHN MIDDLETON, guard, "Potsy" Ross Scholar-Athlete; THOMAS VERNON, end, Oil Can (Humorist); CLIFF LAROSE, tackle, Frederick W. Danziger (Detroit area).

THE SCORES

7	Texas A&M*	9
34	Michigan	8
8	Iowa	37
19	Notre Dame*	0
14	Indiana*	6
24	Ohio State	30
15	Purdue*	0
15	Northwestern*	10
13	Miami (Fla.)	18

5-4-0
Big Ten; 4-2-0, 2nd

THE STANDINGS

	W	L	T
Wisconsin	5	2	0
Michigan State	4	2	0
Purdue	4	2	1
Illinois	4	2	1
Northwestern	4	3	0
Iowa	3	3	0
Michigan	3	4	0
Indiana	2	4	1
Ohio State	2	4	1
Minnesota	1	6	0

THE STAFF

1959 Coaching staff, lt. to rt.: Hank Bullough, ass't.; Cal Stoll, ends; Burt Smith, def. line; Bill Yeoman, off. backs; Dan Boisture, def. backs; Lou Agase, off. line; Gordie Serr, freshmen; Duffy Daugherty, head coach.

THE TEAM

1959 Spartan football team. See pages 309-321 for player identification.

SPARTAN ITEM

JACK HEPPINSTALL retired after 45 years as trainer for the Spartans. He had been a member of the 1948 U.S. Olympic boxing and wrestling teams. He was inducted into the NATA Hall of Fame in 1962 and the Michigan Athletic Trainers Hall of Fame in 1990.

GREEN & WHITE HIGHLIGHTS

- Runners-up in the Big Ten with a 4-2 record; 5-4 overall.

- State shut out Notre Dame and #14 Purdue while thumping Michigan, 34-8, and defeating #6 Northwestern, 15-10.

- Senior quarterback DEAN LOOK named All-America.

- Coach "Biggie" Munn was inducted into the College Football Hall of Fame, becoming Michigan State's first representative in the Hall.

Sophomore halfback GARY BALLMAN (14, East Detroit High) churns away from Texas A & M tackle Gayle Oliver in the '59 season opener, won by A & M, 9-7. Ballman gained 244 yards rushing during the season.

Spartan Moments

Senior halfback BOB BERCICH (43) carries against Texas A & M.

SPARTAN SALUTE

DEAN LOOK earned All-Big Ten and All-America gridiron accolades in 1959 as the Spartans' quarterback. Dean was also the MVP of the 1958 baseball squad, finishing third in the Big Ten with a .412 batting average! He tied for the conference lead in home runs (4) and RBIs (14). He began officiating high school football games in 1967 and has been officiating NFL games since 1978.

★ MSU ALL-STARS ★

Lt. to rt.: junior right halfback HERB ADDERLEY, senior fullback BLANCHE MARTIN (River Rouge High), junior left halfback JON MARX and senior quarterback DEAN LOOK.

OTHER AWARD WINNERS

All-Big Ten honorees, first team: DEAN Z. LOOK, quarterback; honorable mention: FREDERICK V. ARBANAS, end; WILLIAM P. PYLE, tackle; DONALD M. WRIGHT, center; DAVID F. MANDERS, center; LARRY L. CUNDIFF, tackle; HERBERT A. ADDERLEY, back; GARY J. BALLMAN, back; BLANCHE MARTIN, fullback, Academic All-Big Ten, "Potsy" Ross Scholar-Athlete, and Frederick W. Danziger (Detroit area); DEAN LOOK, quarterback, MVP and 6th in balloting for Heisman Trophy; EDWIN MCLUCAS, guard, Oil Can (Humorist).

1960-1969

MICHIGAN STATE UNIVERSITY
SPARTAN
FOOTBALL
100 Seasons
MAC - MSC - MSU

1960

THE SCORES

7	Pittsburgh	7
24	Michigan*	17
15	Iowa*	27
21	Notre Dame	0
35	Indiana	0
10	Ohio State*	21
17	Purdue	13
21	Northwestern	18
43	Detroit*	15

6-2-1
Big Ten: 3-2-0, 4th

THE STANDINGS

	W	L	T
Iowa	5	1	0
Minnesota	5	1	0
Ohio State	4	2	0
Michigan State	3	2	0
Illinois	2	4	0
Michigan	2	4	0
Northwestern	2	4	0
Purdue	2	4	0
Wisconsin	2	5	0
Indiana	-	-	-

THE STAFF

1960 Coaching staff, lt. to rt.: Gordie Serr, off. line; Hank Bullough, freshmen; Vince Carillot, ass't. backfield; Dan Boisture, def. backs; Duffy Daugherty, head coach; Cal Stoll, ends; Burt Smith, def. line; Bill Yeoman, off. backs.

THE TEAM

1960 Spartan football team. See pages 309-321 for player identification.

SPARTAN ITEM

Senior running back and defensive back HERB ADDERLEY would complete his MSU career and become the No. 1 draft pick (25th player overall, which netted him a contract of $15,000 with a $5,500 signing bonus) of the NFL Green Bay Packers. In 1968, Adderley became the first defensive player in history to score in a Super Bowl game (Super Bowl II). A member of the NFL Hall of Fame since 1980, he came to MSU and wore the number 26 of his idol, former Spartan star Clarence Peaks.

GREEN & WHITE HIGHLIGHTS

- Registered a 6-2-1 season with shutout victories over Notre Dame and Indiana. It was the second straight blanking of the Irish.

- State became the first team ever to defeat Notre Dame five times in a row.

- State played Detroit for the last time in a terrific 14-game rivalry. State won, 43-15 giving MSU a 7-6-1 edge in the series.

Spartan Moments

ART BRANDSTATTER, JR. (88, East Lansing High), was one of the team's top receivers, catching five for 95 yards and two TDs.

Junior RON HATCHER (Carnegie, Pennsylvania) led MSU rushers with 36 yards. Hatcher gained 109 yards and scored a touchdown (51-yd. run in the 4th qtr.) in 10 carries against Northwestern to help State overcome a 12-point halftime deficit to beat the Wildcats, 21-18.

Spartan List

All-Time Spartan Defensive Team

(selected in 1969-1970 from ballots in the MSU football game program, MSU Alumni Magazine and State News)

Ends	Sam Williams	1958
	"Bubba" Smith	1966
Linemen	Ed Bagdon	1949
	Jerry Rush	1964
	Harold Lucas	1965
Linebackers	Dan Currie	1957
	Frank Kush	1952
Backs	George Webster	1966
	Lynn Chandnois	1949
	Herb Adderley	1960
	George Saimes	1962

SPARTAN SALUTE

GAYLE ROBINSON, long-time Spartan, became head trainer. He served State in that capacity from 1960-83 after 14 years as the assistant trainer from 1946-59. "Robby" served as trainer for the 1972 U.S. Olympic Team and in the 1976 Pan American Games. He was inducted into the NATA Hall of Fame in 1976. As a student-athlete, he lettered in track (1937-39) and was co-holder of the indoor varsity record for the 70-yard low hurdles.

★ MSU ALL-STARS ★

Tri-captains, lt. to rt., senior guard FRED BOYLEN (Grand Rapids Catholic Central), senior halfback HERB ADDERLEY, and senior end FRED ARBANAS (Detroit St. Mary's).

OTHER AWARD WINNERS

All-Big Ten honorees, first team: HERBERT A. ADDERLEY, back; second team: FREDERICK V. ARBANAS, end; honorable mention: FREDERICK J. BOYLEN, guard; DAVID W. BEHRMAN, guard; GARY J. BALLMAN, back; ED RYAN, halfback, Academic All-Big Ten and Academic All-America; TOM WILSON, qb, MVP and "Potsy" Ross Scholar-Athlete; RON GRIMSLEY, guard, Oil Can (Humorist); MICKEY WALKER, tackle, Frederick W. Danziger (Detroit area).

1961

THE SCORES

20	Wisconsin	0
31	Stanford *	3
28	Michigan	0
17	Notre Dame*	7
35	Indiana*	0
0	Minnesota	13
6	Purdue	7
21	Northwestern*	13
34	Illinois*	7

7-2-0
Big Ten: 5-2-0, 3rd

THE STANDINGS

	W	L	T
Ohio State	6	0	0
Minnesota	6	1	0
Michigan State	5	2	0
Purdue	4	2	0
Wisconsin	4	3	0
Michigan	3	3	0
Iowa	2	4	0
Northwestern	2	4	0
Indiana	0	6	0
Illinois	0	7	0

THE STAFF

1961 Coaching staff: Duffy Daugherty, head coach; Hank Bullough, def. line; Dan Boisture, def. backs; Vince Carillot, ass't. backs; Gordie Serr, off. line; Cal Stoll, ends; Burt Smith, freshmen; and Bill Yeoman, off. backs.

THE TEAM

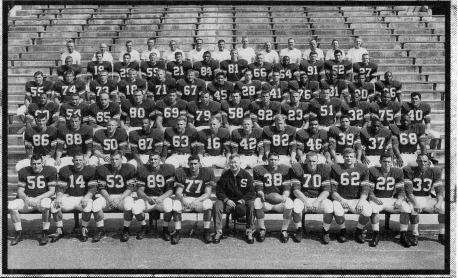

1961 Spartan football team. See pages 309-321 for player identification.

SPARTAN ITEM

DUFFY DAUGHERTY poses with 1961 captain ED RYAN, a defensive specialist from Chicago. "Rocky," a transfer from Notre Dame, was one of the hardest hitters for the Spartans.

GREEN & WHITE HIGHLIGHTS

- The '61 defense still holds the school record for scoring defense, allowing just 5.6 points per game during a 7-2 season. State shut out Wisconsin, Michigan and Indiana. The two losses were to Minnesota, 13-0, and Purdue, 7-6.

- Junior guard DAVE BEHRMAN was named All-America.

- Coach "BIGGIE" MUNN became MSU's first inductee into the Michigan Sports Hall of Fame.

Spartan Moments

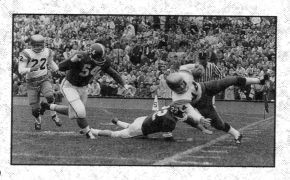

Senior defensive back BOB SUCI (22, Grand Blanc) knocks Notre Dame halfback Angelo Dabiero out of bounds as State prevailed, 17-7. TOM JORDAN (54, Bethlehem, Pennsylvania) is MSU's other player, while ND's George Sefcik trails the play.

Spartan List

MSU's Top 10 Nationally Ranked Teams

1.	1952	#1 AP	#1 UPI
2.	1965	#2 AP	#1 UPI
3.	1966	#2 AP	#2 UPI
	1951	#2 AP	#2 UPI
	1955	#2 AP	#2 UPI
6.	1953	#3 AP	#3 UPI
	1957	#3 AP	#3 UPI
8.	1987	#8 AP	#8 UPI
9.	1961	#8 AP	#9 UPI
	1950	#8 AP	#9 UPI

SPARTAN SALUTE

A tackle on the 1957 club and a member of State's boxing team, TOM McNEELEY came to State (with his brother, Brian) as the amateur heavyweight boxing champion of Massachusetts and an All-America prep football player. Winner of 24 straight fights, he graced the cover of *Sports Illustrated* prior to his fight with Floyd Patterson for the world heavyweight championship on December 4, 1961, in Toronto, Canada. Three decades later, his son, Peter, fought Mike Tyson for the heavyweight title.

★ MSU ALL-STARS ★

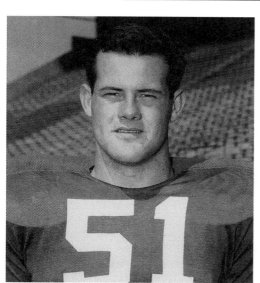

Junior guard DAVE BEHRMAN.

OTHER AWARD WINNERS

All Big Ten honorees, first team: GEORGE SAIMES, fullback; DAVID W. BEHRMAN, tackle; second team: SHERMAN P. LEWIS, back; honorable mention: ARTHUR F. BRANDSTATTER, JR., end; CHARLES E. BROWN, guard; DAVID F. MANDERS, center; EDWARD L. BUDDE, guard; ANTHONY L. KUMIEGA, guard; DEWEY R. LINCOLN, back; GEORGE SAIMES, fullback, MVP; PETE KAKELA, tackle, "Potsy" Ross Scholar-Athlete; WAYNE FONTES, halfback, Oil Can (Humorist); GARY BALLMAN, halfback, Frederick W. Danziger (Detroit area).

1962

THE SCORES

13	Stanford	16
38	North Carolina*	6
28	Michigan*	0
31	Notre Dame	7
26	Indiana	8
7	Minnesota*	28
9	Purdue*	17
31	Northwestern	7
6	Illinois	7

5-4-0
Big Ten: 3-3-0, T-5th

THE STANDINGS

	W	L	T
Wisconsin	6	1	0
Minnesota	5	2	0
Northwestern	4	2	0
Ohio State	4	2	0
Michigan State	3	3	0
Purdue	3	3	0
Iowa	3	3	0
Illinois	2	5	0
Indiana	1	5	0
Michigan	1	6	0

THE STAFF

1962 Coaching staff, front row, lt. to rt.: John McVay, ass't. backs; Duffy Daugherty, head coach; Burt Smith, freshmen. Back row, lt. to rt., Gordie Serr, off. line; Vince Carillot, def. backs; Cal Stoll, ends; Henry Bullough, def. line; Dan Boisture, off. backs.

THE TEAM

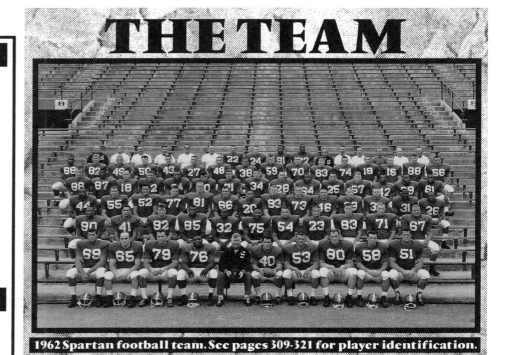

1962 Spartan football team. See pages 309-321 for player identification.

SPARTAN ITEM

The huge, paper mache Spartan head, worn by CYRUS STEWART, from the Sigma Phi Epsilon fraternity, appeared in its fourth football season after its introduction in 1959. Today, Dr. Stewart is a professor in the MSU School of Criminal Justice.

GREEN & WHITE HIGHLIGHTS

- Reserve RON RUBICK becomes first Spartan ever to gain over 200 yards rushing in a single game, with 207 in 14 carries vs. North Carolina.
- Registered second consecutive 28-0 shutout of Michigan.
- Completed four straight lopsided wins over North Carolina (38-6), Michigan (28-0), Notre Dame (31-7) and Indiana (26-8).
- Three seniors earned All-America acclaim: center DAVE BEHRMAN (second straight year), tackle ED BUDDE and captain and fullback GEORGE SAIMES.
- RALPH YOUNG is inducted into the Michigan Sports Hall of Fame.

Spartan Moments

A trio of blockers swing out in front of MSU halfback RON RUBICK (33) in a demonstration of why the Spartans were among the nation's top rushing teams in '62. Blockers are JOE BEGENY (34, Tonawanda, N.Y.), PETE SMITH (23, Ecorse St. Francis) and GEORGE AZAR (58, Johnstown, Pennsylvania). The loyal Spartan fans set a Spartan Stadium attendance record at this Michigan game: 77,501.

Junior tailback SHERM LEWIS (below) gains seven yards around left end against the Wolverines. Lewis gained 590 yards rushing with nine TDs in '62 with a team-high 6.0 yards-per-carry average.

Spartan List

Top Single Game Leaders in Points Scored (20 or more)

Blake Ezor, Northwestern, '89	36
Scott Greene, Illinois, '95	26
Craig Thomas, Central Michigan, '93	24
Craig Thomas, Indiana, '92	24
Tico Duckett, Purdue, '90	24
Blake Ezor, Indiana '89	24
Clinton Jones, Iowa, '65	24
Bud Crane, Hawaii, '47	24
Eric Allen, Purdue, '71	24
Eric Allen, Minnesota, '71	24
Derek Hughes, Minnesota, '79	24
Steve Smith, Northwestern, '80	24
Bob Apisa, Northwestern, '65	20
Sherman Lewis, Michigan, '62	20
Evan Slonac, Marquette, '52	20
Bob Carey, Oregon State, '50	20

SPARTAN SALUTE

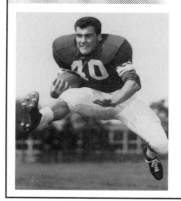

Senior fullback GEORGE SAIMES was named to All-America teams by AP, UPI, Football Writers Association, Football Coaches Association, CBS-TV, New York News and Look Magazine. Saimes led State with 642 yards rushing and nine TDs on 122 attempts (5.3 avg.). He became an All-Pro safety for Buffalo in 1965, playing there from 1963-69. George later played for the Denver Broncos from 1970-72.

★ MSU ALL-STARS ★

Senior tackle ED BUDDE.

Senior fullback GEORGE SAIMES paced the ground game with 642 yards and nine TDs in 122 rushes (5.3 yds.) At left are Saimes (40) and senior center DAVE BEHRMAN.

OTHER AWARD WINNERS

All-Big Ten honorees, first team: GEORGE SAIMES, fullback; DAVID W. BEHRMAN, center; second team: H. MATTHEW SNORTON, end; SHERMAN P. LEWIS, back; honorable mention: ERNEST R. CLARK, end; JAMES BOBBITT, tackle; EDWARD L. BUDDE, guard; STEPHEN T. MELLINGER, guard; DEWEY R. LINCOLN, back; GEORGE SAIMES, fullback, MVP, and 7th in balloting for Heisman Trophy; GEORGE AZAR, guard, "Potsy" Ross Scholar-Athlete; DEWEY LINCOLN, halfback, Oil Can (Humorist); ED BUDDE, tackle, Frederick W. Danziger (Detroit area).

1963

THE SCORES

31	North Carolina*	0
10	Southern California	13
7	Michigan	7
20	Indiana*	3
15	Northwestern	7
30	Wisconsin*	13
23	Purdue	0
12	Notre Dame*	7
0	Illinois*	13

6-2-1
Big Ten: 4-1-1, T-2nd

THE STANDINGS

	W	L	T
Illinois	5	1	1
Michigan State	4	1	1
Ohio State	4	1	1
Purdue	4	3	0
Northwestern	3	4	0
Wisconsin	3	4	0
Michigan	2	3	2
Iowa	2	3	1
Minnesota	2	5	0
Indiana	1	5	0

THE STAFF

1963 Coaching staff, front row, lt. to rt.: John McVay, ass't. backs; Duffy Daugherty, head coach; Burt Smith, freshmen. Back row, lt. to rt., Gordie Serr, off. line; Vince Carillot, def. backs; Cal Stoll, ends; Henry Bullough, def. line; Dan Boisture, off. backs.

THE TEAM

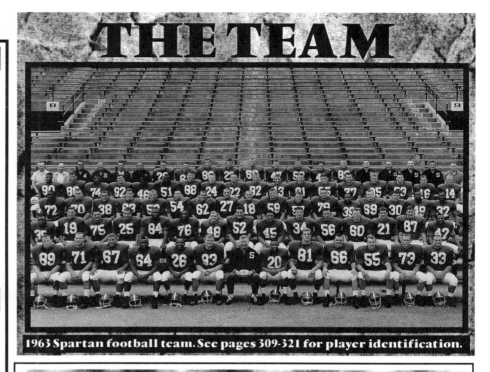

1963 Spartan football team. See pages 309-321 for player identification.

SPARTAN ITEM

President JOHN F. KENNEDY was assassinated 24 hours prior to the scheduled game between MSU and Illinois in the Game of the Week. Even as fans entered the stadium at 11 a.m., no day of mourning had been declared. Then, less than two hours before kickoff, the game was postponed until the following Thursday, Thanksgiving Day. Illinois won the game, 13-0, and knocked MSU out of the Rose Bowl.

GREEN & WHITE HIGHLIGHTS

- Spartans completed a 6-2-1 overall season, 4-1-1 in the Big Ten, good for a second-place tie.
- One of the most outstanding defensive units ever at State, allowing just 174.1 yards of total offense per game, ranking fourth in the nation as well as the second best mark in 100 seasons of Spartan football. State yielded just 82 yards per game rushing, the fourth best mark in the nation in '63 and the fourth best seasonal effort in Spartan history. Opponents could muster only seven points per game, the fourth best average in the country and the third best in State annals.
- MSU ran its streak to eight straight games without a loss to Michigan (6-0-2 in eight years) or Notre Dame (8-0 in nine years).

Spartan Moments

Senior back DEWEY LINCOLN (26, Hamtramck) climbs aboard Wisconsin halfback LOU HOLLAND as the Spartans registered a 30-13 victory. Holland scored both of the Badgers' touchdowns.

Spartan List

Top 10 Longest Runs from Scrimmage

Lynn Chandnois, Arizona, '49 (TD)	90
Tico Duckett, Minnesota, '91 (TD)	88
Levi Jackson, Ohio State, '74 (TD)	88
Dick Panin, Notre Dame, '51 (TD)	88
Sherman Lewis, Northwestern, '63 (TD)	87
George Guerre, Iowa State, '47 (TD)	87
Sherman Lewis, Notre Dame, '63 (TD)	85
Craig Thomas, Purdue, '92	82
Clinton Jones, Ohio State, '65 (TD)	80
Bruce Reeves, Wisconsin, '79 (TD)	79

SPARTAN SALUTE

SHERMAN LEWIS, the 152-pound halfback from Louisville, Kentucky, enjoyed one of the most productive days ever for a Spartan in 1963 against Northwestern. MSU was trailing, 7-0, as Lewis grabbed a 29-yard touchdown pass from Steve Juday. He then went 87 yards for a third-quarter TD and followed that with an 84-yard punt that sealed MSU's 15-7 victory. After a brief stint in pro football, Lewis returned to MSU as an assistant coach from 1969 through 1982.

★MSU ALL-STARS★

Senior halfback SHERMAN LEWIS (below) and senior guard EARL LATTIMER (right) were recognized as MSU All-Americans in 1963.

OTHER AWARD WINNERS

All Big Ten honorees, first team: SHERMAN P. LEWIS, back; DANIEL D. UNDERWOOD, end; second team: EARL B. LATTIMER, guard; ROGER LOPES, fullback; honorable mention: EDWARD D. LOTHAMER, end; H. MATTHEW SNORTON, end; S. RAHN BENTLEY, tackle; DAVID J. HERMAN, tackle; JOHN J. KARPINSKI, guard; ALTON L. OWENS, tackle; RICHARD J. PROEBSTLE, quarterback; DEWEY R. LINCOLN, back; RONALD R. RUBICK, back; LOUIS L. BOBICH, back; SHERM LEWIS, halfback, MVP and 3rd in balloting for Heisman Trophy; ED YOUNGS, center, "Potsy" Ross Scholar-Athlete; EARL LATTIMER, guard, Oil Can (Humorist) DEWEY LINCOLN, halfback, Frederick W. Danziger (Detroit area).

1964

THE SCORES

15	North Carolina	21
17	Southern California*	7
10	Michigan*	17
20	Indiana	27
24	Northwestern*	6
22	Wisconsin	6
21	Purdue*	7
7	Notre Dame	34
0	Illinois	16

4-5-0
Big Ten: 3-3-0, 6th

THE STANDINGS

	W	L	T
Michigan	6	1	0
Ohio State	5	1	0
Purdue	5	2	0
Illinois	4	3	0
Minnesota	4	3	0
Michigan State	3	3	0
Northwestern	2	5	0
Wisconsin	2	5	0
Iowa	1	5	0
Indiana	1	5	0

THE STAFF

1964 Coaching staff, front row, lt. to rt.: John McVay, ass't. backs; Duffy Daugherty, head coach; Burt Smith, freshmen. Back row, lt. to rt., Gordie Serr, off. line; Vince Carillot, def. backs; Cal Stoll, ends; Henry Bullough, def. line; Dan Boisture, off. backs.

THE TEAM

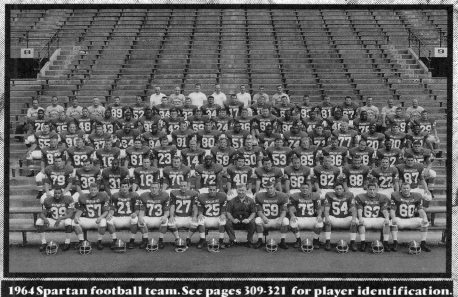

1964 Spartan football team. See pages 309-321 for player identification.

SPARTAN ITEM

Sophomore DICK KENNEY (Aiea, Hawaii) attracted widespread attention as one of the early barefoot kickers in football. He kicked a school-record 49-yard field goal in his first game appearance, scoring the first points of the 17-7 victory over second-ranked Southern Cal.

GREEN & WHITE HIGHLIGHTS

- Team finished 4-5, 3-3 in the Big Ten.
- Suffered first loss to Notre Dame or Michigan since 1955.
- State still placed three players on the All-Big Ten First Team — the most in seven years since 1954 — halfback DICK GORDON, tackle JERRY RUSH and roverback CHARLIE MIGYANKA.
- MSU stunned No. 2-ranked Southern Cal, 17-7. The Trojans came to East Lansing with a 2-0 record, with wins over Oklahoma and Colorado.

Spartan Moments

Senior halfback DICK GORDON — the team's top rusher with 741 yards (6.0 avg.) — gains yardage in the Purdue game, won by State, 21-7.

Spartan List

100-Yard-Plus Receiving Games by Spartan Players

11	Andre Rison
9	Mark Ingram
7	Kirk Gibson
6	Gene Washington
6	Courtney Hawkins
4	Frank Foreman
4	Mill Coleman
4	Muhsin Muhammad

SPARTAN SALUTE

USC head coach John McKay praised the effective and intelligent performance of Spartan defensive back DON JAPINGA. "We tried everything we could to fool him and couldn't," McKay said. "He was the difference in the game." In addition to being one of the defensive stalwarts in 1964, Japinga also ended the 1964 season as MSU's top punt returner with a 9.4 yard average on 13 returns.

★MSU ALL-STARS★

More stalwarts of '64, lt. to rt., soph. CHARLIE THORNHILL, junior RON GOOVERT and senior CHARLIE MIGYANKA.

OTHER AWARD WINNERS

All-Big Ten honorees, first team: RICHARD F. GORDON, back; JERRY M. RUSH, tackle; CHARLES MIGYANKA, roverback; second team: DONALD L. JAPINGA, back; HERMAN A. JOHNSON, back; honorable mention: GEORGE D. WEBSTER, roverback; STEPHEN A. JUDAY, quarterback; LOUIS L. BOBICH, back; DICK GORDON, halfback, MVP, Academic All-Big Ten and Academic All-America; GENE WASHINGTON, end, Academic All-Big Ten and Academic All-America; RICHARD FLYNN, tackle, "Potsy" Ross Scholar-Athlete; LARRY MACKEY, fullback, Oil Can (Humorist); JERRY RUSH, tackle, Frederick W. Danziger (Detroit area).

1965

National Champions!

THE SCORES

13	UCLA*	3
23	Penn State	0
22	Illinois*	12
24	Michigan	7
32	Ohio State*	7
14	Purdue	10
49	Northwestern*	7
35	Iowa	0
27	Indiana*	13
12	Notre Dame	3

Rose Bowl

12	UCLA	14

10-1-0
Big Ten: 7-0-0, 1st

THE STANDINGS

	W	L	T
Michigan State	7	0	0
Ohio State	6	1	0
Purdue	5	2	0
Minnesota	5	2	0
Illinois	4	3	0
Northwestern	3	4	0
Michigan	2	5	0
Wisconsin	2	5	0
Indiana	1	6	0
Iowa	0	7	0

Ranking
AP: 2nd
UPI: 1st

THE STAFF

1965 Coaching staff, front row, lt. to rt.: Ed Rutherford, freshmen; Duffy Daugherty, head coach; Al Dorow, ass't; back row, lt. to rt., Dan Boisture, off. backs; Henry Bullough, def. line; Cal Stoll, ends; Vince Carillot, def. backs; Gordie Serr, off. line

THE TEAM

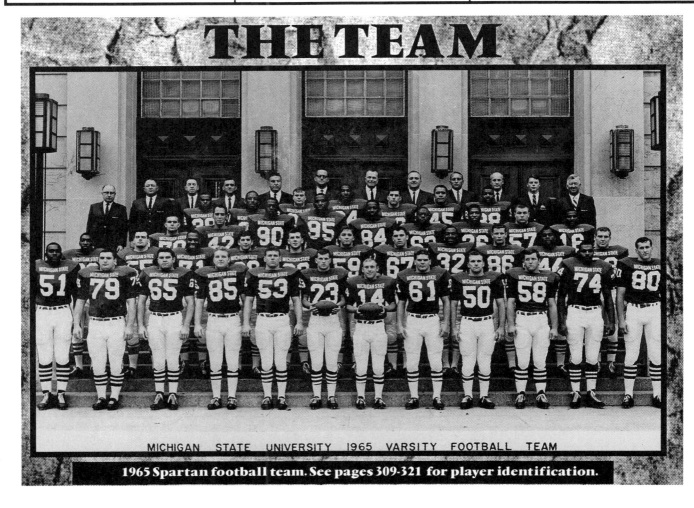

MICHIGAN STATE UNIVERSITY 1965 VARSITY FOOTBALL TEAM

1965 Spartan football team. See pages 309-321 for player identification.

Spartan Moments

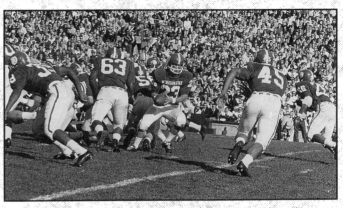

BOB APISA (45, Honolulu, Hawaii), MSU's brilliant Hawaiian fullback known as the "Samoan Bull," is about to take the handoff from STEVE JUDAY during the Illinois game, won by State, 22-12. Typical of the great blocking for Spartan ball carriers is the work here of DRAKE GARRETT (39, Dayton, Ohio), NORM JENKINS (63, West Mifflin, Pennsylvania), JERRY WEST (67, Durand; barely visible), JOHN KARPINSKI (58, Buchanan), and CLINT JONES (26, Cleveland, Ohio).

GEORGE WEBSTER (90) at his best against Michigan, as CHARLIE "MAD DOG" THORNHILL (Roanoke, Virginia) is about to complete the Wolverine "sandwich". Michigan's total rushing offense was -51 yards.

Defensive end BUBBA SMITH (95) belts hard-driving Illinois fullback Jim Grabowski (31) in second quarter action of the 22-12 victory over the Illini.

GREEN & WHITE HIGHLIGHTS

- Duffy's defensive juggernaut won the Big Ten championship on the way to the national title and a No. 1 ranking in the final UPI poll (#2 in the AP poll), ending with a perfect 10-0 mark before falling to UCLA, 14-12, in the '66 Rose Bowl. State also received the MacArthur Bowl, symbolic of the nation's best college football team.
- MSU topped the nation in rushing defense, allowing an amazing total of just 45.6 yards per game. That mark still stands as the school standard. The '65 defense also was second in the country in total defense permitting only 169.9 yards per opponent — another school record that has withstood the test of 30 years. The Spartans yielded just 6.2 points per game, the best in the nation in '65 and MSU's second-best mark in history.
- Held Michigan, Ohio State, and Notre Dame to negative rushing yardage: (-51 vs. UM; -22 vs. OSU; -12 vs. ND). Also limited Northwestern to 7 yards rushing and Iowa to 1 yard!
- Eight Spartans earned All-America accolades: sophomore FB BOB APISA, senior LB RON GOOVERT, junior HB CLINT JONES, senior QB STEVE JUDAY, senior MG HAROLD LUCAS, junior DE CHARLES "BUBBA" SMITH, junior end GENE WASHINGTON and junior LB GEORGE WEBSTER.
- DUFFY DAUGHERTY was voted "Coach of the Year" by the Football Writers Association of America (first man ever to be named twice), as the Spartans go undefeated in the regular season.
- State outscored its opponents in the fourth quarter by 115 to 7.
- STEVE JUDAY became the first (of four) Spartans to earn a National Football Foundation Hall of Fame Graduate Fellowship Award.

One of MSU's great photos. Five stalwarts of Duffy's 1965-66 championship teams and five of the greatest Spartans ever to don the Green and White — All-Americans (lt. to rt., BOB APISA, CLINT JONES, BUBBA SMITH, GENE WASHINGTON and GEORGE WEBSTER. Other All-Americans include LB RON GOOVERT, QB STEVE JUDAY, and MG HAROLD LUCAS.

OTHER AWARD WINNERS

All-Big Ten honorees, first team: EUGENE WASHINGTON, end; CLINTON C. JONES, back; CHARLES A. SMITH, end; GEORGE D. WEBSTER, roverback; STEPHEN A. JUDAY, quarterback; RONALD E. GOOVERT, linebacker; DONALD L. JAPINGA, back; HAROLD W. LUCAS, guard; second team: JOHN J. KARPINSKI, guard; ROBERT APISA, fullback; JERRY F. WEST, tackle; BORIS N. DIMITROFF, center; honorable mention: ROBERT W. VINEY, end; DONALD J. BIEROWICZ, tackle; ALTON L. OWENS, tackle; DAVID G. TECHLIN, guard; DWIGHT L. LEE, back; DUFFY DAUGHERTY, coach, Coach of the Year; DON JAPINGA, halfback, Academic All-Big Ten and Academic All-America; DON BIEROWICZ, tackle, Academic All-Big Ten and Academic All-America; JIM PROEBSTLE, end, Academic All-Big Ten and President's Outstanding Senior; STEVE JUDAY, quarterback, MVP, Academic All-Big Ten, 6th in voting for Heisman Trophy, and "Potsy" Ross Scholar Athlete; CLINT JONES, halfback, 13th in voting for Heisman Trophy; ROBERT VINEY, end, "Biggie" Munn Most Inspirational; DRAKE GARRETT, halfback, Oil Can (Humorist); HAROLD LUCAS, middle guard, Frederick W. Danziger (Detroit area).

Spartan List

Top 10 Career Leaders in Passing Yardage

Dave Yarema,
1982-83-84-85-86 5,809
Ed Smith,
1976-77-78 5,706
Jim Miller,
1990-91-92-93 5,037
Tony Banks,
1994-95 4,129
John Leister,
1979-80-81-82 3,999
Dan Enos,
1987-88-89-90 3,837
Bobby McAllister,
1985-86-87-88 3,194
Bryan Clark,
1978-79-80-81 2,725
Steve Juday,
1963-64-65 2,576
Charlie Baggett,
1973-74-75 2,335

SPARTAN SALUTE

GENE WASHINGTON established the school record for pass receptions (40) and reception yardage (677) in a single season in 1965, as well as for career catches (102) and reception yardage (1,857; still 6th on the MSU list).

BOWL
Highlights

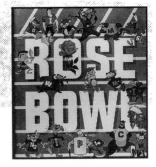

The MSU CHEERLEADERS (left) ride the Big Ten float in the Rose Bowl Parade. More than 2,000 MSU students turned Disneyland into an MSU annex on the Friday before the game.

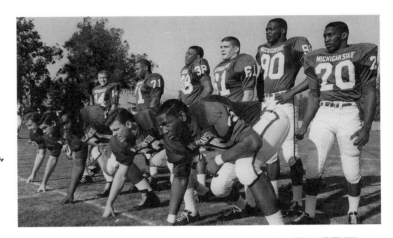

The greatest defensive unit in Spartan history (right) , and clearly, one of the best in NCAA history. Front lt. to rt.: end BOB VINEY, tackle BUDDY OWENS, end CHARLES "BUBBA" SMITH. Back, lt. to rt.: halfback DON JAPINGA, linebacker CHARLIE "MAD DOG" THORNHILL, halfback JESS PHILLIPS, linebacker RON GOOVERT, roverback GEORGE WEBSTER and halfback JIM SUMMERS.

The Spartans visit Disneyland.

BOB APISA runs 38 yards in the fourth quarter for State's first touchdown, making the score 14-6, UCLA.

STEVE JUDAY squeezes in from one-yard out to bring State to within two points at 14-12, but the extra point run failed. Blockers include JERRY WEST (67) and NORM JENKINS (63).

1966

THE SCORES

28	North Carolina State*	10
42	Penn State*	8
26	Illinois	10
20	Michigan*	7
11	Ohio State	8
41	Purdue*	20
22	Northwestern	0
56	Iowa*	7
37	Indiana	19
10	Notre Dame*	10

9-0-1
Big Ten: 7-0-0, 1st

THE STANDINGS

	W	L	T
Michigan State	7	0	0
Purdue	6	1	0
Michigan	4	3	0
Illinois	4	3	0
Minnesota	3	3	1
Ohio State	3	4	0
Northwestern	2	4	1
Wisconsin	2	4	1
Indiana	1	5	1
Iowa	1	6	0

Ranking
AP: 2nd
UPI: 2nd

THE STAFF

1966 Coaching staff, front row l. to r.: Ed Rutherford, freshmen; Duffy Daugherty, head coach; Al Dorow, ass't. backs. Back row, l. to r.: Dan Boisture, off. backs; Henry Bullough, def. line; Cal Stoll, ends; Vince Carillot, def. backs; Gordie Serr, off. line.

THE TEAM

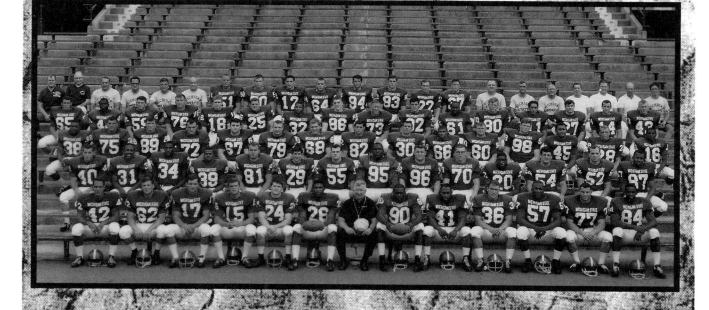

1966 Spartan football team. See pages 309-321 for player identification.

Spartan Moments

MSU quarterback JIMMY RAYE (16, Fayetteville, N.C.), an expert at running the ball on option plays, enjoys the potent blocking escort of TONY CONTI (67, Mt. Clemens, St. Mary) and BOB APISA (45) in the Michigan game. State won the game, 20-7. Michigan defenders include Jon Kramer (84) and Dick Williamson (75).

The talented Spartan defense pressures Purdue All-American Bob Griese. Defensive linemen GEORGE CHATLOS (82, Hunker, Pennsylvania) and PAT GALLINAGH (55, Detroit Servite) penetrate the Boilermakers' offense.

The Iowa game belonged to senior co-captain and All-American halfback CLINT JONES, who rushed for 268 yards and three scores in 21 rushes to pace MSU to the big 56-7 blowout.

GREEN & WHITE HIGHLIGHTS

- Spartans continue at the apex of the college football world, turning in an undefeated 9-0-1 mark. The tie was the famous 10-10 "Game of the Century" with Notre Dame and Irish coach Ara Parseghian that will be debated for eternity. Some still refer to this game as the greatest game ever played. Looking at the talent on the field that day, it would be tough to argue the point!
- State finished #2 in both wire service polls, but was awarded the MacArthur Bowl, along with Notre Dame, by the National Football Foundation Hall of Fame.
- The tremendous MSU defense nearly matched the '65 stats, permitting only 51.4 rushing yards per game. That figure was third in the nation and still ranks second in MSU history to the '65 squad. The Spartans outgained their opponents on the ground, 230-51 yards per game.
- State yielded just 9.9 points per game while the offense racked up 29.3 per outing, including 56 against Iowa, 42 vs. Penn State and 41 against Purdue. Other than the 10-10 tie and a three-point win over Ohio State, the smallest victory margin was 13 points.
- MSU placed a remarkable 11 players on the All-Big Ten first team.

★ MSU ALL-STARS ★

Six Spartans were accorded All-America honors, including four first-round draft picks. In fact, MSU enjoyed four of the first eight selections in the National and American Football League's spring (1967) draft.

"BUBBA" SMITH, the #1 NFL draft pick (Baltimore).

CLINT JONES, the #2 NFL draft selection (Minnesota)

GEORGE WEBSTER, #5 NFL/AFL draft pick (Houston)

GENE WASHINGTON, #8 NFL draft pick (Minnesota)

BOB APISA, junior fullback, who would be drafted after the '67 season by Green Bay.

JERRY WEST, who signed with the British Columbia Lions in the Canadian Football League.

OTHER AWARD WINNERS

All-Big Ten honorees, first team: EUGENE WASHINGTON, off. end; JERRY F. WEST, off. tackle; CLINTON C. JONES, halfback; CHARLES A. SMITH, def. end; CHARLES E. THORNHILL, def. back; GEORGE D. WEBSTER, def. back; RICHARD K. KENNEY, kicker; ROBERT APISA, fullback; J. NICHOLAS JORDAN, def. tack;e; ANTHONY CONTI, off. guard; JESS W. PHILLIPS, def. back; second team: PATRICK F. GALLINAGH, def. tackle; JAMES A. RAYE, quarterback; PHILLIP M. HOAG, def. end; JOSEPH R. PRYZBYCKI, off. tackle; JEFFREY RICHARDSON, off tackle; honorable mention: GEORGE R. CHATLOS, def. end; ALLEN R. BRENNER, off. end; DWIGHT L. LEE, off. back; DRAKE F. GARRETT, def. back; REGIS CAVENDER, fullback; ALLEN BRENNER, end, Academic All-Big Ten and Academic All-America; PATRICK GALLINAGH, tackle, Academic All-Big Ten and Academic All-America, "Potsy" Ross Scholar-Athlete, Frederick W. Danziger (Detroit area); CLINT JONES, halfback, 6th in balloting for Heisman Trophy; GEORGE WEBSTER, roverback, MVP; JEFF RICHARDSON, guard, President's Outstanding Senior; JERRY JONES, halfback, "Biggie" Munn Most Inspirational; DRAKE GARRETT, halfback, Oil Can (Humorist).

"BUBBA" SMITH, GEORGE WEBSTER and GENE WASHINGTON were named to the American Football Coaches 1966 All-American Team. MSU's trio, along with the rest of the squad, appeared on the Ed Sullivan television show.

Spartan List

Top 10 Single-Season Receiving Averages
(Yards per catch— Min. 20 recs.)

Gene Washington, 1966	25.0
Andre Rison, 1988	24.6
Frank Foreman, 1969	24.4
Kirk Gibson, 1977	24.1
Andre Rison, 1987	23.1
Mark Ingram, 1984	22.7
Mark Ingram, 1985	21.9
Daryl Turner, 1981	21.1
Bob Carey, 1949	20.1
Daryl Turner, 1983	19.6

SPARTAN SALUTE

Two-time All-American CHARLES "BUBBA" SMITH became the focus of the national college football scene. The "Bubba" craze swept the country and "KILL, BUBBA, KILL" buttons appeared everywhere in East Lansing. One of the most dominating defensive players ever to play college football, he was the first player selected in the spring NFL draft.

NOTRE DAME ACTION 1966

The top two teams in the land collided in Spartan Stadium. MSU fullback REGIS CAVENDER (25, Detroit Cathedral) hurdled past the Notre Dame defensive front on his way to an 11-yard gain to the Irish 9-yardline.

Three plays later, Cavender (25) blasts over from the 4-yardline to give MSU a 6-0 lead. Moving in for the celebration are ALLEN BRENNER (86, Niles High), DWIGHT LEE (34, New Haven), JOE PRZYBYCKI (79, Detroit Notre Dame) and CLINT JONES (26).

Notre Dame's QB Terry Hanratty runs against MSU's defense before being knocked out of action. State defenders are "BUBBA" SMITH (95), PAT GALLINAGH (55) and GEORGE WEBSTER (90).

The scoreboard as the games clock runs down to 0:00. The crowd expresses a variety of emotions, but mostly, perhaps, bewilderment.

1967

THE SCORES

7	Houston*	37
17	Southern California*	21
35	Wisconsin*	7
34	Michigan	0
0	Minnesota	21
12	Notre Dame	24
7	Ohio State*	21
13	Indiana*	14
7	Purdue	21
41	Northwestern*	27

3-7-0
Big Ten: 3-4-0, T-5th

THE STANDINGS

	W	L	T
Indiana	6	1	0
Minnesota	6	1	0
Purdue	6	1	0
Ohio State	5	2	0
Illinois	3	4	0
Michigan	3	4	0
Michigan State	3	4	0
Northwestern	2	5	0
Iowa	0	6	1
Wisconsin	0	6	1

THE STAFF

1967 Coaching Staff: front row, lt. to rt.: Gordie Serr, off. line; Cal Stoll, ends; Dave Smith, ass't. backs; Henry Bullough, def. line. Back row, lt. to rt., Al Dorow, off. backs; George Perles ass't.; Head Coach Duffy Daugherty; Ed Rutherford, freshmen; Vince Carillot, def. backs.

THE TEAM

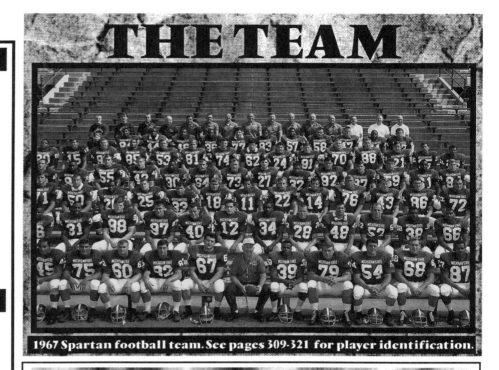

1967 Spartan football team. See pages 309-321 for player identification.

SPARTAN ITEM

GEORGE WEBSTER was voted as State's greatest Spartan gridiron performer. He has been regarded by many as the greatest defensive football player ever to play the game. Here he is pictured with Biggie Munn and Duffy Daugherty as his No. 90 is retired in his honor.

GREEN & WHITE HIGHLIGHTS

- State endured a 3-7 season, but rose to the occasion with a 35-7 romp over Wisconsin and a 34-0 blitzing of Michigan in consecutive weeks.

- Battled 1968 Heisman Trophy winner O.J. Simpson and USC to the end, before dropping a 21-17 decision.

- Played Big Ten champion Indiana to a standoff, before falling, 14-13.

Spartan Moments

USC's O.J. Simpson turned in a typically great day versus MSU, gaining 190 yards on 31 carries, scoring two TDs and passing for another. The Spartans' DON LAW (95, Brownsville, Pennsylvania) and NICK JORDAN (72, Ashland, Kentucky) try to head Simpson off as Trojan QB Steve Sogge watches and Mike Taylor (74) blocks.

Spartan List

Top 10 Career Leaders in Fumble Recoveries

George Chatlos, 1966	7
Tom Kronner, 1973	5
Tom Standal, 1975	5
Matt Vanderbeek, 1989	5
Myron Bell, 1993	4
Dan Bass, 1979	4
Dan Bass, 1977	4
Larry Savage, 1978	4
Larry Savage, 1976	4
23 players on 23 occasions	3

SPARTAN SALUTE

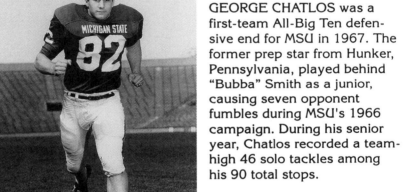

GEORGE CHATLOS was a first-team All-Big Ten defensive end for MSU in 1967. The former prep star from Hunker, Pennsylvania, played behind "Bubba" Smith as a junior, causing seven opponent fumbles during MSU's 1966 campaign. During his senior year, Chatlos recorded a team-high 46 solo tackles among his 90 total stops.

★ MSU ALL-STARS ★

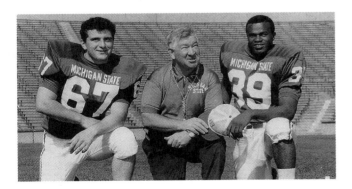

Duffy with 1967 co-captains TONY CONTI (67) and DRAKE GARRETT (39).

OTHER AWARD WINNERS

All-Big Ten honorees, first team: GEORGE R. CHATLOS, def. end; second team: JOSEPH R. PRYZBYCKI, off. tackle; honorable mention: RONALD A. RANIERI, center; ALLEN R. BRENNER, off. end; CHARLES A. BAILEY, def. tackle; DRAKE F. GARRETT, def. back; DWIGHT LEE, halfback, MVP; TONY CONTI, guard, "Potsy" Ross Scholar-Athlete; ROBERT LANGE, linebacker, President's Outstanding Senior; FRANK WATERS, halfback, "Biggie" Munn Most Inspirational; Drake Garrett, halfback, Oil Can (Humorist); Ron Ranieri, center, Frederick W. Danziger (Detroit area).

1968

THE SCORES

14	Syracuse*	10
28	Baylor*	10
39	Wisconsin	0
14	Michigan	28
13	Minnesota*	14
21	Notre Dame*	17
20	Ohio State	25
22	Indiana*	24
0	Purdue*	9
31	Northwestern	14

5-5-0
Big Ten: 2-5-0, 7th

THE STANDINGS

	W	L	T
Ohio State	7	0	0
Michigan	6	1	0
Purdue	5	2	0
Minnesota	5	2	0
Indiana	4	3	0
Iowa	4	3	0
Michigan State	2	5	0
Illinois	1	6	0
Northwestern	1	6	0
Wisconsin	0	7	0

THE STAFF

1968 Coaching staff, kneeling, lt. to rt.: Gordie Serr, off. line; Al Dorow, off. backs; George Perles ass't.; Cal Stoll, ends; Ed Rutherford, freshmen. Standing, lt. to rt., Dave Smith, ass't. backs; Henry Bullough, def. line; Duffy Daugherty, head coach; Vince Carillot, def. backs; Don Coleman, ass't.

THE TEAM

1968 Spartan football team. See pages 309-321 for player identification.

SPARTAN ITEM

Sophomore TOMMY LOVE (Sylva, N.C.) burst onto the scene in '68 as he led State with 729 yards and five touchdowns in 177 carries. Against Minnesota, he enjoyed his finest day, carrying the ball 18 times for 114 yards. Love suffered a fatal heart attack in 1971 at the age of 22. MSU's most improved player award is named the Tommy Love Award.

GREEN & WHITE HIGHLIGHTS

- The Spartans opened the season with three straight wins, including a 39-0 thrashing of Wisconsin before ending the year at 5-5.
- State defeated fifth-ranked Notre Dame, 21-17, to improve MSU's record against the Irish to 13-3-1 since 1950 (the last 17 games).
- Split end and safety Al Brenner joined the list of Spartan All-Americans. He also earned a National Football Foundation Hall of Fame Graduate Fellowship Award.
- Spartan Stadium sported a new synthetic surface, called Tartan Turf.
- JOHN PINGEL was inducted into the College Football Hall of Fame and John Kobs was inducted into the Michigan Sports Hall of Fame.

Spartan Moments

Senior quarterback BILL FERACO (Irwin, Pennsylvania) ran for six TDs and threw for another to lead MSU in scoring with 42 points. He completed 55% of his passes (33-of-60) for 478 yards.

Spartan List

Top 10 Career Leaders in QB Sacks

Larry Bethea, 1975-76-77
(208 yds.) 33
Kelly Quinn, 1982-83-84-85
(183 yds.) 24
Travis Davis, 1986-87-88-89
(217 yds.) 24
Mark Nichols, 1983-85-86-87
(90 yds.) 15
Mel Land, 1975-76-77-78
(65 yds.) 15
Carl Banks, 1980-81-82-83
(84 yds.) 14
Ron Curl, 1968-69-70-71
(73 ys.) 14
Larry Savage, 1976-77-78-79
(84 yds.) 12
John Shinsky, 1970-71-72-73
(67 yds.) 11
Juan Hammonds, 1991-92-93-94
(63 yds.) 10

SPARTAN SALUTE

CHARLES WEDEMEYER has been an inspiration for most of his life. The senior quarterback and slotback from Hawaii was MSU's outstanding offensive back in 1968 and appeared in the East-West Shrine Game and the Hula Bowl. In 1977 he was diagnosed with Lou Gehrig's disease. Yet, with the help of his wife, Lucy, he was a highly successful high school football coach in California through 1985. In 1987, Wedemeyer returned to East Lansing to receive the Varsity Alumni "S" Club's second annual Jack Breslin Life Achievement Award.

★ MSU ALL-STARS ★

Senior All-America end ALLEN BRENNER caught 25 passes for 413 yards and a TD, with a team-high 16.5 yards-per-catch average.

OTHER AWARD WINNERS

All-Big Ten honorees, first team: ALLEN R. BRENNER, safety; CHARLES A. BAILEY, def. tackle; second team: RICHARD R. SAUL, def. guard; RONALD R. SAUL, off. guard; ALLEN R. BRENNER, off. end; honorable mention: EDWARD MCLOUD, center; WILLIAM TRIPLETT, quarterback; FRANK WATERS, JR., off. halfback; THOMAS LOVE, off. halfback; ALLEN BRENNER, end/safety, MVP, Academic All-Big Ten and Academic All-America and "Potsy" Ross Scholar-Athlete; DAVE VANELST, tackle, Academic All-Big Ten; DON BAIRD, guard, Academic All-Big Ten; RICH SAUL, middle guard, Academic All-Big Ten; RICHARD BERLINSKI, fullback, President's Outstanding Senior; EDDY MCLOUD, center, "Biggie" Munn Most Inspirational, Oil Can (Humorist), KEN HEFT, halfback, Frederick W. Danziger (Detroit area).

1969

THE TEAM

1969 Spartan football team. See pages 309-321 for player identification.

See pages 309-321 for player identification.

THE SCORES

27	Washington*	11
23	Southern Methodist*	15
28	Notre Dame	42
21	Ohio State	54
23	Michigan*	12
18	Iowa	19
0	Indiana*	16
13	Purdue	41
10	Minnesota*	14
39	Northwestern	7

4-6-0
Big Ten: 2-5-0, 9th

THE STANDINGS

	W	L	T
Michigan	6	1	0
Ohio State	6	1	0
Purdue	5	2	0
Minnesota	4	3	0
Indiana	3	4	0
Iowa	3	4	0
Northwestern	3	4	0
Wisconsin	3	4	0
Michigan State	2	5	0
Illinois	0	7	0

THE STAFF

1969 Coaching staff, kneeling, lt. to rt.: Dave Smith, linebackers; Al Dorow, passing game; George Perles, def. backs; Joe Carruthers, ass't. line; Henry Bullough, def. coord. and def. line. Standing, lt. to rt., George Paterno (Joe's brother), running backs; Ed Rutherford, freshmen; Duffy Daugherty, head coach; Gordie Serr, off. line; Sherman Lewis, ass't. backfield.

SPARTAN ITEM

GOVERNOR MILLIKEN, along with Athletic Director BIGGIE MUNN, signs the proclamation for the 100 Years of College Football. The Spartans wore "100" decals on their helmets to commemorate the celebration.

GREEN & WHITE HIGHLIGHTS

- State opened the season 2-0 with wins over Washington and Southern Methodist before settling for a 4-6 record.
- MSU defeated #13 Michigan, 23-12, in Bo Schembechler's first year as UM head coach. That was the year — after two big losses the previous two weeks — Duffy closed practices and MSU came out in the Wishbone offense, totally catching the Wolverines by surprise. The offensive game ball was awarded to BILL TRIPLETT and the defensive game ball to coach HENRY BULLOUGH.
- Guard RON SAUL was accorded All-America honors.

Spartan Moments

Senior halfback DON HIGHSMITH (40, New Brunswick, N.J.) was the star in the '69 Michigan game, rushing for 129 yards and two touchdowns, to hand the Wolverines their only Big Ten loss that year. UM went on to tie Ohio State for the conference crown.

Spartan List

Top 10 Leaders in Single-Game Receiving Yardage

Andre Rison, Georgia '89	252
Courtney Hawkins, Minnesota '89	197
Andre Rison, Indiana '86	19
Courtney Hawkins, Purdue '89	193
Kirk Gibson, North Carolina State '76	173
Muhsin Muhammad, Louisiana State '95	171
Andre Rison, Wisconsin '87	162
Eugene Byrd, Iowa '79	159
Andre Rison, Western Michigan '86	155
Frank Foreman, Purdue '69	155

SPARTAN SALUTE

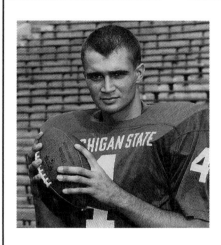

DAN WERNER was the first Michigan State player to pass for more than 300 yards in a single game. He did it against Purdue in 1969. Replacing starter Steve Piro, Werner completed 16-of-35 passes for 314 yards, just two yards shy of the then-Big Ten record. But the Spartans lost the game, 41-13. Werner went on to serve as business manager for the NFL's Dallas Cowboys.

★MSU ALL-STARS★

Sr. guard RON SAUL (70) earned All-America recognition in '69. He is pictured with twin brother RICH (88). Ron and Rich were both named to the First-Team Academic All-America squad. Rich led the '68 team with 84 tackles.

OTHER AWARD WINNERS

All-Big Ten honorees, first team: RONALD R. SAUL, off. guard; RICHARD R. SAUL, def. end/LB; RONALD C. CURL, def. tackle; second team: DONALD LAW, linebacker; honorable mention: DONALD C. HIGHSMITH, halfback; ERIC B. ALLEN, halfback; FRANKLIN S. FOREMAN, off. end; DONALD G. BAIRD, off. guard; RON SAUL, guard, MVP, Academic All-Big Ten and Academic All-America; RICH SAUL, def. end, Academic All-Big Ten and Academic All-America; DON BAIRD, guard, "Potsy" Ross Scholar-Athlete; BRUCE KULESZA, end, President's Outstanding Senior; DON HIGHSMITH, halfback, "Biggie" Munn Most Inspirational; CLIFTON HARDY, halfback, Oil Can (Humorist); CRAIG WYCINSKY, tackle, Frederick W. Danziger (Detroit area).

1970-1979

MICHIGAN STATE UNIVERSITY

SPARTAN FOOTBALL

100 Seasons

MAC - MSC - MSU

1970

THE SCORES

16	Washington	42
28	Washington State*	14
0	Notre Dame*	29
0	Ohio State	29
20	Michigan	34
37	Iowa*	0
32	Indiana	7
24	Purdue*	14
13	Minnesota	23
20	Northwestern*	23

4-6-0
Big Ten: 3-4-0, T-5th

THE STANDINGS

	W	L	T
Ohio State	7	0	0
Michigan	6	1	0
Northwestern	6	1	0
Iowa	3	3	1
Wisconsin	3	4	0
Michigan State	3	4	0
Minnesota	2	4	1
Purdue	2	5	0
Illinois	1	6	0
Indiana	1	6	0

THE STAFF

1970 Coaching staff, kneeling, lt. to rt.: Gordie Serr, off. line; Duffy Daugherty, head coach; Ed Rutherford, freshmen; Al Dorow, staff coord. Standing, lt. to rt., Joe Carruthers, linebackers; George Perles, def. line; Sherm Lewis, def. backs; Dave Smith, receivers.

THE TEAM

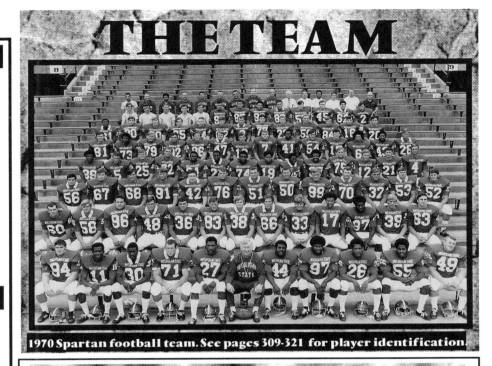

1970 Spartan football team. See pages 309-321 for player identification.

SPARTAN ITEM

Senior split end GORDON BOWDELL (Allen Park Cabrini) topped the receiving corps with an impressive 34 catches for 495 yards and four TDs.

GREEN & WHITE HIGHLIGHTS

- State struggled through its second straight 4-6 season, but improved to 3-4 in the Big Ten, good for a fifth-place tie.

- MSU rolled to three consecutive convincing victories in mid-season: 37-0 over Iowa, 32-7 versus Indiana and 24-14 against Purdue.

- Junior placekicker BORYS SHLAPAK (Park Ridge, Ilinois) set the school record with a 54-yard field goal against Northwestern — a standard he would tie twice the next season.

Standing at the entrance way to Michigan State's athletic establishment is the "Spartan."

The "Sparty" mascot

The Wharton Center for the Performing Arts

Spartan Stadium

A spring scene on the MSU campus

MICHIGAN STATE UNIVERSITY
SPARTAN
FOOTBALL
100 Seasons

*Even in the winter,
MSU's campus remains
beautiful.*

The world-famous Spartan Marching Band

The elusive Lorenzo White (34).

George Perles served as the Spartans' head coach for 12 seasons.

Bobby Morse's 87-yard punt return versus Michigan in 1984 helped catapult Michigan State to a 19-7 victory in Ann Arbor. (photo courtesy of Sportech Productions)

In his first season, Nick Saban directed the Spartan football team to a victory over Michigan and a berth in the Independence Bowl.

Coach Saban leads his Spartans onto the field.

Spartan Moments

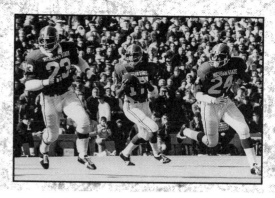

Senior back BILL TRIPLETT (left) was the No. 2 rusher, gaining 200 yards. Here he picks up blockers ERIC ALLEN (24) and HENRY MATTHEWS (23, Akron, Ohio).

Spartan List

All-Time Spartan Offensive Team

(named in 1969-70 by ballots from the MSU game programs, MSU Alumni Magazine, and State News)

Ends	Gene Washington	1966
	Bob Carey	1951
Linemen	Don Coleman	1951
	Norm Masters	1955
	Jerry West	1966
	Ed Budde	1962
	Dave Behrman	1962
Backs	Earl Morrall	1955
	Clint Jones	1966
	John Pingel	1938
	"Sonny" Grandelius	1950

SPARTAN SALUTE

DR. JAMES S. FEURIG, served as physician for the MSU football team for 22 years until he passed away from an apparent heart attack in 1975. Feurig was also the director of MSU's Olin Health Center. MSU presents an annual athletic award bearing his name (The Dr. James S. Feurig Achievement and Service Award) to the graduating senior involved in athletics as a competitor or in a supporting role who carries at least a 3.0 grade-point-average and demonstrates involvement in school/campus and community activities. He played three years with the Green Bay Packers out of high school in order to finance his college education at Marquette University.

★ MSU ALL-STARS ★

Junior ERIC ALLEN (Georgetown, S.C.) paced the ground attack with 811 yards and eight touchdowns in 186 rushes. He was tuning up for his sensational season in 1971.

OTHER AWARD WINNERS

All-Big Ten honorees, second team: GORDON B. BOWDELL, off. end; JOE M. DeLAMIELLEURE, off. guard; THOMAS L. BEARD, center; ERIC B. ALLEN, off. halfback; honorable mention: MICHAEL J. RASMUSSEN, quarterback; WILTON J. MARTIN, def. end; BRAD A. VANPELT, def. back; JOE DeLAMIELLEURE, guard, Academic All-Big Ten; ERIC B. ALLEN, tailback, MVP; VICTOR MITTELBERG, tackle, "Potsy" Ross Scholar-Athlete; GARY PARMENTIER, guard, President's Outstanding Senior; CALVIN FOX, end, "Biggie" Munn Most Inspirational; MIKE TOBIN, linebacker, Oil Can (Humorist); GORDON BOWDELL, split end, Frederick W. Danziger (Detroit area).

1971

THE SCORES

10	Illinois*	0
0	Georgia Tech	10
31	Oregon State*	14
2	Notre Dame	14
13	Michigan*	24
28	Wisconsin	31
34	Iowa*	3
43	Purdue	10
17	Ohio State	10
40	Minnesota*	25
7	Northwestern	28

6-5-0
Big Ten: 5-3-0, T-3rd

THE STANDINGS

	W	L	T
Michigan	8	0	0
Northwestern	6	3	0
Ohio State	5	3	0
Illinois	5	3	0
Michigan State	5	3	0
Wisconsin	3	5	0
Minnesota	3	5	0
Purdue	3	5	0
Indiana	2	6	0
Iowa	1	8	0

THE STAFF

1971 Coaching staff, top, lt. to rt.: Joe Carruthers, receivers; Sherm Lewis, secondary; Carl (Buck) Nystrom, off. line; George Perles, def. line. Bottom, lt. to rt., Ed Rutherford, freshmen; Gordie Serr, backfield; Denny Stolz, def. coordinator; Ed Youngs, line-backers. Duffy Daugherty, head coach.

THE TEAM

1971 Spartan football team. See pages 309-321 for player identification.

SPARTAN ITEM

In the record-setting Purdue game, ERIC ALLEN had rolled up 189 rushing yards by halftime. At the end of three quarters he was clearly within range of the record 347-yard game of Michigan's Ron Johnson. When Jim Bond was substituted for Allen early in the fourth quarter, the MSU sports information staff quickly got word to the Spartan coaches in the press box of how close Allen was to the record. Two carries later, Allen had the NCAA single-game rushing record (In 1978, Eddie Lee Ivery (Georgia Tech) gained 356 yds. vs. Air Force).

GREEN & WHITE HIGHLIGHTS

- The year of ERIC "THE FLEA" ALLEN, who amassed 1,494 yards and 18 touchdowns (second highest TD total in MSU history) in 259 carries for a sterling 5.7 yards-per-carry average.
- In the Purdue game, Allen established six school records, including 350 yards rushing (29 rushes) as State won, 43-10. Allen's heroics also broke the NCAA record of 347 yards in a single game, and Allen sat out the final 8:19 of the game! Triggered by Allen's fabulous day, the Green & White also set MSU's single-game rushing record of 573 yards. MSU's single game total offense also had a standard set that day, totaling 698 yards. All three records still stand. Also, Boris Shlapak kicked a 53-yard field goal, the third of four career FGs he would kick of 54 or 53 yards.
- Senior tailback ERIC ALLEN, senior def. tackle RON CURL and junior safety BRAD VANPELT were all accorded first-team All-America honors.

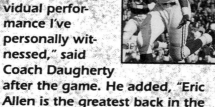

Against Purdue, ERIC ALLEN (24), turned in "the greatest individual performance I've personally witnessed," said Coach Daugherty after the game. He added, "Eric Allen is the greatest back in the country."

The leading tackler for State was junior linebacker GAIL CLARK (98, Bellefontaine, Ohio), who recorded 58 solos and 65 assists for a total of 123 tackles.

Spartan Moments

Spartan List

Top 10 Single-Game Rushing Yardage

Eric Allen, Purdue '71 (29 att.) 350
Lorenzo White, Indiana '87
  (56 att.) 292
Lorenzo White, Indiana '85
  (25 att.) 286
Clinton Jones, Iowa '66 (21 att.) 268
Blake Ezor, Indiana '88 (44 att.) 250
Eric Allen, Wisconsin '71 (21 att.) 247
Lorenzo White, Purdue '85
  (53 att.) 244
Tico Duckett, Minnesota '91
  (30 att.) 241
Marc Renaud, Minnesota '95
  (35 att.) 229
Tico Duckett, Rutgers '90
  (33 att.) 229
Steve Smith, Northwestern '80
  (30 att.) 229

SPARTAN SALUTE

Senior All-America defensive tackle RON CURL (Chicago, Ill.) ranks as one of the top defensive linemen to play at MSU. A two-time All-Big Ten selection, he was third on the squad in '71 with 89 tackles (45 solo hits) and tied for the team lead with seven tackles behind the line of scrimmage.

★ MSU ALL-STARS ★

All-American senior ERIC ALLEN (Left, accepting the Chicago Tribune Silver Football Trophy) , was also the runner-up in the 1971 Big Ten triple jump. Another All-American, junior safety BRAD VANPELT was second on the team with 92 tackles, added four interceptions (returned two for TDs) and was State's top punt returner with an average return of 11.5 in 10 attempts.

OTHER AWARD WINNERS

All Big Ten honorees, first team: JOE DeLAMIELLEURE, off. guard; ERIC B. ALLEN, off. halfback; RONALD C. CURL, def. tackle; BRAD A. VANPELT, def. back; second team: BILLY JOE DuPREE, tight end; ERNEST HAMILTON, linebacker; honorable mention: WILLIAM DAWSON, def. tackle; GAIL A. CLARK, linebacker; MARK W. NIESEN, safety; MARVIN E. ROBERTS, off. tackle; MICHAEL J. RASMUSSEN, quarterback; ERIC ALLEN, tailback, MVP, 10th in voting for Heisman Trophy; ERROL ROY, tackle, Tommy Love Most Improved; MIKE RASMUSSEN, quarterback, "Potsy" Ross Scholar-Athlete; DOUG BARR, halfback, President's Outstanding Senior; RON CURL, def. tackle, "Biggie" Munn Most Inspirational; DAN KOVACS, manager, Oil Can (Humorist); RALPH WIELEBA, end, Frederick W. Danziger (Detroit area).

1972

THE SCORES

24	Illinois	0
16	Georgia Tech*	21
6	Southern California	51
0	Notre Dame*	16
0	Michigan	10
31	Wisconsin*	0
6	Iowa	6
22	Purdue*	12
19	Ohio State*	12
10	Minnesota	14
24	Northwestern*	14

5-5-1
Big Ten: 5-2-1, 4th

THE STANDINGS

	W	L	T
Michigan	7	1	0
Ohio State	7	1	0
Purdue	6	2	0
Michigan State	5	2	1
Minnesota	4	4	0
Indiana	3	5	0
Illinois	3	5	0
Iowa	2	6	1
Wisconsin	2	6	0
Northwestern	1	8	0

THE STAFF

1972 Coaching staff, kneeling, lt. to rt.: Gordie Serr, backfield; Herb Paterra, def. ass't; Denny Stolz, def. coord. & linebackers; Jimmy Raye, receivers. Standing, lt. to rt., Duffy Daugherty, head coach; Ed Rutherford, freshmen; Sherm Lewis, def. backs; Ed Youngs, def. line; Joe Carruthers, off. line.

THE TEAM

1972 Spartan football team. See pages 309-321 for player identification.

SPARTAN ITEM

Duffy and senior co-captains and All-Americans BILLY JOE DuPREE(89) and BRAD VANPELT. DuPree was a standout with the Dallas Cowboys for 11 years while VanPelt strengthened the New York Giants for 11 years before finishing his career with three years in Los Angeles (Raiders) and Cleveland.

GREEN & WHITE HIGHLIGHTS

- Duffy's 19th and final season as head coach at MSU . The Spartans were fourth in the Big Ten with a 5-2-1 record, 5-5-1 overall.
- Upset No. 5 Ohio State, 19-12, in Duffy's final game against the Buckeyes.
- State surrendered an average of 8.5 and a maximum of 14 points against its defense in the Big Ten season, including two shutouts of Illinois and Wisconsin (the Badgers' only blanking of 1972).
- Senior safety BRAD VANPELT, a consensus All-American, was awarded the (Robert W.) Maxwell Award as the outstanding player of the year in college football.
- In addition to co-captain VanPelt, sr. co-captain and tight end BILLY JOE DuPREE and sr. guard JOE DeLAMIELLEURE (Center Line St. Clement) were named All-Americans.

Spartan Moments

Sophomore halfback DAVID E. BROWN (26, Bloomington, Indiana) topped State's ground game with 575 yards and one score in 123 attempts (4.6 avg.). Here he tries to pull away from a defender as All-America guard JOE DeLAMIELLEURE seeks his next block.

Junior QB MARK NIESEN (14, Manistee Catholic Central), was State's #2 rusher, compiling 467 yards and four TDs in 105 carries (4.4 avg.). He quarterbacked MSU to a 31-0 rout of Wisconsin, netting 114 yards in 20 rushes.

Spartan List

Top 10 Career Leaders in Pass Interceptions

John Leister, 1979-80-81-82	35
Dave Yarema, 1982-83-84-85-86	33
Ed Smith, 1976-77-78	32
Charlie Baggett, 1973-74-75	30
Jim Miller, 1990-91-92-93	29
Dan Enos, 1987-88-89-90	25
Steve Juday, 1963-64-65	24
Al Dorow, 1949-50-51	23
Tony Banks, 1994-95	21
Bill Triplett, 1968-69-70	21

SPARTAN SALUTE

Junior strong safety PAUL HAYNER (27, Detroit St. Ambrose) combined with Brad VanPelt to give the Spartans a truly outstanding pair of safeties. Hayner picked off six opponent passes to tie Bill Simpson (Royal Oak Shrine) for the team lead in '72, and recorded 71 tackles (sixth on the team) with 46 solos and 25 assists. Backfield coach Sherm Lewis was duly impressed with Hayner. "Paul Hayner is the best strong safety in the country," Lewis said in 1972. "He teams with VanPelt to give us a safety combination that I wouldn't trade for any in the nation."

★ MSU ALL-STARS ★

Senior guard and All-American JOE DeLAMIELLEURE went on to a fine 13-year NFL career with Buffalo and Cleveland.

OTHER AWARD WINNERS

All-Big Ten Honorees, first team: JOE DeLAMIELLEURE, off. guard; GAIL A. CLARK, linebacker; BRAD A. VANPELT, def. back; WILLIAM T. SIMPSON, def. back; BILLY JOE DuPREE, tight end; second team: GARY L. VANELST, def tackle, JAMES NICHOLSON, off. tackle, BRIAN T. McCONNELL, def. end; honorable mention: MARVIN E. ROBERTS, off. tackle; JOHN E. SHINSKY, def. tackle; MARK W. NIESEN, quarterback; BRAD VANPELT, safety, Columbus Touchdown Club College Defensive Back of the Year, 13th in the voting for the Heisman Trophy; GAIL CLARK, linebacker, MVP; BILLY JOE DuPREE, tight end, Tommy Love Most Improved; MARK GRUA, halfback, "Potsy" Ross Scholar Athlete; JOE DeLAMIELLEURE, tackle, President's Outstanding Senior; GARY VANELST, tackle, "Biggie" Munn Most Inspirational; BILL SIMPSON, halfback, Frederick W. Danziger (Detroit area).

DENNIS E. STOLZ
(1973-75)

Denny Stolz, defensive coordinator under Duffy Daugherty, was the 16th man to direct Spartan football fortunes. The graduate and former head coach at Alma College started off slowly at MSU, but soon built the Spartans into a Big Ten challenger. Stolz' second club finished a half-game behind Michigan and Ohio State in the 1974 Big Ten standings, earning him Conference "Coach of the Year" honors. The highlight that year was an unforgettable upset victory over the top-ranked Buckeyes at Spartan Stadium. His final MSU team tied for third in the Conference standing with the major accomplishment an upset victory at Notre Dame. Stolz left MSU following the 1975 season. He coached at Bowling Green State, 1977-85, and then served as Head Coach at San Diego State, 1986-88.

Career Record: 19-13-1

1973

THE SCORES

10	Northwestern	14
14	Syracuse	8
21	UCLA*	34
10	Notre Dame	14
0	Michigan*	31
3	Illinois*	6
10	Purdue	7
21	Wisconsin*	0
0	Ohio State	35
10	Indiana*	9
15	Iowa	6

5-6-0
Big Ten: 4-4-0, T-4th

THE STANDINGS

	W	L	T
Ohio State	7	0	1
Michigan	7	0	1
Minnesota	6	2	0
Illinois	4	4	0
Michigan State	4	4	0
Purdue	4	4	0
Northwestern	4	4	0
Wisconsin	3	5	0
Indiana	0	8	0
Iowa	0	8	0

THE STAFF

1973 Coaching staff, kneeling, lt. to rt.: Jimmy Raye, passing game; Andy MacDonald, off. coordinator; Charlie Butler, off. line; Sherm Lewis, def. backs. Standing, lt. to rt., Ed Rutherford, admin. ass't.; Howard Weyers, def. ends; Dan Underwood, linebackers; William Davis, off. backs; Ed Youngs, def. coordinator; Denny Stolz, head coach.

THE TEAM

1973 Spartan football team. See pages 309-321 for player identification.

SPARTAN ITEM

Junior fullback CLARENCE BULLOCK (33, Ft. Wayne, Ind.) was a three-year letterwinner who enjoyed his best season in 1973 as MSU's leading ground gainer with 496 yards in 113 attempts for a 4.4 average.

GREEN & WHITE HIGHLIGHTS

- Dennis E. Stolz, defensive coordinator under Duffy Daugherty, took over the reins of the football program as State's 16th head coach. He would coach MSU to a 19-13-1 record in three seasons, including two third place finishes in the Big Ten.
- This team still holds the school record for Passing Defense Per Game Average. The '73 defensive unit gave up just 55.7 yards per game through the air, the second-best mark in the nation.
- After a slow start, the Spartans won four of the last five Big Ten games to finish 4-4 in the conference, tied for fourth.
- Senior defensive back BILL SIMPSON earned All-America status.
- JOHN PINGEL was inducted into the Michigan Sports Hall of Fame.

The total offense leader for State in 1973 was a young sophomore quarterback named CHARLES BAGGETT (16). Baggett threw for 516 yards and ran for another 313 and three TDs for a total offense of 829 yards, despite missing three games due to injury.

Spartan Moments

Senior linebacker RAY NESTER (97, Mt. Clemens Clintondale) set an MSU single season record with 129 tackles in 1973. He finished his career as State's No. 2 all-time leading tackler with 265 stops.

Spartan List

Top 10 Career Field Goals Scored

John Langeloh, 1987-88-89-90	57/79
Morten Anderson, 1978-79-80-81	45/72
Hans Nielsen, 1974-75-76-77	44/70
Ralf Mojsiejenko, 1982-83-84	35/53
Chris Gardner, 1994-95	26/37
Bill Stoyanovich, 1992-93	22/35
Dick Kenney, 1964-65-66	19/36
Chris Caudell, 1985-86	16/35
Dirk Kryt, 1972-73	15/27
Jim DelVerne, 1991-92	13/21
Borys Shlapak, 1970-71	13/34

SPARTAN SALUTE

State's top two signal-callers in 1973 were a pair of sophomore roommates from North Carolina, CHARLIE BAGGETT (16, Fayetteville, N.C.) and TYRONE WILLINGHAM (Jacksonville, N.C.). The two friends competed against one another in high school and have now moved on to outstanding coaching careers. Baggett is currently the assistant head coach and receivers coach at Michigan State and Willingham is the head coach at Stanford.

★MSU ALL-STARS★

Senior defensive back BILL SIMPSON (left) earned first-team All-Big Ten honors for the second straight year as well as All-America recognition in '73. He contributed 64 tackles and led the team in interceptions (5) and passes broken up (7). Simpson went on to a successful career in the NFL with the L.A. Rams and the Buffalo Bills.

OTHER AWARD WINNERS

All-Big Ten honorees, first team: BILL SIMPSON, def. back; second team: JOHN E. SHINSKY, def. tackle; RAYMOND NESTER, linebacker; TERRENCE G. McCLOWRY, linebacker; MARK W. NIESEN, def. back; honorable mention: OTTO SMITH, def. end; CLARENCE BULLOCK, fullback; JOHN SHINSKY, tackle, Academic All-Big Ten, Academic All-America, President's Outstanding Senior; BRUCE HARMS, def. back, Academic All-Big Ten, "Potsy" Ross Scholar-Athlete; RICHARD PAWLAK, tackle, Academic All-Big Ten and Academic All-America; RAY NESTER, linebacker, MVP; MIKE HOLT, tailback, Tommy Love Most Improved; PAUL HAYNER, halfback, "Biggie" Munn Most Inspirational; BILL SIMPSON, def. back, Frederick W. Danziger (Detroit area).

1974

THE SCORES

41	Northwestern*	7
19	Syracuse*	0
14	UCLA	56
14	Notre Dame*	19
7	Michigan	21
21	Illinois	21
31	Purdue*	7
28	Wisconsin	21
16	Ohio State*	13
19	Indiana	10
60	Iowa*	21

7-3-1
Big Ten: 6-1-1, 3rd

THE STANDINGS

	W	L	T
Ohio State	7	1	0
Michigan	7	1	0
Michigan State	6	1	1
Wisconsin	5	3	0
Illinois	4	3	1
Purdue	3	5	0
Minnesota	2	6	0
Iowa	2	6	0
Northwestern	2	6	0
Indiana	1	7	0

THE STAFF

1974 Coaching staff, kneeling, lt. to rt.: Andy MacDonald, off. coord. - QBs; Jimmy Raye, receivers; Charles Butler, guards-centers; Ron Chismar, tackles-tight ends. Standing, lt. to rt., Howard Weyers, def. ends; Ed Youngs, def. coord. - interior line; Denny Stolz, head coach; Bill Davis, running backs; Sherm Lewis, def. backs; Dan Underwood, linebackers.

THE TEAM

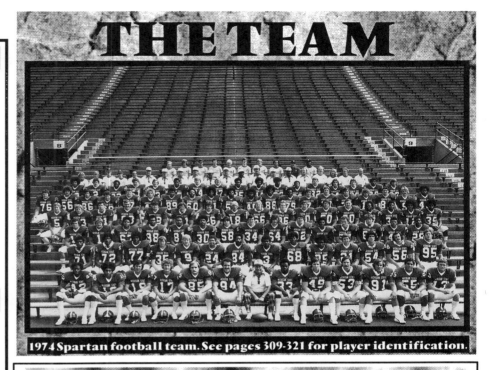

1974 Spartan football team. See pages 309-321 for player identification.

SPARTAN ITEM

One of the great pictures in Spartan gridiron history, during the unforgettable upset victory of top-ranked Ohio State, 16-13. Sophomore fullback LEVI JACKSON (40, Detroit Kettering) races down the Spartan sideline during his 88-yard touchdown run that proved to be the winning fourth-quarter points in one of the great highlights in Spartan gridiron annals (3:17 left on clock when he scored). Jackson was MSU's top rusher in '74 with 942 yards and four TDs in 153 carries, for an impressive 6.2 average gain! Jackson's run is still tied for the second-longest rushing play in MSU history.

GREEN & WHITE HIGHLIGHTS

- Stolz' second-year program turned the corner with a 7-3-1 overall record, 6-1-1 in the Big Ten, just one-half game behind Michigan and Ohio State.
- The Spartans upset No. 1-ranked Ohio State, 16-13, in Spartan Stadium.
- Coach Stolz earns Big Ten "Coach of the Year" honors.
- State won the final five games of the season, capped by a 60-21 blowout of Iowa.
- BOB McCURRY wins NCAA Silver Anniversary Award (25-year achievement award).

Junior CHARLIE BAGGETT led the Spartans in total offense for the second year in a row, this time with 1,713 yards and a whopping 21 touchdowns. When Baggett graduated after the '75 season, he owned the Spartans' record for career total offense with 4,041 yards.

Junior defensive end OTTO SMITH (71, Columbia, S.C.) turned in a terrific year in '74. He was second in total tackles with 114 (65 solos) and paced the defense with 12 tackles for losses of 50 yards!

Spartan Moments

Spartan List

Top 10 Career Touchdown Passes Caught

Kirk Gibson, 1975-76-77-78 24
Andre Rison, 1985-86-87-88 20
Gene Washington,
  1964-65-66 16
Eugene Byrd,
  1975-76-77-78-79 15
Mark Ingram, 1983-84-85-86 ... 14
Bob Carey, 1949-50-51 14
Daryl Turner, 1980-81-82-83 13
Courtney Hawkins,
  1988-89-90-91 12
Otis Grant, 1980-81-82-83 12
Ellis Duckett, 1951-52-53-54 10

SPARTAN SALUTE

Senior receiver MIKE HURD (42, Jackson Parkside) was an outstanding two-sport athlete for State, winning three letters each in football and track. His best football season was '74, catching a team-high 18 passes for 373 yards and three scores (nearly 21 yards per catch). He also captured a 1973 Big Ten indoor hurdles title.

★MSU ALL-STARS★

Senior linebacker TERRY McCLOWRY (49, Dearborn Sacred Heart) led the Spartan defenders with a lofty 129 tackles, including 67 solo hits. He recorded 102 tackles his junior season for a two-year sum of 231 tackles.

OTHER AWARD WINNERS

All-Big Ten honorees, first team: THOMAS HANNON, def. back; MICHAEL COBB, tight end; second team: GREGORY J. SCHAUM, def. tackle; honorable mention: LEVI JACKSON, fullback; CHARLES W. BAGGETT, quarterback; OTTO SMITH, def. end; KIM A. ROWEKAMP, linebacker; LARRY BETHEA, def. tackle; TOM STANDAL, mid. guard, Academic All-Big Ten, Academic All-America, "Potsy" Ross Scholar-Athlete; LEVI JACKSON, fullback, MVP; DANE FORTNEY, split end, Tommy Love Most Improved; CHARLIE BAGGETT, quarterback, President's Outstanding Senior; GREG SCHAUM, tackle, "Biggie" Munn Most Inspirational; MIKE COBB, tight end, Gerald R. Ford Up Front (off. lineman); GREG CROXTON, guard, Downtown Coaches Outstanding Sr. on offense; Frederick W. Danziger (Detroit area); GREG SCHAUM, tackle, Downtown Coaches Outstanding Sr. on defense; ED BUDDE, K. C. Chiefs, Daugherty Award (Distinguished Football Alumnus).

1975

THE SCORES

0	Ohio State*	21
14	Miami (Ohio)*	13
37	North Carolina State*	15
10	Notre Dame	3
6	Michigan*	16
38	Minnesota	15
19	Illinois*	21
10	Purdue	20
14	Indiana	6
47	Northwestern*	14
27	Iowa	23

7-4-0
Big Ten: 4-4-0, T-3rd

THE STANDINGS

	W	L	T
Ohio State	8	0	0
Michigan	7	1	0
Michigan State	4	4	0
Illinois	4	4	0
Purdue	4	4	0
Wisconsin	3	4	1
Minnesota	3	5	0
Iowa	3	5	0
Northwestern	2	6	0
Indiana	1	6	1

THE STAFF

1975 Coaching staff: Denny Stolz, head coach; Andy MacDonald, off. coord.—QBs; Ed Youngs, def. coord. —interior line; Sherm Lewis, def. backs; Jimmy Raye, receivers; Bill Davis, running backs; Dan Underwood, linebackers; Charles Butler, guards-centers; Howard Weyers, def. ends; Ron Chismar, off. tackles-tight ends.

THE TEAM

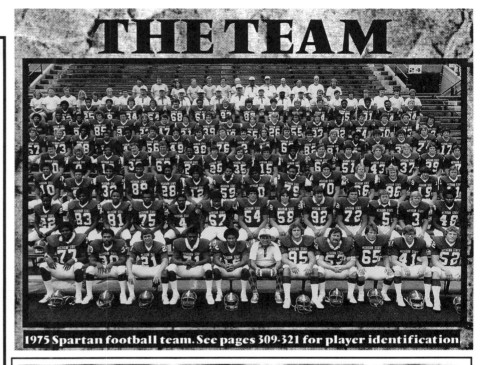

1975 Spartan football team. See pages 309-321 for player identification.

SPARTAN ITEM

A pair of freshmen receivers began to excite the Spartan faithful. Split end EUGENE BYRD (84, East St. Louis, Illinois) and flanker KIRK GIBSON (23, Waterford Kettering) stole the passing-game spotlight with unbelievable reception-yardage averages. Byrd caught 10 aerials for 266 yards (26.6 avg.) and one Touchdown, while Gibson gathered in nine passes for 262 yards (29.1 avg.) and four scores!

GREEN & WHITE HIGHLIGHTS

- State completed its second straight seven-victory season, this time 7-4 overall, 4-4 in the Big Ten (tied for third).
- The Spartans upset #8 Notre Dame in South Bend, 10-3.
- DON COLEMAN was inducted into the College Football Hall of Fame.
- Former Spartan Frank Kush, head coach at Arizona State, is named Coach of the Year by the American Football Coaches Association.
- Hugh Duffy Daugherty inducted into the Michigan Sports Hall of Fame.

Spartan Moments

Sophomore placekicker HANS NIELSEN (8, Vejle, Denmark), pictured here in action against Illinois, booted 10-of-14 field goal attempts and added 22-of-24 extra point conversions to lead State in scoring with 52 points. By the time he left State, he would hold the career record for field goals with 44 (of 70).

Spartan List

Top 10 Career Passes Attempted

Ed Smith, 1976-77-78	789
Dave Yarema, 1982-83-84-85-86	767
Jim Miller, 1990-91-92-93	746
John Leister, 1979-80-81-82	686
Tony Banks, 1994-95	496
Dan Enos, 1987-88-89-90	478
Bryan Clark, 1978-79-80-81	409
Bobby McAllister, 1985-86-87-88	386
Steve Juday, 1963-64-65	384
Charlie Baggett, 1973-74--75	287

Spartan Salute

J. BURT SMITH held the post of MSU's Athletic Director for 3 1/2 years from 1972-75. He was appointed after Biggie Munn suffered a stroke. Burt came to MSU in 1954 as an assistant football coach to Duffy Daugherty. In '65 he became an assistant A.D. A University of Michigan grad, he played two years of pro hockey and base-ball. He was a highly successful football coach at Flint Northern before coming to State.

★ MSU ALL-STARS ★

In his junior campaign, LEVI JACKSON (left) led State's rushing game again. He powered his way to 1,063 yards and five touchdowns in 230 attempts (4.6 avg.), becoming only the third runner in Spartan history to surpass the 2,000-yard career rushing plateau. He ended his career with 2,043 yards, behind only Eric Allen and Lynn Chandnois. His 1974 and '75 season totals marked two of the four highest seasonal rushing totals in the MSU record book.

OTHER AWARD WINNERS

All-Big Ten honorees, first team: THOMAS HANNON, def. back; MICHAEL COBB, tight end; second team: GREGORY J. SCHAUM, def. tackle; honorable mention: LEVI JACKSON, fullback; CHARLES W. BAGGETT, quarterback; OTTO SMITH, def. end; KIM A. ROWEKAMP, linebacker; LARRY BETHEA, def. tackle; TOM STANDAL, mid. guard, Academic All-Big Ten, Academic All-America, "Potsy" Ross Scholar-Athlete; LEVI JACKSON, fullback, MVP; DANE FORTNEY, split end, Tommy Love Most Improved; CHARLIE BAGGETT, qb, President's Outstanding Senior; GREG SCHAUM, tackle, "Biggie" Munn Most Inspirational; MIKE COBB, tight end, Gerald R. Ford Up Front (off. lineman); GREG CROXTON, guard, Downtown Coaches Outstanding Sr. on offense; Frederick W. Danziger (Detroit area); GREG SCHAUM, tackle, Downtown Coaches Outstanding Sr. on defense; ED BUDDE, K. C. Chiefs, Daugherty Award (Distinguished Football Alumnus).

DARRYL D. ROGERS
(1976-79)

Darryl Rogers joined the Spartan football staff following stints at Hayward State and San Jose State in California. Like the two men who preceeded him at Michigan State, Rogers' first team struggled a bit, but he bounced back big in season number two. The Spartans, who set a conference record for offensive proficiency, finished a half-game behind Michigan and Ohio State with a 6-1-1 Big Ten record. In 1978, MSU shared the Big Ten title with the Wolverines. However, NCAA probation prohibited State from going to the Rose Bowl. That performance won Rogers Coach-of-the-Year honors in the Big Ten. Following the 1979 season, he left Michigan State for the head coaching position at Arizona State, 1980-84. Following his stint with the Sun Devils, Rogers signed as head coach of the Detroit Lions, 1985-88. During the 1991 season, he served as the head coach of the Winnipeg Blue Bombers of the Canadian Football League. He is now the athletic director at Southern Connecticut State.

Career Record: 24-18-2

1976

THE SCORES

21	Ohio State	49
21	Wyoming*	10
31	North Carolina State	31
6	Notre Dame*	24
10	Michigan	42
10	Minnesota*	14
31	Illinois	23
45	Purdue*	13
23	Indiana*	0
21	Northwestern	42
17	Iowa*	30

4-6-1
Big Ten: 3-5-0, T-7th

THE STANDINGS

	W	L	T
Michigan	7	1	0
Ohio State	7	1	0
Minnesota	4	4	0
Purdue	4	4	0
Illinois	4	4	0
Indiana	4	4	0
Iowa	3	5	0
Wisconsin	3	5	0
Michigan State	3	5	0
Northwestern	1	7	0

THE STAFF

1976 Coaching staff, kneeling, lt. to rt.: Ray Greene, receivers; Ron Chismar, off. tackles-tight ends; Darryl Rogers, head coach; Leon Burtnett, inside linebackers; Dan Underwood, outside linebackers. Standing, lt. to rt., C.T. Hewgley, centers-guards; Marv Braden, off. coordinator; Sherm Lewis, def. backs; Bob Padilla, def. coordinator.

THE TEAM

1976 Spartan football team. See pages 309-321 for player identification.

SPARTAN ITEM

Athletic Director JOE KEARNEY (lt.) hired Spartan basketball coach Jud Heathcote (rt.) (as well as football coach Darryl Rogers) to come to MSU. Here, Kearney and Heathcote are pictured with long-time Big Ten Commissioner Wayne Duke (center) at a State football game.

GREEN & WHITE HIGHLIGHTS

- DARRYL ROGERS became the 17th head football coach in the 80-year history of the sport at MSU.

- Won three games in a row near the end of the year, including a 45-13 romp over Purdue and a 23-0 shutout of Indiana, to finish 4-6-1 overall, 3-5 in the Big Ten.

- GIBSON and BYRD combined to catch 70 aerials for 1,287 yards and 10 TDs.

- Former Spartan LYMAN FRIMODIG was inducted into the Michigan Sports Hall of Fame.

Spartan Moments

Sophomore flanker KIRK GIBSON established himself as one of the top receivers in the nation. His rare combination of size, speed and strength led to 39 catches for 748 yards and seven scores, including an 82-yard pass-run play from MARSHALL LAWSON against Ohio State in the season opener.

The top rusher was senior tailback RICH BAES who gathered 931 yards and 7 scores in 187 carries.

Spartan List

Top 10 Career Rushing Attempts

Lorenzo White,
1984-85-86-87 1,082
Tico Duckett,
1989-90-91-92 836
Blake Ezor, 1986-87-88-89 800
Steve Smith, 1977-78-79-80 524
Eric Allen, 1969-70-71 521
Rich Baes, 1973-74-75-76 474
Duane Goulbourne,
1992-93-94 414
Charlie Baggett,
1973-74--75 406
Clinton Jones, 1964-65-66 396

SPARTAN SALUTE

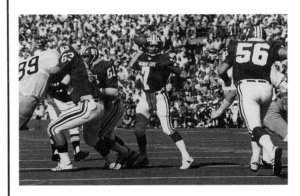

The offense was led by a young sophomore quarterback named EDDIE SMITH (7, Pittsburgh, Pennsylvania). He threw for 1,749 yards and 13 TDs (132-of-257) as the Smith-to-Gibson connection began to build a head of steam. Smith would end his career as the passing yardage leader in MSU history. His 5,706 passing yards is second only to Dave Yarema.

★ MSU ALL-STARS ★

Outstanding senior on defense TOMMY HANNON (45, Massillon, Ohio) was the #2 tackler on the squad with 108, including a team-high 68 solo hits.

OTHER AWARD WINNERS

All-Big Ten honorees, first team: MICHAEL COBB, tight end; THOMAS HANNON, def. back; second team: ALFRED E. PITTS, center; KIRK H. GIBSON, flanker; LARRY BETHEA, def. tackle; ANTON BRUGGENTHIES, off. tackle; honorable mention: RICHARD W. BAES, halfback; OTTO SMITH, def. end; TOM COLE, guard, Academic All-Big Ten; DAVE DUDA, def. back, Academic All-Big Ten, Academic All-America; CRAIG FEDORE, out. linebacker, Academic All-Big Ten; RICH BAES, tailback, MVP, Downtown Coaches Outstanding Sr. on offense; ANTHONY MAREK, guard, Tommy Love Most Improved (co-winner) MEL LAND, def. tackle, Tommy Love Most Improved (co-winner); DAVE RADELET, split end, "Potsy" Ross Scholar-Athlete; MIKE COBB, tight end, President's Outstanding Senior Lineman; OTTO SMITH, linebacker, President's Outstanding Senior Back; TY WILLINGHAM, flanker, "Biggie" Munn Most Inspirational; KIRK GIBSON, flanker, Outstanding Underclass Back; LARRY BETHEA, def. tackle, Outstanding Underclass Lineman; TONY BRUGGENTHIES, tackle, Gerald R. Ford Up Front (off. lineman); TOMMY HANNON, def. back, Downtown Coaches Outstanding Sr. on defense; DEAN LOOK, business/NFL official Daugherty Award (Distinguished Football Alumnus).

THE SCORES

19	Purdue*	14
21	Washington State*	23
34	Wyoming*	16
6	Notre Dame	16
14	Michigan*	24
13	Indiana	13
9	Wisconsin	7
49	Illinois*	20
29	Minnesota	10
44	Northwestern*	3
22	Iowa	16

7-3-1
Big Ten: 6-1-1, 3rd

THE STANDINGS

	W	L	T
Michigan	7	1	0
Ohio State	7	1	0
Michigan State	6	1	1
Indiana	4	3	1
Minnesota	4	4	0
Purdue	3	5	0
Iowa	3	5	0
Wisconsin	3	6	0
Illinois	2	6	0
Northwestern	1	8	0

THE STAFF

1977 Coaching staff, kneeling, lt. to rt.: Ron Chismar, tackles-tight ends; Sherm Lewis, def. backs; George Dyer; inside linebackers; Bob Baker, off. backs. Standing, lt. to rt., Ray Greene, receivers; Bob Padilla, def. coordinator; Darryl Rogers, head coach; Dan Underwood, outside linebackers; C. T. Hewgley, guards-centers.

THE TEAM

1977 Spartan football team. See pages 309-321 for player identification.

SPARTAN ITEM

Sophomore linebacker DAN BASS (49, Bath) — pictured here in the 49-20 romp over Illinois — led the defensive charge with 134 tackles. He also paced the defense his freshman year with 111 stops. The '77 season was the first of three straight years in which Bass would set the Spartans' single-season tackle record.

GREEN & WHITE HIGHLIGHTS

- DARRYL ROGERS' second squad bounced back big in 1977 with a 7-3-1 overall record.
- Finished one-half game behind Michigan and Ohio State with a 6-1-1 conference ledger.
- Won the last five games of the season and went undefeated in the last six, including routs of Illinois (49-20), Minnesota (29-10) and Northwestern (44-3).
- LARRY BETHEA was voted the Big Ten's Most Valuable Player.
- DON COLEMAN was chosen for NCAA Silver Anniversary Award.

Spartan Moments

EDDIE SMITH threw for another 1,731 yards and 10 TDs. In the foreground is senior fullback JIM EARLEY (48, Dayton, Ohio), who was State's #2 ground gainer with 668 yards and three TDs on 109 carries for a fine 6.1 average.

Receivers were plentiful with five in double figures for catches and three — GIBSON, BRAMMER and EDGAR WILSON (41, Dowagiac) —with over 20 receptions each. Wilson, here escaping a Wyoming defender, was second in receptions to Brammer with 23 for 418 yards and two scores.

Spartan List

Top 10 Career Receiving Yardage

Andre Rison,
1985-86-87-88 2,992
Kirk Gibson,
1975-76-77-78 2,347
Courtney Hawkins,
1988-89-90-91 2,210
Eugene Byrd,
1975-76-77-78-79 2,082
Mark Ingram,
1983-84-85-86 1,944
Gene Washington,
1964-65-66 1,857
Mill Coleman,
1991-92-93-94 1,813
Ted Jones, 1980-81-82 1,678
Daryl Turner,
1980-81-82-83 1,577
Otis Grant, 1980-81-82 1,358

SPARTAN SALUTE

LARRY BETHEA, winner of the 1977 Chicago Tribune Silver Football Award as the Big Ten's Most Valuable Player, examines the award with coach Rogers. As a junior defensive end in '76, Bethea performed yeoman's duty with 63 tackles, including a team-high 12 stops behind the line of scrimmage for 77 yards in losses.

★ MSU ALL-STARS ★

OTHER AWARD WINNERS

All-Big Ten honorees, first team: RAYMOND M. STACHOWICZ, punter; LARRY BETHEA, def. tackle; ALFRED E. PITTS, center; second team: MARK A. ANDERSON, def. back; KIRK H. GIBSON, flanker; MARK D. BRAMMER, tight end; PAUL G. RUDZINSKI, linebacker; honorable mention: JAMES EARLEY, fullback; JAMES A. HINESLY, off. tackle; HANS J. NIELSEN, placekicker; JIM SCIARINI, guard, Academic All-Big Ten, Academic All-America; CRAIG FEDORE, linebacker, Academic All-Big Ten, Academic All-America; LARRY BETHEA, def. tackle, MVP, Downtown Coaches Outstanding Senior on defense; MIKE DEAN, linebacker, Tommy Love Most Improved; DAVE RADELET, def. back, "Potsy" Ross Scholar-Athlete; AL PITTS, center, President's Outstanding Senior Lineman, Gerald R. Ford Up Front (off. lineman); PAUL RUDZINSKI, linebacker, President's Outstanding Senior Back; JEROME STANTON, def. back, "Biggie" Munn Most Inspirational; MARK BRAMMER, tight end, Outstanding Underclass Lineman (co-winner); MEL LAND, def. tackle, Outstanding Underclass Lineman (co-winner); MARK ANDERSON, def. back, Outstanding Underclass Back; JIM EARLEY, fullback, Downtown Coaches Outstanding Senior on offense; EARL MORRALL, NFL veteran, Daugherty Award (Outstanding Football Alumnus).

1978

THE SCORES

14	Purdue	21
49	Syracuse*	21
9	Southern California	30
25	Notre Dame*	29
24	Michigan	15
49	Indiana*	14
55	Wisconsin*	2
59	Illinois	19
33	Minnesota*	9
52	Northwestern	3
42	Iowa*	7

8-3-0
Big Ten: 7-1-0, T-1st

THE STANDINGS

	W	L	T
Michigan State	7	1	0
Michigan	7	1	0
Purdue	6	1	1
Ohio State	6	2	0
Minnesota	4	4	0
Wisconsin	3	4	2
Indiana	3	5	0
Iowa	2	6	0
Illinois	0	6	2
Northwestern	0	8	1

THE STAFF

1978 Coaching staff, front, lt. to rt.: Walt Harris, inside linebackers; C.T. Hewgley, centers-guards; Darryl Rogers, head coach; Sherm Lewis, def. backs; Ron Chismar, tackles-tight ends. Back, lt. to rt., Bob Baker, off. backs; Mo Forte, receivers; Matt Means, grad. ass't.; George Dyer, def. coordinator; Dan Underwood, outside linebackers; Kurt Schottenheimer, grad. ass't.

THE TEAM

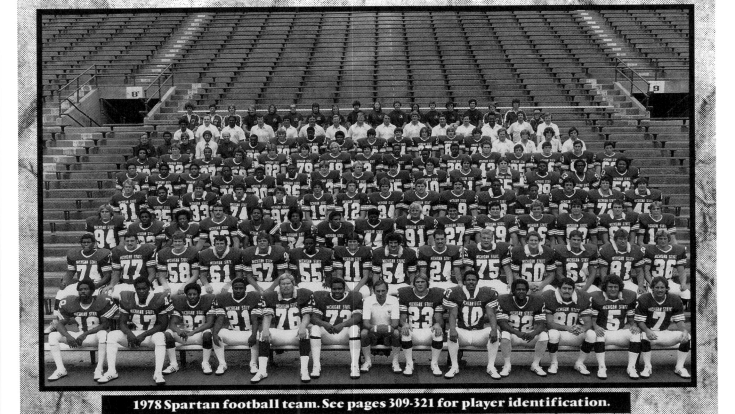

1978 Spartan football team. See pages 309-321 for player identification.

Spartan Moments

The talk of the Big Ten was the amazing senior pass-catch combination of EDDIE SMITH to KIRK GIBSON. In '78, Smith completed 169-of-292 passes for 2,226 yards and 20 touchdowns — six to Gibson (and six to Byrd). His 369 passing yards vs. Indiana is still the MSU standard.

Four TD passes to KIRK GIBSON (right) came in the first quarter of four different games (Indiana, 86 yds.; Purdue, Northwestern and Iowa, 54 yds.). "Gibby" is pictured here in the Michigan game, hauling in one of his five receptions for 82 yards in the 24-15 win in Michigan Stadium.

GREEN & WHITE HIGHLIGHTS

- MSU shared the Big Ten title with Michigan, compiling a 7-1 Big Ten slate, 8-3 overall. However, NCAA probation prohibited the Spartans from going to the Rose Bowl.
- This unit set the Big Ten record for offensive proficiency by averaging 481.3 yards of total offense per game, third in the nation in '78. The Spartans also were the third highest scoring team in the land with 37.4 points per game. Both marks are still MSU standards.
- The only Big Ten defeat was the season opener at Purdue, 21-14. State then ran the table with seven straight league wins, including a 24-15 victory in Ann Arbor over 5th-ranked Michigan. State was unstoppable on offense, averaging 44.9 points per game over the last seven wins while yielding an average of just 9.8.
- DARRYL ROGERS won Big Ten Coach of the Year honors as well as The Sporting News' Coach of the Year.
- KIRK GIBSON was named the Outstanding Offensive End in the nation by the Downtown Athletic Club of New York.
- DAN BASS returned an interception 99 yards for a TD against Wisconsin — the longest pass interception return in Spartan history.
- Charlie Bachman was inducted into the College Football Hall of Fame.

★ MSU ALL-STARS ★

EDDIE SMITH (left), established Big Ten career records for yards gained passing (5,706), passes attempted (789) and passes completed (418). He led the nation with 7.0 total offense yards per play. Eddie was second in TD passes (20) and second in interception avoidance (2.6%). He finished 5th in the NCAA in pass completions per game (16.9), and 4th in total offense (224.7).

OTHER AWARD WINNERS

All-Big Ten honorees, first team: EUGENE W. BYRD, off. end; MARK D. BRAMMER, tight end; JIM HINESLY, off. tackle; KIRK H. GIBSON, flanker; MELVIN LAND, def. tackle; THOMAS E. GRAVES, def. back; RAYMOND M. STACHOWICZ, punter; second team: EDWARD L. SMITH, quarterback; MARK A. ANDERSON, def. back; DAN E. BASS, linebacker; honorable mention: D. STEVE SMITH, halfback; MICHAEL R. DENSMORE, off. guard; ED SMITH, quarterback, MVP, Downtown Coaches Outstanding Sr. on offense; MATT FOSTER, center, Tommy Love Most Improved; CHARLES SHAFER, tight end, "Potsy" Ross Scholar-Athlete; JIM HINESLY, tackle, President's Outstanding Senior Lineman, Gerald R. Ford Up Front (off. lineman); KIRK GIBSON, flanker, President's Outstanding Senior Back; MIKE HANS, fullback, "Biggie" Munn Most Inspirational (co-winner); JEROME STANTON, def. back, "Biggie" Munn Most Inspirational (co-winner); MARK BRAMMER, tight end, Outstanding Underclass Lineman; STEVE SMITH, tailback, Outstanding Underclass Back; MEL LAND, def. tackle, Downtown Coaches Outstanding Sr. on defense; JOHN WILKS, business, Daugherty Award (Distinguished Football Alumnus).

Spartan List

Top 10 Single-Season Passes Attempted

Jim Miller, 1993	336
Dave Yarema, 1986	297
Ed Smith, 1978	292
Tony Banks, 1995	258
Ed Smith, 1976	257
John Leister, 1982	251
John Leister, 1980	247
Dan Enos, 1989	240
Ed Smith, 1977	240
Tony Banks, 1994	238

SPARTAN SALUTE

KIRK GIBSON, a junior centerfielder, completed one of the most amazing athletic careers in Spartan history. In 1978, he was the No. 1 draft choice of the Detroit Tigers following his only season of collegiate baseball (and first season of baseball since his senior year in high school), earning All-America honors. "Gibby" hit .390, collected 16 home runs and 52 RBIs, and stole 21 bases to lead MSU to a Big Ten runner-up finish and a spot in the NCAA District Five tournament in Tulsa, Oklahoma. He then returned to football in the fall of '78 for a brilliant final season with the Spartans in their Big Ten co-championship season when he earned All-America recognition in that sport as well.

BIG TEN CHAMPIONS!

JOE KEARNEY, Director of Athletics, holds the Big Ten championship trophy during a basketball half-time ceremony.

All-American KIRK GIBSON (left) ended his MSU career as State's leader in pass receptions (112), reception yardage (2,347), yardage per reception (21.0) and TD passes caught (24). He is still 6th, 2nd, 1st and 1st, respectively, in those categories in the MSU record book. When he left State, he began to intimidate baseball pitchers even more often than he did defensive backs.

All-American MARK BRAMMER left State as the #3 performer in receptions (107) and is still 7th in the MSU record book and the top career receiver among Spartan tight ends.

1979

THE SCORES

33	Illinois*	16
41	Oregon*	17
24	Miami (Ohio)*	21
3	Notre Dame	27
7	Michigan*	21
29	Wisconsin	38
7	Purdue*	14
0	Ohio State	42
42	Northwestern	7
31	Minnesota*	17
23	Iowa	33

5-6-0
Big Ten: 3-5-0, T-7th

THE STANDINGS

	W	L	T
Ohio State	8	0	0
Purdue	7	1	0
Michigan	6	2	0
Indiana	5	3	0
Iowa	4	4	0
Minnesota	3	5	1
Michigan State	3	5	0
Wisconsin	3	5	0
Illinois	1	6	1
Northwestern	0	9	0

THE STAFF

1979 Coaching staff, front row lt. to rt.: Ron Chismar, tackles-tight ends; Walt Harris, inside linebackers; Darryl Rogers, head coach; George Dyer, def. coordinator; Mo Forte, receivers; Matt Means, grad. ass't. Back row, lt. to rt., Dan Underwood, outside linebackers; Ron Marciel, volunteer ass't., Bob Baker, off. backs; Sherm Lewis, def. backs; Kurt Schottenheimer, grad. ass't.; C.T. Hewgley, guards-centers.

THE TEAM

1979 Spartan Football Team. See pages 309-321 for player identification.

SPARTAN ITEM

Senior flanker EUGENE BYRD was the top receiver with 30 catches for 559 yards and four TDs. He left State as its career leader in receptions (114, eclipsing Gibson's 112 catches) and was #2 in reception yardage (behind Gibson).

GREEN & WHITE HIGHLIGHTS

- Opened the season 3-0 before falling to a 5-6 overall record, 3-5 in the Big Ten.
- Senior DAN BASS set the school record for the third straight year with 160 tackles—still 5th on the Spartans' single-season tackle chart.
- EUGENE BYRD topped all Big Ten receivers in single-game reception yardage with 159 yards (on five catches) against Iowa.
- State's defense held Purdue to -5 yards rushing and no first downs rushing.

Spartan Moments

Junior tailback STEVE SMITH (20, Louisville, Ky.) led the team in rushing for the second straight season, gaining 972 yards and four TDs on 204 rushes (4.8 avg.).

Spartan List

Top 10 Career Reception Yardage Averages

Kirk Gibson, 1975-76-77-78 .... 21.0
Andre Rison, 1985-86-87-88 .... 20.5
Mark Ingram, 1983-84-85-86 .... 20.5
Daryl Turner, 1980-81-82-83 ..... 20.2
Dave Kaiser, 1955-56-57 .... 19.5
Frank Foreman, 1967-68-69 ...... 18.5
Eugene Byrd, 1975-76-77-78-79 18.3
Gene Washington, 1964-65-66 . 18.2
Mike Hurd, 1971-72-73-74 .... 18.2
Nigea Carter, 1993-94-95 .... 18.0

SPARTAN SALUTE

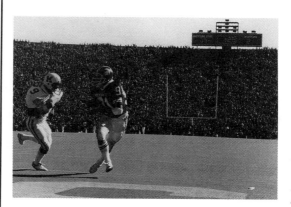

Senior tight end MARK BRAMMER scored the game-winning touchdown on this pass reception as State defeated Miami (Ohio), 24-21. Brammer hauled in a six-yard pass from QB Bert Vaughn to give the Spartans their third straight victory of the season without a loss. He led all receivers that afternoon with five catches for 69 yards.

Brammer ended his MSU career with 107 receptions, third on State's all-time list at the time—behind only Gibson and Byrd—and still ranks 7th.

★ MSU ALL-STARS ★

All-American junior punter RAY STACHOWICZ (left), after finishing 8th in the nation in 1978, led the Big Ten and was 5th in the nation in 1979 with a 44.3 punting average.

OTHER AWARD WINNERS

All-Big Ten honorees, first team: RAY STACHOWICZ, punter; DAN E. BASS, linebacker; MARK D. BRAMMER, tight end; second team: ANGELO B. FIELDS, off. tackle; MORTEN ANDERSEN, placekicker; BERNARD B. HAY, def. tackle; honorable mention: EUGENE BYRD, off. end; D. STEVE SMITH, halfback; DEREK P. HUGHES, halfback; JAMES E. BURROUGHS, def. back; MATTHEW FOSTER, center; LARRY E. SAVAGE, linebacker; MARK A. ANDERSON, def. back; ALAN DAVIS, def. back, Academic All-Big Ten, Academic All-America, "Potsy" Ross Scholar-Athlete; DAN BASS, linebacker, MVP, Downtown Coaches Outstanding Sr. on defense; STEVE OTIS, linebacker, Tommy Love Most Improved (co-winner); BRYAN CLARK, quarterback, Tommy Love Most Improved (co-winner); MARK ANDERSON, def. back, President's Outstanding Senior Back; MARK BRAMMER, tight end, President's Outstanding Senior Lineman, Downtown Coaches Outstanding Sr. on offense; MATT FOSTER, center, "Biggie" Munn Most Inspirational, Gerald R. Ford Up Front (off. lineman); BERNARD HAY, mid. guard, Outstanding Underclass Lineman; STEVE SMITH, tailback, Outstanding Underclass Back; JIM NINOWSKI, business, NFL Daugherty Award (Distinguished Football Alumnus).

FRANK "MUDDY" WATERS
(1980-82)

Frank "Muddy" Waters became only the second former Michigan State player to coach the Spartans. The personable coach was named head man at MSU one day before his 57th birthday, following a highly successful career at Hillsdale and Saginaw Valley State. State failed to post a winning record in any of Waters' three seasons with the Spartans, but fielded a potent offensive unit most of the time. Three players — Ray Stachowicz, Morten Andersen and James Burroughs — won All-America honors during Muddy's stint at MSU. He and his wife, Mary Lou, currently reside in East Lansing.

Career Record: 10-23-0

1980-1989

MICHIGAN STATE UNIVERSITY

SPARTAN FOOTBALL

100 Seasons

MAC - MSC - MSU

1980

THE SCORES

17	Illinois	20
7	Oregon	35
33	Western Michigan*	7
21	Notre Dame*	26
23	Michigan	27
7	Wisconsin*	17
25	Purdue	36
16	Ohio State*	48
42	Northwestern*	10
30	Minnesota	12
0	Iowa*	41

3-8-0
Big Ten: 2-6-0, 9th

THE STANDINGS

	W	L	T
Michigan	8	0	0
Ohio State	7	1	0
Purdue	7	1	0
Iowa	4	4	0
Minnesota	4	5	0
Indiana	3	5	0
Wisconsin	3	5	0
Illinois	3	5	0
Michigan State	2	6	0
Northwestern	0	9	0

THE STAFF

1980 Coaching staff, kneeling, lt. to rt.: Joe Pendry, off. coordinator; Frank "Muddy" Waters, head coach; Sherm Lewis, ass't. head coach and def. coordinator. Standing, lt. to rt., Ty Willingham, def. backs; Dick Comar, off. line; Dave Driscoll, off. backs; Matt Means, receivers; Kurt Schottenheimer, out. linebackers; Ted Guthard, def. line.

THE TEAM

1980 Spartan football team. See pages 309-321 for player identification

SPARTAN ITEM

Two of MSU's great kickers! Two-time All-America punter RAY STACHOWICZ (lt.) was MSU's career leader in punting average (43.3) when he graduated in 1980. Here he is pictured with 1981 All-America field goal kicker MORTEN ANDERSEN who left for the professional ranks as State's career leader in field goals (45) and still owns the longest FG in Spartan history—63 yards vs. OSU in 1981.

GREEN & WHITE HIGHLIGHTS

- FRANK "MUDDY" WATERS became only the second former Michigan State player to ascend to the Spartans' head coach position.
- The '80 passing attack accounted for 199 yards per game, still the fifth highest seasonal average at MSU.
- Two freshmen led State to the first Big Ten victory of the season, 42-10 over Northwestern. Linebacker CARL BANKS was named Defensive Player of the Game and defensive back TIM CUNNINGHAM, who has become a popular local musician, (saxophone player), was voted the #2 defensive star of the game.

Spartan Moments

Senior tailback **STEVE SMITH** completed an excellent career by leading the ground game for the third consecutive season with 667 yards and five touchdowns. He was also the team's second-leading receiver with 26 receptions for 333 yards and four TDs.

Sophomore quarterback **JOHN LEISTER** (Great Falls, Montana), threw for 1,559 yards on 103 completions of 247 attempts. He entered the MSU record book with 54 passes thrown during a 36-25 loss to Purdue.

Spartan List

Top 10 Single-Season Passing Yardage

Dave Yarema, 1986	2,581
Jim Miller, 1993	2,269
Ed Smith, 1978	2,226
Tony Banks, 1995	2,084
Dan Enos, 1989	2,066
Tony Banks, 1994	2,040
Ed Smith, 1976	1,749
Ed Smith, 1977	1,731
Dan Enos, 1990	1,677
John Leister, 1980	1,559

SPARTAN SALUTE

DOUG WEAVER became the 15th Director of Athletics and served the school for 10 years. He developed the revenue-producing sports of football, basketball and hockey while building a strong cash reserve for the athletic department. A 1953 graduate of MSU and a three-year football letterwinner, Weaver took over at the age of 49. He was a former head football coach at Kansas State and Southern Ilinois. He served as A.D. at SIU and Georgia Tech prior to coming back to MSU. Weaver also earned a law degree from the U. of Kansas.

★ MSU ALL-STARS ★

Punter RAY STACHOWICZ became a two-time All-American in 1980. He departed State as the school's career leader in punting average (43.3) and the first Big Ten player to earn All-Big Ten first team honors for four years.

OTHER AWARD WINNERS

All-Big Ten honorees, first team: RAY STACHOWICZ, punter; second team: RODNEY L. STRATA, off. guard; MORTEN ANDERSEN, placekicker; honorable mention: TED D. JONES, off. end; JOHN W. LEISTER, quarterback; D. STEVE SMITH, halfback; SMILEY L. CRESWELL, def. tackle; THOMAS L. MORRIS, safety; TODD LANGERVELD, def. back, Academic All-Big Ten; STEVE SMITH, tailback, MVP, President's Outstanding Senior Back, Downtown Coaches Outstanding Sr. on offense; ALAN KIMICHIK, tight end, Tommy Love Most Improved, MIKE SCIARINI, center, "Potsy" Ross Scholar-Athlete; ROD STRATA, off. guard, President's Outstanding Senior Lineman, Iron Man (strength and conditioning), Gerald R. Ford Up Front (off lineman); JOHNNY LEE HAYNES, def. tackle, "Biggie" Munn Most Inspirational; GREG LAUBLE, linebacker, Oil Can (Humorist); SMILEY CRESWELL, def. end, Outstanding Underclass Lineman, THOMAS MORRIS, def. back, Outstanding Underclass Back (co-winner); JOHN LEISTER, quarterback, Outstanding Underclass Back (co-winner); JOHN McCORMICK, linebacker, Downtown Coaches Outstanding Sr. on defense; JEFF WISKA, off. tackle, Frederick W. Danziger (Detroit area); JOHN PINGEL, advertising exec., Daugherty Award (Distinguished Football Alumnus).

1981

THE SCORES

17	Illinois*	27
13	Ohio State	27
10	Bowling Green State *	7
7	Notre Dame	20
20	Michigan*	38
33	Wisconsin*	14
26	Purdue	27
26	Indiana*	3
61	Northwestern	14
43	Minnesota*	36
7	Iowa	36

5-6-0
Big Ten: 4-5-0, T-6th

THE STANDINGS

	W	L	T
Ohio State	6	2	0
Iowa	6	2	0
Michigan	6	3	0
Illinois	6	3	0
Wisconsin	6	3	0
Minnesota	4	5	0
Michigan State	4	5	0
Purdue	3	6	0
Indiana	3	6	0
Northwestern	0	9	0

THE STAFF

1981 Coaching staff, kneeling, lt. to rt.: Ted Guthard, def. line; Sherm Lewis, ass't. head coach & def. coordinator; "Muddy" Waters, head coach; Joe Pendry, off. coordinator; Ty Willingham, def. backs; Mike Imhoff, grad. ass't. Standing, lt. to rt., Dick Comar, off. line; Dave Driscoll, off. backs; Matt Means, receivers; Kurt Schottenheimer, out. linebackers; Dave Arnold, grad. ass't.; Steve Schottel, grad. ass't.

THE TEAM

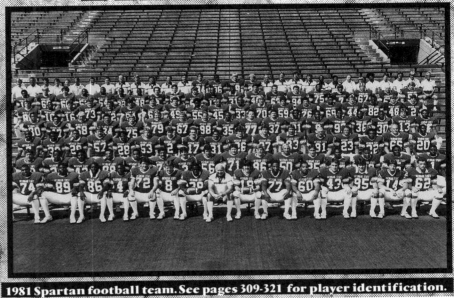

1981 Spartan football team. See pages 309-321 for player identification.

SPARTAN ITEM

Junior split end TED JONES (21, Akron, Ohio) enjoyed a big year with 44 catches for 624 yards and five TDs to lead all Spartan receivers for the second straight year. Here he hauls in a 28-yard scoring strike from Bryan Clark against Michigan.

GREEN & WHITE HIGHLIGHTS

- The most prolific passing game in State's history in terms of passing yards per game. The '81 unit rolled up 251.9 aerial yards per game — still MSU's record—which was 12th in the nation.
- Team improved over 1980 by two victories to 5-6 overall, 4-5 in MSU's first nine-game Big Ten schedule.
- State upset #14 Wisconsin, 33-14.
- DARYL TURNER was considered the nation's #1 long-ball threat. He closed the season with a 70-yard TD catch vs. Minnesota (from BRYAN CLARK) to go with other 1981 TD catches of 63, 5, 54, 49, and 45 yards!

Spartan Moments

The defense was led by CARL BANKS (54, Flint Beecher), a sophomore linebacker who registered 97 tackles, including 46 unassisted takedowns and a team-high 10 tackles for losses of 42 yards. Banks went on to become one of the all-time great linebackers in the NFL as well as MSU.

Senior QB BRYAN CLARK (14, Bloomfield Hills), the son of former Detroit Lions coach Monte Clark, completed 109-of-204 passes (.536) for 1,521 yards and 14 TDs to earn MVP honors.

Spartan List

MSU's Longest Field Goals
(53 yards or longer)

Morten Andersen, Ohio State '81	63
Ralf Mojsiejenko, Illinois '82	61
Ralf Mojsiejenko, Purdue '83	59
Morten Andersen, Michigan '80	57
Borys Shlapak, Iowa '71	54
Borys Shlapak, Northwestern '70	54
Borys Shlapak, Minnesota '71	54
Morten Andersen, Iowa '79	54
Ralf Mojsiejenko, Purdue '84	54
Morten Andersen, Minnesota '79	53
Hans Nielsen, Wyoming '77	53
Borys Shlapak, Purdue '71	53

SPARTAN SALUTE

Senior All-America PK MORTEN ANDERSEN set MSU and Big Ten placekicking records with 45 FGs in his career. He set the MSU and Big Ten records with an astonishing 63-yard field goal at Ohio State in 1981 (John Leister holds). Andersen kicked a school record 57-yard field goal vs. Michigan in 1980. He also booted FGs of 49 and 35 yards in that game.

★ MSU ALL-STARS ★

OTHER AWARD WINNERS

Senior All-America cornerback JAMES BURROUGHS (Pahokee, Florida) set the school record of 13 passes broken up in the '81 season.

All-Big Ten honorees, first team: MORTEN ANDERSEN, placekicker; THOMAS M. PIETTE, center; CARL E. BANKS, linebacker; JAMES E. BURROUGHS, def. back; honorable mention; DARYL TURNER, off. end; TED D. JONES, off. end; ALAN W. KIMICHIK, tight end; JEFFREY R. WISKA, off. tackle; SMILEY L. CRESWELL, def. tackle; GEORGE J. COOPER, linebacker; STEVE K. MAIDLOW, linebacker; TIMOTHY W. CUNNINGHAM, safety MORTEN ANDERSEN, placekicker, Academic All-Big Ten; TODD LANGERVELD, def. back, Academic All-Big Ten; BRYAN CLARK, quarterback, MVP; WALTER SCHRAMM, off. tackle, Tommy Love Most Improved (co-winner); STEVE MAIDLOW, linebacker, Tommy Love Most Improved (co-winner); BRYAN BOAK, off. tackle, "Potsy" Ross Scholar-Athlete; JEFF WISKA, off. tackle, President's Outstanding Sr. Lineman, Iron Man (strength & conditioning), Gerald R. Ford Up Front (off. lineman), Frederick W. Danziger (Detroit area); BRYAN CLARK, quarterback, President's Outstanding Sr. Back, Downtown Coaches Outstanding Sr. on offense; GEORGE COOPER, linebacker, "Biggie" Munn Most Inspirational; GREGG LAUBLE, linebacker, Oil Can (Humorist); CARL BANKS, linebacker, Outstanding Underclass Back; TED JONES, split end, Outstanding Underclass Lineman; JAMES BURROUGHS, corner back, Downtown Coaches Outstanding Sr. on defense; DON COLEMAN, MSU administrator, Daugherty Award (Distinguished Football Alumnus).

1982

THE STANDINGS

	W	L	T
Michigan	8	1	0
Ohio State	7	1	0
Iowa	6	2	0
Illinois	6	3	0
Wisconsin	5	4	0
Indiana	4	5	0
Purdue	3	6	0
Northwestern	2	7	0
Michigan State	2	7	0
Minnesota	1	8	0

THE STAFF

1982 Coaching staff, kneeling, lt. to rt.: Mike Vite, quarterbacks-receivers; Sherm Lewis, ass't. head coach & def. coordinator; "Muddy" Waters, head coach; Steve Schottel, off. coordinator; Ty Willingham, def. backs. Standing, lt. to rt., Dave Driscoll, off. backs; Robert "Turf" Kauffman, def. line; Matt Means, tackles-tight ends; Ted Guthard, def. line; Kurt Schottenheimer, linebackers; Dick Comar, centers-guards.

THE TEAM

1982 Spartan football team. See pages 309-321 for player identification.

SPARTAN ITEM

One of the most incredible plays in the history of college football occurred in the Iowa game. MSU trailed, 17-0, in the second quarter and faced a third-and-10 from the Iowa 21 yardline. QB DAVE YAREMA (Birmingham Brother Rice) overthrew DARRYL TURNER in the end zone when Iowa safety Ron Hawley crashed into the goalpost, knocking it down and breaking the cross bar. The grounds crew held the goal posts up for the field goal attempt (which RALF MOJSIEJENKO made).

GREEN & WHITE HIGHLIGHTS

- The Spartans defeated Indiana and Minnesota but dipped to a 2-9 record, 2-7 in the Big Ten, losing three games by a total differential of seven points. Other than the Michigan and Ohio State games, State's largest margin of defeat was eight points (the other seven losses were by 7, 3, 8, 1, 3, 4 and 6 points).
- Coach "Muddy" Waters was so loved by the players and fans, that even after enduring a 2-9 season which ended his coaching career, he was carried off the field on the shoulders of the fans. When he reached the locker room, he was greeted with a standing ovation from the team.

Spartan Moments

Senior running back TONY ELLIS (5, Coolidge, Arizona) showed the way on the ground with 671 yards and seven touchdowns in '82.

Spartan List

Top 12 Single-Season Passes Completed

Jim Miller, 1993	215
Dave Yarema, 1986	200
Ed Smith, 1978	169
Tony Banks, 1995	156
Dan Enos, 1989	153
Tony Banks, 1994	145
Dan Enos, 1990	137
Tony Banks, 1994	145
Dan Enos, 1990	137
Ed Smith, 1976	132
Jim Miller, 1991	130
Jim Miller, 1992	122

SPARTAN SALUTE

Another top senior receiver was TED JONES who added 34 receptions for 486 yards and one score. Jones eclipsed the career reception marks of Kirk Gibson and Eugene Byrd to leave MSU as its all-time pass-catching leader with 118 (in three seasons)! Against Michigan, Jones caught nine aerials for 123 yards.

★MSU ALL-STARS★

Senior linebacker JIM NEELY (above) (58, South Bend, Indiana) enjoyed a superb year with 130 tackles, including 77 solo tackles. CARL BANKS was second with 71 hits, 36 unassisted tackles.

OTHER AWARD WINNERS

All-Big Ten honorees, first team: CARL E. BANKS, linebacker; second team: SMILEY L. CRESWELL, def. tackle; honorable mention: TED D. JONES, off. end; RANDY J. LARK, off. guard; WALTER SCHRAMM, off. tackle; RALF MOJSIEJENKO, punter/placekicker; OTIS GRANT, flanker; MARVIN M. MANTOS, off. guard; JIM NEELY, linebacker; JIM NEELY, linebacker, MVP, Downtown Coaches Outstanding Sr. on defense; JIM MORRISSEY, linebacker, Tommy Love Most Improved; DARRIN McCLELLAND, fullback, "Potsy" Ross Scholar-Athlete, President's Outstanding Senior Back (co-winner), Frederick W. Danziger (Detroit area); TONY ELLIS, halfback, President's Outstanding Senior Back (co-winner); SMILEY CRESWELL, def. tackle, President's Outstanding Senior Lineman, Iron Man (strength & conditioning); TONY GILBERT, split end, "Biggie" Munn Most Inspirational (posthumously); GREGG LAUBLE, linebacker, Oil Can (Humorist); CARL BANKS, linebacker, Outstanding Underclass Back; RANDY LARK, tackle, Outstanding Underclass Lineman; WALT SCHRAMM, tackle, Gerald R. Ford Up Front (off. lineman); OTIS GRANT, flanker, Downtown Coaches Outstanding Sr. on offense; ROBERT McCURRY, auto. exec., Daugherty Award (Distinguished Football Alumnus).

GEORGE J. PERLES
(1983-94)

George Perles with sons
John (left) and Pat

Former Spartan gridder and assistant coach George Perles saw his dream of becoming head coach of the MSU football program come true when he was appointed to the position December 3, 1982. After posting just 10 wins in three seasons prior to his arrival, Perles helped restore the MSU program to national prominence with two bowl appearances in his first three seasons. In 1987, Perles and the Spartans captured the Big Ten title and made the program's first Rose Bowl appearance since 1966. The Spartans topped Southern Cal, 20-17, ending the year at 9-2-1, the most victories by an MSU squad since 1966, along with a No. 8 national ranking. His efforts that season earned him *Football News'* Coach of the Year honors. The Rose Bowl began a string of four straight bowl appearances that included triumphs in the 1989 John Hancock Bowl. The architect of the dominating Pittsburgh Steelers' defense during their Super Bowl years (1974-75-78-79), 50 of his players were selected in the NFL draft including nine first-rounders. He guided the Spartans to a Big Ten slate of 57-38-3, and to seven bowl games.

Career Record: 73-62-4

1983

THE SCORES

23	Colorado*	17
28	Notre Dame	23
10	Illinois*	20
29	Purdue	29
0	Michigan*	42
12	Indiana	24
11	Ohio State	21
34	Minnesota*	10
9	Northwestern	3
6	Iowa*	12
0	Wisconsin	32

4-6-1
Big Ten: 2-6-1, 7th

THE STANDINGS

	W	L	T
Illinois	9	0	0
Michigan	8	1	0
Iowa	7	2	0
Ohio State	6	3	0
Wisconsin	5	4	0
Purdue	3	5	1
Michigan State	2	6	1
Indiana	2	7	0
Northwestern	2	7	0
Minnesota	0	9	0

THE STAFF

1983 Coaching staff, kneeling, lt. to rt.: Nick Saban, def. backs; "Buck" Nystrom, off. line; George Perles, head coach; Norm Parker, out. linebackers. Standing, lt. to rt., Bill Rademacher, quarterbacks; Ted Guthard, inside linebackers; Steve Furness, def. line; Larry Bielat, running backs; Charlie Baggett, receivers.

THE TEAM

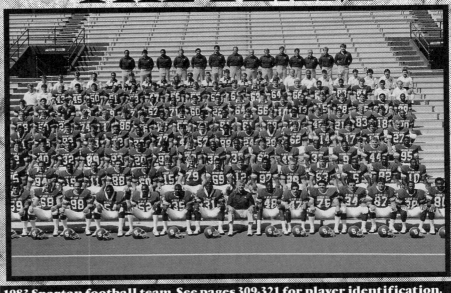

1983 Spartan football team. See pages 309-321 for player identification.

SPARTAN ITEM

State defeated Notre Dame in South Bend, 28-23, in George Perles' first try. Sophomore QB DAVE YAREMA threw three touchdown passes, including an 81-yard pass play to DARYL TURNER.

GREEN & WHITE HIGHLIGHTS

- Former Spartan gridder and assistant coach George Perles realized his dream of becoming head coach of the MSU program when he was appointed as State's 19th head coach on December 3, 1982. Perles helped restore the MSU program to national prominence with two bowl appearances in his first three seasons.
- State greeted the Perles era with upsets over Colorado (23-17) and #4 Notre Dame (28-23) in South Bend.
- CARL BANKS and RALF MOJSIEJENKO were accorded All-America honors.

Spartan Moments

Senior DARYL TURNER (38, Flint Southwestern) was the go-to guy with 28 receptions for 549 yards (team-high 19.6 yards per catch) and five touchdowns. Turner grabbed six passes for 128 yards in the season-opening victory over Colorado. Turner's 78 career catches ranked 7th on MSU's list in 1983.

Junior free safety PHIL PARKER (32, Lorain, Ohio) intercepted seven passes in '83 (MSU's 3rd highest seasonal mark at the time) on the way to the first of two years as an All-Big Ten performer. He returned the seven INTs for a lofty 209 yards, including a 72-yard return for a score vs. Illinois.

Spartan List

Top 10 Single-Season Pass Completion Percentage

Dave Yarema, 1986 (297-200)	.673
Jim Miller, 1993 (215-336)	.640
Jim Miller, 1992 (191-122)	.639
Dan Enos, 1989 (240-153)	.638
Todd Schultz, 1995 (83-52)	.627
Dan Enos, 1990 (220-137)	.623
Tony Banks, 1994 (238-145)	.609
Tony Banks, 1995 (258-156)	.605
Jim Miller, 1991 (218-130)	.596
Clark Brown, 1983 (141-82)	.582

SPARTAN SALUTE

Senior All-America linebacker CARL BANKS was congratulated by Big Ten Commissioner Wayne Duke as Carl displays his MVP trophy. Banks was honored by the Columbus Touchdown Club as College Linebacker of the Year, after completing his career with 279 tackles, which ranked third in Spartan history at the time.

★ MSU ALL-STARS ★

Junior All-America punter/placekicker RALF MOJSIEJENKO (Bridgman) booted this 59-yard field goal in the 4th quarter to tie Purdue, 29-29. In '82, he powered a 61-yarder versus Illinois.

OTHER AWARD WINNERS

All-Big Ten honorees, first team: CARL E. BANKS, linebacker; PHILLIP J. PARKER, safety; second team: RALF MOJSIEJENKO, punter; RALF MOJSIEJENKO, placekicker; honorable mention: DARYL TURNER, off. end; SCOTT E. AUER, off. tackle; JAMES M. MORRISSEY, linebacker; TIMOTHY W. CUNNINGHAM, safety; CARL BANKS, MVP, Downtown Coaches Outstanding Sr. on defense; TOM ALLAN, def. end, Tommy Love Most Improved; TIM CUNNINGHAM, safety, "Potsy" Ross Scholar-Athlete; JIM BOB LAMB, off. tackle, President's Outstanding Senior Lineman, NATE HANNAH, cornerback, President's Outstanding Senior Back; JIM RINELLA, def. tackle, "Biggie" Munn Most Inspirational; DARRYL DIXON, safety, Oil Can (Humorist); RANDY LARK, guard, Iron Man (strength & conditioning); KELLY QUINN, def. end, Outstanding Underclass Lineman; PHIL PARKER, safety, Outstanding Underclass Back; SCOTT AUER, tackle, Gerald R. Ford Up Front (off. lineman); DARYL TURNER, split end, Downtown Coaches Outstanding Sr. on offense; MARK NAPOLITAN, center, Frederick W. Danziger (Detroit area); GEORGE WEBSTER, business, Daugherty Award (Distinguished Football Alumnus).

1984

THE SCORES

24	Colorado	21
20	Notre Dame*	24
7	Illinois	40
10	Purdue*	13
19	Michigan	7
13	Indiana*	6
20	Ohio State*	23
20	Minnesota	13
27	Northwestern*	10
17	Iowa	16
10	Wisconsin*	20

Cherry Bowl

| 6 | Army | 10 |

6-6-0
Big Ten: 5-4-0, T-6th

THE STANDINGS

	W	L	T
Ohio State	7	2	0
Illinois	6	3	0
Purdue	6	3	0
Iowa	5	3	1
Wisconsin	5	3	1
Michigan	5	4	0
Michigan State	5	4	0
Minnesota	3	6	0
Northwestern	2	7	0
Indiana	0	9	0

THE STAFF

1984 Coaching staff, kneeling, lt. to rt.: "Buck" Nystrom, off. line; Norm Parker, out. linebackers; Ted Guthard, inside linebackers; George Perles, head coach; Nick Saban, def. coordinator - def. backs; Ed Rutherford, admin. ass't.; Steve Beckholt, tight ends - special teams. Standing, lt. to rt., Rick Kaczmarek, grad. ass't.; Charlie Baggett, receivers; Bill Rademacher, quarterbacks; Dave Kaple, grad. ass't.; Steve Furness, def. line; Randy Zimmerman, grad. ass't.; Larry Bielat, running backs; Greg Croxton, grad. ass't.; Brian Wood, volunteer ass't.

THE TEAM

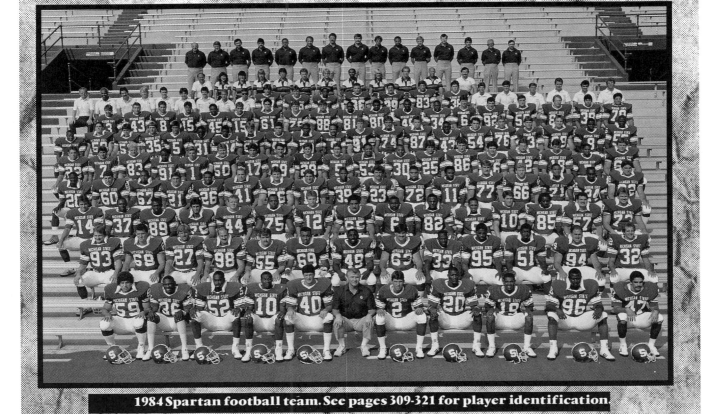

1984 Spartan football team. See pages 309-321 for player identification.

Spartan Moments

After an injury in 1983, sophomore quarterback DAVE YAREMA returned to lead State to 1,477 passing yards with 11 TDs while completing 119-of-222 aerials (.536).

YAREMA's top target was sophomore flanker MARK INGRAM (85, Flint Northwestern) who caught 22 passes for 499 yards and four scores, including a 75-yard touchdown catch and run against #8 Ohio State.

Spartan fans got their first look at freshman tailback LORENZO WHITE (34, Ft. Lauderdale). White played in 11 games, starting just three, and led MSU with 616 rushing yards and four TDs on 142 rushes (4.3 avg.). Against Northwestern, White carried 26 times for 170 yards and two TDs.

The defense was paced again by senior linebacker JIM MORRISSEY (40, Flint Powers) who compiled a career-best 137 tackles. He left MSU after the '84 season as the school's #2 all-time tackler, and is still #5 on the career tackles chart.

GREEN & WHITE HIGHLIGHTS

- GEORGE PERLES' second season was the first step back into the national scene with a 6-5 regular season (5-4 in the Big Ten) and a bid to play in the inaugural Cherry Bowl in the Pontiac Silverdome.

- The Spartans upset #13 Michigan, 19-7, which ignited a series of five wins in six weeks.

- JIM MORRISSEY and PHIL PARKER are named to the All-Big Ten defensive team. Morrissey went on to play in the Super Bowl with the Chicago Bears and Parker began a college coaching career.

- BOBBY MORSE led the Big Ten punt returners with a 12.0 return average.

- DUFFY DAUGHERTY was inducted into the College Football Hall of Fame.

★ MSU ALL-STARS ★

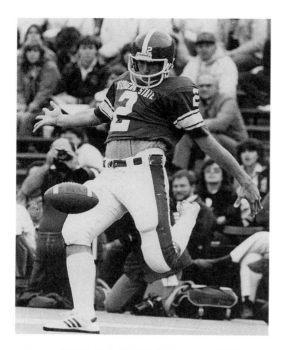

Senior RALF MOJSIEJENKO punted 76 times for a 44.7 average. His career average of 43.8 is still second to GREG MONTGOMERY. His 35 career field goals ranks 4th all-time at State.

OTHER AWARD WINNERS

All-Big Ten honorees, first team: JAMES M. MORRISSEY, linebacker; PHILLIP J. PARKER, free safety; second team: RALF MOJSIEJENKO, placekicker; KELLY QUINN, def. end; RALF MOJSIEJENKO, punter; CARL BUTLER, tailback; MARK R. NAPOLITAN, center; honorable mention: DONALD D. (BUTCH) ROLLE, tight end; JOHN WOJCIECHOWSKI, off. guard; MARK J. INGRAM, flanker; ROBERT W. MORSE, fullback; S. JAMES RINELLA, def. tackle; ANTHONY D. BELL, linebacker; VENO L. BELK, tight end; LONNIE YOUNG, cornerback; TERRANCE L. LEWIS, cornerback.

Spartan List

Top 10 Career Touchdown Passes Thrown

Dave Yarema, 1982-83-84-85	43
Ed Smith, 1976-77-78	43
Steve Juday, 1963-64-65	21
Tony Banks, 1994-95	20
John Leister, 1979-80-81-82	20
Bryan Clark, 1978-79-80-81	20
Al Dorow, 1949-50-51	19
Gene Glick, 1946-47-48-49	18
Tom Yewcic, 1951-52-53	18
Jim Miller, 1990-91-92-93	17

SPARTAN SALUTE

STEVE GARVEY and KIRK GIBSON — two of State's highest-profile athletic heroes —posed for this photo prior to a 1984 World Series game in Detroit between Gibson's Detroit Tigers and Garvey's San Diego Padres. Gibson (lt.) donned his MSU #23 jersey while Garvey wears his former #24. Gibson (1975-78) starred as a Spartan All-America receiver in football (1978) and All-America centerfielder in baseball (1978). Garvey earned a football letter in '67 as a defensive back in addition to his baseball status as an All-America third baseman in 1968.

BOWL
Highlights

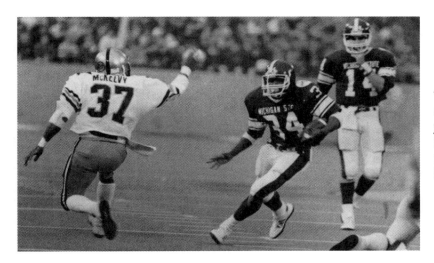

The Pontiac Silverdome was the scene of MSU's first bowl game in nearly 18 years, as the Spartans met Army in the inaugural Cherry Bowl. Lorenzo White (above) gained 103 yards, but State lost a tough 10-6 decision.

Junior defensive end KELLY QUINN (93, Stone Mountain, Georgia) was relentless on defense, setting a Spartan record with 15 tackles-for-loss (totaling 96 yards), including 12 QB sacks which ranked second at the time and is still third on the single-season sack list.

The Spartans were rewarded with a bid to the inaugural Cherry Bowl — State's first bowl game in nearly 19 years. In spite of a 10-6 loss to Army, the game signaled State's return to the national scene.

MSU spoiled the Rose Bowl plans of Iowa with a 17-16 victory in Iowa City, thanks to this successful last-minute defensive stand at the Hawkeyes' goal line on a two-point conversion attempt to win the game. JIM MORRISSEY makes the initial hit on QB Chuck Long, who tried the right end, while soph. linebacker SHANE BULLOUGH (41, Cincinnati, Ohio) makes the final stop.

1985

THE SCORES

12	Arizona State*	3
10	Notre Dame	27
7	Western Michigan*	3
31	Iowa	35
0	Michigan*	31
17	Illinois*	31
31	Purdue	24
31	Minnesota*	26
35	Indiana	16
32	Northwestern*	0
41	Wisconsin	7

All-American Bowl
| 14 | Georgia Tech | 17 |

7-5-0
Big Ten: 5-3-0, T-4th

THE STANDINGS

	W	L	T
Iowa	7	1	0
Michigan	6	1	1
Illinois	5	2	1
Ohio State	5	3	0
Michigan State	5	3	0
Minnesota	4	4	0
Purdue	3	5	0
Wisconsin	2	6	0
Indiana	1	7	0
Northwestern	1	7	0

THE STAFF

1985 Coaching staff: George Perles, head coach; Charlie Baggett, running backs; Steve Beckholt, tight ends - special teams; Larry Bielat, quarterbacks; Steve Furness, def. line; Ted Guthard, inside linebackers; "Buck" Nystrom, off. line; Norm Parker, out. linebackers; Bill Rademacher, receivers; Nick Saban; def. coordinator - def. backs.

THE TEAM

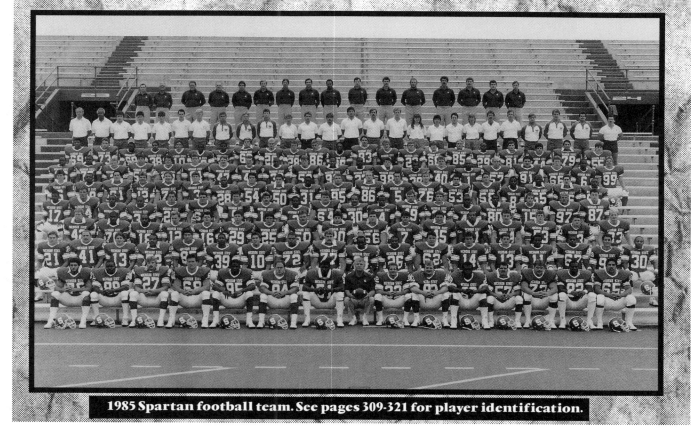

1985 Spartan football team. See pages 309-321 for player identification.

Spartan Moments

Senior free safety PHIL PARKER was the "quarterback" on defense. He was third on the team with 99 tackles, including 58 unassisted. Parker is the school's #1 career tackler among defensive backs (276). He added three interceptions in '85, bringing his career INT total to 16, second on State's all-time list at the time and currently third. He is also 4th on MSU's career list of passes broken up (20).

Another weapon was sophomore punter GREG MONTGOMERY (left) (23, Shrewsbury, N.J.), who averaged 44.1 yards per punt including a then-school record 80-yarder against Indiana and a 75-yard punt vs. Michigan.

Junior MARK INGRAM led the team in receptions for the second straight year, this time with 34 catches for 745 yards and five TDs. He could catch it in traffic, as witnessed during the Purdue game when he grabbed six passes for 102 yards.

GREEN & WHITE HIGHLIGHTS

- State registered a 7-4 regular season record (5-3 in the Big Ten) and secured its second straight bowl bid — this time the All-American Bowl in Birmingham, Alabama.
- MSU won its last five games of the regular season, before falling to Georgia Tech, 17-14, in the All-American Bowl.
- Sophomore sensation LORENZO WHITE was a consensus first-team All-American as he set the all-time single-season NCAA rushing record for sophomores with 1,908 yards (386 attempts, 11 games); the fourth-best yardage total in NCAA records. He was the 1985 NCAA rushing leader and set the all-time single-season Big Ten rushing record. Including the bowl game, Lorenzo amassed 2,066 yards and 17 TDs in 419 carries (4.9 avg.).

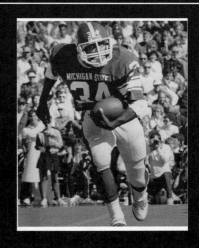

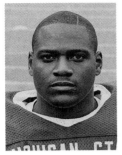

Sophomore All-America tailback LORENZO WHITE sprinted his way to an historic season. One of his greatest games, in terms of yardage, was against top-ranked Iowa in a 35-31 defeat. White carried 39 times for 226 yards and two TDs. Another was the 28-24 win over Purdue, in which Lorenzo did yeoman's duty with 53 totes for 244 yards and two scores. But his #1 game came in Bloomington as State defeated Indiana, 35-16, behind White's 286 yards and three touchdowns on 25 carries. He turned in four games of 200+ rushing yards in '85.

OTHER AWARD WINNERS

All-Big Ten honorees, first team: LORENZO M. WHITE, tailback; PHILLIP J. PARKER, free safety; JOHN WOJCIECHOWSKI, off. guard; GREG MONTGOMERY, punter; second team: STEVEN J. BOGDALEK, off. tackle; SHANE H. BULLOUGH, linebacker; GREGORY H. MONTGOMERY, punter; KELLY QUINN, def. end; honorable mention: MARK J. INGRAM, flanker; JOHN JONES, def. end; DONALD D. (BUTCH) ROLLE, tight end; DEAN ALTOBELLI, def. back, Academic All-Big Ten, Academic All-America; STEVE BOGDALEK, tackle, Academic All-Big Ten, "Potsy" Ross Scholar-Athlete; SHANE BULLOUGH, linebacker, Academic All-Big Ten, Academic All-America; LORENZO WHITE, tailback, Columbus Touchdown Club Running Back of Year, 4th in voting for the Heisman Trophy, MVP, Outstanding Underclass Back (co-winner); MARK INGRAM, flanker, Tommy Love Most Improved (co-winner); MARK NICHOLS, def. tackle, Tommy Love Most Improved (co-winner); JOE CURRAN, def. tackle, President's Outstanding Senior Lineman; PHIL PARKER, safety, President's Outstanding Senior Back, Downtown Coaches Outstanding Senior on defense; BOBBY MORSE, fullback, "Biggie" Munn Most Inspirational (co-winner); MARK BEAUDOIN, def. end, "Biggie" Munn Most Inspirational (co-winner); JOHN JONES, def. end, Oil Can (Humorist); KELLY QUINN, def. end, Iron Man (strength & conditioning); TONY MANDARICH, tackle, Outstanding Underclass Lineman; SHANE BULLOUGH, linebacker, Outstanding Underclass Back (co-winner); JOHN WOJCIECHOWSKI, guard, Gerald R. Ford Up Front (off. lineman), Frederick W. Danziger (Detroit area); VENO BELK, tight end, Downtown Coaches Outstanding Senior on offense; BUTCH ROLLE, tight end, Downtown Coaches Outstanding Senior on offense; ROLLIE DOTSCH, pro fb coach, Daugherty Award (Distinguished Football Alumnus); DAVE YAREMA, quarterback, Outstanding Underclass Back (co-winner).

Spartan List

Top 10 Career Leaders in Total Touchdowns

Lorenzo White,
1984-85-86-87 43
Blake Ezor,
1986-87-88-89 34
Lynn Chandnois,
1946-47-48-49 31
Eric Allen,
1969-70-71 30
Tico Duckett,
1989-90-91-92 28
Scott Greene,
1992-93-94-95 27
Kirk Gibson,
1975-76-77-78 26
Leroy Bolden,
1951-52-53-54 26
Craig Thomas,
1990-91-92-93 25
Steve Smith,
1977-78-79-80 25

SPARTAN SALUTE

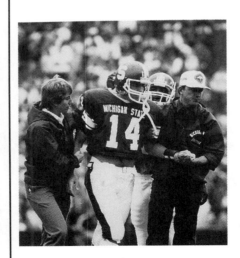

JEFF MONROE (rt.) became the Spartans' head athletic trainer in the fall of 1985 from the University of Minnesota. His responsibilities include coordination of all MSU student athletic care. Assistant trainer SALLY NOGLE (lt), who came to MSU from San Diego State in 1983, was hired by then-athletic director Doug Weaver to supervise the athletic training staff for women's sports. She has worked football with Monroe since 1985. In 1986, she worked the U.S. Olympic Sports Festival and in '88 served for the Olympic Games in Seoul, Korea. Here, Monroe and Nogle assist Spartan QB Dave Yarema from the field.

BOWL Highlights

One of the more important events at this bowl (and several others) is the visitation by players and coaches to Birmingham Children's Hospital.

Michigan Governor and MSU alumnus JIM BLANCHARD, MSU President JOHN DIBIAGGIO and Head Coach GEORGE PERLES pose with the Birmingham Motorcycle Police who escorted the Spartans throughout the city during bowl week.

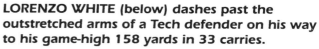

LORENZO WHITE (below) dashes past the outstretched arms of a Tech defender on his way to his game-high 158 yards in 33 carries.

MARK INGRAM (left) was the game's MVP scoring both of State's touchdowns. He caught three passes for 70 yards. He caught a six-yard TD pass from YAREMA in the second quarter and had this 27-yard scoring play in the third quarter, which put MSU ahead, 14-7. Georgia Tech rallied for 10 points in the fourth quarter for a 17-14 win.

1986

THE SCORES

17	Arizona State	20
20	Notre Dame*	15
45	Western Michigan*	10
21	Iowa*	24
6	Michigan	27
29	Illinois	21
37	Purdue*	3
52	Minnesota	23
14	Indiana*	17
21	Northwestern	24
23	Wisconsin*	13

6-5-0
Big Ten:
4-4-0, T-5th

THE STANDINGS

	W	L	T
Michigan	7	1	0
Ohio State	7	1	0
Iowa	5	3	0
Minnesota	5	3	0
Michigan State	4	4	0
Indiana	3	5	0
Illinois	3	5	0
Northwestern	2	6	0
Purdue	2	6	0
Wisconsin	2	6	0

THE STAFF

1986 Coaching staff, kneeling, lt. to rt.: Bill Rademacher inside linebackers; Morris Watts, off. coordinator - quarterbacks; George Perles, head coach; Nick Saban, def. coordinator - def. backs; Steve Beckholt, tight ends - special teams. Standing, lt. to rt., "Buck" Nystrom, off. line; Charlie Baggett, receivers; Steve Furness, def. line; Larry Bielat, running backs; Norm Parker, out. linebackers; Ed Rutherford, admin. ass't.

THE TEAM

1986 Spartan football team. See pages 309-321 for player identification.

Spartan Moments

DAVE YAREMA's senior season set the school record for passing yardage with 2,581 yards. His 16 TD passes remains second only to the 20 thrown by EDDIE SMITH in 1978.

Junior tailback LORENZO WHITE led the ground game with 633 yards and six TDs in spite of missing considerable action due to injury. Here is a familiar scene, with fullback BOBBY MORSE (21) leading the way for White.

Sophomore wide receiver ANDRE RISON (1, Flint Northwestern) dazzled defenders with 54 receptions for 966 yards and five scores. Here is a photo of Rison, (left) MSU's all-time leading receiver (receptions and reception yardage), and YAREMA, the Spartans' all-time leader in passing yardage.

SHANE BULLOUGH, (left) senior middle linebacker and son of former Spartan player and coach Henry Bullough, was the No. 1 tackler with 118 stops, 51 unassisted.

Junior defensive end JOHN BUDDE (87, Kansas City, Mo.), son of former Spartan player and NFL star Ed Budde, accounted for 12 tackles behind the line of scrimmage to pace the team in that category. He was tied for fifth on the team in tackles with 57.

Junior outside linebacker TIM MOORE was second to BULLOUGH with a personal season best 101 total tackles. Moore was a significant cog in the '87 championship team defense and ended his career with 332 tackles, second at the time (to DAN BASS) and currently 4th.

GREEN & WHITE HIGHLIGHTS

- The Spartans upset #20 Notre Dame and completed a 6-5 season (4-4 in the Big Ten), the third straight year with at least six wins in the regular season.

- Junior punter GREG MONTGOMERY earned All-America recognition in 1986 and again in '87.

- Senior safety DEAN ALTOBELLI became the third (of four) Spartans to earn a National Football Foundation Hall of Fame Graduate Fellowship Award.

- MARK INGRAM had perhaps the most spectacular play of the season—a 71-yard reverse run with 6:50 to play in the Illinois game to seal a 29-21 victory.

195

All-American junior punter GREG MONTGOMERY (left) established the school standard in '86 with a booming average of 47.8 yards per punt. In Big Ten games, "Monty" averaged a Big Ten-record 49.7 yards per punt, breaking the mark of Iowa's Reggie Roby (47.8). He crushed 12 punts 60 or more yards in his MSU career, including the school record 86-yarder vs. Michigan in '86. Greg is the son of former MSU quarterback Greg Montgomery, Sr. of East Lansing who played in the 1950s. Another son, Steve, became an outstanding fullback in 1987, '88, and '89. Steve was also elected co-captain in '89.

OTHER AWARD WINNERS

All-Big Ten honorees, first team: ANDRE RISON, wide receiver; GREG MONTGOMERY, punter; SHANE BULLOUGH, linebacker; second team: DAVE YAREMA, quarterback; LORENZO WHITE, tailback; MARK NICHOLS, def. tackle; MARK INGRAM, flanker; honorable mention: JOHN BUDDE, def. end; PAT SHURMUR, center; BOBBY MORSE, fullback; MIKE SARGENT, tight end; TONY MANDARICH, off. tackle; DOUG ROGERS, off. guard; TODD KRUMM, cornerback; DEAN ALTOBELLI, safety, Academic All-Big Ten, Academic All-America; "Potsy" Ross Scholar-Athlete; SHANE BULLOUGH, linebacker, Academic All-Big Ten, Academic All-America, Downtown Coaches Outstanding Senior on defense; PAT SHURMUR, center, Academic All-Big Ten, Gerald R. Ford Up Front (off. lineman) (co-winner); DAVE YAREMA, quarterback, MVP (co-winner), President's Outstanding Senior Back, Frederick W. Danziger (Detroit area); MARK INGRAM, flanker, MVP (co-winner), Downtown Coaches Outstanding Senior on offense; JOHN BUDDE, def. end, Tommy Love Most Improved (co-winner); ANDRE RISON, wide receiver, Tommy Love Most Improved (co-winner); DAVE WOLFF, def. tackle, President's Outstanding Senior Lineman; BOBBY MORSE, fullback, "Biggie" Munn Most Inspirational, Iron Man (strength & conditioning); PETE HRISKO, quarterback, Oil Can (Humorist); TONY MANDARICH, tackle, Gerald R. Ford Up Front (off. lineman) (co-winner); HENRY BULLOUGH, NFL coach, Daugherty Award (Distinguished Football Alumnus).

Spartan List

Top Players of the '80s and '90s Who Earned Academic All-Big Ten Honors

1. **Rob Fredrickson,** 1990-91-92-93
2. **Courtney Hawkins,** 1989
3. **Mill Coleman,** 1991-92-93-94
4. **Jim Miller,** 1990-91-92
5. **Pat Shurmur,** 1986-87
6. **Shane Bullough,** 1985-86
7. **Mitch Lyons,** 1989-90
8. **Dean Altobelli,** 1985-86
9. **Steve Wasylk,** 1990-91-92-93
10. **Toby Heaton,** 1989-90-91-92

SPARTAN SALUTE

One of the greatest sources of pride in coach Perles' career was the rare academic achievement of not one, but two, Spartans from '86. DEAN ALTOBELLI (left) and SHANE BULLOUGH (right) were both two-time Academic All-Americans, repeating from 1985. Bullough was second team in '85 and first team in '86. Altobelli, a former Rhodes Scholar candidate who is campaigning for the United States Senate in 1996, was a first-team selection both years.

LORENZO WHITE Highlights

- Finished career as No. 2 rushing leader in Big Ten history.
- 1987 recipient of Silver Football Award as Big Ten MVP.
- 1987 consensus first-team All-American as senior.

- Set MSU career records for carries (1,082), yards gained (4,887) and touchdowns (43).
- Fourth in Heisman Trophy voting in both 1987 and 1985.
- Finished career as No. 14 all-time NCAA rushing leader.

LORENZO WHITE appeared with Bob Hope on his All-America TV special.

WHITE was named to the 1985 Kodak/American Football Coaches Association All-America Team.

LORENZO receives his *Chicago Tribune* Silver Football Trophy, symbolic of the Big Ten Conference MVP.

LORENZO and Kodak All-America team member Deion Sanders (top) of Florida State met up with Universal Studio's Laurel and Hardy during the Kodak All-America Weekend activities in Los Angeles, California.

1987

THE SCORES

27	Southern California*	13
8	Notre Dame	31
3	Florida State*	31
19	Iowa	14
17	Michigan*	11
38	Northwestern	0
14	Illinois*	14
13	Ohio State	7
45	Purdue*	3
27	Indiana*	3
30	Wisconsin	9
	Rose Bowl	
20	Southern California	17

9-2-1
Big Ten: 7-0-1, 1st

THE STANDINGS

	W	L	T
Michigan State	7	0	1
Iowa	6	2	0
Indiana	6	2	0
Michigan	5	3	0
Ohio State	4	4	0
Minnesota	3	5	0
Purdue	3	5	0
Illinois	2	5	1
Northwestern	2	6	0
Wisconsin	1	7	0

THE STAFF

1987 Coaching staff, kneeling, lt. to rt.: Bill Rademacher, inside linebackers; Norm Parker, out. linebackers; Morris Watts, off. coordinator - quarterbacks; George Perles, head coach; Nick Saban, def. coordinator - def. backs; Pat Morris, off. line; Steve Beckholt, tight ends - special teams. Standing, lt. to rt., Gary Raff, volunteer ass't.; Phil Parker, grad. ass't.; Larry Bielat, running backs; Greg Colby, grad. ass't.; Dave McLaughlin, grad. ass't.; Steve Furness, off. line; Charlie Baggett, receivers; Jeff Marron, grad. ass't.; Ed Rutherford, admin. ass't.

THE TEAM

1987 Spartan football team. See pages 309-321 for player identification.

Spartan Moments

After losses to #9 Notre Dame and #7 Florida State, MSU came from behind in the second half to win at Iowa, 19-14. Sophomore defensive tackle TRAVIS DAVIS (75, Warren, Ohio) came up with three tackles for losses. He led the team with 16 TFLs for the season (second only to Bethea's 18 in 1977), including a dozen QB sacks (second only to Bethea's 16 in 1977). The defense pinned a minus-47 yards rushing on the Hawks in the second half and a minus-16 for the day! Later in the season, Davis set a school record with five QB sacks (-37 yds.) versus Ohio State as MSU defeated the Bucks for the first time since 1974, 13-7.

The following week, the Spartans hosted Michigan and tied a Big Ten team record with seven interceptions on the way to a 17-11 conquest. Senior strong safety JOHN MILLER (44, Farmington Hills Harrison) set a school record and tied a Big Ten mark with four interceptions.

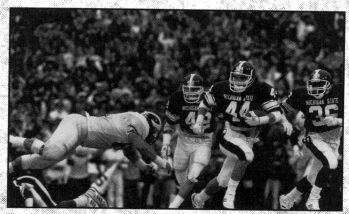

Senior free safety TODD KRUMM (below) (35, West Bloomfield) led the team with nine INTs in '87, including a pair against the Wolverines. Krumm and MILLER combined for 17 interceptions in '87.

Sophomore middle linebacker PERCY SNOW (48, Canton Ohio) — '88 Rose Bowl MVP — led MSU with 127 emphatic tackles.

GREEN & WHITE HIGHLIGHTS

- In PERLES' fifth year as head coach, State won the Big Ten championship, made its first journey to the Rose Bowl in 22 years and captured its first Rose Bowl victory in 32 years. Perles is voted Big Ten Coach of the Year and the Football News' national Coach of the Year.
- MSU defeated Michigan (17-11) in East Lansing for the first time in nine games since 1969 and beat Ohio State for the first time in nine games since 1974 (and the first time in Ohio Stadium since 1971).
- State marched to its first undefeated Big Ten season (7-0-1) since 1966. The overall record of 9-2-1 was the best winning percentage since 9-0-1 in 1966 and good for a #8 ranking nationally.
- State romped to eight wins and a tie after a 1-2 start. The "Gang Green" defense smothered opponent ground games to the tune of 61.5 yards per game — a figure that led the nation (and is 3rd in the MSU record book). In the Big Ten, the Spartans yielded a near-record 37.6 yards against the run. MSU was #2 in the NCAA in total defense (225.6) and topped the Big Ten (184.5) in league encounters.
- Indicative of MSU's powerful ground attack, the Spartans set a team record for rushing attempts in a Big Ten game with 77. In that game, EZOR rushed for 151 yards and WHITE accounted for 144 more, to mark the first time since 1976 that MSU had two players rush for 100 or more yards in the same game.
- TONY MANDARICH (79, Oakville), GREG MONTGOMERY and LORENZO WHITE all earn All-America honors.
- GEORGE WEBSTER is inducted into the College Football Hall of Fame.

★ MSU ALL-STARS ★

All-American junior offensive tackle TONY MANDARICH (left) became one of the nation's most dominant and feared linemen in college football. Two-time All-American GREG MONTGOMERY culminated his fine career with an average of 45.0 yards per punt and still placed 13 punts inside the opponents' 20 yard line. His strong leg and tremendous hang-time made him a sure-fire NFL star.

OTHER AWARD WINNERS

All-Big Ten honorees, first team: TODD KRUMM, safety; TONY MANDARICH, off. tackle; LORENZO WHITE, tailback; JOHN MILLER, safety; GREG MONTGOMERY, punter; PAT SHURMUR, center; PERCY SNOW, linebacker; second team: TRAVIS DAVIS, def. tackle; TIM MOORE, linebacker; MARK NICHOLS, def. tackle; ANDRE RISON, split end; honorable mention: JOHN BUDDE, def. end; BLAKE EZOR, tailback; JOHN LANGELOH, placekicker; KURT LARSON, linebacker; BOBBY McALLISTER, quarterback; KEVIN ROBBINS, tackle, Academic All-Big Ten; PAT SHURMUR, center, Academic All-Big Ten, "Potsy" Ross Scholar-Athlete, President's Outstanding Senior Lineman; LORENZO WHITE, tailback, Chicago Tribune Silver Football (Big Ten MVP), 4th in the voting for the Heisman Trophy (2nd time), Downtown Coaches Outstanding Senior on offense; PERCY SNOW, linebacker, Tommy Love Most Improved; MIKE SARGENT, tight end, President's Outstanding Senior Back; TIM MOORE, linebacker, "Biggie" Munn Most Inspirational; GREG MONTGOMERY, punter, Oil Can (Humorist); DAVID HOULE, tackle, Iron Man (strength & conditioning); JOHN BUDDE, def. end, Outstanding Underclass Lineman (co-winner); TRAVIS DAVIS. def. tackle, Outstanding Underclass Lineman (co-winner); BOBBY McALLISTER, quarterback, Outstanding Underclass Back (co-winner); ANDRE RISON, split end, Outstanding Underclass Back (co-winner); TONY MANDARICH, tackle, Gerald R. Ford Up Front (off. lineman), Big Ten Broadcasters Lineman of the Year; MARK NICHOLS, def. tackle, Downtown Coaches Outstanding Sr. on defense (co-winner); TODD KRUMM, safety, Downtown Coaches Outstanding Senior on defense (co-winner); JOHN MILLER, safety, Frederick W. Danziger (Detroit area); JOHN WILSON, president, Washington & Lee Univ., Daugherty Award (Distinguished Football Alumnus).

Spartan List

Top 10 Career Rushing Yardage Leaders

Lorenzo White,
1984-85-86-87 4,887
Tico Duckett,
1989-90-91-92 4,212
Blake Ezor,
1986-87-88-89 3,749
Steve Smith,
1977-78-79-80 2,676
Eric Allen,
1969-70-71 2,654
Levi Jackson,
1973-74-75-76 2,287
Rich Baes,
1973-74-75-76 2,234
Lynn Chandnois,
1946-47-48-49 2,093
Clinton Jones,
1964-65-66- 1,921
Duane Goulborne,
1992-93-94 1,906

SPARTAN SALUTE

Two-time All-American LORENZO WHITE capped his home career in style with a personal-best 292 yards (and two TDs) in 56 carries, one short of the NCAA single-game record. Here he scores one of his two TDs against Michigan.

He remains State's all-time leader in: rushing attempts (1,082), rushing yardage (4,887), all-purpose yardage (5,152), total touchdowns scored (43), rushing touchdowns (43), single-season rushing attempts (419) and single-season rushing yardage (2,066).

BOWL
Highlights

The Rose Bowl Parade included the MSU cheerleaders riding the Big Ten float.

Grand Marshall Gregory Peck tosses the coin in the pre-game ceremony at mid-field.

Rose Bowl MVP PERCY SNOW (48), along with outside linebackers CARLOS JENKINS (51, Boynton Beach, Fla.) and DIXON EDWARDS (57, Cincinnati, Ohio), smother the USC ballcarrier.

Placekicker JOHN LANGELOH (above and left) (10) and holder GREG MONTGOMERY (23) celebrate Langeloh's fourth-quarter, game-winning field goal (with 4:14 left) over Southern Cal in the 74th Rose Bowl game.

1988

THE SCORES

13	Rutgers*	17
3	Notre Dame*	20
7	Florida State	30
10	Iowa*	10
3	Michigan	17
36	Northwestern*	3
28	Illinois	21
20	Ohio State*	10
48	Purdue	3
38	Indiana	12
36	Wisconsin*	0
	Gator Bowl	
27	Georgia	34

6-5-1
Big Ten: 6-1-1, 2nd

THE STANDINGS

	W	L	T
Michigan	7	0	1
Michigan State	6	1	1
Iowa	4	1	3
Illinois	5	2	1
Indiana	5	3	0
Purdue	3	5	0
Ohio State	2	5	1
Northwestern	2	5	1
Minnesota	0	6	2
Wisconsin	1	7	0

THE STAFF

1988 Coaching staff, lt. to rt.: Ed Rutherford, admin. ass't.; Anthony "Dino" Folino, def. backs; Bill Rademacher, inside linebackers; Steve Furness, def. line; Norm Parker, def. coordinator - out. linebackers; George Perles, head coach; Morris Watts, off. coordinator - quarterbacks; Charlie Baggett, running backs; Steve Beckholt, tight ends - special teams; Pat Morris, off. line; Larry Bielat, receivers.

THE TEAM

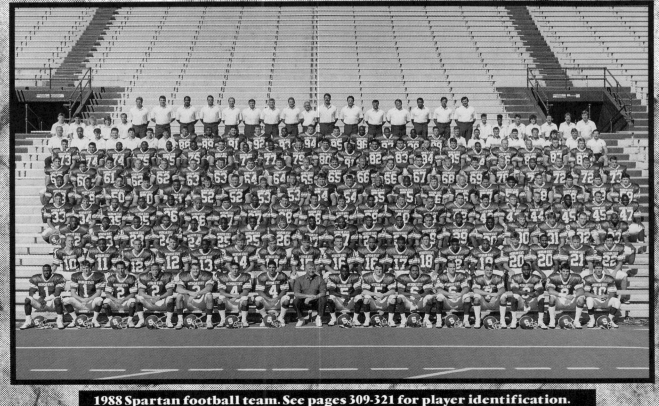

1988 Spartan football team. See pages 309-321 for player identification.

Spartan Moments

Junior tailback BLAKE EZOR (26, Las Vegas, Nevada), was described by Coach Perles as "pound for pound, the toughest player I've ever coached." Ezor ripped off 1,496 yards and 11 scores as the workhorse in the backfield (322 rushes, 4.7 avg.). Blake rang up some huge games in his career, but none bigger than the '88 Indiana game in Bloomington when he carried 44 times for 250 yards and three TDs — the Big Ten's best effort of the season by a running back and still the 5th-highest single-game rushing total in MSU history.

State's top two tacklers in '88 are pictured here in the 36-0 hammering of Wisconsin. Junior middle linebacker PERCY SNOW (48) set a then-school record with 164 tackles (with

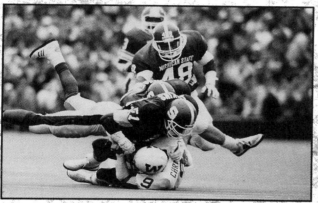

Senior OLB KURT LARSON (3, Waukesha, Wisconsin) picked off eight interceptions to tie JOHN MILLER and JESSE THOMAS for second place on MSU's single-season list, just one shy of TODD KRUMM's 1987 total.

an amazing 97 unassisted tackles) to lead the squad. Sophomore outside linebacker CARLOS JENKINS (51) contributed 99 big hits (70 solo tackles) to the defense.

GREEN & WHITE HIGHLIGHTS

- After a start of 0-4-1, the Spartans rallied to win six straight Big Ten games to close the regular season at 6-4-1 — 6-1-1 in the Big Ten (second place) — and attract a bid to play Georgia on New Year's Day in the Mazda Gator Bowl in Jacksonville, Florida. It marked the second straight New Year's Day game for the Spartans.
- During the six-game winning streak, MSU dominated by outscoring its opponents by an average of 34.3 to 8.2 ppg.
- MSU ended the season with the 1989 Gator Bowl, which was the final game for Georgia head coach Vince Dooley. In 25 seasons, Dooley was 201-77-10.
- In the 20-10 victory over Ohio State, BLAKE EZOR rushed for 147 yards and HYLAND HICKSON added a game-high 187 for a school record 334 yards by two 100-yard rushes in a single game. The former 100-yard tandem record of 310 yards was held by RICH BAES (159) and CHARLIE BAGGETT (151) in 1974.
- "BUBBA" SMITH was inducted into the College Football Hall of Fame.

Senior co-captain and All-American TONY MANDARICH (left) capped a brilliant career in '88 before moving on to the NFL as the No. 2 pick (Green Bay) in the first round of the draft.

Junior All-American PERCY SNOW enjoyed a record season in '88 and reaped most of the rewards after the '89 season when he became a two-time All-American.

OTHER AWARD WINNERS

All-Big Ten honorees, first team: ANDRE RISON, wide receiver; TONY MANDARICH, off. tackle; PERCY SNOW, linebacker; JOHN MILLER, safety; KEVIN ROBBINS, off. tackle; second team: BOB KULA, off. guard; BLAKE EZOR, tailback; TRAVIS DAVIS, def. tackle; KURT LARSON, linebacker; DERRICK REED, def. back; honorable mention: JOSH BUTLAND, punter; MATT VANDERBEEK, def. end; JOHN BUDDE, def. end; TONY BRININGSTOOL, linebacker, Academic All-Big Ten; JOSH BUTLAND, punter, Academic All-Big Ten; JOHN KIPLE, safety, Academic All-Big Ten; CHRIS WILLERTZ, def. end, Academic All-Big Ten;TONY MANDARICH, tackle, Big Ten Broadcasters Lineman of the Year, Columbus Touchdown Club's College Offensive Lineman of the Year, Fiesta Bowl Samaritan All-American of the Year, 6th in the balloting for the Heisman Trophy, Iron Man (strength & conditioning), Gerald R. Ford Up Front (off. lineman); KURT LARSEN, linebacker, MVP, Downtown Coaches Outstanding Senior on defense; MATT VANDERBEEK, def. end, Tommy Love Most Improved; DAVE MARTIN, center, "Potsy" Ross Scholar-Athlete; JASON RIDGEWAY, def. tackle, President's Outstanding Senior Lineman (co-winner); VINCE TATA, guard, President's Outstanding Senior Lineman (co-winner); DERRICK REED, def. back, President's Outstanding Senior Back; RICH GICEWICZ, tight end, "Biggie" Munn Most Inspirational; STEVE MONTGOMERY, fullback, Oil Can (Humorist); TRAVIS DAVIS,def. tackle, Outstanding Underclass Lineman (co-winner); BOB KULA, guard, Outstanding Underclass Lineman (co-winner); BLAKE EZOR, tailback, Outstanding Underclass Back; ANDRE RISON, split end, Downtown Coaches Outstanding Senior on offense; JOHN MILLER, safety, Frederick W. Danziger (Detroit area); FRANK KUSH, college FB coach, Daugherty Award (Distinguished Football Alumnus).

Spartan List

Top 10 Career Reception Leaders

Andre Rison, 1985-86-87-88	146
Courtney Hawkins, 1988-89-90-91	138
Mill Coleman, 1991-92-93-94	126
Ted Jones, 1980-81-82	118
Eugene Byrd, 1975-76-77-78	112
Kirk Gibson, 1975-76-77-78	112
Scott Greene, 1992-93-94-95	110
Mark Brammer, 1976-77-78-79	107
Gene Wahington, 1964-65-66	102
Bobby Morse, 1983-84-85-86	102

SPARTAN SALUTE

Senior All-American ANDRE RISON tied Bob Carey's 1949 record of eight touchdown receptions in '88. He went on to lead the team with 39 catches for 961 yards. His lofty average gain of 24.6 yards per catch remains second (20 or more catches) only to Gene Washington's 25.0 in 1966! He ended his MSU career as State's career leader in reception yardage (2,992).

BOWL
Highlights

Head Coach **GEORGE PERLES** and Georgia boss **VINCE DOOLEY** pose for the cameras with the Gator Bowl trophy at the pre-game luncheon.

The offensive star for the Spartans was **ANDRE RISON** who re-wrote the MSU record book for single-game pass reception yardage with 292 yards and three touchdowns on nine catches in the '89 Gator Bowl. One of Rison's scores was an amazing 50-yard grab on a third-and-46 situation. It was a sterling performance from a very special talent.

BOBBY McALLISTER (left) closed out his senior campaign in grand style, throwing for a career-high 288 yards on 14-of-24 passing in the Gator Bowl. McAllister threw for 1,406 yards and nine TDs in '88. His deft running netted another 351 yards on the ground. In his final two seasons he added 649 rushing yards and 2,577 passing yards to the Spartans' offense.

1989

THE SCORES

49	Miami (Ohio)*	0
13	Notre Dame	21
20	Miami (Fla.)*	26
17	Iowa	14
7	Michigan*	10
10	Illinois*	14
28	Purdue	21
51	Indiana	20
21	Minnesota*	7
76	Northwestern*	14
31	Wisconsin	3

Aloha Bowl

33	Hawaii	13

8-4-0
Big Ten: 6-2, T-3rd

THE STANDINGS

	W	L	T
Michigan	8	0	0
Illinois	7	1	0
Michigan State	6	2	0
Ohio State	6	2	0
Minnesota	4	4	0
Indiana	3	5	0
Iowa	3	5	0
Purdue	2	6	0
Wisconsin	1	7	0
Northwestern	0	8	0

THE STAFF

1989 Coaching staff, seated, lt. to rt.: Bill Rademacher, inside linebackers; Ed Rutherford, admin. ass't.; Marcelle Carruthers, grad. ass't.; "Dino" Folino, def. backs; Morris Watts, off. coordinator - quarterbacks; George Perles, head coach; Norm Parker, def. coordinator - out. linebackers; Gary Raff, volunteer ass't.; Mike Denbrock, grad. ass't. Standing, lt. to rt., Steve Furness, def. line; Greg Pscodna, grad. ass't.; Pat Morris, off. line; Larry Bielat, receivers; Charlie Baggett, running backs; Steve Beckholt, tight ends; Gary Van Dam, grad. ass't.; Jim Nudera, grad. ass't.

THE TEAM

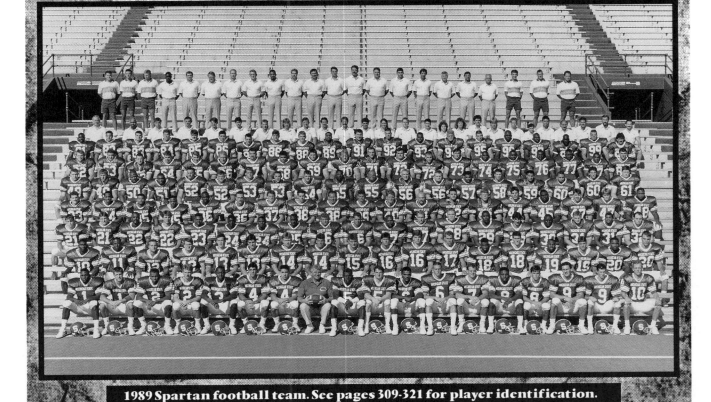

1989 Spartan football team. See pages 309-321 for player identification.

Spartan Moments

Junior quarterback DAN ENOS (4, Dearborn Edsel Ford) took over for BOBBY McALLISTER and led the offense to consecutive bowl victories. In '89, he became only the third Spartan QB to throw for 2,000 yards in a season. Enos amassed 2,066 yards and 9 TDs while completing nearly 64 percent of his passes (153-of-240), and is still 4th on the seasonal passing yardage list.

ENOS' favorite target was sophomore wide receiver COURTNEY HAWKINS (5, Flint Beecher), who exploded onto the scene by breaking ANDRE RISON's single-season school records in receptions (60) and reception yardage (1,080). Six of his catches were for touchdowns.

Senior tailback BLAKE EZOR led the ground game again, this time with 1,299 yards and a Spartan single-season record 19 touchdowns! Ezor tallied the MSU single game mark of six TDs against Northwestern. He ended his career as State's #2 ground gainer (behind White) with 3,749 yards and 34 touchdowns on 800 carries.

JOHN LANGELOH, now a junior following two record seasons of converting a combined 35 field goals, set the MSU single game record of 10 PATs vs Northwestern. In 1988, sophomore Langeloh established the MSU single-season record for most field goals with 18 (of 27 attempts). He led the team in scoring in '88 with 83 points.

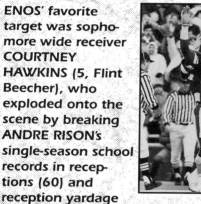

Senior defensive tackle TRAVIS DAVIS wound up his fine career as the top tackler among D-linemen with 72 and eight tackles for losses, including five QB sacks. He is still #2 on MSU's all-time chart of tackles for losses (39) and tied for #2 (with KELLY QUINN) in career QB sacks (24).

GREEN & WHITE HIGHLIGHTS

- State turned in the first of two consecutive 8-win seasons, a third straight bowl game and the fifth bowl game in the last six seasons.
- After a 2-4 start — which included close losses to #1 Notre Dame, 21-13, #2 Miami (Florida) 26-20, and #5 Michigan 10-7 — State steamrolled six consecutive opponents, including Hawaii in the Aloha Bowl, to finish 8-4 overall, 6-2 in the Big Ten (tied for third).
- MSU scored a modern-day school-record 76 points against Northwestern, crushing the 'Cats, 76-14.
- State finished the year as the 16th-ranked team in the country.
- PERCY SNOW became a two-time All-American and two other Spartans joined the All-America ranks: offensive tackle BOB KULA (West Bloomfield) and strong safety HARLON BARNETT (Cincinnati, Ohio).
- JOHN WILSON was inducted into the second annual class of the GTE Academic All-America Hall of Fame — the highest honor paid to a very select group of scholar-athletes across America.

★MSU ALL-STARS★

All-America senior safety HARLON BARNETT (left) made a host of ferocious tackles in his career. Barnett was 4th on the team and the top defensive back with 73 tackles, including 51 solo tackles. Another All-American, senior tackle BOB KULA was voted the Offensive Lineman of the Year by the Big Ten Broadcasters — the third straight year that award was captured by a Spartan.

OTHER AWARD WINNERS

All-Big Ten honorees, first team: BOB KULA, off. tackle; TRAVIS DAVIS, def. tackle; PERCY SNOW, linebacker; HARLON BARNETT, def. back; COURTNEY HAWKINS, wide receiver; second team: JOSH BUTLAND, punter; DUANE YOUNG, tight end; COURTNEY HAWKINS, wide receiver; ERIC MOTEN, off. guard; BLAKE EZOR, tailback; JOHN LANGELOH, placekicker; honorable mention; DAN ENOS, quarterback; MATT VANDERBEEK, def. end; CARLOS JENKINS, linebacker; VENTSON DONELSON, def. back; DIXON EDWARDS, linebacker; TONY BRININGSTOOL, linebacker, Academic All-Big Ten; COURTNEY HAWKINS, receiver, Academic All-Big Ten, Outstanding Underclass Back (co-winner); TOBY HEATON, guard, Academic All-Big Ten; JOHN KIPLE, safety, Academic All-Big Ten, "Potsy" Ross Scholar-Athlete; MITCH LYONS, tight end, Academic All-Big Ten; CHRIS WILLERTZ, def. end, Academic All-Big Ten, Academic All-America, Tommy Love Most Improved; PERCY SNOW, linebacker, 8th in voting for Heisman Trophy, MVP; MATT VANDERBEEK, def. end, President's Outstanding Senior Lineman; HARLON BARNETT, safety, President's Outstanding Senior Back; TIM RIDINGER, def. tackle, "Biggie" Munn Most Inspirational; STEVE MONTGOMERY, fullback, Oil Can (Humorist); BOB KULA, tackle, Iron Man (strength and conditioning), Gerald R. Ford Up Front (off. lineman); ERIC MOTEN, guard, Outstanding Underclass Lineman (co-winner); DUANE YOUNG, tight end, Outstanding Underclass Lineman (co-winner); DAN ENOS, quarterback, Outstanding Underclass Back (co-winner); BLAKE EZOR, tailback, Downtown Coaches Outstanding Senior on offense; TRAVIS DAVIS, def. tackle, Downtown Coaches Outstanding Senior on defense; VENTSON DONELSON, cornerback, Frederick W. Danziger (Detroit area); DOUG WEAVER, MSU Athletic Director, Daugherty Award (Distinguished Footbal (Alumnus).

Spartan List

Top 10 Single-Season Reception Leaders

Courtney Hawkins, 1989	60
Andre Rison, 1986	54
Derrick Mason, 1995	53
Muhsin Muhammad, 1995	50
Mill Coleman, 1993	48
Courtney Hawkins, 1991	47
Ted Jones, 1981	44
Eugene Byrd, 1978	43
Scott Greene, 1994	42
Kirk Gibson, 1978	42

SPARTAN SALUTE

PERCY SNOW broke his own single-season record with 172 tackles (still #2) while tying Mike Iaquaniello (Dearborn Fordson) for the team lead with four interceptions. Percy's personal best came against Illinois with 23 tackles. Snow became the most decorated Spartan of all-time by becoming the first player ever to win both the Lombardi Award and the Butkus Award.

BOWL
Highlights

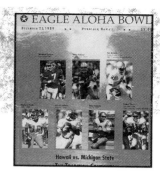

BLAKE EZOR's (left and below, right) last game was a memorable one as he led all rushers with 179 yards (110 in the second half) and three TDs in 41 carries to pace State's 33-13 victory.

JOHN LANGELOH (above) did double duty — and how! He kicked two-of-two field goals and punted three times for an average of 50.7 yards per punt!

Two future NFL stars—DIXON EDWARDS (lt.) and CARLOS JENKINS—race downfield on kickoff coverage during State's Aloha Bowl win over Hawaii.

1990-1995

MICHIGAN STATE UNIVERSITY

SPARTAN FOOTBALL

100 Seasons

MAC - MSC - MSU

1990

THE SCORES

23	Syracuse	23
19	Notre Dame*	20
34	Rutgers	10
7	Iowa*	12
28	Michigan	27
13	Illinois	15
55	Purdue*	33
45	Indiana *	20
28	Minnesota	16
29	Northwestern	22
14	Wisconsin*	9

John Hancock Bowl

| 17 | Southern California | 16 |

8-3-1
Big Ten: 6-2, T-1st

THE STANDINGS

	W	L	T
Michigan	6	2	0
Michigan State	6	2	0
Illinois	6	2	0
Iowa	6	2	0
Ohio State	5	2	1
Minnesota	5	3	0
Indiana	3	4	1
Northwestern	1	7	0
Purdue	1	7	0
Wisconsin	0	8	0
Penn State	-	-	-

THE STAFF

1990 Coaching staff, seated, lt. to rt.: Larry Bielat, admin. ass't.; Bobby Williams, running backs; "Dino" Folino, def. backs; Morris Watts, off. coordinator—quarterbacks; George Perles, head coach; Norm Parker, def. coordinator - out. linebackers; Gary Raff, volunteer ass't.; Bill Rademacher, inside linebackers; Larry Smith, grad. ass't. Standing, lt. to rt., Steve Furness, def. line; Pat Morris, off. line; Billy Davis, grad. ass't.; Kip Waddell, grad. ass't.; Charlie Baggett, receivers; Jim Nudera, grad. ass't.; Walt Bazylewicz, grad. ass't.; Pat Shurmur, tight ends; Gary Van Dam, recruiting coordinator.

THE TEAM

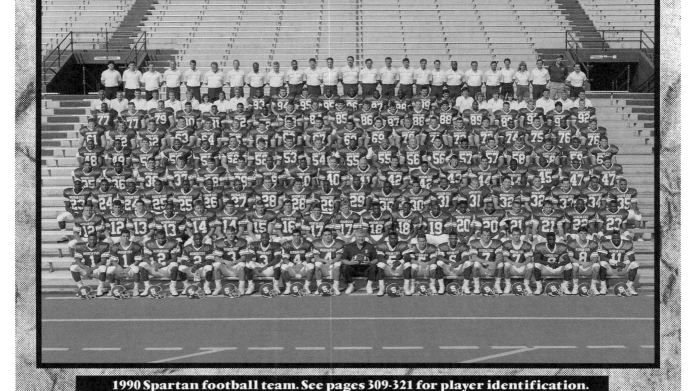

1990 Spartan football team. See pages 309-321 for player identification.

Spartan Moments

It was a big year for the powerful MSU rushing game with sophomore tailback TICO DUCKETT (left) (35, Kalamazoo Loy-Norrix) and senior tailback HYLAND HICKSON (below) (30, Ft. Lauderdale) combining for 2,590 yards on the ground. State doubled its opponents on the ground, 2,877 to 1,401 in 12 games. In the 45-20 Indiana victory, pictured here, the dynamic duo sprinted for 320 yards and four TDs on 49 carries. Duckett gained 150 yards and a TD in 24 rushes while Hickson tallied 170 yards and three scores in 25 attempts. For the season, Duckett piled up 1,394 yards and 10 TDs while Hickson added 1,196 yards and 14 scores.

Junior CHUCK BULLOUGH (left) (41, Orchard Park, N.Y.) — younger brother of Shane — took over the middle linebacker position for PERCY SNOW and proceeded to ring up 164 tackles to lead the team. Chuck registered 19 tackles vs. Wisconsin (14-9 win) and matched that single game output three more times in 1991. In this photo, Bullough helps limit Indiana's Vaughn Dunbar to 63 yards in 15 carries.

The top receiver in 1990 was senior wide receiver JAMES BRADLEY (3, Orrville, Ohio) who collected 32 passes for 517 yards and a team-leading 16.2 yards per catch.

GREEN & WHITE HIGHLIGHTS

- MSU was Big Ten co-champion with a 6-2 league ledger, 8-3-1 overall.
- State defeated Southern Cal, 17-16, in the John Hancock Bowl in El Paso, Texas, for MSU's fourth straight bowl appearance and third win in that stretch.
- 1990 marked the sixth consecutive winning season (seventh straight non-losing season), the second eight-win season in a row and the school's second Big Ten title in four years.
- The Spartans upset top-ranked Michigan, 28-27, in Ann Arbor, in one of the most thrilling games in the long history of the series.
- State narrowly missed the upset of then-#1 ranked Notre Dame in the home opener. MSU held a 19-7 lead heading into the fourth quarter, but lost on an Irish TD with 34 seconds left in the game, three plays after the "Immaculate Deflection" of a pass off the shoulder pads of Todd Murray and into the arms of Adrian Jarrell at the MSU two-yard line.
- The Spartans ended the season as the No. 14 team in the nation by UPI, 16th by AP.
- A school record 23 Spartans were honored at the end of the season by being voted to the All-Big Ten team — either first team (6), second team (8) or honorable mention (9). Another MSU standard of 12 Academic All-Big Ten performers were so honored in 1990.
- BOB CAREY was inducted into the Michigan Sports Hall of Fame.
- STEVE JUDAY won the NCAA Silver Anniversary Award.

★MSU ALL-STARS★

OTHER AWARD WINNERS

All-Big Ten honorees, second team: TONY BANKS, quarterback; BOB DENTON, off. tackle; honorable mention: FLOZELL ADAMS, off. tackle; YAKINI ALLEN, def. tackle; REGGIE GARNETT, mid. linebacker; DERRICK MASON, wide receiver; MATT BEARD, center, Academic All-Big Ten, Gerald R.Ford Up Front (off. lineman); GARETT GOULD, fullback, Academic All-Big Ten; DAVE KEHR, tackle, Academic All-Big Ten; BRIAN MOSALLAM, guard, Academic All-Big Ten; DAVE MUDGE, tackle, Academic All-Big Ten; CHRIS SALANI, punter, Academic All-Big Ten, "Potsy" Ross Scholar-Athlete; SCOTT GREENE, fb/tb, MVP, "Biggie" Munn Most Inspirational; MARVIN WRIGHT, safety, Tommy Love Most Improved (co-winner); FLOZELL ADAMS, tackle, Tommy Love Most Improved (co-winner); MUHSIN MUHAMMAD, receiver, President's Outstanding Senior Back; BOB DENTON, tackle, President's Outstanding Senior Lineman; YAKINI ALLEN, de/dt, Doug Weaver Oil Can (Humorist); Downtown Coaches Outstanding Senior on defense (co-winner); CHRIS SMITH, dt, Iron Man (strength & conditioning); REGGIE GARNETT, mlb, Outstanding Underclass Lineman (co-winner); IKE REESE, linebacker, Outstanding Underclass Lineman (co-winner); DERRICK MASON, receiver, Outstanding Underclass Back (co-winner); MARC RENAUD, tailback, Outstanding Underclass Back (co-winner); TONY BANKS, quarterback, Downtown Coaches Outstanding Senior on offense; DEMETRICE MARTIN, cb, Downtown Coaches Outstanding Senior on defense(co-winner); ROBERT McBRIDE, de/dt, Frederick W. Danziger (Detroit area); HERB ADDERLEY, NFL Hall of Fame, Daugherty Award (Distinguished Football Alumnus); TONY POPOVSKI, guard, Jim Adams Award (Unsung Hero).

Spartan List

Top 10 Career Passes Completed

Jim Miller,
1990-91-92-93 467
Dave Yarema,
1982-83-84-85-86 464
Ed Smith, 1976-77-78 418
John Leister,
1979-80-81-82 313
Tony Banks, 1994-95 301
Dan Enos, 1987-88-89-90 297
Bryan Clark,
1978-79-80-81 204
Steve Juday, 1963-64-65 198
Bobby McAllister,
1985-86-87-88 194
Charlie Baggett,
1973-74-75 128

SPARTAN SALUTE

THE SEVEN MOST EXCITING MINUTES IN SPARTAN FOOTBALL HISTORY! State upset top-ranked Michigan, 28-27, in Ann Arbor. The teams tallied four TDs in the final seven minutes (6:03). With the score tied 14-14 in the fourth quarter, State was driving with seven minutes to play. Hyland Hickson's spectacular 26-yard run with 6:03 to play gave MSU a 21-14 lead. On the ensuing kickoff, UM's Desmond Howard raced 95 yards to tie the game at 21-all. State mounted another drive culminated by a Tico Duckett nine-yard TD run for a 28-21 Spartan lead with 1:59 remaining. Michigan's last-ditch drive ended with a seven-yard TD pass from Elvis Grbac to Derrick Alexander with six seconds on the clock. The controversial two-point conversion pass to Howard fell incomplete in the end zone and State had captured the upset!

BOWL Highlights

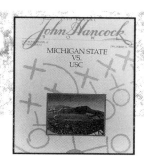

A record crowd of 50,562 filled Sun Bowl Stadium in El Paso, as the Spartans handed USC another defeat — the third in three games since 1987 — 17-16. According to the bowl officials, it was the hardest-hitting game in the bowl's history (Sun Bowl prior to John Hancock Bowl).

Senior signal-caller DAN ENOS continued his accurate passing with 137 completions in 220 attempts (.623) for 1,677 yards and four TDs. In the 1990 John Hancock Bowl versus USC, Enos completed 9-of-17 passes for 131 yards and a TD. Enos graduated as MSU's all-time leader in career pass completion percentage (.621, 297-of-478) and is currently second behind only JIM MILLER's .629.

Two of the top defenders in the Hancock Bowl and all season long were senior outside linebackers CARLOS JENKINS (above) and DIXON EDWARDS (right) (57, Cincinnati, Ohio). Jenkins was second on the team with 116 tackles and Dixon was third with 112. Jenkins totaled eight tackles for losses, Edwards had seven. Jenkins is still the No. 6 career tackler at State with 314, while Edwards is 12th with 277. Against the Trojans, Jenkins made eight stops and Edwards turned in nine.   As a junior outside linebacker in '89, Edwards enjoyed a break-through year with 111 tackles (second to PERCY SNOW) and 11 TFLs, including three QB sacks.

THE SCORES

3	Central Michigan*	20
10	Notre Dame	49
7	Rutgers*	14
0	Indiana	31
28	Michigan*	45
20	Minnesota*	12
17	Ohio State	27
13	Northwestern*	16
20	Wisconsin	7
17	Purdue	27
27	Illinois*	24

3-8
Big Ten: 3-5, T-6th

THE STANDINGS

	W	L	T
Michigan	5	3	0
Iowa	7	1	0
Ohio State	5	3	0
Indiana	5	3	0
Illinois	4	4	0
Purdue	3	5	0
Michigan State	3	5	0
Wisconsin	2	6	0
Northwestern	2	6	0
Minnesota	1	7	0
Penn State	-	-	-

THE STAFF

1991 Coaching staff, front, lt. to rt.: Larry Bielat, admin. ass't.; Bill Rademacher, inside linebackers; Norm Parker, def. coordinator - out. linebackers; George Perles, head coach; Charlie Baggett, receivers - passing game coordinator; Pat Morris, off. line - running game coordinator; Bobby Williams, running backs. Second row, lt. to rt., "Dino" Folino, def. backs; Ed Zaunbrecher, quarterbacks; Walt Bazylewicz, grad. ass't.; Gary Raff, volunteer ass't.; Kip Waddell, def. line; Pat Shurmur, tight ends; Gary Van Dam, recruiting coordinator. Third row, lt. to rt., Tim Johns, grad. ass't.; Billy Davis, grad. ass't.; Dan Enos, grad. ass't.; Dan O'Brien, grad. ass't.

THE TEAM

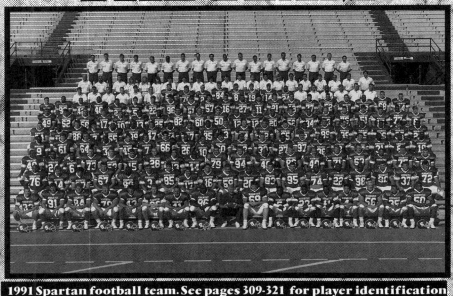

1991 Spartan football team. See pages 309-321 for player identification.

SPARTAN ITEM

Senior COURTNEY HAWKINS (5) and junior TICO DUCKETT (35) carried the offensive load. Here the two offensive stars pose with the trophies, awards, and bowl game t-shirts accumulated through 1990 during the Perles era. Hawkins was the #1 receiver with 47 catches for 656 yards and five touchdowns. A second-round NFL selection, Hawkins also left MSU as the school record holder for career kickoff return yards (1,571). Duckett added 1,204 yards and five scores in 1991. He was also the team's #2 receiver with 17 for 136 yards. 1991 was his second-straight 1,000-yard rushing season.

GREEN & WHITE HIGHLIGHTS

- State won two of the last three games of the season, but dipped to 3-8 overall, 3-5 in the Big Ten.
- The Spartans kept their winning streak over Minnesota alive by winning for the 13th straight time (20-12) in the series — a string that has now reached 15.
- CHUCK BULLOUGH set the Spartans' single-season record for tackles with 175.
- TICO DUCKETT's single-game high-water mark was 241 yards and two TDs on 30 carries in a 20-12 win over Minnesota. It remains the 8th-highest single-game rushing total in MSU history.
- Senior punter JOSH BUTLAND (88, Troy) concluded his career averaging 40.2 yards per punt in 1991 and 40.7 for his career—5th on the Spartans' career punting average list.

Spartan Moments

Sophomore QB JIM MILLER (16, Waterford Kettering) became the starting quarterback in the fourth game of the '91 season and was the signal-caller for the rest of his fine career. He threw for 1,368 yards and six TDs on 130 completions in 218 passes (.596). He became just the fifth different quarterback to throw for over 300 yards in a game when he completed 30-of-39 passes for 302 yards and three TDs in a 45-28 loss to Michigan.

Senior MLB CHUCK BULLOUGH was a busy man, setting a Spartan single season record with 175 tackles, placing him solidly in 3rd place (behind DAN BASS and PERCY SNOW) on State's all-time tackles list with 391.

Spartan List

Top 10 Single-Season Rushing Attempts

Lorenzo White, 1985	419
Lorenzo White, 1987	357
Blake Ezor, 1988	322
Tico Duckett, 1991	272
Blake Ezor, 1989	267
Eric Allen, 1971	259
Tico Duckett, 1990	257
Hyland Hickson, 1990	234
Levi Jackson, 1975	230
Marc Renaud, 1995	216

SPARTAN SALUTE

CLARENCE UNDERWOOD returned to MSU when then-athletic director George Perles hired him from the Big Ten Conference to be Assistant Athletic Director for Compliance. Underwood served the Big Ten as Deputy Commissioner from 1983-90. Underwood returned to State where he had been Assistant Athletic Director for Academics from 1972-82. Today he is the Spartans' Senior Associate Athletic Director.

★ MSU ALL-STARS ★

OTHER AWARD WINNERS

All-Big Ten honorees, first team: COURTNEY HAWKINS, flanker; CHUCK BULLOUGH, linebacker; second team: TICO DUCKETT, tailback; JOSH BUTLAND, punter; BILL JOHNSON, def. end; honorable mention: ROB FREDRICKSON, linebacker; TOBY HEATON, off. guard; JIM JOHNSON, off. tackle; JIM DELVERNE, placekicker; ALAN HALLER, def. back; MYRON BELL, safety; MILL COLEMAN, QB/receiver, Academic All-Big Ten; COLIN CRONIN, guard, Academic All-Big Ten; ROB FREDRICKSON, linebacker, Academic All-Big Ten; TODD GRABOWSKI, linebacker, Academic All-Big Ten; TOBY HEATON, guard, Academic All-Big Ten; MARK MACFARLAND, receiver, Academic All-Big Ten; MIKE MADDIE, linebacker, Academic All-Big Ten; JIM MILLER, quarterback, Academic All-Big Ten; Doug Weaver Oil Can (Humorist); BRIAN VOOLETICH, safety, Academic All-Big Ten, "Potsy" Ross Scholar-Athlete, STEVE WASYLK, safety, Academic All-Big Ten; CHUCK BULLOUGH, linebacker, MVP (co-winner), Downtown Coaches Outstanding Senior on defense; COURTNEY HAWKINS, receiver, MVP (co-winner), Downtown Coaches Outstanding Senior on offense; MITCH LYONS, tight end, Tommy Love Most Improved (co-winner); JOHN MACNEILL, def. end, Tommy Love Most Improved (co-winner); ALAN HALLER, cornerback, President's Outstanding Senior Back; CHRIS PIWOWARCZYK, center, President's Outstanding Senior Lineman (co-winner); BILL JOHNSON, def. end, President's Outstanding Senior Lineman (co-winner); ED O'BRADOVICH, def. tackle, "Biggie" Munn Most Inspirational; JIM JOHNSON, tackle, Iron Man (strength & conditioning), Gerald R. Ford Up Front (off. lineman); TICO DUCKETT, tailback, Outstanding Underclass Back; BILL REESE, def. tackle, Outstanding Underclass Lineman; JOSH BUTLAND, punter, Frederick W. Danziger (Detroit area); SONNY GRANDELIUS, coach/business, Daugherty Award (Distinguished Football Alumnus).

1992

THE SCORES

20	Central Michigan*	24
31	Notre Dame*	52
0	Boston College	14
42	Indiana*	31
10	Michigan	35
20	Minnesota	15
17	Ohio State*	27
27	Northwestern	26
26	Wisconsin*	10
35	Purdue*	13
10	Illinois	14

5-6
Big Ten: 5-3, 3rd

THE STANDINGS

	W	L	T
Michigan	6	0	2
Ohio State	5	2	1
Michigan State	5	3	0
Illinois	4	3	1
Iowa	4	4	0
Indiana	3	5	0
Wisconsin	3	5	0
Purdue	3	5	0
Northwestern	3	5	0
Minnesota	2	6	0
Penn State	-	-	-

THE STAFF

1992 Coaching staff: George Perles, head coach; Morris Watts, ass't. head coach - off. coordinator; Norm Parker, def. coordinator — out. linebackers; Charlie Baggett, receivers; "Dino" Folino, def. backs; Pat Morris, off. line; Pat Shurmur, tight ends; Kip Waddell, def. line; Bobby Williams, running backs; Ed Zaunbrecher, inside linebackers.

THE TEAM

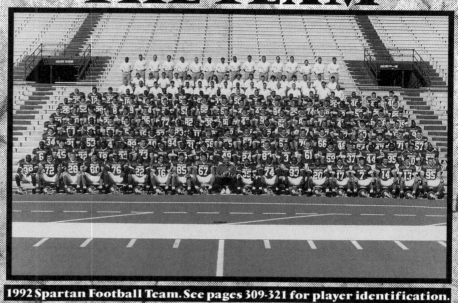

1992 Spartan Football Team. See pages 309-321 for player identification.

SPARTAN ITEM

Jim Miller threw primarily to sophomore MILL COLEMAN (6, Farmington Hills Harrison) and senior tight end Mitch Lyons. Coleman caught 37 passes for 586 yards and three TDs. The most memorable play of 1992—the one that turned an 0-3 start into a 5-3 finish—was the late second-quarter fake field goal against Indiana in the Big Ten opener. Trailing 21-7 and facing a 4th-and-5 from the IU 16 with 32 seconds remaining until halftime, State called a timeout. Coleman entered the game as the holder for an apparent field-goal attempt. Instead, Coleman swept left end for a 16-yard TD and a 21-14 score that swung the momentum entirely to the Spartans. Coleman caught six passes for 98 yards as State won, 42-31.

GREEN & WHITE HIGHLIGHTS

- MSU finished 5-3 in the Big Ten to tie for 3rd place. The Spartans' 5-6 record narrowly missed out on a bowl opportunity when they dropped the season finale at Illinois, 14-10.
- Middle linebacker TY HALLOCK, who moved from fullback for the 1992 season, registered in 10 solo tackles to help hold Purdue to 16 yards rushing in a 35-13 victory. The defense caused four turnovers.
- TOBY HEATON became MSU's first four-time Academic All-Big Ten performer.
- FRANK "MUDDY" WATERS was inducted into the Michigan Sports Hall of Fame.

Spartan Moments

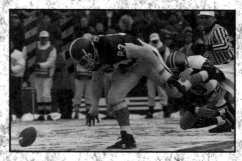

Junior linebacker ROB FREDRICKSON (83, St. Joseph) not only was one of the top defensive stoppers with 102 tackles, he also made Spartan history. Pictured at left, Fredrickson is about to scoop up the extra point kick which he blocked and returned 82 yards for the first defensive extra points in school history. At the time MSU led 10-6 and Purdue hoped to make it 10-7 in the second quarter. Instead, Fredrickson's heroics made it 12-6 at halftime and MSU won, 35-13.

MITCH LYONS grabbed 36 aerials for 400 yards, including his record performance at Michigan when he caught a Spartan single-game record 12 passes (for 119 yards) in a 35-10 defeat in Ann Arbor.

Spartan List

Top 10 Single-Season Rushing Touchdown Leaders

Blake Ezor, 1989	19
Eric Allen, 1971	18
Scott Greene, 1995	17
Lorenzo White, 1985	17
Lorenzo White, 1987	16
Craig Thomas, 1992	15
Hyland Hickson, 1990	14
Sonny Grandelius, 1950	11
Blake Ezor, 1988	11
Charlie Baggett, 1974	11

SPARTAN SALUTE

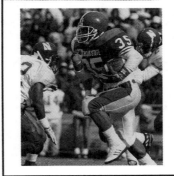

Senior TICO DUCKETT (35) became the only back in Spartan football history to rush for over 1,000 yards in three consecutive seasons. He churned out another 1,021 yards and seven TDs in 204 carries for a fine 5.0 average rush. His top game in '92 was a 172-yard effort with one six-pointer on 31 attempts as State edged Northwestern, 27-26, in Evanston. Incidentally, Tico is his given name and not a nickname. Tico claims it was the name of a cartoon character that his family was watching on television.

★ MSU ALL-STARS ★

OTHER AWARD WINNERS

All-Big Ten honorees, first team: TICO DUCKETT, tailback; second team: TY HALLOCK, linebacker; TOBY HEATON, offensive guard; MITCH LYONS, tight end; CRAIG THOMAS, tailback; honorable mention: MYRON BELL, cornerback; MILL COLEMAN, FL/QB; WILLIAM REESE, def. tackle; STEVE WASYLK, strong safety; MITCH LYONS, tight end; MIKE EDWARDS, defensive end; JUAN HAMMONDS, def. end ; MILL COLEMAN, flanker/QB, Academic All-Big Ten, MVP; ROB FREDRICKSON, linebacker, Academic All-Big Ten;TODD GRABOWSKI, tight end, Academic All-Big Ten; TOBY HEATON, guard, Academic All-Big Ten, Iron Man (strength and conditioning), Gerald R. Ford Up Front (off. lineman); MARK MacFARLAND, receiver, Academic All-Big Ten, "Potsy" Ross Scholar-Athlete; JIM MILLER, quarterback, Academic All-Big Ten; Doug Weaver Oil Can (Humorist), Outstanding Underclass Back (co-winner); STEVE WASYLK, safety, Academic All-Big Ten; Academic All-America, Tommy Love Most Improved (co-winner); MIKE EDWARDS, def. end, Tommy Love Most Improved (co-winner); MITCH LYONS, tight end, President's Outstanding Senior Lineman; TONY ROLLIN, fullback, President's Outstanding Senior Back (co-winner); BRET JOHNSON, quarterback, President's Outstanding Senior Back (co-winner); JEFF GRAHAM, center, "Biggie" Munn Most Inspirational; JUAN HAMMONDS, def. end, Outstanding Underclass Lineman; MYRON BELL, cornerback, Outstanding Underclass Back (co-winner); CRAIG THOMAS, tailback, Outstanding Underclass Back (co-winner); TICO DUCKETT, tailback, Downtown Coaches Outstanding Senior on offense; TY HALLOCK, linebacker, Downtown Coaches Outstanding Senior on defense; BRICE ABRAMS, fullback, Frederick W. Danziger (Detroit area); "BUCK" NYSTROM, coach, Daugherty Award (Distinguished Football Alumnus).

1993

THE SCORES

31	Kansas*	14
14	Notre Dame	36
48	Central Michigan*	34
17	Michigan*	7
21	Ohio State	28
24	Iowa*	10
0	Indiana	10
31	Northwestern*	29
27	Purdue	24
37	Penn State*	38
20	Wisconsin	41
	(at Tokyo, Japan)	

Liberty Bowl

7	Louisville	18

6-6
Big Ten: 4-4, 7th

THE STANDINGS

	W	L	T
Ohio State	6	1	1
Wisconsin	6	1	1
Penn State	6	2	0
Indiana	5	3	0
Michigan	5	3	0
Illinois	5	3	0
Michigan State	4	4	0
Iowa	3	5	0
Minnesota	3	5	0
Northwestern	0	8	0
Purdue	0	8	0

THE STAFF

1993 Coaching staff, front row, lt. to rt.: "Dino" Folino, def. backs; Norm Parker, def. coordinator-out. linebackers; George Perles, head coach; Morris Watts, assistant head coach - offensive coordinator - quarterbacks; Pat Shurmur, tight ends. Second row, lt. to rt., Steve Beckholt, strength & conditioning; Bobby Williams, running backs; Gary Van Dam, recruiting coordinator; Ed Zaunbrecher, inside linebackers; Willie "Skip" Peete, receivers; Pat Morris, off. line. Back row, lt. to rt., Chris Kolbak, grad. ass't.; Larry Ballew, grad. ass't.; Dan Enos, grad. ass't.; Pat Perles, grad. ass't.; Bill Rademacher, admin. ass't.; Dean Olson, ass't. video; Tom Shepard, video coordinator; Kip Waddell, def. line.

THE TEAM

1993 Spartan football team. See pages 309-321 for player identification.

Spartan Moments

Senior fullback BRICE ABRAMS (49, Detroit Henry Ford) was all the Wolverines could handle, and then some, during the Spartans' 17-7 upset in East Lansing. Known for his crushing blocks, a fired-up Abrams opened the scoring on this three-yard run on his first carry of the season behind a great block from SCOTT GREENE (47, Canandaigua, NY)! He also was State's #1 receiver in the game, catching five passes for 39 yards.

Junior tight end BOB ORGAN (94, Ludington) hauled in 33 passes for 306 yards to rank second behind COLEMAN. In the 28-21 loss to Ohio State, Organ was a big load for the Buckeye defense with eight receptions for 61 yards.

Senior CRAIG THOMAS (below, right) complemented DUANE GOULBOURNE with 889 yards and nine touchdowns. He matched Goulbourne with a career-high 195 yards in the CMU game, scoring four times.

GREEN & WHITE HIGHLIGHTS

- Team responded with a 6-5 regular season and a bid to the Liberty Bowl, State's seventh bowl game in the last 10 years under PERLES.

- A 17-7 victory over #9 Michigan gave State a 2-2 record versus the Wolverines over the last four years.

- MSU stood 6-3 before the two final game losses to Penn State (38-37) and Big Ten champion Wisconsin (41-20) in the 18th annual Coca-Cola Bowl in Tokyo, Japan.

- CHARLES "BUBBA" SMITH was inducted into the Michigan Sports Hall of Fame.

- Sophomore tailback DUANE GOULBOURNE (27, Detroit Northern), topped the ground game with 973 yards and eight TDs. His two big days were 195 yards and two scores in 28 carries and a TD in 29 attempts in the 24-10 win over Iowa.

OTHER AWARD WINNERS

All-Big Ten honorees, second team: SHANE HANNAH, off. tackle; JIM MILLER, quarterback; ROB FREDRICKSON, out. linebacker; honorable mention: MYRON BELL, def. back; MARK BIRCHMEIER, center; JUAN HAMMONDS, def. end; MILL COLEMAN, flanker; BOB ORGAN, tight end; STEVE WASYLK, def. back; Academic All-Big Ten, Frederick W. Danziger (Detroit area); PETER DRZAL, def.back, Academic All-Big Ten; BRIAN MOSALLAM, guard, Academic All-Big Ten; ROB FREDRICKSON, linebacker, Academic All-Big Ten, Downtown Coaches Outstanding Senior on defense; CHRIS SALANI, punter, Academic All-Big Ten; STEVE WASYLK, safety, Academic All-Big Ten, Academic All-America, Nat'l Football Foundation Hall of Fame Graduate Fellowship, NCAA Post-Graduate Scholarship, Anson Mount Scholar-Athlete of the Year, "Potsy" Ross Scholar-Athlete; BRICE ABRAMS, fullback, MVP (co-winner), "Biggie" Munn Most Inspirational; JIM MILLER, quarterback, MVP (co-winner); Doug Weaver Oil Can (Humorist), Downtown Coaches Outstanding Senior on offense; RICH GLOVER, def. end, Tommy Love Most Improved; BRETT LORIUS, guard, President's Outstanding Senior Lineman, Iron Man (strength & conditioning); CRAIG THOMAS, tailback, President's Outstanding Senior Back; JUAN HAMMONDS, def. end, Outstanding Underclass Lineman (co-winner); MARK BIRCHMEIER, center, Outstanding Underclass Lineman (co-winner); DUANE GOULBOURNE, tailback, Outstanding Underclass Back; SHANE HANNAH, tackle, Gerald R. Ford Up Front (off. lineman), MYRON BELL, cornerback, Downtown Coaches Outstanding Senior on defense; KIRK GIBSON, major league baseball, Daugherty Award (Distinguished Football Alumnus).

Spartan List

Oakland Press All-Time Offensive Team
(selected by the Oakland Press sports staff in 1994)

QB	Earl Morrall	1953-55
RB	Lorenzo White	1984-87
RB	Eric Allen	1969-71
WR	Andre Rison	1985-88
WR	Kirk Gibson	1975-78
TE	Billy Joe DuPree	1970-72
T	Tony Mandarich	1985-88
T	Don Coleman	1949-51
G	Ed Bagdon	1946-49
G	Joe DeLamielleure	1970-72
C	Dan Currie	1955-57

SPARTAN SALUTE

PETER McPHERSON is named President of Michigan State University. Here, he is pictured at the press reception on the Friday night prior to State's first Big Ten Conference game against Penn State University. President McPherson unveiled the "Land Grant Trophy," established by MSU coach George Perles and PSU mentor Joe Paterno. The trophy honors the two institutions' unique places in history as the two pioneer land-grant schools in the nation. Michigan Agricultural College (MAC) and PSU were each founded in 1855 — MAC on Feb. 12, and PSU 10 days later, on February 22. These were the prototypes after which the trophy was appropriately dubbed "The Land-Grant Trophy" by MSU Sports Information Director Ken Hoffman.

BOWL
Highlights

The Spartans played Wisconsin in the regular season Big Ten finale in the Tokyo Dome in Tokyo, Japan. The game marked the first time MSU played a football game outside of the United States (MSU played two games outside of the continental U.S. defeating Hawaii, 58-19 in 1947, and 33-13 in the 1989 Aloha Bowl — both in Hawaii).

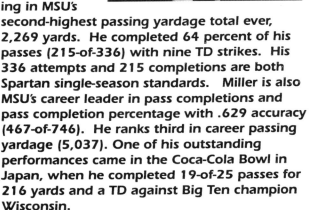

Senior linebacker ROB FREDRICKSON capped his State career with 13 tackles in the Liberty Bowl game. He compiled a team-leading 98 tackles, 74 of the solo variety. Fredrickson became a first-round pick of the NFL Raiders.

Senior QB JIM MILLER engineered an outstanding season, resulting in MSU's second-highest passing yardage total ever, 2,269 yards. He completed 64 percent of his passes (215-of-336) with nine TD strikes. His 336 attempts and 215 completions are both Spartan single-season standards. Miller is also MSU's career leader in pass completions and pass completion percentage with .629 accuracy (467-of-746). He ranks third in career passing yardage (5,037). One of his outstanding performances came in the Coca-Cola Bowl in Japan, when he completed 19-of-25 passes for 216 yards and a TD against Big Ten champion Wisconsin.

Junior flanker MILL COLEMAN snared six passes for 100 yards in the Liberty Bowl. For the season, he caught 48 passes for 671 yards and three TDs. The 48 receptions rank third on State's single-season list, behind only COURTNEY HAWKINS and ANDRE RISON.

1994

THE SCORES

10	Kansas	17
20	Notre Dame*	21
45	Miami (Ohio)*	10
29	Wisconsin*	10
20	Michigan	40
7	Ohio State*	23
14	Iowa	19
27	Indiana*	21
35	Northwestern	17
42	Purdue*	30
31	Penn State	59

5-6
Big Ten: 4-4, T-5th

THE STANDINGS

	W	L	T
Penn State	8	0	0
Ohio State	6	2	0
Michigan	5	3	0
Wisconsin	4	3	1
Illinois	4	4	0
Michigan State	4	4	0
Iowa	3	4	1
Indiana	3	5	0
Purdue	2	4	2
Northwestern	2	6	0
Minnesota	1	7	0

THE STAFF

1994 Coaching staff, front, lt. to rt.: "Skip" Peete, receivers; Henry Bullough, def. coordinator; George Perles, head coach; Morris Watts, ass't. head coach - off. coordinator - quarterbacks; Bobby Williams, running backs. Middle row, lt. to rt., Norm Parker, out. linebackers; "Dino" Folino, def. backs; Kip Waddell, def. line; Pat Shurmur, tight ends; Bill Rademacher, admin. ass't. Back row, lt. to rt., Brad Salem, grad. ass't.; Mark Rhea, grad. ass't.; Gary Van Dam, admin. ass't.; Pat Morris, off. line; Steve Beckholt, strength & conditioning.

THE TEAM

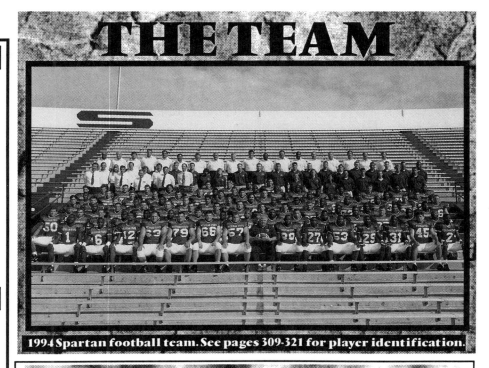

1994 Spartan football team. See pages 309-321 for player identification.

SPARTAN ITEM

Against Ohio State, senior flanker MILL COLEMAN was on the receiving end of a season-high seven aerials for 109 yards before suffering what proved to be a season-ending knee sprain. "The Thrill's" career reception total of 126 is third on the Spartans' all-time list.

GREEN & WHITE HIGHLIGHTS

- Won three of the last four games, losing only to #2-ranked and Rose Bowl-bound Penn State, to wind up 5-6 overall, 4-4 in the Big Ten, in George PERLES' 12th and final season (MSU would later forfeit the five wins as part of the school's self-imposed sanctions in response to the findings of the school's and NCAA's investigation of the football program).
- State crushed #15 Wisconsin in the Big Ten opener, 29-10, to notch MSU's fifth straight Homecoming victory.
- The Spartans built a 20-7 halftime lead over Notre Dame before the Irish pulled out a 21-20 decision. State's defense picked off four (Irish QB) Ron Powlus passes.
- Junior tailback DUANE GOULBOURNE was just short of the 1,000-yard plateau again in '94, claiming 930 yards and eight touchdowns in 214 carries (4.3 avg.) "Goldy" turned in four 100-yard rushing games with the highlight being his 181 yards and two TDs in the 35-17 romp over Northwestern.

Spartan Moments

Sophomore wide receiver and kick return specialist DERRICK MASON (80, Detroit Mumford), not only caught 14 passes for 262 yards (18.7 avg.) and two scores, he also became the first Spartan to return a kickoff for a touchdown (100 yds. vs. Penn State) since 1984. Mason's 966 kickoff return yards in '94 shattered the school record of 598 by ERIC ALLEN (1969) and was ranked fifth in the nation. It marked the second-highest single-season total in Big Ten history and just the second time a player reached 900 kickoff return yards in conference history.

Spartan List

Top 10 Single-Season Leaders in Kickoff Return Yardage

Derrick Mason, 1994 (36 ret.)	966
Derrick Mason, 1995 (35 ret.)	947
Eric Allen, 1969 (20 ret.)	598
Eric Allen, 1970 (24 ret.)	549
Courtney Hawkins, 1991 (21 ret.)	548
Larry Jackson, 1984 (20 ret.)	522
Larry Jackson, 1983 (23 ret.)	500
Derek Hughes, 1979 (16 ret.)	497
Tyrone Willingham, 1976 (23 ret.)	454
Courtney Hawkins, 1989 (18 ret.)	454

SPARTAN SALUTE

GEORGE PERLES, pictured here taking the field for the last time as MSU's head football coach, served the University for 12 years as head football boss — the second-longest tenure in Spartan grid history, behind only his mentor, Duffy Daugherty. Perles joined Munn and Daugherty as the three coaches who have led State to the Rose Bowl.

★MSU ALL-STARS★

OTHER AWARD WINNERS

All-Big Ten honorees, first team: BRIAN DEMARCO, off. guard; DEMETRICE MARTIN, def. back; second team: SHANE HANNAH, off. tackle; honorable mention: MARK BIRCHMEIER, center; MATT CHRISTENSEN, out. linebacker; REGGIE GARNETT, mid. linebacker; JUAN HAMMONDS, def. end; IKE REESE, out. linebacker; MILL COLEMAN, flanker, Academic All-Big Ten, "Potsy" Ross Scholar-Athlete, Downtown Coaches Outstanding Senior on offense; ANTHONY FOLINO, def. back, Academic All-Big Ten; SCOTT GREENE, fullback, MVP, "Biggie" Munn Most Inspirational; DEMETRICE MARTIN, cornerback, Tommy Love Most Improved (co-winner); MUHSIN MUHAMMAD, receiver, Tommy Love Most Improved (co-winner); MATT CHRISTENSEN, linebacker, President's Outstanding Senior Back, (co-winner); BOB ORGAN, tight end, President's Outstanding Senior Back (co-winner); SHANE HANNAH, tackle, President's Outstanding Senior Lineman (co-winner); AARON JACKSON, def. tackle, President's Outstanding Senior Lineman (co-winner); NIGEA CARTER, receiver, Doug Weaver Oil Can (Humorist); MARK BIRCHMEIER, center, Iron Man (strength & conditioning) (co-winner); BRIAN DEMARCO, tackle, Iron Man (strength & conditioning) (co-winner), Gerald R. Ford Up Front (off. lineman); TONY BANKS, quarterback, Outstanding Underclass Back (co-winner); DUANE GOULBOURNE, tailback, Outstanding Underclass Back (co-winner); IKE REESE, linebacker, Outstanding Underclass Back (co-winner); BOB DENTON, guard, Outstanding Underclass Lineman; JUAN HAMMONDS, def. end, Downtown Coaches Outstanding Senior on defense; DERRICK MASON, receiver, Frederick W. Danziger (Detroit area); WAYNE FONTES, NFL coach, Daugherty Award (Distinguished Football Alumnus); PETER DRZAL, def. back, Jim Adams Award (Unsung hero).

NICK SABAN
(1994-present)

Nick Saban (left) with former coach George Perles

In just one season at the helm of the Michigan State University football team, head coach Nick Saban put his stamp of success on the program, guiding MSU to a 6-5-1 mark and a berth in the Independence Bowl in 1995, the school's first winning season since 1990. Saban previously coordinated MSU from 1983-87 as defensive coordinator and secondary coach. Though many experts had tabbed MSU for a low second-division finish in the Big Ten, the Spartans rose to a fifth-place (4-3-1) standing in 1995, and were in a position to finish third entering the final weekend of the season. The revitalization began with Saban's hiring as MSU's 20th head coach on Dec. 5, 1994. From Kent State to Michigan State, from the Houston Oilers to Cleveland Browns, Saban brought a wealth of success to MSU founded on an aggressive, disciplined leadership and a no-nonsense philosophy on football and academics.

Career Record: 15-7-1

1995

THE SCORES

10	Nebraska*	50
30	Louisville	7
35	Purdue	35
25	Boston College*	21
7	Iowa*	21
27	Illinois	21
34	Minnesota*	31
14	Wisconsin	45
28	Michigan*	25
31	Indiana	13
20	Penn State*	24

Independence Bowl
| 26 | Louisiana State | 45 |

6-5-1
Big Ten: 4-3-1, 5th

THE STANDINGS

	W	L	T
Northwestern	8	0	0
Ohio State	7	1	0
Penn State	5	3	0
Michigan	5	3	0
Michigan State	4	3	1
Iowa	4	4	0
Illinois	3	4	1
Wisconsin	3	4	1
Purdue	2	5	1
Minnesota	1	7	0
Indiana	0	8	0

THE STAFF

1995 Coaching staff, front, lt. to rt.: Jim Bollman, off. line; Dean Pees, def. coordinator - inside linebackers; Gary Tranquill, off. coordinator - quarterbacks; Nick Saban, head coach; Charlie Baggett, ass't. head coach - receivers; Glenn Pires, out. linebackers - recruiting coordinator. Second row, lt. to rt., Greg Colby, def. line; Mark Dantonio, def. backs; Bobby Williams, running backs; Pat Shurmur, tight ends; Gary VanDam, football operations; Ken Mannie, strength & conditioning. Back row, lt. to rt., Mark Rhea, grad. ass't.; Brad Salem, grad. ass't.; Jason Ridgeway, grad. ass't.; Brian Wilt, grad.ass't.; Trent Clark, grad. ass't.

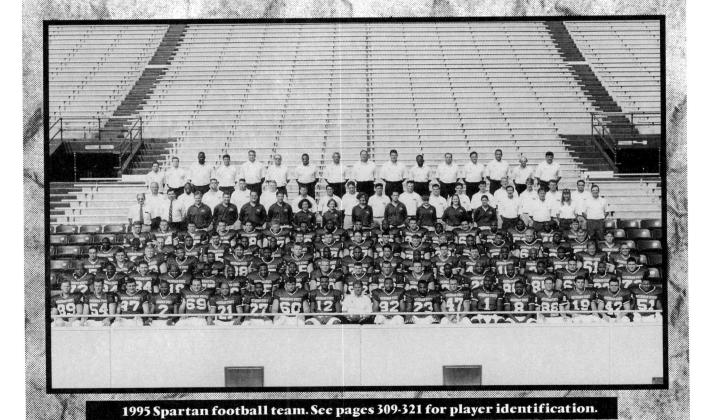

THE TEAM

1995 Spartan football team. See pages 309-321 for player identification.

Spartan Moments

The heart and soul of the '95 squad was senior fullback/tailback SCOTT GREENE whose determination to succeed was undeniable. He was the team's No. 2 rusher with 590 yards and a whopping team-high 17 touchdowns. He was the #3 receiver, as well, with 33 catches for 291 yards. Here he is pictured scoring a touchdown against Michigan while literally dragging a UM's defender into the endzone with him. State pulled off a big upset in the intrastate rivalry, 28-25.

The offense was engineered by senior QB TONY BANKS (12, San Diego, Calif.). Banks missed three games due to injury and still managed to pass for 2,089 yards and nine TDs on 156-of-258 passing (.605). His passing numbers represent the 4th highest seasonal total in MSU history. Although competing only two years at State after transferring from Mesa Junior College, Banks threw for 4,129 yards (4th on State's career list) and 20 TDs (tied for 4th on MSU's career list). At that pace, Banks would have become MSU's all-time leader in passing yardage in just one more year.

Senior defensive tackle YAKINI ALLEN (Detroit Mumford) led the team with six QB sacks for 49 yards in losses. He was also one of the team's leading tacklers with 54, including 33 first hits. Allen played defensive tackle, defensive end and linebacker during his career.

GREEN & WHITE HIGHLIGHTS

- NICK SABAN was named MSU's 20th head football coach on Dec. 3, 1994 and fielded his first Spartan team in 1995.
- State fooled all the prognosticators who had picked MSU for an 8th-10th place finish in the Big Ten. Saban led the Spartans to a 6-4-1 regular season (4-3-1 in the Big Ten for 5th place) and a berth in the 1995 Independence Bowl.
- MSU knocked off Michigan, 28-25, in East Lansing.
- Sophomore MARC RENAUD (Deerfield Beach, Florida) became State's first 1,000-yard rusher since 1992 (Duckett) when he collected 1,057 yards and three TDs on 216 carries (4.9 avg.) to lead the ground attack. It marked the 10th-highest rushing total on MSU's single-season list. Renaud also proved valuable as a receiver with 24 catches for another 226 yards. His total offense in '95 (including 35 yds. on two kickoff returns) was 1,318 yards.
- Junior receiver and kickoff return specialist DERRICK MASON broke a 100-yard kickoff return for a touchdown in the Independence Bowl against Louisiana State. It was his second kickoff return for a score in 1995. Mason also established the Big Ten record for career kickoff return yardage.

OTHER AWARD WINNERS

All-Big Ten honorees, second team: TONY BANKS, quarterback; BOB DENTON, off. tackle; honorable mention: FLOZELL ADAMS, off. tackle; YAKINI ALLEN, def. tackle; REGGIE GARNETT, mid. linebacker; DERRICK MASON, wide receiver; MATT BEARD, center, Academic All-Big Ten, Gerald R.Ford Up Front (off. lineman); GARETT GOULD, fullback, Academic All-Big Ten; DAVE KEHR, tackle, Academic All-Big Ten; BRIAN MOSALLAM, guard, Academic All-Big Ten; DAVE MUDGE, tackle, Academic All-Big Ten; CHRIS SALANI, punter, Academic All-Big Ten, "Potsy" Ross Scholar-Athlete; SCOTT GREENE, fb/tb, MVP, "Biggie" Munn Most Inspirational; MARVIN WRIGHT, safety, Tommy Love Most Improved (co-winner); FLOZELL ADAMS, tackle, Tommy Love Most Improved (co-winner); MUHSIN MUHAMMAD, receiver, President's Outstanding Senior Back; BOB DENTON, tackle, President's Outstanding Senior Lineman; YAKINI ALLEN, de/dt, Doug Weaver Oil Can (Humorist); Downtown Coaches Outstanding Senior on defense (co-winner); CHRIS SMITH, dt, Iron Man (strength & conditioning); REGGIE GARNETT, mlb, Outstanding Underclass Lineman (co-winner); IKE REESE, linebacker, Outstanding Underclass Lineman (co-winner); DERRICK MASON, receiver, Outstanding Underclass Back (co-winner); MARC RENAUD, tailback, Outstanding Underclass Back (co-winner); TONY BANKS, quarterback, Downtown Coaches Outstanding Senior on offense; DEMETRICE MARTIN, cb, Downtown Coaches Outstanding Senior on defense(co-winner); ROBERT McBRIDE, de/dt, Frederick W. Danziger (Detroit area); HERB ADDERLEY, NFL Hall of Fame, Daugherty Award (Distinguished Football Alumnus); Tony Popovski, guard, Jim Adams Award (Unsung Hero).

Spartan List

Academic All-Big Ten Peformers (1985-95; except Penn State)

1.	Minnesota	72
2.	Ohio State	71
3.	Indiana	68
4.	Michigan State	62
5.	Northwestern	59
6.	Iowa	49
7.	Illinois	47
8.	Wisconsin	45
9.	Michigan	42
10.	Purdue	25

SPARTAN SALUTE

MERRITT J. NORVELL, JR., Ph.D., took over the reins as MSU's 18th Director of Intercollegiate Athletics on May 25, 1995. A football and baseball letterman at Wisconsin, Norvell played for the 1963 Big Ten champions and Rose Bowl representative Badgers. Norvell served IBM for 14 years (1979-93) and the University of Wisconsin for nine years (1969-77) as Assistant Dean for Graduate School Administration and Assistant Vice-Chancellor for Student Affairs. From 1993-95, he was Chairman and President of the Norvell Group, a national marketing and distribution firm. From 1990-94, he served UW as a member of its Athletic Board.

BOWL Highlights

MSU played Louisiana State in the 20th Independence Bowl game in Shreveport, Louisiana. This aerial shot depicts the first sell-out crowd in the bowl's history.

Senior offensive tackle BOB DENTON, the team's leader on the offensive line, was one of the Spartans who visited the children at the Willis-Knighton Medical Center.

Senior wide receiver MUHSIN MUHAMMAD (Lansing) (above and left) electrified the sellout crowd of 48,835 on the second play of the game when he lined up on the left side, beat the cornerback and hauled in a 78-yard catch and run for a touchdown to give the Spartans a 7-0 lead just 47 seconds into the game. Muhsin caught nine passes from BANKS for 171 yards (both game-highs) and a TD. That combination would end up as consecutive second-round picks in the spring NFL draft.

MICHIGAN STATE FOOTBALL
ALL-TIME LETTER WINNERS LIST

Spartan All-Time Letter winners are listed by Name: Yrs. Lettered; Position; Jersey No.; Hometown/High School; *Info not available.

A

Abrams, Brice; '90-91-92-93 CoC; FB; #49; Detroit/Henry Ford
Abdo, Edward S; '38-39-40; OG; #12; Detroit/Northwestern
Abraham, Stephen R; '75; LB; #86; Ashtabula, Ohio/St. John
Abrecht, Jeffrey L; '62; #92; Dover, Ohio/Same
Adams, A. Gordon, Jr.; '41; Mgr.; *
Adams, Flozell; '94-95; OT; #76; Bellwood, Ill./Proviso West
Adams, Howard J.; '52; G; #62; Jackson/Same
Adderley, Herb A.; '58-59-60 CoC; HB; #26; Philadelphia, Pa./Northeast
Adolph, Bruce E.; '67; Mgr.; Union City/*
Agett, Albert H.; '34-35-36; HB; Kingsport, Tenn./Same
Agnew, Thomas G.; '02; *; Corunna/*
Akana, Alan; '84-85; OG; #65; Garden Grove, Calif./Costa Mesa Estancia
Alderson, Kenith O.; '70-71-72; FB/LB; #41; Baytown, Tex./Sterling
Alfson, Albert H.; '99; T; #*; Long Rapids/*
Allan, E. Thomas.; '82-83-84; C/DT/DE; #59; Cincinnati, Ohio/Moeller
Allen, Eric B.; '69-70-71C; HB; #24; Georgetown, S.C./Howard
Allen, Gerald H.; '07-08; *; #*; Detroit/*
Allen, Yakini; '92-93-94-95 CoC; DT/LB/DE; #23; Detroit/Mumford
Alling, Ronald V.; '37-38-39; C; #3; Lansing/Central
Allman, Robert M.; '34-35; E; #27; Bay City/Central
Altobelli, Dean M.; '83-84-85-86; FB/DB; #13; Escanaba/Same
Alward, Brad; '89; Mgr.; Gladwin/Same
Amacker, Matt; '91-92; OT; #76; Detroit/Mackenzie
Ammon, Harry R.; '63-64; HB; #38; Holt/Same
Amon, Jack R.; '39-40; FB; #43; Grand Rapids/Union
Ammori, Charles; '78-79-80; Mgr.; Farmington/*
Andersen, Morten; '78-79-80-81; PK; #8; Struer, Denmark/Indianapolis, Ind./Ben Davis
Anderson, Earl; '68-70; FB/TB; #44; Tifton, Ga./Tift City
Anderson, Greg; '92-93-94; DB; #16; Warren/De LaSalle
Anderson, John H.; '26-27-28; E; #*; Lansing/*
Anderson, Mark A.; '76-77-78-79; DB; #16; Akron, Ohio/Springfield
Anderson, Michael; '86-87-88; TE/OT; #97/65; Sun Prairie,Wis./Same
Anderson, Paul J.; '24; E; #*; Lansing/*
Andrews, C. Ward; '19; E; #*; Napolean/*
Ane, Charles T.; '72-73-74; C; #55; Honolulu, Hawaii/Punahou
Angel, Anthony J.; '65; #86; Honolulu, Hawaii/*
Apisa, Bob; '65-66-67; FB; #45; Honolulu, Hawaii/Farrington
Arbanas, Frederick V.; '58-59-60; E; #84; Detroit/Redford St. Mary
Arbury, James N.; '60-61; Mgr.; Detroit/*
Archbold, Harold K.; '21; HB/QB; #9; Massillon, Ohio
Archer, Laurence C.; '17-18-19; C; #16; Benton Harbor/Same
Arena, Anthony G.; '39 41; C; #4/58; Detroit/Northwestern
Arend, Donald H.; '56-58; FB; #44; Baroda/Benton Harbor
Armstrong, Robert E.; '32-33-34; HB; #38; Benton Harbor/*
Armstrong, Sterling A.; '65-66-67; DB; #31; Detroit/Central
Arnson, Donald R.; '44-45-46 47; G; #68; Muskegon/Same
Aronson, Fred; '44; HB; #14; Chicago, Ill./Austin
Amtz, Arthur B.; '44; E; #80; Benton Harbor/St. Johns
Arthurs, Jeffrey; '76-77; Mgr.; *
Ashley, Amos A.; '03-04; E; #'; Lansing/*
Audas, Sedric L.; '77-79; C; #59; Saginaw/Arthur Hill
Auer, Scott E.; '80-81-82-83; TE/OT; Ft. Wayne, In./Elmhurst
Austin, Charles O.; '49; Mgr.; Rutherford, N.J./*
Azar, George J.; '60-61-62; G; #58; Johnstown, Pa./Central

B

Babich, Richand W.; '84; OLB; #98; Mt. Clemens/Same
Badaczewski, Joseph; '53-54-55; C; #56; Seanor, Pa./Conemaugh Twp.
Baes, Richard W.; '74-75-76 CoC; TB; #3; Brookfield, Wis./Central
Bagdon, Edward; '46-47-48-49; G; #65; Dearborn/Fordson
Baggett, Charles A.; '73-74-75; QB; #i6; Fayetteville, N.C./Smith
Bailey, Charles A.; '66-67-68; DT; #61; Dayton, Ohio/Dunbar
Bailey, Phillip F.; '17; G; #18; Ludington/Same
Bailey, Terry L.; '80-81; MLB; #77; San Francisco, Calif./Wilson
Baird, Donald G.; '67-68-69; OG; #59; Tecumseh/Same
Baker, Albert H.; '34; *; #*; *
Baker, Corey; '93-94; LB/FB; #48; East Kentwood/Same
Baker, Park F.; '58-59; FB; #32; Seanor, Pa./Conemaugh
Balasis, Michael; '86; PK; #99; East Lansing/Same
Baldwin, Ernest W.; '10; G; *; Midland/*
Baldwin, William W.; '46; T; #72; Lansing/Central
Balge, Kenneth E.; '42-46C; T/E; #70/80; Dearborn/Fordson
Ball, Elton E.; '20; *; #*; Albion/*
Ball, Walter; '40; HB; #56; Lansing/Eastern
Ballard, Clint V.; '11; *; #*; East Lansing/*
Ballman, Gary J.; '59-60-61; HB; #14; East Detroit/ Same
Bancroft, Harry L.; '11; Mgr.; Lansing
Banks, Carl E.; '80-81-82-83 CoC; OLB; #54; Flint/Beecher
Banks, Tony; '94-95 CoC; QB; #12; San Diego, Calif. Mesa JC
Barbas, Constantino J.; '45; E; #89; Detroit/Cooley
Barker, Homer L.; '73; OG; #62; Denver, Colo./Manual
Barker, Richard A.; '57-58; FB/E; #46/89; Lansing/Eastern
Barnett, Harlon; '86-87-88-89 TnC; DB; #36; Cincinnati, Ohio/Princeton
Bamett, William D.; '09; *; #*; Pittsburgh, Pa./*
Barnum, Thomas E.; '69-70; LB/DDG; #49; Woodland/Lake Odessa Lakewood
Barr, Douglas E.; '69-70-71; RB/CB; #25; Canton, Ohio/Glenwood
Barratt, Fred W.; '29; C; #*; Lansing/*
Barrie, Joseph H.; '35; *; #*; *
Bass, Dan E.; '76-77-78-79; ILB; #49; Bath/Same
Bassett, Charles F.; '17-19-20; HB/E; #*; Flint/*
Batchelor, William L.; '39-40; C; #2; Buchanan/Same
Beale, John A.; '39; Mgr; Rockford Ill./*
Beard, Thomas L.; '69-70; C, #51; Battle Creek/Central
Beardsley, William W.; '42; FB; #35; Beaverton, Pa./Same
Beatty, Howard E.; '15; HB; #*; Petoskey/*
Beaubien, Paul J.; '36; G; #29; Flint/Central
Beaudoin, Mark S.; '82-83-84-85; LB/DE; #27; Charlevoix/Same
Beck, Jordan; '85; WR; #10; Milwaukee, Wis./Nicolet
Becker, Henry L.; 1896-97; *; #*; Hesperia/*
Beckley, Arthur K.; '22-23-24; HB; #*; Bay City/*
Beery, Robert L.; '69; Mgr.; Traverse City/*
Begeny, Joseph Jr.; '62-63; FB; #34; Tonawanda, N.Y./Geistown, Pa. Richland
Behrman, David W.; '60-61-62; T/C; #51; Dowagiac/Same
Belk, Veno; '82-83-84-85; LB/TE; #95; Flint/Northwestern
Bell, Anthony D.; '82-83-84-85; LB; #51; Fort Lauderdale, Fla./Anderson
Bell, Chris L.; '81; LB; #45; Cincinnati, Ohio/Wyoming
Bell, Myron; '90-91-92-93; DB; #24; Toledo, Ohio/Macomber-Whitney
Bell, Robert F.; '02-03C-04; T; #*; Mason/*
Bell, Theodore; '75; TB; #20; Youngstown, Ohio/Cardinal
Bencie, Luke; '94-95; FS/TE; #19; Sarasota, Fla./Riverview
Benedict, Richard R; '67-68; OG/DT; #68; East Lansing/Same
Bennett, Ralph E.; '38-39; E; #24; Mt. Clemens/Same

Benson, Hubert E.; '63; G; #89; Oak Park, Ill./River Forest
Benson, Wayne E.; '50-51; HB/FB; #17; Flint/Central
Bentley, S. Rahn; '62-63-64; G/T; #75; Grand Rapids/South
Bercich, Robert E.; '57-58-59; FB/HB; #43; Summit, Ill./Argo
Berger, Donald; '55-56-57; C; #54; Philadelphia, Pa./Staunton Military, Va.
Bergin, Joseph; '86-87; DE; #45; Elmhurst, Ill./York
Berlinski, Richard A.; '66-67-68; HB/FB; #22; Quinnesec/Kingsford
Bernard, Lacey; '56; E; #80; Flint/Central
Besanceney, Chris; '89-90-91; Mgr; East Lansing/*
Bethea, Larry; '74-75-76-77CoC; TE/DT; #88; Newport News, Va./Ferguson
Beyer, Howard; '42; C; #53; Muskegon/Same
Bielat, Lawrence J.; '57-58-59; QB; #21; Center Line/Same
Bielat, Scott; '83-84-85-86-87; Mgr.; Uniontown, Pa./*
Bierowicz, Donald J.; '64-65; DT; #65; Chicago, Ill./St. Rita
Bigelow, Rolla L.; 1898; *; #*; Owosso/*
Biondo, Michael H.; '60; G; #77; Detroit/St. Catherine's
Birchmeier, Mark; '92-93-94; C; #57; Wexford, Pa./North Allegheny
Birney, Thomas F.; '74-75-76-77; P/PK; #3; Detroit/Bishop Borgess
Bishop, Judson E.; 1896; *; #*; Dimondale/*
Black, Don D.; '45; G; #63; Toledo, Ohio/Libbey
Black, Steve; '88-90; OLB; #30; New York, N.Y./Bronx High School of Science
Blackburn, Bruce F.; '38-39-40; E; #33; Flint/Northern
Blacklock, Hugh; '13-14-15; T; #*; Grand Rapids/Central
Blackman, Mark S.; '45-46-47-48; T/G; #54; Jackson/Same
Blanchard, Charles M.; '00-01; *; #*; Chesaning/*
Blank, Steven D.; '80-81; MLB/OG; #57; Grand Rapids/Northview
Blenkhorn, James C.; '46-47-48-49; HB/FB; #10/31; Saginaw/Sam
Boak, W. Bryan; '81; OT; #62, New Castle, Pa./Same
Bobbitt, James L.; '60-61-62; T; #76; Buchanan/Same
Bobbitt, Paul V.; '83-84-85-86; DB; #39; Southfield/Lathrup
Bobich, Louis L.; '62-63-64; QB/FB/PK; #27; Woodville, Pa./Scott Twp.
Bobo, Douglas M.; '51-52; E; #84; Reed City/Same
Boehringer, Rudolph E.; '25-26; *; #*; Bay City/'
Bogdalek, Steven J.; '83-84-85; DT/OT; #92/68; Naperville, Ill./Central
Bohn, Ted R.; '67; C; #50; Glenview, Ill./South
Bolden, LeRoy, Jr.; '51-52-53-54 CoC; HB; #39; Flint/Northern
Bolte, Gregory; '83; TE; #88; Joliet, Ill. West
Bond, James A.; '71-72; HB; #35; Fond du Lac, Wis./Goodrich
Bongiorni, Mario; '90; DB; #7; Burgettstown, Pa./Same
Boomsliter, George P.; '04-05; *; #*; Grand Haven/*
Boron, Kevin; '92; DE; #71; Monroe/Same
Bos, John; '18-19-20-21C; E/T; #22; Grand Rapids/Central
Bourna, Robert D.; '67; Mgr.; Grand Rapids/*
Boutell, William H.; '57; Mgr.;*
Bouyer, Willie; '86-87-88; WR; #17; Detroit/Chadsey
Bowdell, Gordon B.; '68-69-70C; SE; #83; Allen Park/Cabrini
Bowditch, John J.; '06; *; #*; Hillsdale/*
Boyce, Gary C.; '68-69; PK; #3; St. Johns/Same
Boyd, Leo J.; '51-52; FB/HB; #23; Saginaw/Sts. Peter IL Paul
Boyle, Jesse G.; '05-06; *; #*; Glendora/*
Boylen, Frederick J.; '58-59-60 CoC; G; #55; Grand Rapids/Catholic Central
Brady Jacob O.; '20-21-22; QB/HB; #2; Allegan/Same
Bradley, James; '89-90; WR; #3; Orrville, Ohio/Same
Bradley, Michael W.; '66; OG; #66; Ypsilanti/Same
Brainard, Walton K.; 1897; C-01; *; #*; Brady/*
Brakeman, James R.; '34; *; #*;
Brammer, Mark D.; '76-77-78-79; TE; #91; Traverse City/Same

Brand, Louis J.; '42; QB; #29; Grand Rapids/South
Brandstatter, Arthur F., Sr.; '34-35-36; FB; #31; Ecorse/Same
Brandstatter, Arthur L., Jr.; '59-60-61; ;E; #88; East Lansing/Same
Brawley, Robert L.; '65-66; DG/LB; #62; Sault Ste. Marie/Same
Breen, Gerald; '29-30; HB; #48; Holland/*
Bremer, Ernest K.; '36-37-38; E/T; #25; East Lansing/Same
Breniff, Robert G.; '52; G; #64; Maumee, Ohio/Same
Brenner, Allen R.; '66-67-68C; E/DB; #86; Niles/Same
Breslin, Jacweir Jr.; '68-69-70; LB/S; #42; East Lansing/Same
Breslin, John T.; '74-75-76; DB; #5; East Lansing/Same
Brewton, Gregory; '74-75; OT; #77; Ft. Lauderdale, Fla./Dillard
Briningstool, Tony; '88-89-90-91; MLB; #54/43; Northville/Same
Broadway, William V.; '75; DB; #25; Flint/Northern
Brogan, Timothy; '87; OLB; #50; Springville, N.Y./Griffith Institute
Brown, Arthur L.; '16; HB; #5; Hastings/*
Brown, Charles E.; '61-62-63; G/T; #64; Pontiac/Central
Brown, Charles M.; '33; FG; #*; *
Brown, Clark D.; '83-84; QB; #23; Portage/Northern
Brown, David E.; '72-73; TB; #26; Bloomington, Ind./Same
Brown, Eddie; '89-90; WR/DB; #17; Muskegon/Same
Brown, Thomas B.; '71-72; TE; #82; Royal Oak/Kimball
Brown, William L; '74; OT; #73; McKeesport, Pa./Same
Bruckner, Leslie C.; '37-38-39; QB; #31; Milan/Same
Bruggenthies, Anton; '74-75-76; OT; #70; Denver, Colo./Mullen
Bryan, Tim; '90-91-92; WR; #14; Tecumseh/Same
Buckridge, Francis P.; 1900; *; #*; *
Budde, Edward L.; '60-61-62; G/T; #79; Detroit/Denby
Budde, John; '85-86-87-88; LB/DE; #87; Kansas City, Mo./Rockhurst
Budinski, John; '38; HB; #51; Litchfield/Same
Bufe, Noel; '55-56; E; #81; Wyandotte/Roosevelt
Buggs, Travis; '54; HB; #28; East Chicago, Ill./Washington
Bullock, Clarence; '72-73-74CoC; FB; #33; Fort Wayne, Ind./Central
Bullough, Charles; '88-89-90-91; OLB/MLB; #41; Orchard Park, NY/Same
Bullough, Henry; '52-53-54; G; #67; Canton, Ohio/Timken Voc.
Bullough, Shane H.; '83-84-85-86C; LB; #41; Cincinnati, Ohio/Moeller
Bunbury, J. Chris; '77; OT; #71; Grand Rapids/Rockford
Bunch, Derek; '80-83-84; OLB; #52; Dayton, Ohio/Meadowdale
Burge, Frederick L.; '38; Mgr.; *
Burke, Patrick F.; '55-56-57C; T; #71; Lawrence, Mass./Staunton Military, Va.
Burke, Thomas W.; '69; Mgr.; Okemos/*
Burrington, Gray K.; '02; *; #*; Lansing/*
Burroughs, Charles G.; '05-06-08; *; #*; Frontier/*
Burroughs, James E.; '77-78-79-81; CB; #28; Pahokee, Fla./Same
Buss, Arthur T.; '31-32-33; T; #6; Benton Harbor/Same
Butland, Josh; '88-89-90-91; P; #88; Troy/Same
Butler, Carl; '83-84; FB; #49; Elroy, Ariz./Santa Cruz
Butler, Charles O.; '15-16; E; #21; Bellevue/*
Butler, Frank A., Jr.; '71; SE; #87; Chicago, Ill./Leo
Butler, Frank J.; '32-33; C; #20; Chicago, Ill./*
Byrd, Eugene W.; '75-76-78-79; SE/FL; #84; East St. Louis, Ill./Same

C

Callendar, Stan; '91-92-93-94; DB; #32; Fayetteville, N.C./E.E. Smith
Campbell, Arthur L.; '06-07-08-09; *; #*; Cheat Haven, Pa.
Campbell, James F.; '08-09-10; T; #*; Charlevoix/*
Campbell, Jon; '90; LB; #77; Detroit/Bishop Borgess
Campbell, Leroy J.; '11-12; G/T; #*; Grand Rapids/*
Cantrell, Dan; '95; LB; #54; New Canaan, Conn./Same
Cappaert, Carl W.; '46-47-48-49; QB; #20; Clare/Same
Carey, Charles L.; '40; HB; #53; Charlevoix/Same
Carey, Owen; '09; E; #*; Harbor Springs/*
Carey, Robert W.; '49-50-51; C; E; #88; Charlevoix/Same
Carey, William R.; '49-50-51; QB/E; #85/21; Charlevoix/Same
Carnaghi, Bnan; '93; Mgr.; Mt. Clemens/*
Carrigan, Cornelius R.; '47; E; #89; East Pittsburgh, Pa./Same
Carruthers, Joseph D.; '55-56-57; E; #65; Detroit/Western
Carter, Fred L.; '39-40-41; T; #27/79; Elsie/Same
Carter, Nigea; '93-94-95; WR; #17/#81; Coconut Grove, Fla./Coconut Creek
Case, Albert H.; '99-00; G; #*; Springville/*

Case, Athol A.; '03; G; #*; Marengo/*
Case, Ralph W.; '99; HB; #*; Mt. Pleasant/*
Cauddell, Christopher; '85-86; PK; #7; Novi/Same
Caukins, Elmer A.; '12; G; #*; Sparta/*
Cavender, Regis; '66-67-68; FB; #25; Detroit/Cathedral
Chada, William H.; '71; DE; #95; West Natrona, Pa./Natrona Heights Highlands
Chaddock, Frank G.; '12-14; G/E; #*; Lansing/*
Chamberlain, Maunce L.; '85-86-87; DB; #31; Jeanette, Pa./Same
Chamberlain, Ralph G.; '12; C; #*; Grand Rapids/*
Chandnois, Lynn E.; '46-47-48 49; HB; #14; Flint/Central
Chapman, Marcus; '95; TE; #87; Toledo, Ohio/Rogers
Charette, Mark S.; '70-71-72; FB/LB; #45; Flint/Southwestern
Charon, Carl H.; '59-60-61; FB/HB; #33; Boyne City/Same
Chartos, William; '39; C; #5; Hammond, Ind./Same
Chastian, James M.; '58-59; C/T; #50; Waynesburg, Pa./Same
Chatlos, George R.; '65-66-67; DE; #82; Hunker, Pa./Hempfield
Cherocci, James; '86; LB; #77; Bloomfield Hills/Birmingham Brother Rice
Chesney, M. James; '60; QB; #27; Bay City/Central
Childs, Donald M.; '02; *; #*; Lansing/*
Childs, Dennis; '64; OT; #75; Chicago, Ill./Sullivan
Childs, Harold A.; '02; *; #*; Lansing/*
Christensen, Koester L.; '26-27-26; E; #*; Escanaba/*
Christensen, Matt; '91-92-93-94; OLB; #45; Libertyville, Ill./Same
Ciolek, Eugene S.; '37-36; HB; #45; Michigan City, Ind./Same
Ciolek, Robert; 49-51; QB/E; #28; Michigan City, Ind./Same
Clark, M. Bryan; '78-79-80-81; QB; #14; Bloomfield Hills/Los Altos, Calif.
Clark, Emest R.; '60-61-62; E; #65; Lockport, NY/Medina
Clark, Gail A.; '70-71-72; LB; #98; Bellefontaine, Ohio/Same
Clouse, Sean; '87; OLB; #81; Lake Orion/Orchard Lake St. Mary's
Clupper, Steven R.; '68; Mgr.; Dowagiac/*
Cobb, Leslie A.; '14; FB; #'; Grand Rapids/
Cobb, Michael; '73-74-75-76; TE; #89; Youngstown, Ohio/North
Colina, Richard W.; '33-34-35; QB; #40; Detroit/Northern
Cole, Thomas C.; '74-75-76; C/OT; #72; Howell/Same
Coleman, Don E.; '49-50-51; T; #78; Flint/Central
Coleman, Mill; '91-92-93-94; WR/QB; #6; Farmington Hills/Harrison
Colwell Fred E., Jr.; '40; Mgr.;*
Confer, Clifford; '87-88-89-90; DE; #62; New Lothrop/Same
Connor, Alger V.; '42-46; G; #63; Pontiac/Same
Conti, Anthony F.; '66-67CoC; OG; #67; Mt. Clemens/St.Mary's
Conti, Dominic F.; '45; QB; #23; Niagara Falls, NY/Same
Contos, Steve G.; '45; HB; #18; Toledo, Ohio/Waite
Converse, Craig M.; '77-78-79; MG; #97; Utica/Eisenhower
Convertini, Fred E.; '65; OG; #70; Downey, Calif./Same
Conway, Lynn V.; '46; E; #96; Bay City/Same
Coolidge, John K., Jr.; '36-37; HB; #34; Traverse City/Same
Cooper, George J.; '78-79-80CoC-81CoC; OLB; #39; Detroit/Northern
Cordery, James W.; '73; TE; #80; Louisville, Ky./Flaget
Corgiat, James G.; '59; E; #82; Bessemer/Same
Corless, Rex E.; '51-52; HB; #49; Coldwater/Same
Cortright, Ion J.; '07-08-09-10C; HB; #*; Mason/*
Cortright, Wesley H.; '02; *; #*; Hillsdale/*
Corwin, Christopher C.; '70; Mgr.; Plymouth/*
Coryell, Sherman H.; '16-17C-19; E; #29/12; Chicago, Ill./*
Costanzo, Louis; '54; HB; #12; Dunmore, Pa./Same
Costello, Brad; '94; PK; #40; Delran, N.J./Holy Cross
Cotton, Eddie; '64-65; FB; #44; New York, N.Y./DeWitt Clinton
Covey, William D.; '84; OG; #55; Jackson/Northwest
Cowing, Frank P., Jr.; '38; Mgr.; Homewood, Ill./*
Crabill, C. Joseph; '26-27-28; C; #*; Battle Creek/*
Crall, Max B.; '29; HB/E; #*; Dimondale/*
Crane, Bud C.; '47-48-49; FB/HB; #40; Highland Park/Same
Crane, LeRoy R.; '48-49-50C; FB; #36; Mt. Pleasant/Same
Crary, John R.; '35; Mgr.; Detroit/*
Creager, Basil J.; '33; Mgr.; Three Rivers/*
Creamer, James E.; '50-51; C; #50; Flint/Northern
Crenshaw, Tyrone; '95; TB; #30; Pacoima, Calif./Sylmar
Creswell, Smiley L.; '80-81-82; DE/DT; #91; Monroe, Wash./Same
Cronin, Colin; '91-92-93-94; OT; #66; St. Joseph/Same
Crosby, Matt A.; '98-99-00-01; HB; #*; East Lansing/*
Crosthwaite, Duane T.; '39; HB; #45; Detroit/Cooley
Croxton, Gregory; '73-74-75; OG; #67; Highland Park/Same
Culp, Steve; '92-93; Mgr.; Wilmington, Calif./*
Culver, Edward G.; '10-11; G; #*; Midland/*

Cundiff, Larry L.; '57-58-59; T/C; #99/79; Honolulu, Hawaii/Iolani
Cunningham, Timothy W.; '80-81-82-83; OLB/SS; #35; Lansing/Everett
Curl, Ronald C.; '68-69-71C; DT; #94; Chicago, Ill./DeLaSalle
Curran, Joseph W.; '82-83-84-85; NG/DT; #94; Elmhurst, Ill./Immaculate Conception
Currie, Daniel G.; '55-56-57; G/C; #55; Detroit/St. Anthony
Currie, Michael J.; '61-63; C; #55; Detroit/St. Ambrose
Currie, Tim; '89; LB; #47; Utica/Eisenhower
Curtis, Fred S.; '98-99; FB; #*; White Pigeon/*
Cutler, Donald E.; '52; T; #90; East Jordan/Same

D

Dahlgren, Gordon A.; '34-35-36C; G; #22; Chicago, Ill./Lindblom
Dahlke, Craig A.; '72-73; OG; #64; Port Huron/Same
Danciu, George W.; '40-41; G; #20/69; East Chicago, Ind./Washington
Danielewicz, Michael A.; '72-73; HB/FL; #11; Detroit/Hamtramck St. Ladislaus
Danziger, Fred W.; '26-28-29 CoC; FB; #*; Detroit/*
DePrato, Neno J.; '12-14-15; HB; #*; Iron Mountain/*
Darby, Keith A.; '53; Mgr.; Ft. Wayne, Ind./*
Daubenmeyer, John P.; '75; DE; #93; West Bloomfield/North Farmington
Davis, Alan W.; '77-78-79; DB; #27; Bloomfield Hills/Berkeley
Davis, Bayley; '89-90; Mgr.; Shrewsbury, N.J./*
Davis, Frank R.; '11; *; #*; Detroit/*
Davis, Hugh G.; '42; HB; #13; Lansing/Central
Davis, Randolph, Jr.; '70; FL; #19; Matawan, N.J./Matawan Regional
Davis, Travis; '86-87-88-89; DT; #75; Warren, Ohio/Harding
Davis, Wilford D.; '39-40-41C; QB; #48/28; Dundee/Same
Davis, Wyman D.; '39-4041; HB; #54/49; Dundee/Same
Dawson, William, Jr.; '68-69-71; MG/DT; #96; Tucson, Ariz./Same
Deacon, Fred E.; '26-27; B; #*; Lansing/*
Dean, Michael A.; '74-75-76-77; DE/OLB; #82; Dayton, Ohio/Dunbar
DeBrine, Thomas R.; '63-64; Mgr.; Sodus, N.Y./*
Decker, Arthur R.; '00; *; #*; Utica/*
Decker, John W.; '02-03; C; #*; Three Oaks/*
Decker, Michael; '77-78-79; LB; #50; Roseville/LaSalle
DeGraw, Al; '83-84-85; Mgr.; */*
Deibert, Glenn E.; '4142; E/T; #84/78; Pontiac/Same
Dekker, Paul N.; '51-52; E; #81; Muskegon/Same
DeLamielleure, Joseph M.; '70-71-72; OG; #59; Center Line/St. Clement
Delgrosso, Daniel J.; '58; T; #97/77; Chicago, Ill./Mt. Carmel
DelVerne, Jim; '91-92; PK; #7; Toledo, Ohio/St. John's
DeMarco, Brian; '91-92-93-94; OT; #79; Lorain, Ohio/Admiral King
Demarest, Ben H.; '33-34; *; #*; Lansing/*
Demos, Constantine S.; '63-64; Mgr.; Muskegon/*
Dendel, Charles T.; '12; HB; #*; Detroit/*
Dendrino, Peter C.; '44; T; #70; Muskegon Heights/Same
Densmore, Michael R.; '76-77-78-80; OG; #66; Lapeer/West
Denton, Robert; '92-93-94-95; OT/OG; #60; Martinsville, Ind./Same
DeRose, Daniel P.; '76; FL/SE; #19; East Lansing/Same
Derrickson, Paul W.; '38-39; FB; #59/50; Cranbrook Prep
Dersnah, Bernard E.; '06; *; #*; Mt. Pleasant/*
Dibble, Dorne A.; '49-50; F; #82; Adrian/Same
Dickeson, Verne C.; '27-28-29; HB; #*; Highland Park/*
Dickinson, James; '87; DT; #89; Portage/Northern
Diebold, Allen O.; 36-37-38C; QB; #44; Jackson/Same
Diehl, David D.; '36-37-38C; E; #27; Dansville/Same
Diener, Carl A.; '53-54; E; #88; Saginaw/Arthur Hill
Dietz, William H.; '98; *; #*; Lansing/*
Dignan, John; '90-91; LB; #87; Ypsilanti/Same
Dill, Reuben E.; '28-29-31; T/G; #16; Saginaw/Same
Dimitroff, Boris N.; '64-65; c; #50; Livonia/Bentley
Dixon, Darryl; '81-82-83; CB/S; #31; East St. Louis, Ill./Same
Dohoney, Donald C.; '51-52-53C; E; #80/Ann Arbor/Same
Donelson, Venson; '87-88-89; DB; #25; Detroit/Henry Ford
Donnahoo, Roger J.; '57-58; HB; #40; Lincoln Park/Redford St. Mary
Dorow, Albert R.; '49-50-51; HB/QB; #47; Imlay City/Same
Dotsch, Roland D.; '53-54; G/T; #63; Alpena/Lansing Resurrection
Doty, Stephen W.; '03-04-05-06; FB; #*; Lockport, N.Y./*
Dozier, Robert; '93-94; FB; #43; Muskegon/Muskegon Catholic
Drake, Gerald A.; '38-39; HB; #52/47; East Lansing/Same
Drew, Franklin F.; '02; *; #*; Highland Park, Ill./*

Drew, Kenneth L.; '25-26-27; B/E; #*; Tipton/*
Drobot, Richard T.; '71; Mgr.; Grand Rapids/*
Drzal, Peter; '92-93-94; DB; #38; Okemos/Same
Duckett, Ellis; '52-53-54; E; #32; Grand Rapids/*
Duckett, Tico; '89-90-91-92; TB; #35; Kalamazoo/Loy-Norrix
Duda, David; '74-75-76; DB; #15; Mt. Clemens/Same
Duda, Michael C.; '72-73-74; DE; #91; Mt. Clemens/Same
Dudley, Darwin C.; '36-37; G; #15; Christopher, Ill./Same
Dukes, Harold C.; '56-57; E; #92; Detroit/Eastern
Dunlap, Charles W.; '06; *; #*; Mt. Pleasant/*
Dunphy, Herbert; '18; HB; #*; Lansing/Central
DuPree, Billy Joe; '70-71-72CoC; TE; #89; West Monroe, La./
Richardson

E

Earley, James; '74-75-76-77; FB; #48; Dayton, Ohio/Dunbar
Eaton, Darrin; '88-89-90-91; WR; #11; Lansing/Sexton
Eaton, James P.; '60; HB; #24; Newport, R.I./Rogers
Ebey, Warren W.; '59; Mgr.; Detroit/*
Echols, Brian; '93-94-95; DB; #35; Benton Harbor/Benton
Harbor
Eckel, Clifford B.; '41; FB; #36; Dundee/Same
Eckerman, Harold; '22-23-24; C; #*; Muskegon/*
Eckert, Edward C.; '22-23-24; T; #*; Grand Rapids/*
Eddy, Howard J.; '20; *; #*; East Lansing/*
Edgar, Oliver W.; '00; *; #*; Lakeview/*
Edmunds, Allen T.; '23; E; #*; Bedford/*
Edwards, Dixon; '87-88-89-90; OLB; #57; Cincinnati, Ohio/
Aiken
Edwards, Michael; '90', '92; DE; #93; Columbus, Ohio/Marion
Edwards, Richard A.; '34-35; HB; #37; Williamston/Same
Eisner, Gerald R.; '80; Mgr.; Fayetteville, N.Y./
Eliowitz, Abe.; '30-31-32CoC; FB #30; Detroit/*
Elliott, James E.; '96; *; #*; Hickory Corners/*
Ellis, Anthony T.; '79-80-81-82; FB; #5; Coolidge, Ariz./Same
Ellis, James; '51-52-53; HB; #11; Saginaw/Same
Enos, Daniel; '87-88-89-90; QB; #4; Dearborn/Edsel Ford
Epolito, James C.; '73-74-76; DB/OLB; #87; McKeesport,
Pa./Same
Ernsberger, Scott; '95; S; #49; Portage/Central
Esbaugh, Ernest K.; '45-48-49; T; #70/76; Grand Rapids/
South
Exelby, Leon C.; '07-08-09-10; FB; #*; Britton/*
Exo, Lester W.; '29-30; G/L; #1; Holland/*
Ezor, Blake; '86-87-88-89; TB; #26; Las Vegas, Nev./Bishop

F

Fairbanks, Charles L; '54; E; #82; Grand Rapids/Charlevoix
Farrell, James; '84-85; Mgr.; */*
Fase, Jacob P.; '29-30-31; E; #28; Grand Haven/Same
Fata, Robert; '87-89; TE; #82; Lansing/Catholic Central
Faulman, Duane L.; '40; QB; #39; Flint/Central
Featherstone, William; '80-81-82; Mgr.; Fremon/Same
Fedore, Craig A.; '74-75-78-77; DE/OLB; #38; East Lansing/
Same
Feeney, Todd; '93-94-95; TE; #86; Henderson, Nev./
Raynham (Mass.)
Feigelson, Arthur; '46; Mgr.; East Lansing/*
Fenton, Jack W.; '40-41-42; HB; #49/19; Richmond/Same
Feraco, William A.; '67-68; QB; #14; Irwin, Pa./Greensburg
Central Catholic
Ferrari, George D.; '27-28-29; T; #*; Bessemer/*
Ferrari, Joseph C.; '32; G; #21; Bessemer/Same
Ferris, Dean V.; '18; QB; #*; Swarthmore/Prep
Ferris, Henry M.; '47; T; #32; Utica, N.Y./Same
Fertig, Nomman; '36; G; #23; Far Rockaway, N.Y./Same
Fick, Hilmar A.; '15-16; HB; #15; Wilmette, Ill./*
Fields, Angelo B.; '76-77-78-79; OT/DT; #53; Washington
D.C./ Wilson
Fincher, Mark A.; '83-85-88; OT; #72; Toledo, Ohio/Libby
Fischer, Robert H.; '46; QB; #21; Benton Harbor/Same
Fisher, Keith L.; '84-85; DB; #43; Baden, Pa./Ambridge Area
Fisk, James E.; '04-05; *; #*; Colling/*
Flynn, Richard O.; '62-63-64; E/T; #88; Mt. Pleasant/Same
Flynn, Walter H.; '98; Mgr.; St. Thomas, Ont./*
Fogg, Cecil C.; '28-29-30; E; #29; Jackson/*
Follis, Daniel S.; '58; #26/86; Grosse Pointe/Same
Folino, Anthony; '94; #10; FS; Okemos, Mich./Same
Foltz, Dale; '54; C; #53; Flint/Central
Fomenko, Joseph; '57; C; #51; Detroit/Pershing
Fontes, Wayne H.; '60-61; HB/E; #39; Canton, Ohio/McKinley
Foreman, Franklin J.; '67-68-69CoC; SE; #84; Louisville, Ky./
DuPont Manual
Fornari, Peter A.; '41-42; HB; #16; Detroit/Southwestern
Forman, Walter H.; '65; C; #59; Ft. Lauderdale, Fla./Same
Forsythe, Pete; '90-91-92-93; Mgr.; Charlottesville, Va./
Albemarle

Fortney, Dane E.; '73-74-75; SE/FL #21; Ypsilanti/Same
Foster, Matthew; '76-77-78-79; C; #67; Livonia/Churchill
Fouts, Leslie J.; '25; B; #*; South Haven/*
Fowler, Larry D.; '51-52-53; T. #70; Lansing/Eastern
Fox, Calvin J.; '68-69-70; DE/LB; #50; Battle Creek/Central
Fracassa, Albert; '54; QB; #22; Detroit/Northeastern
Fraleigh, Royden G.; '41-42; E; #85; Detroit/Mackenzie
Francis, Milton J.; '25; Mgr.; Ontonagon/*
Frank, Charles W.; '51-52-53; T; #72; Detroit/Wyandotte
Roosevelt
Franson, Harry E.; '17-18-19C; *; #*; Iron Mountain/Same
Frazer, William D; '06-07-08; *; #*; Buffalo, N.Y./*
Fredrickson, Rob; '90-91-92-93CoC; OLB; #83; St. Joseph/
Same
Freeman, Josh; '95; DL; #98; Adrian/Same
Fremont, Perry J.; '24; QB; #*; Bad Axe/*
Friedlund, Robert M.; '39-40-41; E; #38/88; Peekskill, N.Y./
Peekskill Military Academy
Frimodig, Lyman L.; '15-16; C; #7; Calumet/Same
Fuller, Merrill S.; '15; Mgr.; Paw Paw/*
Fusi, Peter; '46-47-48; C/T; #51/77; Flint/Northern)

G

Gaddini, Rudy, J.; '55-56; HB/FB; #40; Chicago, Ill./Fenwick
Gaines, Frank; '35-36-37; E; #28; Lansing/Central
Galinagh, Patrick F.; '65-66; MG/DT; #55; Detroit/Servite
Gardner, Chris; '94-95; PK; #14; Plantation, Fla./Same
Gargett, George G.; '38-39; T; #29; St. Clair Shores/Lakeview
Garland, Tyrone; '94-95; LB; #37; Cliffwood, N.J./Matawan
Regional
Garner, Deane H.; '50-51; G; #62; Jackson/Same
Garnett, Reggie; '93-94-95; MLB; #22; Akron, Ohio/Buchtel
Garrett, Drake, F.; '65-66-67; HB/DB; #39; Dayton, Ohio/
Dunbar
Garrett, James T.; '65; HB; #32; Columbia, S.C./Johnson
Garver, John E.; '24-25-26; G; #*; Caro/*
Garvey, Steve P.; '67; DB; #24; Tampa, Fla./Chamberlain
Gasser, Harold E.; '47-48-49; T/C; #54; Birmingham/Same
Gates, Keith; '83-84-85; FB; #26; Belleville/Same
Gauthier, George C.; '12-13; QB; #*; Detroit/*
Gibson, Kirk H.; '75-76-77-78; FL; #23; Waterford/Kettering
Gicewicz, E. Richard; '85-86-87-88; TE; #86; Getzville, N.Y./
St. Joseph
Gieselman, John; '89', '92; QB; #13; Rochester/Birmingham
Brother Rice
Gifford, Chester W.;'11-12-13C; T; #*; South Westport Mass./
*
Gilbert, Donald D.; '55-56-57; FB; #42; DuBois, Pa./Same
Gilbert, M. Anthony; '80; SE; #24; Santa Barbara, Calif./Same
Gilliland, William O; '33; HB; #24; Gladwin/*
Gilman, John L.; '47-46-49; E; #83; Clinton/Same
Gilpin, Russell L.; '42-46-47; QB/G; #26/61; Detroit/Cooley
Gingrass, Morgan J.; '41-42; HB/FB; #18/33; Marquette/
Graverae
Gingrich, Wayne A.; '20-21; E; #4; Trout Creek/*
Glick, Eugene R.; '46-47-48-49; HB/QB; #43/23; Saginaw/
Arthur Hill
Glover, Richard; '90-91-92-93; OLB; #55; Lima, Ohio/Same
Godfrey, Robert E.; '44-45; G; #67; Mt. Clemens/Same
Goode, Benjamin L.; '24; HB; #*; Charleston, W. Va./*
Goovert, Ronald E.; '63-64-65; G/LB; #61; Ferndale/Hazel
Park
Gordon, Richard F.; '63-64; HB; #39; Cincinnati, Ohio/Wal-
nut Hills
Gorenflo, Elmer F.; '11-12; E; #*; Detroit/*
Gortat, Thomas A.; '35-36-37; G; #7; Muskegon/Same
Goulbourne, Duane; '92-93-94; TB; #27; Detroit/Northern
Gould, Garett; '95; FB; #45; Troy/Troy
Grabenhorst, Ted J.; '77-78-79; OT; #75; Mt. Morns/Jack-
son
Grabowski, Todd; '90-91-92; TE; #80; Brunswick, Ohio/Same
Graham, Jeff; '90-91-92; OT; #72; Westland/John Glenn
Grandelius, Everett; '48-49-50; HB/FB; #24; Muskegon
Heights/Same
Grannell, James M.; '74; DB; #13; Benton Harbor/Same
Grant, Otis; '80-81-82; QBvFL; #9; Atlanta, Ga./Carver
Graves, Harry C.; '18-21-22; FB; #6; Pratt, Kan./Same
Graves, Thomas E.; '74-75-77-78; DB; #10; Norfolk, Va./
Lake Taylor
Greene, Bill; '95; FB; #34; Canandaigua, N.Y./Academy
Greene, Jay; '93-94; TE; #80; Flint/Central
Greene, Scott; '92-93-94-95CoC; FB; #47; Canandaigua,
N.Y./ Same
Griffeth, Paul L.; '38-39-40; G; #8; Sturgis/Same
Griffin, Curtis D.; '76-78-79; DB/OLB/TE; #24; Novi/ Bir-
mingham Brother Rice

Griffin, Isaac C.; '78-79-80-81; DT/TE/DE; #89; Gary, Ind./
Wallace
Grim, Bohn W. '25-26; *; #*; Sturgis/*
Grimes, Ogden E.; '26-27; G; #*; Des Moines, Iowa/*
Grimsley, R. Ike; '59-60; QB/G; #25; Canton, Ohio/McKinley
Grondzak, Donald; '44; E; #83; Saginaw/Same
Gross, Milton C.; '29-30-31; C/G; #14; Saline/Same
Grove, Roger R.; '28-29-30; HB/QB; #36; Sturgis/*
Grua, R. Mark; '72; HB; #18; East Lansing/*
Grzibowski, Chester; '87; OT; #62; Norwich, N.Y./Same
Guerre, George T.; '46-47-46; HB; #45; Flint/Central
Gunderson, LeRoy E.; '45; E; #85; Lapeer/Same
Guthard, Ted C.; '62; C; #53; Detroit/Denby

H

Haas, Christopher; '85; Mgr.; */*
Haas, Greg; '89-90-91; Mgr.; Holt/Same
Hackenbracht, Dan; '95; S; #28; Massillon, Ohio/Washing-
ton
Hackett, Paul M.; '23-24-25; G; #*; Saginaw/*
Haftenkamp, Joseph P.; '03-04; Mgr.; Grand Rapids/*
Hagbom, Gregory A.; '75; DE; #92; Grand Rapids/Central
Hahn, Harvey D.; '04; *; #*; Brookfield/*
Hahn, Oscar C.; '58-59-60; G; #68; Midland/Same
Haidys, Leo T.; '55; T; #75; Detroit/Chadsey
Halbert, Charles J.; '36-37; QB; #39; Grand Rapids/Central
Haller, Alan; '88-89-90-91; DB; #23; Lansing/Sexton
Halliday, Douglas G.; '69-70-71; OG/DE; #91; Royal Oak/
Kimball
Hallmark, Ferris; '52-53-54; T/G; #55; Flint/Grand Blanc
Hallock, Ty; '89-90-91-92; FB/TE; #28; Greenville/Same
Hamilton, Ernest; '70-71-72; DE/MG; #61; Greenville, S.C./
Beck
Hammes, John H.; '17-19-20; FB; #2; Newberry/*
Hammonds, Juan; '91-92-93-94; LB; #89; Louisville, Ky./
Fern Creek
Handloser, Robert A.; '56-58; HB/FB; #18; Detroit/Catholic
Central
Handy, George B.; '30-31-32; G; #15; Detroit/*
Haney, Usif; '36-37-38; FB; #38; Kinsport, Tenn./Dobyns-
Bennett
Hannah, Nathaniel; '80-81-82-83; CB; #48; Pahokee, Fla./
Same
Hannah, Shane; '91-92-93-94; OT; #63; Carlisle, Ohio/Val-
ley View
Hannon, Thomas; '73-74-75-76CoC; DB; #45; Massillon,
Ohio/Washington
Hans, Micheal; '77-78; FB; #5; Pittsburgh, Pa./Central Catholic
Harding, Lawrence F.; '56-57; E; #84; Detroit/Denby
Hardy, Clifton; '68-69-70; DB; #30; E. Chicago, Ind./Roosevelt
Hardy, Dante; '94; OLB; #87; Cincinnati, Ohio/Princeton
Hare, Bill; '88; P; #22; Romeo/Same
Harewicz, Joseph; '81; OLB; #68; Pittsburgh, Pa./Upper St.
Clair
Harms, Bruce C.; '72-73; DB; #36; Utica/Same
Harness, Jason E.; '58-59-60; E; #93; St. Joseph/Same
Hariatte, Cheadrick; '72; CB; #3; Conway, S.C./Whittemore
Harris, Barry K.; '77-78; FL; #83; San Diego, Calif./Crawford
Harris, Michael H.; '62; Mgr.; Traverse City/*
Hart, Shon; '94-95; DB; #17; Elizabeth, N.J./Same
Harvey, Terry; '92-95; LB; #51; Detroit/Denby
Haskins, Donald A.; '23-24-25C; T; #*; Grand Rapids/*
Hatcher, Ronald A.; '59-60-61; FB; #46; Carnegie, Pa./Same
Hatfield, Glen J.; '44; G; #65; Flint/Same
Hauck, Thomas; '86; DB; #29; Grand Rapids/Forest Hills
Haun, Harold E.; '29; E; #26; Charlotte/*
Hauptli, Clifford H.; '26; Mgr.; Sault Ste. Marie/*
Hawkins, Courtney; '88-89-90-91; WR; #5; Flint/Beecher
Hawkins, Dwayne; '95; LB; #56; Pompano Beach, Fla./Ely
Hawkins, Terry; '81-82; FB; #33; Cincinnati, Ohio/Woodward
Hay, Bernard; '77-78-79-80; MG/DT; #93; Riviera
Beach,Fla./Palm Beach Gardens
Hayden, James G.; '29; G; #*; Cassopolis/* Hayner, Paul
M.; '71-72-73; CB; #27; Detroit/St. Ambrose
Haynes, Johnny Lee; '78-79-80-81; DT/OLB; #86; Delray
Beach, Fla./Boca Raton
Haynes, A. Maurice; '66-67; E; #87; Baton Rouge, La./South-
ern
Hayes, Orion; '94-95; DE; #97; Kettering, Ohio/Fairmont
Heaton, Toby; '89-90-91-92; OG; #67; Redford/Catholic Cen-
tral
Hecker, Gene P.; '57; T; #63; Grand Rapids/Central
Heft, Kenneth; '67-68; DB; #28; Birmingham/Seaholm
Helstowski, Jerry; '87; DE; #73; Trenton/Same
Hendricks, Donald R.; '45; HB; #35; Muskegon Hts./Same
Hendrie, Leland J.; '58; Mgr.; */*
Henning, Ralph B.; '13-14-15-16C; E; #1; Bay City/*

Henry, Aldi; '93-94-95; DB; #36; Montreal, Quebec/Cegep Du Vieux
Henry, Bob; '89-90; OT; #70; Cudahy, Wis./Same
Hepler, James; '93; DB; #3; Smithton, Pa.Nough
Herbert, Fred W.; '95; Mgr.; */*
Herman, David J.; '61-62-63; T; #67; Edon, Ohio/Same
Hickson, Hyland; '88-89-90; TB; #30; Ft. Lauderdale, Fla./Dillard
Highsmith, Donald C.; '68-69; TB; #40; New Brunswick, N.J./Same
Hill, Brian; '88-89; DT; #56; Chicago, Ill./Notre Dame
Hill, Leon, J.; '09-10-11; HB; #-; Benton Harbor/*
Hill, Mark; '86-87; OG; #53; Holland/West Ottawa
Hill, Ray; '95; CB; #10; Detroit/Chadsey
Hill, Willie; '90-91; DT; #45; Palm Beach, Fla./Cardinal Newman
Hinesly, James, '54-55-56; E; #90; Detroit/Miller
Hinesly, James A.; '75-76-77-78; OT; #61/73; Detroit/Country Day
Hiram, Damien; '95; QB; #4; Jackson/Same
Hitchcock, Lytton B.; '05; Mgr.; Jackson/*
Hitchings, Glenn E.; '26-27-28; T; #'; Petoskey/*
Hoag, Philip M.; '64-66; QB/DE; #36; Toledo, Ohio/Central Catholic
Hodo, James; '81; HB; #22; Flint/Southwestern
Hoffman, Michael A.; '80; MLB; #49; Burgoon, Ohio/ Kansas Lake
Hogan, Michael P.; '68-89-70C; LB; #66; Kettering, Ohio/Alter
Holdsworth, Wilbert G.; '04-05; *; #*; Detroit
Holland, Robert; '80; FB; #44; Kalamazoo/Central
Hollem, Dale F.; '53-54-55; G; #60; Ashville, Pa./Cresson
Holman, Stephen; '92-93; TB; #41; Indianapolis/Ben Davis
Holt, Michael E.; '71-72-73C; CB/TB; #1; Highland Park/Detroit Henry Ford
Hood, Robert L.; '62; Mgr.; Detroit/*
Hornbeck, Lewis A.; '26-27-28C; E; #*; Lansing/*
Horrell, William G.; '49-50-51; T; #63; New Kensington, Pa ./Same
Houle, David; '85-88-87; OL; #74; Plymouth/Salem
Howard, Brian; '90-93; WR; #1/81; Chicago, Ill./Julian
Howard, Samson E.; '78-79-81; SE; #4; Miami, Fla./Northwestern
Hrisko, Peter A.; '85-86; QB; #16; Cleveland Hts.Ohio/Cleveland Benedictine
Hudas, Larry J.; '60-61; HB/E; #86; Detroit/Denby
Huebel, Robert R.; '15-16; QB; #47; Menominee/*
Huey, Warren B.; '45-46-47-48; E; #84; Punxsutawney, Pa./Same
Hughes, Derek P.; '78-79-81; TB; #42; Charleston, S.C./Bishop England
Hughes, Timothy; '91; DB; #36; Ft. Wayen, Ind./Northrup
Hughes, William L.; '50-51; T/C; #77; Lewiston, Pa./Same
Hulkow, Richard J.; '72-73; DT; #92; Attleboro, Mass./Same
Hultman, Vivian J.; '22-23-24C; E; #*; Grand Rapids/*
Hunt, Joseph; '74-75; DB; #32; Toledo, Ohio/Scott
Hunter, Kam D.; '79-80-81; Mgr; Ionia/Same
Hurd, Michael H.; '71-73-74; SE; #42; Jackson/Parkside
Hurt, John W.; '83-84; FL; #19; Chicago, Ill./Simeon
Hutton, Kenneth W.; '12; T; #*; Ludington/*

I

Iaquaniello, Mike; '87-88-89-90; DB; #9/44; Dearborn/Fordson
Imhoff, Michael A.; '74-75-76-77; DB; #11; Union Lake/ Walled Lake Central
Ingram, Mark J.; '83-84-85-86; FL; #85/11; Flint/Northwestern
Ivey, Ross; '91-92; C; #54; Monroe/Catholic Central

J

Jacks, Frederick H.; '16; HB; #*; *
Jackson, Aaron; '91-92-93-94; DE; #75; Pittsburgh, Pa./Penn Hills
Jackson, Alvin F.; '33; *; #*; *
Jackson, Larry; '73; DB; #25; Clermont, Fla./Same
Jackson, Larry; '83-84; FL; #33; Compton, Calif./La Mirada
Jackson, Cleveland L.; '75; TE; #86; Detroit/Northwestern
Jackson, Levi; '73-74-75-76; FB; #40; Detroit/Kettering
Jackson, Ricardo; '92-93-94; DB; #25; Lansing/Sexton
Jacobs, Jeffrey; '87; WR; #14; Dallas, Tex./Franklin D. Roosevelt
Jacquemain, Joseph M.; '79-80-81; C/OG; #51; Mt. Clemens/L'AnCreuse
Jansen, Ronald J.; '52; Mgr; Geneva, Ohio/*
Japinga, Donald L.; '63-64-65CoC; DB; #14; Wayland/Same
Jebb, James; '53; T; #73; Grand Rapids/Cathoilc Central

Jenkins, Carlos; '87-88-89-90; OLB; #51; Boynton Beach, Fla./Santaluces
Jenkins, Norman F.; '65; OG; #63; West Mifflin, Pa./North
Jenkins, William R.; '60; Mgr.; Flint/*
Jewett, Robert G.; '55-56-57; E; #86; Mason/Same
Johns, J. Edward; '18; G; #*; Lansing/Central
Johnson, Arthur L.; '56-57-58; HB; #30; Flint/Northern
Johnson, Bill; '88-89-90-91; DE; #96; Chicago, Ill./Simeon
Johnson, Bret; '91-92; QB; #3; Mission Viejo, Calif./El Toro
Johnson, Carl V.; '51; Mgr; Ludington/*
Johnson, Craig T.; '85-86-87; TB/DB; #28; Massilon, Ohio/Washington
Johnson, David B.; '36; Mgr.; *
Johnson, Glenn H.; '41-45; QB; #21/24; Grosse Ile/Same
Johnson, Harold C.; '44; HB; #18; DuBois, Pa./Same
Johnson, Herman A.; '61-62-64; HB; #31; Plainfield, N.J./Same
Johnson, Jim; '88-89-90-91; OT; #59/69; Alto/Lowell
Johnson, Leon G.; '09; Mgr.; Cadillac/*
Johnson, Thomas A.; '40-41; T; #22/73; Detroit/Northeastern
Johnson, William C.; '20-21-22C; HB/E; #8; Newberry/*
Johnson, William M.; '44; C; #58; Wyandotte/Same
Jones, Allen, Jr.; '61; QB; #26; Washington, D.C./Staunton Academy
Jones, Brian; '87-89; MLB; #32; Akron, Ohio/St. Vincent-St. Mary
Jones, Clinton; '64-65-66CoC; HB; #26; Cleveland, Ohio/Cathedral Latin
Jones, Eric L.; '76-77-78-79; DT; #64; Grosse Pointe/South
Jones, Gerald R.; '31-32; QB; #36; Bay City/*
Jones, Jeffrey; '89-90; OLB/DL; #92; Waterford/Detroit Country Day
Jones, Jerald L.; '64-65-66; DB; #29; Grand Ledge/Same
Jones, Joel; '55-56; E, T; #79; Weirton, W. Va./Same
Jones, John; '83-84-85; ILB/DT; #6/88; Barberton, Ohio/Same
Jones, Kenneth; '74-75-76; DB; #28; Detroit/Kettering
Jones, Mark A.; '77-78-79-80; SE; #6; Ypsilanti/Same
Jones, Michael; '73-74; SE; #84; Detroit/Kettering
Jones, Michael; '80-81; FL; #25; South Haven/Same
Jones, Milford H.; '45; FB; #33; Eaton Rapids/Same
Jones, Ted D.; '80-81-82; SE; #21; Akron, Ohio/East
Jones, Zeb; '91-93; LB/DL; #58; Zeeland/ Zeeland
Jordan, Thomas W.; '61-62; C; #54; Bethlehem, Pa./Same
Jordan, J. Nicholas; '66-67-68; DT; #72; Ashland, Ky./Blazer
Joseph, Ronald J.; '68-69; OT/DT; #7; New Orleans, La./St. Augustine
Joslin, Manon I.; '27-28-29; T; #*; Grand Rapids/*
Jubenville, Mike; '88-89; LB; #58; Flint Powers
Juday, James R.; '67; DE; #89; Northville/Same
Juday, Stephen A.; '63-64-65 CoC; QB; #23; Northville/Same
Julian, George E; '11-12-13-14C; FB; #*; Rochester, N.Y./*
Justice, Morgan A.; '69; C; #52; Trenton/Same

K

Kaae, William K.; '55; HB; #39; Honolulu, Hawaii/Farrington
Kaczmarek, Mark W.; '82; C; #50; Hobart, Ind./Same
Kaiser, David M.; '55-56-57; E; #89; Alpena/Same
Kakela, Peter.J.; '59-60-61; T; #62; Toledo, Ohio/Libbey
Kalakailo, Andy; '90; DB; #4; Ann Arbor/Pioneer
Kalman, Kazmer C.; '57; Mgr.; *
Kaman, Roman J.; '39; FB; #60; Grand Rapids/Central
Kamana, Carter L.; '81-82-83-84; CB; #47; Honolulu, Hawaii/Kamehameha
Kanicki, James H.; '60-61-62; C/T; #69; Bay City/Central
Kanitz, Hugo F.; '26-27; T; #*; Muskegon/*
Kanu, Sorie; '95; S; #6; Alexandria, Va./Williams
Kapral, Frank S.; '50-51; G; #56; Courtdale, Pa./Wyoming Sem.
Kaminski, John J.; '63-64-65; OG; #58; Buchanan/Same
Karas, Frank J.; '39-40-41; T; #13/78; Escanaba/Same
Kauth, Donald; '52-53-54CoC; E; #89; Paducah, Ky./Same
Keast, Roger; '32; E; #34; Lansing/*
Kehr, Dave; '95; OT; #70; Grandville/Grandville
Keller, Mathew; '87-88-89-90; OG; #52; Austintown, Ohio/Fitch
Kellogg, Orson T.; '17; QB; #6; Reading/*
Kelly, Ellison L.; '56-57-58; G; #57; Sandusky, Ohio/Same
Kelly, Martin J.; '48; HB; #12; Detroit/Holy Redeemer
Kelly, Russell W.; '57; G; #73; Fruitport/Muskegon
Kennedy, J. Martin; '75; OG; #69; Dearborn Hts./Detroit Bishop Borgess
Kennedy, William J.; '39-40-41; FB/C/G; #44/3/67; Detroit/Northwestern
Kenney, Richard K.; '64-65-66; C/K; #42; Aiea, Hawaii/Iolani
Kepple, Ted W.; '54; T; #58; Jeannette, Pa./Same

Ketchman, Samuel H.; '36; C; #1; Battle Creek/Central
Ketchman, James P.; '50; Mgr.; East Lansing/*
Ketzko, Alexander G.; '38-39; T; #17; Mattawan/Same
Keur, Josh; '94-95; TE; #83; Muskegon/Orchard View
Keyes, Corey; '90-91; DB; #2; Pittsburgh, Pa./Steel Valley
Keyton, Kerry; '88-90; OT; #55; Lansing/Eastern
Kiel, David; '87; OT; #76; Chelsea/Same
Kieppe, Richard N.; '40-41-42; HB; #41/18; Lansing/Central
Kimichik, Alan W.; '79-80-81; TE; #95; Norway/Same
Kinek, Michael; '37-39C; E; #26; Whitting, Ind./Same
King, Christopher J.; '70-71-72; MG/OG; #65; Bronx, N.Y./DeWitt Clinton
King, James M.; '50; E; #86; Gary, Ind./Emerson
Kingsley, Chris; '92-'93; Mgr.; Kalamazoo/*
Kipke, Raymond L.; '23-24; E; #*; Lansing/*
Kiple, John; '88-89; DB; #38; Elk Grove, Ill./Same
Kircher, Alton S.; '32-33; QB; #47; Gladstone/*
Kirkling, Jack M.; '79-80-81; DT/OT; #60; Greensburg, Pa./Hempfield Area
Klein, Joseph A.; '49-50-51; G/T; #61; New Kensington, Pa/Same
Klewicki, Edward L.; '32-33-34; E; #28; Hamtamck/Same
Klewicki, Herman A.; '39; QB; #49; Hamtramck/Same
Klott, Scott; '89-90-91; Mgr.; East Detroit/*
Knight, Dale W.; '53; E; #93; St. Johns/Same
Kolodziej, Anthony W.; '55-56-57; E; #93; Florence, Mass./Northampton
Kolodziej, Joseph A.; '78-80; ILB/OG; #67; Nashville, Tenn./Overton
Kolb, J. Richard; '83; QB; #15; Plantation, Fla./S. Plantation
Kolch, Frank E.; '71; QB; #8; Warren/Detroit Servite
Kough, Stephen J.; '69-70-71; FL/WR; #33; Dearborn/Edsel Ford
Kouri, John E.; '81-82; C; #70; Roseville/Same
Kovacich, George T.; '36-37-38; FB; #32; Whiting, Ind./Same
Kovacs, M. Dan; '72; Mgr.; */*
Kowalczyk, Walter J.; '55-56-57; HB; #14; Westfield, Mass./Same
Kowalski, Kendall; '89; CB; #5; Troy/Athens
Kowatch, Joseph; '30-31-32; QB; #31; Ionia/*
Kozikowski, Renaldo; '50; T; #72; New Kensington, Pa./Same
Kratz, Frank J.; '01-02-03-04; T; #**; Albion/*
Kratz, Oscar A.; '05; *; #*; Albion/*
Krestel, Robert D.; '47-48; QB; #25; Swissvale, Pa./Same
Kronner, Thomas G.; '71-72-73; DE; #93; Detroit/St. David
Krumm, Todd; '84-85-86-67; DB; #35; West Bloomfield/Same
Kryt, Dirk; '72-73; PK; #5; Bergen, Netherlands
Krzemienski; Thomas J.; '63-64; E; 382; Beaver Falls, Pa./Same
Kuh, Richard E.; '50-51; T/G; #75; Chicago, Ill./Leo
Kuhl, K. Robert; '55; Mgr.; St. Paul, Minn./*
Kuhn, Gany; '93-94; LB; #84; Toledo, Ohio/Start
Kuhne, Kurt H.; '35; FB; #24; Pontiac /Central
Kula, Bob; '86-67-88-89TriC; OL; #63; West Bloomfield/ Birmingham Brother Rice
Kulesza, Bruce A.; '66-69; TE; #61; Muskegon/Catholic
Kulikowski, Dan J '70-71; LB; #53; Muskegon/Orchard View
Kumiega, Anthony L.; '59-60-61; E/G; #69; Chicopee, Mass.
Kumiega, Ronald W.; '71-72-73; LB/DE; #47; Chicopee, Mass./Same
Kurrie, Harry A.; '26-27-28; B; #*; Owosso/*
Kush, Frank J.; '50-51-52; G; #60; Windber, Pa./Same
Kutchins, Henny S.; '34-35-36C; E; #20; Hamtramck /*
Kutchins, Walter S.; '39-40; E G; #40/7; Hamtramck/Same
Kutschinski, Thomas A.; '66-69-70; OE DB; #38; East Grand Rapids/Same

L

Lacy, Mark; '91; DT; #42; Medina, Ohio/Same
Laitner, Cass B.; '96; *#*; Detroit *
Lalain, Scott; '91; DT; #50; Bloomfield Hills/Brother Rice
Lamb, Jim Bob; '62-83; OT; #79; Linden/Same
Lampke, Louis J.; '03; G; #*; Durand/*
Lamssies, Robert R.; '44-45; G; #76/60; South Haven/Same
Land, Melvin; '75-76-77-76 CoC; DT; #47; Campbell, Ohio/Memorial
Landry, J. Chnstopher; '81; DE; #92; Rochester/Brecksville, Ohio
Landreth, Tom; '88; OG; #64; Battle Creek/Harper Creek
Landry, Patrick; '87; MLB; #86; Rochester/Same
Lange, Robert P.; '67; LB; #48; Chicago, Ill./Lane Tech
Langeloh, John; '87-88-89-90; PK; #10; Sterling Heights/Utica
Langerveld, Todd L.; '80; SS; #23; Portage/Central
Lantz, Douglas J.; '76; MG; #85; Canton, Ohio/Massilon Perry
Lark, Randy J.; '80-82-83; DT/OG; #76; Wyoming/Lee

LaRose, Clifford E.; '56-57-58; G/T; #58; Grosse Pointe/Detroit Catholic Central
Larson, Kurt; '85-86-67-88CoC; OLB; #3; Waukesha, Wis. / North
Lartigue, Kevin; '91-92-93; Mgr; Lansing Everett
Lattimer Earl B.; '61-62-63; HB/FB; #44/76; Dallas, Tex./ Lincoln
Lauble, Gregory F.; '81-82; MLB; #37; Pittsburgh, Pa./ Central Catholic
Lavelle, Denis C.; '82; QB; #17; Rocky River, Ohio/Lakewood St. Edward
Law, Donald; '67-68-69; DT/LB; #95; Brownsville, Pa./Same
Lawson, Marshall L.; '75-76-77; QB; #12; Lake Charles, La./ Boston
Lawson R. Paul; '66-67; S; #37; Detroit/Thurston
Lay, Russell M.; '32-33; G; #7; Williamston/*
LeClair, Donald D.; '41-42-46; G; #66; Wyandotte/Roosevelt
Ledlow, Ryan; '93; Mgr.; Schoolcraft/*
Ledyard, Courtney; '95; LB; #53; Shaker Heights, Ohio/Same
Lee, Alvin R.; '54-55; G; #61; Gary, Ind./Roosevelt
Lee, Dwight L.; '65-66-67; HB; #34; New Haven/Same
Lee, Martin E.; '08; *; #*; Hart/*
LeFevre, Neil; '41; Mgr.; *
Lefler, Martin J.; '17-19; G; #14; Boyne City/*
Lehnhardt, Milton O.; '35-36; HB/E; #33; Detroit/Cass Tech
Leister, John W.; '80-81 CoC-82 CoC; QB; #18; Great Falls, Mont./Russell
Lekenta, Eugene E.; '52; FB; #42; Grand Rapids/Union
Lemmon, Charles A.; '08-09; *; #*; Lansing/*
Lenardson, Faunt V.; '10-13; G; #*; Britton/*
Lester, Warren; '83-84-85; OLB/DE; #82; Racine, Wis./St. Catherine's
Lewis, Floyd W.; '29; E; #*; Midland/*
Lewis, John R.; '53-54-55; E; #87; Fremont, Ohio/Ross
Lewis, Robert J.; '61-62-63CoC; HB; #20; Louisville, Ky./ duPont Manual
Lewis, Terrance L.; '81-82-83-84; CB; #10; Highland/*
Lickley, Ralph M.; '99; Mgr.; Hudson/*
Lilly, Richard J.; '72-73; Mgr.; *
Limber, Peter E.; '44; Mgr.; *
Lincoln, Dewey R.; '61-62-63; HB; #26; Hamtramck/Same
Lindemann, Edward C.; '10; Mgr.; St. Clair/*
Lioret, Ernest L.; '22-23-24; FB; #*; Ishpeming/*
Little, Kenneth E.; '67-68-69; DG/DE/LB; #85; Youngstown, Ohio/East
Lofgren, Bruce E.; '56; Mgr.; Detroit/*
Logan, Leonard G.; '31; Mgr.; Detroit/*
Long, Octavis; '95; WR; #20; Lansing/Sexton
Lonce, Craig T.; '76-77-78; MG/DT/OT; #76; Canton, Ohio/ Catholic Central
Look, Dean Z.; '57-58-59; HB; #24; Lansing/Everett
Loper, Mark M.; '70-71; OG; #56; Cambridge, Ohio/Same
Lopes, Roger; '61-62-63; FB; #45; Honolulu, Hawaii/Iolani
Lorius, Brett; '90-91-92-93; OG; #61; Akron, Ohio/St. Vincent-St. Mary
Lothamer, Edward D.; '62-63; E; #81; Detroit/Redford
Love, Robert; '86; LB; #84; Dearborn/Same
Love, Thomas E.; '68; TB; #26; Sylva, N.C./Sylva-Webster
Loveland, Clarence W.; '14; G; #*; Grand Rapids/*
Lowe, Gary R.; '54-55; HB/FB; #20; Trenton/Same
Lowther, Charles M.; '66; DB; #24; Royal Oak/Shrine
Lucas, Harold V.; '63-64-65; C/T/MG; #51; Detroit/Southwestern
Ludwig, Robert H.; '45; HB; #41; Muskegon/Same
Lueck, Walter H.; '36-37; G; #9; Dundee, Ill./Same
Lukasik, Lawrence F.; '64-66; DB; #17; Cleveland, Ohio/ Shaker Hts.
Luke, Edwin E.; '50-51-52; E; #85/82; Flint/Northern
Lumsden, David H.; '48-49; C; #51; Statesville, N.C./Same
Lundy, Charles, B.; '98; *; #*; *
Luplow, Alvin D., Jr.; '58; HB; #42; Saginaw/St. Andrew
Lyman, Richard P., Jr.; '23-24-25; QB; #*; East Lansing/*
Lyons, Mitch; '89-90-91-92; TE; #85; Grand Rapids/Forest Hills Northern

M

MacCarthy, Kevin M.; '80-81; Mgr.; St. Joseph/*
MacFarland, Mark; '90-91-92; WR; #17; Rochester/Same
Macholz, Dennis; '70-71-72; TE/OT/OG; #66; Bethpage, NY/ Same
Mackey, Lawrence L.; '64; HB; #26; Akron, Ohio/St. Vincent
MacMillan, Roy A.; '20-22; OB; #*; Mt. Clemens/*
MacNeill, John; '90-91; DE; #84; Marshfield, Mass./Same
Macuga, Edward J.; '64; G; #60; Dixonville, Pa./Purchase Line
Mahoney, Earl L.; '46; T; #77; Chicago, Ill./Austin
Maidlow, Steven K.; '79-80-81-82; MLB/OLB; #43; East Lansing/Same

Malinosky, John M.; '75-76-77; OT/DT; #63; Vancouver, B.C./ Notre Dame
Malinowski, Joseph S.; '75; FB; #35; Wyandotte/Roosevelt
Maliskey, Don C.; '38; T; #23; Lansing/Eastern
Mandarich, Tony; '85-86-87-88 CoC; OT; #79; Oakvlle Ont./ Kent, Ohio Roosevelt
Manderino, Paul A.; '71-73-74; BF/DT/DE; #85; Arlington, Mass./Same
Manders, David F.; '59-60-61; C; #71/50; Kingsford/Same
Mangnum, Richard W.; '41-42C; T; #76; Durand/Same
Manley, Tony C.; '84; CB; #9; Newark, N.J./Weequahic
Manson, Damian; '91-92-93-94; DB; #31; Riviera Beach, Fl/ Same
Mantos, Marvin M.; '79-80-81-82; OG; #71; Bloomingdale, Ohio/Wintersville
Marek, Anthony J.; '78; OG; #60; Warren/Cousino
Marino, Carlos; '88-89-90; TE; #89; Detroit/Central
Markham, Arthur G.; '11; HB; *#*;
Marshall, Eric R.; '67; QB; #19; Oxford, Miss./Central
Marshall, Lemar; '95; DB; #29; Cincinnatti, Ohio/St Xavier
Marshall, Michael B.; '76-78-79-80; CB; #6/2; Detroit/Southwestern
Martin, Arthur D.; '20; *; #*; Corunna/*
Martin, Blanche; '56-57-59; HB/FB; #31; River Rouge/Same
Martin, David; '86-87-88; C; #58; Bloomfeild Hills/ Birmmingham Brother Rice
Martin, Demetrice; '92-93-94-95; WR/DB; #12/#21; Pasadena, Calif./Muir
Martin, John E.; '72; DE; #48; East Lansing/Same
Martin, Stanley A.; '11; *; #*; Fredonia/*
Martin, Wilton J.; '68-69-70C; DE/DT; #97; St. Louis, Mo./ Ancor Bay, Mich.
Martinek, Julius A.; '48; Mgr.; Traverse City/*
Marvin, Virgil I.; '29; Mgr.; Toledo, Ohio/*
Maskill, William R.; '44; HB; #15; Detroit/DeLaSalle
Masny, Myron M.; '38; G; #10; Arlington Hts., Ill./Same
Mason, Derrick; '93-94-95; WR; #13/#80; Detroit/Mumford
Mason, Donald L.; '48-49; G; #60; Wayne/Same
Massuch, Richard C.; '44-45; T/E; #71/88; Lansing/Eastern
Masters, Norman D.; '53-54-55; G/T; #57; Detroit/Redford St. Mary
Matsko, John; '54-55-56; C; #49; St. Micheal, Pa./Adams Twp.
Matsock, John J.; '53-54; HB/QB; #43; Detroit/Pershing
Matson, Edward I.; '20-21; G; #21; Dollar Bay/*
Matsos, Emil G.; '55-56-58; G; #63; Detroit/Redford
Matthews, Henry; '70-71; TB/FB; #23; Akron, Ohio/South
May, Frank C.; '47; Mgr.; Dearborn/*
Mays, Damond; '72-73; HB/FL; #22; Phoenix, Ariz./Hayden
Mazza, Orlando J.; '51; E; #46; Niagara Falls, N.Y./Same
McAdoo, Howard J.; '80-81-82; DT; #55; Rancho Palos Verdes, Calif./Rolling Hills
McAllister, Robert; '85-86-87-88CoC; QB; #8; Pompano Beach, Fla./Ely
McAuliffe, Donald F.; '50-51-52C; HB; #40; Chicago, Ill./Leo
McBride, Robert; '92-93-94-95; DT; #92; Detroit/Northern
McCarthy, Kevin J.; '76-77; Mgr.; *
McClelland, Albert L.; '16; HB; #9; Holland/*
McClelland, Darrin L.; '79-81-82; FB; #41; Detroit/Central
McClowry, Patrick G.; '73-74; LB; #53; Dearborn/Sacred Heart
McClowry, Robert J.; '70-71-72; OT/C; #57; Dearborn/Sacred Heart
McClowry, Terrence G.; '72-73-74; LB; #49; Dearborn/Sacred Heart
McComb, J. Robert; '37; G; #30; Muskegon Hts./Same
McConnell, Brian T.; '70-71-72; TE/OT/DE; #85; Smoke Rise, N.J./Hightstown Peddle
McCool, Paul F.; '17; *; #*; Cameron, Mo./*
McCormick, David M.; '63-64; QB; #16; Chicago, Ill./St. Rita
McCormick, John P.; '77-78-79-80; OLB; #40; Marquette/ Same
McCosh, James A.; '25-26-27; B; #*; Detroit/*
McCrary, James L.; '33-34; HB; #46; Flint/*
McCue, Charles A.; '98-99C; E; #*; Cass City/*
McCulloh, James A.; '77-78; OG; #55; Youngstown, Ohio/ Cardinal Mooney
McCurdy, Russell J.; '12-13; G; #*; Lansing/*
McCurry, Robert B.; '46C-47C-48C; C; #52; Lewistown, Pa./ Same
McDermid, Frank H.; '11; C; #*; Battle Creek/*
McDermid, H.B.; '04-05; *; #*; Battle Creek/*
McDowell, John; '83-84-85; OT/C; #77; Ann Arbor/*
McFadden, Marvin G.; '50-51; T; #74; Lansing/Eastern
McFarland, Jerome; '58; T; #67; Birmingham, Ala./Parker
McGee, E. Leroy; '77-78; TB; #22; El Cajon, Calif./Same
McGillivray, Lodiwic A.; '08; *; #*; Valley City, N.D./*

McGiness, John M.; '79; Mgr.; *
McIntyre, Malcomb M.; '00; *; #*; *
McKenna, Edward B.; '03-04-05C; HB; #*; Quinnesec/*
McKenna, Parnell G.; '06-07-08-09C; *; #*; Quinnesec/*
McLaughlin, Duane J.; '70-71; DB/DT; #99; Auburn Hts./ Avondale
McLaughery, DeArmand O.; '11; T; #*; *
McLee, Bradley M.; '69-70; S/RB; #35; Uniontown, Pa./Same
McLoud, Eddy W.; '67-68; OT/C; #75; Fairborn, Ohio/Same
McLouth, Aldrich L.; '98-99; C; #*; Medina/*
McLucas, Edwin; '59; T; #76; Newark, N.J./Central
McNeil, Robert A.; '40-41-42; E; #25/78/88; Phoenix, Ariz./ Same
McNutt, Bernard G.; '32-33C; FB; #23; Allegan/*
McQuaide, Regis G.; '77-78-79; OG/OT; #77; Pittsburgh, Pa./ Brentwood
McRae, Stanley P.; '38-39; T/E; #13/21; Pellston/Same
McShannock, Thomas G.; '37-38; C; #4; Muskegon/Same
McWilliams, James E; '10-11; C; #*; *
Meadows, Clinton L.; '67; DT; #98; Okemos/Same
Meek, Harry C.; '01-02; *; #*; Manton/*
Meiers, Francis H.; '30-31; C; #25; Muskegon/*
Mellinger, Stephen T.; '61-62-64; G; #73; South Bend, Ind./ Adams
Mencotti, Edo; '42; FB; #37; Detroit/Cooley
Mendyk, Dennis A.; '55-56; HB; #38; St. Charles/St. Peter and Paul
Merkel, William J.; '97; Mgr.; Manistee/*
Mervin, Clyde E.; '07; Mgr.; Moscow/*
Meyer, Donald H.; '54-55; Mgr.; W. Lafayette, Ind./*
Middleton, Alonzo D.; '76-77-78-79; FB; #44; Orangeburg, S.C./Orangeburg-Wilkinson
Middleton, John L.; '56-57-58; G; #61; Duluth, Minn./Central
Migyanka, Charles, Jr.; '62-63-64C; QB; #25; E. Conemaugh, Pa./Same
Mihaiu, George M.; '70-71-72; QB; #20; River Rouge/Same
Miketinac, Mike N.; '42; G; #68; Hemmansville/Same
Miknavih, Norbert A.; '36-37; C; #8; Grand Rapids/Union
Milhizer, Richard M.; '79-80; SS; #13; Farmington/Same
Millar, Wilson F.; '03; HB; #'; Ray Center/*
Miller, Charles D.; '23; Mgr.; Eaton Rapids/*
Miller G. Devere; '96; *; #*; Cadillac/*
Miller, H. Hewett; '13-14-15; HB; #*; Tonawanda, N.Y./*
Miller, John; '85-86-87-88CoC; DB; #44; Farmington Hills/ Harrison
Miller, Jim; '90-91-92-93; QB; #16; Waterford/Kettering
Miller, Oscar R.; '13-14; E/QB; #*; Saginaw/*
Miller, Patrick F.; '69-70; P; #14; Menominee/Same
Miller, Roger L.; '66; Mgr.; Dearborn/*
Miller, W. Blake; '12-13-14-15C; E/HB; #*; Tonawanda, N.Y./*
Miller Wilbert E.; '17-19;G/T;#24;Bay City/*
Mills, Robert E.; '71-72-73; C; #52; Lakewood, Colo./Denver Alameda
Milliken, William F.; '41-42; QB; #25; Chicago, Ill./Senn
Mittenberger, Bcon A; '71; OT; #73; Monroe, Ohio/Lemon-Monroe
Minahan, Jeffrey M.; '77-78; Mgr.;*
Minark, Henry J.; '48-49-50; E; #80; Flint/Central
Mineweaser, Richard L.; '44; E; #79; Pontiac/St. Michael
Mitchell, Brian; '86; OL; #70; Toledo, Ohio/DeVilbiss
Mitchell, Kerry; '89-90; C; #72/59; Detroit/
Mitchell, Robert B.; '58; Mgr.; *
Mitchem, Ronald G.; '79-80-81; DT/DE; #88; South Bend, Ind./Adams
Mittelberg, Victor; '69-70; OT; #71; Skokie, Ill./Niles East
Mitten, Patrick J.; '79; DT; #92; Naperville, Ill./Central
Moeller, William F.; '26-27-28; G; #-; Detroit/
Mojsiejenko, Ralf; '81-82-83-84; P/Pk; #2; Bridgman/Same
Monnett, Robert C.; '30-31-32CoC; HB; #33; Bucyrus, Ohio/*
Monroe, William R.; '42; C; #59; Three Rivers/Same
Montford, Roy M.; '10; E; #10; #*; Benton Harbor/*
Montgomery, Clayton Jr.; '72; HB; #44; Stockon, Calif./Edison
Montgomery, Greg H., Sr.; '57-58; QB; #23; Grand Rapids/ East Lansing
Montgomery, Greg H., Jr.; '85-86-87; P; #23; Shrewsbury, N.J./Little Silver Red Bank Regional
Montgomery, Russell F.; '17; Mgr.; Detroit
Montgomery, Stephens; '87-88-89 TriC; FB; #43; Shrewsbury, N.J./Little Silver Red Bank
Moore, Allen; '81-83-84; DE; #69; Detroit/Cooley
Moore, Clyde D.; '06-07-08-09; *; #*; Freeport/*
Moore, Glenn B.; '45; Mgr.;
Moore, James; '86-87-88; FB; #33; Lansing/Sexton
Moore, Rex W.; '44; QB; #25; Muskegon/Same
Moore, Timothy S.; '84-85-86-87; OLB; #42; St. Johns/Same

237

Moore, Wendell; '74; DT; #72; Port Arthur, Tex./Lincoln
Morabito, Daniel L.; '40; T; #18; Buffalo, N.Y./Hutchinson
Morgado, Arnold Jr.; '72; FB; #24; Ewa, Hawaii/Honolulu Punahou
Morgan, Jack D.; '50-51-52; T; #79; Detroit/Denby
Morrall, Earl E.; '53-54-55; QB; #21; Muskegon/Same
Morris, Thomas L.; '80-81; FS; #27; Long Beach, Calif./Millikan
Morrison, Russell H.; '20-21-22; C; #23; Alpena/*
Morrissey, Harry; '53; Mgr.; Pittsburgh, Pa./*
Morrissey, James M.; '81-82-83-84C; TE/ILB; #40; Flint/Powers
Morse, Robert W.; '83-84-85-86; TB/FB; #21; Muskegon/Catholic Central
Mosallam, Brian; '93-95; OG; #62/#63; Dearborn/Fordson
Mosher, Richard W.; '46; Mgr.; East Lansing/*
Moten, Eric; '87-88-89-90; DT/OG; #77; Cleveland, Ohio/Shaw
Mouch, Robert W.; '82; OT; #73; Redford/Union
Mroz, Vincent; '42; E; #89; East Chicago, Ind./Washington
Mudge, Dave; '95; OT; #65; Whitby, Ont./Henry Street
Muhammad, Muhsin; '92-94-95; WR; #19/#1; Lansing/Waverly
Mullen, John M.; '64-66; QB; #15; Toledo, Ohio/Central Catholic
Murphy, Morley; '52-53-54; T; #71; Detroit/Chadsey
Murray, Craig; '73-74; Mgr.; *
Murray, Todd; '89-90-91-92; CB; #20; Bloomington, Minn./Jefferson
Musetti, Gerald A.; '54-55; HB; #47; Detroit/Denby
Muster, Michael; '81; OG; #50; Utica/Eisenhower

N

Napolitan, Mark R.; '83-84; C; #63; Trenton/Same
Neal, James E.; '52-53; C; #51; Muskegon/Same
Needham, George W.; '27; T; #*; Saginaw/*
Neely, James A.; '79-80-81-82; MLB; #58; South Bend, Ind./Adams
Neller, Elton G.; '22-23-24; HB; #*; Lansing/*
Nelson C. Walter; '36-37-38; E; #21; Chicago, Ill./Hirsch
Nern, Carl R.; '02: *; #*; Port Huron/*
Nester, Raymond; 71-72-73; OG/MG/LB; #97; Mt. Clemens/Clintondale
Nestor, Carl N.; '47 G #67; East Chicago, Ill./Same
Neubert, Bernard E.; '42; G #65; Chicago, Ill./Thornton
Neumann, Harrison H.; '35-36; OB #36; Lansing/Central
Newman, Mitchell L.; '61; HB #42 Detroit/Denby
Nichols, Mark E.; '85-86-87CoC; DT #83; Bloomfield Hills/Birmingham Brother Rice
Nicholson, James B.; '70-72 OT #72 77; Honolulu, Hawaii/St. Louis
Nielsen, Hans J.; '74-75-76-77; PK #8 Vejle, Denmark Manistee, Mich.
Niesen, Mark W.; '71-72-73; S/QB/DB; #14 Manistee/Catholic Central
Ninowski, James; '55-56-57; QB; #41; Detroit Pershing
Noblett, Ubold J.; '19-20-21; HE: #10; Gladston/*
Nordberg, Carl A.; '28-29-30; HB #39; St. Joseph/*
Norman, Dempsey; '84; SE; #4; Chicago, Ill. Tilden
Northcross, David C.; '57-58-59; E #90; Highland Park/Same
Nowak, Gary W.; '68-69-70 DE/OT; #82 76; St. Clair Shores/Detroit St Ambrose
Nystie, Charles V.; '48-49; T; #73; Detroit/Northwestern
Nystrom, Carl W.; '53-54-55C; T/G; #68; Marquette/Gravareat

O

Oas, Reginald G.; '17: HB #8 Ishpeming/*
O'Bradovich, Ed; '90-91; DL #88 Chicago, Ill./Friend
O'Gara, Francis; '06: Mgr. Ottawa, Ont./*
O'Brien, Francis J.; '56-57-58; T #62 Holyoke, Mass./Same
O'Keefe, Kevin; '86; OL: #59; Lakewood, Ohio/St. Edward
Olman, Norman A.; '36-37; G #16 Grand Rapids/Union
Olmstead, Clifford G.; '00: *; #*; *
Omerod, Craig K.; '72: OT #50: Dearborn Hts./Dearborn Divine Child
Organ, Bob; '91-92-93-94; FB TE; #43/94; Ludington/Same
Organek, Brett; '93; DT; #91; Grandville/Same
Orr, James B.; '66; Mgr.; Mt. Pleasant/*
Otis, Steven J.; '76-77-78-79; DT/OLB/ILB; #52; Chicago, Ill./Gordon Tech
Otting, Robert W.; '42-46 QB; #28: Lapeer/Same
Outlaw, Napoleon; '92-93-94-95; WR #8 West Palm Beach, Fla./Cardinal Newman
Oviatt, Clarence R.; '15- E #/ Bay City/*
Owens, Alton L.; '63-64-65; C/DT; #53; Ft. Worth, Tex./Paschal
Oxendine, Richard C.; '60: E #87 Aliquippa, Pa./Same

P

Pagel, William M.;. '45: C; #74; Blissfield/Same
Paior, John J.; '54 C; #50: Latrobe, Pa./Same
Pajokowski, Joseph A.; '45: G; #61; South Bend, Ind./Washington
Palmateer, Bernard B.; '62: E #83 Port Huron/Same
Palmer, Jeffrey; '87; OG; #67; Detroit/Chadsey
Panin, L. Richard; '50-51-52 FB; #38; Detroit/Denby
Panitch, Michael B.; '56-57-58; QB; #16 Chicago, Ill./Austin
Parker, Frederick; '87; DB; #37; Jackson/Same
Parker, Phillip J.; '82-83-84-85; CB/S; #32; Lorain, Ohio/Amherst Steele
Parker, Ward H.; '06-07; *; #*; Holly/*
Parks, Warren A.; '21; T; #20; Cheboygan/*
Parks, William T.; '97-98-99; T; #*; Pipestone/*
Parmentier, Gary; '68-70; DB/DG; #48; East Detroit/Detroit Denby
Parrott, Roy E.; '61; C; #53; Detroit/Cooley
Parsell, Rex. J.; '47-48-49; E; #81; Flint/Central
Partchenko, Pete; '92; OT; #73; Toronto, Ont./Power
Paterra, Herbert E.; '62; G; #60; Glassport, Pa./Same
Paterra, Jeffrey; '86; DB; #9; Diamond Bar, Calif./Walnut
Patrick, Antwain; '94-95; TB; #32; Wilmington, N.C./New Hanover
Pattison, Benjamin P.; '09-10; T; #*; Caro/*
Pawlak, Richard L.; '73; OT; #60; Detroit/DeLaSalle
Pawlowski, Walter L.; '40-41-42C; HB; #47; Calumet City, Ill./Thornton
Paxson, Avery B.; '33; C; #52; Saginaw/*
Payne, Wade D.; '67; DB; #40; Garden City/Same
Payton, Lenier; '87-88; DB; #24; Highland Park/Same
Peaks, Clarence E.; '54-55-56; QB/HB; #26; Flint/Central
Pearce, Edward J.; '37-38-39; HB; #41; Flint/Northern
Pearson, Helge E.; '37; T; #22; Norway/Same
Pearson, Jeff; '89-90; C; #68; Chicago, Ill./St. Laurence
Peck, Clair B.; '03; G; #*; Belding/*
Perkins, Calvin A.; '80-81-82; OT/DT; #74; Atlanta, Ga./Harper
Perles, George J.; '58; T; #65; Allen Park/Detroit Western
Perles, John W.; '82-83-84; LB; #44; Upper St. Clair, Pa./Same
Person, Dale; '92-93-94; DL; #53; Chicago, Ill./Vocational
Peters, Arthur D.; '01-02C-03; E; #*; Springport/*
Peterson, Carl H.; '14; Mgr.; Lucas/*
Peterson, Thomas H.; '75-76; DB; #31; Ann Arbor/Huron
Pettit, Arvilee W.; '80-81; Mgr.; Grand Ledge/Same
Pettit, Nick; '93; Mgr.; Grand Ledge/Same
Petzold, Rudolf H.; '54-55; Mgr.; Vassar/*
Phelps, Brian F.; '83; QB; #12; Camarillo, Calif./Same
Phillips, Harold B.; '68-69-70; DB; #27; Detroit/Southeastern
Phillips, Jess, Jr.; '65-66; DB; #38; Beaumont, Tex./Pollard
Piette, Thomas M.; '78-80-81-82; C; #56; Redford Twp./Union
Pingel, John S.; '36-37-38; HB; #37; Mt. Clemens/Same
Piro, Steven P.; '69; QB; #16; Iowa City, Iowa/Same
Pirronello, William G.; '44; FB; #39; Detroit/Catholic Central
Pisano, Vincent F.; '50-51-52; HB; #12; New Kensington, Pa./Same
Pitts, Alfred E.; '74-75-76-77 CoC; #56; Hubbard, Ohio/Same
Pitts, Jack N.; '67; DB; #26; Decatur, Ga./Trinity
Piwowarczyk, Chris; '88-89-90-91; OL; #56; Fenton/Same
Planutis, Gerald R.; '53-54-55; FB; #45; W. Hazelton, Pa./Same
Pletz, John E.; '46; T; #74; Turtle Creek, Pa./Same
Pobur, Edward J.; '82; LB; Livonia/Detroit Catholic Central
Pogor, Edmund F.; '39; G; #11; Dunkirk, N.Y./Same
Polonchek, John N.; '47-48-49; HB; #41; E. Chicago, Ind./Roosevelt
Popovski, Tony; '95; OG; #69; Mt. Clemens/Utica Eisenhower
Popp, Robert; '57; QB; #25; Conemaugh, Pa./Franklin
Porter, Anthony E.; '75-76; OT; #79; New York, N.Y./Dewitt Clinton
Postula, Victor A.; '54; FB; #34; Marshall/Same
Postula, William J.; '53; E; #86; Marshall/Same
Potter, James; '84; DT; #76; Mt. Clemens/Clintondale
Pound, Howard J.; '39; E; #32; Grand Rapids/Central
Powers, John F. III; '75-76; P; #41; Lansing/Catholic Central
Prashaw, Milton F.; '44; T; #78; Massena, N.Y./Same
Price, H. Eugene; '96-97; *; #*; Ithaca/*
Prins, Kurt; '89-90-91-92; TE; #92; Muskegon/Reeths-Puffer
Proebstle, Richard J.; '61-63-64; QB; #21; Canton, Ohio/Central Catholic
Proebstle, James M.; '65; E; #80; Canton, Ohio/Central Catholic
Pruder, David; '84-85; Mgr.; Ann Arbor/*
Pruiett, Mitchell W.; '65-66-67; OG; #60; Benton Harbor/Same
Pryor, Corey; '88-89-90; RB/DB; #18; Jackson/Same

Pryzbycki, Joseph R.; '65-66-67; OT; #79; Detroit/Notre Dame
Pugh, Joseph; '86-87; FB; #38; Grand Rapids/Central
Pyle, W. Palmer; '57-58-59; T; #69; Winnetka, Ill./New Trier

Q

Quigley, Fred K.; '39; HB; #51; Grand Rapids/Central
Quinlan, William D.; '52-53; E; #83; N. Andover, Mass./Same
Quinn, Kelly B.; '82-83-84-85; LB/DE; #13/93; Stone Mountain, Ga./Same

R

Radelet, David P.; '75-76-77; SE/DB; #29; East Lansing/Same
Radewald, Karl B.; '20; *; #*; Niles/*
Radford, Fred L.; '00; Mgr.; Pine Creek/*
Radulescu, George; '42; *; #61; Imlay City/Same
Ralph, Donald H.; '55; Mgr.; Sault Ste. Marie/*
Ramsey, Clarence F.; '16-17-19; T; #23/10; Ludington/*
Ramsey, Kenneth T.; '76; TE; #83; Detroit/Milwaukee, Wis. King
Ranieri, Ronald A.; 66-67; C; #54; Royal Oak/Shrine
Ranney, Ellis W.; '97-98C; HB; #*; Belding/*
Ransom, Brian; '91-92-93; Mgr.; Livonia/Stevenson
Rasmussen, Michael J.; '70-71; QB; #12; Fresno, Calif./Same
Ray, Harlan C.; '27; Mgr.; Manistee/*
Ray, Jonathan S.; '74; OG; #66; Beaver, Pa./Same
Raye, James A.; '65-66-67; QB; #16; Fayetteville, N.C./Smith
Reader, Russell B.; '45-46; HB; #46; Dearborn/Same
Reaveley, Gordon G.; '32-33-34; T; #18; Durand/*
Reaves, Carl; '94-95; OLB; #55; Oxford/Same
Redd, Keith L.; '66; C; #53; Detroit/Denby
Redfern, Scott J.; '96; Mgr.; Maple Rapids/*
Reece, Travis; '94-95; FB/LB; #41; Detroit/Denby
Reed, Derrick; '87-88; DB; #6; Dallas, Tex./Lake Highlands
Reese, Elroy; '95; TE; #85; Detroit/Bishop Gallagher
Reese, Ike; '94-95; OLB; #44; Cincinnati, Ohio/Aiken
Reese, William; '89-90-91-92; DE; #74; Cincinnati, Ohio/Princeton
Reeves, M. Bruce; '77-78-79; HB; #30; Irmo, S.C./Same
Reid, Greg; '95; DT; #67; Tinley Park, Ill./Andrew
Renaud, Marc; '94-95; TB; #26; Deerfield Beach, Fla./Same
Repko, Stephen M.; '73; Mgr.; *
Reynolds, Russell H.; '33-34C; HB; #39; Flint/*
Rhodes, Tyrone D.; '83-84-85-86; OG; #67; Cincinnati, Ohio/Moeller
Riba, Micheal S.; '82; FL; #25; Arlington Hts., Ill./Buffalo Grove
Ribby, Robert; '93; C; #51; Eaton Rapids/Same
Riblet, William R.; '10-11-12C; QB; #*; Elkhart, Ind./*
Ricamore, Wilford W.; '99-00-01; E; #*; Berryville, Va./*
Richards, Rolland G.; '22-23-24; QB/HB; #*; Lansing/*
Richardson, Jeffrey; '66; C/OG; #57; Johnstown, Pa./Central
Richendollar, Melvin; '86; OT; #65; Belleville/Same
Rickens, Ronald F.; '56-57-58; G; #74; Cresson, Pa./Same
Ricucci, Robert J.; '59; HB; #47; Maumee, Ohio/Chicago Leo
Ridgeway, Jason; '85-86-87-88; DT; #55; Detroit/Chadsey
Ridinger, Tim; '86-87-88-89; LB/DT; #40; Ferndale/Hazel Park
Ridler, Don G.; '28-29-30; T; #2; Detroit/*
Rinella, S. James; '82-83-84-85; NG/DT; #57; Plantation,Fla./S. Plantation
Ripmaster, P. Edward; '40-42; FB; #44/36; Grand Rapids/Central
Rison, Andre; '85-86-87-88; SE; #1; Flint/Northwestern
Robbins, Kevin; '87-88; OT; #71; Washington, D.C./H.D. Woodson
Roberts, Aaron M.; '81-82-83-84; HB/FB; #20; Detroit/Catholic Central
Roberts, Douglas W.; '63-64; E; #87; Detroit/Cooley
Roberts, Marvin E.; '70-71-72; TE/OT/PK; #64; Akron, Ohio/Springfield
Robinson, Embry L.; '54-55; T/G; #77; Pittsburgh, Pa./Fifth Ave.
Robinson, Hugh A.; '22-23-24; E; #; Detroit/*
Robinson, Kenneth E.; '77; DB; #9; Ypsilanti/Same
Robinson, Theodore K.; '59; Mgr.; Okemos/Same
Robinson, Thomas D.; '82-83; TE; #34; Birmingham/Seaholm
Rochester, Paul G.; '58-59; T; #72; Midland/Sewanhaka Floral Park, N.Y.
Rockenbach, Paul G.; '37-38=39C; G; #14; Crystal Lake Ill./Same
Rody, Frederick A.; '53-54; C; #66; Detroit/Anaconda, Mont.
Rogers, Douglas S.; '83-84-85-86; DT/OT; #71; Youngstown, Ohio/Ursuline
Rolle, Donald D. (Butch); '82-83-84-85; TE; #89; Hallandale, Fla./Same
Rollick, Nicholas P.; '76-77; TB; #26; Skokie, Ill./Niles Twp.

Rollin, Tony; '90-91-92; RB; #22; Akron, Ohio/St. Vincent-St. Mary
Rollins, James; '89-90; DB; #34; Anaheim, Calif./Servite
Rork, Frank C.; '99-01; E; #*; Lansing/*
Roseboro, Ronald; '84; SE; #37; Detroit/Mumford
Roskopp, Bernard G.; '42-46-47; E; #84/82; Mt. Clemens/Same
Ross, Archie F.; '34-35; *; #16; Grand Rapids/South
Ross, Donald L.; '63-64; C; #59; East Lansing/Same
Ross, Ronald R.; '62; T; #65; Detroit/Catholic Central
Ross, Ward F.; '25-26-27; G/C; #*; Port Huron/*
Ross, William L.; '52; G; #69; Niagara Falls, N.Y./Same
Rossi, Donald A.; '38-39; QB; #36; Detroit/Mackenzie
Rowe, Ronald; '85-86; DB; #18; San Diego, Calif./Lincoln
Rowekamp, Kim A.; '73-74-75-76; LB/MG; #43; Kalamazoo/Central
Roy, Errol A.; '69-70-71; OG/C; #55; New Orleans, La./St. Augustine
Roy, Rob; '88-89-90; FB; #27; Chicago, Ill./Gordon Tech
Rubick, Ronald R.; '61-62-63; HB; #27/33; Manistique/Same
Rudzinski, Paul G.; '74-75-76-77 CoC; ILB; #37; Detroit/Catholic Central
Ruff, Timothy W.; '74-75; OG; #62; Bridgman/Same
Rugg, Gary L.; '64; FB; #42; Battle Creek/Pennfield
Ruhl, Jack W.; '28; *; #*; Detroit/*
Ruminski, Roger J.; '66; OT; #76; Walled Lake/*
Rummell, Martin F.; '24-25-26C; *; #*; Saginaw/*
Rupp, William, Jr.; '39-40-41C; G; #15/68; Louisville, Ky./Male
Rush, Jerry M.; '62-63-64; T; #72; Pontiac/Central
Russell, William E.; '97-98-99; HB; #*; Benton Harbor/*
Rutledge, Leslie E.; '55-56-57; T; #95; El Paso, Tex./Austin
Ruzich, John L.; '73; OT; #79; Pittsfield, Ill./Same
Ryan, Edward J.; '60-61C; HB; #38; Chicago, Ill./Leo

S

Saidock, Thomas; '55-56; T; #69; Dearborn/Fordson
Saimes, George; '60-61-62C; FB; #40; Canton, Ohio/Lincoln
Salani, Chris; '92-93-94-95; P; #88; Hancock/Same
Salani, Richard A.; '72; WR; #15; Hancock/Central
Sanders, Lonnie, Jr.; '60-61-62; E/WB; #90; Detroit/Pershing
Sargent, Michael W.; '84-85-86-87; TE; #49/88; Flint/Powers
Saul, Richard R.; '67-68-69C; DE/LB; #88; Butler, Pa./Same
Saul, Ronald R.; '67-68-69; OT/OG; #70; Butler, Pa./Same
Savage, Larry E.; '76-77-78-79; ILB/OLB; #57; Warren, Ohio/Howland
Scarlett, Todd A.; '80-81; CB; #26; Okemos/Same
Schario, Richard S.; '78-81-82; PK; #3; Lyndhurst, Ohio/Brush
Schau, Henry W.; '27-28-29; FB; #*; Schererville, Ind./*
Schaum, Gregory J.; '73-74-74C; DT; #95; Baltimore, Md./Polytech
Schelb, Michael W.F.; '39-40-41; HB; #59/14; Allegan/Same
Schiesswohl, Donald A.; '52-53; G; #65; Saginaw/Arthur Hill
Schinderle, Jack W.; '64-65; DT; #79; Iron River/Same
Schloss, Harvey J.; '70; Mgr.; *
Schmyser, Verne J.; '23-24; HB; #*; Bad Axe/*
Schrader, Nelson C.; '36-37; *; #6; Northville/Same
Schramm, Andrew J.; '77-78-79-80; FB; #45; Findlay, Ohio/Same
Schramm, Walter; '81-82; OT; #61; Findlay, Ohio/Same
Schrecengost, Fred A.; '52-53-54; T; #76; Ford City, Pa./Same
Schroeder, Fred A.; '36-37; T; #12; Clawson/Same
Schroeder, Robert E.; '44; QB; #88; Flint/Same
Schulgen, George F.; '20-21; E; #*; Traverse City/*
Schultz, Carl F.; '23-24; E; #*; Lansing/*
Schultz, Todd; '95; QB; #9; Morris, Ill./Community
Schwei, John J.; '18-19-20; E; #*; Iron Mountain/Same
Sciarini, James M.; '75-76-77; C; #51; Fort Wayne, Ind./Bishop Dwenger
Sciarini, Michael P.; '78-79-80; OG; #65; Fort Wayne, Ind./Bishop Dwenger
Scott, Chris; '90; LB; #52; Troy/Same
Sebo, Steve; '34-35-36; HB; #41; Battle Creek/Central
Sedelbauer, Norman J.; '56; Mgr.; Grand Rapids/*
Seelig, Scott; '83-84-85; Mgr.; *
Sell, Joseph P., Jr.; '40; Mgr.; *
Selzer, Scott; '88-89; TB; #21; Farmington Hills/North Farmington
Serr, Gordon H.; '50-51-52; G; #56; Corunna/Same
Servis, Lawrence R.; '12; HB; #*; St. Joseph/*
Shafer, Charles L.; '77-78; TE; #80; Stevensville/Lakeshore
Shapiro, Mark; '89; C; #53; Farmington Hills/Farmington Harrison
Sharp, John E.; '59-61; HB/FB; #37; Flint/Northern
Shaw, Harold; '03; E; #*; Detroit/*

Shaw, Scott; '95; OG; #73; Sterling Heights/Henry Ford II
Shaw, Steve J.; '36-37-39; *; #*; *
Shedd, Bert; '05-06-07-08C-09; *; #*; Tekonsha/*
Shedd, John G.; '39; Mgr.; Rockford, Ill./*
Shedd, Robert W.; '42; Mgr.; *
Shedd, Ward R.; '00-01; *; #*; Tekonsha/*
Shepherd, Leroy; 81-82-83; DE; #97; New Castle, Pa./Same
Sherman, Robert G.; '39-40-41; QB; #57/26; Lansing/Eastern
Shinsky, John E.; '70-72-73C; DT; #88; Lyndhurst, Ohio/Cleveland St. Joseph
Shlapak, Borys W.; '70-71; K; #5; Park Ridge, Ill./Maine South
Shumay, Guy W.; '19; G; #*; Grand Rapids/*
Shurelds, Robert; '92-93-94-95; DB; #38/2; Cincinnati, Ohio/Western Hills
Shurmur, Joe; '89; Mgr.; Dearborn Heights/Divine Child
Shurmur, Patrick; '83-85-86-87CoC; C/OG; #60; Dearborn Heights/Divine Child
Shuttlesworth, Earl H.; '11; *; #; Lansing/*
Sieminski, Adam C.; '55; T; #70; Swoyerville, Pa./Same
Sieradzki, Stephen H.; '46-47; FB; #36; Muskegon/Same
Siler, William M.; '44; QB; #21; Dundee/Same
Silverstone, Michael; '83; PK; #7; Bloomfield Hills/Andover
Simonsen, Ronald W.; '50; Mgr.; Toledo, Ohio/*
Simpson, David; '87; OT; #68; Temperance/Bedford
Simpson, William T.; '71-72-73; DB/P; #29; Royal Oak/Shrine
Sinner, J. Hackley; '98-99; G; #; Cooper/*
Skinner, Ralph L.; '67; HB; #23; Battle Creek/St. Philip
Skuce, Thomas W.; '21; Mgr.; Charleston, W. Va./*
Slank, Ronald J.; '69-70; FB; #36; Detroit/Harper Woods Notre Dame
Slater, Eugene B.; '34; Mgr.; Saginaw/*
Sleder, Julius C.; '34-35-36; T; #20; Traverse City/Same
Slonac, Evan J.; '51-52-53; FB; #33; St. Michael, Pa./Adams Twp.
Small, Walter H.; '03-04-05-06-07; QB; #*; Charlevoix/*
Small, Sebastian; '90-91; RB; #44; Fayetteville, N.C./E.E. Smith
Smead, Harold E.; '28-29-30C; C; #*; Sturgis/*
Smiley, Lewis N.; '39-40-41; E; #37/89; Ferndale/Lincoln
Smith, Charles A.; '64-65-66; DE; #95; Beaumont Tex./Pollard
Smith, Chester; '27; *; #*; Detroit/*
Smith, Chris; '93-94-95; DT; #96; Clinton Twp./Clintondale
Smith, D. Steve; '77-78-79-80CoC; TB; #20; Louisville, Ky./duPont Manual
Smith, Earl I; '97-98; FB; #*; Lansing/*
Smith, Edward I.; '76-77-78CoC; QB; #7; Hallandale, Fla./Pittsburgh Central Catholic
Smith, George B.; '47-48-49; QB; #21; Wayne/Same
Smith, Gideon E.; '13-14-15; T; #*; Lansing/*
Smith, Gregory; '84-85; LB; #80; Detroit/Henry Ford
Smith, Horace; '46-47-48-49; E/HB; #18; Jackson/Same
Smith, Howard R.; '02; *; #*; Ludington/*
Smith, James; '81-82; FS; #81; Royal Oak/Shrine
Smith, Kermit; '67-68-69; FB; #41; Baytown, Tex./Carver
Smith, Lawrence J.; '37; Mgr.; Lake Odessa/*
Smith, Lawrence J.; '66-67; C; #52; Chicago, Ill./St. Rita
Smith, Louis A.; '51; HB; #43; Greenville/Same
Smith, Michael R.; '72; TE; #87; Detroit/Denby
Smith, Otto; '73-74-76; DE/OLB; #71; Columbia, S.C./Washington
Smith, Paul M.; '25-26-27C; B; #*; Saginaw/*
Smith, Peter H.; '61-62; QB; #23; Ecorse/St. Francis Xavier
Smith, William C.; '75-77; ILB; #39; Inkster/Dearborn Robichaud
Smith, William E.; '52; Mgr.; Detroit/*
Smolinski, Brian; '87-88-89-90; SE; #12; Farmington Hills/Harrison
Smolinski, Philip C.; '73; OT; #74; Allen Park/Same
Smolinski, Theodore C.; '41; T; #77; Rogers City/Same
Snider, Irving J.; '17-18-19; HB; #28; Richmond/Same
Snorton, Matthew H.; '61-62-63; E; #84; Detroit/Northwestern
Snow, Percy; '86-87-88-89; MLB; #48; Canton, Ohio/McKinley
Snyder, Robert W.; '70; Mgr.; Toledo, Ohio/*
Soave, John; '57; HB; #35; Detroit/Pershing
Sobczak, Edward E.; '46-48; E; #53/85; Pittsburgh, Pa./Langley
Soehnlen, Christopher; '87-88-89; DT; #64; Canton, Ohio/Thomas Aquinas
Sohacki, Edward; '47; G; #63; Detroit/*
Sokoll, Mark R.; '70; DB; #9; Winston-Salem, N.C./Okemos, Mich.
Soltys, Charles J.; FB; #29; Lansing, Ill./Thorton Frac. South
Sommer, Robert J.; '76' Mgr.; *

Speelman, Harry E.; '35-36-37C; T; #18; Lansing/Central
Speerstra, Herbert A.; '44-48; HB/E; #48/88; Saginaw/Eastern
Spencer, Raymond; '73-74-75; OG/OT; #59; Detroit/Central
Spiegel, William S.; '46-47-48; HB; #11; Birmingham/Baldwin
Spiekerman, Roy P.; '23-24-25; T; #*; Saginaw/*
Spragg, Clayton W. III; '82-84; Mgr.; Mt. Pleasant/Same
Springer, Harold A.; '15-19-20C; QB; #40; Port Huron/*
Squier, George G.; '32; T; #22; Benton Harbor/*
Stachowicz, Raymond M.; '77-78-79-80; P; #19; Broadview Hts., Ohio/Brecksville
Stafford, Jermaine; '95; WR; #25; Rochester, N.Y./Franklin
Standal, Thomas P.; '74-75; MB; #66; Flint/Beecher
Stansbery, Kevin; '92-93; FS; #39; Battle Creek/Harper Creek
Stanton, Edmund A.; '77-78; OT; #61; Battle Creek/Lakeview
Stanton, Jerome; '76-77-78; DB; #l; Detroit/Central
Stark, Elbert J.; '42; HB; #49; Geneva, Ill./Same
Stevens, Dewey D.; '50; T; #70; Flint/Central
Stevens, Joseph A.; '79-80-81-82; TE/DE; #83; Mentor, Ohio/Same
Stevenson, George A.; '60; G; #31; River Rouge/Same
Steward, Ernest; '89-90-91-92; LB; #98; Flint/Beecher
Stewart, Donald M.; '45; C; #22; Toledo, Ohio/Waite
Stewart, Donald W.; '59-60-61; HB/QB; #16; Muskegon/Same
Stockwell, Kenneth; '81-82-83; C; #53; Grosse Pointe/South
Stone, Fred A.; '09-10-IIC; E; #*; Clare/*
Stoyanovich, Bill; '92-93; PK; #10; Dearborn Heights/Crestwood
Stradley, Robert; '84-85-86-87 CoC; FS/LB; #22; Hartville, Ohio/Uniontown Lake
Straight, Herbert D.; '14-15-16; G; #44; Holland/*
Strand, William C.; '02; *; #*; Otsego/*
Strata, Rodney L.; '77-78-79-80 CoC; OG; #69; Canton, Ohio/Massillon Perry
Strauch, Clark M.; '24; Mgr.; Durand/*
Streb, Claude R.; '29-30; G; #17; Birmingham/*
Stroia, Eugene J.; '50; T; #76; River Rouge/*
Stump, Jeffrey; '84-85; OG; #64; Lansing/Waverly
Suci, Robert L.; '59-60-61; HB; #22; Grand Blanc/*
Sullivan, Thomas B.; '44C; C; #56; Steubenville, Ohio/Same
Summers, James; '65-66; DB; #20; Orangeburg, S.C./Wilkinson
Super, Robert V.; '66-67-68; QB/LB/DB; #12; Ferndale/Same
Sutilla, Edward D.; '58; T; #96; Revioc, Pa./Edensburg-Cambria
Swanson, Hugo T.; '20-21-22; G; #19; Ishpeming/*
Swartz, Howard R.; '35-36-37; T; #19; LaGrange, Ill./Lyons
Szwast, Robert F.; '60-61; T/G; #63; Chicago, Ill./Leo
Szymanski, James; '86-87-89; DE; #91; Sterling Heights/Stevenson

T

Tamburo, Richard P.; '50-51-52; C; #52; New Kensington, Pa./Same
Tanker, Terrence P.; '82-83; TE; #87; Westlake, Ohio/Lakewood
Tapling, Mark E.; '77-78-79; C; #54; Chicago, Ill./Gordon Tech
Tata, Vincent P.; '85-86-87-88; OG; #61; Fenton/Linden
Tate, Charles G.; '97; *; #*; Altoona, Pa./*
Tate, Mark T.; '58; G; #60; New Castle, Pa./Same
Taubert, James K.; '72-73-74CoC; DT; #94; Weymouth, Mass./Same
Taylor, Donavon, '85; DB; #24; Jamestown, Ohio/Greenview
Taylor, Maurice R.; '22-23C; G; #*; East Cleveland, Ohio/*
Terlaak, Robert T.; '32-33; G; #5; Cleveland, Ohio/*
Thayer, Robert F.; '24; G; #*; Williamston/*
Teufer, Philip H.; '22; T; #*; Eaton Rapids/*
Thayer, Robert F.; '24; G; #*; Williamston/*
Theuerkauf, Robert W.; '73; DB; #34; Menominee/Same
Thomas, Craig; '91-92-93; TB; #33; Braddock, Pa./Woodland Hills
Thomas, David W.; '68-69-70; OG/DE; #63; Warren/East Detroit
Thomas, Deane A.; '50; G; #71; Chicago, Ill./Leo
Thomas, E. James; '74-75-76-77; DT/OG; #76; Akron, Ohio/St. Vincent
Thomas, Jesse L.; '48-49-50; HB; #42; Flint/Central
Thomas, LaMarr; '67; HB; #36; Markham, Ill./Harvey-Thornton
Thomson, Charles J.; '17-19-20; E; #34; Eau Claire/*
Thomson, Elmer L.; '96; *; #*; Dansville/*
Thornhill, Charles E.; '64-65-66; G/LB; #41; Roanoke, Va./Addison
Thornton, Gregory L.; '84; DE; #96; Louisville, Ky./Butler
Thorpe, Gustave A.; '20-21-22; T; #24; Stephenson/*
Threats, Jabbar; '95; DE; #94; Garden City, Kan./Garden City CC

Thrower, Willie L.; '52; QB; #27; New Kensington, Pa./Same
Timmerman, Edward G.; '50-51-52; FB; #30; Grand Rapids/ Union
Timmons, Frank D.; '71-72; CB; #43; Winter Haven, Pa./ Jewitt
Tinnick, John F.; '64; HB; #22; Patton, Pa./Cambria Hts.
Tipton, Norman E.; '45; T; #77; Dearborn/Same
Tobin, John; '84; Mgr.; Taylor/Same
Tobin, John F.; '48-49-50; G; #66; Dearborn/Same
Tobin, Micheal G.; '68-69-70; OG/C; #60; Detroit/Bordertown, N.J. Military
Todd, Jerry; '88-89; TB/DB; #12; Flushing/Flint Powers
Toney, Marcus L.; '80-81-82; SS/FB; #1; Muskegon Hts./ Catholic Central
Toth, Kenneth A.; '85; LB; #85; New Baltimore/Algonac
Tower, Gordon E.; '99; T; *; Otisco/*
Townsend, Anthony; '79-80; FS; #36; Grand Rapids/Union
Travis, William E.; '99; E; #*; Milford/*
Traylor, Frank Jr.; '67; DT; #57; Beaumont, Tex./Pollard
Triplett, Howard; '92-93; CB; #11; Lansing/Sexton
Triplett, William L.; '68-69-70; TB/QB; #17; Vicksburg, Miss./ Temple
Trueman, John J.; '59; E; #80; Bakerton, Pa./Carrolltown
Tryon, Dugald J.; '65; Mgr.; East Lansing/Same
Turner, Daryl; '80-81-82-83; SE; #38; Flint/Southwestern
Turner, Joseph E.; '16-17; E/HB; #4; Whitney/*
Tyree, Thomas M.; '83-84; OLB; #28; Fort Wayne,Ind./South Side
Tyrell, Milford A.; '22; Mgr.; Detroit/*

U

Underwood, Dan D.; '61-62-63CoC; G/E; #59/93; Dowagiac/ Same
Underwood, Dimitrius; '95; DE; #99; Fayetteville, N.C./E.E. Smith

V

Van Buren, Earl C.; '25; *; #*; Jackson/*
Vanderburg, Vincent I.; '34-35-36; G; #2; Muskegon/Same
Vanderbeek, Matthew; '86-87-88-89; LB/DE; #66; Holland/ West Ottawa
Vanderbush, Randy; '89; QB; #15; Franklin, Ind./Same
Vanderhoef, Wilfred R.; '96C; *; #*; Washington, D.C./*
Vandermeer, Myrton L.; '30-31-32; E; #27; Grand Rapids/*
Vanderstolpe, John H.; '96-97-98; *; #*; Grand Rapids/*
Vandervoort, Adelbert D.; '14-15-16-19; G; #13; Lansing/*
VanElst, Gary L.; '69-71-72; LB/DT; #70; Middleville/Same
VanElst, G. David; '68-69; OT; #74; Middleville/Same
VanOrden, Richard O.; '18-19; G; #*; Corvallis, Ore./Same
VanPelt, Brad A.; '70-71-72CoC; S; #10; Owosso/Same
Van Pelt, Christopher J.; '79-80-81-82; CB; #7; Fort Wayne, Ind./Elmhurst
Vaughn, Bert R.; '77-78-79-80-81; QB; #15; Magasore,Ohio/ Same
Vaughn, Ernest; '07; *; #*; Detroit/*
Vaughn, Lawrence F.; '13-14; C; #*; Reading/*
Vershinksi, Thomas F.; '59; E; #94; Mt.Carmel, Pa./Same
Vezmar, Walter; '45; T; #58; Detroit/Northeastern
Veilhaber, John T.; '79; FL; #11; Findlay, Ohio/Same
Viney, Robert W.; '63-64-65; DE; #85; Pittsburgh, Pa./North Catholic
Vissing, William C.; '42; Mgr.; *
Vogel, Alfred R.; '24-25; *; #*; Evanston, Ill./*
Vogler, Harold L.; '47-48-49C; T; #72; Detroit/Cooley
Vogt, Ray A.; '50-51-52; HB; #48; Duquesne, Pa./Same
Vollrath, Mark; '73; Mgr.; *
Vooletich, Brian; '90-91; DB; #33; Ann Arbor/Pioneer
Vorkapich, Mike; '94; OLB; #50; Leamington, Ont./Same

W

Wachman, Mitchell; '83-84-85; OG; #62; Lauderdale Lakes, Fla./Anderson
Wagner, Roosevelt; '89-90-91; OG; #50; Ravenna, Ohio/Same
Wagner, Sidney P.; '33-34-35C; G; #17; Lansing/Central

Waldron, Donald; '46; HB; #47; Milwaukee, Wis./Shorewood
Walker, Don; '94-95; OG; #72; Detroit/Martin Luther King
Walker, G. Mickey; '58-59-60; G/T; #59; East Detroit/Same
Waller, Joel S.; '83; SE; #13; Miami, Fla./Miami Beach
Walsh, John J.; '62-64; G; #63; Chicago, Ill./Brother Rice
Ware, William H., Jr.; '67; DB; #32; Beaumont, Tex./Pollard
Warmbein, Kurt C.; '33-34-35; HB; #45; St. Joseph/Same
Wasczenski, Robert; '84; FL; #15; Farmington Hills/Harrison
Washington, Eugene; '64-65-66; SE; #84; LaPorte, Tex./ Baytown Carver
Washington, Richard; '74-75; DE; #75; Pontiac/Northern
Wasylk, Steve; '90-91-92-93; DB; #37; Tawas City/Same
Waters, Franklin D.; '46-47-48-49; HB/FB; #31/43; Wallingford, Conn./Same
Waters, Frank D. III; '66-67-68; HB/FL; #43; Hillsdale/Same
Watkins, Ronald A.; '62; TB; #32; Flint/Central
Weatherspoon, Donald; '65; DT; #74; Vandalia/Cassopolis
Weaver, Douglas W.; '50-51-52; C; #54; Goshen, Ind./Same
Webb, Tanya W.; '78-79; DT; #98; Augusta, Ark./Same
Webster, George D.; '64-65-66CoC; E/LB; #90; Anderson, S.C./Westwide
Weckler, Charles A.; '21; HB; #3; Lansing/*
Wedemeyer, Charles W.; '66-68; QB/FL; #11; Kailua, Hawaii/ Honolulu Punahon
Weeks, Kenneth B.; '27; *; #*; St. Louis/*
Weill, Norman O,; '16; Mgr.; Cleveland, Ohio/*
Weller, Paul R.; '73-75; Mgr.; *
Wells, George B.; '96-97; *; #*; Ithaca/*
Wells, William P.; '51-52-53; HB; #14; Chicago, Ill./ Menominee
Wenger, Ralph D.; '45-48-49; C; #56; Saginaw/Arthur Hill
Wenner, Elwyn A.; '26; T; #*; Brooklyn/*
Werner, Daniel L.; '69-72; QB; #4; Rocky River, Ohio/Cleveland St. Ignatius
West, Jerry F.; '64-65-66; OT; #77; Durand/Same
Wheeler, John P.; '46; T; #78; Kankakee, Ill./Same
Wheeler, Roy S.; '07-08; *; #*; Athens/*
White, Eric; '91; DE; #94; Indianapolis, Ind./Lawrence North
White, Lorenzo M.; '84-85-86-87CoC; TB; #34; Fort Lauderdale, Fla./Dillard
Whittemore, Olin S.; '51; Mgr.; East Lansing/*
Whittle, David D.; '79-80; OT; #63; Seattle, Wash./Shoreville
Wielba, Ralph C.; '69-70-71; LB/DB/DE; #39; Dearborn/ Fordson
Wietecha, Raymond W.; '46; C; #56; E. Chicago, Ill./Roosevelt
Wilcox, Frederick E.; '20-21; QB/HB; #1; Rockford, Ill./*
Wilks, John J.; '57-59; C; #53; Grand Rapids/Catholic Central
Willertz, Christopher; '86-87-88-89; DE; #99; Bay City/Handy
Williams Carl A.; '79-80-81-82; SS; #29; Detroit/Royal Oak Shrine
Williams, Fred T.; '97; *; #*; Petoskey/*
Williams, J.C.; '48-49-50; G; #69; Jackson/Same
Williams, James A.; '78-79-80; SE/FL; #85; San Diego, Calif./Madison
Williams, Jesse D.; '71; TB; #40; Bellefontaine, Ohio/Same
Williams, Leon L.; '74-75-76; TB; #22; Norfolk, Va./Lake Taylor
Williams, Samuel F.; '56-57-58C; E; #88; Dansville/Same
Williams, Terence L.; '77-78; DB; #18; Cincinnati, Ohio/ Princeton
Williams, P. Van; '79-80; CB; #32; Delray Beach, Fla./Boca Raton
Williamson, Herbert H.; '34; *; #*; *
Willingham, L. Tyrone; '73-74-76; QB/FL; #4; Jacksonville, N.C./Same
Wilson, Bernard; '85-86-87-88; SE/FL; #81; Patterson, N.J./ Eastside
Wilson, Bobby; '89-90; DL; #97; Chicago, Ill./Austin
Wilson, Charles A.; '73-74; OG; #68; Amityville, NY/Memorial
Wilson, Edgar; '77; SE; #41; Dowagiac/Union

Wilson, Freddie; '88-89-90; DB; #19; Boynton Beach, Fla./ Santaluces
Wilson, John; '27; *; #*; Asbury Park, N.J./*
Wilson, John D.; '50-51-52; HB/QB; #45; Lapeer/Same
Wilson, Miles M.; '34-35; G; #13; Kalamazoo/Central
Wilson, Patrick J.; '54-55-56; QB; #24; Lapeer/Same
Wilson, Thomas R.; '58-59-60; QB; #28; Lapeer/Same
Wilson, Tyrone C.; '73-74-75; TB/FB; #30; Wilkinsburg, Pa./ Same
Winiecki, Thomas S.; '60-61; T; #70; Chicago, Ill./Leo
Winters, Brian; '90-91; WR; #82; Toledo, Ohio/Macomber-Whitney
Wiseman, Donald R.; '34-35; FB; #32; Cadillac/Same
Wiska, Jeffrey R.; '79-80-81; OG/OT; #72; Farmington Hills/ Catholic Central
Wittig, Jeff; '88-89; OT; #60; Grand Rapids/Forest Hills Central
Wojciechowski, John; '81-82-84-85; DT/NG/OG; #93/73; Warren/Fitzgerald
Wolf, Clyde M.; '98; *; #*; Frontier/*
Wolff, David A.; '83-84-85-86; DT; #56; Southgate/Aquinas
Won, Douglas; '72; S; #39; Honolulu, Hawaii/St. Louis
Woods, Anthony E.; '81-82; SE; #80; Chicago, Ill./Sullivan
Woodworth, Fred L.; '97; *; #*; Caseville/*
Woodworth, Thomas L.; '30; Mgr.; *
Woody, Troy; '88; DB; #23; Flint/Northwestern
Wright, Donald M.; '57-58-59C; C/G; #68/54; Dearborn/Same
Wright, Harry A.; '05; *; #*; Iron Mountain/*
Wright, Marvin; '93-94-95; FB; #18; Saginaw/Arthur Hill
Wulff, James F.; '55-56-58; HB; #22; Chicago, Ill./Evanston St. George
Wycinsky, Craig P.; '68-69; OT; #77; Farmington/N. Farmington

Y

Yarema, David A.; '82-84-85-86; QB; #14; Warren/Birmingham Brother Rice
Yarlan, Stephen E.; '64; G; #69; Huntington, W. Va./Same
Yewcic, Thomas; '51-52-53; HB/QB; #41; Conemaugh, Pa./ Same
Yocca, John A.; '48-50; G; #67; Windber, Pa./Same
Young, Duane; '87-88-89-90; OL/FB/TE; #29; Kalamazoo/ Central
Young, Edmund C.; '18; E; #*; Mason/Same
Young, Gregory T.; '75; LB; #96; Bloomfield Hills/Rochester, N.Y. Brighton
Young, H. Earl; '01; Mgr.; Mason; *
Young, Hendricks, M.; '58; HB; #17; Detroit/Chicago Carver
Young, Lonnie; '81-82-83-84; CB; #36; Mt. Morris/Flint Beecher
Young, Michael S.; '67-68; DB/DT; #64; Detroit/Holy Redeemer
Youngs, Edward W.; '61-62-63; T/C; #71; Jackson/Same
Yuhse, Frank J.; ' 13; Mgr.; Manistee/*

Z

Zagers, Bert A.; '52-53-54; HB; #19; Cadillac/Same
Zalar, Edward J.; '55; E; #51; Barberton, Ohio/Same
Zarza, Louis F.; '33-34-35; E; #25; E. Chicago, Ind ./Washington
Ziegel, Frederick K.; '34-35-36; QB; #42; Detroit/Northwestern
Ziegler, Nicholas J.; '45; E; #83; Cleveland, Ohio/West Tech
Zimmer, Mark T.; '81-82; Mgr.; Cadillac/*
Zimmer, Michael J.; '80-81-82; Mgr.; Cadillac/*
Zindel, Barry L.; '59; E; #81; Williamston/Same
Zindel, Howard C.; '34-35-36; T; #11; Grand Rapids/Union
Zindel, Jack D.; '68; MG; #65; East Lansing/Same
Zito, James J.; '46-47; T; #73; Geneva, Ohio/Same
Zorn, William L.; '62; T; #80; Massillon, Ohio/Same
Zucco, Victor A.; '56; FB; #36; Renton, Pa./Plum Twp.
Zysk, Donald H.; '55-56-57; HB; #34; Grand Haven/Same

240

ALL-TIME SPARTAN SUMMARY

Year	Games	Won	Lost	Tied	Pts.	Opp. Pts.	Coach	Captain (position)
1896	4	1	2	1	26	42	No Established Coach	Wilfred R. Vanderhoef (Tackle)
1897	7	4	2	1	146	106	Henry Keep	Walton K. Brainard (Halfback)
1898	7	4	3	0	142	127	Henry Keep	J. H Vanderstolpe (Guard)
1899	7	2	4	1	81	101	Charles O. Bemies	Ellis W. Ranney (Quarterback)
1900	4	1	3	0	51	67	Charles O. Bemies	Charles A. McCue (End)
1901	8	3	4	1	120	94	George Denman	Albert H. Case (Guard)
1902	9	4	5	0	93	206	George Denman	Arthur D. Peters (Tackle)
1903	8	6	1	1	178	24	Chester L. Brewer	Frank J. Kratz (Tackle)
1904	9	8	1	0	380	16	Chester L. Brewer	Frank J. Kratz (Tackle)
1905	11	9	2	0	280	75	Chester L. Brewer	Edward B. McKenna (Halfback)
1906	11	7	2	2	195	28	Chester L. Brewer	Stephen W. Doty (Fullback)
1907	7	4	2	1	127	60	Chester L. Brewer	Walter H. Small (Quarterback)
1908	8	6	0	2	205	22	Chester L. Brewer	Bert Shedd (Tackle)
1909	9	8	1	0	233	17	Chester L. Brewer	Parnell G. McKenna (Halfback)
1910	7	6	1	0	168	8	Chester L. Brewer	Ion J. Cortright (Halfback)
1911	6	5	1	0	93	30	John F. Macklin	Fred A. Stone (End)
1912	8	7	1	0	297	98	John F. Macklin	William R. Riblett (Quarterback)
1913	7	7	0	0	180	28	John F. Macklin	Chester W. Gifford (Tackle)
1914	7	5	2	0	188	51	John F. Macklin	George E. Julian (Fullback)
1915	6	5	1	0	258	38	John F. Macklin	W. Blake Miller (Halfback)
1916	7	4	2	1	126	26	Frank Sommers	Ralph B. Henning (End)
1917	9	0	9	0	23	179	Chester L. Brewer	Sherman Coryell (Tackle)
1918	7	4	3	0	134	68	George E. Gauthier	Lawrence C. Archer (Center)
1919	9	4	4	1	132	99	Chester L. Brewer	Harry E. Franson (Tackle)
1920	10	4	6	0	270	166	George "Potsy" Clark	Harold A. Springer (Quarterback)
1921	8	3	5	0	68	126	Albert M. Barron	John Bos (Tackle)
1922	10	3	5	2	111	135	Albert M. Barron	William C. Johnson (Halfback)
1923	8	3	5	0	57	144	Ralph H. Young	Maurice R. Taylor (Guard)
1924	8	5	3	0	210	48	Ralph H. Young	Vivian J. Hultman (Guard)
1925	8	3	5	0	105	106	Ralph H. Young	Donald H. Haskins (Tackle)
1926	8	3	4	1	97	171	Ralph H. Young	Martin F. Rummel (Tackle)
1927	9	4	5	0	111	128	Ralph H. Young	Paul M. Smith (Fullback)
1928	8	3	4	1	153	66	Harry G. Kipke	Lewis A. Hornbeck (End)
1929	8	5	3	0	244	104	James H. Crowley	Fred W. Danziger (Halfback) Vern C. Dickeson (Halfback)
1930	8	5	1	2	151	32	James H. Crowley	Harold E. Smead (Center)
1931	9	5	3	1	291	61	James H. Crowley	Milton C.Gross (Guard)
1932	8	7	1	0	220	64	James H. Crowley	Abe Eliowitz (Fullback) Robert C. Monnett (Halfback)
1933	8	4	2	2	73	49	Charles W. Bachman	Bernard G. McNutt (Fullback)
1934	9	8	1	0	153	56	Charles W. Bachman	Russell H. Reynolds (Quarterback)
1935	8	6	2	0	207	57	Charles W. Bachman	Sidney P. Wagner (Guard)
1936	9	6	1	2	143	40	Charles W. Bachman	Gordon A. Dahlgren (Guard) Henry S. Kutchins (End)
1937	10	8	2	0	117	42	Charles W. Bachman	Harry E. Speelman (Tackle)
1938	9	6	3	0	133	59	Charles W. Bachman	Allen O. Diebold (Quarterback) David D. Diehl (End)
1939	9	4	4	1	102	92	Charles W. Bachman	Michael Kinek (End) Lyle J. Rockenbach (Guard)
1940	8	3	4	1	108	76	Charles W. Bachman	Jack R. Amon (Fullback) Paul J. Griffeth (Guard)

Year	Games	Won	Lost	Tied	Pts.	Opp. Pts.	Coach	Captain (position)
1941	9	5	3	1	150	77	Charles W. Bachman	Wilford D. Davis (Quarterback)
1942	9	4	3	2	120	99	Charles W. Bachman	Richard Mangrum (Tackle)
1943				Football terminated (war restrictions)				
1944	7	6	1	0	167	31	Charles W. Bachman	Thomas B. Sullivan (Center)
1945	9	5	3	1	120	128	Charles W. Bachman	Jacweir Breslin (Halfback)
1946	10	5	5	0	181	202	Charles W. Bachman	Robert B. McCurry (Center)
								Kenneth E. Balge (End)
1947	9	7	2	0	167	101	Clarence L. Munn	Robert B. McCurry (Center)
1948	10	6	2	2	359	130	Clarence L. Munn	Robert B. McCurry (Center)
1949	9	6	3	0	309	107	Clarence L. Munn	Harold L. Vogler (Tackle)
1950	9	8	1	0	243	107	Clarence L. Munn	LeRoy R. Crane (Fullback)
1951	9	9	0	0	270	114	Clarence L. Munn	Robert Carey (End)
1952	9	9	0	0	312	84	Clarence L. Munn	Donald McAuliffe (Halfback)
1953	10	9	1	0	240	10	Clarence L. Munn	Donald Dohoney (End)
1954	9	3	6	0	177	149	Hugh Duffy Daugherty	LeRoy Bolden (Halfback)
								Don Kauth (End)
1955	10	9	1	0	253	83	Hugh Duffy Daugherty	Carl Nystrom (Guard)
1956	9	7	2	0	239	87	Hugh Duffy Daugherty	John Matsko (Center)
1957	9	8	1	0	264	75	Hugh Duffy Daugherty	Patrick Burke (Tackle)
1958	9	3	5	1	117	123	Hugh Duffy Daugherty	Sam Williams (End)
1959	9	5	4	0	149	118	Hugh Duffy Daugherty	Donald Wright (Guard)
1960	9	6	2	1	193	118	Hugh Duffy Daugherty	Fred Arbanas (End)
								Fred Boylen (Guard)
								Herb Adderley (Halfback)
1961	9	7	2	0	192	50	Hugh Duffy Daugherty	Ed Ryan (Halfback)
1962	9	5	4	0	184	96	Hugh Duffy Daugherty	George Saimes (Fullback)
1963	9	6	2	1	148	63	Hugh Duffy Daugherty	Dan D. Underwood (End)
								Sherman P. Lewis (Halfback)
1964	9	4	5	0	136	141	Hugh Duffy Daugherty	Chas. Migyanka, Jr. (Linebacker)
1965	11	10	1	0	263	76	Hugh Duffy Daugherty	Donald Japinga (Halfback)
								Stephen Juday (Quarterback)
1966	10	9	0	1	293	99	Hugh Duffy Daugherty	Clinton Jones (Halfback)
								George Webster (Roverback)
1967	10	3	7	0	173	193	Hugh Duffy Daugherty	Anthony Conti (Tackle)
								Drake Garrett (Halfback)
1968	10	5	5	0	202	151	Hugh Duffy Daugherty	Allen Brenner (End)
1969	10	4	6	0	202	231	Hugh Duffy Daugherty	Franklin Foreman (End)
								Richard Saul (Linebacker)
1970	10	4	6	0	19	215	Hugh Duffy Daugherty	Gordon Bowdell (End)
								Michael Hogan (Linebacker)
1971	11	6	5	0	225	169	Hugh Duffy Daugherty	Eric Allen (Halfback)
								Ron Curl (Tackle)
1972	11	5	5	1	158	156	Hugh Duffy Daugherty	Brad VanPelt (Safety)
								Billy Joe DuPree (Tight End)
1973	11	5	6	0	114	164	Dennis Stolz	Michael Holt (Tailback)
								John Shinsky (Tackle)
1974	11	7	3	1	270	196	Dennis Stolz	James Taubert (Tackle)
								Clarence Bullock (Fullback)
1975	11	7	4	0	222	164	Dennis Stolz	Gregory Schaum (Tackle)
								Charles Baggett (Quarterback)
1976	11	4	6	1	236	278	Darryl Rogers	Rich Baes (Tailback)
								Tom Hannon (Safety)
1977	11	7	3	1	260	162	Darryl Rogers	Larry Bethea (Tackle)
								Al Pitts (Center)
								Paul Rudzinski (Linebacker)

Year	Games	Won	Lost	Tied	Pts.	Opp. Pts.	Coach	Captain (position)
1978	11	8	3	0	411	170	Darryl Rogers	Ed Smith (Quarterback)
1979	11	5	6	0	240	253	Darryl Rogers	Mel Land (Tackle)
								Dan Bass (Linebacker)
1980	11	3	8	0	221	279	Frank (Muddy) Waters	Mark Brammer (Tight End)
								Rodney Strata (Guard)
								Steve Smith (Halfback)
								George Cooper (Linebacker)
1981	11	5	6	0	263	249	Frank (Muddy) Waters	Bernard Hay (Defensive Tackle)
								George Cooper (Linebacker)
1982	1	2	9	0	202	242	Frank (Muddy) Waters	John Leister (Quarterback)
								John Leister (Quarterback)
								Carl Banks (Linebacker)
1983	11	4	6	1	162	233	George Perles	Carl Banks (Linebacker)
1984	12	6	6	0	193	203	George Perles	Jim Morrissey (Linebacker)
1985	12	7	5	0	258	219	George Perles	Anthony Bell (Linebacker)
								John Wojciechowski (Guard)
1986	11	6	5	0	285	197	George Perles	Shane Bullough (Linebacker)
								Dave Yarema (Quarterback)
1987	12	9	2	1	262	153	George Perles	Mark Nichols (Defensive Tackle)
								Pat Shurmur (Center)
								Rob Stradley (Linebacker)
1988	12	6	5	1	269	177	George Perles	Lorenzo White (Tailback)
								Kurt Larson (Linebacker)
								John Miller (Safety)
								Tony Mandarich (Offensive Tackle)
1989	12	8	4	0	356	163	George Perles	Bobby McAllister (Quarterback)
								Harlon Barnett (Defensive Back)
								Bob Kula (Offensive Tackle)
1990	12	8	3	1	312	223	George Perles	Steve Montgomery (Fullback)
								Dan Enos (Quarterback)
								Mike Iaquaniello (Def. Back)
								Carlos Jenkins (Linebacker)
1991	11	3	8	0	162	272	George Perles	Eric Moten (Off. Guard)
								Alan Haller (Def. Back)
								Courtney Hawkins (Wide Receiver)
								Bill Johnson (Def. end)
								Jim Johnson (Offensive Tackle)
								Brian Vooletich (Def. Back)
1992	11	5	6	0	238	261	George Perles	Tico Duckett (Tailback)
								Toby Heaton (Tackle)
								William Reese (Def. Tackle)
1993	12	6	6	0	277	289	George Perles	Brice Abrams (Fullback)
								Rob Fredrickson (Outside Linebacker)
1994	11	0	11#	0	280	267	George Perles	Mark Birchmeier (Center)
								Mill Coleman (Flanker)
								Juan Hammonds (Defensive End)
1995	12	6	5	1	287	338	Nick Saban	Yakini Allen (Defensive Tackle)
								Tony Banks (Quarterback)
								Scott Greene (Fullback)
Totals	915	527	344#	44	19,160	12,089		

#Reflects five 1994 wins forfeited by MSU as part of 1996 self-imposed sanctions.

The 1921-22 Aggie Yell Team.

The 1949 Michigan State Cheerleaders.

MSU Cheerleaders circa 1950s.

MSU ALUMNI CHEERLEADER CLUB MEMBERS

Karen Able Kolschowsky
Tim Abler
Alan Ammesmaki
Kenneth Andrews Jr.
Bambi Austin Cole
Gail Ayala
Julie Bader
Joan Banks
Bonnie Barnes Cole
Barbara Barrett Sutton
Jack Bates
Dick Beals
Sue Beekman Mills
Debra Benson
Peter Betrus
Nan Blasy
William Boughner
Sue Brabbs Ritchie
L'Tonya Braceful
Clark Brown
Diane Brown
Kurt Broock
Eppie Bruckner Garland
Patricia Bondshua Barid
Dr. Richard Burg
Alphonza Burgess
Dr. Thomas Carlson
Nancy Carter
Judith Casturo
Joe Cesar

Dan Charboneau
Laura Cheney Gladwin
Marjorie Chesney
Elaine Chilimigras
Brian Clark
Howard Clark
Kay Clark Miller
Paul Cline
Kevin Cole
Charlie Costantini
Kathleen Craine Duda
Dan Crowder
Kevin Cummings
Tim Dameron
John Darling
Roberta Davidson Colaner
Harriet Davidson Vaugeois
Jeff Davis
Jack DeBarr
Sue Deller
Warren DeYoung
David Dobbins

Maudine Dobbins
John Dodds
Jill Drader-Skrzynski
Wayne Dugger
Bob Easterly
Thomas Eble
James Ehle

The 1975 Spartan Cheerleaders.

David Ernst
Kent Esbaugh
Lori A. Evans
Patti Farhat
Gary Faust
Penny Faustyn
Claire Ferguson
Theresa Flattery
Vicki L. Foster
Stacey Gartee
Kim Gavigan Caldwell
David Gradison
Jill Graham Baston
Susan Grayum Deller
David Green
Deena Green Powell
Joyce Grenfel Spade
Jerry C. Gross Ph.D.
Ernest Guy
Charles Guzak
David Hannah
Gary Hanpel
Robert Harris
Melissa Hess
Kristin Hoeksema

The 1980 Michigan State Cheerleading Squad.

The 1979 MSU Cheerleaders.

Tracy Hogan Davis
Margaret Hoohhout
Jody Houf Eberly
Martin Johnson
William Jones
Anthony Kandt
Debby Karabees Betts
Ted Kiesling
Bert Kinner
Mary Kluiber Flynn
Rodger Kolasinski
Jill Krause Bianco
Kendra Kurz
Jim Labus
Gina LaFace
Douglas Lamb
Pat Leblanc
Caroline Lettas Cook
Cathy Lilly Belknap
Bob Lockwood II
Miki Look
Casey Lowe
Bob Luberto
Nancy Mack Spring
Steven Mawf
Jim McCabe
Tim McCall
Karen McDonald
Keith McElroy
Rae McIntyre
Jaqueline Milzow
Lisa Morrow
Celeste Moy
Ginny Nancarrow Unold
Dave Nicely
Robert Nole
Robert Norris

Sue Nottingham-Misner
Julie Olds Maclachlan
Missy Otterbein Hess
Michele Ouellette Henson
Mary Lu Pelton
Margie Poplawski Riley
Mary Jo Poplawski Rulewicz
Kristin Powell
Mary Rademacher
Monique Ramirez
Linda Raymond Dice
Jan Richter
Deb Rodgers Beaudry
Bob Rorich
Loren Rosenberg
Julie Rowe Powell
Mike Rowe
Ed Rutherford, Director
Robin Sanford
Molly Sapp
Nancy Sayers Ginns
Nancy Schlichting Morley
Mike Schmitt
Lara Schaden
Kayce Shepard
Jennifer Shriver
Sherry Simons Kohlman
Greg Skipper
Diana Skrzycki Moher
Bob Smith
Christine Smith
Congressman Nick Smith
Steve Smith
Tom Smith
John Southerland
Henry Sparapani
Maurice Spencer
Richard Stafford

Joe Staser
Lynn & Mike Stenback
Michael Stern
Anne Stimson Davis
Suzanne Stimson Leech
Teisha Struik
Barb Sutton
Eric Swanson
Fred Teich Jr.
Dr. Thomas Terry
Jonathan Thomson
Kathy Tiplady Torphy
Tamara Trimmer Bammell
Paul Troth
Ron Turkus
Kevin Twining
Patrick Vachon
Janet Voss
John Walker
Roger Walker
William Warner
Lynn Weaver Sykes
Nancy Welford Hidlay
William Wells
Michael J. Wessely
Max Widawer
Toni Willson
Lorie Wile Donlan
Todd Winston
Lanney Wixson
Vikki Wiegand Hill
Jeanne Wrase Morris
Sam Yeiter
Michael Yockey
Rollie Young
Sue Zachariason Boice

The 1994 Michigan State Spartan Cheerleaders.

MSU ALUMNI BAND

Band member, instrument (if available), year participated (if available)

A

Abell, Sharyl
Achenbach, Scott, Trombone
Acre, Keri, Flag Color Guard
Acre, Lori, Flag Color Guard, 1983
Acre, Timothy
Adamec, Jeremy, Trombone, 1989
Adams, Charles A.
Adams, Ken, Trombone, 1971
Adams, Ralph, French Horn
Adams, Terry
Addleman, Robert Jr., Trumpet
Ahrens, Harry, Trumpet, 1961
Aikman, Mariella, Alto Clarinet
Alberts, Donna, Trumpet, 1986
Aldredge, Debra L.
Alan, Carrie (Blanchette), Tuba
Alleman, John E., Clarinet
Allen, Barbara, Clarinet, 1962
Allen, Carey
Allen, David, Baritone, 1986
Allen, Kevin, 1988
Allen, Ronald D.
Allen, Steven T., Saxophone
Allhands, Ken, Tuba, 1989
Allum, Jeffrey R., Trombone, 1993
Alpert, Lawrence, S., Trumpet, 1970
Altovilla, Anthony R., Trumpet, 1982
Altovilla, Lynda (English), Flute, 1986
Alward, George A., Flag, 1983
Alway, Thomas J., Trombone, 1987
Amabebe, Anna
Ambrose, Shirley
Ambrose, William D., Trumpet
Ambs, Cheryl, Mellophone, 1986
Ambs, Susan, Flute
Amsterburg, Thomas P., Trumpet
Amstutz, Keith, Trumpet
Anderson, Dennis D., Trumpet, 1970
Anderson, John A.
Anderson, John A. Jr.,
Anderson, Mark E., Trumpet, 1993
Anderson, Paul
Anderson, Robert, Cornet
Anderson, Sigfrid M., Tuba
Andringa, Jill, Flute, 1991
Anibal, John D.
Anibal, Paul M., Trumpet
Antieau, Chris, Trumpet, 1996
Arent, Christopher, Saxophone, 1991
Arnold, Hubert E., Baritone, piano
Arnold, Michelle, Alto Saxophone
Arnold, Rebecca F., Clarinet
Arny, Francis V.
Ash, Jeffrey, Trombone, 1993
Askeland, Chris, Percussion

Astalos, Richard, Clarinet, 1953
Atkins, Sandra L.
Aula, Susan, Trumpet, 1989
Aurand, Charles H. Jr., Clarinet, 1954
Ausdemore, Jeff, Percussion
Austin, Virginia J.
Austin, William L., Clarinet
Autrey, Byron, Trumpet
Arsdemore, Jeffrey, Percussion
Aylesworth, Kay Billings, French Horn, 1961
Aylesworth, Martha B., French Horn

B

Babcock, Kim, Baritone
Backstrom, Sharon, French Horn
Bacon, Lawrence D., Baritone, 1973
Bailey, Roger, Percussion, 1960
Baker, Barry J., Trumpet, 1977
Baker, Lyman R., Trombone, 1969
Baker, Ronald C.
Baker, Steven, W., Trumpet
Baldwin, Eric, Percussion, 1986
Bale, Lisa A. (Wagner), Flag, 1982
Balkus, Charles A.
Ball, Hermann F. Jr., Trombone
Bango, Anthony M., Percussion
Bangs, Michael, Flag, 1992
Banny, Jim, Flag
Barann, Kristine (Knas), Trumpet, 1988
Baranowski, James, Trombone
Barger, Dave, Trumpet
Bargner, Judy, Alto Saxophone
Barker, Angela, Alto Saxaphone
Barkman, Renae, Clarinet, 1995
Barnes, Carol J., Clarinet, 1985
Baron, Gary W. Alto Saxopphone, 1964
Barosko, James M., French Horn
Barrett, Richard R., Trumpet
Barry, Jeanne, Trumpet, 1995
Barry, Jim, Trumpet, 1973
Barry, Karen, Flag Color Guard, 1989
Barry, Linda, Flute, Twirler, 1974
Bartholomew, Craig A., Baritone, 1975
Bartholomew, Karen J., Clarinet
Bartlett, Dale, French Horn, 1955
Bartlett, Dan, Mellophone, 1991
Bartlett, Deborah K.
Bartlett, Gerald, Trumpet
Bartley, Linda L., Clarinet
Basrai, Margaret, Trombone, 1991
Bassett, Nancy A.
Bastien, Mary, Trombone
Batdorff, Steven L., Flag
Bauer, Mike, Flag, 1973
Bauer, Shelly, Clarinet, 1995
Baumann, Carol, Flag, 1993
Baumgarten, Kristyne, 1975
Baumgartner, J. Scott, Tenor Sax, 1992

Baumgartner, Steve, Baritone, 1994
Bauries, Suzette L. , Baritone
Bausano, Liz, Flag Color Guard, 1988
Bawol, Stan, Trumpet
Beador, David A., Flag
Beagley, David C., 1977
Beam, John P., French Horn, 1967
Bean, Bruce W., Twirler, Drum
Beaumont, Derek, Percussion
Beaumont, Larry
Beauvais, JoAnne, Flag Color Guard, 1994
Beaver, Dennis, Bassoon, Contra, 1995
Beck, Donna, Flute, 1976
Beck, Stephanie L., French Horn
Becker, John H.
Beem, Herb, Clarinet/Saxophone, 1954
Beery, Michael, Oboe, Alto Saxophone
Begian, Harry, Director of Bands
Behnke, Bruce E. Trumpet
Behnke, Bruce I.
Behrend, Roger, Baritone
Behrend, Sandy
Behrens, Gene A.
Beimer, Daniel J.
Bell, Karin D.
Bell, Larry W., Baritone
Bell, Michael E., Baritone, 1971
Belser, Douglas M., Tenor Saxophone, 1989
Bembenek, James, French Horn
Bemish, Joel, Percussion
Benda, Ann, Trumpet, 1988
Bender, Donald R., Percussion, 1984
Bender, Jeanetta Z.
Benedict, Frank A.
Benedict, Vernon L., Clarinet, 1950
Beneker, Carrie, Mellophone, 1994
Benfer, Thomas
Benison, James, Baritone, 1992
Benner, Laurence, French Horn
Bennett, Dennis K.
Benson, Gregory, Trombone
Benson, Mark, Trombone, 1983
Benstein, Harvey G., Clarinet, 1972
Benzing, Pamela J.
Berg, Sidney
Berggren, John L. Sr.
Bergman, Lisa, French Horn, 1993
Bergren, Richard J., Trumpet
Berndt, William C., Trumpet
Beroza, Richard P., Tuba
Berriman, Robert, Percussion, 1993
Berry, Clare, Flute, 1995
Berry, David W., French Horn
Bertolini, Philip R., Tuba
Berz, Rita, Flute
Berz, William, Clarinet
Besinger, Donna M. (Keilen), Mellophone, 1985

Beson, Dennis, Tuba, 1992
Beson, Kevin M., Tuba, 1980
Beson, Patricia (Neff), Baritone, 1986
Beson, William M., Alto Saxophone, 1986
Best, Richard C., Baritone, 1969
Betz, Alice, Flag, 1978
Betz, Jim, Flag, 1975
Beyersdorf, Michael L.
Bickel, Philip, Trombone, 1968
Bicking, David, M.
Bielski, Kristen (Miller), Mellophone, 1988
Bienias, Lynnea, Color Guard, 1988
Bilkie, Robert, W., Flag, 1986
Billig, T. Patrick, Baritone, 1979
Binkowski, Matt, Trumpet, 1993
Biondo, Mary F., Trumpet, 1981
Bischoff, James A., Tenor Saxophone
Bishop, Julie (Rio), Saxophone, 1990
Bitterman, Hannah L.
Black, Gary D., Flag, 1976
Black, Sue, Bassoon, 1994
Blackson, John H.
Blaess, Kenneth D.
Blair, Geoffrey, Tenor Saxophone, 1989
Blake, Roger, Trombone, 1989
Blakemore, John, Percussion, 1991
Blanch, Christina
Blanchard, Steve, Trombone, 1986
Bliss, Steve, Baritone, 1993
Blohm, Alan J., 1979
Bloomquist, Ann, Soprano
Bloomquist, Kenneth G., Trumpet, Director
    of Bands
Blound Kristen A., Trumpet, 1989
Bloye, Dawna L.
Bobrow, Andy, Tuba, 1986
Bodeau, John, Trombone
Bodnar, Brent, Alto Saxophone, 1989
Bogart, James E., 1967
Boissoneau, Ross, Trumpet, 1981
Boitel, Earl C. Jr., 1956
Boley, John, Trumpet, 1992
Bolinsky, Steve, Trombone
Bolley, Shane, Saxophone
Bolzman, Deana, Flag Color Guard
Bond, Mark E., Trumpet, 1974
Bond, Tracy, Alto Horn, 1981
Bonnette, Jean, Flag Color Guard
Bonnette, Stephen J., Tuba
Booth, Becky, Trombone
Borden, Richard S., Trombone, 1968
Boren, John, Trombone
Boron, Julie (Chrisenberry), Mellophone,
    1989
Boron, Michael A., Tuba, 1993
Borton, Michelle (Rabey), Baritone, 1989
Bortz, Michael G., Trumpet
Boruta, Howard J.
Bos, Troy E., Tuba, 1991
Bosch, Mary
Bosse, Joanna, Clarinet, 1991
Bough, Michael, Mellophone, 1988
Boulton, John, B., Flute
Bousfield, Beth, Saxophone, 1991

Bovenschen, Kathleen S. (Melnick)Alto
    Saxophone, 1984
Bovenschen, Tricia (Bailey), Percussion,
    1992
Bovenschen, Wayne E., Percussion, Snare,
    1987
Bowers, Ray D., French Horn
Bowman,Theo E., Trumpet, 1942
Bowyer, John M., Baritone, 1980
Boyd, Albert C.
Boyer, Kathy, M., Clarinet
Braciszeski, Terry, L., Trumpet, 1979
Braden, Patrick, Flag Color Guard, 1995
Bradley, Karen (Downey), Trumpet, 1986
Bradley, Leon C., Trombone
Bradley, Roger, Trombone, 1986
Braman, Russ, Baritone, 1994
Brandt, James S., Percussion
Brandt, Stacy, Flag Color Guard 1993
Brasseur, Vicky
Braun, Jack C., Clarinet, 1952
Bredwell, Bryan R., Tenor Saxophone,
    1994
Bredwell II, Harold D., Baritone
Breed, Marie, Bassoon, 1995
Brehm, Shirley, Trombone, 1948
Breneman, Brian, Trumpet, 1994
Breon, John A.
Breyer, Christopher, Tuba
Breza, Mark J., Trumpet
Brezinski, Beth, Flute, 1993
Brisbin, John D., French Horn
Brisbin, Margot
Broadbent, Tawny, Twirler
Brockington, Howard B.
Brockington, Joseph, L., French Horn,
    1972
Broka, Derrick, Flute
Broka, Stephanie, Trumpet
Broka, Thomas G., Baritone
Bronson, Burton, B., Tuba, 1950
Bronson, James G., Trumpet, 1982
Brook, Roger C., Trombone
Brooks, Clara, Clarinet
Brooks, Joseph P.
Brough, Glen, Drum Major, 1979
Brower, Ross G., Trombone
Brown, B. Lynn, flute, 1973
Brown, Bill, Baritone, 1993
Brown, Bruce F., 1982
Brown, David L., Tuba, 1979
Brown, Douglas D.
Brown, Jeffrey D., French Horn
Brown, Jere, Trombone, 1969
Brown, Ken, Tuba, 1987
Brown, Kenneth M.
Brown, Marnie, Alto Saxophone
Brown, Robert M.
Brownell, David R., French Horn
Bruce, Craig E., Percussion, 1971
Bruning, Thomas R., Trombone, 1974
Bruns, Jay C., Alto Saxophone
Buck, Christopher, Alto Saxophone
Buck, Marsha K.

Bullock, R.J., Alto Saxophone, 1975
Bunce, Mark, Saxophone, 1995
Bunch Jr., Fred, Saxophone
Burdick, Jerry, Drum Major, 1995
Burgess, William, Baritone
Burnett, Greg, percussion, 1985
Burnett, Charles E., Jr., 1982
Burnett, Ray
Burroughs, Beverly, Clarinet, 1979
Burroughs, Stanley H., Jr., Clarinet, 1964
Burtt, Charlie, Trombone, 1988
Bush, Dan, Trumpet, 1963
Bushnell, Herman, Trombone, 1950
Butler, James R., Baritone, 1974
Butrick, Darla, Trumpet, 1993
Butts, David R., Trumpet, 1974
Buyarski, Linda J., French Horn
Byam, Charles, Percussion, 1989
Byl, Carolyn, Flute/Alto Saxophone, 1981
Byrd, David, Trumpet, 1977

C

Cabib, Lana B. (Rayburg)
Calhoun, Ron, Percussion
Callewaert, John H.
Callow, Patrick, Trumpet, 1994
Calme, Nancy (Hassan), French Horn,
    1978
Campbell, Leslie, Trumpet, 1977
Canan, Mike, Trombone, 1980
Cannons, Kyle, C., Flag, 1980
Capelli, Shanna (Mosher), Flag Color
    Guard, 1993
Carless, Lori L., Trombone, 1989
Carlson, Diane M., Clarinet, 1971
Carlson, Melanie, Flag Color Guard
Carlson, Melissa, Flag Color Guard, 1995
Carlson, Wayne, Trumpet, 1973
Carp, Steven S., Percussion, 1983
Carpenter, Dan, Trumpet, 1993
Carter, Brian D., French Horn
Case, Andrew C., Mellophone, 1989
Case, Christopher, Trombone
Casey, Janis, French Horn
Casey, William R., Alto Saxophone/French
    Horn, 1974
Casola, Damien, Percussion, Bass
Cassiday, Todd, Baritone, 1985
Catey, Joe S., Bassoon
Catherman, Rick L., Trumpet, 1990
Catron, David
Catt, Stephen R.
Cayce, James L.
Cesarz, Candace D., Trumpet, 1977
Chabot, Michele (Engler), Trumpet, 1991
Chadderdon, Donald, 1946
Chadwick, David P., Clarinet, 1956
Chamberlain, Richard L.
Champion, Kim, Flute
Chan, Bonnie, Percussion
Chapman, Elizabeth L. French Horn
Chapman, Kelly, Flag Color Guard
Chatfield, Henry E., Tuba, 1929
Chausse, Kari, French Horn, 1995

Cheal, Jennifer P., Flute
Cheal, William J. Jr., Trombone
Chelekis, Philip, Percussion, 1991
Chen, Kelvin L., Trumpet, 1976
Cheney, Douglas P., Percussion, 1972
Cheng, Hans H.
Chersack, Walter J.
Chevallard,Philip C., Baritone
Chezick, Beverly J., Clarinet
Chirgwin, Martin E., Cornet, 1965
Chissus, Craig M., Trumpet, 1991
Christensen, Doug, Trombone, 1996
Christner, Richard, S.
Christopherson, Frederick A., Tuba
Christopherson, Gerald M.
Church, Jane, Alto Saxophone, 1975
Church, William R., 1968
Cilwa, Michelle, Alto Saxophone, 1994
Cisler, Lisa, Trumpet
Clark, Ann Marie (Scalia), Alto Saxophone, 1987
Clark, Barbara
Clark, Dalin, Tenor Saxophone, 1988
Clark II, Donald J., Baritone/ Piano
Clark, Jeff, Trumpet, 1983
Clark, Kenneth, Trumpet, 1980
Clark, Lisa, Flute, 1993
Clark, Robert D.
Clarke, Anne, Flute, Piccolo
Clarke, Theresa, Trumpet, 1992
Clavette, Gary, Tenor Saxophone
Clavette, Robert C.
Clee, Susan, Alto Saxophone, 1993
Clemens, Leroy S., Oboe
Clement, Timothy G., Baritone
Cleveland, David, Baritone, 1991
Clickard, Carrie L., Flag Color Guard
Clickard, Kyle S., Flag Color Guard
Close, Robert, Baritone
Coats, Dorothy H.
Cobb, Robert L.
Cockrell, Richard, Arranger, 1949
Cogsdill, Cherie L.
Cohrs, Nancy
Colby, Chuck, Tuba, 1993
Colby, Jennifer P., Trumpet, 1992
Cole, Greg, Percussion, 1993
Cole, Kimberly, Clarinet, 1994
Cole, Roy D.
Collar, Hiram D. Jr.
Collins, Bill, Trombone, 1990
Collins, David, Percussion, 1996
Collins, James S., 1968
Collins, Michael, Tuba, 1982
Collins, William, Trombone, 1994
Coltrane, Charles E., Flute
Coltrane, Linda A., Clarinet
Colwell, Jack, Flag,1988
Compton, Brian R., Tuba, 1992
Conklin, David, Trumpet, 1976
Conrad, Pete, Trumpet, 1986
Conway, Don
Cooke, June (Hale), Widow James
Coon, David M., Trombone, 1976

Coons, Martin G., French Horn
Cooper, Deni Jean, Flag Color Guard, 1988
Cooperider, John, Trombone, 1989
Copelin, Stephen J., French Horn
Corcoran, Mike J., Trombone, 1983
Cornell, Tom, Flag, 1976
Corns, David A.
Cosens, Lynne M., Alto Saxophone, 1989
Costar, Deborah, Alto Saxophone, 1981
Costar, Jim
Costello, Clarissa (Majors), Flag Corp, 1984
Cote, Richard G., Percussion, 1975
Court, Gayle
Cousins, Dennis A.
Cowelchuk, Glen, Tenor Saxophone, 1992
Cowell, Robert
Cox, Becky (Brown), Mellophone, 1991
Cox, Kevin, Alto Saxophone
Craig, John E., Percussion, 1971
Crandall, Tim, Trumpet, 1984
Crane, Donald E., Trumpet, 1942
Crawford, Marsha, Baritone
Crean, Joseph, Trumpet
Creaven, Terry
Cribbs, Mary L., French Horn
Cribbs, Steven R., Percussion, 1991
Crisp, Lisa, Flag Color Guard, 1994
Crissman, Molly, Trumpet, 1988
Crites, Russell G., Tuba, 1955
Cross, Cindy L.
Crowe, Elton, Trombone
Crownover, Charles A.
Crutcher, Damien, Mellophone, 1990
Cubbage, Donna, Alto Saxophone, 1984
Cubbage, Robert, Alto Saxophone, 1987
Cummings, Robert W.
Cunningham, Joshua, Percussion
Curnow, James E., Baritone
Curtis, Betsy A., Trombone, 1986

D

D'Arcangelis, Aurelio, Clarinet
D'Arcangelis, Judith, Flute
D'Arcangelis, Richard, Clarinet, 1972
Dailey, Janine, Flag Corps
Dailey, Steven, Percussion
Dale, Les, Percussion, Bass, 1974
Dalton, Darin, Alto Saxophone
Dalton, Scott, Trombone, 1994
Danner, Tracy, Mellophone, 1993
Darin, Karl, Trumpet, 1993
Darin, Keith, Trombone, 1993
Darling, Benjamin, Alto Saxophone, 1988
Das Gupta, Kolyan, Percussion, 1992
Davey, James H., Percussion, 1964
David, Shawn, Trombone, 1976
Davidson, Gail E.
Davies, Richard H.
Davis, Arthur, Trombone, 1994
Davis, Bradford G.
Davis, Edith L., Flute, 1978
Davis, Deland M. Jr., Clarinet, 1960
Davis, Richmond C. Jr.

Davis, Margaret
Davis, Mary (Shaw)
Dawson, Jerry E., Clarinet, 1956
Deacon, Brad, Bass Clarinet, 1993
Deal, William, Trumpet, 1975
Debutts, Dwane
Decamp, James C.
Deeb, Edward, Clarinet, 1960
Dekoning, David B., French Horn, 1966
DeKuiper, Mitzi, Flag Color Guard, 1993
DeLaFuente, Joe, Tuba
Dell, Heather, Flag/Big Ten
Dell, John, Trumpet, 1972
Delpup, Sue, Alto Saxophone, 1978
Delvecchio, Patty, Tuba, 1985
Demint, Jeanne, Alto Saxophone, 1984
Demos, Peter J., Clarinet
Dempsey, Thomas P.
Denbrock, William B., Alto Saxophone, 1984
DePlonty, Brian, Trumpet, 1996
Derby, Gail M., French Horn
Dermody, Erin, Trumpet, 1995
Derr, Tom, 1958
Desmet, Karen, (Laird) Flag, 1979
Detgen, Stacie, Mellophone, 1986
Deuby, Shawn P., French Horn
Devera, Leslie, Trumpet, 1988
Devey, Richard E., Clarinet
DeVoll, Joyce (Esch), Baritone, 1957
DeWalt, Dave, Percussion, 1979
DeWitt, Lori, Alto Saxophone, 1984
Diamond, Larry M., Alto Saxophone
Dickens, Bonnie W., Trombone, 1981
Dickens, Edward H., Trombone, 1979
Dickie, Jennifer (Topic), Flag Color Guard, 1991
Dietlin, Jean, Clarinet, 1993
Dietz, Norman C., Baritone
Dike, Donald K., Snare Drum, 1985
Dike, Karen, Alto Saxophone, 1985
Dillard, Lea P., Clarinet
Dilley, Allen L., Clarinet
Dineen, Michael, Trumpet, 1984
Divish, Daniel E., Clarinet
Dixon, Anne, E.
Dixon, Jonathan, Trumpet
Dobbertin, James H., French Horn
Dobbs, William D.
Docksey III, Frank, Trumpet, 1969
Docksey, Nancy, Flute, 1971
Dodd, Michelle, Flag Color Guard, 1993
Dodge, Michael J.
Doerr, Jan, Alto Saxophone
Doherty, Richard T., 1984
Dolson, Kathleen M., Percussion, 1984
Domanski, Mona, Flag Corp
Dombroske, Carol, Alto Saxophone
Dombroske, Olan C., Alto Saxophone, 1973
Dombroske, Paul G., Alto Bassoon, 1977
Dominik, William C.
Donnellon, John P., Trumpet
Donovan, Ryan, Trumpet, 1993

Dorvinen, Michael C.
Doss, Dean, Tuba, 1992
Dougherty, Don, Trumpet, 1979
Dowling, Eugene A., Tuba
Downey, Brian R., Trombone, 1970
Downey, Carlyn, Flag Corp
Doyle, Brian, Saxophone, 1995
Draeger, Rachel (Hyde), Flag, 1989
Draeger, Tim, Tuba, 1986
Dragosh, Pam, Trombone
Drenth, Michael J., Trombone, 1994
Drinjak, Christopher, Oboe, 1994
Driver, James R.
Driver, Martha (Hess), French Horn
Droscha, Jeanna, French Horn, 1995
Droscha, Jon, Tuba, 1991
Droscha, Ruben, Cornet, 1965
Drummond, Burton J., Trombone
Drury, Kara (O'Dell), Flag Color Guard,
    1985
Dryfoos, Robin J., Alto Saxophone, 1982
Dubach, Chris, Percussion, 1989
Dudley, Laurie, Trumpet
Dudley, Leitha G.
Dukes, Carla'nne, Flag Color Guard
Dulan, Amy J., 1991
Dunbar, George A.
Duncan, James R., Percussion
Duncan, John W.
Duncan Leslie (DeVera), Trumpet, 1988
Duncan, Thomas, Flag, 1984
Duncan, Tim, Alto Saxophone, 1994
Dunham, Dirk, Baritone, 1978
Dunham, Penny (Beckerson), Trombone,
    1979
Dunlop, Nancy (Kalso), Flute, 1976
Dunn, Ron, Alto Saxophone, 1956
Du Puis, Tania, Mellophone, 1994
Dura, Michelle, Saxophone, 1991
Durham, Dennis, Tuba, 1990
Durham, Geanna (Schlueter), Twirler, 1989
Durham, Robert, Trumpet, 1987
Durham, Scott, Trombone, 1993
Durkee, Eldon, Clarinet, 1936
Dutchik, Jim
Dux, Robert D.
Dye, Bruce H., Trumpet, 1967
Dye, James, B., Trumpet/Drums

E

Eareckson, Sue, Flute
Earp, Janice, Flag/Flute, 1991
Easterday, B.C., Clarinet, 1952
Eastham, Glenn D., Clarinet, 1926
Ebbeson, Dalton, Baritone, 1946
Ebenhoeh, Carol L.
Ebersole, Richard W., Trombone
Eckstrom, Jeff
Eddy, Mel
Eddy, Tom
Edwards, Douglas, Trumpet, 1979
Eidam, Porter B., Percussion, 1991
Eidson, John C.
Eilerson, Sally (Webb)

Eklund, Coy G.
Eldredge, David, Tuba
Eldridge, Barry C.
Elie, Albert H., Tenor Saxophone
Elie, Mary L., Tenor Saxophone
Ellickson, Kim, Horn
Elliot, Fred O., Trumpet, 1943
Elliot, Betty (Lowe), Alto Saxophone
Elliot, Matt, Trumpet, 1989
Ellis, Donna J., Oboe
Ellis, Emil G., Trumpet, 1947
Elmhirst, Dennis, Trombone, 1993
Elmore, Mike C., Tuba
Elmore, Frederick D.
Elmore, Mike
Elsenheimer, Denise E.
Elton, Cheryl, Percussion, 1989
Elwell, Roy, Trumpet, 1949
Emery, Marianne E.
Emery, Thomas J., Trumpet, 1965
Emmons, Dennis L., Clarinet, 1965
Emmons, Kimberly L., Trumpet, 1987
Emmons, Susan S., Flute
Engelhardt, Jack D.
English, Sam
Epperly, Michael, S.
Erdman, James W., Trombone
Erickson, Alan J.
Erickson, Ken, 1975
Erickson, Martin D., Tuba
Ernst, Alice (Renton), Mellophone, 1988
Ernst, Garret M., Alto Saxophone, 19910
Esch, Andrew, Horn, 1986
Esch, Kimberly G., Flag Color Guard
Esch, Victor E., Trumpet
Essenberg, Randy, Trombone, 1980
Ethington, Bradley P., Trumpet, 1978
Evans, Bradley A.
Evans, Robert W., Trumpet, 1992
Everett, Cindy L., Flag, 1981
Everhart, Viki, Trumpet, 1982
Everson, Dana F., Alto Saxophone, 1976
Eyke, David, Percussion, 1983

F

Faber, Benton, Baritone, 1993
Facktor, Patricia L., 1962
Facktor, Ronald D., 1962
Fadie, Steven F.
Falcoff, Monte L., Trumpet
Falcone, Baryl, French Horn, 1962
Falcone, Cecilia Y., French Horn
Falconer, Dave, Percussion, 1977
Falkinburg, Eric L., Alto Saxophone, 1992
Fan, Sheau-Ru, Flute, 1994
Farhat, Ray, Trumpet, 1988
Farley, Thomas
Farrell, Michael, Trumpet, 1995
Farwell, Bruce, Trumpet, 1987
Faulstick, Luke, Trumpet, 1985
Fauth, Greg, Cornet, 1969
Fee, William C.
Feeney, Kathleen A., Flag Corp, 1984
Feeney, Sharon J., French Horn

Feiler, Matt, Percussion, 1989
Feist, Timothy J., Tenor Saxophone, 1985
Fellabaum, William M.
Ferrari, Michael R.
Ferris, Clement J.
Fettig, James H.
Fickett, Jean, Clarinet, 1954
Findlay, Elizabeth, Clarinet, 1991
Fink, Robert R., French Horn
Fink, Ruth J.
Fink, Stephanie, Baritone TC, 1993
Finnicum, Qunde, Percussion
Fischer, Joan
Fish, James E., Trombone
Fisher, Kenneth M., Alto Saxophone
Fisher, Allen, Flag, 1993
Fisher, Barbara J. (Wagner), Baritone,
    1960
Fisher, Michael, Baritone
Fisk, Al, Trombone, 1978
Fisk, Fred, Baritone TC, 1982
Fisk, Howland W., Baritone TC, 1959
Fisk, John, Trombone, 1985
Fitts, Ann E.
Fitts, David, Bassoon
Fitzgerald, Dennis K.
Fitzgerald, Russell, Trumpet, 1985
Fitzko, John, Baritone, 1985
Flahiv, Craig R., Percussion
Fleckenstein, Donna L.
Flegel, Dane R.
Flounders, Leslie P. Jr., 1960
Fluder, John E., Baritone
Foerch, David B.
Fogarsi, Darcy
Fogle, Becky, Alto Saxophone
Foley, Leann M., Flag Corp
Folkertsma, James
Fordon, Ann, Alto Saxophone, 1986
Fornari, David G., Trumpet, 1991
Forsyth, Kevin, Mellophone, 1992
Foss, Eric M.
Foster, Brian E., Alto Saxophone, 1995
Foster, Richard
Foster, Stacey, Mellophone, 1989
Fowler, Brad, Trumpet, 1982
Fowler, Pamela, K., Trombone, 1982
Fox, Laurine C., Trumpet
Fox, Timothy M., Flag, 1985
Fox, Tracey, Alto Saxophone/Flute, 1984
Frame, Robert W., 1958
Francis, John J., 1975
Francis, John, Trumpet, 1989
Francke, Leonard N. Jr.,
Frank, Mary Kay, (Bronson), 1978
Frankena, Frederick, L.
Franklin, Larry R., Clarinet, 1959
Franklin, Susan E., Bass Clarinet
Fraser, Bruce M.
Fraser, Rodney K., Trombone, 1975
Frayer, David J., Saxophone, 1988
Fredericks, Thomas S., Trumpet, 1976
Freedman, Thomas P., French Horn
Freel, Susan (Reece), Oboe, 1960

Freeman, Deborah, Clarinet, 1973
Friebe, John W., Trumpet, 1984
Fringer, Bradley, Trumpet
Frisch, Bill, Tuba
Fritz, Ben P., Trombone, 1985
Fritz, Tracey, Flag Color Guard, 1993
Fritz, William A.
Frommer, Larry, Percussion, 1988
Fry, Leonard D.
Fuller Gene E., Tuba, 1969
Fuller, John, Clarinet, 1951
Fuller, Steven D.
Fullerton, Charles, H.
Fulton, Lisa, Trumpet
Furbush, John P., Clarinet, 1954

G

Gage, Marjorie, French Horn
Gaines, David, Trumpet
Galbraith, Glenn, Tuba, 1981
Gallihugh, Margaret, Alto Saxophone, 1983
Gallihugh, Mike, Alto Saxophone, 1984
Galm, James D., French Horn
Gammicchia, Kim
Gardner, Dwain P., Alto Saxophone, 1972
Gardner, William G., Clarinet
Gardstrom, Susan, Flute
Garlock, Ann, Alto Saxophone, 1987
Garlock, Diedra, Flute, 1984
Garlock, Gary, Trumpet, 1986
Garvin, Jo Ann N., Trumpet, 1967
Garvin, Melford, Trumpet, 1966
Gates, William H., Percussion, 1943
Gause, Patricia A.
Gawart, Susan (Rosenkranz)
Geers, Bob, Trumpet
Geis, Karl, Trombone, 1991
Geminder, Philip H.
Gentile, Joseph F., Trumpet, 1964
German, Lawrence L., Trombone, 1941
Gerold, Noel, Trumpet, 1982
Gettings, Janet K.
Ghilani, Patrick, Percussion, 1989
Gholson, James Jr., Clarinet
Gibbs, Ronald, Baritone, 1964
Gibson, Marikay, Alto Saxophone, 1980
Gilbert, Dean S., Trombone, 1986
Gillan, Michael A.
Gillett, Jeffrey R., Trumpet, 1986
Gillette, Deborah
Gillette, Donald, R.
Gillette, James R.
Gillette, Tom, Bariton
Gillies, Peter C., Tuba
Gilpin, Bryan, Trumpet, 1993
Gilzow, Douglas F.
Gingrich, Fredric D., Bassoon
Ginther, Jennifer (Vincent), French Horn, 1991
Girand, Matt, Trumpet
Girand, Mike, Trumpet, 1991
Girard, Rita, Percussion Bass, 1989
Gitersonke, Matt, Flag
Gludstone, Paul, Alto Saxophone, 1975

Glass, Jeff, J., Tuba, 1984
Gleason, James R., Trumpet
Gleason, Nancy
Glenn, Chris W., Trombone
Glidden, Randle
Glovac, Barbara (Duncan), Alto Saxophone, 1980
Goetz, Ann, Baritone BC, 1989
Goff, Danforth O., Percussion, 1966
Goff, Iris, Flute
Golden, Patricia A., Clarinet, 1991
Golden, Sandra C., 1961
Goldsworthy, Richard, Trombone
Goodburne, Christopher, Trombone, 1993
Goodburne, Stuart, Trombone, 1988
Goodman, Amy (Heisler), Alto Saxophone, 1993
Goodrich, Douglas, Baritone BC
Goodrich, Jane, Flute/Piccolo
Goodrich, Lawrence J.
Goodridge, Gary R., Percussion Bass, 1979
Goodsell, Robert J., Trumpet, 1979
Goodstein, Richard K., Clarinet, 1961
Goodwin, Debra S., Percussion/Bass, 1984
Goodwin, Suzanne (Kuenzli), Percussion, 1984
Gordon, Gary P., Alto Saxophone, 1973
Gorsuch, Diane, Trumpet, 1991
Gotko, Vincent J., Tenor Saxophone, 1985
Gott, Sara G., Flute, 1992
Gottschalk, Claytin K., 1959
Gould, Bob, Trumpet, 1990
Gould, Susan (Wiengandt), Alto Saxophone/Flute, 1991
Gould, Todd, 1991
Gourley, William W., Trumpet, 1976
Gouth, Pauline V., Alto Saxophone, 1982
Gradowski, Elaine (Tucker), Flute, 1969
Gradowski, John W., Alto Saxophone, 1969
Grafius, Edward J., French Horn
Graham, Carol M.
Graham, Craig C., Trumpet, 1984
Grainger, George
Gram, Eric, Trombone, 1993
Gramer, Russel A.
Grant, Charles (Bud), Alto Saxophone, 1954
Grant, Ronald B.
Granthen, Gary, Trumpet, 1985
Grattan, Kristin, Alto Saxophone, 1994
Gray, James, Baritone
Gray, John, Bass Clarinet
Green, Charles, Trumpet, 1978
Green, Robert, Baritone, 1994
Greene, Kathryn A., 1967
Greenlee, Joe W.
Grewe, Angela
Grieve, Harold R., Alto Saxophone, 1960
Grieve, Nadine R., Bassoon, 1960
Griffith, Janet, Trumpet
Griffith, Michael, Oboe
Griffiths, Jim, Trombone
Griffiths, Julie B., French Horn

Grindall, Ron, Percussion, 1992
Gringorten, Reesa, Clarinet
Grischke, Paul R., Clarinet
Grochowski, Catherine, French Horn
Gronda, Amy, Mellophone, 1992
Grove, James H., Trombone, 1984
Grove, Roger L., Baritone
Gruber, Dale C., Saxophone, 1978
Guijio, Jessica, Clarinet, 1993
Guibault, Denise M.
Guitar, Marianne E., Trumpet
Guitar, Ralph M., Trumpet
Gulash, Mary K., Saxophone
Gulick, Kristine, Alto Saxophone
Gulick, Matt L., Trombone
Gulick, Terri, Flag Color Guard, 1992
Gulick, Traci, Flag Color Guard, 1992
Gulliver, Richard, Trombone
Gulliver, Robert S., Clarinet, 1940
Guthaus, Cindy, Alto Saxophone, 1981

H

Haering, Richard, Trumpet
Hagan, Steve, Trombone, 1986
Hagan, Thomas, Trumpet, 1985
Hageman, Elizabeth, 1989
Hager, Harry S., French Horn
Hagy, Brian, Clarinet, 1991
Haines, Kari, Flag Color Guard, 1993
Haines, William C., Trumpet, 1964
Halinski, Donna, Alto Saxophone, 1986
Hall, Richard W.
Haller, Dan, Tuba
Halls, Brad, Percussion, 1987
Halls, Heather (Spry), Alto Saxophone, 1988
Hally, Enver, Flag, 1987
Halvas, Duane, Percussion, 1978
Ham, Rodney A., Trombone, 1962
Hamlin, Jennifer, Trombone
Hammar, Eric, Trombone, 1976
Hammond, R. Michael, Percussion, 1986
Hanson, Eugene R., Percussion
Hanushek, Phil, Trumpet, 1989
Harbour, Charles E., Alto Saxophone, 1987
Harding, Scott, Percussion, 1994
Hardoin, Jennifer (Dobbs), Flag Color Guard, 1993
Hardoin, Kevin M., Trumpet, 1985
Hardoin, Rebecca, Flag Color Guard, 1992
Harrington, Vicky S., Flag Corp, 1991
Harris, Dustin, Tuba, 1994
Harris, Kimberlee, Flag Color Guard, 1990
Harrison, Tim, Percussion, 1995
Hart, Mary S., French Horn
Hart, Thomas, Tuba, 1976
Hart, William, Trumpet
Hartner, David A., French Horn
Hartsoe, Brad, Percussion
Harvey, Robert, Percussion, 1985
Hass, Kathleen S.
Hasselhuhn, Johanna, Tenor Saxophone, 1993
Haston, Jeffrey L., Trumpet, 1978

Haston, Lisa, Alto Saxophone, 1978
Hatch, Colleen
Hatfield, Jason, Tuba
Hathaway, Roger J., Tuba, 1960
Hatton, James D.
Haubenstricker, Cathy (King), Alto
    Saxophone, 1982
Haughey, Christopher L., Trombone, 1985
Haupricht, Christine M., Alto Saxophone,
    1989
Hautau, Richard, Tuba, 1966
Haven, John, Tuba, 1992
Hays, Laurie, French Horn
Hayward, Patty, Flag, 1983
Hazlett, Leslie (Videan), French Horn, 1981
Hazlett, Timothy J., Drum Major, 1982
Healey, Michael, Percussion, 1987
Heavener, Blain, Trombone, 1993
Heckert, William F.
Hedlund, Denise (Oakley), Alto Saxophone,
    1991
Hedlund, Thomas, Trombone, 1991
Heemer, A.R., Baritone, 1966
Hegerberg, Thad, Clarinet
Heide, Renee (Hatch), Trumpet, 1988
Helmbold, Chris N., Trombone, 1970
Helmboldt, Bruce A.
Helmer, Bruce G., Clarinet, 1948
Helmsley, Kathy
Hemsworth, Douglas
Henderson, Robert A.
Henderson, William, Percussion, 1980
Henry, Margaret, Flag Color Guard, 1995
Henry, Teri L., Flag Color Guard, 1988
Hercik, James S., Trumpet, 1973
Herrell, Richard, Tenor Saxophone
Herrington, Dan B., Clarinet, 1961
Herrington, Mike, Tenor Saxophone
Herrinton, Dan B., 1961
Herrinton, Lisa (Rumple), Twirler
Herscher, Dale C.
Herscher, Ellen, French Horn
Hershman, Edward, Trumpet, 1975
Heskitt-Heiser, Pamela J., French Horn
Hess, Bruce T., Trumpet, 1957
Hess, Carol, Trumpet, 1957
Hewitt, Michael, Trumpet
Hicks, Carolle (Thompson), Tenor Saxo-
    phone, 1989
Hicks, Gary L., Flag, 1976
Hicks, Todd, Trumpet, 1988
Higgins, Ronald J., Trumpet, 1965
Hilarides, Jeffrey C., Alto Saxophone
Hilgendorf, Chris, Trumpet, 1989
Hill, Vaughn, Trombone
Hilliker, Curt, Alto Saxophone, 1988
Hillstrom, Phil, French Horn
Hilton, Russ, Trumpet, 1988
Himelhoch, David
Hirt, Harry C., Baritone
Hobart, Tavia, Tuba, 1998
Hodges, Daniel, Tuba, 1993
Hodson, William, Trombone
Hoey, Timothy J., Trombone, 1983

Hoffer, Charles R. J., Flute/Clarinet
Hoffman, Dave, French Horn, 1987
Hoffman, Steward B. Jr.
Hoffman, Stephan
Hofmeister, Karl
Hogan, Melissa, Alto Saxophone, 1988
Holcombe, George, Tuba, 1991
Holleman, James A., French Horn
Holley, Darin, Trumpet
Hollinger, Paul
Hollingsworth, Richard
Holmes, Jonathan, Trombone
Holmes, Mark
Holzhei, Greg, Trombone, 1993
Hondorp, Kevin, Trumpet, 1991
Honsinger, James
Hood, Laura, French Horn
Hooper, Dennis, French Horn, 1964
Hooper, Patricia (Belleville), 1972
Hoover, Jennifer (Northrup), Trumpet,
    1989
Hoppe, Rene, Percussion, 1991
Hora, Otto J., Saxophone
Horness, Joseph W., Flute, 1949
Hornung, Cynthia, Mellophone, 1994
Horsic, Lori A., Bass Clarinet
Horton, William S.
Hoshield, Dennis, Baritone TC
Hoskins, Gary, Trumpet, 1969
Hosmer, Margaret A.
Hostetter, Paul H., Trombone
Hough, Raymond, Drum Major
Houghton, Aimee M., Trombone, 1980
Houghton, Mike, Trombone, 1993
House, Harold D., Trumpet, 1969
House, Kimberly L., Flag Color Guard,
    1992
Houston, Eileen, Trombone, 1962
Houston, Robert, Trumpet, 1967
Howe, Larry, Alto Saxophone, 1989
Howse, Dennis P., Trombone, 1968
Hraba, Michelle, Flag Color Guard, 1993
Hrabowecki, Diana, Trombone, 1986
Hribek, Craig, Tenor Saxophone, 1984
Hruska, John R. Jr., Trombone, 1982
Hudson, Keith, Clarinet, 1968
Hudson, Jean (Brack), Flute
Huey, Jerry, Trumpet
Hufford, David, Tuba, 1987
Hufford, Denise (Rau), Flag Color Guard,
    1987
Hughes, John P., Alto Horn, 1973
Huibley, Scott, 1988
Huizinga, Sue (Townley), Tenor Saxo-
    phone, 1989
Hulbert, Warren, Trumpet, 1989
Hull, Richard, Big Ten Flag
Hunt, Dennis
Hunter, George, Trumpet, 1994
Hurlbert, Deanna, Baritone
Hussey, Stephanie, Flute, 1993
Huston, Geovany, Baritone, 1993
Hyler II, David S., Alto Saxophone, 1984

I

Ifkovits, Joyce, Flag Color Guard
Illman, Richard, Trumpet
Irish, Gerald E.
Irish, Shirley A.
Iuele, John, Trumpet
Iverson, Michael, Alto Saxophone, 1992

J

Jackson, Cheryl, Bass Clarinet, 1996
Jackson, Mark, Clarinet, 1991
Jackson, Patricia (Keilen), Alto Saxophone,
    1979
Jackson, Timothy, Tuba, 1978
Jackson, Todd, Flag, 1991
Jacob, Joseph F.
Jacobs, Julie, French Horn, 1993
Jaksa, Tracy A. (Gardner), Alto Saxo-
    phone, 1983
James, Matthew C.
Jardot, Bernard R.
Jarrard, Dennis J., Alto Saxophone, 1988
Jarrett, Bruce, Tuba, 1994
Jed, Laurie A., French Horn
Jed, Timothy, Trumpet, 1988
Jefferson, Cedric T.
Jenks, Earle, Clarinet, 1960
Jennings, Howard H.
Jeschke, David, Percussion
Jeschke, Kathy, Trumpet
Jeschke, Martin, Trombone
Jessup, James R.
Jewett, Jennifer, Tenor Saxophone, 1994
Johnkoski, Stephen V., Trombone, 1976
Johnson, Amy, Trumpet, 1991
Johnson, Andrew P.
Johnson, Bill, Trumpet, 1957
Johnson, Clifford
Johnson, Curtis A.
Johnson, Donald, Alto Saxophone, 1976
Johnson, Elwyn K.
Johnson, Kenneth W.
Johnson, Mark, Trombone, 1979
Johnson, Ronald, Alto Saxophone, 1967
Johnson, Terry, Percussion, 1972
Johnson, Thalia
Johnson, William E.
Johnston, Albert K., Percussion
Johnston, Brigitte
Johnston, Gerald, Trombone, 1963
Jones, Charles L, Tuba, 1983
Jones, Chuck, Trumpet
Jones, David V.
Johnson, Donald G. Trumpet, 1983
Jones, Harold R., Trumpet
Jones, Jeffery R., Flag, 1972
Jones, Kenneth R., French Horn
Jones, Travis, Percussion, 1988
Jordan, Jamie, Trumpet, 1995
Jorgensen, Robert D., Baritone
Joseph, Otis
Judson, Nathan L., Mellophone, 1984
Juenemann, Julie A.
Jupp, Ropert P., Percussion 1966

K

Kaiser, Barb (Patterson), Baritone, 1993
Kaiser, Chris, Tuba, 1992
Kaiser, Richard, Trombone
Kajor, Carol M.
Kalcevic, Christine E., Percussion, 1975
Kamish, Michael, Trombone, 1986
Kamlay, James A.
Kanicki, Carolyn J. (Ward), French Horn
Kapolka, Dave, Trumpet, 1989
Kapuska, Janice O.
Karoub, Jeff, Alto Saxophone, 1991
Karpinen, Joanne, Percussion, 1992
Karriker, Galen, Percussion, 1994
Kaskey, Monica A., Percussion
Kates, Robert, Baritone, 1991
Kato, Joel, Trumpet, 1991
Kato, Matt, Drum Major, 1994
Kaufman, Beth (Mylnarek), Twirler, 1975
Kaufman, Alford G. Jr., Tuba
Kaufman, Michael, Alto Horn, 1976
Kay, Karl W.
Keech, Robert R., Trumpet
Keenan, Susana (Woloson), Trombone, 1985
Kehler, David T., Drum
Keller, Dee (Whitacker), Percussion 1987
Keller, Rick, Percussion/Bass, 1987
Kelly, Cindi (Rosner), Clarinet
Kelly, Kathleen, Flag Corp, 1987
Kempf, Susan (Shoemaker), Trumpet, 1986
Kendall, Corinna, Alto Saxophone, 1993
Kendig, Sean C., Flag Color Guard, 1994
Kerastas III, John W., Trombone
Kerbleski, Julie L., Trumpet, 1983
Kerby, Natalie M.
Kern, Andrew J., Baritone BC, 1991
Kern, Matt, Percussion, 1989
Kersten, Scott, Tenor Saxophone, 1995
Kestenholtz, Sam, Percussion, 1991
Kiel, Christine
Kim, Walter, Percussion, 1995
Kimball, Alan E., Clarinet, 1968
Kimble, Lori, French Horn
King, Daniel R., Trumpet, 1980
King, Shari A., Trumpet, 1987
King, Sherry
King, Tamara
Kionka, Riina R., Trumpet
Kirby, Brett, Trumpet, 1990
Kirby, Paul H.
Kiter, Steven W., Trumpet, 1990
Kitzman, Christine E., French Horn
Kitzman, Howard C., Trumpet, 1949
Kjellberg, David, Tuba
Klass, James C., Alto Saxophone, 1977
Klass, Michael L., Tuba, 1981
Klein, David, Trombone, 1986
Klein, Jeff, Mellophone, 1995
Kleist, Mary L., Percussion
Kline, Paul D., Alto Saxophone, 1975
Klink, Brian, Trombone, 1987
Kloha, John A., Clarinet

Klump, Brian, Alto Saxophone
Knakal, Richard, Tuba, 1981
Knapp, Marnie, Trumpet, 1991
Knappe, Edmund F. Jr.,
Knas, Karl, Tuba, 1994
Knas, Ken, Alto Saxophone, 1981
Knazik, Stephen, R., Trombone, 1979
Knecht, Dina, Trumpet
Knight, Andrew L, Trombone, 1973
Knipe, Carl E., Trumpet, 1974
Knitter, Scott, Alto Saxophone, 1983
Knowlton, Christopher B., Baritone BC, 1991
Koch, Heather, Flute
Koch, Linda, Clarinet, 1984
Kocher, Jeff, Trumpet, 1984
Koepele, Brian J., 1986
Koepele, Debra A., Trumpet, 1985
Kohlenberg, Ken, Trumpet, 1979
Kokochak, Cherie L., Trumpet, 1983
Koning, Paul D.,1981
Korpi, Ed, Tuba, 1989
Korte, Don, Tenor Saxophone, 1948
Kostas, Emmanuel, French Horn
Kostoff, John S., Clarinet, 1960
Kot, Eric
Kot, James R.
Kotter, Laurie
Kozachik, Michael, Baritone, 1972
Kozyra, Michelle, Alto Saxophone, 1994
Kraman, Michael F., French Horn
Kramer, Ronald D., Tuba, 1988
Kraus, Randy, Trombone
Krause, Gerald G., Tuba, 1979
Kressler, David S., Trumpet, 1970
Kressler, Jeffrey A., Trumpet, 1969
Kressler, Peter B.
Klrieger, Corey, Mellophone, 1982
Krieger, Kevin J., Saxophone, 1985
Krill, Susan J.
Kriner, Robert, French Horn
Krive, Kent J., Clarinet
Krolczyk, James, Trombone
Kroopnick, Richard E.
Krukemyer, Darlene (Kanitz), Percussion, 1988
Krupp, Carrie J., Flag Color Guard
Kucharek, Kelly J., French Horn
Kuehn, Mark A., Trumpet, 1975
Kuehnl, Deborah, Trumpet, 1988
Kuenker, Kay, French Horn
Kuhn, Kurt D., Tuba, 1987
Kulp, Dannene, Clarinet, 1995
Kurth, Thomas C., Alto Saxophopne, 1990
Kurzyna, Laura, Mellophone, 1988
Kurzyna, Susan J., Alto Saxophone, 1986
Kusek, Tom, Tuba, 1985
Kutscher, Susan L.
Kuzmich, John A., French Horn

L

LaBarge, James A., French Horn
Ladd, Michelle (Caruso)
LaDuke, Lance, Baritone, 1990

LaFountaine, David, Baritone, 1976
Laird, James J., Alto Saxophone
Laird, Rhonda N., Tenor Saxophone
Lammers, Jeffrey P., Baritone
Lampman, Nathaniel, Trombone, 1995
Lampman, Nicole (Kropf), Mellophone, 1995
Land, Colleen R., Trumpet, 1988
Landree, James H., Baritone/Trumpet, 1949
Langdon, Gary C., Trumpet, 1965
Langenberg, David, Baritone BC, 1976
Lapinski, Michael, Trumpet, 1978
LaPrise, Darren, Trombone, 1995
Lark, Susan, Mellophone
LaRowe, Todd, Trumpet, 1989
Larsen, Tage, Trumpet
Lauxman, Cindy, Clarinet, 1991
Lavery, Sharon, Alto Saxophone, 1991
Lawson, David, Alto Saxophone, 1985
Lawson, Jay, Percussion, 1994
Lawson, Kay, Bassoon, 1991
Lawson, Steve, French Horn, 1991
Leach, Joel T., Percussion
Leahy, David, Trumpet, 1988
Leavens, Glen P., Trumpet, 1981
Lebow, Susan H.
Leckrone, Jan H., French Horn
Lecy, Melissa (Mason), Trombone, 1985
Lederer, Robert, Alto Saxophone, 1993
Lefebvre, Audra, Trumpet, 1993
Leimback, Joe, Alto Saxophone, 1978
Leipprandt, John, Baritone, 1954
Leith, Stephen S.
Lemmons, Keith, Clarinet
Leonard, Kati, Alto Saxophone, 1996
Leopard, Jack M.
Lepard, John, Percussion
Lerandowski, Paul, Tuba, 1992
LeRoy, Ann, Mellophone, 1992
Leslie, Warren P., Baritone, 1985
Leson, Aaron, Trumpet, 1989
Letton, Lucy T., French Horn
Levia, Beth, Oboe
Levine, Ian, Percussion
Levine, Joseph, Clarinet, 1962
Levine, Rhonda (Vesta), Alto Saxophone, 1986
Lewis, Charles R.
Lewis, Cheryl E.
Lewis, David, Baritone, 1989
Lewis, Lynn C., Percussion/Snare, 1964
Lewis, Patricia, Clarinet, 1970
Lewis, Steve, Trumpet, 1970
Liao, Ju-hsin, Clarinet, 1993
Lichau, Jason, Trumpet, 1995
Liddle, Wayne C., Clarinet, 1956
Lightfoot, Brent, Flag, 1992
Lighthiler, Mark, Percussion
Lilly, Steven, Trombone, 1993
Lin, Tsuhsin, Clarinet, 1994
Lindsey, Gregory J., Trombone, 1975
Linehan, Leslie A., Flag Color Guard, 1982

Linley, Sarah (Lewis), Flag Color Guard, 1992
Linley, Steven, Percussion, 1991
Lipa, Paul J., Alto Saxophone
Lipson, Daniel J., Trumpet, 1981
Livingstone, John E., Percussion
Lloyd, Alex H., Trumpet, 1995
Locke, Ian, Tuba, 1994
Lockwood, Jane E., Bassoon
Lockwood, Kathryn, Alto Saxophone, 1990
Lockyer, Tom, Twirler, 1969-1971
Lodge, Richard D., Percussion, 1969
Long, Michelle (Jackson), Flag Color Guard, 1989
Long, Richard L., Trumpet
Lopez, Angela, Alto Saxophopne, 1995
Lopez, Daniel, Trumpet, 1994
Lorah, Theodore R., Jr., Tuba
Lott, Paul L., Percussion/Bass, 1978
Louden, Vertis, Band Manager
Louder, Earle L., Baritone
Lounsbury, Heather (Towsley), Trumpet, 1988
Love, Kent, Tuba, 1993
Lovy, Jordan
Lower, Dave, Trombone, 1976
Lower, John A.
Lucia, Christina M.
Luckenbill, John W. Jr., Tuba
Luckenbill, Robert R.
Luedtke, Kevin T., Tuba, 1981
Lunde, Robert, Baritone BC, 1993
Lundgren, Carl S.
Luntz, William
Luoma, James R.
Lutsch, Andy, Trombone, 1985
Lutz, Merrit M., Percussion, 1967
Lynch, Thomas, Saxophone, 1995
Lyon, C.K., Flute, 1973

M

Maccani, Lee W., 1956
MacDonald, Margaret A.
Mace, David, Percussion/Snare
Mack, Andrea, Trombone, 1989
Mackay, Lachlan R. Trumpet, 1988
MacKay, Tamra, Flag Color Guard, 1989
Mackenzie, Mark S.
Mackey, Melissa (Brown), Alto Saxophone, 1988
Madden, John T., Trumpet
Madden, Joseph P., Baritone TC, 1989
Madden, Shelly, Flag Color Guard, 1985
Magee, Terry N., Baritone
Magistro, Amy, Flag Big Ten, 1986
Mahar, Angela, Flag Color Guard
Maksimchuk, Thomas G., Alto Saxophone, 1972
Mallires, Stephen, Trumpet, 1985
Malott, Krista, Mellophone, 1989
Mandel, Adam J., Percussion
Manderfield, William E.
Manett, Sheri (Dolson), Trumpet, 1981
Mangon, Steve

Manthe, Ellen, French Horn, 1995
Maples, Roger W.
Marklewitz, John W.
Markley, Greg, Percussion, 1989
Marks, Brad, Tuba, 1989
Markwick, Jack, Trumpet, 1970
Marque, Marjorie, French Horn
Marrah, James A., Alto Horn, 1989
Marshall, Gerald F.
Marshall III, Herbert (Butch) D., French Horn, 1985
Marshall, Jerry R., Baritone, BC, 1965
Marshall, Larry, Alto Saxophone, 1991
Martel-Miller, Alice, French Horn, 1965
Martin, Lee Anne, Tenor Saxophone, 1992
Martin, Mark A.
Martin, Mindy, Flag Color Guard, 1993
Martinek, Ken, Tuba, 1981
Martinson, Todd, Trumpet, 1988
Martzke, Gary L, Trumpet
Martzke, Rich, Trumpet, 1969
Marwede, Kelly, Mellophone, 1988
Marwede, Leif P., Percussion
Marwick, John N., Trumpet, 1970
Marx, Gary, Trumpet, 1973
Marx, Linda, Alto Horn, 1979
Mason, Melody, Trombone, 1983
Masters, Jay T., Percussion, 1983
Mathews, Robert W.
Matkin, Robert J.
Matson, Kevin
Mattson, Dan, Trombone, 1993
Mattson, John, Trombone
Mattson, Morton E., Baritone, 1968
Matyanawski, Marie L., Flute, 1993
Matzen, Thomas O., Trumpet, 1982
Matzen, Wendy (Judson)
Mau, Robert Jr., Tuba, 1986
Mawby, Carolyn, Trumpet
Mayne, Joe, Alto Saxophone, 1993
McAnulty, Carol L., Clarinet
McCaffrey, James E., Percussion, 1980
McCaffrey, Kevin P., Percussion
McCaffrey, Mindy (Nash), Alto Saxophone, 1991
McCaffrey, Susan L., Alto Saxophone, 1981
McCall, Bruce, Oboe
McCargar, Wright B., French Horn, 1977
McClay, Diane, Trumpet, 1989
McCluer, Mac, Flute
McClure, Norman C.
McConnell, Lynn T., Baritone BC, 1960
McCorkle, Donald, Clarinet
McCormick, Ann (Barrett) Flag Color Guard, 1986
McCormick, Dan H., Trumpet
McCoy, Kimberly, Trumpet, 1994
McCoy, Randall L., Flag
McCririe, Dale R.
McCubbrey, Douglas S., Flag,1980
McCulloch, Bryson, Alto Saxophone
McCullough, Pineabrim Jr., Trumpet, 1990
McCurdy, Lynn (Herrington), Trombone
McDaniel, Arlene P., Alto/Baritone, 1984

McDaniel, John T., Baritone BC, 1981
McDonald, David R.
McDonald, Edward, Percussion, 1989
McDonald, John, Percussion, 1967
McDonough, Ronald E.
McFarlin, Bill, Trumpet
McGee, Robert C., Trumpet
McGeen, Jody A.
McGowan, Patrick J., Percussion
McGreen, Donald, Bassoon
McGuire, Carol (Begian), Flute
McGuire, Mary, Trombone
McIntosh,Robert, Percussion, 1935
McIntyre, Janice E., Alto Horn, 1978
McKay, Donald W.
McKay, Robert W., Trombone, 1972
McKellar, Erin, Flag Color Guard, 1996
McKenna, Karen
McKenzie, Don, Alto Saxophone, 1995
McKinney, Michael A.
McKinney, Peter J., Percussion/Bass, 1986
McKoin, Sarah
McLaughlin, Daniel
McMahon, Karen, Tenor Saxophone, 1987
McManus, Mark E., Tenor Saxophone
McMurtry, Anthony H., Percussion
McNeal, Peggy J.
McNeilly, Paul, Trumpet, 1992
McPherson, Andrea, Alto Saxophone, 1995
McPherson, Cindy (Gould), Flag Color Guard, 1989
McWhorter, Ann E., Alto Saxophone
Mead, Jon A., Baritone, 1963
Mehne, John L., Bass Clarinet
Mehne, Wendy L., Flute
Melkin, David, Baritone/Trumpet, 1995
Melnick, Michael, Trombone
Melnick, Vickie, Alto Saxophone, 1991
Merz, Lisa, Alto Saxophone, 1984
Messina, Matthew, J., French Horn
Mette, Barbara J., French Horn
Metzger, Gary, Trombone, 1979
Meyer, John, Trombone
Meyer, Judith A., Oboe
Meyers, Mary, French Horn
Meyers, Robert F., Trumpet
Michael, Bruce
Michaud, Matthew, Trumpet, 1992
Middleton, James B.
Midgley, Cynthia, Alto Saxophone, 1989
Mike, Seraphime, Clarinet
Milano, Donald J.
Milch, Heather (Kane), Alto Saxophone, 1993
Milch, Kenneth, Baritone, 1993
Milchus, Sharon, Oboe, 1993
Miles, Martin L., Alto Saxophone
Miller, David, Baritone, 1991
Miller, Donald, Trumpet, 1968
Miller, Gerald K.
Miller, Glen, Trombone
Miller, Gregory
Miller, James E., French Horn
Miller, John, Baritone, 1989

Miller, Keith W.
Miller, Larissa (Bien), Tenor Saxophone, 1992
Miller, Laura
Miller, Matt, Percussion, 1991
Miller, Richard, Trombone, 1981
Miller, Robert K., Percussion, 1965
Miller, Sue, Saxophone, 1981
Miller, William L., Drum Major, 1958
Millikin, Betsy (Bartko), Baritone, 1993
Milikin, Kevin, Baritone, 1993
Mills, Kerry (Kappes), 1972
Milnarich, Gary, Percussion, 1970
Miltenberger, Cheryl A.
Milton, David, Oboe
Minkley, Charles G., Trumpet, 1962
Minkley, Pam, Flute, 1962
Minkley, Verne H.
Minster, Henry, Trombone
Minster, Todd, 1989
Mirochna, Conrad J., French Horn
Missal, Joseph P., Trumpet
Missavage, Karen R.
Mistele, Paul E.
Mitchel, Thomas O., Trumpet, 1964
Mitchell, Dwain M.
Mitchell, Lee, Percussion, 1995
Mitchell, Mark
Mixter, Keith E., Trombone, 1947
Modiba, Elisha, Tuba, 1994
Modlin, Ron, Trumpet, 1972
Moehlman, Jennifer, Flute/Alto Saxophone, 1991
Moffitt, Bill, 1969
Mohr, Loretta A., French Horn
Moleski, Desmond C., Tenor Saxophone
Moline, Betsy (Green), Alto Saxophone, 1989
Moline, Christopher, Alto Saxophone, 1990
Monit, Skip, Trombone,
Monroe, Bill, Trombone, 1981
Monzo, Abigail, Percussion, 1991
Moon, Louis F., Trumpet, 1988
Mooney, Connie
Moore, Bonnie L., Alto Saxophone, 1986
Moore, Gayle A., French Horn
Moore, Jeffrey W., Trombone, 1977
Moore, Jill, Flag Color Guard, 1989
Moots, Gregory, Trombone, 1990
Moran, James (Mike), Alto Saxophone
Moran, Shawn L., Flag Color Guard, 1991
Mordan, Kathleen A., Clarinet
Morehouse, Robert L., French Horn, 1956
Morell, Todd, Percussion, 1979
Morency, Robert L.
Morgan, David, Baritone, 1994
Morgan, Paula, Flag Color Guard, 1978
Morie, Wayne G.
Morin, Rick, Alto Saxophone
Morill, Dennis G.
Morris, Dan, Trumpet, 1992
Morris, David A., Percussion
Morris, Douglas, Trombone, 1986
Morris, Terri, Flag, 1992

Morris, Wendell C.
Morris, William S., Clarinet
Morrison, Brent, Percussion
Morrissey, Bill, Mellophone, 1975
Morrissey, Johanna
Mors, J. Scott, Mellophone, 1995
Morse, Gretchen, Oboe, 1993
Mortensen, James W., Trombone, 1982
Mortlock, Laura, Clarinet, 1994
Morton, Brent, Baritone, 1992
Morton, Don, Baritone
Moser, Lawrence D.
Moss, Keith, Trumpet, 1991
Motz, Ronald T., Baritone
Mowen, Gregg G., Tuba
Moyle, Larry A.
Mracna, Albert M. Jr., 1965
Mucha, Tim, Trumpet, 1992
Mucha, Tom, Trumpet, 1991
Mueller, Frances, Flute
Mueller, Maurice, Trumpet
Muethel, Christopher, Alto Saxophone, 1989
Munro, Michael
Munroe, Dick
Muratzki, James M., Percussion, 1986
Murawski, Mark D.
Murdock, Deborah M., French Horn
Murray, Maryann, Flag Corp, 1982
Mutch, Misty, Percussion, 1994
Myers, Heather, Trumpet, 1993
Myrick, George A., French Horn

N

Naperalsky, Janette, Tenor Saxophone, 1993
Nash, Gary P., Saxophone, 1986
Nash, Julie M.
Neal, Elizabeth, Flag Color Guard, 1989
Needham, James C.
Neff, Jenny L. (Stogner), French Horn
Nehls, Paul, Percussion, 1988
Nellson, Julie, Trumpet
Nelson, Betsy (Cobb), Clarinet
Nelson, Christine M., Flute, 1970
Nelson, Henry, Flute/Piccolo, 1947
Nelson, Jack, Alto Saxophone, 1974
Nelson, Maynard F.
Nelson, Nancy L., Alto Saxophone, 1977
Nelson, Phyllis J., Clarinet, 1944
Nelson, Susie, Trumpet, 1992
Nesbary, Dale, Trombone, 1977
Nestor, Thomas E.
Neuder, David L.
Neuendorf, Kimberly A., Flag Color Guard, 1977
Neuendorf, Robert O., Trombone, 1979
Neuman, Devin, Flute, 1994
Neuman, Gordon, French Horn, 1945
Newman, Ronald E., Alto Saxophone
Newton, Joanne, Alto Saxophone
Newton, Thomas L., Alto Saxophone
Niblock, Howard E., Oboe
Nicar, L. Howard Jr., French Horn

Nichols, Janet, Flute
Nichols, Jon P., Percussion
Nido, Michael E.
Niebling, Jim, Tuba, 1985
Nightingale, Ronald J.
Nigrelli, Pete, Trombone, 1993
Nixon, Thomas J.
Nolan, Laura, Flag Corps, 1988
Noll, Steven H.
Noppenberg, Cathy
Norberg, Dan, Baritone, 1987
Norberg, John, Trombone, 1989
Norman, David E.
Norsworthy, Michael, Clarinet, 1995
Norton, David, Baritone, 19528
Notestine, Thomas P.
Novak, Jeffrey L., Trumpet
Noyes, Jerry, Tuba, 1995
Nye, Harland F.
Nygren, Dennis Q., Clarinet
Nymeyer, Rich, Flag Big Ten, 1991
Nyquist, Lois B.

O

O'Brien, Terrence P., Baritone
O'Connell, Kevin M., Trumpet, 1993
O'Connor, Brian P., Drum Major
O'Donnell, Don, Baritone, 1994
O'Shea, Patrick, Drum Major
O'Toole, Martin P. Saxophone, 1987
Oakes, Gregory, Clarinet, 1993
Oakley, Tonya, Alto Saxophone
Oatley, Nancy A., Trombone
Odelli, Terry E., Trumpet
Ohl, Nicole M., Trombone, 1994
Ohrt, Cynthia L., Percussion
Ohrt, James D., Percussion
Okun, Seymour, Flute, 1943
Oliphant, James D., Saxophone, 1969
Oliphant, Kathy, Flute/Piccolo, 1969
Oliver, Tim, Trumpet, 1973
Olmstead, Debra
Olmstead, Randal L.
Onachuk, Paul N., Alto Saxophone
Onachuk, Sylvia A.
Onufer, Erik V., French Horn
Opatich, Bona M., Baritone, 1985
Optholt, Timothy B.
Orcutt, Pamela A.
Osborn, Michael K., Tuba, 1992
Osborne, Christopher J.
Osborne, Charles E.
Oshnock, Jeffrey R., Percussion
Osler, Thomas M.
Osmer, Robert L.
Ososkie, Terrence J., Clarinet
Ostien, J. Keith, Baritone, 1968
Ostien, Philip A.
Ostler, Mike, Baritone
Ostrofsky, Jeff, Trumpet
Othmer, Dawn, Flute, 1995
Ott, Debbie, Flag Color Guard, 1992
Overholt, Robert L., Trumpet, 1943
Overton, David, Trumpet, 1960

Overton, Greg, Trombone
Overton, Ken, Baritone
Oviatt, Stanley, Euphonium
Owen, Steven L., Flag, 1973

P
Padden, Jeff, Trombone
Pagani, Marc, Percussion, 1991
Paige, Steven H., French Horn
Paksi, Craig, Mellophone
Palazzola, Joseph V., Trumpet
Paluszewski, Richard E., Tuba
Pankhurst, Jerry G.
Papineau, Bill, Trumpet
Pappas, Linda
Parish, Sandra L.
Park, John H.
Parker, Gene, French Horn
Parker, Robert
Parkhurst, Douglas, Alto Saxophone, 1971
Parks, Heather, Flag Color Guard
Parks, Jeanne, Alto Saxophone, 1980
Parmalee, Chad M., Trumpet, 1989
Parmalee, Roschenne W., Trumpet, 1989
Parrott, Herbert I., Trumpet
Parry, Timothy L., Trumpet, 1973
Parsons, Gilbert A.
Partenheimer, Kay
Pasley, Mark, Trumpet, 1991
Patenge, Holly, Alto Saxophone, 1986
Patenge, James W., Percussion, 1986
Patterson, Charles M., Tenor Saxophone, 1995
Patterson, Joseph, H., French Horn
Patton, Archie N. Jr., Drum Major, 1957
Patton, Mary L., Trumpet, 1987
Paulus, Ross T.
Pavlivac, Jon P.
Peabody, Frank R., Clarinet, 1942
Peabody, Margaret, Baritone, 1946
Pearks, Alison, Flag Big Ten, 1992
Pearson, Daniel E., Band Manager, 1961
Pecora, Jim, Percussion, 1989
Peebles, Will, Bassoon, 1994
Pell, Greg, Trumpet, 1966
Pelton, Dorothy B., Flute
Pelton, Gary M., Trumpet
Pelton, Maurice D., Trumpet
Pemberton, James R., Trombone, 1964
Pendergraft, Fred, Percussion, 1987
Penhollow, Erik J., Trumpet, 1988
Peppel, Albert W., Clarinet
Perkins, Tommy, Oboe
Perry, Dennis A., Trombone, 1969
Person, Terry (McKenney), Alto Saxo-phone, 1980
Peshek, Charles A., Trumpet
Peters, Herbert A., Baritone
Peters, Keith, 1985
Peters, Kelvin
Petersen, Jacqueline, Flute, 1991
Petersen, Raymond, Baritone, 1974
Peterson, Daniel E.
Peterson, Judyth L., Percussion, 1981

Peterson, Ron, Tuba, 1983
Petipren, David, Trombone, 1991
Petipren, Susan M., French Horn
Petras, Donna M. (Fisher)
Petras, Pam, Alto Saxophone, 1989
Petrella, Robert L., Clarinet, 1966
Petrillo, Linda J., French Horn
Petroff, Nancy L. (Catron), Clarinet
Petto, Scott T.
Petty, Timothy M., 1969
Pfannenstein, Mary Jo, Clarinet, 1991
Phillips, Daniel H., French Horn
Phillips, Ronald, Trumpet
Piatt, Bob, Tuba, 1960
Piatt, Gerald F.
Piche, Steven A., Trumpet
Pierce, Kimberly, Alto Saxophone, 1991
Pierce, Rick, Trombone, 1974
Pike, Delbert, Tuba
Pilmore, Barb, Baritone, 1994
Pinter, Christina A.
Place, Kelley (Eyer), Flag, 1991
Platt, Mary A., Trumpet, 1979
Pogasic, Janet (Murray), Alto Saxophone, 1992
Poirier, Steven C., Trumpet, 1982
Polk, Harold K. Jr.
Pollack, Peter, Percussion
Pollok, Keith, Trombone, 1970
Polzin, Johanna, Trumpet, 1995
Pompos, William S.
Poole, Mary E., French Horn
Poreda, Bradley, Trumpet, 1994
Porsch, Chris, 1988
Porter, Carol J.
Porter, Teresa, Color Guard, 1988
Porter, William J. Jr., Trombone, 1932
Poteet, James A., Bass/Clarinet, 1956
Potter, Bruce, Tuba
Potts, Diana J., French Horn
Potts, Richard G.
Povich, Edward, Tenor Saxopoone, 1970
Powers, Margaret, French Horn
Prange, Larry, Trombone, 1992
Pratt, Robert S.
Preadmore, Scott D., Trumpet, 1986
Prezewodek, Kevin, Percussion, 1989
Price, Gene M.
Price, Jeffrey K., Baritone
Price, William L. Jr.
Prierce, Patricia A., Alto Saxophone
Prichard, Greg, Bassoon, 1993
Prodger, Robert G.
Proko, Donald, Trumpet, 1953
Propft, Andrea (Sexton), Flag Color Guard, 1986
Pryor, Byron L., Baritone
Psaros, Catherine, Flag Color Guard, 1995
Ptashnik, Martha (Heenan), Tenor Saxo-phone, 1989
Pulter, Daniel L.
Purcell, Craig C.
Purslow, Gordon, Trumpet
Puryear, Gary W., 1967

Pushman, Kristen, Trumpet
Pushman, Todd, Tuba

Q
Quick, Edward P. Jr., Clarinet
Quick, Todd, Mellophone, 1986
Quigley, William, Flag, 1994
Quinn, Timothy

R
Rabey, Chip, Trombone, 1993
Rafferty, David W., Trumpet, 1964
Rafferty, Deborah P., Flute, 1970
RaJala, John R. Jr.
Randalls, Jerome, Flag
Rantz, Mark E.
Rapp, Jessica S., Alto Saxophone
Ratte, Stephanie, Clarinet
Rau, Stephen, Percussion/Bass, 1994
Rawlinson, Arlene M., Oboe
Rayl, Robert, Trumpet, 1993
Read, James F.
Read, Leslie, Trombone, 1991
Reaume, Jeanine, Alto Saxophone, 1980
Reaume, Tom, Percussion, 1980
Redman, Ralph A.
Redman, Renee
Reed, Christopher, Alto Saxophone, 1993
Reed, Greg, Euphonium, 1970
Reed, Jodi, Flag Color Guard, 1988
Reed Thomas B. Jr., Trombone, 1975
Reed, Leslie
Reeves, Jodi, French Horn, 1985
Rehanek, Dorothy, Flag Color Guard, 1992
Rehberg, Milton, Trombone, 1984
Rehmus, Philip F.
Reid, David, Alto Saxophone, 1978
Reid, Lisa
Reinbold, Thomas, Baritone
Reindehl, John
Relyea, Marcia, Flute, 1962
Remisiewicz, Joseph, Trombone, 1993
Rensland, Linda L., Flag, 1985
Replogle, Paul H.
Reuss, Dale, Trumpet
Revord, Terry Joseph, Trumpet, 1989
Reynolds, Brian K., Trumpet, 1989
Rhoades, Constance, French Horn
Rhoades, Dean, Mellophone, 1990
Rice, Bob, Tuba, 1972
Rice, Leanna C., Clarinet, 1974
Rice, Robert L., Trumpet, 1972
Rice, William, Tuba
Richard, Ted A., Trumpet
Richards, Floyd R., French Horn
Richards, Linda, Flag Color Guard
Richardson, Daniel L., Trumpet, 1983
Richardson, Gordon, Flag, 1994
Richardson, Peter W.
Richtmeyer, Lorin, C.
Ricker, Ramon L.
Ridenour, Jack B. Sr., Tuba, 1948
Rider, Daniel C., Alto Saxophone
Riedel, Arthur E., Clarinet, 1960

Riedel, Susan K., French Horn
Riegel, Bob, Percussion, 1989
Riggs, Richard J.
Riley, Beth (Vitale), Flag Color Guard, 1989
Riley, Greg, Alto Saxophone, 1990
Rillema, Kurt, Trombone, 1994
Rimpau, Joy A., Baritone, 1975
Rinderspacher, Carol
Rinderspacher, George A., Trumpet
Ringlein, Linda, Flag, 1994
Rittenhouse, Ann R., Clarinet, 1977
Robbins, Brian D., Color Guard
Roberge, Lisa, Trumpet
Roberson, Blanchard P.
Roberts, Charles L.
Roberts, D.J., Trombone
Roberts, Lori A., Alto Saxophone, 1992
Robertson, William J.
Robinson, John T., Trumpet, 1993
Robinson, Richard C.
Robison, David, Trumpet, 1987
Robison, Philip, Trumpet, 1992
Rockwood, Melissa, Mellophone, 1995
Rodgers, Chris
Rodner, Darren, Trombone, 1993
Rodriguez, Krista, Flute, 1993
Roelofs, Don H., French Horn, 1957
Rogers, Chris, Trombone, 1988
Rogers, David, Mellophone, 1995
Rogers, Jim, Trombone
Roghan, Carl, Percussion
Rohrback, April, Flag Color Guard, 1989
Root, Denise, French Horn
Root, George, Trumpet, 1983
Root, Kyle, Trombone, 1994
Rorick, Charyl, Tenor Saxophone, 1993
Rorick, Kathy, Alto Saxophone, 1989
Rose, Andrew, Baritone BC, 1989
Rose, Terri (Garlock), Flag Color Guard, 1988
Rosegart, Eldon C., Drum, 1941
Roser, Filiz (Bilge), Trumpet
Roshak, Craig, Tuba
Rosier, David, Percussion, 1981
Ross, Scott, Trumpet
Roster, David D.
Roth, Ray, Low Brass
Rowan, Roger A.
Royer, Michael, French Horn
Ruiz, Joseph C.
Rummel, Greg K., Flag Big Ten, 1990
Rush, Chris, Flute
Rush, Tim, Percussion
Rushing, Melissa, Tenor Saxophone, 1993
Ruska, John
Rygell, Dave F., Trumpet, 1994

S

Saar, Laura E., French Horn
Sabin, Gordon L.
Sabin, Matt, Percussion, 1993
Sabourin, Robert C., Saxophone
Sachs, William E., Alto Saxophone, 1967
Sack, Robert A., Clarinet, 1957

Safran, John M., Percussion/Snare, 1984
Safran, Laura S., Percussion, 1984
Sakala, Roxanne, Flag Color Guard, 1989
Salciccioli, Gino, Mellophone, 1989
Salow, Elaine, Trombone
Salow, Ronald F., Clarinet/Trumpet, 1951
Sambrano, Kristine (Weyersberg), Flag Corps, 1986
Sameilippo, Joseph
Sams, Ronald F., Trombone, 1972
Sanborn, Clio F., Tuba, 1952
Sanders, Kenneth L.
Sang, Dr. Richard C., French Horn, 1970
Sarata, William, French Horn
Saska, Ronald, Clarinet
Sather, Nancy R.
Sawatzke, Mark
Sayen, Sandra K.
Scates, Berry, Clarinet/Piano, 1979
Schaberg, Albert L., French Horn
Schack, Victoria, Flag Color Guard, 1989
Schadel, Richard G. Jr.
Schadel, Robert B. Sr., Baritone, 1966
Schadel, Robert S., Trumpet, 1992
Schaefer, Irving
Schaefer, Al, Flag Big Ten, 1984
Schafer, Dennis
Schaffer, Lisa, Alto Saxophone, 1993
Schallert, David W.
Schallert H. W.
Schaner, Charles, Percussion, 1979
Schaner, Gary A.
Schaner, Marcia J., Flute
Scharchburg, Martha, Trombone, 1971
Schark, Rhonda, Trumpet, 1984
Scharsse, Bill, Percussion, 1996
Schartow, Chuck, Trumpet, 1975
Schartow, Page, Trumpet
Scheid, Lynn D., Clarinet
Scheid, Patricia L., Flute
Scheid, Steven L., Clarinet
Schemm, Bonnie, Alto Saxophone, 1968
Schemm, Leonard E., Alto Saxophone, 1969
Schenkel, Joseph H., Trumpet, 1965
Schewe, Peter K., French Horn
Schiller, Richard M.
Schimmel, Amy, Mellophopne, 1987
Schleif, Julie M., French Horn
Schlesinger, Perry, Clarinet, 1941
Schley, F. Craig, Alto Saxophone, 1964
Schlosser, Shannon, Flag Color Guard, 1993
Schmeltekopf, Duane, French Horn, 1964
Schmeltekopf, Gerhart, Tuba/Trombone, 1964
Schmid, Andy, Tuba, 1979
Schmid, Jonathan A.
Schmidt, John, Alto Saxophone, 1947
Schmitz, Darryl, Tuba
Schnizlein, Mark A., Percussion, 1975
Scholberg, Samuel R., Bassoon
Scholfield, David B.
Schott, Michael W., Baritone BC, 1979

Schrader, Timothy D.
Schrauben, Philip, Alto Saxophone
Schroeder, Joseph
Schuler, Herbert T.
Schult, Kristie L., Flag Color Guard, 1988
Schultz, Amy, Percussion, 1996
Schultz, David R.
Schultz, Raymond C.
Schult, Robert S., 1988
Schumaker, Derek, Trombone
Schuster, Myles, Percussion, 1991
Schwab, Jenny, Oboe
Scoggins, Dana (Schueller), Alto Saxophone, 1989
Scott, Craig L., Tenor Saxophone, 1974
Scott, Donel W.
Scott, Joseph D., Tuba
Scott, Lisa M., Alto Horn, 1987
Scott, Raymond C.
Scott, Robert A., Clarinet, 1971
Scott, Todd, Mellophone, 1985
Scott, Vince, Tenor Saxophone, 1985
Scully, Susan, 1985
Scurto, Robin M., Clarinet
Sears, Kingsley, Tuba
Seastrom, Bill, French Horn
Sebald, David C., Clarinet
Secord, Brian, Trombone, 1982
Sedan, Harry M.
Seebeck, Meredith, Flute, 1991
Seeger, Donna (Miller), Flag Corp, 1988
Seel, Melinda S., Flag Color Guard
Seel, Michael D., Drum Major
Seely, Tom
Segedy, James A., Tenor Saxophone, 1973
Seifert, William M., Clarinet
Seitz, Mark, Trumpet
Selanders, Louise C., Flute, 1969
Senkmajer, Erick, Tenor Clarinet
Seymore II, Bruce A., Trombone, 1986
Shackelford, Andrew
Shafer, Shirley, Baritone, 1955
Shannon, Cheryl C., Percussion
Shanon, Leslie, Trumpet, 1977
Shapton, Warren W., Baritone, 1939
Sharpe, Tammy, Flag Color Guard, 1987
Sheahan, Nancy (Skelton)
Sheedlo, Monte L., Trumpet, 1964
Sheedlo, Scott, Trombone, 1992
Sheehy, Michael, Alto Saxophone, 1993
Shelp, Gordon H., Trombone
Shepard, William G.
Sherman, Craig B.
Sherman, Robert W.
Sherman, William D., Percussion, 1943
Sherrill, Carolyn, Clarinet, 1981
Shier, Adam, Trumpet, 1989
Shinall, J. Scott, Tenor Saxophone, 1992
Shipman, Edward, Trombone, 1993
Shipman, Lance, Percussion, 1994
Shirey, DeAnn, Trumpet
Showerman, Linette, Trumpet, 1981
Shulick, Tony
Shultis, Chris L., Percussion

Shultis, Terry, Percussion, 1957
Shuster, Jeff, Percussion/Bass, 1978
Sibley, Forbes S.
Sicheneder, Carol, Alto Saxophone, 1986
Sikorski, Jake, Trombone
Silbernagel, Joseph J., Percussion/Bass, 1972
Silverman, Steve, Alto Saxophone, 1993
Silvestros, Nick, Tuba, 1987
Simmons, Larry, Percussion
Simon, Carl, Trumpet, 1961
Simoncic, Tara, Trumpet
Simons, Kevin E.
Simpson, Richard L., Trumpet, 1958
Sims, Pete, Trumpet, 1991
Sinclair, Laura, Trumpet, 1991
Sines, Lori ., Alto Saxophone, 1985
Singer, Jon, Trumpet, 1989
Singer, Kurt A., Trombone
Singer, Philip W.
Sironen, Gary, Trumpet, 1974
Sisco, Keith, Tuba
Sisk, Maryanne, French Horn
Sisunik, Chuck, Trumpet, 1989
Sjoberg, Steven, Flag, 1992
Skelton-Schimpk, Kathy, Twirler
Skerratt, Howard
Skidmore, David L., Baritone, 1992
Skinkle, Brian S., Baritone
Skinner, John, Percussion, 1993
Skubick, Timothy C., Clarinet
Skutnick, Jeffrey, Tenor Saxophone, 1988
Slagle, Zoe L.
Slaughter, Gail, French Horn, 1990
Slesinski, Sandi, Alto Saxophone, 1984
Sloan, Allison, Saxophone, 1994
Small, William C.
Smeader, Chris, Trumpet, 1988
Smeltekop, Hugh, Baritone BC, 1993
Smeltekop, Roger A., Trombone, 1968
Smith, Brian P., Trombone, 1982
Smith, Debbie D., Alto Saxophone, 1980
Smith, Duane P., Baritone, 1954
Smith, Felicia, Oboe
Smith, Gary C.
Smith, Guy R., Tuba, 1968
Smith IV, Mahlon C., Trumpet
Smith, Jennifer, Flag Color Guard, 1992
Smith, Joe, Trombone
Smith, Dannelly C. Jr.
Smith III, Leslie E., Flag Big Ten, 1993
Smith, Lindsey, Trombone, 1980
Smith, Lora, Alto Saxophone, 1988
Smith, Marc K., Bass Clarinet, 1976
Smith, Max H., Clarinet
Smith, Patricia A.
Smith, Smolenyak, Lynn (Price), Alto Saxophone, 1978
Snoeck-Greene, Elise L.
Snow, Marie (Miller), 1983
Snyder, Patricia
Snyder, Shelly, Flag Color Guard, 1995
Sobell, Jeff, Trumpet, 1992
Soloko, Jenine "Chip," Tuba, 1983

Solomon, Peter, Trombone
Sommerness, Martin D., Trumpet, 1979
Somoncic, Tara
Sonneberger, Jamie, Trumpet
Sordyl, Ralph A.
Sorensen, Kristi A., French Horn
Spangler, Amanda M., French Horn
Sparks, Amy E. (Thuemmel), Baritone, 1987
Sparks, Laura L., Trumpet, 1979
Spataro, Angela, Oboe, 1991
Spataro, Lawrence O., Baritone, 1986
Speck, John W.
Spees, Steve, Tenor Saxophone
Spence, Robert, Trombone, 1995
Spencer, David, Trumpet, 1987
Spencer, Mark
Spencer, Tina, Baritone/Trumpet, 1987
Spink, Dorothy, Clarinet
Spink, Edward, Clarinet
Spink, Gordon, Trumpet
Spink, Jerry, Trombone
Splittberger-Rose, Andrea, Clarinet
Sprague, James T., Percussion, 1964
Springer, Kathy, Alto Saxophone, 1991
Springgay, Bret
Spry, Gerald K., Percussion Bass
St. Clair, Angela, Alto Saxophone, 1994
Stacey, Brian, Trumpet, 1991
Staelens, Ronald L., Tuba, 1987
Staffeld, Glenn D.
Staib, Eric, Percussion
Stainbrook, Dennis W.
Staley, Greg
Stanley, Kurt E., Trumpet, 1977
Stansburg, John, Oboe
Stansell, Derrick, Baritone, 1979
Stansell, Fritz, Baritone
Stansell, Gretchen, Flute
Stanton, Philip J., French Horn
Starkey, Jim, Baritone, 1989
Staron, Ben, Trumpet, 1994
Stauffer-Selm, Patricia
Stautz, Douglas L.
Stavros, Matthew, Flag Color Guard
Steel, Philip C.
Steffensky, Lee F., Trombone, 1983
Steggall, Todd, Trombone, 1995
Steiner, Jeff, Flag
Stene, Virginia (Peckens), Mellophone, 1981
Stepp, Kevin, Trumpet, 1994
Stevens, Christine
Stevens, Julie M., Saxophone, 1984
Stevens, Roger, Percussion/Tenor, 1978
Stevenson, Ronald T., Trumpet
Stewart, Amy (Yanz), Trumpet
Stewart, Ann M., Flute, 1993
Stewart, Gary F., Trumpet, 1975
Stewart, Jan C., Baritone BC, 1994
Stewart, Ken C., Trombone, 1978
Stewart, William R.
Stillwell, Sean, Alto Saxophone
Stimson, Greg, Trumpet, 1995

Stocum, Paul T., Percussion, 1984
Stoeckle, Douglas, Trombone, 1994
Stone, Sara W., Alto Saxophone, 1978
Stoner, Becky L., Alto Saxophone, 1987
Stoner, Tim A., Alto Saxophone
Stouffer, Anne, Percussion
Strager, Alana A., Percussion/Bass, 1993
Strahle, Gail E., Flute/Piccolo, 1976
Strecher, Victor G.
Strong, Melissa, Trumpet, 1994
Strouf, Ralph, Clarinet
Struble, Edgar, Trombone
Struble, Theresa, Clarinet, 1991
Stubbs, Richard W.
Stuckey, Howard
Stuit, Jeffrey
Stukey, Howard, Trumpet, 1968
Stults, Russell G., Trombone
Stutler, Bill, Drum Major, 1960
Stutler, Yvonne, Clarinet, 1961
Sullivan, Florence, Oboe, 1944
Sullivan, Gary T., Baritone, 1975
Sullivan, Marie, Alto Saxophone, 1988
Sullivan, Murry L., Clarinet
Sullivan, Pamela, French Horn
Sullivan, Taimur, Saxophone, 1994
Sundstedt, Oscar E.
Sutherland, Don, Trombone, 1990
Sutherlay, Hallie, Flag Color Guard, 1993
Suttles, Charles M.
Sutton, Gary L., Trombone, 1967
Swanson, Dana, Saxophone, 1987
Swanson, Mark, Tuba, 1989
Swikoski, Donald E.

T
Tallis, Jay E.
Tallman, Larry, Trumpet,
Tamblin, Tracy, Flag Color Guard, 1993
Tamex, Azael C., Trumpet
Tatseos, Paul, Trumpet
Taylor, Chris, Trumpet
Taylor, Percussion
Taylor, Norman L., Trumpet, 1976
Taylor, Philip, Trumpet, 1987
Taylor, Stewart
Taylor, Teresa M., French Horn, 1991
Teare, Daniel B.
Tedesco, Dawn, Alto Saxophone
Teel, William, Oboe, 1956
Teitle, Sue, Flag, 1990
Tennant, Rusty, Trumpet
Tennant, William E., Clarinet
TerBurgh, William, Baritone TC, 1992
Terrill, Jeff M., Trumpet, 1989
Tevis, Royce, Trumpet, 1992
Texter, Tracy (Irish), Trumpet, 1982
Thamer, Todd, Trumpet, 1995
Thar, James W., Trombone, 1959
Thar, William (Bud), Baritone, 1964
Thar, William E., Trombone
Thelen, Glenn, Trumpet, 1995
Thelen, Stephanie L. (Atkinson), Flag Color Guard, 1989

Thoede, Donald, Alto Saxophone, 1993
Thoma, August J., Alto Saxophone/
    Clarinet, 1976
Thomas, Dale J.
Thomas, Kelland, Saxophone, 1994
Thomas, Richard, Tuba, 1964
Thomas, Robert M., Baritone, 1982
Thomas, Scott G.
Thompson, Brad, Trumpet, 1981
Thompson, Julie, Alto Saxophone
Thompson, Karan (Fekete), Alto Saxo-
    phone, 1982
Thompson, Kristen, Flute
Thompson, Larry K., Alto Saxophone,
    1981
Thompson, Laura (Burk), Baritone TC,
    1993
Thompson, Laurel, Flute, 1981
Thompson, Ted, Clarinet, 1953
Thornburg, Donald L., Trombone, 1957
Thurow, John
Timlin, Tom, Trumpet, 1979
Timm, Dave, Baritone
Timmons, David E., Tenor Saxophone
Timmons, Leslie J.
Timmons, Michael L., Trumpet, 1970
Tindall, Mary A., Clarinet, 1986
Todd, Carol, French Horn
Toenniges, Jeffrey N., Trumpet, 1985
Toenniges, Lisa (Merz), Alto Saxophone,
    1984
Tolhurst, Charles R. Jr., Alto Saxophone,
    1982
Tolsma, Heather, Percussion
Tomaras, Ted, Trumpet, 1991
Topliff, Roger J., Clarinet, 1959
Topoleski, Marc, Trumpet, 1993
Topolevski, Timothy, Trombone
Topolewski, Brian, Trombone
Topping, Laura C. Baritone/Tuba, 1949
Topping, Sue M., Baritone
Toskey, George A., Trumpet
Toth, Lois A.
Toth, Mary, Alto Saxophone, 1986
Toulmin, Marnie
Towne, Thomas, Trumpet, 1973
Townley, Art, Trombone, 1989
Townsend, Brandi (Anderson), Mellophone,
    1990
Townsend, Kathy A.
Townsend, Nancy, Clarinet, 1994
Tracey, Robert M.
Travis, Denise, Mellophone
Trezise, Christine (Pinter) Flag, 1985
Trezise, Douglas, Trombone, 1985
Tribby, James L., Alto Saxophone
Trierweiler, Virginia, Alto Saxophone, 1982
Trojan, Joe, Percussion, 1987
Troxel, Ronald K., Alto Saxophone, 1965
Trudgen, S. Earle, Trumpet, 1939
Tucker, Eileen A.
Tundo, Claudia, Trumpet, 1994
Turkus, Peter J., Percussion, 1976
Turmell, Robert L.

Turnage, Lois W., Bassoon
Turner, Katherine L., French Horn, 1988
Turner, Mistene, Trumpet
Turner, Suzanne, Flag
Tusan, Michelle, Alto Horn, 1985
Tushman, David A., Flag, 1985
Tuson, Mike, Trumpet, 1986
Tymes, Doug, Trumpet, 1993
Tymes, Norlin, Baritone, 1959
Tyrrell, Christine (Stark), Mellophone, 1992

U
Underwood, John F., Clarinet, 1950
Ungerman, Ed, Mellophone, 1992
Urbane, Katherine (Squires), Tuba
Urick, Dennis M., Tenor Saxophone, 1969

V
Vader, Randy, Trombone, 1973
Vagasky, Debra K.
Valade, David, Trumpet
Valasek, John C.
VanInwagen, Nancy
VanRiper, Susan
VanSchagen, John, Trombone, 1983
VanVleck, Lynn
Vanaman, Norm, Trumpet
Vanderbeek, Rick, Trombone, 1987
Vanderboegh, Scott L., Baritone, 1984
Vandermolen, Robert H.
Vanderwaerden, Anne M.
Vandette, Steven J.
Vandevelde, James A.
VanDyke, Harrison, Trumpet, 1976
Van Houten, Jennifer, Flute, 1990
Vanhouten, Thomas J.
Vanneman, Debra M., Baritone, 1980
Vanosdall, Frederick E., French Horn, 1952
VanRemmen, Pat, Trumpet, 1991
VanSchagen, John, Trombone, 1983
Vantine, James G. Jr., Tuba, 1975
VanVleck, Peter, L.
VanWingen, Jeff, Tuba, 1993
Varaprath, Prasanth, Trumpet
Vaughn, Lauren, Trumpet, 1975
Vechinski, Lance, Saxophone, 1980
Veenendall, Thomas L.,Twirler/Drum
Velderman, Pat, Twirler/Drum
Verdun, Willard, French Horn
Vernier, Lawrence, Trumpet, 1982
Vernier, Tom, Tuba, 1982
Vernon, Sandra (Gillmann), Clarinet, 1981
Vickery, Jean M. (Rice)
Vince, Kenneth W., Trumpet, 1953
Vincent, Jerry W. Jr., Baritone
Vittoz, Irene
Vivio, Frank M.
Voelker, Andy, Trombone
Vogelreuter, Rudy D.
Vogie, Lona, Trumpet
Vogler, Jonathan E., Trumpet, 1980
Voketz, Daniel, Trombone, 1981
Vondrasek, Jean (Hruby), Trumpet, 1988

Voss, Heather
Vreeland, Charles, French Horn

W
Wade, Clarence H., Trumpet, 1951
Wade, Sandra, Clarinet, 1993
Wagner, Brian, Trombone, 1991
Wagner, John R.
Wagner, Mike, Tuba
Wagner, Richard, Tuba
Wait, Gregory F.
Wakefield, George, Trumpet, 1967
Wakenhut, Anne W., Percussion, 1966
Wakenhut, Gary W., Clarinet, 1962
Walbeck, William M.
Waldecker, Bruce J., Trumpet
Waldmann III, Clement J., Percussion
Wall, Brad, Percussion
Walling, Michelle, Trombone
Walsh, Brian E., Baritone TC, 1986
Walsh, Michael, Tuba, 1995
Walters, Bob, Trumpet, 1971
Walters, Douglas, French Horn
Walters, Judith, Clarinet, 1969
Walters, Mark, Baritone, 1988
Waltzer, Andrian A.
Waltzer, Rosemary, French Horn
Wangler, Frank, Bassoon
Ward, Chris, Flag Color Guard, 1989
Ward, Nancy L.
Ward, Robert K., Trombone, 1980
Warle, Clifford J.
Warnaar, Steven J.
Warner, Thomas, Percussion, 1981
Warner, Gary
Warren, Ron, Flag Big Ten, 1988
Warrington, Denise (Wagner), Flag Color
    Guard, 1988
Warthen, John
Watkins, Heather, Flag Color Guard, 1994
Watkins, Shelley L.
Watkins, Willis, Trumpet
Watson, Richard B.
Watson, Ted
Watson, Thomas G.
Waun, James, Tuba
Weaver, David J.
Weaver, Lori A.
Webb, John B., Baritone TC, 1964
Webb, Richard, Alto Saxophone, 1974
Webb, Susan C., Flute
Weber, Carolyn, Saxophone
Webster, Richard S.
Webster, Sherry (Rice), Trombone, 1989
Weigel, Jane, Clarinet
Weiss, Edward, French Horn
Weiss, Jane (Dombroski), Alto Saxophone
Weiss, Jeff, Tenor Saxophone, 1989
Weisse, Cynthia A.
Weitzmann, Janice G.
Welch, Myron, French Horn
Welch, Richard A., Snare Drum, 1981
Welch, Robert, Tenor Saxophone, 1979
Welch, Robert D.

Wellman, Emory
Wellman, Ron, Percussion, 1991
Wellmeter, Jennifer L., Flag Color
    Guard, 1995
Welter, Bob
Welton, Harper, Flute
Welton, Roger, Flute/Piccolo, 1950
Welty, Robert
Wendlandt, Eric W.
Wendt, Robert E.
Wendzel, Bradley M.
Wenyel, Lorelei A. (Widmar), French
    Horn
Werner, Robert E., Trumpet
Wernette, David, Alto Saxophone, 1975
Werth, David, Baritone, 1991
Wesley, Craig, Trombone, 1980
Wesseldyk, Michael, Trombone, 1978
Westby, Gary, Alto Saxophone
Westcott, John W.
Weyersberg, Kurt G., Baritone BC, 1981
Weyersberg, Nadine, Clarinet/Oboe,
    1974
Weyersberg, Roger, Trombone, 1973
White, Arnie, Trumpet, 1994
White, Dawn, Alto Saxophone, 1991
White, John C.
White, Robert, 1971
White, Stephen, Trombone, 1989
White, Timothy L., Trombone, 1984
White, William R., Percussion, 1975
Whitehead, Collin, Trumpet, 1994
Whitlock, Janet K. (Gettings), Trumpet,
    1984
Widenhofer, Amy, Mellophone
Wieckowski, Chris, Clarinet
Wieckowski, Paul, Percussion
Wiedrich, William W., Percussion
Wifler, Raymond C., Clarinet
Wiggers, Jarvis
Wikman, William C., Clarinet, 1949
Wilbert, Edward J., Alto Saxophone, 1979
Wilcox, John, Alto Saxophone, 1976
Wiley, Steven J.
Wilhelms, Tybo
Wilks, Ted, Trumpet
Willett, Dan L., Oboe
Williams, Heidi, Trumpet, 1995
Willett, Dan L., Oboe
Williams, Jane A., Trumpet
Williams, Jennifer, Flag Color Guard
Williams, Marilyn
Williams, Mark A., Bassoon, 1994
Williams, Moya (Terry), Alto Saxophone,
    1979
Williams, Nancy, Euphonium
Williams, Russell
Williams, Shelaen, Tenor Saxophone, 1992
Williamsen, Robert, Tuba, 1985
Williamson, William R., Trumpet, 1982
Willis, Sharon, French Horn
Wilson, Jessica

The 1966 edition of the MSU marching band.

Wilson, Lisa, Trumpet, 1987
Wilson, Michael R., Trumpet, 1983
Wilson, Steve, Percussion, 1989
Wing, Eric, Trombone, 1989
Wing, Rachelle, Alto Saxophone, 1992
Winga, John A. Jr., Clarinet, 1956
Winslow, Carolyn (Diehl)
Winter, Dean, Trumpet, 1938
Winters, Gerald, Trombone
Wirgau, Carol, Flag Color Guard
Wirtanen, William W.
Wirth, Bradley M., Percussion, 1983
Wittz, Barbara A., Alto Saxophone, 1981
Wiscombe, Randy
Wise, Deborah L.
Wise, Shirley E.
Wishart, Roschenne, Trumpet, 1989
Wisner, David, Trumpet, 1959
Wisser, Jeff, Drum Major, 1992
Wisser, Susan, Clarinet, 1970
Witman, Keri, Flag Color Guard, 1989
Witucki, Nancy, Flute/Piccolo, 1978
Witucki, Paul, Trumpet, 1974
Witzig, David, Trumpet
Wojciechowski, Dan
Wolan, Diana (Bayles)
Wolfe-Richards, Terril L.
Woll, Brad, Percussion/Snare, 1993
Wolters, Robert O.
Wood, Colleen, Flag Color Guard, 1994
Wood, Shelli, Tenor Saxophone, 1989
Woodhull, Lin, Clarinet, 1994
Woodin, Richard, L., Trombone
Woodin, Signe J., Trombone
Woodrum, Karen J.

Woods, Bill, Tuba, 1990
Woods, Donna K.
Woods, Tony, Saxophone, 1994
Wooten, Ronnie, Grad assistant, 1989
Wortman, John F.
Wotring, C. Edward
Woznicki, Dennis T.
Wright, Jeffrey S.
Wright, Sharon K.
Wullaert, Dave, Trombone
Wygant, Dave, Flute, 1960
Wyskowski, Darci
Wysocki, Daniel A., Tenor Saxophone

Y
Yarger, Timothy D., Trumpet
Yodhes, David, Trombone, 1983
Yoskovick, Michael, Flag, 1991
Young, Frank, Trumpet
Young, Suzanne (Monroe), Flag, 1984

Z
Zagorski, Marcus, Percussion, 1994
Zednik, Lou, Trombone, 1979
Zeisler, Kathleen, Flute
Zenas, Joe, Trumpet, 1988
Ziek, Gary, Trumpet, 1994
Zimmer, Dale L., Trumpet, 1970
Zimmerman, Cheryl (Lewis), Alto Saxo-
    phone, 1974
Zimmerman, Dennis R.
Zimmerman, Lynn L.
Zimmerman, Nancy E.
Zimmerman, Bob, Clarinet, 1950
Zirk, Willard D., French Horn
Zugger, Tom, Trombone, 1993

MSU ALL-TIME INDIVIDUAL RECORDS

(CAREER/SEASON/GAME/PLAY)
Career statistics include postseason bowl games

CAREER

Rushing Attempts

Lorenzo White, 1984-85-86-87	1,082
Tico Duckett, 1989-90-91-92	836
Blake Ezor, 1986-87-88-89	800
Steve Smith, 1977-78-79-80	524
Eric Allen, 1969-70-71	521
Rich Baes, 1973-74-75-76	507
Levi Jackson, 1973-74-75-76	474
Duane Goulbourne, 1992-93-94	414
Charlie Baggett, 1973-74-75	406
Clinton Jones, 1964-65-66	396
Hyland Hickson, 1988-89-90	384
Craig Thomas, 1990-91-92-93	362

Rushing Yardage

Lorenzo White, 1984-85-86-87	4,887
Tico Duckett, 1989-90-91-92	4,212
Blake Ezor, 1986-87-88-89	3,749
Steve Smith, 1977-78-79-80	2,676
Eric Allen, 1969-70-71	2,654
Levi Jackson, 1973-74-75-76	2,287
Rich Baes, 1973-74-75-76	2,234
Lynn Chandnois, 1946-47-48-49	2,093
Clinton Jones, 1964-65-66	1,921
Duane Goulbourne, 1992-93-94	1,906
Hyland Hickson, 1988-89-90	1,906
Craig Thomas, 1990-91-92-93	1,823
George Guerre, 1946-47-48	1,721

Rushing Average

(Yards per attempt min. 150 atts.)

George Guerre, 1946-47-48	6.75
Lynn Chandnois, 1946-47-48-49	6.52
Sherman Lewis, 1961-62-63	6.21
Sonny Grandelius, 1948-49-50	6.09
Derek Hughes, 1978-79-80-81	6.04
Jim Earley, 1974-75-76-77	5.78
Leroy Bolden, 1952-53-54	5.75
Walt Kowalczyk, 1955-56-57	5.58
Dick Panin, 1950-51-52	5.45
Evan Slonac, 1951-52-53	5.42

Passes Attempted

Ed Smith, 1976-77-78	789
Dave Yarema, 1982-83-84-85-86	767
Jim Miller, 1990-91-92-93	746
John Leister, 1979-80-81-82	686
Tony Banks, 1994-95	496
Dan Enos, 1987-88-89-90	478
Bryan Clark, 1978-79-80-81	409
Bobby McAllister, 1985-86-87-88	386
Steve Juday, 1963-64-65	384
Charlie Baggett, 1973-74-75	287
Mike Rasmussen, 1970-71	287
Al Dorow, 1949-50-51	259

Passes Completed

Jim Miller, 1990-91-92-93	467
Dave Yarema, 1982-83-84-85	464
Ed Smith, 1976-77-78	418
John Leister, 1979-80-81-82	313
Tony Banks, 1994-95	301
Dan Enos, 1987-88-89-90	297
Bryan Clark, 1978-79-80-81	204
Steve Juday, 1963-64-65	198
Bobby McAllister, 1985-86-87-88	194
Charlie Baggett, 1973-74-75	128
Al Dorow, 1949-50-51	125
Mike Rasmussen, 1970-71	123

Pass Interceptions

John Leister, 1979-80-81-82	35
Dave Yarema, 1982, 1983, 1984, 1985, 1986	33
Ed Smith, 1976-77-78	32
Charlie Baggett, 1973-74-75	30
Jim Miller, 1990-91-92-93	29
Dan Enos, 1987-88-89-90	25
Steve Juday, 1963-64-65	24
Al Dorow, 1949-50-51	23
Tony Banks, 1994-95	21
Bill Triplett, 1968-69-70	21
Gene Glick, 1946-47-48-49	20
Bryan Clark, 1978-79-80-81	20
Mike Rasmussen, 1970-71	18
Jimmy Raye, 1965-66-67	18

Pass Completion Percentage

(Min. 100 atts.)

Jim Miller, 1990-91-92-93 (746-467)	629
Dan Enos, 1987-88-89-90 (478-297)	621
Tony Banks, 1994-95 (496-301)	607

Dave Yarema, 1982-83-84-85-86 (767-464)	605
Clark Brown, 1983 (141-82)	582
Ed Smith, 1976-77-78 (789-418)	530
Steve Juday, 1963-64-65 (384-198)	516
Jim Ninowski, 1955-56-57 (124-63)	508
Bobby McAllister, 1985-86-87-88 (386-194)	503
Bryan Clark, 1978-79-80-81 (409-204)	499
Earl Morrall, 1953-54-55 (198-98)	495
Bill Ferraco, 1966-67-68 (142-70)	493
Marshall Lawson, 1975-76-77 (101-49)	485

Passing Yardage

Dave Yarema, 1982-83-84-85-86	5,809
Ed Smith, 1976-77-78	5,706
Jim Miller, 1990-91-92-93	5,037
Tony Banks, 1994-95	4,129
John Leister, 1979-80-81-82	3,999
Dan Enos, 1987-88-89-90	3,837
Bobby McAllister, 1985-86-87-88	3,194
Bryan Clark, 1978-79-80-81	2,725
Steve Juday, 1963-64-65	2,576
Charlie Baggett, 1973-74-75	2,335
Earl Morrall, 1953-54-55	2,015
Mike Rasmussen, 1970-71	1,986
Al Dorow, 1949-50-51	1,875
Gene Glick, 1946-47-48-49	1,748

Receptions

Andre Rison, 1985-86-87-88	146
Courtney Hawkins, 1988-89-90-91	138
Mill Coleman, 1991-92-93-94	126
Ted Jones, 1980-81-82	118
Eugene Byrd, 1975-76-78-79	114
Kirk Gibson, 1975-76-77-78	112
Scott Greene, 1992-93-94-95	110
Mark Brammer, 1976-77-78-79	107
Gene Washington, 1964-65-66	102
Bobby Morse, 1983-84-85-86	102
Mark Ingram, 1983-84-85-86	95
Otis Grant, 1980-81-82	79
Daryl Turner, 1980-81-82-83	78
Allen Brenner, 1966-647-68	73
Muhsin Muhammad, 1992-93-94-95	69
Derrick Mason, 1993-94-95	67

Receiving Yardage

Andre Rison, 1985-86-87-88	2,992
Kirk Gibson, 1975-76-77-78	2,347

Courtney Hawkins, 1988-89-90-91 ... 2,210
Eugene Byrd, 1975-76-77-78-79 2,082
Mark Ingram, 1983-84-85-86 1,944
Gene Washington, 1964-65-66 1,857
Mill Coleman, 1991-92-93-94, ... 1,813
Ted Jones, 190-81-82 1,678
Daryl Turner, 1980-81-82-83 1,577
Otis Grant, 1980-81-82 1,358
Mark Brammer, 1976-77-78-79 1,305
Allen Brenner, 1966-67-68 1,232

Receiving Average

(Yards per attempt—Min. 30 recs.)
Kirk Gibson, 1975-76-77-78 .... 21.0
Andre Rison, 1985-86-87-88 .... 20.5
Mark Ingram, 1983-84-85-86 .... 20.5
Daryl Turner, 1980-81-82-83 .... 20.2
Dave Kaiser, 1955-56-57 .... 19.5
Frank Foreman, 1967-68-69 .... 18.5
Eugene Byrd, 1975-76-78-79 .... 18.3
Gene Washington, 1964-65-66 .... 18.2
Mike Hurd, 1971-73-74 .... 18.2
Nigea Carter, 1993,1994,1995 .... 18.0
Billy Joe DuPree, 1970-71-72 .... 17.7
James Bradley, 1989-90 .... 17.7
Otis Grant, 1980-81-82 .... 17.2

Rushing-Passing Attempts

Lorenzo White, 1984-85-86-87 1,083
Dave Yarema, 1982-83-84-85-86 960
Jim Miller, 1990-91-92-93 875
Ed Smith, 1976-77-78 875
Tico Duckett, 1989-90-91-92 863
John Leister, 1979-80-81-82 830
Blake Ezor, 1986-87-88-89 802
Dan Enos, 1987-88-89-90 723
Charlie Baggett 1973-74-75 693
Bobby McAllister, 1985-86-87-88 683
Tony Banks, 1994-95 635

Rushing-Passing Yardage

Ed Smith, 1976-77-78 5,556
Dave Yarema, 1982-83-84-85-86 5,269
Lorenzo White, 1984-85-86-87 4,887
Jim Miller, 1990-91-92-93 4,748
Dan Enos, 1987-88-89-90 4,301
Tico Duckett, 1989-90-91-92 4,212
Tony Banks, 1994-95 4,105
John Leister, 1979-80-81-82 4,073
Charlie Baggett, 1973-74-75 4,041
Bobby McAllister, 1985-86-87-88 3,871
Blake Ezor, 1986-87-88-89 3,749
Bryan Clark, 1978-79-80-81 2,755
Steve Smith, 1977-78-79-80 2,676
Eric Allen, 1969-70-71 2,654

Rushing-Passing Average

(Yards per attempt in. 200 atts.)
Earl Morrall, 1953-54-55 .... 7.41
Tom Yewcic, 1951-52-53 .... 6.64
George Guerre, 1946-47-48 .... 6.57
Tony Banks, 1994-95 .... 6.46
Lynn Chandnois, 1946-47-48-49 .... 6.35
Ed Smith, 1976-77-78 .... 6.35
Sonny Grandelius, 1948-49-50 .... 6.17
Sherman Lewis, 1961-62-63 .... 6.16
Dan Enos, 1987-88-89-90 .... 5.95
Charlie Baggett, 1973-74-75 .... 5.83
Bobby McAllister, 1985-86-87-88 .... 5.67
Dave Yarema, 1982-83-84-85-86 .... 5.49
Jim Miller, 1990-91-92-93 .... 5.43

All-Purpose Yardage

(Includes rushing, receiving and all returns)
Lorenzo White, 1984-85-86-87 5,152
Tico Duckett, 1989-90-91-92 4,511
Blake Ezor, 1986-87-88-89 4,475
Eric Allen, 1969-70-71 4,446
Steve Smith, 1977-78-79-80 4,060
Courtney Hawkins, 1988-89-90-91 ... 3,946
Derrick Mason, 1993-94-95 3,413
Andre Rison, 1985-86-87-88 3,270
Lynn Chandnois, 1946-47-48-49 3,205
Mill Coleman, 1991-92-93-94 2,815

Total Touchdowns

Lorenzo White, 1984-85-86-87 43
Blake Ezor, 1986-87-88-89 34
Lynn Chandnois, 1946-47-48-49 31
Eric Allen, 1969-70-71 30
Tico Duckett, 1989-90-91-92 28
Scott Greene, 1992-93-94-95 27
Kirk Gibson, 1975-76-77-78 27
Leroy Bolden, 1951-52-53-54 26
Craig Thomas, 1990-91-92-93 25
Steve Smith, 1977-78-79-80 25
Clinton Jones, 1964-65-66 23
Sherman Lewis, 1961-62-63 23
Charlie Baggett, 1973-74-75 21
Hyland Hickson, 1988-89-90 20
Andre Rison, 1985-86-87-88 20
Rich Baes, 1973-74-75-76 20
Don McAuliffe, 1950-51-52 20
Sonny Grandelius, 1948-49-50 20

Rushing Touchdowns

Lorenzo White, 1984-85-86-87 43
Blake Ezor, 1986-87-88-89 34
Lunn Chandnois, 1946-47-48-49 29
Eric Allen, 1969-70-71 28
Tico Duckett, 1989-90-91-91 26
Craig Thomas, 1990-91-92-93 25
Leroy Bolden, 1951-52-53-54 23

Steve Smith, 1977-78-79-80 21
Charlie Baggett, 1973-74-75 21
Clinton Jones, 1964-65-66 20
Rich Baes, 1973-74-75-76 20
Scott Greene, 1992-93-94-95 19
Hyland Hickson, 1988-89-90 19
Sonny Grandelius, 1948-49-90 19
Don McAuliffe, 1950-51-52 18
Duane Goulbourne, 1992-93-94 16
Sherman Lewis, 1961-62-63 16

Touchdown Passes Thrown

Dave Yarema, 1982-83-84-85-86 43
Ed Smith, 1976-77-78 43
Steve Juay, 1963-64-65 21
Tony Banks, 1994-95 20
John Leister 1979-80-81-82 20
Bryan Clark, 1978-79-80-81 20
Al Dorow, 1949-50-51 19
Gene Glick, 1946-47-48-49 18
Tom Yewcic, 1951-52-53 18
Jim Miller, 1990-91-92-93 17
Bobby McAllister, 1985-86-87-88 17

Touchdown Passes Caught

Kirk Gibson, 1975-76-77-78 24
Andre Rison, 1985-86-87-88 20
Gene Washington, 1964-65-66 16
Eugene Byrd, 1975-76-78-79 15
Mark Ingram, 1983-84-85-86 14
Bob Carey, 1949-50-51 14
Daryl Turner, 1980-81-82-83 13
Courtney Hawkins, 1988-89-90-91 12
Otis Grant, 1980-81-82 12
Ellis Duckett, 1951-52-53-54 10
Mill Coleman, 1991-92-93-94 8
Scott Greene, 1992-93-94 7
Sherman Lewis, 1961-62-63 7
Ed Sobczak, 1946-48 7
Frank Foreman, 1967-68-69 7

Points Scored

John Langeloh, 1987-88-89-90 308
Morten Andersen, 1978-79-80-81 261
Lorenzo White, 1984-85-86-87 258
Hans Nielsen, 1974-75-76-77 230
Blake Ezor, 1986-87-88-89 204
Lynn Chandnois, 1946-47-48-49 186
Eric Allen, 1969-70-71 182
Tico Duckett, 1989-90-91-92 168
Scott Greene, 1992-93-94-95 166
Kirk Gibson, 1975-76-77-78 156
Leroy Bolden, 1951-52-53-54 156
Steve Smith, 1977-78-79-80 150
Craig Thomas, 1990-91-92-93 150
Ralf Mojsiejenko, 1982-83-84 149

P.A.T. Scored

John Langeloh, 1987-88-89-90 ... 137/140
Morten Andersen,1978-79-80-81 . 126/129
Hans Nielsen, 1974-75-76-77 .... 98/105
George Smith, 1947-48-49 .... 94/116
Chris Caudell, 1985-86 .... 60/69
Evan Slonac, 1951-52-53 .... 55/63
Chris Gardner, 1994-95 .... 55/58
Dick Kenney, 1965-66 .... 50/58
Bill Stoyanovich, 1992-93 .... 49/52
Bob Carey, 1949-50-51 .... 47/68
Ralf Mojsiejenko, 1982-83-84 .... 44/53
Borys Shlapak, 1970-71 .... 43/47

Field Goals Scored

John Langeloh, 1987-88-89-90 .... 57/79
Morten Andersen, 1978-79-80-81 .... 45/72
Hans Nielsen, 1974-75-76-77 .... 44/70
Ralf Mojsiejenko, 1982-83-84 .... 35/53
Chris Gardner, 1994-95 .... 26/37
Bill Stoyanovich, 1992-93 .... 22/35
Dick Kenney, 1964-65-66 .... 19/36
Chris Caudell, 1985-86 .... 16/35
Dirk Kryt, 1972-73 .... 15/27
Jim DelVerne, 1991-1992 .... 13/21
Borys Shlapak, 1970-71 .... 13/34

Tackles

Dan Bass, 1976-77-78-79 541
Percy Snow, 1986-87-88-89 473
Chuck Bullough, 1988-89-90-91 391
Tim Moore, 1984-85-86-87 332
Jim Morrissey, 1981-82-83-84 329
Carlos Jenkins, 1987-88-89-90 314
Shane Bullough, 1983-84-85-86 311
Paul Rudzinski, 1974-75-76-77 298
Matt Christensen, 1991-92-93-94 289
Rob Fredrickson, 1990-91-92-93 281
Carl Banks, 1980-81-82-83 279
Dixon Edwards, 1987-88-89-90 277
Phil Parker, 1982-83-84-85 276
Tom Hannon, 1973-74-75-76 275
Reggie Garnett, 1993-94-95 272
Don Law, 1967-68-69 266
Ray Nestor, 1971-72-73 265
James Neely, 1979-80-81-82 263
Gail Clark, 1970-71-72 262
Otto Smith, 1973-74-75-76 261

Tackles for Losses

Larry Bethea, 1975-76-77 (208 yds.) 43
Travis Davis, 1986-87-88-89
  (248 yds.) 39
Juan Hammonds, 1991-92-93-94
  (120 Yds.) 33
Kelly Quinn, 1982-83-84 (214 yds.) 31

Mark Nichols, 1983-85-86-87
  (136 yds.) 29
Mel Land, 1975-76-77-78 (116 yds.) 29
Bill Johnson, 1988-89-90-91 (77 yds.) .. 27
Tim Moore, 1984-85-86-87 (135 yds.) .. 27
Matt Christensen, 1991-92-93-94
  (79 yds.) 25
Carl Banks, 1980-81-82-83 (122 yds.) .. 25
Ernie Hamilton, 1970-71-72
  (168 yds.) 25
Ron Curl, 1968-69-71 (128 yds.) 25
John Shinsky, 1970-71-72-73
  (136 yds.) 24
Larry Savage, 1976-77-78-79
  (115 yds.) 23
Otto Smtih, 1973-74-75-76 (107 yds.) .. 23

Quarterback Sacks

Larry Bethea, 1975-76-77 (208 yds.) 33
Kelly Quinn, 1982-83-84-85
  (183 yds.) 24
Travis Davis, 1986-87-88-89
  (217 yds.) 24
Mark Nichols, 1983-85-86-87
  (90 yds.) 15
Mel Land, 1975-76-77-78 (65 yds.) 15
Carl Banks, 1980-81-82-83 (84 yds.) 14
Ron Curl, 1968-69-70-71 (73 yds.) 14
Larry Savage, 1976-77-78-79
  (84 yds.) 12
John Shinsky, 1970-71-72-73
  (67 yds.) 11
Juan Hammonds, 1991-92-93-94
  (63 Yds.) 10
Tim Moore, 1984-85-86-87 (79 yds.) 10
Ernie Hamilton, 1970-71-72 (73 yds.) ... 10
Aaron Jackson, 1991-92-93-94
  (60 yds.) 10

Pass Interceptions

Lynn Chandnois, 1946-47-48-49 20
Todd Krumm, 1984-85-86-87 18
Phil Parker, 1982-83-84-85 16
Brad VanPelt, 1970-71-72 14
John Miller, 1985-86-87-88 14
Kurt Larson, 1985-86-87-88 14
Mark Anderson, 1976-77-78-79 12
Bill Simpson, 1971-72-73 12
Jesse Thomas, 1948-49-50 12
Demetrice Martin, 1992-93-94-95 10
John Polonchek, 1947-48-49 10

Pass Interception Yardage

Lynn Chandnois, 1946-47-48-49 384
Brad VanPelt, 1970-71-72 268
Phil Parker, 1982-83-84-85 267
Jesse Thomas, 1948-49-50 212
Todd Krumm, 1984-85-86-87 198

John Polonchek, 1947-48-49 189
Bob Suci, 1959-60-61 152
John Miller, 1985-86-87-88 145
Brad McLee, 1969-70 145
Dan Bass, 1976-77-78-79 138
Earl Morrall, 1953-54-55 132

Fumble Recoveries

Dan Bass, 1976-77-78-79 12
Larry Savage, 1976-77-78-79 8
Carlos Jenkins, 1987-88-89-90 7
Smiley Creswell, 1980-81-82 7
John McCormick, 1977-78-79-80 7
Mel Land, 1975-76-77-78 7
George Chatlos, 1966-67 7
Matt Vanderbeek, 1986-87-88-89 6
Ike Reese, 1994-95 5
Myron Bell, 1990-91-92-93 5
Lonnie Young, 1981-82-83-84 5
Larry Bethea, 1975-76-77 5
Kim Rowekamp, 1973-74-75-77 5
Tom Standal, 1973-74-75 5
Ray Nester, 1971-72-73 5
Bill Simpson, 1971-72-73 5
Ernie Hamilton, 1970-71-72 5
Tom Kronne, 1971-72-73 5

Passes Broken Up

James Burroughs, 1977-78-79-81 28
Todd Krumm, 1984-85-86-87 21
Nate Hannah, 1980-81-82-83 21
Phil Parker, 1982-83-84-85 20
Stan Callender, 1991-92-93-94 18
Lonnie Young, 1981-82-83-84 18
Bill Simpson, 1971-72-73 17
Mark Niesen, 1971-72-73 17
Myron Bell, 1990-91-92-93 16
Mark Anderson, 1976-77-78-79 16
Paul Hayner, 1971-72-73 15
Tom Hannon, 1973-74-75-76 15
Harlon Barnett, 1986-87-88-89 15
Matt Christensen, 1991-92-93-94 14
Mike Iaquaniello, 1987-88-89-90 14
Brad VanPelt, 1970-71-72 14

Punts

Ralf Mojsiejenko, 1981-82-83-84 279
Ray Stachowicz, 1977-78-79-80 230
Chris Salani, 1992-93-94-95 224
Josh Butland, 1988-89-90-91 220
Bill Simpson, 1971-72-73 196
Greg Montgomery, 1985-86-87 184
John Pingel, 1937-38 .... *150
Tom Yewcic, 1951-52-53 123
Lou Bobich, 1962-63-64 107
Dick Berlinski, 1967-68 99
Dick Kenney, 1965-66 85
* 1936 punting statistics unavailable

Punting Average
(Min. 50 atts.)

Greg Montgomery, 1985-86-87 .... 45.2
Ralf Mojsiejenko, 1981-82-83-84 .... 43.8
Ray Stachowicz, 1977-78-79-80 .... 43.3
John Pingel, 1937-38 .... *42.1
Josh Butland, 1988-89-90-91 .... 40.7
Bill Simpson, 1971-72-73 .... 39.8
Earl Morrall, 1953-54-55 .... 39.2
Lou Bobich, 1962-63-64 .... 39.0
Tom Yewcic, 1951-52-53 .... 38.7
Tom Birney, 1974-75-76 .... 37.8
* 1936 punting statistics unavailable

Punt Return Yardage

Jim Ellis, 1951-52-53
    (55 rets.) 619
Bobby Morse, 1983-84-85-86
    (70 rets.) 584
Todd Krumm, 1984-85-86-87
    (64 rets.) 561
George Guerre, 1946-47-48
    (35 rets.) 513
Jesse Thomas, 1948-49-50
    (27 rets.) 490
Frank Waters, Jr. 1967-68
    (44 rets.) 434
Mill Coleman, 1991-92-93-94
    (39 rets.) 411
Sherman Lewis, 1961-62-63
    (32 rets.) 355
Dean Look, 1957-58-59
    (20 rets.) 349
Tom Hannon, 1974-75-76
    (41 rets.) 332
Horace Smith, 1946-47-48-49
    (21 rets.) 329
DERRICK MASON, 1993-94-95
    (30 rets.) 308
Lynn Chandnois, 1946-47-48-49
    (16 rets.) 308
Thomas Morris, 1980-81
    (43 rets.) 293

Kickoff Return Yardage

DERRICK MASON, 1993-94-95
    (78 rets.) 2,051
Courtney Hawkins, 1988-89-90-91
(65 rets.) 1,571
Eric Allen, 1969-70-71
    (62 rets.) 1,340
Larry Jackson, 1983-84
    (43 rets.) 1,022
Derek Hughes, 1979-80-81
    (36 rets.) 898
Bruce Reeves, 1977-78-79-80
    (45 rets.) 863
Steve Holman, 1992-93
    (29 Rets.) 625

Mark Ingram, 1983-84-85-86
    (27 rets) 585
Steve Smith, 1977-78-79-80
    (30 rets.) 563
Otis Grant, 1980-81-82
    (27 rets.) 554
Craig Johnson, 1985-86-87-88
    (34 rets.) 541
Blake Ezor, 1986-87-88-89
    (27 rets.) 540
Jim Ellis, 1951-52-53
    (24 rets.) 515

SEASON

Rushing Attempts

Lorenzo White, 1985 419
Lorenzo White, 1987 357
Blake Ezor, 1988 322
MARC RENAUD, 1995 312
Tico Duckett, 1991 272
Blake Ezor, 1989 267
Eric Allen, 1971 259
Tico Duckett, 1990 257
Hyland Hickson, 1990 234
Levi Jackson, 1975 230
Duane Goulbourne, ... 214
Don Highsmith, 1969 209
Tico Duckettt, 1992 204
Steve Smith, 1979 204
Duane Goulbourne, 1993 196
Craig Thomas, 1993 193
Rich Baes, 1976 187
Eric Allen, 1970 186

Rushing Yardage

Lorenzo White, 1985 2,066
Lorenzo White, 1987 1,572
Blake Ezor, 1988 1,496
Eric Allen, 1971 1,494
Tico Duckett, 1990 1,394
Blake Ezor, 1989 1,299
Tico Duckett, 1991 1,204
Hyland Hickson, 1990 1,196
Levi Jackson, 1975 1,063
MARC RENAUD, 1995 1,057
Sonny Grandelius, 1950 1,023
Tico Duckett, 1992 1,021
Duane Goulbourne, 1993 973
Steve Smith, 1979 972
Levi Jackson, 1974 942
Don Highsmith, 1969 937
Rich Baes, 1976 931

Rushing Average
(Yards per attempt . Min. 90 atts.)

Lynn Chandnois, 1948 .... 7.48
George Guerre, 1946 .... 7.03
Lynn Chandnois, 1949 .... 6.86
Steve Smith, 1978 .... 6.71
Sherman Lewis, 1963 .... 6.41
Sonny Grandelius, 1950 .... 6.27
George Guerre, 1948 .... 6.22
Levi Jackson, 1974 .... 6.16
Jim Earley, 1977 .... 6.12
Dick Gordon, 1964 .... 6.02

Passes Attempted

Jim Miller, 1993 336
Dave Yarema, 1986 297
Ed Smith, 1978 292
Tony Banks, 1995 258
Ed Smith, 1976 257
John Leister, 1982 251
John Leister, 1980 247
Dan Enos, 1989 240
Ed Smith, 1977 240
Tony Banks, 1994 238
Dave Yarema, 1984 222
Dan Enos, 1990 220
Jim Miller, 1991 218
Bryan Clark, 1981 204
Mike Rasmussen, 1970 199
Jim Miller, 1992 191

Passes Completed

Jim Miller, 1993 215
Dave Yarema, 1986 200
Ed Smith, 1978 169
Tony Banks, 1995 156
Dan Enos, 1989 153
Tony Banks, 1994 145
Dan Enos, 1990 137
Ed Smith, 1976 132
Jim Miller, 1991 130
Jim Miller, 1992 122
John Leister, 1982 119
Dave Yarema,1984 119
Ed Smith, 1977 117
Bryan Clark, 1981 109
John Leister, 1980 103

Pass Interceptions Thrown

Tony Banks, 1995 15
Dave Yarema, 1984 15
Ed Smith, 1977 14
John Leister, 1980 14
Jim Miller, 1991 11
Dan Enos, 1989 12
Charlie Baggett, 1975 12
Bill Triplett, 1969 12

Dan Enos, 1990 11	Kirk Gibson, 1978 42
Dave Yarema, 1986 11	Ted Jones, 1980 40
John Leister, 1982 11	Gene Washington, 1965 40
Mike Rasmussen, 1970 11	Andre Rison, 1988 39
Jim Miller, 1993 10	Kirk Gibson, 1976 39
Bryan Clark, 1981 10	Bobby Morse, 1986 39
Steve Juday, 1964 10	Al Kimichik, 1981 39
John Leister, 1981 10	
Ed Smith, 1976 10	

Pass Completion Percentage
(Min. 75 atts.)

Dave Yarema, 1986 (297-200) 673	
Jim Miller, 1993 (215-336) 640	
Jim Miller, 1992 (191-122) 639	
Dan Enos, 1989 (240-153) 638	
Dan Enos, 1990 (220-137) 623	
Tony Banks, 1994 (238-145) 609	
Tony Banks, 1995 (258-156) 605	
Jim Miller, 1991 (218-130) 596	
Clark Brown, 1983 (141-82) 582	
Ed Smith, 1978 (292-169) 579	
Dave Yarema, 1982 (80-46) 575	
Jim Ninowski, 1957 (79-45) 570	
Dave Yarema, 1985 (116-66) 569	
Al Dorow, 1951(114-64) 561	
Bryan Clark, 1981 (204-109) 536	
Dave Yarema, 1984 (222-119) 536	

Receiving Yardage

Courtney Hawkins, 1989 1,080
Andre Rison, 1986 966
Andre Rison, 1988 961
Muhsin Muhammad, 1995 867
Kirk Gibson, 1978 806
Derrick Mason 1995 787
Andre Rison, 1987 785
Kirk Gibson, 1976 748
Mark Ingram, 1985 745
Eugene Byrd, 1978 718
Gene Washington, 1966 677
Mark Ingram, 1986 672
Mill Coleman, 1993 671
Courtney Hawkins, 1991 656
Gene Washington, 1965 638

Rushing-Passing Yardage

Dave Yarema, 1986 2,359
Ed Smith, 1978 2,247
Dan Enos, 1989 2,219
Jim Miller, 1993 2,109
Tony Banks, 1994 2,100
Lorenzo White, 1985 2,066
Tony Banks, 1995 2,005
Dan Enos, 1990 1,810
Bobby McAllister, 1988 1,757
Ed Smith, 1976 1,738
Charlie Baggett, 1974 1,713
John Leister, 1980 1,658
Bryan Clark, 1981 1,640
Lorenzo White, 1987 1,572
Ed Smith, 1977 1,571
Jimmy Raye, 1966 1,546

Passing Yardage

Dave Yarema, 1986 2,581
Jim Miller, 1993 2,269
Ed Smith, 1978 2,226
Tony Banks, 1995 2,089
Dan Enos, 1989 2,066
Tony Banks, 1994 2,040
Ed Smith, 1976 1,749
Ed Smith, 1977 1,731
Dan Enos, 1990 1,677
John Leister, 1980 1,559
Bryan Clark, 1981 1,521
Dave Yarema, 1984 1,477
Bobby McAllister, 1988 1,406
Jim Miller, 1992 1,400
Jim Miller, 1991 1,368
Mike Rasmussen, 1970 1,344
John Leister, 1982 1,321

Receiving Average
(Yards per attempt . Min. 20 recs.)

Gene Washington, 1966 .... 25.0
Andre Rison, 1988 .... 24.6
Frank Foreman, 1969 .... 24.4
Kirk Gibson, 1977 .... 24.1
Andre Rison, 1987 .... 23.1
Mark Ingram, 1984 .... 22.7
Mark Ingram, 1985 .... 21.9
Daryl Turner, 1981 .... 21.1
Bob Carey, 1949 .... 20.1
Daryl Turner, 1983 .... 19.6
Mark Ingram, 1986 .... 19.2
Kirk Gibson, 1978 .... 19.2
Kirk Gibson, 1976 .... 19.1

Rushing-Passing Average
(Yards per attempt . Min. 100 atts.)

Charlie Baggett, 1974 .... 7.08
Ed Smith, 1978 .... 7.00
Dave Yarema, 1986 .... 6.96
Bobby McAllister, 1988 .... 6.78
George Guerre, 1946 .... 6.72
Steve Smith, 1978 .... 6.71
Lynn Chandnois, 1949 .... 6.66
Bryan Clark, 1981 .... 6.51
Tony Banks, 1995 .... 6.47
Tony Banks, 1994 .... 6.46
Dan Enos, 1989 .... 6.34
Jimmy Raye, 1966 .... 6.31
Sonny Grandelius, 1950 .... 6.28
Ed Smith, 1976 .... 6.27

Receptions

Courtney Hawkins, 1989 60
Andre Rison, 1986 54
Derrick Mason, 1995 53
Muhsin Muhammad, 1995 50
Mill Coleman, 1993 48
Courtney Hawkins, 1991 47
Ted Jones, 1981 44
Eugene Byrd, 1978 43
Scott Greene, 1994 42

Rushing-Passing Attempts

Lorenzo White, 1985 420
Jim Miller, 1993 377
Lorenzo White, 1987 357
Dan Enos, 1989 350
Dave Yarema, 1986 339
Tony Banks, 1994 325
Blake Ezor, 1988 323
Ed Smith, 1978 321
Dan Enos, 1990 311
Tony Banks, 1995 310
John Leister, 1980 301
Dave Yarema, 1984 301
John Leister, 1982 300
Ed Smith, 1977 277
Ed Smith, 1976 277
Bobby McAllister, 1987 275

Total Touchdowns

Blake Ezor, 1989 19
Scott Greene, 1995 18
Eric Allen, 1971 18
Lorenzo White, 1985 17
Lorenzo White, 1987 16
Craig Thomas, 1992 15
Hyland Hickson, 1990 15
Clinton Jones, 1965 12
Sonny Grandelius, 1950 12
Lynn Chandnois, 1948 12
Tico Duckett, 1990 11
Blake Ezor, 1988 11
Charlie Baggett, 1974 11
Derek Hughes, 1979 11
Eric Allen, 1970 10
Lynn Chandnois, 1949 10

Rushing Touchdowns

Blake Ezor, 1989 19
Eric Allen, 1971 18
Scott Greene, 1995 17

Lorenzo White, 1985	17
Lorenzo White, 1987	16
Craig Thomas, 1992	15
Hyland Hickson, 1990	14
Sonny Grandelius, 1950	11
Blake Ezor, 1988	11
Charlie Baggett, 1974	11
Clinton Jones, 1965	10
Lynn Chandnois, 1948	10
Tico Duckett, 1990	10
Lynn Chandnois, 1949	10

Touchdown Passes Thrown

Ed Smith, 1978	20
Dave Yarema, 1986	16
Bryan Clark, 1981	14
Ed Smith, 1976	13
Tony Banks, 1994	11
Gene Glick, 1948	11
Dave Yarema, 1984	11
Ed Smith, 1977	10
John Leister, 1980	10
Charlie Baggett, 1974	10
Jimmy Raye, 1966	10
Tom Yewcic, 1952	10
Dave Yarema, 1985	10

Touchdown Passes Caught

Andre Rison, 1988	8
Bob Carey, 1949	8
Eugene Byrd, 1978	7
Kirk Gibson, 1976	7
Kirk Gibson, 1978	7
Gene Washington, 1966	7
Kirk Gibson, 1977	6
Courtney Hawkins, 1989	6
Courtney Hawkins, 1991	6
Ted Jones, 1981	5
Gene Washington, 1964	5
Otis Grant, 1981	5
Daryl Turner, 1983	5
Mark Ingram, 1985	5
Mark Ingram, 1986	5
Andre Rison, 1986	5
Andre Rison, 1987	5

Points Scored

Blake Ezor, 1989	114
Scott Greene, 1995	112
Eric Allen, 1971	110
Lorenzo White, 1985	102
Lorenzo White, 1987	96
Craig Thomas, 1992	90
Hyland Hickson, 1990	90
John Langeloh, 1988	83
John Langeloh, 1987	79
Hans Nielsen, 1977	78
John Langeloh, 1990	74
Clinton Jones, 1965	74

Morten Andersen, 1978	73
Morten Andersen, 1981	73

P.A.T. Scored

Morten Andersen, 1978	52/54
John Langeloh, 1989	42/44
George Smith, 1948	39/50
John Langeloh, 1990	38/38
George Smith, 1949	38/41
Evan Slonac, 1952	37/43
Bill Stoyanovich, 1993	32/34
Chris Caudell, 1986	31/36
Chris Gardner, 1994	30/30
Dick Kenney, 1966	30/35
John Langeloh, 1988	29/30
Chris Caudell, 1985	29/33
John Langeloh, 1987	28/28
Morten Andersen, 1981	28/28
Hans Nielsen, 1976	27/27
Hans Nielsen, 1977	27/30
Bob Carey, 1950	27/35

Field Goals Scored

John Langeloh, 1988	18/27
John Langeloh, 1987	17/24
Hans Nielsen, 1977	17/28
Morten Andersen, 1981	15/20
Chris Gardner, 1994	14/21
Ralf Mojsiejenko, 1982	14/20
Chris Gardner, 1995	12/16
Jim DelVerne, 1991	12/17
John Langeloh, 1990	12/15
Morten Andersen, 1980	12/18
Bill Stoyanovich, 1993	11/21
Bill Stoyanovich, 1992	11/14
Morten Andersen, 1979	11/18
Dick Kenney, 1965	11/17
Ralf Mojsiejenko, 1983	11/17
Hans Nielsen, 1976	11/20
Hans Nielsen, 1975	10/14
Ralf Mojsiejenko, 1984	10/16
Chris Caudell, 1986	10/19
John Langeloh, 1989	10/13

Tackles

Chuck Bullough, 1991	175
Percy Snow, 1989	172
Chuck Bullough, 1990	164
Percy Snow, 1988	164
Dan Bass, 1979	160
Shane Bullough, 1985	156
Ty Hallock, 1992	144
Jim Morrissey, 1984	137
Dan Bass, 1978	136
Dan Bass, 1977	134
James Neely, 1982	130
Jim Morrissey, 1983	130
Ray Nester, 1973	129
Terry McClowry, 1974	129

Tackles for Losses

Larry Bethea, 1977 (93 yds.)	18
Travis Davis, 1987 (113 yds.)	16
Bill Johnson, 1990 (33 yds.)	15
Tim Moore, 1987 (73 yds.)	15
Kelly Quinn, 1984 (96 yds.)	15
Juan Hammonds, 1993 (61 Yds.)	14
Mel Land, 1978 (57 yds.)	14
Bobby Wilson, 1990 (48 yds.)	13
Kelly Quinn, 1983 (101 yds.)	13
Larry Bethea, 1975 (60 yds.)	13
Howard McAdoo, 1982 (40 yds.)	13
Otto Smith, 1974 (50 yds)	12
Larry Bethea, 1976 (77 yds.)	12
Rich Saul, 1969 (89 yds.)	12
John Jones, 1985 (66 yds.)	12
Mark Nichols, 1985 (50 yds.)	12
John Budde, 1986 (42 yds.)	12

Quarterback Sacks

Larry Bethea, 1977 (90 yds.)	16
Travis Davis, 1987 (105 yds.)	12
Kelly Quinn, 1984 (84 yds.)	12
Kelly Quinn, 1983 (84 yds.)	10
Larry Bethea, 1976 (61 yds.)	9
Larry Bethea, 1975 (57 yds.)	8
Juan Hammonds, 1993 (43 Yds.)	7
Mel Land, 1978 (32 yds.)	7
Yakini Allen, 1995 (49 yds.)	6
Tim Moore, 1987 (46 yds.)	6
Mark Nichols, 1985 (36 yds.)	6
Mark Nichols, 1986 (34 yds.)	6
Mel Land, 1977 (29 yds.)	6

Pass Interceptions

Todd Krumm, 1987	9
Kurt Larson, 1988	8
John Miller, 1987	8
Jesse Thomas, 1950	8
Demetrice Martin, 1994	7
Lynn Chandnois, 1949	7
Phil Parker, 1983	7
Jim Ellis, 1951	6
Mark Anderson, 1977	6
Paul Hayner, 1972	6
Bill Simpson, 1973	6
Lynn Chandnois, 1947	6
Brad VanPelt, 1970	6

Pass Interception Yardage

Phil Parker, 1983	203
Lynn Chandnois, 1949	183
Todd Krumm, 1987	129
Brad VanPelt, 1971	129
Earl Morrall, 1955	109
John Polonchek, 1949	108
George Guerre, 1948	106

Brad McLee, 1970 106
John Miller, 1988 101
Dan Bass, 1978 101
Brad VanPelt, 1970 100

Fumble Recoveries

George Chatlos, 1966 7
Tom Kronner, 1973 5
Tom Standal, 1975 5
Matt Vanderbeek, 1989 5
Myron Bell, 1993 4
Dan Bass, 1979 4
Dan Bass, 1977 4
Larry Savage, 1978 4
Larry Savage, 1976 4
23 players on 23 occasions 3

Passes Broken Up

James Burroughs, 1981 13
Clifton Hardy, 1969 12
Nate Hannah, 1983 12
Harold Phillips, 1969 11
Mark Niesen, 1971 11
Lonnie Young, 1984 10
Stan Callender, 1992 9
Todd Krumm, 1985 9
James Burroughs, 1979 9
Mark Anderson, 1977 9
Bill Simpson, 1972 9
Ray Hill, 1995 8
Tom Hannon, 1976 8
Harlon Barnett, 1987 8

Punts

John Pingel, 1938 99
Ralf Mojsiejenko, 1982 77
Ralf Mojsiejenko 1984 76
Greg Montgomery, 1985 75
Ralf Mojsiejenko, 1983 74
Josh Butland, 1991 73
Bill Simpson, 1972 73
Ray Stachowicz, 1980 71
Greg Montgomery, 1987 70
Bill Simpson, 1973 67
Ray Stachowicz, 1979 62
Josh Butland 1988 61
Chris Salani, 1992 58
Ray Stachowicz, 1977 58

Punting Average
(Min. 20 atts.)

Greg Montgomery, 1986 .... 47.8
Ray Stachowicz, 1980 .... 46.2
Greg Montgomery, 1987 .... 45.0
Ralf Mojsiejenko, 1984 .... 44.7
Ralf Mojsiejenko, 1982 .... 44.6

Ray Stachowicz, 1979 .... 44.3
Greg Montgomery, 1985 .... 44.1
Ralf Mojsiejenko, 1983 .... 43.9
Ray Stachowicz, 1978 .... 43.1
Josh Butland, 1989 .... 43.1
Earl Morrall, 1955 .... 42.9
John Pingel, 1937 .... 42.6

Punt Return Yardage

Jesse Thomas, 1950 (18 ret.) 358
Todd Krumm, 1987 (36 ret.) 322
Jim Ellis, 1951 (24 ret.) 305
Bill Simpson, 1972 (21 ret.) 286
Frank Waters Jr., 1967 (24 rets.) 264
Derrick Mason, 1995 (24 ret.) 260
Allen Brenner, 1966 (22 ret.) 256
George Guerre, 1946 (16 ret) 253
Steve Smith, 1978 (22 ret.) 224
Bobby Morse, 1984 (20 ret.) 218
Todd Krumm, 1986 (22 ret.) 211
Drake Garrett, 1965 (18 ret.) 210

Kickoff Return Yardage

Derrick Mason, 1994 (36 ret.) 966
Derrick Mason, 1995 (35 ret.) 947
Eric Allen, 1969 (20 ret.) 598
Eric Allen, 1970 (24 ret.) 549
Courtney Hawkins, 1991 (21 ret.) 548
Larry Jackson, 1984 (20 ret.) 522
Larry Jackson, 1983 (23 ret.) 500
Derek Hughes, 1979 (16 ret.) 497
Tyrone Willingham, 1976 (23 ret.) 454
Courtney Hawkins, 1989 (18 ret.) 454
LaMarr Thomas, 1967 (17 ret.) 392
Bruce Reeves, 1977 (19 ret.) 387
Mark Ingram, 1986 (17 ret.) 359
Steve Holman, 1993 (15 Ret.) 344
Otis Grant, 1982 (14 ret.) 307
Derek Hughes, 1981 (17 ret.) 307

SINGLE-GAME

Rushing Attempts

Lorenzo White, Indiana '87
    (292 yds.) 56
Lorenzo White, Purdue '85
    (244 yds) 53
Lorenzo White, Minnesota '85
    (172 yds.) 49
Blake Ezor, Indiana '88
    (250 yds.) 44
Tico Duckett, Wisconsin '91
    (216 yds.) 42
Lorenzo White, Wisconsin '85
    (223 yds.) 42
Lorenzo White, Notre Dame '86
    (147 yds.) 41

Blake Ezor, Northwestern, '89
    (228 yds.) 41
Blake Ezor, Hawaii '89
    (179 yds.) 41

Rushing Yardage

Eric Allen, Purdue '71 (29 att.) 350
Lorenzo White, Indiana '87 (56 att.) 292
Lorenzo White, Indiana '85 (25 att.) 286
Clinton Jones, Iowa '66 (21 att.) 268
Blake Ezor, Indiana '88 (44 att.) 250
Eric Allen, Wisconsin '71 (21 att.) 247
Lorenzo White, Purdue '85 (53 att.) 244
Tico Duckett, Minnesota '91 (30 att.) ... 241
Marc Renaud, Minnesota '95
    (35 att.) 229
Tico Duckett, Rutgers '90 (33 att.) 229
Steve Smith, Northwestern '80
    (30 att.) 229
Blake Ezor, Minnesota '89 (41 att.) 228
Lorenzo White, Iowa '85 (39 att.) 226
Lorenzo White, Wisconsin '85
    (42 att.) 223
Tico Duckett, Wisconsin '91
    (42 att.) 216
Duane Goulbourne, Iowa '93
    (29 att.) 213
Derek Hughes, Minnesota '79
    (31 atts.) 213
Tico Duckett, Purdue '90 (34 att.) 210
Don Highsmith, Northwestern '69
    (37 att.) 209

Passes Attempted

John Leister, Purdue '80
    (18 comp.) 54
John Leister, Michigan '82
    (32 comp.) 46
John Leister, Wisconsin '82
    (25 comp.) 45
Dave Yarema, Northwestern '86
    (30 comp.) 45
Tony Banks, Louisiana State '95
    (22 comp.) 44
Bryan Clark, Minnesota '81
    (21 comp.) 43
Jim Miller, Ohio State '93
    (31 Comp.) 42
Ed Smith, Minnesota '78
    (26 comp.) 42
Jim Miller, Notre Dame '92
    (23 Comp.) 41
Ed Smith, Notre Dame '78
    (27 comp.) 41
Jim Miller, Michigan '91
    (30 Comp.) 39
Ed Smith, Wyoming '76
    (16 comp.) 39
Bryan Clark , Michigan '81
    (21 comp.) 38

Passes Completed

John Leister, Michigan '82 (46 att.) 32
Jim Miller, Ohio State '93 (42 att.) 31
Jim Miller, Michigan '91 (39 att.) 30
Dave Yarema, Northwestern '86
    (45 att.) 30
Ed Smith, Notre Dame '78 (41 att.) 27
Ed Smith, Minnesota '78 (42 att.) 26
Dave Yarema, Arizona State '86
    (33 att.) 26
Dave Yarema, Minnesota '86 (30 att.) 25
John Leister, Wisconsin '82 (45 att.) 25
Jim Miller, Notre Dame '92 (41 att.) 23
Dave Yarema, Iowa '86 (36 att) 23
John Leister, Indiana '81 (37 att.) 23
Three quarterbacks on four occasions 21

Passing Yardage

Ed Smith, Indiana '78 (30-20) 369
Jim Miller, Ohio State '93 (42-31) 360
Dave Yarema, Northwestern '86
    (45-30) 352
Tony Banks, LSU '95 (44-22) 348
Ed Smith, North Carolina State '76
    (29-18) 324
Dave Yarema, Minnesota '86
    (30-25) 321
Ed Smith, Wisconsin '78 (29-19) 320
Bryan Clark, Minnesota '81 (43-21) 318
Bryan Clark, Michigan '81 (38-21) 316
Dan Werner, Purdue '69 (35-16) 306
Jim Miller, Michigan '91 (39-30) 302
Ed Smith, Wyoming '77 (39-16) 296
Ed Smith, Minnesota '78 (42-26) 296

Receptions

Mitch Lyons, Michigan '92 12
Andre Rison, Indiana '86 11
Darrin McClelland, Michigan '82 10
Ted Jones, Illinois '80 10
Muhsin Muhammad,
    Louisiana State '95 9
Andre Rison, Georgia '89 9
Gene Washington, Notre Dame '64 9
Darrin McClelland, Wisconsin '82 9
Ted Jones, Michigan '82 9
Andre Rison, Wisconsin '86 9
Courtney Hawkins, Minnesota '89 9
Derrick Mason, Iowa '95 8
Scott Greene, Penn State, '94 8
Bob Organ, Ohio State '93 8
Mill Coleman, Kansas '93 8
Courtney Hawkins, Rutgers '91 8
Courtney Hawkins, Michigan '89 8
Courtney Hawkins, Northwestern '89 8
Bobby Morse, Arizona State '86 8
Otis Grant, Illinois '82 8
Al Kimichik, Indiana '81 8
Ted Jones, Wisconsin '80 8

Kirk Gibson, Minnesota '78 8
Mark Brammer, Notre Dame '77 8
Billy Joe DuPree, Southern Cal '72 8
Billy Joe DuPree, Illinois '71 8
Frank Waters, Jr., Notre Dame '67 8

Receiving Yardage

Andre Rison, Georgia '89 252
Courtney Hawkins, Minnesota '89 197
Andre Rison, Indiana '86 196
Courtney Hawkins, Purdue '89 193
Kirk Gibson,
    North Carolina State '76 173
Muhsin Muhammad,
    Louisiana State '95 171
Andre Rison, Wisconsin '87 162
Eugene Byrd, Iowa '79 159
Andre Rison, Western Michigan '86 155
Frank Foreman, Purdue '69 155
Allen Brenner, Baylor '68 153
Gene Washington, Notre Dame '64 150
Mark Ingram, Iowa '85 148
Kirk Gibson, Minnesota '77 148

Rushing-Passing Yardage

Bryan Clark, Minnesota '81 372
Ed Smith, Indiana '78 369
Eric Allen, Purdue '71 350
Bryan Clark, Wisconsin '81 343
Dave Yarema, Northwestern '86 342
Dan Enos, Purdue '89 330
Ed Smith, North Carolina State '76 324
Tony Banks, Louisiana State '95 320
Dave Yarema, Minnesota '86 318
Dan Werner, Purdue '69 314
Ed Smith, Wisconsin '78 314
Bryan Clark, Michigan '81 303
John Leister, Michigan '82 300

Total Touchdowns*

Blake Ezor, Northwestern '89 6
Scott Greene, Illinois '95 4
Craig Thomas, Central Michigan '93 4
Craig Thomas, Indiana '92 4
Tico Duckett, Purdue '90 4
Blake Ezor, Indiana '89 4
Clinton Jones, Iowa '65 4
Bud Crane, Hawaii '47 4
Eric Allen, Purdue '71 4
Eric Allen, Minnesota '71 4
Derek Hughes, Minnesota '79 4
Steve Smith, Northwestern '80 4
(*The above are modern-day records:
George E. "Carp" Julian, scored seven TDs
in a 75-6 win over Akron in 1914.)

Rushing Touchdowns

Blake Ezor, Northwestern '89 6
Scott Greene, Illinois '95 4
Craig Thomas, Central Michigan '93 4
Craig Thomas, Indiana '92 4
Tico Duckett, Purdue '90 4
Blake Ezor, Indiana '89 4
Clinton Jones, Iowa '65 4
Eric Allen, Purdue '71 4
Eric Allen, Minnesota '71 4
Derek Hughes, Minnesota '79 4
Steve Smith, Northwestern '80 4

Touchdown Passes Thrown

Gene Glick, Iowa State '48 4
Mike Rasmussen, Indiana '70 4
Ed Smith, Wisconsin, '78 4
11 players on 21 occasions 3

Touchdown Passes Caught

Gene Washington, Indiana '65 3
Mark Ingram, Iowa '86 3
Andre Rison, Georgia '89 3

Points Scored

Blake Ezor, Northwestern '89 36
Scott Greene, Illinois '95 26
Craig Thomas, Central Michigan '93 24
Craig Thomas, Indiana '92 24
Tico Duckett, Purdue '90 24
Blake Ezor, Indiana '89 24
Clinton Jones, Iowa '65 24
Bud Crane, Hawaii '47 24
Eric Allen, Purdue '71 24
Eric Allen, Minnesota '71 24
Derek Hughes, Minnesota '79 24
Steve Smith, Northwestern '80 24
Bob Apisa, Northwestern '65 20
Sherman Lewis, Michigan '62 20
Evan Slonac, Marquette '52 20
Bob Carey, Oregon State '50 20

PAT Scored

John Langeloh, Northwestern '89 10
George Smith, Hawaii '48 8
George Smith, Temple '49 8
George Smith, Arizona '49 8
Evan Slonac, Marquette '52 8
Morten Andersen, Illinois '78 8
Morten Andersen, Northwestern '81 7
John Langeloh, Miami(O.) '89 7
John Langeloh, Purdue '90 7

Field Goals Scored

John Langeloh, Wisconsin '88 5
Ralf Mojsiejenko, Minnesota '82 4
Dirk Kryt, Ohio State '72 4
Hans Nielsen, Purdue '77 4
Morten Andersen, Illinois '79 4
Morten Andersen, Indiana '81 4
Chris Gardner, Lousiville '95 3
Chris Gardner, Wisconsin, '94 3
Ralf Mojsiejenko, Indiana '82 3
Dick Kenney, Penn State '65 3
Hans Nielsen, North Carolina State '75 3
Hans Nielsen, Indiana '76 3
Morten Andersen, Iowa '79 3
Morten Andersen, Michigan '80 3
Morten Andersen, Minnesota '80 3
Ralf Mojsiejenko, Colorado '83 3
Ralf Mojsiejenko, Purdue '83 3
John Langeloh, Wisconsin '87 3
John Langeloh, Northwestern '88 3
John Langeloh, Syracuse '90 3
Jim DelVerne, Ohio State '91 3

Tackles

Dan Bass, Ohio State '79 32
Don Law, Ohio State '69 28
Dan Bass, Notre Dame '79 24
Percy Snow, Illinois '89 23
Ty Hallock, Minnesota '92 21
Shane Bullough, Indiana '85 21
Brad VanPelt, Notre Dame '71 21
Doug Barr, Ohio State '69 21
Don Law, Indiana '67 21
Steve Otis, Wisconsin '79 20
Otto Smith, Wisconsin '74 20
Rich Saul, Notre Dame '68 20
Tim Moore, Iowa '85 19
Mike Hogan, Iowa '69 19
Jim Morrissey, Purdue '83 19
Derek Bunch, Notre Dame '83 19
Shane Bullough, Indiana '86 19
Percy Snow, Purdue '88 19
Percy Snow, Notre Dame '89 19
Chuck Bullough, Wisconsin '90 19
Chuck Bullough, Central Michigan '91 ... 19
Chuck Bullough, Notre Dame '91 19
Chuck Bullough, Indiana '91 19
Ty Hallock, Ohio State '92 19

Tackles for Loss

Travis Davis, Ohio State '87 (37yds.) 5
Rich Saul, Iowa '68 (14 yds.) 5
Matt Christensen, Indiana '93 (16 Yds.) 4
Brian McConnell, Northwestern '72
    (34 yds.) 4
Ray Nester, Iowa '72 (22 yds.) 4
Kelly Quinn, Illinois '83 (18 yds.) 4
Kelly Quinn, Colorado '84 (24 yds.) 4
Kelly Quinn, Northwestern '84
    (26 yds.) 4

John Miller, Northwestern '87 (8 yds.) 4
Carlos Jenkins, Indiana '89 (28 yds.) 4
John MacNeill, Northwestern '91
    (35 yds.) 4
Several players with three tackles for loss

Quarterback Sacks

Travis Davis, Ohio State '87 (37 yds.) 5
Kelly Quinn, Northwestern '84
    (26 yds.) 4
Rich Saul, Iowa '69 (13 yds.) 4
Kelly Quinn, Colorado '84 (22 yds.) 3
Kelly Quinn, Illinois '83 (15 yds.) 3

Pass Interceptions

John Miller, Michigan '87 4
Jim Ellis, Oregon State '50 3
Jesse Thomas, Indiana '50 3
Jesse Thomas, Michigan '50 3
John Polonchek, William & Mary '49 3
Brad VanPelt, Washington State '70 3
Mark Anderson, Notre Dame '77 3

Fumble Recoveries

Phil Hoag, Illinois '66 3
Ernie Clark, Illinois '61 3
Matt Vanderbeek, Hawaii '89 3
Several players with two fumble recoveries

Passes Broken Up

James Burroughs, Purdue '79 4
Several players with three passes
    broken up

Punt Return Yardage

Allen Brenner, Illinois '66 (3 ret.) 117
Jesse Thomas, Minnesota '50
    (4 ret.) 113
Derrick Mason, Michigan '95
    (3 ret.) 106
Jesse Thomas, William & Mary '50
    (3 ret.) 105
John Matsock, Illinois '54 (4 ret.) 104
Sherman Lewis, Northwestern '63
    (4 ret.) 103

Kickoff Return Yardage

Derrick Mason, Penn State '94
    (5 ret.) 186
Larry Jackson, Ohio State '84
    (4 ret.) 168

Derrick Mason, Michigan '94
    (7 ret.) 156
Derrick Mason, Indiana '95
    (7 ret.) 148
Eric Allen, Washington '70
    (5 ret.) 136
Derrick Mason, LSU '95
    (4 ret.) 132
Courtney Hawkins, Central Michigan '91 (3
    ret.) 131
Derrick Mason, Minnesota '95
    (5 ret.) 129
Derrick Mason, Purdue '94
    (4 ret.) 125
Russ Reader, Miami Fla. '45 (5 ret) 122
Eric Allen, Ohio State '69 (7 ret.) 119
Derrick Mason, Nebraska '95
    (6 ret.) 115
John Matsock, Notre Dame '54
    (4 ret.) 112
Derek Hughes, Wisconsin '79
    (3 ret.) 110
Mark Ingram, Purdue '85
    (4 ret.) 108
Blake Ezor, Indiana '87
    (2 ret.) 107

PLAY

Rushing Yardage

Lynn Chandnois, Arizona '49 (TD) 90
Tico Duckett, Minnesota '91 (TD) 88
Levi Jackson, Ohio State '74 (TD) 88
Dick Panin, Notre Dame '51 (TD) 88
Sherman Lewis, Northwestern '63
    (TD) 87
George Guerre, Iowa State '47 (TD) 87
Sherman Lewis, Notre Dame '63 (TD) ... 85
Craig Thomas, Purdue '92 82
Clinton Jones, Ohio State '65 (TD) 80
Bruce Reeves, Wisconsin '79 (TD) 79
Clinton Jones, Iowa '66 (TD) 79
Blake Ezor, Indiana '89 (TD) 79
Rich Baes, Northwestern '76 (TD) 76
Tyrone Wilson, Notre Dame '75 76

Passing Yardage

Tony Banks to Nigea Carter, Ind. '94 (TD)93
Steve Juday to Sherman Lewis, So. Cal '63
    (TD) 88
Steve Juday to Sherman Lewis, Wisconsin
    '63 (TD) 87
Ed Smith to Kirk Gibson, Indiana '78
    (TD) 86
Ed Smith to Kirk Gibson, Minnesota '77
    (TD) 85
Bill Feraco to Allen Brenner, Baylor '68
    (TD) 83

Gene Glick to Lynn Chandnois, Notre Dame '49 (TD) 83
Ed Smith to Kirk Gibson, Wyoming '77 (TD) 82
Marshall Lawson to Kirk Gibson, Ohio State '76 (TD) 82
Charlie Baggett to Kirk Gibson, Iowa '75 (TD) 82
Clark Brown to Carl Butler, Purdue '83 (TD) 82

Field Goal Yardage

Morten Andersen, Ohio State '81 63
Ralf Mojsiejenko, Illinois '82 61
Ralf Mojsiejenko, Purdue '83 59
Morten Andersen, Michigan '80 57
Borys Shlapak, Iowa '71 54
Borys Shlapak, Northwestern '70 54
Borys Shlapak, Minnesota '71 54
Morten Andersen, Iowa '79 54
Ralf Mojsiejenko, Purdue '84 54

Morten Andersen, Minnesota '79 53
Morten Andersen, Notre Dame '79 53
Hans Nielsen, Wyoming '77 53
Borys Shlapak, Purdue '71 53

Interception Return Yardage

Dan Bass, Wisconsin '78 (pass-TD) 99
Bob Suci, Michigan '59 (pass-TD) 93
Earl Morrall, Purdue '55 (fumble-TD) 90
Allen Brenner, Minnesota '68 (pass-TD) 84
Carl Williams, Northwestern '81 (pass-TD) 83
Brad McLee, Washington '70 (pass-TD) 80
Dave Kaiser, Minnesota '57 (fumble-TD) 77
Phil Parker, Illinois '83 (pass-TD) 72
Don Law, Washington '69 (pass-TD) 70
Mike Marshall, Purdue '80 (pass-TD) 57

Punt Return Yardage

Allen Brenner, Illinois '66 (TD) 95
Dean Look, Michigan '58 (TD) 92
Jesse Thomas, William & Mary '50 (TD) 90
Bobby Morse, Michigan '84 (TD) 87
Blanche Martin, Illinois '57 (TD) 86
Horace Smith, Santa Clara '47 (TD) 85
Sherman Lewis, Northwestern '63 84
Scott Greene, Indiana '95 (TD) 76
Bill Simpson, Georgia Tech '72 (TD) 74
Derrick Mason, Michigan '95 (TD) 70
Tom Hannon, Northwestern '74 70

Punt Yardage

Greg Montgomery, Michigan '86 86
Chris Salani, Nebraska '95 83
Greg Montgomery, Indiana '85 80
Greg Montgomery, Michigan '85 75
Ray Stachowicz, Notre Dame '78 75
Ray Stachowicz, Wisconsin '80 73
Ray Stachowicz, Purdue '79 73
Ray Stachowicz, Purdue '78 72
Ralf Mojsiejenko, Iowa '84 72
Earl Morrall, Stanford '55 71
Ralf Mojsiejenko, Notre Dame '83 71
Ralf Mojsiejenko, Wisconsin '83 71
Ralf Mojsiejenko, Ohio State '84 70
Greg Montgomery, Indiana '86 70

Kickoff Return Yardage

Derrick Mason, LSU '95 (TD) 100
Derrick Mason, Penn State '94 (TD) 100
Derek Hughes, Oregon '79 (TD) 100
Derek Hughes, Wisconsin '79 (TD) 98
Russ Reader, Wayne State '46 (TD) 98
Mike Holt, UCLA '73 (TD) 95
Dwight Lee, Northwestern '67 (TD) 93
Larry Jackson, Ohio State '84 (TD) 93
Blake Ezor, Indiana '87 90
Derrick Mason, Indiana '95 (TD) 87
Courtney Hawkins, Illinois '89 85
Derrick Mason, Purdue '94 81
Jim Ellis, Michigan '51 79
Courtney Hawkins, Central Michigan '91 66
Blanche Martin, Wisconsin '57 65
Ron Rubick, Minnesota '62 64
Jim Ellis, Indiana '52 64

MICHIGAN STATE IN THE RANKINGS

Michigan State football teams have ranked in the nation's top 10 in Associated Press and United Press International polls 12 times in the last 45 years. They have also been in the second 10 on six other occasions.

State made the elite group for the first time in 1950, and was ranked No. 1 in both polls in 1952 and by UPI in 1965. State was second in both polls in 1951, 1955 and 1966, and third in 1953 and 1957.

The Spartans also made their first appearance in the CNN/USA poll in 1987, ranking eighth.

THE RANKING YEARS

	AP	UPI
1950	8th	9th
1951	2nd	2nd
*1952	1st	1st
1953	3rd	3rd
1955	2nd	2nd
1956	9th	10th
1957	3rd	3rd
1960	15th	13th
1961	8th	9th
1963	9th	9th
1964	—	20th
#1965	2nd	1st
+1966	2nd	2nd
1974	12th	18th
1978	12th	—
1987	8th	8th
1989	16th	t-16th
1990	16th	14th

*consensus national champions
#National champions UPI, No. 2 AP
+MSU awarded MacArthur Bowl with Notre Dame; Bowl is presented annually by National Football Foundation Hall of Fame and is emblematic of the national championship.

MISCELLANEOUS HONORS

Heisman Trophy Balloting Involving MSU Spartans

Year	Place, Player, Position (Winner)
1952	8th, Don McAuliffe, HB (Billy Vessels, Oklahoma)
1955	4th, Earl Morrall, QB (Howard Cassady, Ohio State)
1957	3rd, Walt Kowalczyk, HB (John Crow, Texas A & M) 8th, Dan Currie, C
1959	6th, Dean Look, QB (Billy Cannon, LSU)
1962	7th, George Saimes, FB (Terry Baker, Oregon St.)
1963	3rd, Sherman Lewis, HB (Roger Staubach, Navy)
1965	6th, Steve Juday, QB (Mike Garrett, Southern California) 13th, Clinton Jones, HB
1966	6th, Clinton Jones, HB (Steve Spurrier, Florida)
1971	10th, Eric Allen, HB (Pat Sullivan, Auburn)
1972	13th, Brad VanPelt, S (Johnny Rogers, Nebraska)
1985	4th, Lorenzo White, TB (Bo Jackson, Auburn)
1987	4th, Lorenzo White, TB (Tim Brown, Notre Dame)
1988	6th, Tony Mandarich, OT (Barry Sanders, Oklahoma State)
1989	8th, Percy Snow, LB (Andre Ware, Houston)

National Coach of the Year (AFCA)

Clarence L. Munn, 1952
Hugh Duffy Daugherty, 1955

National Coach of the Year (FWAA)

Hugh Duffy Daugherty, 1955, 1965

The Sporting News Coach of the Year

Darryl Rogers, 1978

Butkus Award

Percy Snow, 1989

Outland Award

Ed Bagdon, 1949

Lombardi Award

Percy Snow, 1989

UPI Lineman of the Year

Charles "Bubba" Smith, 1966

Robert W. Maxwell Award

Brad VanPelt, 1972

Walter Camp Trophy

Don McAuliffe, 1952

Big Ten Coach of the Year

Dennis Stolz, 1974 (Midwest Writers and Broadcasters)
Darryl Rogers, 1978 (Midwest Writers and Broadcasters)
George Perles, 1987 (UPI)

UPI Big Ten Most Valuable Player

Lorenzo White, 1985 (co-MVP with Iowa's Chuck Long)
Lorenzo White, 1987

Chicago Tribune Big Ten Most Valuable Player

Eric Allen, 1971
Larry Bethea, 1977
Lorenzo White, 1987

Big Ten Broadcasters Lineman of the Year

Offensive — Tony Mandarich, 1987, 1988
Offensive — Bob Kula, 1989

Pro Football Hall of Fame

Herb Adderley, 1980

College Football Hall of Fame (Coaches)

Clarence L. Munn, 1959
Charles W. Bachman, 1978
Hugh Duffy Daugherty, 1984

(Players)

John S. Pingel, 1968
Don E. Coleman, 1975
George Webster, 1987
Charles "Bubba'" Smith, 1988

Michigan Sports Hall of Fame

Clarence L. Munn, 1961
Ralph H. Young, 1962
John H. Kobs, 1968
John S. Pingel, 1973
Hugh Duffy Daugherty, 1975
Lyman L. Frimodig, 1976
Earl E. Morrall, 1979
Charles P. Davey, 1980
Don L. Ridler, 1981
Glenn Johnson, 1987
Lynn Chandnois, 1987
Bob Carey, 1990
Frank "Muddy" Waters, 1992
Charles "Bubba" Smith, 1993
Herb Adderley, 1996

CoSIDA Academic All-America

*Indicates first- team selection
1952 —	*John Wilson, back
1953 —	*Donald Dohoney, end
	Carl Diener, end
1954 —	Donald Kauth, end
1955 —	*Carl Nystrom, guard
1957 —	*Blanche Martin, back
	Robert Jewett, end
1958 —	Richard Barker, end
	Ellison Kelly, guard
	Blanche Martin, back (honorary)
1960 —	Edward Ryan, roverback
1964 —	Eugene Washington, end
	Richard Gordon, back
1965 —	*Donald Japinga, back
	*Donald Bierowicz, tackle
1966 —	*Patrick Gallinagh, tackle
	Allen Brenner, end
1968 —	*Allen Brenner, end-safety
1969 —	*Ronald Saul, guard
	*Richard Saul, end
1973 —	*John Shinsky, tackle
	Richard Pawlak, tackle
1974 —	Richard Baes, back
1975 —	Thomas Standal, middle guard
1976 —	David Duda, defensive back
1977 —	James Sciarini, guard
	Craig Fedore, linebacker
1979 —	*Alan Davis, defensive back
1985 —	*Dean Altobelli, defensive back
	Shane Bullough, linebacker
1986 —	*Dean Altobelli, strong safety
	*Shane Bullough, linebacker
1989 —	Chris Willertz, defensive end
1992 —	*Steve Wasylk, strong safety
1993 —	*Steve Wasylk, strong safety

GTE Academic All-America Hall of Fame

1989 — John Wilson

Toyota Leadership Award

1989—Chris Willertz, Notre Dame game

Downtown Athletic Club, New York

Outstanding Offensive End
1978 —   Kirk Gibson, flanker

Cleveland Touchdown Club Player Award

Clinton Jones, 1966

Columbus Touchdown Club

Brad VanPelt, 1972 (College Defensive Back of the Year)
Carl Banks, 1983 (College Linebacker of the Year)
Lorenzo White, 1985 (College Running Back of the Year)
Tony Mandarich, 1988 (College Offensive Lineman of the Year)

Washington, D.C. Touchdown Club

Lorenzo White, 1985 (College Running Back of the Year)
Tony Mandarich, 1988 (College Lineman of the Year)

Fiesta Bowl Samaritan All-American of the Year

Tony Mandarich, 1988

Honda Scholar-Athlete Award

Pat Shurmur, USC game, 1987
Mill Coleman, Kansas game, 1993

National Football Hall of Fame Graduate Fellowship Award

Steve Juday, 1965
Allen Brenner, 1968
Dean Altobelli, 1986
Steve Wasylk, 1993

NCAA Post-Graduate Scholarship

Allen Brenner, 1968
Donald Baird, 1969
Steve Wasylk, 1993

Playboy's Anson Mount Scholar-Athlete of the Year

Steve Wasylk, 1993

Sports Illustrated Silver Anniversary All-American

Clarence L. Munn, 1956
Arthur F. Brandstatter, 1961
Frank Gaines Jr., 1962

NCAA Silver Anniversary Award

Bob McCurry, 1974
Don Coleman, 1977
Steve Juday, 1990

NCAA College Athletics Top Ten

Robert McCurry, 1974

Players of the Game Chevrolet Scholarship Award

Ron Curl, defensive winner Michigan game, 1971, $1,000
Brad VanPelt, defensive winner Notre Dame game, 1971, $1,000
Brad VanPelt, defensive winner of the year, 1972, $5,000
Mark Niesen, offensive winner Ohio State game, 1972, $1,000
Gail Clark, defensive winner Notre Dame game, 1972, $1,000
Paul Hayner, defensive winner Syracuse game, 1973, $1,000
Charles Baggett, offensive winner Ohio State game, 1974, $1,000
Levi Jackson, offensive winner North Carolina St. game, 1975, $1,000
Larry Bethea, defensive winner North Carolina St. game, 1975, $1,000
Derek Hughes, offensive winner Minnesota game, 1979, $1,000
Steve Smith, offensive winner Michigan game, 1979, $1,000
Ted Jones, offensive winner Illinois game, 1980, $1,000
John Leister, MSU player of game Illinois game, 1982, $1,000
Phil Parker, MSU player of game Illinois game, 1983, $1,000
Clark Brown, MSU player of game Purdue game, 1983, $1,000
Phil Parker, MSU player of game, Cherry Bowl game vs. Army, 1984, $1,000
Lorenzo White, MSU player of game Iowa game, 1985, $1,000
Phil Parker, MSU player of game Michigan game, 1985, $1,000
Todd Krumm, MSU player of game Notre Dame game, 1986, $1,000
Mark Ingram, MSU player of game Iowa game, 1986, $1,000

Players of the Game Chevrolet
Scholarship Award, cont.

Lorenzo White, MSU player of game, USC game, 1987, $1,000

Lorenzo White, MSU player of game Michigan game, 1987, $1,000

Bobby McAllister, MSU player of game Ohio State game, 1987, $1,000

Lorenzo White, MSU player of game Indiana game, 1987, $1,000

Blake Ezor, MSU player of game Iowa game, 1988, $1,000

Blake Ezor, MSU player of game Indiana game, 1988, $1,000

Percy Snow, MSU player of game Notre Dame game, 1989, $1,000

Percy Snow, MSU player of game Miami (Fla.) game, 1989, $1,000

Travis Davis, MSU player of game Michigan game, 1989, $1,000

Chuck Bullough, MSU player of the game Notre Dame game, 1990, $1,000

Dan Enos, MSU player of the game Michigan game, 1990, $1,000

John Langeloh, MSU player of the game Illinois game, 1990, $1,000

Courtney Hawkins, MSU player of the game Notre Dame game, 1991, $1,000

Jim DelVerne, MSU player of the game Ohio State game, 1991, $1,000

Craig Thomas, MSU player of game Notre Dame game, 1992, $1,000

Steve Wasylk, MSU player of game Michigan game, 1992, $1,000

Bret Johnson, MSU player of game Ohio State game, 1992, $1,000

Craig Thomas, MSU player of game Kansas game, 1993, $1,000

Mill Coleman, MSU player of game Notre Dame game, 1993, $1,000

Rob Fredrickson, MSU player of game Michigan game, 1993, $1,000

Jim Miller, MSU player of game Ohio State game, 1993, $1,000

Steve Holman, MSU player of game Penn State game, 1993, $1,000

Robert Shurelds, MSU player of game Notre Dame game, 1994, $1,000

Mill Coleman, MSU player of game Ohio State game, 1994, $1,000

Tony Banks, MSU player of game Nebraska game, 1995, $1,000

Scott Greene, MSU player of game Purdue game, 1995, $1,000

Todd Schultz, MSU player of game Boston College game, 1995, $1,000

Tony Banks, MSU player of game Michigan game, 1995, $1,000

SPARTAN FIRST-TEAM
ALL-AMERICA SELECTIONS

ABBREVIATIONS

AFC- American Football Coaches
AP - Associated Press
B - All-American Board
CBS-TV - CBS Television Sports
CP- Central Press
CTP - Chicago Tribune Players
FCAK - Football Coaches Association Kodak
FD - Football Digest
FN - Football News
FWA - Football Writers Association
GNS - Gannett News Service
INS - International News Service
MSN - Medalist Sports News
MTV - Mizlou TV Sports (Seniors)
NEA - Newspaper Enterprise Association
NYN - New York News
NYS - New York Sun
PN- Paramount News
SN- Sporting News
UP - United Press
UPI - United Press International
US - Universal Sports
WC - Walter Camp

1915	* Neno Jerry DaPrato, halfback — INS, Detroit Times, W. Blake Miller, end — Atlanta Constitution
1935	*Sidney P. Wagner, guard — UP, INS, NYS, Liberty Magazine
1936	Arthur Brandstatter, fullback — B
1938	*John S. Pingel, halfback — AP
1949	*Lynn E. Chandnois, halfback — INS, UP, CP, FN, Collier's
	Donald L. Mason, guard — PN, FN
	*Edward Bagdon, guard — Look, UP, SN, NYN, CP, NEA, Tele-News
1950	*Dorne A. Dibble, end — Look
	*Everett Grandelius, halfback — AP, INS, CP
1951	*Robert W. Carey, end — UP, AP, SN, NEA, NYN, B
	*Don E. Coleman, tackle — AP, UP, Collier's, Look, SN, NYN, FN, NEA, CP, Tele-News, INS, CTP, B
	*Albert R. Dorow, quarterback — INS
	James Ellis, halfback — CTP
1952	*Frank J. Kush, guard — AP, Look, NYN, Fox Movietone, Athletic Publications, All-Catholic
	*Donald F. McAuliffe, halfback — UP, Collier's, FD, PN, All-Catholic

	*Richard P. Tamburo, center — AP, CP, NEA, INS, NYN, FD, PN, Athletic Publ.
	Ellis Duckett, Jr., end — NBC-TV
	Thomas Yewcic, quarterback — NBC-TV
	James Ellis, halfback — CTP
1953	*Donald C. Dohoney, end — AP, UP, Collier's, Look, SN, FN, NEA, CP, NBC-TV
	LeRoy Bolden, Jr., halfback — NBC-TV
	Larry D. Fowler, guard — NBC-TV
1955	*Earl E. Morrall, quarterback — AP, Collier's, Look, INS, SN, PN, NBC-TV, Hearst Syndicate, Frank Leahy
	*Norman D. Masters, tackle — UP, Look, INS, NEA, NBC-TV, CP, Fox Movietone
	Carl W. Nystrom, guard — Radio-TV Guide, Frank Leahy
	Gerald R. Planutis, fullback — Jet
1957	*Walter J. Kowalczyk, halfback — FWA, SN, NEA, UP, CP, FCAK, NBC-TV, FD
	*Daniel G. Currie, center — FWA, AP, INS, FCA, NBC-TV
1958	*Samuel F. Williams, end — UPI, FCA, NYN, Time
1959	*Dean Z. Look, quarterback — FWA, FN
1961	*David W. Behrman, guard — AP, FWA
1962	Dave Behrman, guard — CBS TV
1962	*George Saimes, fullback — AP, UPI, FWA, FCA, NYN, SN, CBS-TV, Look
	Edward L. Budde, guard — Time
1963	*Sherman P, Lewis, halfback — AP, UPI, CP, FWA, NYN
	Earl P. Lattimer, guard — NYN
1965	Robert Apisa, fullback — FN
	*Ronald E. Goovert, linebacker — FWA
	*Clinton Jones, halfback — FWA
	*Stephen A. Juday, quarterback — AP
	*Harold W. Lucas, middle guard — NEA
	*Charles A. Smith, def. end — AFC, UPI
	*Eugene Washington, end — CP, FN, FD
	*George Webster, roverback — AP, NEA, AFC, UPI, FN, NYN
1966	Robert Apisa, fullback — FN, NYN
	*Clinton Jones, halfback — AP, CP, NEA, SN
	*Charles A. Smith, def. end — AP, UPI, FWA, AFC, NEA, SN, CP, FN, NYN
	*Eugene Washington, end — UPI, AFC, SN
	*George Webster, roverback — AP, UPI, AFC, FWA, NEA, SN, CP, FN, NYN
	*Jerry West, tackle — NEA

1968	*Allen Brenner, safety — AFC, NEA	1985	*Lorenzo White, tailback — AP, UPI, FVVA, WC, AFC, SN
1969	*Ronald R. Saul, guard — NEA, Time, SN	1986	*Greg Montgomery, punter — FWA
1971	*Eric B. Allen, tailback — AFC	1987	Tony Mandarich, offensive tackle—FN
	*Brad A. VanPelt, safety — UPI, FN		Greg Montgomery, punter—FN, GNS, MTV
	*Ronald C. Curl, tackle — AFC		*Lorenzo White, tailback—FN, WC, FWA, GNS, UPI, FCAK, MTV
1972	*Brad A. VanPelt, safety — AP, UPI, AFC, FWA, Time, SN, US, WC, Gridiron	1988	*Tony Mandarich, offensive tackle — AP, UPI, FCAK, WC, FWA, SN, GNS, FN, MTV
	*Joseph DeLamielleure, guard — SN		Andre Rison, split end — GNS
	Billy Joe DuPree, end — Time		*Percy Snow, linebacker — SN
1973	*William T. Simpson, def. back — SN, US	1989	Harlon Barnett, defensive back — SN, MTV
1978	*Kirk H. Gibson, flanker — UPI, SN, FN, NEA		*Bob Kula, offensive tackle — FCAK, AP
	*Mark D. Brammer, tight end — FWA		*Percy Snow, linebacker — FCAK, AP, UPI, FWA, FN, SN, WC, MTV
1979	Raymond Stachowicz, punter — FN		
1980	Raymond Stachowicz, punter — FN, NEA, WC, MSN		
1981	*Morten Andersen, placekicker — SN, UPI, WC		
	*James Burroughs, def. back — SN		
1983	*Carl Banks, linebacker — AP, UPI, SN		
	*Ralf Mojsiejenko, punter — SN		

SPARTAN TEAM AWARDS

Governor of Michigan Award

Given annually since 1931 to the player who is voted the most valuable on the team by the men on the football squad. Presentation made each year by the governor of Michigan.

1931 — Abe Eliowitz, fullback
1932 — Robert Monnett, halfback
1933 — Arthur Buss, tackle
1934 — Edward Klewicki, end
1935 — Sid Wagner, guard
1936 — Sam Ketchman, center
1937 — Harry Speelman, tackle
1938 — John Pingel, halfback
1939 — Lyle Rockenbach, guard
1940 — Jack Amon, fullback
1941 — Anthony Arena, center
1942 — Richard Kieppe, halfback
1943 — No award
1944 — Jack Breslin, fullback
1945 — Steve Contos, halfback
1946 — George Guerre, halfback
1947 — Warren Huey, end
1948 — Lynn Chandnois, halfback
1949 — Eugene Glick, quarterback
1950 — Everett Grandelius, halfback
1951 — Don Coleman, tackle
1952 — Richard Tamburo, linebacker
1953 — LeRoy Bolden, halfback
1954 — John Matsock, halfback
1955 — Carl Nystrom, guard
1956 — James Hinesly, end
1957 — Dan Currie, center
1958 — Sam Williams, end
1959 — Dean Look, quarterback
1960 — Thomas Wilson, quarterback
1961 — George Saimes, fullback
1962 — George Saimes, fullback
1963 — Sherman Lewis, halfback
1964 — Richard Gordon, halfback
1965 — Stephen Juday, quarterback
1966 — George Webster, roverback
1967 — Dwight Lee, halfback
1968 — Allen Brenner, end-safety
1969 — Ronald Saul, guard
1970 — Eric Allen, tailback
1971 — Eric Allen, tailback
1972 — Gail Clark, linebacker
1973 — Ray Nester, linebacker
1974 — Charles Baggett, quarterback
1975 — Levi Jackson, fullback
1976 — Richard Baes, tailback
1977 — Larry Bethea, defensive tackle
1978 — Edward Smith, quarterback

1979 — Dan Bass, linebacker
1980 — Steve Smith, halfback
1981 — Bryan Clark, quarterback
1982 — James Neely, linebacker
1983 — Carl Banks, linebacker
1984 — Jim Morrissey, linebacker
1985 — Lorenzo White, tailback
1986 — Dave Yarema, quarterback
　　　　Mark Ingram, flanker
1987— Lorenzo White, tailback
1988— Kurt Larson, linebacker
1989— Percy Snow, linebacker
1990— Dan Enos, quarterback
　　　　Hyland Hickson, tailback
1991— Chuck Bullough, linebacker
　　　　Courtney Hawkins, wide receiver
1992— Mill Coleman, flanker/quarterback
1993—Brice Abrams, fullback
　　　　Jim Miller, quarterback
1994—Scott Greene, fullback
1995—Scott Greene, fullback

Love Award

Award given annually in the name of late Spartan football letterman Tommy Love, to the most improved player on the varsity team.

1971 — Errol Roy, tackle
1972 — Billy Joe DuPree, end
1973 — Michael Holt, tailback
1974 — Mike Duda, defensive end
1975 — Dane Fortney, split end
1976 — Anthony Marek, guard
　　　　Melvin Land, defensive tackle
1977 — Michael Dean, outside linebacker
1978 — Matthew Foster, center
1979 — Steve Otis, linebacker
　　　　Bryan Clark, quarterback
1980 — Alan Kimichik, tight end
1981 — Walter Schramm, offensive tackle
　　　　Steve Maidlow, linebacker
1982 — Jim Morrissey, linebacker
1983 — Tom Allan, defensive end
1984 — Anthony Bell, linebacker
1985 — Mark Ingram, flanker
　　　　Mark Nichols, def. tackle
1986 — John Budde, defensive end
　　　　Andre Rison, wide receiver
1987— Percy Snow, linebacker
1988— Matt Vanderbeek, defensive end
1989— Chris Willertz, defensive end
1990— Freddie Wilson, safety
　　　　Eddie Brown, cornerback

1991—Mitch Lyons, tight end
    John MacNeill, defensive end
1992— Steve Wasylk, strong safety
    Mike Edwards, defensive end
1993—Rich Glover, defensive end
1994—Demetrice Martin, def. back
    Muhsin Muhammad, flanker
1995—Flozell Adams, off. tackle
    Marvin Wright, safety

Cowing Award

This award, named for Frank P. Cowing, Jr., Spartan football manager in 1938, has been presented annually since 1969 to the outgoing head manager.

1969 — Robert Beery
1970 — Robert Snyder
1971 — Richard Drobot
1972 — Richard Lilly
1973 — Steve Repko
1974 — Craig Murray
1975 — Paul Weller
1976 — Robert Sommer
1977 — Jeffrey Arthurs
1978 — Jeffrey Minahan
1979 — Joseph McGiness
1980 — No award
1981 — Kam Hunter
    Kevin MacCarthy
1982 — Bill Featherstone
    Mike Zimmer
1983 — Mark Zimmer
1984 — Clay Spragg
    John Tobin
1985 — No award
1986 — Scott Bielat
    Dave Pruder
1987— Scott Bielat
1988— Chris Haas
1989— Brad Alward
    Joe Shurmur
1990 — Chris Besanceney
1991 — Chris Besanceney
    Scott Klott
1992 — No Award
1993 — No Award
1994 — Kevin Lartigue
1995 — No Award

Ross Award

Given annually since 1949 to the player who has made the best contribution to the team both athletically and scholastically. Named for the late F. Ward Ross, football letterman in 1925-26-27, and contributed by his wife, Mrs. Dorothy Ross.

1949 — John Polonchek, halfback
1950 — John Yocca, guard
1951 — Frank Kapral, guard
1952 — John Wilson, halfback
1953 — James Neal, center
1954 — Don Kauth, end
1955 — Carl Nystrom, guard
1956 — Pat Wilson, quarterback
1957 — Don Zysk, halfback
1958 — John Middleton, guard
1959 — Blanche Martin, fullback
1960 — Thomas Wilson, quarterback
1961 — Pete Kakela, tackle
1962 — George Azar, guard
1963 — Ed Youngs, center
1964 — Richard Flynn, tackle
1965 — Stephen Juday, quarterback
1966 — Patrick Gallinagh, guard
1967 — Anthony Conti, guard
1968 — Allen Brenner, end-safety
1969 — Donald Baird, guard
1970 — Victor Mittelberg, tackle
1971 — Michael Rasmussen, quarterback
1972 — Mark Grua, halfback-wide receiver
1973 — Bruce Harms, defensive back
1974 — Charles Wilson, guard
1975 — Thomas Standal, middle guard
1976 — David Radelet, split end
1977 — David Radelet, defensive back
1978 — Charles Shafer, tight end
1979 — Alan Davis, defensive back
1980 — Mike Sciarini, center
1981 — Bryan Boak, offensive tackle
1982 — Darrin McClelland, fullback
1983 — Tim Cunningham, safety
1984 — Bill Covey, guard
1985 — Steve Bogdalek, off. tackle
1986 — Dean Altobelli, strong safety
1987 — Pat Shurmur, center
1988 — Dave Martin, center
1989 — John Kiple, defensive back
1990 — Mike Iaquaniello, safety
1991 — Brian Vooletich, safety
1992 — Mark MacFarland, wide receiver
1993 — Steve Wasylk, defensive back
1994 — Mill Coleman, flanker
1995 — Chris Salani, punter

Presidents Award

This award, named for the University president, is now expanded to go to the outstanding senior lineman and senior back.

1965 — James Proebstle, end
1966 — Jeffrey Richardson, guard
1967 — Robert Lange, linebacker
1968 — Richard Berlinski, fullback
1969 — Bruce Kulesza, end
1970 — Gary Parmentier, guard
1971 — Doug Barr, halfback
1972 — Joseph DeLamielleure, tackle
1973 — John Shinsky, tackle
1974 — Mike Jones, flanker
1975 — Charles Baggett, quarterback
1976 — Michael Cobb, tight end
        Otto Smith, linebacker
1977 — Alfred Pitts, center
        Paul Rudzinski, inside linebacker
1978 — James Hinesly, offensive tackle
        Kirk Gibson, flanker
1979 — Mark Anderson, defensive back
        Mark Brammer, tight end
1980 — Rodney Strata, offensive guard
        Steve Smith, halfback
1981 — Jeff Wiska, offensive tackle
        Bryan Clark, quarterback
1982 — Darrin McClelland, fullback
        Tony Ellis, halfback
        Smiley Creswell, defensive tackle
1983 — Jim Bob Lamb, offensive tackle
        Nate Hannah, cornerback
1984 — Tom Allan, defensive end
        Terry Lewis, cornerback
        Lonnie Young, cornerback
1985 — Joe Curran, defensive tackle
        Phil Parker, free safety
1986 — Dave Wolff, defensive tackle
        Dave Yarema, quarterback
1987 — Pat Shurmur, center
        Mike Sargent, tight end
1988 — Jason Ridgeway, defensive tackle
        Vince Tata, guard
        Derrick Reed, defensive back
1989 — Matt Vanderbeek, defensive end
        Harlon Barnett, defensive back
1990 — Rob Roy, fullback
        Duane Young, tight end
1991— Alan Haller, def. back
        Chris Piwowarczyk, center
        Bill Johnson, defensive end
1992 — Mitch Lyons, tight end
        Tony Rollin, fullback
        Bret Johnson, quarterback

1993 — Brett Lorius, offensive guard
        Craig Thomas, tailback
1994 — Matt Christensen, linebacker
        Shane Hannah, off. tackle
        Aaron Jackson, def. tackle
        Bob Organ, tight end
1995 — Bob Denton, off. tackle
        Muhsin Muhammad, wide receiver

Munn Award

This award given annually in the name of the late MSU Athletic Director Clarence Biggie Munn to the team's most inspirational player.

1965 — Robert Viney, end
1966 — Jerry Jones, halfback
1967 — Frank Waters, halfback
1968 — Eddy McLoud, center
1969 — Donald Highsmith, halfback
1970 — Calvin Fox, end
1971 — Ronald Curl, tackle
1972 — Gary VanElst, tackle
1973 — Paul Hayner, halfback
1974 — Jim Taubert, defensive tackle
1975 — Gregory Schaum, tackle
1976 — Tyrone Willingham, flanker
1977 — Jerome Stanton, defensive back
1978 — Michael Hans, fullback
        Jerome Stanton, defensive back
1979 — Matthew Foster, center
1980 — Johnny Lee Haynes, defensive tackle
1981 — George Cooper, linebacker
1982 — Tony Gilbert, split end (posthumously)
1983 — Jim Rinella, defensive tackle
1984 — Jim Rinella, defensive tackle
1985 — Bobby Morse, fullback
        Mark Beaudoin, defensive end
1986 — Bobby Morse, fullback
1987 — Tim Moore, linebacker
1988 — Rich Gicewicz, tight end
1989 — Tim Ridinger, defensive tackle
1990 — Hyland Hickson, tailback
1991 — Ed O'Bradovich, defensive tackle
1992 — Jeff Graham, center
1993 — Brice Abrams, fullback
1994 — Scott Greene, fullback
1995 — Scott Greene, fullback

Doug Weaver Oil Can Award

This annual award goes to the player or manager who contributes most in a humorous way to the team.

1949 — Peter Fusi, tackle
1950 — Jack Morgan, tackle
1951 — Douglas Weaver, center
1952 — Gordon Serr, guard
          Doug Weaver, center
1953 — Larry Fowler, tackle
1954 — Henry Bullough, guard
1955 — Embry Robinson, guard
1956 — Joseph Carruthers, tackle
1957 — Robert Popp, quarterback
1958 — Thomas Vernon, end
1959 — Edwin McLucas, guard
1960 — Ronald Grimsley, guard
1961 — Wayne Fontes, halfback
1962 — Dewey Lincoln, halfback
1963 — Earl Lattimer, guard
1964 — Larry Mackey, fullback
1965 — Drake Garrett, halfback
1966 — Drake Garrett, halfback
1967 — Drake Garrett, halfback
1968 — Eddy McLoud, center
1969 — Clifton Hardy, halfback
1970 — Michael Tobin, linebacker
1971 — Dan Kovacs, manager
1972-79 — No award given
1980 — Gregg Lauble, linebacker
1981 — Gregg Lauble, linebacker
1982 — Gregg Lauble, linebacker
1983 — Darryl Dixon, safety
1984 — John Jones, defensive tackle
1985 — John Jones, defensive end
1986 — Pete Hrisko, quarterback
1987 — Greg Montgomery, punter
1988 — Steve Montgomery, fullback
1989 — Steve Montgomery, fullback
1990 — Dan Enos, quarterback
1991 — Jim Miller, quarterback
1992 — Jim Miller, quarterback
1993 — Jim Miller, quarterback
1994 — Nigea Carter, wide receiver
1995 — Yakini Allen, def. tackle

Iron Man Award

Presented annually to the player who has made the most noteworthy accomplishments in strength and conditioning.

1980 — Rodney Strata, offensive guard
1981 — Jeff Wiska, offensive tackle

1982 — Smiley Creswell, defensive tackle
1983 — Randy Lark, offensive guard
1984 — Mark Napolitan, center
1985 — Kelly Quinn, defensive end
1986 — Bobby Morse, fullback
1987 — David Houle, offensive tackle
1988 — Tony Mandarich, offensive tackle
1989 — Bob Kula, offensive tackle
1990 — Matt Keller, offensive guard
1991 — Jim Johnson, offensive tackle
1992 — Toby Heaton, offensive guard
1993 — Brett Lorius, offensive guard
1994 — Mark Birchmeier, center
          Brian DeMarco, off. guard
1995 — Chris Smith, def. tackle

Band-Aid Award

Presented annually to the player who shows greatest desire over adversity of injury.

1977 — Edgar Wilson, split end
1978 — Rodney Strata, offensive guard
1979 — Mark Anderson, safety
1980 — Mike Densmore, offensive guard
1981 — Johnny Lee Haynes, defensive tackle
1982 — Calvin Perkins, defensive nose guard
1983-95 — No award given

Spring Game Outstanding Player Award

Outstanding performers in spring windup game have been honored since 1948.

1948 — Lynn Chandnois, halfback
1949 — Lynn Chandnois, halfback
1950 — Everett Grandelius, halfback
1951 — Wayne Benson, fullback
1952 — Billy Wells, halfback
1953 — James Ellis, halfback
1954 — Gerald Planutis, fullback
          Howard Graves, halfback
1955 — Patrick Wilson, quarterback
          James Ninowski, quarterback
1956 — Clarence Peaks, halfback
1957 — James Ninowski, (Varsity), quarterback
          Gerald Planutis (Old Timers), fullback
1958 — Blanche Martin (Varsity), fullback
          Robert Jewett (Old Timers), end
1959 — Thomas Wilson (Varsity), quarterback
          James Ninowski (Old Timers), quarterback
1960 — Herb Adderley (Varsity), halfback
          Thomas Yewcic (Old Timers), quarterback
1961 — Sherman Lewis (Varsity), halfback
          Clarence Peaks (Old Timers), halfback

1962 — George Saimes (Varsity), fullback,
shared with Charles Migyanka (Varsity),
quarterback
Robert Ricucci (Old Timers), halfback
1963 — Richard Proebstle, quarterback, shared Stephen J
uday, quarterback
Matthew Snorton, end
1964 — Dave McCormick, quarterback, Green
John Walsh, guard, White
1965 — Jimmy Raye, quarterback, Green
Phil Hoag, end, White
1966 — Clinton Jones, halfback, Green
Richard Berlinski, halfback, White
1967 — Jimmy Raye, quarterback, Green
Gordon Bowdell, end, White
1968 — Allen Brenner, end, Green, offense
Wilt Martin, end, Green, defense
Gordon Longmire, quarterback, White, offense
Michael Hogan, linebacker, White, defense
1969 — William Triplett, back, Green
Frank Foreman, lineman, Green
Steven Piro, back, White
Frank Butler, lineman, White
1970 — Henry Matthews, back, Green
Wilt Martin, lineman, Green
George Mihaiu, back, White
Gordon Bowdell, lineman, White
1971 — Gail Clark, back, Green
Gary VanElst, lineman, Green
Mike Rasmussen, back, White
Frank Butler, lineman, White
1972 — George Mihaiu, offense, Green
Gary VanElst, defense, Green
James Bond, offense, White
Brian McConnell, defense, White
1973 — Charles Baggett, offense, Green
John Shinsky, defense, Green
David E. Brown, offense, White
Greg Schaum, defense, White
1974 — No Spring Game Played
1975 — No Spring Game Played
1976 — Ed Smith, quarterback, Green
Larry Bethea, defensive tackle, Green
1977 — Kirk Gibson, offense, Varsity
Paul Rudzinski, defense, Varsity
George Mihaiu, offense, Alumni
Paul Hayner, defense, Alumni
1978 — Ed Smith, offense, Varsity
Dan Bass, defense, Varsity
Rich Baes, offense, Alumni
Paul Hayner, defense, Alumni
1979 — Bryan Clark, offense
Craig Converse, defense
1980 — Samson Howard, offensive back
Jack Kirkling/Marv Mantos, off. line
Terry Bailey, defensive line
Marcus Toney, defensive back

1981 — John Leister, offensive back
Daryl Turner, offensive line
Ron Mitchem, defensive line
Jim Smith, defensive back
1982 — Aaron Roberts, halfback, Green, offense
Walter Schramm, tackle, Green, offense
Tim Cunningham, safety, White, def.
Rodney Parker, split end, White, offense
1983 — Carl Banks, linebacker, Green
Tim Cunningham, safety, White
1984 — Dave Yarema, quarterback
Jim Morrissey, linebacker
1985 — Lorenzo White, tailback
Joe Curran, defensive tackle
1986 — Andre Rison, split end
Dave Yarema, quarterback
Tony Mandarich, defensive end
1987 — Travis Davis, defensive tackle
Blake Ezor, tailback
1988 — Rich Gicewicz, tight end
Andre Rison, split end
1989 — John Gieselman, quarterback, white team
Todd Murray, def. back green team
1990 — Jim Miller, quarterback, white team
Craig Thomas, tailback, green team
1991 — Brice Abrams, fulllback, green team
Randy Vanderbush, outside linebacker, white team
1992 — Craig Thomas, tailback, green team
Mill Coleman, FL/QB, white team
1993 — Dale Person, def. tackle, green team
Hickey Thompson, tailback, white team
1994 — No Spring Game
1995 — Scott Greene, fullback, green team
Reggie Garnett, linebacker, green team

Outstanding Underclassmen Awards

Presented to outstanding varsity underclass lineman and
back.

1976 — Kirk Gibson, flanker
Larry Bethea, defensive tackle
1977 — Mark Brammer, tight end
Melvin Land, defensive tackle
Mark Anderson, defensive back
1978 — Mark Brammer, tight end
Steve Smith, tailback
1979 — Bernard Hay, middle guard
Steve Smith, tailback
1980 — Smiley Creswell, defensive end
Tie between Thomas Morris, def. back and John
Leister, quarterback
1981 — Carl Banks, linebacker
Ted Jones, split end
1982 — Carl Banks, linebacker
Randy Lark, tackle

1983 — Kelly Quinn, defensive end
       Phil Parker, safety
1984 — Kelly Quinn, defensive end
       Lorenzo White, tailback
1985 — Tony Mandarich, offensive tackle
       Shane Bullough, linebacker
       Lorenzo White, tailback
       Dave Yarema, quarterback
1986 — Mark Nichols, defensive tackle
       Dave Houle, offensive tackle
       Todd Krumm, cornerback
1987 — John Budde, defensive end
       Travis Davis, defensive tackle
       Bobby McAllister, quarterback
       Andre Rison, split end
1988 — Travis Davis, defensive tackle
       Blake Ezor, tailback
       Bob Kula, offensive guard
1989 — Eric Moten, offensive guard
       Duane Young, tight end
       Dan Enos, quarterback
       Courtney Hawkins, wide receiver
1990 — Tico Duckett, tailback
       Bill Johnson, defensive end
1991 — Tico Duckett, tailback
       William Reese, defensive tackle
1992 — Juan Hammonds, defensive end
       Myron Bell, cornerback
       Jim Miller, quarterback
       Craig Thomas, tailback
1993 — Juan Hammonds, defensive end
       Mark Birchmeier, center
       Duane Goulbourne, tailback
1994 — Tony Banks, quarterback
       Bob Denton, off. guard
       Duane Goulbourne, tailback
       Ike Reese, linebacker
1995 — Reggie Garnett, mid. linebacker
       Derrick Mason, wide receiver
       Ike Reese, out. linebacker
       Marc Renaud, tailback

Gerald R. Ford Up-Front Award

This award annually goes to the Spartan offensive lineman who most exemplifies the courage and integrity displayed by the nation's 38th President, Grand Rapids' own Jerry Ford. He personally approved the award, The winner receives a personalized plaque with a letter from Mr. Ford.

1975 — Michael Cobb, tight end
1976 — Tony Bruggenthies, offensive tackle
1977 — Alfred Pitts, center
1978 — James Hinesly, offensive tackle
1979 — Matthew Foster, center
1980 — Rodney Strata, offensive guard
1981 — Jeff Wiska, offensive tackle

1982 — Walt Schramm, offensive tackle
1983 — Scott Auer, offensive tackle
1984 — Mark Napolitan, center
1985 — John Wojciechowski, offensive guard
1986 — Tony Mandarich, offensive tackle
       Pat Shurmur, center
1987 — Tony Mandarich, offensive tackle
1988 — Tony Mandarich, offensive tackle
1989 — Bob Kula, offensive guard
1990 — Eric Moten, offensive guard
1991 — Jim Johnson, offensive tackle
1992 — Toby Heaton, offensive guard
1993 — Shane Hannah, offensive tackle
1994 — Brian DeMarco, offensive guard
1995 — Matt Beard, center

Football Bust Radio Network Awards

Awarded at the MSU Football Bust by WXYT Radio, these honored the most outstanding offensive and defensive stars.
*Awards presented at Detroit Bust through 1988

Offensive Player

1977 — James Hinesly, tackle
1978 — James Hinesly, tackle
1979 — Mark Brammer, tight end
1980 — Steve Smith, halfback
1981 — Bryan Clark, quarterback
1982 — Otis Grant, flanker
1983 — Daryl Turner, split end
1984 — Mark Ingram, flanker
1985 — Lorenzo White, tailback
1986 — Dave Yarema, quarterback
1987 — Lorenzo White, tailback
1988 — Tony Mandarich, offensive tackle
1989 — Blake Ezor, halfback
1990 — James Bradley, split end
       Dan Enos, quarterback
1991 — Courtney Hawkins, wide receiver
       Tico Duckett, tailback

Defensive Player

1977 — Paul Rudzinski, linebacker
1978 — Jerome Stanton, back
1979 — Dan Bass, linebacker
1980 — Thomas Morris, back
1981 — Carl Banks, linebacker
1982 — James Neely, linebacker
       Smiley Creswell, tackle
1983 — Carl Banks, linebacker
1984 — Jim Morrissey, linebacker
1985 — Phil Parker, free safety
1986 — Shane Bullough, linebacker
1987 — Todd Krumm, safety
1988 — John Miller, safety
       Percy Snow, linebacker

1989 — Percy Snow, linebacker
1990 — Dixon Edwards, linebacker
        Carlos Jenkins, linebacker
1991 — Chuck Bullough, linebacker

Downtown Coaches Club Awards

These awards, presented by the Downtown Coaches Club, the area booster club for football, go to the most outstanding Spartan senior defensive player and the most outstanding Spartan senior offensive player.

Offensive player
1975 — Gregory Croxton, guard
1976 — Richard Baes, tailback
1977 — James Earley, fullback
1978 — Edward Smith, quarterback
1979 — Mark Brammer, tight end
1980 — Steve Smith, halfback
1981 — Bryan Clark, quarterback
1982 — Otis Grant, flanker
1983 — Daryl Turner, split end
1984 — Mark Napolitan, center
1985 — Veno Belk, tight end
        Butch Rolle, tight end
1986 — Mark Ingram, flanker
1987 — Lorenzo White, tailback
1988 — Andre Rison, wide receiver
1989 — Blake Ezor, tailback
1990 — Jeff Pearson, center
1991 — Courtney Hawkins
1992 — Tico Duckett, tailback
1993 — Jim Miller, quarterback
1994 — Mill Coleman, flanker
1995 — Tony Banks, quarterback

Defensive Player
1975 — Gregory Schaum, tackle
1976 — Thomas Hannon, back
1977 — Larry Bethea, tackle
1978 — Melvin Land, tackle
1979 — Dan Bass, linebacker
1980 — John McCormick, linebacker
1981 — James Burroughs, back
1982 — James Neely, linebacker
1983 — Carl Banks, linebacker
1984 — Jim Morrissey, linebacker
1985 — Phil Parker, free safety
1986 — Shane Bullough, linebacker
1987 — Mark Nichols, defensive tackle
        Todd Krumm, free safety
1988 — Kurt Larson, linebacker
1989 — Travis Davis, defensive tackle
1990 — Skip Confer, defensive end
1991 — Chuck Bullough, linebacker

1992 — Ty Hallock, linebacker
1993 — Myron Bell, defensive back
        Rob Fredrickson, outside linebacker
1994 — Juan Hammonds, defensive end
1995 — Yakini Allen, defensive tackle
        Demetrice Martin, defensive back

Daugherty Award

This award, named in honor of the former Michigan State head football coach, goes annually to an MSU football alumnus who's distinguished himself in endeavors on and off the field since his graduation.

1975 — Edward L. Budde, Kansas City Chiefs
1976 — Dean Look, insurance exec./NFL Official
1977 — Earl Morrall, 21-Year NFL veteran
1978 — John Wilks, business exec. (posthumous)
1979 — James Ninowski, NFL player, business exec.
1980 — John S. Pingel, advertising exec.
1981 — Donald Coleman, MSU administrator
1982 — Robert McCurry, automobile exec.
1983 — George Webster, business exec.
1984 — Jack Breslin, MSU administrator
1985 — Rollie Dotsch, pro football coach
1986 — Henry Bullough, pro football coach
1987 — John Wilson, president, Washington and Lee University
1988 — Frank Kush, former college head coach
1989 — Doug Weaver, MSU Athletic Director
1990 — John McConnell, President, Worthington Industries
1991 — Sonny Grandelius, former college head coach and current business exec.
1992 — "Buck" Nystrom, former MSU All-American and assistant coach
1993 — Kirk Gibson, former MSU All-American and current major league baseball player
1994 — Wayne Fontes, MSU alumnus, former Spartan freshman coach; current head coach of Detroit Lions
1995 — Herb Adderley, former MSU great and lone Spartan in the Pro Football Hall of Fame

Danziger Award

Given annually from 1954 through 1975, and reinstated in 1980, this award goes to the player from the Detroit area who made the most outstanding contribution to the team. From 1976 through 1979, the award went to the players voted team captains at the end of the season. Named for the late Frederick W. Danziger, football letterman in 1926-28-29 and team captain in 1929, and contributed by his family.

1954 — Al Fracassa, quarterback
1955 — Norman Masters, tackle
1956 — James Hinesly, end
1957 — Jim Ninowski, quarterback
1958 — Cliff LaRose, tackle
1959 — Blanche Martin, fullback
1960 — Mickey Walker, tackle
1961 — Gary Ballman, halfback
1962 — Ed Budde, tackle
1963 — Dewey Lincoln, halfback
1964 — Jerry Rush, tackle
1965 — Harold Lucas, middle guard
1966 — Patrick Gallinagh, guard
1967 — Ronald Ranieri, center
1968 — Kenneth Heft, halfback
1969 — Craig Wycinsky, tackle
1970 — Gordon Bowdell, split end
1971 — Ralph Wieleba, end
1972 — William Simpson, halfback
1973 — William Simpson, halfback
1974 — Terry McClowry, linebacker
1975 — Gregory Croxton, guard
1980 — Jeff Wiska, offensive tackle
1981 — Jeff Wiska, offensive tackle
1982 — Darrin McClelland, fullback
1983 — Mark Napolitan, center
1984 — Mark Napolitan, center
1985 — John Wojciechowski, offensive guard
1986 — Dave Yarema, quarterback
1987 — John Miller, strong safety
1988 — John Miller, safety
1989 — Ventson Donelson, defensive back
1990 — John Langeloh, placekicker
1991 — Josh Butland, punter
1992 — Brice Abrams, fullback
1993 — Mill Coleman, flanker
1994 — Derrick Mason, wide receiver
1995 — Robert McBride, defensive end

Jim Adams Award

This award, named in honor of long-time MSU broadcaster Jim Adams, goes to the unsung player on each Spartan team, beginning with the 1994 season.

1994 — Peter Drzal, defensive back
1995 — Tony Popovski, offensive guard

SPARTAN FIRST-ROUND DRAFT PICKS

Since 1936, Michigan State University has had 29 players selected in the first round of the National Football League draft. The most memorable draft for Michigan State players came in 1967 when four Spartans were tabbed in the first round. Linebacker Rob Fredrickson was the most recent first-round draftee, selected by the Los Angeles (now Oakland) in 1994. The Spartans have had eight first-round selections in the last 11 years.

1936 — Sid Wagner, G, Detroit
1939 — John Pingel, B, Detroit
1950 — Lynn Chandnois, B, Pittsburgh
1952 — Bob Carey, E, Los Angeles Rams
1956 — Earl Morrall, QB, San Francisco
1957 — Clarence Peaks, B, Philadelphia
1958 — Walt Kowalczyk, B, Philadelphia
1958 — Dan Currie, C, Green Bay
1961 — Herb Adderley, DB, Green Bay
1963 — Dave Behrman, C, Buffalo (AFL)
1964 — Ed Budde, G, Kansas City (AFL),
        Chicago (NFL) & Philadelphia (NFL)
1965 — Jerry Rush, DE, Boston (AFL)
1967 — Clinton Jones, RB, Minnesota
1967 — Gene Washington, WR, Minnesota
1967 — George Webster, LB, Houston
1967 — Bubba Smith, DT, Baltimore
1973 — Joe DeLamielleure, OG, Buffalo
1973 — Billy Joe DuPree, TE, Dallas
1977 — Mike Cobb, TE, Cincinnati
1978 — Larry Bethea, DE, Dallas
1984 — Carl Banks, LB, New York Giants
1986 — Anthony Bell, LB, St. Louis

1987 — Mark Ingram, FL, New York Giants
1988 — Lorenzo White, RB, Houston
1989 — Tony Mandarich, OT, Green Bay
1989 — Andre Rison, WR, Indianapolis
1990 — Percy Snow, LB, Kansas City
1991 — Bobby Wilson, DT, Washington
1994 — Rob Fredrickson, LB, Los Angeles Raiders

SPARTANS IN BOWL GAMES

1938 ORANGE BOWL GAME

MSU vs. Auburn
January 1, 1938, Miami, Fla.
Auburn 6, Michigan State 0

MSU		**Auburn**
Ernie Bremer	LE	Rex McKissick
Harry Speelman (C)	LT	Bo Russell
Lyle Rockenbach	LG	James Sivell
Tom McShannock	C	Lester Antley
Walt Lueck	RG	Milton Howell
Howard Swartz	RT	Fred Holman
Frank Gaines	RE	Stancil Whatley
Allen Diebold	QB	Osmo Smith
John Pingel	LH	H.E. Kelly
Steve Szasz	RH	Jimmy Fenton
Usif Haney	FB	Walter Heath

	MSU	**AU**
First Downs	2	13
Rushing Yards	32	233
Passing Yards	25	79
Passes (Att-Comp-Int)	12-2-3	10-4-2
Punts-Average	12-35.2	10-33.7
Fumbles-Lost	0-0	0-0
Penalties-Yards	-35	-50

FIRST QUARTER: No scoring.
SECOND QUARTER — AU - Ralph O'Gwynne caught George Kenmore's short pass and skirted three yards around left to score, capping a 36-yard drive. Garth Thorpe's conversion attempt was wide.
THIRD QUARTER: No scoring.
FOURTH QUARTER: No scoring.
OFFICIAL ATTENDANCE: 18,970.

1954 ROSE BOWL GAME

MSU vs. UCLA
January 1, 1954, Pasadena, Calif.
Michigan State 28, UCLA 20

MSU		**UCLA**
Bill Quinlan	LE	Rommie Loudd
Jim Jebb	LT	Jack Ellena
Ferris Hallmark	LG	Sam Boghosian
Jim Neal	C	Ira Pauly
Henry Bullough	RG	Rudy Feldman
Larry Fowler	RT	Chuck Doud
Don Dohoney (C)	RE	Myron Berliner
Tom Yewcic	QB	Don Foster
Leroy Bolden	LH	Paul Cameron
Billy Wells	RH	Bill Stits
Evan Slonac	FB	Pete Dailey

	MSU	**UCLA**
First Downs	14	16
Rushes-Yards	53-195	40-90
Passing Yards	11	152
Punt Returns (No-Yds)	5-80	3-31
KO Returns (No-Yds)	4-60	4-100
Passes (Att-Comp-Int)	10-2-1	24-9-2
Punts-Average	5-35.4	6-38.7
Fumbles-Lost	4-4	4-3
Penalties-Yards	2-15	4-30

INDIVIDUAL STATS
RUSHING: Billy Wells (MSU) 14-80, Bill Stits (UCLA) 5-25
PASSING: Tom Yewcic (MSU) 2-S-1 1, Paul Cameron (UCLA) 9-22-152
RECEIVING: Leroy Bolden (MS) 1-18, Bill Stits (UCLA) 2-46

FIRST QUARTER: UCLA — Bill Stits took 13-yard pass from Paul Cameron on goal line and scored, 11:10 (37 yards in six plays), John Hermann converted.
SECOND QUARTER: UCLA— Paul Cameron slanted off left tackle for two yards and scored, 4:04 (13 yards in seven plays),John Hermann converted. MSU — Ellis Duckett blocked Paul Cameron's punt (scrimmage UCLA 25) and ran six yards for TD, 10:04, Evan Slonac converted.
THIRD QUARTER: MSU — LeRoy Bolden ran over guard from one-yard line to score, 6:13 (78 yards in 14 plays), Evan Slonac converted. MSU — Billy Wells ran over tackle from two-yard line to score, 12:15 (73 yards in 11 plays), Evan Slonac converted.
FOURTH QUARTER: UCLA — Rommie Loudd took 28-yard pass from Paul Cameron on goal line to score, 2:24 (24 yards in two plays), Hermann failed to convert. MSU — Billy Wells took Paul Cameron's punt on his own eight and ran for a TD, 10:09, Evan Slonac converted.
OFFICIAL ATTENDANCE: 101,000.

1956 ROSE BOWL GAME

MSU vs. UCLA
January 2, 1956, Pasadena, Calif.
Michigan State 17, UCLA 14

MSU		UCLA
John Lewis	LE	John Hermann
Norm Masters	LT	Roger White
Dan Currie	LG	Hardiman Cureton
Joe Badaczewski	C	Steve Palmer
Carl Nystrom	RG	Jim Brown
Leo Haidys	RT	Gil Moreno
Dave Kaiser	RE	Rommie Loudd
Earl Morrall	QB	Bruce Ballard
Clarence Peaks	LH	Sam Brown
Walt Kowalczyk	RH	Jim Decker
Gerry Planutis	FB	Bob Davenport

	MSU	UCLA
First Downs	18	13
Rushing-Yards	50-251	42-136
Passing Yards	130	61
Punt Returns (No-Yds)	6-8	2-12
KO Returns (No-Yds)	3-61	2-58
Passes (Att-Comp-Int)	18-6-2	10-2-1
Punts-Average	2-80	7-277
Fumbles-Lost	4-1	2-0
Penalties-Yards	10-98	8-60

INDIVIDUAL STATS
RUSHING: Walt Kowalczyk (MSU) 13-88, Sam Brown (UCLA) 14-63.
PASSING: Earl Morrall (MSU) 4-15-2, Ronnie Knox (UCLA) 2-8-1.
RECEIVING: Clarence Peaks (MSU) 3-40, Jim Decker (UCLA) 1-47

FIRST QUARTER: UCLA — Bob Davenport bucked two yards for score, 3:12 (16 yards in four plays), Jim Decker converted.
SECOND QUARTER: MSU — Clarence Peaks took 13-yard pass on goal line from Earl Morrall to score, 9:08 (60 yards in 13 plays), Gerald Planutis converted.
THIRD QUARTER: No scoring.
FOURTH QUARTER: MSU — John Lewis took pass from Clarence Peaks on 50 and went all the way to score, play covering 67 yards, :49 (50 yards in three plays), Gerald Planutis converted. UCLA — Doug Peters bucked one yard for score, 8:53 (56 yards in five plays), Jim Decker converted. MSU — Dave Kaiser kicked 41-yard field goal with seven seconds left in game.
OFFICIAL ATTENDANCE: 100,809

1966 ROSE BOWL GAME

MSU vs. UCLA
January 1, 1966, Pasadena, Calif.
UCLA 14, Michigan State 12

MSU Offense		UCLA Offense
Jim Proebstle	LR	Kurt Altenberg
Jerry West	LT	Russ Banducci
Norm Jenkins	LG	Rich Deakers
Boris Dimitroff	C	Mo Freedman
John Karpinski	RG	Barry Levanthal
Joe Przybycki	RT	Larry Stagle
Gene Washington	RE	Byron Nelson
Steve Juday	QB	Gary Beban
Dwight Lee	LH	Melvin Farr
Clinton Jones	RH	Dick Witcher
Eddie Cotton	FB	Paul Horgan

MSU Defense		UCLA Defense
Bubba Smith	LE	Jim Colletto
Buddy Owens	LT	Terry Donahue
Harold Lucas	MG/RG	John Richardson
Don Bierowicz	RT/RG	Steve Butler
Bob Viney	RE/RT	Alan Claman
Ron Goovert	LLB/RE	Erwin Dutcher
Charles Thornhill	RLB/LLB	Dallas Grider
George Webster	RB/RLB	Jim Miller
Jim Summers	HB/LH	Bob Stiles
Don Japinga	HB/RH	Bob Richardson
Jess Phillips	S	Tim McAteer

	MSU	UCLA
First Downs	13	10
Rushes-Yards	46-204	41-65
Passing Yards	110	147
Punt Returns (No-Yds)	4-3	2-2
KO Returns (No-Yds)	2-23	3-49
Passes (Att-Comp-Int)	12-8-3	20-8-0
Punts-Average	5-42.4	11-39.9
Fumbles-Lost	3-2	3-2
Penalties-Yards	1-14	9-86

INDIVIDUAL STATS
RUSHING: Clinton Jones (MSU) 20-113, Mel Farr (UCLA) 10-36
PASSING: Steve Juday (MSU) 6-18-3, Gary Beban (UCLA) 8-20-0
RECEIVING: Gene Washington (MSU) 4-81, Kurt Altenberg (UCLA) 3-55

FIRST QUARTER: No scoring.
SECOND QUARTER: UCLA — Gary Beban sneaked one yard to score, :03 (6 yards in two plays), Kurt Zimmerman converted. UCLA — Gary Beban sneaked one yard for score, 3:10 (42 yards in seven plays), Kurt Zimmerman converted.
THIRD QUARTER: No scoring.
FOURTH QUARTER: MSU — Bob Apisa took pitchout from Jim Raye and went 38 yards for the score, 6:47 (80 yards in two plays), Steve Juday failed on two-point pass try. MSU — Steve Juday sneaked half-a-yard for score, 14:29 (51 yards in 15 plays), Bob Apisa failed on two-point run try.
OFFICIAL ATTENDANCE: 100,067.

1984 CHERRY BOWL GAME

MSU vs. Army
December 22, 1984, Pontiac, Mich.
Army 10, Michigan State 6

MSU Offense		Army Offense
Bob Wasczenski	SE	Scott Spellmon
Doug Rogers	LT	Jeff Karsonovich
Jeff Stump	LG	Vince McDermott
Mark Napolitan	C	Ron Rice
John Wojciechowski	RG	Don Smith
Steve Bogdalek	RT	Dave Woolfolk
Butch Rolle	TE	Rob Dickerson
Dave Yarema	QB	Nate Sassaman
Lorenzo White	TB/LH	Jarvis Hollingsworth
Keith Gates	FB	Doug Black
Mark Ingram	FL/RH	Clarence Jones

MSU Defense		Army Defense
Kelly Quinn	LE/DE	Tom Malloy
Jim Rinella	LT/DT	Mike Seals
Dave Wolff	RT/NG	Rob Ulses
Tom Allan	RE/DT	Jim Jennings
Anthony Bell	LOLB/DE	Kurt Gutierrez
Jim Morrissey (C)	ILB/LB	Many Baptiste
Thomas Tyree	ROLB/LB	Jim Gentile
Lonnie Young	LCB/SC	Eric Griffin
Paul Bobbitt	SS	Bob Silver
Phil Parker	FS	Doug Pavek
Terry Lewis	RCB/WC	Kermit McKelvy

	MSU	Army
First Downs	13	15
Rushes-Yards	33-89	71-256
Passing Yards	155	10
Punt Returns (No-Yds)	6-23	2-18
KO Returns (No-Yds)	2-29	0-0
Passes (Att-Comp-Int)	25-11-3	2-1-1
Punts-Average	4-55.8	7-36.7
Fumbles-Lost	3-2	2-1
Penalties-Yards	4-26	1-7

INDIVIDUAL STATS
RUSHING: Lorenzo White (MSU) 23-103, Nata Sassaman (A) 28-136
PASSING: Dave Yarema (MSU) 11 -25-1 55, Nate Sassaman (A) 1-2-10
RECEIVING: Butch Rolle (MSU) 5-65, Jarvis Hollingsworth (A) 1-10

FIRST QUARTER: No scoring.
SECOND QUARTER: Army — Clarence Jones runs off right tackle four yards to score, 6:19 (46 yards in eight plays), Graig Stopa converts.
THIRD QUARTER: No scoring.
FOURTH QUARTER: Army — Graig Stopa kicks 36-yard field goal. MSU — Dave Yarema passes 36 yards to Bob Wasczenski in end zone corner, 10:41 (51 yards in three plays), Yarema pass to Mike Sargent fails on two-point try.
OFFICIAL ATTENDANCE: 70,336.

1985 ALL AMERICAN BOWL GAME

MSU vs. Georgia Tech
December 31, 1985, Birmingham, Ala.
Georgia Tech 17, Michigan State 14

MSU Offense		GT Offense
Andre Rison	SE	Bugs Isom
Tony Mandarich	LT	John Ivemeyer
Doug Rogers	LG	John Thomas
Pat Shurmur	C	Andy Hearn
John Wojciechowski	RG	Sam Bracken
Steve Bogdalek	RT	John Davis
Butch Rolle	TE	Robert Massey
Dave Yarema	QB	Todd Rampley
Lorenzo White	TB	Cory Collier
Bobby Morse	FB	Malcolm King
Mark Ingram	FL	Toby Pearson

MSU Defense		GT Defense
Mark Beaudoin	DE	Pat Swilling
Mark Nichols	DT	Ken Parker
Joe Curran	DT/NG	Ivery Lee
John Jones	DE	Mark Pike
Anthony Bell	OLB/ILB	Ted Roof
Shane Bullough	MLB/ILB	Jim Anderson
Tim Moore	OLB	Mark Hogan
Todd Krumm	CB	Reginald Rutland
Dean Altobelli	SS/R	Cleve Pounds
Phil Parker	FS	Anthony Harrison
Paul Bobbitt	CB	Mike Travis

	MSU	GT
First Downs	14	16
Rushes-Yards	39-148	48-182
Passing Yards	85	99
Punt Returns (No-Yds)	2-14	1-11
KO Returns (No-Yds)	4-47	2-30
Passes (Att-Comp-Int)	15-6-1	23-12-1
Punts-Average	6-36.7	6-37.8
Fumbles-Lost	2-1	2-0
Penalties-Yards	3-28	5-47

INDIVIDUAL STATS
RUSHING: Lorenzo White (MSU) 33-158, Malcolm King (GT) 16-122
PASSING: Dave Yarema (MSU) 6-15-1, Todd Rampley (GT) 12-23-1
RECEIVING: Mark Ingram (MSU) 3-70, Jerry Mays (GT) 3-22

FIRST QUARTER: No scoring.
SECOND QUARTER: MSU — Dave Yarema passes six yards to Mark Ingram in left corner of end zone, 2:03 (48 yards in four plays), Chris Caudell converts.
THIRD QUARTER: GT — Todd Rampley sneaks in from the one, 11:44 (66 yards in four plays), David Bell converts.
MSU — Yarema passes 27 yards to Ingram, 4:41 (38 yards in two plays), Caudell converts.
FOURTH QUARTER: GT — David Bell kicks a 40-yard field goal, 7:08. GT — Malcolm King runs for a five-yard score,1:50 (42 yards in eight plays), Bell converts.

OFFICIAL ATTENDANCE: 45,000.

1988 ROSE BOWL GAME

MSU vs. Southern Cal
January 1, 1988, Pasadena, Calif.
Michigan State 20, Southern Cal 17

MSU Offense		**USC Offense**
Andre Rison	SE	Erik Affholter
Tony Mandarich	LT	John Guerrero
Bob Kula	LG	Brent Parkinson
Pat Shurmur	C	John Katnik
Vince Tata	RG	Mark Tucker
David Houle	RT	Dave Cadigan
Mike Sargent	TE	Paul Green
Bobby McAllister	QB	Rodney Peete
Lorenzo White	TB	Scott Lockwood
James Moore	FB	Leroy Holt
Willie Bouyer	FL	Randy Tanner

MSU Defense		**USC Defense**
Jim Szymanski	DE/OLB	Marcus Cotton
Mark Nichols	DT	Tim Ryan
Travis Davis	DT/NG	Don Gibson
John Budde	DE/DG	Dan Owens

Tim Moore	OLB	Bill Stokes
Percy Snow	MLB/ILB	Scott Ross
Kurt Larson	OLB/ILB	Keith Davis
Derrick Reed	CB/HB	Chris Hale
John Miller	SS/TR	Cleveland Colter
Todd Krumm	FS/FS	Mark Carrier
Harlon Barnett	CB/CB	Greg Coauette

	MSU	USC
First Downs	11	21
Rushes-Yards	60-148	34-161
Passing Yards	128	249
Punt Returns (No-Yds)	2-13	7-90
KO Returns (No-Yds)	4-56	4-60
Passes (Att-Comp-Int)	7-4-1	42-22-4
Punts-Average	8-47.1	4-45.0
Fumbles-Lost	0-0	4-1
Penalties-Yards	5-32	4-20

INDIVIDUAL STATS
RUSHING: Lorenzo White (MSU) 35-113, Rodney Peete (USC) 11-54
PASSING: Bobby McAllister (MSU) 4-7-0, Rodney Peete (USC) 22-41-3
RECEIVING: Andre Rison (MSU) 2-91, Paul Green (USC) 7-58

FIRST QUARTER: USC — Quin Rodriquez kicks 34-yard field goal, 7:32 (52 yards in 12 plays). MSU — Lorenzo White runs left for five-yard score,14:06 (76 yards in 15 plays), Langeloh converts.
SECOND QUARTER: MSU — Lorenzo White runs over left tackle for three-yard score, 5:40 (80 in six plays), Langeloh converts.
THIRD QUARTER: USC — Rodney Peete passes 33 yards to Ken Henry, 5:26 (70 yards in six plays), Quin Rodriquez converts.
FOURTH QUARTER: MSU — John Langeloh kicks 40-yard field goal, 2:21 (45 yards in nine plays). Rodney Peete passes 22 yards to Ken Henry, 6:27 (80 yards in 10 plays), Quin Rodriquez converts. MSU — John Langeloh kicks 36-yard field goal, 10:46 (54 yards in nine plays).

OFFICIAL ATTENDANCE: 103,847.

1989 GATOR BOWL GAME

MSU vs. Georgia
January 1, 1989, Jacksonville, Fla.
Georgia 34, Michigan State 27

MSU Offense		**Georgia Offense**
Andre Rison	SE	John Thomas
Tony Mandarich	LT	Will Colley
Bob Kula	LG	Shelly Anderson
Dave Martin	C	Todd Wheeler
Vince Tata	RG	Scott Adams
Kevin Robbins	RT	Curt Mul
Rich Gicewicz	TE	Troy Sadowski
Bobby McAllister	QB	Wayne Johnson
Blake Ezor	TB	Tim Worley
Steve Montgomery	FB	Alphonso Ellis
Willie Bouyer	FL	Arthur Marshall

MSU Defense		**Georgia Defense**
Matt Vanderbeek	DE/OLB	Aaron Chubb
Jason Ridgeway	DT/NG	Wycliffe Lovelace
Travis Davis	DT/NG	Bill Goldberg
Chris Willertz	DE/OLB	Paul Giles
Carlos Jenkins	OLB	Morris Lewis
Percy Snow	MLB	Demetrius Douglas
Kurt Larson	OLB	Terrie Webster
Alan Haller	LCB	Ben Smth
John Miller	SS	Vince Guthrie
Derrick Reed	FS	Rusty Beasley
Ventson Donelson	RCB	David Hargett

	MSU	UG
First Downs	22	22
Rushes-Yards	51-158	38-182
Passing Yards	288	227
Punt Returns (No-Yds)	0-0	3-27
KO Returns (No-Yds)	5-101	5-74
Passes (Att-Comp-Int)	24-14-0	27-15-0
Punts-Average	6-42.8	4-34.0
Fumbles-Lost	1-0	0-0
Penalties-Yards	8-102	5-25

INDIVIDUAL STATS
RUSHING: Blake Ezor (MSU) 33-146, Rodney Hampton (UG) 10-109
PASSING: Bobby McAllister (MSU) 24-14-0, Wayne Johnson (UG) 27-15-0
RECEIVING: Andre Rison (MSU) 9-252, Rodney Hampton (UG) 4-71
FIRST QUARTER: UG — Wayne Johnson passes six yards to Rodney Hampton, 14:59 (45 yards in eight plays), Kasay converts.
SECOND QUARTER: UG — Steve Crumley kicks 39-yard field goal, 4:00 (39 yards in seven plays). UG — Wayne Johnson passes 30 yards to Rodney Hampton, 7:54 (74 yards in five plays), Kasay converts. MSU — Bobby McAllister passes four yards to Andre Rison, 12:05 (80

yards in 10 plays), Langeloh converts.
THIRD QUARTER: UG — Wayne Johnson passes 18 yards to Kirk Warner, 7:12 (64 yards in six plays), Kasay converts. MSU— Bobby McAllister passes 55 yards to Andre Rison, 11:05 (78 yards in eight plays), Langeloh conversion missed. UG — Steve Crumley kicks 36-yard field goal, 12:44 (51 yards in seven plays).
FOURTH QUARTER: MSU — Blake Ezor rushes three yards over left tackle, :36 (80 yards in eight plays), Langeloh converts. UG — Rodney Hampton scampers 32 yards for score, 3:02 (71 yards in six plays), Kasay converts. MSU — Bobby McAllister passes 50 yards to Andre Rison for score, 11:11 (71 yards in six plays), Langeloh converts.

OFFICIAL ATTENDANCE: 76,236.

1989 ALOHA BOWL GAME

MSU vs. Hawaii
December 25, 1989, Honolulu, Hawaii
Michigan State 33, Hawaii 13

MSU Offense		**Hawaii Offense**
James Bradley	SE/LWR	Chris Roscoe
Bob Kula	LT	Leo Goeas
Eric Moten	LG	Allen Smith
Jeff Pearson	C	Shawn Alivado
Matt Keller	RG	Larry Jones
Jim Johnson	RT	Sean Robinson
Duane Young	TE/RWR	Leonard Lau
Dan Enos	QB	Garrett Gabriel
Blake Ezor	TB/RB	Jamal Farmer
Steve Montgomery	FB/LSB	Dane McArthur
Courtney Hawkins	FL/RSB	Dan Ahuna

MSU Defense		**Hawaii Defense**
Matt Vanderbeek	DE/OLB	Manly Williams
Tim Ridinger	DT	David Slant
Travis Davis	DT/NG	Augie Apelu
Chris Willertz	DE/DT	Delmar Johnson
Carlos Jenkins	OLB	Mark Odom
Percy Snow	MLB/ILB	Louis Randall
Dixon Edwards	OLB/ROV	David Maeva
Alan Haller	LCB	Mike Coulson
Harlon Barnett	SS	Mike Tresler
Mike Iaquaniello	FS	Walter Briggs
Ventson Donelson	RCB	Kim McCloud

	MSU	UH
First Downs	21	19
Rushes-Yards	61-225	28-82
Passing Yards	116	198
Punt Returns (No-Yds)	0-0	2-31
KO Returns (No-Yds)	1-2	7-174
Passes (Att-Comp-Int)	12-7-2	33-20-4
Punts-Average	3-50.7	1-27

			Carlos Jenkins	SOLB/OLB	Craig Hartsuyker
Fumbles-Lost	0-0	7-4	Chuck Bullough	MLB/ILB	Scott Ross
Penalties-Yards	9-85	3-30	Dixon Edwards	WOLB/ILB	Brian Tuliau
			Eddie Brown	CB	Calvin Holmes
			Freddie Wilson	SS	Marcus Hopkins
			Mike Iaquaniello	FS	Stephen Pace
			Alan Haller	CB	Jason Oliver

INDIVIDUAL STATS
RUSHING: Blake Ezor (MSU) 41-179, Dane McArthur (UH), 2-34
PASSING: Dan Enos (MSU) 7-12-2, Garrett Gabriel (UH) 19-31-3
RECEIVING: James Bradley (MSU) 4-85, Chris Roscoe (UH) 6-71

FIRST QUARTER: MSU — Blake Ezor runs left for three-yard TD, 11:01 (65 yards in 10 plays), Langeloh kick is blocked.
SECOND QUARTER: MSU — Blake Ezor takes pitch left for two-yard TD, :07 (48 yards in seven plays), Langeloh converts. MSU — John Langeloh kicks 30-yard field goal, 7:48 (74 yards in 10 plays). MSU — John Langeloh kicks 34-yard field goal, 13:58 (two yards in seven plays).
THIRD QUARTER: UH — Garrett Gabriel passes 11 yards to Chris Roscoe for TD, 5:15 (74 yards in 10 plays), Elam kick blocked.
FOURTH QUARTER: MSU — Hyland Hickson dives right for one-yard TD, 4:47(57 yards in nine plays), Langeloh converts. UH — Garrett Gabriel passes 23 yards to Dane McArthur for TD, 6:53 (67 yards in eight plays), Khan converts. MSU — Blake Ezor runs for 26-yard TD, 9:24 (48 yards in four plays), Langeloh converts.

OFFICIAL ATTENDANCE — 50,000.

1990 JOHN HANCOCK BOWL GAME

MSU vs. Southern Cal
December 31, 1990, El Paso, Tex.
Michigan State 17, Southern Cal 16

MSU Offense / USC Offense

MSU Offense		USC Offense
James Bradley	SE	Johnnie Morton
Roosevelt Wagner	LT/QT	Michael Moody
Eric Moten	LG/QT	Derrick Deese
Jeff Pearson	C	Craig Gibson
Matt Keller	RG/SG	Mark Tucker
Jim Johnson	RT/ST	Pat Harlow
Duane Young	TE	Frank Griffin
Dan Enos	QB	Todd Marinovich
Tico Duckett	TB	Mazio Royster
Rob Roy	FB	Scott Lockwood
Courtney Hawkins	FL	Gary Wellman

MSU Defense / USC Defense

MSU Defense		USC Defense
Skip Confer	DE/OLB	Kurt Barber
Bobby Wilson	DT	Terry McDaniels
William Reese	DT/NG	Gene Fruge
Bill Johnson	DE/DG	Don Gibson

	MSU	USC
First Downs	12	21
Rushes-Yards	35-84	44-156
Passing Yards	131	180
Punt Returns (No-Yds)	1-7	2-27
KO Returns (No-Yds)	5-124	1-17
Passes (Att-Comp-Int)	17-9-1	32-19-3
Punts-Average	5-38.6	1-50
Fumbles-Lost	1-1	2-1
Penalties-Yards	6-54	5-45

INDIVIDUAL STATS
RUSHING: Hyland Hickson (MSU) 14-68, Mazio Royster (USC) 32-125
PASSING: Dan Enos (MSU) 9-17-1, Todd Marinovich (USC) 18-30-3
RECEIVING: Courtney Hawkins (MSU) 6-106, Scott Lockwood, (USC) 5-41
FIRST QUARTER: USC — Todd Marinovich passes seven yards to Gary Wellman for TD, 0:54 (60 yards in eight plays), Rodriguez converts.
SECOND QUARTER: MSU — Hyland Hickson dashes 18 yards on a sprint draw for TD, 2:22 (80 yards in 10 plays), Langeloh converts.
THIRD QUARTER: USC — Quinn Rodriguez kicks 20-yard field goal, 6:00 (80 yards in 18 plays). MSU — Dan Enos passes 21 yards to Courtney Hawkins for TD, 2:53 (71 yards in seven plays), Langeloh converts. MSU — John Langeloh kicks a 52-yard field goal, 0:42 (-1 yard in four plays).
FOURTH QUARTER: USC — Quinn Rodriguez kicks 54-yard field goal, 13:07 (43 yards in nine plays). USC — Quinn Rodriguez kicks 43-yard field goal, 3:07 (31 yards in 12 plays).

OFFICIAL ATTENDANCE — 50,562.

1993 ST. JUDE LIBERTY BOWL GAME

MSU vs. Louisville
December 28, 1993, Memphis, Tenn.
Louisville 18, Michigan State 7

MSU Offense		Louisville Offense
Napoleon Outlaw	SE	Reggie Ferguson
Shane Hannah	LT	Tom Carroll
Colin Cronin	LG	Garin Patrick
Mark Birchmeier	C	Jason Stinson

	RG	Dave Debold
Brett Lorius	RG	Dave Debold
Brian DeMarco	RT	Jermaine Williams
Bob Organ	TE	Jamie Asher
Jim Miller	QB	Jeff Brohm
Craig Thomas	TB/HB	Ralph Dawkins
Brice Abrams	FB	Chris Fitzpatrick
Mill Coleman	FL	Aaron Bailey

MSU Defense		**Louisville Defense**
Juan Hammonds	DE	Kendall Brown
Aaron Jackson	DT	Leonard Ray
Yakini Allen	DT	Jim Hanna
Rich Glover	DE	Joe Johnson
Matt Christensen	SOLB/OLB	Tom Cavallo
Reggie Garnett	MLB/MLB	Vince Dueberry
Rob Fredrickson	WOLB/OLB	Ben Sumpter
Stan Callender	CB	Anthony Bridges
Myron Bell	SS	Terry Quinn
Aldi Henry	FS	Darrius Watson
Demetrice Martin	CB	Kevin Gaines

	MSU	UL
First Downs	18	20
Rushes-Yards	31-114	40-172
Passing Yards	193	197
Punt Returns (No-Yds)	1-3	1-25
KO Returns (No-Yds)	4-59	2-48
Passes (Att-Comp-Int)	28-15-1	31-19-0
Punts-Average	5-29.0	5-36.2
Fumbles-Lost	0-0	1-0
Penalties-Yards	5-60	6-45

INDIVIDUAL STATS
RUSHING: Duane Goulbourne (MSU) 19-63, Ralph Dawkins (UL) 14-88
PASSING: Jim Miller (MSU) 15-28-1, Jeff Brohm (UL) 19-29-0
RECEIVING: Mill Coleman (MSU) 6-100, Ralph Dawkins (UL) 8-68

FIRST QUARTER: MSU — Duane Goulborne slams in from one yard out for TD, 10:10 (79 yards in 11 plays), Stoyanovich converts. UL— David Akers kicks 31-yard field goal; 7:07 (56 yards in 8 plays).
FOURTH QUARTER: UL — Jeff Brohm passes 25 yards to Reggie Ferguson for TD, 12:05 (59 yards in seven plays). UL— Records safety when MSU tailback Craig Thomas is tackled in end zone, 8:53. UL — Ralph Dawkins sweeps 11 yards for TD, 4:57 (54 yards in seven plays), PAT is unsuccessful.

OFFICIAL ATTENDANCE — 34,216

1995 INDEPENDENCE BOWL GAME

MSU vs. Louisiana State
December 29, 1995, Shreveport, La.
Louisiana State 45, Michigan State 26

MSU Offense		**Louisiana State Offense**
Muhsin Muhammad	WR	Eddie Kennison
Dave Mudge	LT	Sean Wells
Tony Popovski	LG	Mark King
Matt Beard	C	Todd McClure
Brian Mosallam	RG	Alan Faneca
Flozell Adams	RT	Ben Bordelon
Josh Keur	TE	David LaFleur
Tony Banks	QB	Herbert Tyler
Marc Renaud	TB	Kevin Faulk
Scott Greene	FB/TE	Nicky Savoie
Derrick Mason	WR	Sheddrick Wilson

MSU Defense		**Louisiana State Defense**
Robert McBride	DE	James Gillyard
Chris Smith	DT	Chuck Wiley
Yakini Allen	DT	Anthony McFarland
Jabbar Threats	DE	Gabe Northern
Carl Reaves	OLB	Allen Stansberry
Reggie Garnett	MLB	Robert Deshotel
Ike Reese	OLB	Pat Rogers
Demetrice Martin	CB	Tory James
Dan Hackenbracht	S	Talvi Crawford
Sorie Kanu	S	Clarence Lenton
Raymond Hill	CB	Denard Walker

	MSU	LSU
First Downs	23	17
Rushes-Yards	35/100	48/272
Passing Yards	348	164
Punt Returns (No-Yds)	2/26	2/3
KO Returns (No-Yds)	7/158	4/150
Passes (Att-Comp-Int)	44/22/3	0/10/1
Punts-Average	6/37.5	4/44.5
Fumbles-Lost	4/3	2/1
Penalties-Yards	9/80	5/42

INDIVIDUAL STATS
RUSHING: Marc Renaud (MSU) 16-79, Kevin Faulk (LSU) 25-234
PASSING: Tony Banks (MSU) 22-44-3—348, Herbert Tyler (LSU) 10-20-1—164
RECEIVING: Muhsin Muhammad (MSU) 9-171, Eddie Kennison (LSU) 5-124<%0>

FIRST QUARTER: MSU — Muhsin Muhammad catches a 78-yard bomb from Tony Banks on the second play from scirmmage, 14:13 (80 yards in 2 plays), Chris Gardner coverts. LSU—Kendall Cleveland bursts six yards for TD, 12:07 (80 yards in 7 plays), Andre Lafleur converts.
SECOND QUARTER: MSU—Scott Greene around right side for 3-yard TD, 14:44 (3 yards in 1 play), Gardner kick

INDIVIDUAL STATS
RUSHING: Marc Renaud (MSU) 16-79, Kevin Faulk (LSU) 25-234
PASSING: Tony Banks (MSU) 22-44-3—348, Herbert Tyler (LSU) 10-20-1—164
RECEIVING: Muhsin Muhammad (MSU) 9-171, Eddie Kennison (LSU) 5-124

FIRST QUARTER: MSU — Muhsin Muhammad catches a 78-yard bomb from Tony Banks on the second play from scirmmage, 14:13 (80 yards in 2 plays), Chris Gardner coverts. LSU—Kendall Cleveland bursts six yards for TD, 12:07 (80 yards in 7 plays), Andre Lafleur converts.
SECOND QUARTER: MSU—Scott Greene around right side for 3-yard TD, 14:44 (3 yards in 1 play), Gardner kick blocked. LSU—Eddie Kennison takes ensuing kickoff 92 yards for TD, 14:30, Lafluer kick is good. MSU—Derrick Mason takes ensuing kickoff 100 yards for TD, 14:17, Greene runs for conversion. LSU—Kevin Faulk races 51 yards for score (13:11), capping an outburst that saw each team score 14 points in a span of 1:33 (57 yards in 2 plays), Lafleur kick good. MSU—Gardner boots a 37-yard field goal, 0:01 (42 yards in 9 plays).
THIRD QUARTER: Faulk sprints five yards for TD, 14:29 (74 yards in 2 plays), Lafleur onverts. LSU—Gabe Northern returns a fumble 37 yards for score, 9:20, Lafleur converts. LSU—Kennison catches a 27-yard scoring strik from Herbert Tyler, 7:13 (14 yards in 3 plays), Lafleur kick is good.
FOURTH QUARTER: LSU—Wade Richey makes a 48-yard field goal, 8:45 (18 yards in 8 plays). MSU—Safety, LSU punter Chad Kessler runs out of endzone.

OFFICIAL ATTENDANCE — 48,835

SPARTAN PLAYERS IN ALL-STAR GAMES

*- won or shared outstanding back or lineman
award +- team captain or co-captain

EAST-WEST

(San Francisco)
Munn, Clarence L., Head Coach,'52,'53
Daugherty, Hugh Duffy, Head
Coach,'58,'59,'66,'68
Rogers, Darryl, Assistant Coach, '80
Perles, George, Head Coach, '88
Adderley, Herb, B, '60
Allen, Eric, B, '71
Anderson, Mark, DB, '80
Andre, Charles, C, '74
Arbanas, Fred, E, '60
Bagdon, Ed, G, '50
Ballman, Gary, B, '61
Bailey, Charles, T, '68
Banks, Tony, QB, '95
Bell, Anthony, LB, '86
Bethea, Larry, T, '77
Bobbitt, James, T, '62
Bobich, Louis, B, '65
Bolden, Leroy, B, '55
Brenner, Allen, B, '68
Breslin, Jack, B, '45, '46
Brogger, Francis, E, '45
Budde, Ed, T, '62
Bullough, Henry, G, '55
Burke, Pat, T, '58
Burroughs, James, DB, '81
Chandnois, Lynn, B, '50
Clark, Gail, LB, '72
Coleman, Don, G, '52
Coleman, Mill, FL, '94
+Curl, Ronald, T, '71
Dekker, Paul, E, '53
DeLamielleure, Joseph, T '72
Dibble, Dorne, E, '51
Dorow, Al, B, '52
Gilbert, Don, B, '58
Gordon, Richard, B, '65
Greene, Scott, FB, '95
Grandelius, Everett, B, '51
Hayner, Paul, B, '73
Hughes, William, G, '52
Ingram, Mark, FL, '86
Jenkins, Carlos, LB, '91
+Jones, Clinton, B, '66
Kelly, Ellison, G, '58
Kenney, Richard, K, '66
Kowalczyk, Walt, B, '58
Krumm, Todd, S, '88
Kula, Robert, OT, '90
Lewis, Sherman, B, '63
Lewis, Terry, DB, '84
Look, Dean, B, '59
Martin, Blanche, B, '59
Martin, Wilton, T, '71
Mason, Don, G, '50
McAuliffe, Don, B, '53
McClowry, Terry, LB, '74

Moten, Eric, OG, '91
Nichols, Mark, DT, '88
O'Brien, Fran, T, '58
Pingel, John, B, '39
Pitts, Alfred, C, '77
Pyle, Palmer, T, '59
Raye, James, QB, '67
Rison, Andre, WR, '89
Saimes, George, FB, '62
Saul, Ronald, G, '69
Simpson, William, B, '73
Snow, Percy LB, '90
Tamburo, Dick, C, '53
Turner, Daryl, SE, '83
Underwood, Dan, E, '63
VanPelt, Brad, B '72
Washington, Eugene, E, '66
*Webster, George, RB, '66
Wedemeyer, Charles, F, '68
White, Lorenzo, TB, '88
*Williams, Sam, E, '58
Wilson, Bobby, DT, '91
Wilson, Tom, B, '60
Wycinsky, Craig, T, '69
Yarema, Dave, QB, '86

NORTH-SOUTH

(Pontiac)
Daugherty, Hugh Duffy, Head Coach,
'56,'57, '61, '72
Azar, George, G, '62
Baker, Park, B, '59
Barker, Dick, E, '58
Behrman, Dave, C, '62
Berlinski, Richard, B, '68
Carruthers, Joe, T, '57
Creamer, Jim, C, '51
Charon, Carl, B, '61
Chatlos, George, E, '67
Conti, Anthony, T, '67
Currie, Dan, C, '57
Dawson, William, T, '71
Fontes, Wayne, B, ' 61
Gallinagh, Pat, T, '66
Grimsley, Ike, G, '60
Hannon, Thomas, DB, '76
Herman, Dave, T, '63
Hinesly, Jim, E, '56
Horrell, Bill, T, '51
Hudas, Larry, E, '61
*Jewett, Bob, E, '57
Johnson, Herman, B, '64
Kaiser, Dave, E, '57
Kakela, Pete, T, '61
King, Chris, LB, '72
Krzemienski, Tom, G, '64
Kuh, Dick, G, '51
Kush, Frank, G, '52
LaRose, Cliff, T, '58

Lee, Dwight, B, '67
Lincoln, Dewey, B, '63
Luke, Ed, E, '52
Macholz, Dennis, G, '72
Matsko, John, C, '56
McClowry, Robert, C, '72
McConnell, Brian, E, '72
McLoud, Eddy, C, '68
Mendyk, Dennis, B, '56
Minarik, Hank, E, '50
Mittelberg, Victor, T, '70
Nester, Ray, LB, '73
*Ninowski, Jim, B, '57
Phillips, Harold, B, '70
Richardson, Jeff, T, '66
Roberts, Marvin, T, '72
Rody, Fred, C, '54
Roy, Errol, T, '71
Rubick, Ron, B, '63
Sanders, Lonnie, E, '62
Saul, Richard, E, '69
Smith, Charles, E, '66
Smith, Otto, LB, '76
+Thornhill, Charles, LB, '66
Waters, Jr., Frank, B, '68
West, Jerry, T, '66
Wilson, John, B, '52
Wulff, Jim, B, '58
Zagers, Bert, B, '54
Zucco, Vic, B, '56

BLUE-GRAY CHRISTMAS

(Montgomery)
Bullough, Hank, Asst. Coach, '94
Perles, George, Asst. Coach '91, '94
Parker, Norm, Asst. Coach '91
Andersen, Morten, K, '81
Banks, Carl, LB, '83
Beard, Thomas, C, '70
Benson, Bill, G, '63
Benson, Wayne, B, '52
Berger, Don, C, '57
Birchmeier, Mark, C, '94
Bowdell, Gordon, E, '70
Carey, Bill, E, '51
Christensen, Matt, LB, '94
Clark, Bryan, QB, '81
Cundiff, Larry, T, '59
DeMarco, Brian, OF, '94
Dotsch, Roland, T, '54
DuPree, Billy Joe, E, '72
Fox, Calvin, E, '70
Garner, Dean, G, '51
Haller, Alan, DB, '91
Harness, Jason, E, '60
Heft, Kenneth, B, '68
Highsmith, Donald, B, '69
Hinesly, James, T, '78
Hoag, Phil, E, '66

Ingram, Mark, FL, '86
Johnson, Bill, DL '91
Kanicki, James, C, '62
Kapral, Frank, G, '51
Kauth, Don, E, '54
Kolodziej, Tony, E, '57
Land, Melvin, T, '78
Lothamer, Ed, E, '63
McFadden, Marv, G, '51
Nicholson, James, G, '72
Postula, Vic, B, '54
Pruiett, Mitch, G, '67
Przybycki, Joseph, T, '67
Rochester, Paul, T, '59
Rutledge, Les, T, '57
Ryan, Ed, B, '61
Saldock, Tom, T, '56
Schaum, Gregory, T, '75
Serr, Gordon, G, '52
Shlapak, Borys, K,'71
*Smith, Ed, QB, '78
Smith, Pete, QB, '62
Summers, James, B, '66
Taubert, James, T, '74
Timmerman, Ed, C, '52
Turner, Daryl, SE, '83
VanElst, Gary, T, '72
Walker, Mickey, T, '60
Wright, Don, G, '59

SENIOR BOWL

(Mobile)
Andersen, Morten, K, ' 81
Arbanas, Fred, E, '61
Bagdon, Ed, C, '50
Banks, Carl, LB, '83
Banks, Tony, QB, '95
Beard, Thomas, C, '71
Bell, Myron, DB, '93
Bercich, Bob, B, '60
Birchmeier, Mark, C, '94
Brammer, Mark, TE, '80
Brandstatter, Art, E, '62
Brenner, Allen, B, '69
Budde, Ed, T, '63
Bullough, Chuck, LB, '92
Bullough, Henry, G, '55
Burroughs, James, DB, '81
Chandnois, Lynn, B, '50
Coleman, Mill, FL, '94
Currie, Dan, C, '58
Davis, Travis, DT, '90
DeLamielleure, Joseph T, '73
DeMarco, Brian, OG, '94
Dibble, Dorne, E, '51
Dohoney, Don, E, '54
Dorow, Al, B, '52
Fields, Angelo, T, '80
Fredrickson, Rob, OLB,
Garrett, Drake, B, '68
*Gordon, Richard, B, '65
*Gibson Kirk, FL '79
Hammonds, Juan, DE, '94
Highsmith, Donald, B, '70
Johnson, Bill, DL, '92

Kanicki, James, C, '63
Kowalczyk, Walt, B '58
Kush, Frank, G, '53
Lowe, Gary, B, '56
Lyons, Mitch, TE, '92
Maidlow, Steve, LB, '82
+Mason, Don, G, '50
McAuliffe, Don, B, '53
Miller, Jim, QB, '93
Moore, Timothy, LB, '88
Neal, Jim, C, '54
Ninowski, Jim, B, '58
Nystrom, Carl, G, '56
Pitts, Alfred, C, '78
+Pryzbycki, Joseph, T, '68
Rison, Andre, WR, '89
Rush, Jerry, T, '65
Ryan, Ed, B, '62
*Smith, Charles, E, '67
Smith, Ed, QB, '79
Tamburo, Dick, C, '53
VanElst, Gary, T, '73
Wells, Billy, B, '54
Wojciechowski, John, OG, '86
Zucco, Vic, B, '57

CANADIAN AMERICAN BOWL

(Tampa)
Daugherty, Duffy, Head Coach, '70
Stolz, Denny, Head Coach North Team, '76
Baggett, Charles, B, '76
Hardy, Clifton, B, '71
Highsmith, Donald, B, '70
Hogan, Michael, LB, '71
Malinosky, John, T, '78
McConnell, Brian, E, '73
Standal, Thomas, LB, '76
Stanton, Jerome, B, '79
Taubert, James, T, '75
Timmons, Frank, B, '73
Wilson, Charles, G, '75
*Wilson, Tyrone, B, '76

HULA BOWL

(Honolulu)
Daugherty, Duffy, Head Coach, '59,'68
Perles, George, Assistant Coach, '91
Rogers, Darryl, Assistant Coach, '79
Adderley, Herb, B, '61
Allen, Eric, B, '72
Ane, Charles, C, '75
Apisa, Robert, FB, '68
Ballman, Gary, B, '62
Banks, Carl, LB, '83
Behrman, Dave, C, '63
Bobich, Louis, B, '65
Bowdell, Gordon E, '71
Brammer, Mark, TE, '80
Brenner, Allen, B, '69
Bullough, Shane, LB, '87
Byrd, Eugene, SE, '80
*Coleman, Don, T, '52
Curl, Ronald, T, '72
Currie, Dan, C, '58
Cundiff, Larry, T, '60

Dekker, Paul, E, '54
DuPree, Billy Joe, E, '73
Foreman, Frank, E, '70
Gibson, Kirk, FL, '79
*Grandelius, Everett, B, '51
Greene, Scott, FB, '95
Hannon, Thomas, DB, '77
Jones, Clinton, B '66
*Juday, Steve, QB, '66
Kelly, Ellison, G, '59
Kula, Robert, OT, '90
Langeloh, John, PK, '91
Lewis, Sherman, B, '64
Land, Melvin, T, '79
Look, Dean, B, '60
Lopes, Roger, B, '64
Lucas, Harold, MG, '66
Masters, Norm, T, '56
Matsko, John, C, '57
McClowry, Terry, LB, '75
Mojsiejenko, Ralf, PK/P, '8
Moten, Eric, OG, '91
Muhammad, Muhsin, WR,
Nicholson, James, G, '73
Ninowski, Jim, B, '58
O'Brien, Fran, T, '59
Parker, Phi, FS, '86
Piette, Tom, C, '82
Planutis, Gerald, B, '56
Raye, James, OB, '68
Rison, Andre, WR, '89
Saimes, George, FB, '63
Saul Ronald, G, '70
Schaum, Gregory, T, '76
Shurmur, Patrick, C, '88
Simpson, William, B, '74
Snow, Percy, LB, '90
VanPelt, Brad, B, '73
Webster, George, B, '66
Wedemeyer, Charles, F,
*Williams, Sam, E, '59
Wilson, Bobby, DT, '91
Wilson, Tom, B, '61
Wiska, Jeff, G, '82

JAPAN BOWL

(Tokyo)
Perles, George, Head Coach, '89; Asst.
Coach, '92
Anderson, Mark, DB, '80
Duckett, Tico, TB, '92
Ezor, Blake, RB, '90
Graves, Thomas, B, '79
Haller, Alan, DB, '92
Hannon, Thomas, DB, '77
Hinesly, James, OT,' 79
Johnson, Bill, DL, '92
Mandarich, Tony, OT, '89
McAllister, Bobby, QB, '89
Miller, John, DB, '89
Mojsiejenko, Ralf, PK/P, '84
Moore, Timothy, LB, '88
Nichols, Mark, DT, '88
Quinn, Kelly, DE, '86

Schaum, Gregory, T, '76
White, Lorenzo, TB, '88
Wiska, Jeff, G, '82

COACHES' ALL-AMERICA

(Lubbock, Texas)
Daugherty, Hugh, Duffy, Head Coach, '66;
Asst. Coach, '70
Adderley, Herb, B, '61
Arbanas, Fred, E, '61
Beard, Thomas, C, '71
Behrman, David, C, '63
Brenner, Allen, B, '69
Curl, Ronald, T, '72
Foreman, Frank, E, '70
Goovert, Ron, LB, '66
Kumiega, Tony, G, '62
Lewis, Sherman, B, '64
Lucas, Harold, MG, '66
McClowry, Terry, LB, '75
Roberts, Marvin, T, '73
Rush, Jerry, T, '65
Ryan, Ed, B, '62
Saimes, George, B, '63
Saul, Ronald, G, '70
Viney, Robert, E, '66
Washington, Eugene, E, '67
Webster, George, LB, '67

COLLEGE ALL-STAR GAME

(Chicago)
Adderley, Herb, B, '61
Agett, Albert, B, '37
Arbanas, Fred, E, '61

Bagdon, Ed, G, '50
+Budde, Ed, T, '63
Bullough, Henry, G, '55
Breslin, Jack, B, '46
Behrman, David, C, '63
Carey, Robert, E, '52
Chandnois, Lynn, B, '50
Clark, Gail, LB, '73
Coleman, Don, T, '52
Currie, Dan, C, '58
Dekker, Paul, E, '53
DeLamielleure, Joseph, T, '73
Dorow, Al, B, '52
Grandelius, Everett, B, '51
Guerre, George, B, '49
Huey, Warren, E, '49
Jewett, Robert, E, '58
Jones, Clinton, B, '67
Kanicki, James, C, '63
Kelly, Ellison, G, '59
Kinek, Michael, E, '40
Kowalczyk, Walt, B, '58
Kush, Frank, G, '53
Lothamer, Ed, E, '64
Matsko, John, C, '57
McAuliffe, Don, B, '53
McClowry, Terry, LB, '75
McCurry, Robert, C, '49
Morrall, Earl, B, '56
*Ninowski, Jim, B, '58
O'Brien, Fran, T, '59
Peaks, Clarence, B, '57
Pingel, John, B, '39
Przybycki, Joseph, T, '68

Rochester, Paul, T, '60
Rush, Jerry, T, '65
Sanders, Lonnie, E, '62
Simpson, William, B, '74
*Smith, Charles, E, '67
Snorton, Matt, E, '64
Tamburo, Dick, C, '53
VanPelt, Brad, B, '73
Washington, Eugene, E,
Webster, George, B, '67
Williams, Sam, E, '59

CHALLENGE BOWL

(Seattle)
Bethea, Larry, T, '78
Earley, James, FB, '78
Nielsen, Hans, K, '78
Pitts, Alfred, C, '78
Rowekamp, Kim, LB, '78

OLYMPIA GOLD BOWL

(San Diego)
Morris, Thomas, DB, '82

MARTIN LUTHER KING CLASSIC

(San Jose, CA)
Barnett, Harlon, DB, '90
Vanderbeek, Matthew, DE, '90

ALL-AMERICAN CLASSIC

(St. Petersburg, FL)
Edwards, Dixon, LB, '91

RETIRED SPARTAN NUMBERS

Three football jersey numbers have been retired in Michigan State's gridiron history. They are No. 78, worn by Don Coleman when he was a consensus All-America tackle in 1951; No. 90, worn by George Webster, All-America roverback in the Big Ten and in the national championship years of 1965 and 1966; and No. 46, as a special tribute to former Michigan State University president Dr. John A. Hannah.

Coleman's 78 was pulled out of circulation by Biggie Munn, then the Spartan head coach, in honor of the young man called the finest lineman to play for State.

Don Coleman #78

The 90 belonging to Webster was set aside by Coach Duffy Daugherty in honor of the player who best symbolized the greatness of the fine Spartan teams during the two big seasons. Daugherty also retired the No. 46 jersey, presenting it to Dr. Hannah in the occasion of his leading the university in 1969 after 46 years of service to become director of the Agency for International Development in President Nixon's administration. Daugherty cited Hannah for important contributions to Spartan athletics over those years.

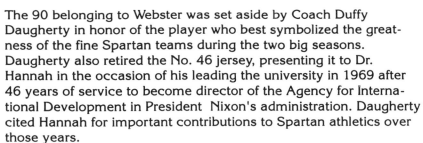

George Webster, #90

Dr. John A. Hannah, #46

SPARTANS IN THE BIG TEN

Michigan State has played in 43 Big Ten football seasons and shows a composite league record of 178 victories, 127 defeats and nine ties for a winning percentage of .581. The Spartans have won three undisputed titles and shared three, finished second four times and shared second once, and have had 29 first-division finishes.

Year	W	L	T	Pct.	Place
1953	5	1	0	.833	Shared first with Illinois
1954	1	5	0	.167	Shared eighth with Northwestern
1955	5	1	0	.833	Second
1956	4	2	0	.667	Shared fourth with Ohio State
1957	5	1	0	.833	Second
1958	0	5	1	.083	Tenth
1959	4	2	0	.667	Second
1960	3	2	0	.600	Fourth
1961	5	2	0	.714	Third
1962	3	3	0	.500	Shared fifth with Iowa & Purdue
1963	4	1	1	.750	Shared second with Ohio State
1964	3	3	0	.500	Sixth
1965	7	0	0	1.000	First
1966	7	0	0	1.000	First
1967	3	4	0	.429	Shared fifth with Illinois & Michigan
1968	2	5	0	.286	Seventh
1969	2	5	0	.286	Ninth
1970	3	4	0	.429	Shared fifth with Wisconsin
1971	5	3	0	.625	Shared fifth with Ohio State & Illinois
1972	5	2	1	.688	Fourth
1973	4	4	0	.500	Shared fourth with Illinois, Northwestern & Purdue
1974	6	1	1	.813	Third
1975	4	4	0	.500	Shared third with Illinois & Purdue
1976	3	5	0	.375	Shared seventh with Iowa & Wisconsin
1977	6	1	1	.813	Third
1978	7	1	0	.875	Shared first with Michigan
1979	3	5	0	.375	Shared seventh with Wisconsin
1980	2	6	0	.250	Ninth
1981	4	5	0	.444	Shared sixth with Minnesota
1982	2	7	0	.222	Shared eighth with Northwestern
1983	2	6	1	.278	Seventh
1984	5	4	0	.556	Shared sixth with Michigan
1985	5	3	0	.600	Shared third with Ohio State
1986	4	4	0	.500	Fifth
1987	7	0	1	.938	First
1988	6	1	1	.812	Second
1989	6	2	0	.750	Shared third with Ohio State
1990	6	2	0	.750	Shared first with Iowa, Michigan & Illinois
1991	3	5	0	.375	
1992	5	3	0	.625	Third
1993	4	4	0	.500	Seventh
1994	4	4	0	.500	Shared fifth with Illinois
1995	4	3	1	.562	Fifth
43 yrs.	**178**	**127**	**9**	**.581**	

MSU RECORDS IN BIG TEN GAMES

LONGEST PLAYS

Rushing — 88 yards, Levi Jackson vs. Ohio State, 1974, TD; Tico Duckett vs. Minnesota, 1991, TD. *Forward Pass* — 93 yards, Tony Banks to Nigea Carter vs. Indiana, 1994, TD. *Interception Return (Pass)* — 99 yards, Dan Bass vs. Wisconsin, 1978, TD. *Interception Return (Fumble)* — 90 yards, Earl Morrall vs. Purdue,1955,TD. *Defensive Extra Point Return* — 82 yards, Rob Fredrickson vs. Purdue, 1992, *2 pts Kickoff Return* — 100 yards, Derrick Mason vs. Penn State, 1994, TD. *Punt Return* — 95 yards, Allen Brenner vs. Illinois, 1966, TD. *Field Goal* — 63 yards, Morten Andersen vs. Ohio State, 1981. *Punt* — 86 yards, Greg Montgomery vs. Michigan, 1986.

INDIVIDUAL IN GAME

Rushing Attempts — 56, Lorenzo White vs. Indiana, 1987. *Yards Gained Rushing* — 350, Eric Allen vs. Purdue, 1971. *Passes Attempted* — 54, John Leister vs. Purdue, 1980. *Passes Completed* — 32, John Leister vs. Michigan, 1982. *Passes Had Intercepted* — 5, John Leister vs. Purdue, 1980. *Yards Gained Passing* — 369, Ed Smith vs. Indiana, 1978. *Total Yards Gained* — 372, Bryan Clark vs. Minnesota, 1981. *Touchdown Passes Thrown* — 4, Mike Rasmussen vs. Indiana, 1970; Ed Smith vs. Wisconsin, 1978. *Passes Caught* — 12, Mitch Lyons vs. Michigan, 1992. *Yards Gained Passes Caught* — 197, Courtney Hawkins vs. Minnesota, 1989. *Touchdown Passes Caught* — 3, Gene Washington vs. Indiana, 1965; Mark Ingram vs. Iowa, 1986. *Pass Interceptions* — 4, John Miller vs. Michigan, 1987. *Punts* — 11, Bill Simpson vs. Ohio State, 1973. *Touchdowns Scored* — 6, Blake Ezor vs. Northwestern, 1989. *P.A.T. Scored* — 10, John Langeloh vs. Northwestern, 1989. Field Goals *Scored* — 5, John Langeloh vs. Wisconsin, 1988. *Points Scored* — 36, Blake Ezor vs. Northwestern, 1989.
Tackles For Loss — 5 (37 yds.), Travis Davis vs. Ohio State, 1987. *Quarterback Sacks* — 5 (37 yds.), Travis Davis vs. Ohio State, 1987.

TEAM OFFENSE IN GAME

Rushing Attempts — 77 vs. Purdue, 1987. Net Yards Rushing — 573 vs. Purdue, 1971. Passes Attempted — 56 vs. Purdue, 1980. Passes Completed — 34 vs. Michigan, 1982. Yards Gained Passing — 369 vs. Indiana, 1978. Total Yards Gained — 698 vs. Purdue, 1971. Touchdown Passes — 5 vs. Northwestern, 1981. Touchdowns Scored — 11 vs. Northwestern, 1989. P.A.T. Scored — 10 vs. Northwestern, 1989. Points Scored — 76 vs. Northwestern, 1989. First Downs by Rushing — 26 vs. Northwestern, 1975. First Downs by Passing — 19 vs. Minnesota, 1978; vs. Michigan, 1982. Total First Downs — 34 vs. Northwestern, 1978; vs. Indiana, 1981, vs. Purdue, 1990. Fumbles Lost — 5 vs. Michigan, 1962; vs. Indiana, 1962; vs. Minnesota, 1981. Yards Penalized — 155 vs. Indiana, 1957. Passes Had Intercepted — 6 vs. Minnesota, 1958.

TEAM DEFENSE IN GAME

Rushing Attempts — 14 by Purdue, 1987. *Net Yards Rushing* — Minus 60 by Northwestern, 1981. *Passes Attempted* — 2 by Michigan, 1955; by Indiana, 1958. *Passes Completed* — 1 by Michigan, 1955; by Indiana, 1958; by Minnesota, 1972. *Yards Gained Passing* — 15 by Michigan, 1955. *Total Yards Gained* — 55 by Northwestern, 1983. *First Downs by Rushing* — 0 by Ohio State, 1965; by Purdue, 1990. *First Downs by Passing* — 1 by 9 different opponents. *Total First Downs* — 4 by Indiana, 1957. *Passes Intercepted* — 7 vs. Michigan, 1987. *Fumbles Recovered* — 7 vs. Purdue, 1955; vs. Illinois, 1971.

ALL-TIME MSU RECORD VS. OPPONENTS

Opponent	G	W	L	T
Adrian	4	4	0	0
Akron	2	2	0	0
Albion	18	11	4	3
Alma	30	22	4	4
Arizona	3	3	0	0
Arizona State	2	1	1	0
Armour Institute	1	1	0	0
Army	2	0	2	0
Auburn	1	0	1	0
Baylor	1	1	1	0
Boston College	5	1	3	1
Bowling Green State	1	1	0	0
Butler	2	1	1	0
California	2	2	0	0
Camp MacArthur	1	0	1	0
CarnegieTech	4	3	0	1
Carroll	2	2	0	0
Case	2	2	0	0
Centre	2	2	0	0
Central Michigan	3	1	2	0
Chicago	1	0	1	0
Chicago YMCA College	3	3	0	0
Cincinnati	2	1	1	0
Colgate	5	1	4	0
Colorado	3	3	0	0
Cornell College	2	1	1	0
Cornell U	1	0	1	0
Creighton	2	0	2	0
Culver Military Academy	1	1	0	0
DePaul	2	1	0	0
DePauw	6	5	1	0
Detroit Athletic Club	8	3	4	1
Detroit	14	7	6	1
Detroit YMCA	1	1	0	0
Eastern Michigan*	3	3	0	0
Florida State	2	0	2	0
Fordham	1	1	0	0
Georgetown	2	1	1	0
Georgia	1	0	1	0
GeorgiaTech	3	0	3	0
Great Lakes Naval Station	2	1	1	0
Grinnell	4	4	0	0
Haskell Institute	1	0	1	0
Hawaii	3	3	0	0
Hillsdale	7	7	0	0
Houston	1	0	1	0
Illinois*	33	15	16	2
Illinois Wesleyan	5	5	0	0
Indiana*	46	32	12	2
Iowa*	31	14	15	2
Iowa State	2	2	0	0
Kalamazoo	17	9	8	0
Kansas	6	5	1	0
Kansas State	6	5	0	1
Kentucky	4	2	2	0
Lake Forest	5	3	1	1
Lansing High School	2	2	0	0
Louisville*	2	1	1	0
Louisiana State	1	0	1	0
Loyola (Cal.)	1	1	0	0
Manhattan	2	1	1	0

Opponent	G	W	L	T
Marietta	1	0	1	0
Marquette	25	18	6	1
Maryland	5	4	1	0
Massachusetts State	1	1	0	0
Miami (Fla.)	4	0	4	0
Miami (Ohio)	4	4	0	0
Michigan*	88	26	57	5
Michigan Frosh	4	4	0	0
Michigan School for Deaf	4	4	0	0
Minnesota*	32	21	11	0
Mississippi State	4	2	1	1
Missouri	6	3	3	0
Mt. Union	4	4	0	0
Nebraska*	3	0	3	0
North Carolina	3	2	1	0
North Carolina State	6	4	1	0
North Central	1	1	0	0
North Dakota State	2	2	0	0
Northwestern	39	29	10	0
Notre Dame	60	18	41	1
Ohio Northern	1	1	0	0
Ohio State	29	10	19	0
Ohio University	1	1	0	0
Ohio Wesleyan	4	2	2	0
Olivet	23	18	4	1
Oregon	2	1	1	0
Oregon State	9	6	2	0
Penn State*	13	8	4	1
Pittsburgh	5	4	0	1
Port Huron YMCA	2	2	0	0
Purdue*	50	27	20	3
Ripon	1	1	0	0
Rutgers	3	1	2	0
Saginaw Naval Brigade	1	1	0	0
St. Louis	2	0	1	1
San Francisco	1	1	0	0
Santa Clara	6	1	3	2
Scranton	1	1	0	0
South Dakota	6	5	0	0
South Dakota State	1	1	0	0
Southern California	8	4	4	0
Southern Methodist	1	1	0	0
Stanford	4	3	1	0
Syracuse	13	9	3	1
Temple	10	7	1	2
Texas A&M	3	2	1	0
Texas Christian	1	1	0	0
Toledo	1	1	0	0
UCLA	6	3	3	0
Wabash	7	5	1	1
Washington	2	1	1	0
Washington (St. Louis)	1	1	0	0
Washington State	7	5	2	0
Wayne State	9	9	0	0
Western Michigan	7	5	2	0
West Virginia	4	4	0	0
William & Mary	2	2	0	0
Wisconsin*	38	24	14	0
Wyoming	2	2	0	0

*Denotes 1996 opponent

Number of Teams Played	120	Number of Games Lost	344#	# Reflects five 1994 wins forfeited by MSU as part
Number of Games Played	915	Number of Games Tied	44	of 1996 self-imposed sanctions.
Number of Games Won	527	Percentage	.605	

MSU IN SEASON OPENERS

(MSU score appears first)

Sept. 26, 1896	Lansing High School (10-0)
Sept. 25, 1897	Lansing High School (28-0)
Oct. 8, 1898	Ypsilanti (11-6)
Sept. 29, 1899	Notre Dame (0-40)
Sept. 29, 1900	Albion (0-23)
Sept. 28, 1901	Alma (5-5)
Sept. 27, 1902	Notre Dame (0-32)
Oct. 3, 1903	Notre Dame (0-12)
Oct. 1, 1904	Michigan Deaf School (47-0)
Sept. 20, 1905	Michigan Deaf School (42-0)
Sept. 29, 1906	Olivet (23-0)
Oct. 3, 1907	Detroit College (17-0)
Oct. 3, 1908	Michigan Deaf School (51-0)
Oct. 7, 1909	Detroit College (27-0)
Oct. 6, 1910	Detroit College (35-0)
Oct. 7, 1911	Alma (12-0)
Oct. 5, 1912	Alma (14-3)
Oct. 4, 1913	Olivet (26-0)
Oct. 3, 1914	Olivet (26-7)
Oct. 2, 1915	Olivet (34-0)
Sept. 30, 1916	Olivet (40-0)
Oct. 6, 1917	Alma (7-14)
Oct. 5, 1918	Albion (21-6)
Oct. 4, 1919	Albion (14-13)
Sept. 25, 1920	Kalamazoo (2-21)
Oct. 1, 1921	Alma (28-0)
Sept. 30, 1922	Alma (33-0)
Sept. 29, 1923	Chicago (0-34)
Sept. 26, 1924	North Central (59-0)
Sept. 26, 1925	Adrian (16-0)
Sept. 26, 1926	Adrian (16-0)
Sept. 24, 1927	Kalamazoo (12-6)
Sept. 29, 1928	Kalamazoo (103-0)
Sept. 28, 1929	Alma (59-6)
Sept. 27, 1930	Alma (28-0)
Sept. 6, 1931	Alma (74-0)
Sept. 24, 1932	Alma (93-0)
Sept. 30, 1933	Grinnell (14-0)
Sept. 29, 1934	Grinnell (33-20)
Sept. 28, 1935	Grinnell (41-0)
Sept. 26, 1936	Wayne State (27-0)
Sept. 25, 1937	Wayne State (19-0)
Sept. 24, 1938	Wayne State (34-6)
Sept. 30, 1939	Wayne State (16-0)
Oct. 5, 1940	Michigan (14-21)
Sept. 27, 1941	Michigan (7-19)
Oct. 3, 1942	Michigan (0-20)
(No games played in 1943 due to WW II)	
Sept. 30, 1944	Scranton (40-12)
Sept. 29, 1945	Michigan (0-40)
Sept. 28, 1946	Wayne State (42-0)
Sept. 27, 1947	Michigan (0-55)

Sept. 25, 1948	Michigan (7-13)
Sept. 24, 1949	Michigan (3-7)
Sept. 23, 1950	Oregon State (38-13)
Sept. 22, 1951	Oregon State (6-0)
Sept. 27, 1952	Michigan (27-13)
Sept. 26, 1953	Iowa (21-7)
Sept. 25, 1954	Iowa (10-14)
Sept. 24, 1955	Indiana (20-13)
Sept. 29, 1956	Stanford (21-7)
Sept. 28, 1957	Indiana (54-0)
Sept. 27, 1958	California (32-12)
Sept. 28, 1959	Texas A&M (7-9)
Sept. 24, 1960	Pittsburgh (7-7)
Sept. 30, 1961	Wisconsin (20-0)
Sept. 29, 1962	Stanford (13-16)
Sept. 28, 1963	North Carolina (31-0)
Sept. 26, 1964	North Carolina (15-21)
Sept. 18, 1965	U.C.L.A (13-3)
Sept. 17, 1966	North Carolina St. (28-10)
Sept. 23, 1967	Houston (7-37)
Sept. 21, 1968	Syracuse (14-10)
Sept. 20, 1969	Washington (27-11)
Sept. 19, 1970	Washington (16-42)
Sept. 11, 1971	Illinois(10-0)
Sept. 17, 1972	Illinois (24-0)
Sept. 15, 1973	Northwestern (10-14)
Sept. 14, 1974	Northwestern (41-7)
Sept. 13, 1975	Ohio State (0-21)
Sept. 11, 1976	Ohio State (21-49)
Sept. 10, 1977	Purdue (19-14)
Sept. 16, 1978	Purdue (14-21)
Sept. 8, 1979	Illinois (33-16)
Sept. 13, 1980	Illinois (17-20)
Sept. 12, 1981	Illinois (17-27)
Sept. 1, 1982	Illinois (16-23)
Sept. 10, 1983	Colorado (23-17)
Sept. 8, 1984	Colorado (24-21)
Sept. 14, 1985	Arizona State (12-3)
Sept. 13, 1986	Arizona State (17-20)
Sept. 7, 1987	Southern California (27-13)
Sept. 10, 1988	Rutgers (13-17)
Sept. 16, 1989	Miami (O.) (49-0)
Sept. 15, 1990	Syracuse (23-23)
Sept. 14, 1991	Central Michigan (3-20)
Sept. 12, 1992	Central Michigan (20-24)
Sept. 11, 1993	Kansas (31-14)
Sept. 10, 1994	Kansas (10-17)
Sept. 9, 1995	Nebraska (10-50)

99 games
63 victories; 34 losses; 2 ties
.646 winning percentage

MSU IN HOMECOMING GAMES

MSU score appears first

Oct. 30, 1915	Oregon State (0-20)
Nov. 18, 1916	Notre Dame (0-14)
Nov. 24, 1918	Syracuse (7-21)
Nov. 8, 1919	South Dakota (13-0)
Oct. 30, 1920	Olivet (109-0)
Nov. 5, 1921	South Dakota (13-0)
Nov. 25, 1922	Massachusetts (45-7)
Oct. 10, 1923	Creighton (27-7)
Oct. 10, 1924	Michigan (0-7)
Nov. 7, 1925	Toledo (58-0)
Nov. 6, 1926	Centre College (42-12)
Oct. 29, 1927	Detroit (7-24)
Oct. 20, 1928	Colgate (0-16)
Oct. 26, 1929	North Carolina State (40-6)
Oct. 17, 1930	Colgate (14-7)
Oct. 31, 1931	Syracuse (10-15)
Nov. 5, 1932	South Dakota (20-6)
Oct. 28, 1933	Syracuse (20-6)
Nov. 3, 1934	Marquette (13-7)
Nov. 9, 1935	Marquette (7-13)
Oct. 17, 1936	Missouri (13-0)
Oct. 22, 1938	Syracuse (19-12)
Nov. 18, 1939	Indiana (7-7)
Oct. 26, 1940	Santa Clara (0-0)
Nov. 1, 1941	Missouri (0-14)
Oct. 10, 1942	Great Lakes (14-0)
(No game played in 1943 due to WWII).	
Nov. 1, 1944	Maryland (33-0)
Nov 3, 1945	Missouri (14-7)
Nov. 16, 1946	Marquette (20-0)
Oct. 18, 1947	Iowa State (20-0)
Oct. 16, 1948	Arizona (61-7)
Oct. 2, 1949	Penn State (24-0)
Oct. 14, 1950	William & Mary (33-14)
Oct. 27, 1951	Pittsburgh (53-26)
Oct. 25, 1952	Penn State (34-7)
Oct. 17, 1953	Indiana (47-18)
Oct. 23, 1954	Purdue (13-27)
Oct. 22, 1955	Illinois (21-7)
Oct. 13, 1956	Indiana (53-6)

Oct. 26, 1957	Illinois (19-14)
Nov. 1, 1958	Wisconsin (7-9)
Oct. 24, 1959	Indiana (14-6)
Oct. 29, 1960	Ohio State (10-21)
Oct. 28, 1961	Indiana (35-0)
Nov. 3, 1962	Minnesota (7-28)
Nov. 2, 1963	Wisconsin (30-13)
Oct. 24, 1964	Northwestern (24-6)
Oct. 30, 1965	Northwestern (49-7)
Oct. 22, 1966	Purdue (41-20)
Nov. 4, 1967	Ohio State (7-21)
Oct. 19, 1968	Minnesota (13-14)
Nov. 1, 1969	Indiana (0-16)
Oct. 23, 1970	Iowa (37-0)
Oct. 23, 1971	Iowa (34-3)
Oct. 21, 1972	Wisconsin (31-0)
Nov. 3, 1973	Wisconsin (21-0)
Oct. 26, 1974	Purdue (31-7)
Oct. 25, 1975	Illinois (19-21)
Oct. 16, 1976	Minnesota (10-14)
Oct. 29, 1977	Illinois (49-20)
Oct. 21, 1978	Indiana (49-14)
Oct. 20, 1979	Purdue (7-14)
Oct. 18, 1980	Wisconsin (7-17)
Oct. 17, 1981	Wisconsin (33-14)
Oct. 23, 1982	Purdue (21-24)
Oct. 29, 1983	Minnesota (34-10)
Oct. 31, 1984	Indiana (13-6)
Oct. 19, 1985	Illinois (17-30)
Oct. 25, 1986	Purdue (37-3)
Oct. 24, 1987	Illinois (14-14)
Oct. 15, 1988	Northwestern (36-3)
Oct. 21, 1989	Illinois (10-14)
Oct. 27, 1990	Purdue (55-33)
Oct. 24, 1991	Minnesota (20-12)
Oct. 3, 1992	Indiana (42-31)
Oct. 23 1993	Iowa (24-10)
Oct. 1, 1994	Wisconsin (29-10)#
Oct. 7, 1995	Iowa (7-21)

80 games
52-25#-3 (.669)

Reflects 1994 forfeit by MSU as part of
1996 self-imposed sanctions.

SPARTAN WINNING STREAKS

All Games

28   From fourth game of 1950 season through the fourth game of the 1953 season. Team coached by Biggie Munn

15   From third game of 1912 season through second game of 1914 season. Team coached by John Macklin

12   From third game of 1955 season through fourth game of 1956 season. Team coached by Duffy Daugherty

10   From first game through final game of 1965 regular season. Team coached by Duffy Daugherty

10   From fifth game of 1978 season through third game of 1979 season. Team coached by Darryl Rogers.

Big Ten Games

16   From first conference game of 1965 season through second conference game of 1967 season. Team coached by Duffy Daugherty

8   From second conference game of 1978 through first conference game of 1979. Team coached by Darryl Rogers

7   From third conference game of 1988 through first conference game of 1989. Team coached by George Perles

6   From third conference game of 1955 through second conference game of 1956. Team coached by Duffy Daugherty

5   From fifth conference game of 1960 through third conference game of 1961. Team coached by Duffy Daugherty

5   From fourth conference game of 1974 through final conference game of 1974. Team coached by Denny Stolz

5   From fourth conference game of 1985 through final conference game of 1985. Team coached by George Perles

5   From fourth conference game of 1990 through final conference game of 1990. Team coached by George Perles

ALL-TIME SPARTAN COACHING STAFFS

BIGGIE MUNN
Head Coach, 1947-1953

ASSISTANT COACHES
Forest Evashevski, 1947-49
Duffy Daugherty, 1947-53
Kip Taylor, 1947-48
John Kobs, 1947-53
Alton Kircher, 1947-49
Robert Flora, 1949
Earle Edwards, 1949-1953
Lowell Dawson, 1950-51
Steve Sebo, 1950-58
Harold Vogler, 1950-51
Dan Devine, 1950-53
Donald Mason, 1952-53
Dewey King, 1952-53
Robert Devaney, 1953

HUGH "DUFFY" DAUGHERTY
Head Coach, 1954-1972

ASSISTANT COACHES
John Kobs, 1954
Donald Mason, 1954-55
Robert Devaney, 1954-56
Dan Devine, 1954
Burt Smith, 1954-64
William Yeoman, 1954-61
Everett Grandelius, 1954-58
Lou Agase, 1955-59
Doug Weaver, 1956-57
Gordon Serr, 1957-72
John Polonchek, 1957-58
Carl "Buck"' Nystrom, 1958,'71
George Perles, 1967-71
Don Coleman, 1968
Joseph Carruthers, 1969-72
George Paterno, 1969-70
Sherman Lewis, 1969-72
Denny Stolz, 1971-72
Ed Youngs, 1971-72
Dan Boisture, 1959-66
Henry Bullough, 1959-69
Cal Stoll, 1959-68
Vince Carillot, 1960-68
John McVay, 1962-64
Edwin Rutherford, 1965-72

Al Dorow, 1965-70
Dave Smith, 1967-70
Woody Widenhofer, 1969-70
Jimmy Raye, 1972
Herb Paterra, 1972

DENNY STOLZ
Head Coach, 1973-1975

ASSISTANT COACHES
Edwin Rutherford, 1973
Sherman Lewis, 1973-75
Ed Youngs, 1973-75
Jimmy Raye, 1973-75
Charles Butler, 1973-75
Daniel Underwood, 1973-75
William Davis, 1973-75
Andy MacDonald, 1973-75
Howard Weyers, 1973-75
Ronald Chismar, 1974-75

DARRYL ROGERS
Head Coach, 1976-1979

ASSISTANT COACHES
Marv Braden, 1976
Ron Chismar, 1976-79
Ray Greene, 1976-77
C.T. Hewgley, 1976-79
Robert Padilla, 1976-77
Leon Burtnett, 1976
Sherman Lewis, 1976-79
Dan Underwood, 1976-79
Robert Baker, 1977-79
George Dyer, 1977-79
Mo Forte, 1973-79
Walt Harris, 1978-79

FRANK "MUDDY" WATERS
Head Coach 1980-1982

ASSISTANT COACHES
Dick Comar, 1980-82

Dave Driscoll, 1980-82
Ted Guthard, 1980-82
Sherman Lewis 1980-82
Matt Means, 1980-82
Joe Pendry, 1980-81
Kurt Schottenheimer, 1980-82
Tyrone Willingham, 1980-82
Steve Schottel, 1982

GEORGE PERLES
Head Coach, 1983-1994

ASSISTANT COACHES
Charlie Baggett, 1983-92
Steve Beckholt, 1983-89
Larry Bielat, 1983-89
Hank Bullough, 1994
Anthony Folino, 1988-94
Steve Furness, 1983-90
Ted Guthard, 1983-85
Pat Morris, 1987-94
Carl "Buck" Nystrom, 1983-86
Willie "Skip" Peete, 1993-94
Norm Parker, 1983-94
Bill Rademacher, 1983-91
Nick Saban, 1983-87
Pat Shurmur, 1990-94
Kip Waddell, 1991-94
Morris Watts, 1986-90; 92-94
Bobby Williams, 1990-94
Ed Zaunbrecher, 1991-93

NICK SABAN
Head Coach, 1995-present

ASSISTANT COACHES
Charlie Baggett, 1995-
Dean Pees, 1995-
Gary Tranquill, 1995-
Jim Bollman, 1995-
Greg Colby, 1995-
Mark Dantonio, 1995-
Todd Grantham, 1996-
Glenn Pires, 1995-
Pat Shurmur, 1995-
Bobby Williams, 1995-

SPARTAN TEAM RECORDS

Team Offense in Game

Rushing Attempts—80 vs. Indiana, 1950.
Net Yards Rushing—573 vs. Purdue, 1971.
Passes Attempted—56 vs. Purdue, 1980.
Passes Completed—34 vs. Michigan, 1982.
Yards Gained Passing—369 vs. Indiana, 1978.
Total Yards Gained—698 vs. Purdue, 1971
Touchdown Passes—5 vs. Northwestern, 1981.
Touchdowns Scored—11 vs. Arizona, 1949; vs.
  Northwestern, 1989.
P.A.T. Scored—10 vs. Northwestern, 1989.
First Downs by Rushing—26 vs. Northwestern, 1975.
First Downs by Passing—19 vs. Minnesota, 1978;
  vs. Michigan, 1982.
Total First Downs—34 vs. Northwestern, 1978; vs.
  Indiana,   1981; vs. Purdue, 1990
Fumbles Lost —9 vs. Kansas State, 1956.
Yards Penalized—155 vs. Indiana, 1967.
Passes Had Intercepted—6 vs. Maryland, 1950;
  vs. Minnesota, 1958.

Team Defense in Game

Rushing Attempts—14 by Purdue, 1987.
Net Yards Rushing—Minus 63 by Pittsburgh, 1950.
Passes Attempted—1 by Maryland, 1944.
Passes Completed—0 by Kansas State, 1944; by
  Maryland, 1944; by Georgia Tech, 1971.
Yards Gained Passing—0 by Kansas State, 1944;
  by Maryland, 1944; by Georgia Tech, 1971.
Total Yards Gained—Minus 11 by Pittsburgh, 1950.
First Downs by Rushing—0 by Wayne State, 1945; by
Wayne State, 1946; by Ohio State, 1965; by
  Purdue, 1990.
First Downs by Passing—0 by 9 different opponents.
Total First Downs—1 by Maryland, 1944.
Passes Intercepted—8 vs. Washington State, 1970.
Fumbles Recovered— 8 vs. Great Lakes, 1945.

THE HISTORY OF SPARTY

The Story Behind the Nickname

Michigan State's first southern baseball training tour in 1926 provided the setting for the birth of the "Spartan" nickname. It all came about when a Lansing sportswriter imposed the silent treatment on a contest-winning nickname and substituted his own choice, the name that has lasted through the years.

In 1925, Michigan State College replaced the name Michigan Agricultural College. The college sponsored a contest to select a nickname to replace "Aggies" and picked "The Michigan Staters."

George S. Alderton, then sports editor of the *Lansing State Journal*, decided the name was too cumbersome for newspaper writing and vowed to find a better one. Alderton contacted Jim Hasselman of Information Services to see if entries still remained from the contest. When informed that they still existed, Alderton ran across the name of "Spartans" and then decided that was the choice. Unfortunately, Alderton forgot to write down who submitted that particular entry, so that part of the story remains a mystery.

Rewriting game accounts supplied by Perry Fremont, a catcher on the squad, Alderton first used the name sparingly and then ventured into the headlines with it. (Incidentally, after two days of spelling the name incorrectly with an "o", Mr. Alderton changed it to Spartan on a tip from a close friend.) Dale Stafford, a sportswriter for the *Lansing Capitol News*, a rival of the *State Journal*, picked up the name for his paper after a couple of days. Alderton called Stafford and suggested that he might want to join the Spartan parade and he did. As Mr. Alderton explains: "No student, alumnus or college official had called up the editor to complain about our audacity in giving the old school a new name, so we ventured into headlines with it. Happily for the experiment, the name took. It began appearing in other newspapers and when the student publication used it, that clinched it."

The School Colors

Details are sketchy as to when Michigan State athletic teams officially began using the school colors green and white. But records of the Athletic Association of the then Michigan Agricultural College show that on April 11, 1899, the organization took steps toward adoption of a green monogram, "to be worn only by athletes who subsequently take part in intercollegiate events."

Two years earlier, at a Michigan Intercollegiate Athletic meeting at Olivet College, MAC shldents decided on green as the college color to wear. The students wore green ribbons and pins of rakes, hoes and spades.

It is generally thought the colors came into wide use with the arrival in 1903 of Chester L. Brewer as the school's first full-time director of athletics. Brewer also coached the Spartan football, basketball, baseball and track teams, the only varsity units in existence at the time.

Sparty

Standing at the entrance way to Michigan State's athletic establishment is "The Spartan," a huge statue which symholized the university's athletic teams.

"The Spartan" was designed and produced by Leonard D. Jungwirth of the art department, and dedicated in June of 1945. It stands ten-feet-six inches, and is mounted on a brick-and-concrete base five-feet-four inches high. The statue weighs three tons and is one of the largest free-standing ceramic figures in the world. Figures representing the 12 sports then included on the varsity program are incised on the base of the statue.

Popularly known as "Sparty," the statue is one of the favorite photo subjects of visitors to the campus.

MSU TEAM PHOTO
PLAYER IDENTIFICATIONS

(Some year listings may not correspond exactly to photos.)

1896

This is the photo of the 1896 MAC football team, the first officially recognized intercollegiate gridiron squad in school history. Only five players have been identified: Front row, second from left is G.D. (Devere) Miller (Cadillac), right halfback; in the middle is James Elliott (Hickory Corners), quarterback; second from the right is Walton K. Brainard (Brady), left halfback. Back row, second from left is Fred Woodworth (Caseville), right tackle ; second from right is Henry Becker (Hesperia), left guard. Other team members were: Elmer Thompson, (Dansville), center; John Vanderstolpe (Grand Rapids), right guard; Wilfred Vanderhoef (Washington, D.C.), right tackle; Eugene Price (Ithaca), left tackle; Judson Bishop (Dimondale), right end; Scott Redfern (Maple Rapids), left end; George Wells (Ithaca), fullback.

1897

No photo exists for this team. Team members included: John Vanderstople, center; Fred Williams (Petoskey), right guard; Henry Becker, left guard; Fred Woodworth, right tackle; Eugene Price, left tackle; William Russell (Benton Harbor), left end; Ellis Ranney (Belding), quarterback; Charles Tate (Altoona, Pa.), right halfback; Walton Brainerd (captain; Brady), left halfback; Earl Smith (Lansing), fullback; William Merkel (Manistee), manager.

1898

Team members: Fred Curtis (White Pigeon), left tackle; Ralph Sinner (Cooper), left guard; John Vanderstolpe, right guard; William Parks (Pipestone), right tackle; William Dietz (Lansing) right end; Charles McCue (Cass City), quarterback; Ellis Ranney, quarterback; William Russell, left halfback; Cylde Wolf (Frontier), right half; Charles Lundy, fullback; Baker, left end; Aldrich McClouth (Medina), center. Ellis W. Ranney is holding the ball in the second row.

1899

H.P. Baker, left end; John Alfsen (Long Rapids), left tackle; Albert Case (Springville), left guard; Aldrich McLouth, center; Hackley Sinner (Cooper), right guard; William Parks, right tackle; Charles McCue, right end; Ellis Ranney (captain), quarterback; William Russell, left halfback; Ralph Case (Mt. Pleasant), right halfback; Earl Smith (Lansing), fullback. Also: Wilford P. Ricamore. Ellis W. Ranney is holding the ball in the second row and coach Charles O. Bemies to Ranney's left.

1900

Albert Case (Springville), right tackle; Charles McCue (Cass City), left end (captain); Charles Blanchard (Chesaning), left halfback; Malcomb McIntyre, right halfback; Wilford Ricamore, right end; Francis Buckridge, fullback & punter; Phillips, left tackle; Oliver Edgar (Lakeview), left tackle; Ward Shedd (Tekonsha), center; Clifford Olmstead, right guard; Arthur Decker (Utica), left guard; McLean, left half-back; Taylor, left end; Taber, center; Gordon Tower (Otisco), right tackle; Ireland, right end.

1901

(Coach George Denman back row, second from right) Matt Crosby, left end; Arthur Peters (Springport), left tackle; Albert Case, left guard (captain); Ward Shedd, center; Wilford Ricamore, right guard/fullback; Frank Kratz (Albion), right tackle; Rourke, right end; Charles Blanchard, quarterback; Walton Brainerd, left halfback; Don Childs (Lansing), right halfback/ fullback; Taylor, fullback; Eaton, left end; Cooper, right halfback; Harry Meek(Manton), right guard; Gordon Tower; Carl Nern (Port Huron), right guard; Ed McKenna, right end; Waterbury; Arthur Decker, left guard; Covell, right end; Ray, right halfback; Brown, fullback.

1902

Front row, lt. to rt., Wesley Bortright (Hillsdale) right end; Gary Burington (Lansing), left end. Row two, lt. to rt., Burr Wheeler (manager, Grand Rapids); Swales, end; William Strand (Otsego), fullback; Don Childs, quarterback; Arthur Peters (captain), left tackle; George Denman, head coach; Harold Childs (Lansing), right halfback. Row three, lt. to rt., Mancl, guard; Frank Kratz, right tackle; Turner, guard; John Decker, center; Harry Meek, right guard; Gunnison, end; Robert Bell (Mason),tackle; George Boomsliter (Grand Haven), tackle; Thomas Agnew (Corunna),fullback.

1903

Team members: Robert Bell (Mason), left tackle (captain); Arthur Peters,left end; Harold Shaw (Detroit) and Amos Ashley (Lansing), right end; Frank Kratz, right tackle; John Decker (Three Oaks), center; Athol A. Case (Marengo),left guard; Walter Small (Charlevoix), quarterback; Louis J. Lampke (Durand) and J.E. "Clair" Peck (Belding), right guard; Wilson F. Millar (Ray Center), left halfback; Ed McKenna (Quinnesec), right halfback; Stephen W. Doty (Lockport,N.Y.), fullback; Joe P. Haftencamp (Grand Rapids), manager; Chester Brewer, coach.

1904

George P. Boomsliter (Grand Haven), right guard; Robert F. Bell, left tackle (captain); Frank Kratz, right tackle; Wilbert Holdsworth (Detroit), left end; Amos A. Ashley, right end; Walter H. Small, quarterback; Ed McKenna (captain-elect), right halfback; Harvey D. Hahn (Brookfield), left halfback; Stephen W. Doty, fullback; Frank "Babe" Kratz, left halfback; Ralph Graham, quarterback;Jesse G. Boyle (Glendora), right end; Harry A. Wright (Iron Mountain); D. Burke,fullback; Charles A. Lemmon (Lansing), Athol A. Case, left guard; Ferguson, right half-back.

1905

Front row, lt. to rt., Lytton B. Hitchcock (Jackson; manager); Stephen W. Doty*(Lockport, N.Y.), Walter H. Small (Charlevoix), Wilbert Holdsworth (Detroit), Coach Chester Brewer. Second row, lt. to rt., William Frazer (Lockport, N.Y.), Bert Shedd (Tekonsha),James E. Fisk (Colling), Ed McKenna (captain), H.B. McDermid (Battle Creek), Jesse G. Boyle (Glendora), Parnell McKenna (Quinnesec). Back row, lt. to rt., Ward H. Parker (Holly), William Strand (Otsego), George P. Boomsliter (Grand Haven), Harry A. Wright (Iron Mountain), Charles G. Burroughs (Frontier), Oscar A. Kratz (Albion).

1906

Team members: Chester Brewer, Coach, John J. Bowditch, Jesse G. Boyle, Charles G. Burroughs, Arthur L. Campbell, Bernard E. Dersnah, Stephen W. Doty, Charles W. Dunlap, William D. Frazer, Edward B. McKenna, Parnell G. McKenna, Clyde D. Moore, Francis O'Gara, Mgr., Ward H. Parker, Bert Shedd, Walter H. Small, Devillo Wood.

1907

First row, lt. to rt., Parnell McKenna, Ion Cortright (Mason), Ernest Vaughn (Detroit), Anderson.Second row, lt. to rt., Clyde Mervin (Moscow; manager), Charles Lemmon, Bert Shedd (captain-elect), Walter Small (captain); Clyde Moore (Freeport), Arthur Campbell, Chester Brewer, coach. Third row, lt. to rt., Gerald Allen (Detroit), Roy Wheeler (Athens), William Frazer (Buffalo, N.Y.), Ward Parker (Holly), James McWilliams, Charles W. Dunlap, Leon Exelby (Britton).

1908

Front row, lt. to rt., Lodiwic McGilvary (Valley City, N.D.); Cogsdill; William Frazer; Bert Shedd (captain); Martin E. Lee (Hart); Clyde Moore; Titus. Second row, lt. to rt., Roy Wheeler; Fred Stone (Clare); Clint Ballard (East Lansing); Ion Cortright; Arthur Campbell; Parnell McKenna; Sorensen. Back row, lt. to rt., Chester Brewer, head coach; Gerald Allen; Leon Exelby; James Campbell (Charlevoix); Charles Burroughs; Maleski; Ben Patterson (Caro). (missing name in back row)

1909

Front row, lt. to rt., Clint Ballard, Frank Davis. Second row, lt. to rt., Emery Horst, William Barnett, Leon Exelby, Ion Cortright, Guy Wooley, Roy Montford. Third row, lt. to rt., Coach Brewer, Arthur Campbell, Charles Lemmon, Captain Parnell McKenna, Clyde Moore, Bert Shedd, Leon Johnson, manager. Back row, lt. to rt., William Riblett, Leon Hill, James Campbell, James McWilliams, Benjamin Pattison, Frank McDermid, Fred Stone, Owen Carey.

1910

Earl H. Shuttleworth (Lansing); Clint Ballard (East Lansing);William R. Riblet (Elkhart, Ind.); Roy M. Montford (Benton Harbor); Elmer Gorenflo (Detroit), Fred A. Stone (Clare); James Campbell; Ion Cortright; Leon Exelby; Ben Patterson; Frank R. Davis (Detroit), Chester Brewer, head coach; James E. McWilliams; E.A. Day; Edward G. Culver (Midland).

1911

Front row, lt. to rt., Frank R. Davis, end; Clint V. Ballard, halfback; Earl H. Shuttleworth, quarterback; A.G. Markham, left halfback.Second row, lt. to rt., Head Coach John Macklin; James E. McWilliams,

center; L.J. "Bubbles" Hill (Benton Harbor), right half-back; Fred A. Stone, left end (captain); William R. Riblet, quarterback; Elmer F. Gorenflo, right end; H.L. Bancroft (Lansing), manager. Back row, lt. to rt., Stanley A. Martin (Fredonia); George E. "Carp" Julian (Rochester, N.Y.), fullback; DeArmand McLaughery, left tackle; Leroy W. "Tex" Campbell (Grand Rapids), left guard; A.E. Day, guard/tackle; Edward G. Culver, right guard; Frank H. McDermid (Battle Creek), center; Chester W. Gifford (South Westport, Mass.), right tackle.

1912

Front row, lt. to rt., Charles T. Dendel (Detroit), left halfback; W.B. "Blake" Miller (Tonawanda, N.Y.), left end; William R. Riblet, left halfback (captain); George Gauthier (Detroit), quarterback; Lawrence R. Servis (St. Joseph), right halfback; Elmer F. Gorenflo, right end. Back row, lt. to rt., Neno Jerry DePrato, right halfback; E.A. Calkins, right guard; George "Carp" Julian, fullback; Leroy W. "Tex" Campbell, left guard; Coach John Macklin; Russell McCurdy Lansing), guard; Frank G. "Fizz" Chaddock (Lansing), left guard; Kenneth W. Hutton (Ludington), right tackle. Other players, not pictured: Ralph G. Chamberlain (Grand Rapids), center; Chester W. Gifford, left tackle (captain-elect).

1913

Front row, lt. to rt., Oscar R. "Dutch" Miller (Saginaw), George Gauthier, Hewitt "Hewie" Miller (Tonawanda, N.Y.). Second row, lt. to rt., Larry Vaughn, Hugh Blacklock, Blake Miller, Chester Gifford (captain), George "Carp" Julian, Ralph B. Henning (Bay City), Russell McCurdy. Row three, lt. to rt., Frank J. "Sun" Yuhse (manager; Manistee), Gideon Smith (Lansing), Coach John Macklin, Faunt V. "Dutch" Lenardson (Britton), Ion Cortright (ass't. coach).

1914

Row one: Leslie A. Cobb (Grand Rapids); Blake Miller, left end; "Hewie" Miller, left halfback.Row two: Frank G. ("Fizz") Chaddock (Lansing), right end; Larry F. Vaughn, center; "Dutch" Miller, quarterback; "Carp" Julian (captain), fullback; Ralph Henning, right end; Neno Jerry DePrato (Iron Mountain), right halfback; Clarence Loveland (Grand Rapids), left guard. Row three: George Gauthier (ass't.), Adelbert "Del" Vandervoort (Lansing), left guard; Herb Straight (Holland), right guard; John Macklin (coach), Hugh Blacklock, left tackle; Gideon Smith, right tackle; Carl H. Peterson (manager, Lucas). Not pictured, Bushnell, right halfback.

1915

Front row, lt. to rt., Clarence R. Oviatt (Bay City), end; Harold "Brownie" Springer (Port Huron), quarterback; Bob Heubel (Menominee), quarterback; Hilmar A. Fick (Wilmette, Ill.), halfback. Second row, lt. to rt., Howard Beatty (Petoskey), halfback; Charles O. Butler (Bellevue), end; Lyman Frimodig (Calumet), center; Blake Miller (captain), left end - halfback; Ralph Henning (captain-elect), end; Neno Jerry DePrato, fullback; "Del" Vandervoort, guard. Back row, lt. to rt., George Gauthier, ass't. coach; Herb D. Straight, guard; Gideon Smith, left tackle; John Macklin, head coach; Hugh Blacklock, tackle; "Hewie" Miller, halfback; Merrill S. Fuller (Paw Paw), manager.

1916

Front row, lt. to rt., Joe E. Turner (Whitney), left end; Bob Heubel, quarterback; Freddy Jacks, left halfback. Second row, lt. to rt., Sherman Coryell (Chicago, Ill.), left tackle; Charles O. Butler, fullback; A.L. McClellan, right halfback; Ralph Henning (captain),

right end; H.A. Fick, right halfback; Clarence "Irish" Ramsey (Ludington), left end; Arthur L. Brown (Hastings), left halfback. Back row, lt. to rt., "Jimmy" Dugan (trainer, Ludington); "Del" Vandervoort, right guard; Lyman Frimodig, center; Frank Sommer, head coach; Norman O. Weil (manager, Cleveland, Oh.); Hugh Blacklock, right tackle; Herb D. Straight, left guard; George Gauthier, ass't. coach.

1917

Front row, lt. to rt., Charles Thomson (Eau Claire); Irving J. Snider (Richmond); Orson T. Kellogg (Reading). Second row, lt. to rt., John H. Hammes (Newberry); Paul F. McCool (Cameron, Mo.); Joseph E. Turner (Whitney); Sherman Coryell (captain); Clarence "Irish" Ramsey (captain-elect); Larry Archer (Benton Harbor); Wilbert E. Miller (Bay City). Back row, lt. to rt., Chester Brewer, head coach; Reginald G. Oas (Ishpeming); Phillip F. Bailey (Ludington); Harry E. "Siwash" Franson (Iron Mountain); Charles F. Bassett (Flint); Martin Lefler (Boyne City); Russell Montgomery (manager, Detroit); George Gauthier, ass't. coach.

1918

Front row, lt. to rt., Jacob Brady (Allegan), QB/half-back; Deaner Ferris (Swarthmore, Pa.), quarterback; Simmons. Second row, lt. to rt., John Bos (Grand Rapids), tackle; Jack Schwei (Iron Mountain), end; Dick Van Orden (Corvalis, Ore.), guard; Irving J. "Shorty" Snider, halfback; Herb Dunphy (Lansing), halfback; Harry Graves (Pratt, Kan.), fullback; Edmund Young (Mason), end; Phillip Bailey. Third row, lt. to rt., Jack Heppinstall (trainer), Ed Johns, guard; Harry "Siwash" Franson (captain-elect), tackle; Larry Archer (captain), center; Ward Andrews (Napoleon), end; Wilson; George Gauthier, head coach. Also on team: Edward Johns (Lansing), guard.

1919

Front row, lt. to rt., John Bos; Wilbert Miller; Irving J. "Shorty" Snider; Harold A. "Brownie" Springer (Port Huron); Jack Schwei; Ubold Noblett (Gladston).Row two, lt. to rt., John Hammes; Larry Archer; A.D. "Del" Vandervoort; Harry "Siwash" Franson (captain); Clarence "Irish" Ramsey; Sherman Coryell; Charles Bassett. Third row: Garrett; Dick Van Orden; Hutchings; Guy Shumay (Grand Rapids); Charles Thomson; Martin Lefler. Back row, lt. to rt., George Gauthier (ass't.); Chester Brewer (head coach); Jack Heppinstall (trainer). Also: Ward Andrews.

1920

Front row, lt. to rt., Thomas Skuse (ass't. manager; behind Noblet; Charleston, W. Va.); Ubold Noblet; John Bos, Charles Thomson, Martin Lefler, Harold Springer (captain), John Hammes, Charles Bassett, John Schwei, Elton Ball (Albion).Second row, lt. to rt., Chester Brewer (coach), Karl Radewald (Niles), Jacob Brady, Edward Matson (Dollar Bay), Roy MacMillian (Mt. Clemens), Fred Wilcox, Hugo Swanson (Ishpeming), "Swede" Rundquist (ass't. coach). Back row, lt. to rt., Jack Heppinstall (trainer), William Johnson (Newberry), Wayne Gingrich (Trout Creek), George Schulgen (Traverse City), Arthur Martin (Corunna), Russell Morrison (Alpena), Gastav Thorpe (Stephenson), George "Potsy" Clark, head coach.

1921

Front row, lt. to rt., Charles A. Weckler (Lansing), halfback; Ubold J. Noblet halfback. Second row, lt.

to rt., Gastav A. "Gus" Thorpe, tackle; Edward I. Matson, guard; Warren Parks (Cheboygan), tackle; John Bos (captain), tackle; Wayne A. "Red" Gingrich, end; George F. Schulgen, end; Harry C. Graves, fullback. Third row, lt. to rt., Jacob O. Brady, quarterback; Harold K. Archbold (Masillon, Oh.), halfback; William C. Johnson, halfback; Russell A. "Bus" Morrison (Alpena), center; Hugo T. Swanson, guard; Frederick E. Wilcox (Rockford, Ill.), quarterback. Back row, lt. to rt., Thomas Skuce (manager), Chester Brewer, coach; Albert Barron, head coach; Jack Heppinstall (trainer).

1922

Front row, lt. to rt., Harry Graves; Jake Brady; Russ Morrison; Bill Johnson (captain); M.R. Taylor; Hugo Swanson; "Gus" Thorpe.Row two, lt. to rt., Nap Lioret; Phil Teufer; Art Beckley; Roy MacMillian; Rollie Richards; Harold Eckerman. Back row, lt. to rt., Albert Barron, head coach; Jack Heppinstall (trainer); Hugh Robinson; Ed Eckert; Elton Neller (Lansing); Viv Hultman; Tyrrell (manager); Dick Rauch (coach).

1923

Front row, lt. to rt., Hugh Robinson (Detroit); Harold Eckerman (Muskegon); Elton Neller (Lansing); M. Taylor (captain); Vivian Hultman (Grand Rapids); Rolland Richards (Lansing); Ernest Lioret (Ishpeming). Second row, lt. to rt., Carl Schultz (Lansing); Paul Hackett (Saginaw); Richard Lyman (East Lansing); Raymond Kipke (Lansing); Edmunds; Arthur Beckley (Bay City). Back row, lt. to rt., J. Taylor; Ralph Young, head coach; Vern Schmyser (Bad Axe); Don Haskins (Grand Rapids); Roy Spiekerman (Saginaw); Jack Heppinstall (trainer); Miller.

1924

Front row, lt. to rt., Edward Eckert (Grand Rapids); Elton Neller; Beckley; Robinson; Vivian Hultman; Harold Eckerman; Rolland Richards; Ernest Lioret; Raymond Kipke.Second row, lt. to rt., Benjamin Goode (Charleston, W. Va.); Vern Schmyser; Robert Thayer (Williamston); Paul "Snoopy" Hackett; Don Haskins; Roy "Zeke" Spiekerman; Alfred Vogel (Evanston, Ill.); Carl Schultz. Back row, lt. to rt., Ralph Young, head coach; Jack Heppinstall (trainer); Martin Rummel (Saginaw); John Garver (Caro); John Anderson (Lansing); Perry Fremont (Bad Axe); Richard Lyman; John Taylor, ass't. coach.

1925

Front row, lt. to rt., Martin Rummel (captain-elect), tackle; Roy Spiekerman, tackle; Donald Haskins (captain), tackle; Christopher Hackett, guard; Richard Lyman, quarterback. Second row, lt. to rt., James McCosh, halfback; Earl VanBuren, fullback; Paul Smith, halfback; Francis Ross, center; John Garver, guard; Rudolph Boehringer, halfback. Back row, lt. to rt., Jack Heppinstall (trainer); Leslie Fouts, quarterback; Ralph Young, head coach; Kenneth Drew, end; Milt Francis (manager). Also, not pictured, Bohn Grim, end; Alfred Vogel, center; Leslie Fouts,quarterback.

1926

Front row, lt. to rt., James McCosh; Bohn Grim; Elwyn Wenner; Martin Rummel (captain); John Garver; Rudolph Boehringer; Paul Smith (captain-elect). Second row, lt. to rt., Glenn Hutchings; Frederick Danziger (Detroit); William Moeller; Kenneth Drew; Harry Kurrie; Ogden Grimes; Ward Ross; Ernesy Deacon. Back row, lt. to rt., Ralph Young, head coach; Casteel, ass't. coach; Kanitz; Joe Crabill; Barratt; Jack Hornbeck; Jack Heppinstall (trainer); Hauptli.

Also, not pictured, Koester Christensen; John Anderson; Hugo Kanitz.

1927

Front row, lt. to rt., George Needham (Saginaw); Harry Kurrie (Owosso); Ogden Grimes (Des Moines, Ia.); James McCosh (Detroit); Paul Smith (captain, Saginaw); Kenneth Drew (Adrian); Ward Ross (Port Huron); Jack Hornbeck (captain-elect, Lansing). Second row, lt. to rt., John Wilson (Asbury Park, N.J.); Marion Joslin (Grand Rapids); Koester Christensen (Escanaba); Hugo Kanitz (Muskegon); John Anderson (Lansing); Joseph Crabill (Battle Creek); Glen Hitchings (Petoskey); William Moeller (Detroit); Ernest Deacon (Lansing). Back row, lt. to rt., Ray Harlen (manager, Manistee); Jack Heppinstall (trainer); Traynor (ass't. coach); Kenneth Weeks (St. Louis, Mich.); Chester Smith (Detroit); George Ferrari (Bessemer); Verne Dickeson (Highland Park); Henry Schau (Schererville, Ind.).

1928

Front row, lt. to rt., Verne Dickeson; Joe Crabil; Glen Hitchings; Jack Hornbeck (captain); Bill Moeller; Koester Christensen; John Anderson. Second row, lt. to rt., Marion Joslin; Reubin Dill (Saginaw); Fred Danziger; Jack Ruhl (Detroit); Roger Grove (Sturgis); Carl Nordberg (St. Joseph). Back row, lt. to rt., Miles Casteel, ass't. coach; Harold Smead (Sturgis); C.C. Fogg (Jackson); Henry Schau; Harry Kipke, head coach; George Ferrari; Don Ridler (Detroit); Jack Heppinstall (trainer). Also, not pictured: Harry Kurrie; Max Crall.

1929

Front row, lt. to rt., James Hayden (Cassopolis); Reuben Dill (Saginaw); George Ferrari (Bessemer); Harold Smead (Sturgis); Marion Joslin (Grand Rapids); Don Ridler (Detroit). Second row, lt. to rt., Milton Gross (Saline); Floyd Lewis (Midland); Lester Exo (Holland); Harold Haun (Charlotte); Claude Streb (Birmingham); Jacob Fase (Grand Haven); Cecil Fogg (Jackson). Third row, lt. to rt., Gerald Breen (Holland); Verne Dickeson (Highland Park);Henry Schau (Schereville, Ind.); Fred Danziger (Detroit); Roger Grove (Sturgis); Max Crall (Dimondale); Carl Nordberg (St. Joseph). Back row, lt. to rt., Virgil Marvin (manager, Toledo, Ohio); Miles Casteel (ass't. coach); Jim Crowley (head coach), Glenn Carberry (ass't. coach); Jack Heppinstall (trainer).

1930

Front row, lt. to rt., Stephenson, Sam Schwartzberg (Detroit), Carl Nordberg (St. Joseph), Joseph Kowatch (Ionia), Gerald Breen (Holland). Second row, lt. to rt., Jack Heppinstall (trainer), Jim Crowley, (head coach), Johnson, DeGurse, Bowen, Myron Vandermeer (Grand Rapids), Olson, Paganelli, Robert Monnett (Bucyrus, Ohio), Willard Friz (Lansing), George Ferrari(Bessemer), Milton Gross (captain-elect, Saline), Donald Warren (St. Joseph), Ardziejewski, Miles Casteel (ass't. coach), Glenn Carberry (ass't. coach). Third row, lt. to rt., Brokaw (ass't. manager), Brigstock (ass't. mgr.), Giffey (ass't. mgr.), Leonard Logan (ass't. mgr., Detroit), Kenneth Lafayette, Lester Exo (Holland), Robert Buskirk, Francis Meiers (Muskegon), Abe Eliowitz (Detroit), Schwartz, Claude Streb (Birmingham), Roger Grove (Sturgis), Ralph Brunette, George Carlson (Iron River), Wojtylo, Thomas Woodworth (manager), Ron Watkins (ass't. mgr., Flint). Back row, lt. to rt., Sweeney, Prendergast, Jacob Fase (Grand Haven), Cecil Fogg (Jackson), Skornia, Maynard Hosler (Kendallville, Ind.), Donald Ridler

(Detroit), Roy Warner (Detroit), George Handy (Detroit), Paul Byers (East Lansing), Fatchett, Harold Haun (Charlotte), Schreur, Louis Handler, List, Charles Gotta (Bessemer), Fisk. Also, Harold Smead; Clifford Liberty.

1931

Front row, lt. to rt., Myron Vandermeer, Joe Kowatch, Abe Eliowitz, Milt Gross (captain), Bob Monnett, Reuben Dill, Brunette. Second row, lt. to rt., Francis Meiers, Jones, Jacob Fase, Buss, George Handy, Les Exo. Back row, lt. to rt., Jack Heppinstall (trainer), Miles Casteel (ass't. coach), Jim Crowley (head coach); Glenn Carberry (ass't. coach). Also, Bernard McNutt, Ralph Brunette.

1932

Front row, lt. to rt., Bob Terlaak, guard (Cleveland, Ohio); Ed Klewicki, end (Hamtrammck); Alton Kircher, quarterback (Gladstone); Bob Monnett, halfback (captain); Abe Eliowitz, halfback (captain); Francis "Bud" Meiers, center; Myron Vandermeer, end; Joe Kowatch, fullback. Second row, lt. to rt., George Squier, tackle (Benton Harbor); Robert Armstrong, halfback (Benton Harbor); Ralph Brunette, tackle (Green Bay, Wis.); George Handy, guard (Detroit); Gerald Jones, halfback (Bay City); Russell Lay, guard (Williamston); Roger Keast, end, (Lansing). Third row, lt. to rt., Morrison (manager), Gordon Reavely (Durand); Frank Butler, center (Chicago, Ill.); Art Buss, tackle (Benton Harbor); Bernard McNutt (captain-elect), fullback (Allegan); Joe Ferrari, guard (Bessemer). Back row, lt. to rt., Miles Casteel, ass't. coach; Jim Crowley, head coach; Glenn Carberry, ass't. coach; Jack Heppinstall (trainer).

1933

Front row, lt. to rt., Bob Terlaak, Russ Lay, Frank Butler, Bernard McNutt, Art Buss, Al Kircher. Second row, lt. to rt., Chuck Brown, Sid Wagner (Lansing), Ed Klewicki, Bob Armstrong, Kurt Warmbein (St. Joseph), Lou Zarza (E. Chicago, Ill.), Charles Muth. Third row, lt. to rt., Gordon Reaveley (Durand), William Gilliland (Gladwin), Ben Demarest (Lansing), Russell Reynolds (Flint), Dick Colina (Detroit), Paxson, Jim McCrary, Jackson.Back row, lt. to rt., Jack Heppinstall (trainer), King (ass't. coach), Charlie Bachman (head coach), Miles Casteel (ass't. coach), Creager. Also, Joe Kowatch.

1934

Front row, lt. to rt., Dennis, Katz, Jim McCrary (Flint), Henry Kutchins (Hamtrammck), Sam Ketchman (Battle Creek), Ed Klewicki (Hamtrammck), Robert Armstrong (Benton Harbor), Milt Lehnhardt, Robert Allmann.Second row, lt. to rt., Leever, Fles, Gordon Dahlgren, Don Wiseman, Julius Sleder (Traverse City), Dick Colina, Kurt Warmbein, Wilson, Brakeman. Third row, lt. to rt., Packowski, Joe Buzolits, Lou Zarza, Harry Wismer, Fred Schroeder (Clawson), Howard Zindel (Grand Rapids), Steve Sebo (Battle Creek), Harrison Neumann, Al Agett. Fourth row, lt. to rt., Richard Edwards (Williamston), Lothamer, Orr, E. Sleder, Creyts, Paul Beaubein (Flint), O'Lear, Art Brandstatter (Ecorse). Fifth row, lt. to rt., Smith, Ralph Bennett (Mt. Clemens), Jones, Knudson, Ruth, Vince Vanderberg, Russ Reynolds (Flint), Fred Ziegel (Detroit), Broome. Back row, lt. to rt., Gordon Reaveley, William Gilliland (Gladwin), Sid Wagner, Ben Demarest (Lansing), Herbert Williamson, Kurt Kuhne (Pontiac), Albert Baker, Archie Ross (Grand Rapids).

1935

Front row, lt. to rt., Joe Buzolits, Archie Ross, Dick Colina, Sid Wagner, Kurt Warmbein, Lou Zarza, Richard Edwards. Second row, lt. to rt., Don Wiseman (Cadillac), Art Brandstatter, Miles Wilson (Kalamazoo), Howard Zindel, Gordon Dahlgren, Julius Sleder, Bob Allmann, Steve Sebo. Third row, lt. to rt., Fred Ziegel, Harrison Neumann, Harry Speelman (Lansing), Tom Gortat (Muskegon), Milt Lehnhardt, Kurt Kuhne, Henry Kutchins. Fourth row, lt. to rt., Jack Heppinstall (trainer), Al Agett (Kingsport, Tenn.), Frank Gaines (Lansing), Howard Swartz (Lagrange, Ill.), Vince Vanderburg (Muskegon), John Crary (manager, Detroit). Back row, lt. to rt., Miles Casteel (ass't. coach), Charlie Bachman (head coach), Tom King (ass't. coach).

1936

Row one, lt. to rt., Norm Fertig, Steve Sebo, Sam Ketchman, Gordon Dahlgren, Henry Kutchins, Julius Sleder, Milt Lehnhardt. Row two, lt. to rt., Art Brandstatter, Vince Vanderburg, Fred Ziegel, Paul Beaubien, Howard Zindel, Al Agett, Walter Lueck, Harrison Neumann. Row three, lt. to rt., Tom Gortat, Frank Gaines, Howard Swartz, Harry Speelman, Charles Halbert, Usif Haney, Fred Schroeder, Ernest Bremer, Dave Diehl. Fourth row, lt. to rt., Walter Nelson, John Pingel, Norm Olman, Norm Miknavitch, Nelson Schrader, John Coolidge, Al Diebold, Steve Szasz, George Kovacich. Back row, lt. to rt., Jack Heppinstall (trainer), Bob Terlaak (ass't.), Charles Bachman (head coach), Tom King (ass't.), David Johnson (manager).

1937

Team members: Al Agett, Paul Beaubien, Art Brandstatter, Ernest Bremer, John Coolidge, Gordon Dahlgren, Al Diebold, Dave Diehl, Darwin Dudley, Norm Fertig, Frank Gaines, Tom Gortat, Charles Halbert, Usif Haney, Sam Ketchman, George Kovacich, Henry Kutchins, Milt Lehnhardt, Walter Lueck, Norm Miknavitch, Walt Nelson, Harrison Neumann, Norm Olman, John Pingel, Nelson Schrader, Fred Schroeder, Steve Sebo, Julius Sleder, Harry Speelman, Howard Swartz, Steve Szasz, Vince Vanderburg, Fred Ziegel, Howard Zindel, Dave Johnson (manager).

1938

Front row, lt. to rt., Gene Ciolek, Ernie Bremer, Usif Haney, John Pingel, Al Diebold (co-captain), Dave Diehl (co-captain), Steve Szasz, George Kovacich, Ole Nelson, Tom McShannock. Second row, lt. to rt., Alex Ketzko, Lyle Rockenbach, Don Rossi, Ralph Bennett, George Gargett, Les Bruckner, Ed Pearce, Mike Masny, Mike Kinek. Third row, Paul Griffeth, Stan McRae, Ron Alling, Ed Abdo, Don Malisky, Bruce Blackburn. Fourth row, Frank Cowing (manager), Gerald Drake, Paul Derrickson, John Budinski, Jack Heppinstall (trainer). Top row, Gordon Dahlgren, Tom King, Charlie Bachman, Miles (Mike) Casteel.

1939

Row one, lt. to rt., Ralph Bennett, George Gargett, Ron Alling, Les Bruckner, Lyle Rockenbach, Mike Kinek, Ed Pearce, Don Rossi, Cas Klewicki, Gerald Drake. Row two, Alex Ketzko, Stan McRae, Paul Derrickson, Ed Abdo, Paul Griffeth, Frank Karas, Bill Chartos, Jack Amon, Ed Pogor. Row three, Roman Kaman, Earl Stevens, Mike Shelb, Walt Kutchins, Willie Davis, Lew Smiley, Wyman Davis, Bill Kennedy, Fred Carter. Row four, Tony Arena, Bob Friedlund, Howard Pound, Fred Quigley, Bill Rupp, Bob Sherman, Bill Batchelor. Top row, Shedd, Gordon

Dahlgren, Tom King, Charlie Bachman, Joe Holsinger, Jack Heppinstall (trainer).

1940

Front row, lt. to rt., Bruce Blackburn, Bill Batchelor, Paul Griffeth, Jack Amon, Ed Abdo, Frank Karas. Row two, Fred Carter, Dan Morabito, Bill Rupp, George Danciu, Mike Shelb, Bob Friedlund, Bill Kennedy. Row three, Walt Kutchins, Tom Johnson, Lew Smiley, Chuck Carey, Bob Sherman, Wy Davis, Wil Davis, Ed Ripmaster. Fourth row, Gordin Dahlgren, Jack Fenton, Bob McNeil, Richard Kieppe, Walt Ball, Walt Pawlowski, Duane Faulman, J. Sell. Top row, Jack Heppinstall, Charlie Bachman, Joe Holsinger, Tom King.

1941

Front, lt. to rt., Wilford Davis, Bill Rupp (co-captains). Row two, Mike Schelb, Cliff Eckel, Fred Carter, Lewis Smiley, Frank Karas, Wyman Davis, Bob Friedlund, Tony Arena, Bill Kennedy, Bob Sherman, George Danciu. Row three, Dave Diehl, Morgan Gingrass, Jack Fenton, Roy Fraleigh, Ted Smolinski, Tom Johnson, Bob McNeil, Richard Mangrum, Richard Kieppe, Neil Lefevre (manager). Top row, Jack Heppinstall (trainer), Joe Holsinger, Walt Pawlowski, Bill Milliken, Pete Fornari, Glenn Johnson, Don LeClair, Charlie Bachman, Al Kawal.

1942

Front, lt. to rt., Walt Pawlowski, Richard Mangrum (co-captains). Row two, Bill Milliken, Bob McNeal, George Radulescu, Jack Fenton, Richard Kieppe, Mike Miketinac, Bernard Neubert, Ed Ripmaster, Bill Monroe. Row three, Bob Shedd (manager), Bill Beardsley, Pete Fornari, Don LeClair, Howard Beyer, Glenn Diebert, Roy Fraleigh, Lou Brand, Morgan Gingrass, Jack Heppinstall (trainer). Back row, Joe Holsinger (ass't.), Charlie Bachman (head coach), Bob Otting, Vince Mroz, Ken Balge, Alger Conner, Elbert Stark, Edo Mencotti, Russ Gilpin, Al Kawal (ass't.).

1943

OFF CAMPUS ENGINEERING FOOTBALL TEAM: Kneeling, lt. to rt., R. Stewart, Willis Boice, F. VonKummer, Ralph Pearson, Asahel Hayes, John Winkel, Joseph Balionis, Bill Matthews, R. Hogoboom, Roy Erickson (captain). Standing, lt. to rt., John Ake, Lundin, Thomas McManus, Leo Spear, Raymond Baumrind, Donald Shapero, Vernon Fenton, Harold Hayner, J. Farrell, Seymour Schwartz, E. Parkes, S. Holloway, J. Baker,

R.O.T.C. FOOTBALL TEAM:
Kneeling, lt. to rt., Paul Carter, Glenn Johnson, Clayton Kowalk, William Beardsley, Gordon Briggs, Peter Fornari, Stanley Gunn, Hubert Bauman. Standing, lt. to rt., Richard Helwig, Robert Drake, Forest Craver, Hugh Zweering, William Johnson, Coach Albert Kawal, Capt. Louis Brand, Capt. Gilliam, William Lorenz, Byron Carpenter, Frank Poulos, John Blanchard, Donald MacPhail, Limber (manager). M. Herder, Coach Joseph Holsinger, G. Doyle, Seymour Brenner.

CIVILIAN FOOTBALL TEAM:
Kneeling, lt. to rt., Robert Ranney, Charles Brown, Norman Dodge, Pergiel, Cecil Vogt, Jack Breslin (captain), Henry Cook, Robert DelSignore, R. Krestel, Norman Pennels. Standing, lt. to rt., Coach Karl Schademan, Peterson, Patrick McAvinchey, Herbert Hackett, James Colville, M. Yarling, G. Rankin, Fred Meyer, Robert Rasmussen, Henry Calkins, J. Godfrey, W. Pearson, R. Kennedy.

ON CAMPUS ENGINEERS FOOTBALL TEAM: Kneeling, lt. to rt., John Brown, Robert Hunt, Robert Ardrey, Eiseman, Stokes, George Pasichuke, Walton Allinger. Standing, lt. to rt., Coach Gordon Dahlgren, John McDonough, Steve Kozak, John Murphy (captain), Charles Marks, David Lofgren, Ralph Schuetz, LerRoy Bilgrav, Weesman, Raymond Gedd, Donald Welsing, Henry Konvicka, Stanley Cohen, Robert Feldner, Paul Libertson, Glenwood Ferry, Robert Grimditch, Barcic, Robert McKenny.

VETERINARIANS FOOTBALL TEAM: Kneeling, lt. to rt., Albert Drury, Ray Krolkiewicz, Harold Bryan, William O'Rourke, Nicole Migliaccio (captain), Phillip Hotchkiss, Warren Roberts, Robert Jewell, Ralph Erkel, Gerald Jansen, Wallace Monson. Standing, lt. to rt., Capt. Atchison, Morris Hathaway, Robert Azelton, Fred Aronson, Jack Preston, Ivan Meyer, William Semtner, Earl Milliman, Roy Westcott, Chris Glenney, Bernard Zeeb, Max Colton, Sherman Byrd, Edward Wallace, Joseph Greer, Thomas Millerick, Coach John Kobs.

1944

Front row, lt. to rt., Bob Schroeder (Flint), quarterback; Jack Breslin (Battle Creek), fullback; Fred Aronson (Chicago, Ill.), halfback; Brady Sullivan (Steubenville, Ohio), halfback; Pete Dendrino (Muskegon), center; Don Grondzik (Saginaw), end; Don Arnson (Muskegon), guard. Second row, lt. to rt., Bill Siler (Dundee); Bob Godfrey (Mt. Clemens); Mike Prashaw (Massena, N.Y.), tackle; Glen Hatfield (Flint), guard; Herb Speersta (Saginaw), halfback; Richard Mineweaser (Pontiac), end. Third row, lt. to rt., Richard Massuch (Lansing), tackle; Bill Pirronello (Detroit); Harold Johnson (DuBois, Pa.); Robert Lamssies (South Haven); Bill Johnson (Wyandotte); Art Arntz (Benton Harbor). Back row, lt. to rt., Jack Heppinstall (trainer); Charlie Bachman, head coach; Karl Schademan, ass't. coach; John Kobs, ass't. coach; Joe Holsinger, ass't.coach; Peter Limber (manager).

1945

Joe Pajakawski, Stanley Wickman, Donald Black, James Smith, Hervey Beutler, Skimley Dusseau, Robert Godfrey, Donald Amson, Carl Drompotich, Kent Esbaugh, Daniel Goldsmith, Donald, Simons, Robert schnitker, William Pagel, Eugene Stroia, Roland Michelson, Norman Tipton, Robert Carson, Robert Maldegen, Richard Peikey, Richard Mineweaser, Robert Malaga, Nicholas Ziegler, Warren Huey, Leroy Gunderson, Donald Cote, Joseph, Emerick, Richard Massuch, Constantino Barbas, Raymond Jobs, John Good, Michael Tesin, Frank Strand, Corlis Foster, Bernard Glowicki, Fred Aronson, Amien Carter, Harry Burns, Francis Cappaert, Steve Contos, Ralph Mazza, William Siler, Donald Steward, Dominic Copati, Glen Hatfield, Tom Hill, John Brooks, Ruby Castellani, Milford Jones, Raymond Boothby, Jacwier Breslin, Robert Ludwid, Joe Bogart, Milton Knight, William Maskilol, Frank Johnson, Jack Lange, Ralph Wenger, Charles Tilse, George Stamas, Brady Sullivan, Walter Vezmar, Edward Topper, Robert Lamssies.

1946

Front row, lt. to rt., George Guerre; Al Connor; Warren Huey; Lynn Chandnois; John Pletz; Ken Balge; Bob McCurry; Russ Gilpin; Ed Bagdon; Mark Blackman; Don Arnson. Second row, lt. to rt., Carl Cappaert; John Harris; Steve Sieradzki; Bill Spiegel; Ed Sobczak; Jim Zito; Bib Fischer; Tony Waldron; Bob Otting. Third row, lt. to rt., Barney Roskopp; Rex

Parsell; Bill Baldwin; Horace Smith; Jim Blenkhorn; Pete Fusi; Gene Glick; Don LeClair; Russ Reader; John Wheeler. Back row, Art Heigelson (manager); Al Kawal, ass't. coach; Charley Bachman, head coach; John Pingel, ass't. coach; Jack Heppinstall (trainer); Lou Zarza, ass't. coach.

1947

Bud O. Crane, George T. Guerre, Robert Kritzer, John Polonchek, Donald Sherrod, Franklin D. Waters, William White, Bryce Brown, Lynn E. Chandnois, Martin Kelly, Horace Smith, William S. Spiegel, James C. Blenkhorn, Henry M. Reffis, Milford H. Jones, Robert E. Heller, Stephen H. Sieradski, Eugene Glick, Robert Krestal, George Smith, Robert Swett, Donald Waldron, Robert W. Otting, George H. Porter, Edward Schacki, Carl W., Cappmart, Alger V. Conners, William G. Cordell, Kent E. Ashbaugh, Mike A. La Magna, Tony Musida, Charles V., Kyustic, Bernard D. Patton, Robert Shaibly, Max D. Thiele, John P. Wheeler, James J. Zitto, Richard M. Alban, Peter Fusi, Harold P. Oasser, Robert B. McCurry, Ralph Wenger, Kenneth E. Balge, Cornelius R. Carrigan, Lynn Conway, Lee H. Dibble, Jack Finn, Robert Gernand, John L. Gilman, Warren B. Huey, Vincent F. Mros, Rex J. Parcell, Barnard G. Boskopp, Edward F. Sobosak, Herbert A. Speerstra, Harold L. Vogler, Howard J. Adams, Donald H. Arnson, Edward, Bagdon, Mark S. Blackman, Carl Mrompotich, Don L. Mason, Carl Hester

1948

David R. Crego, George B. Smith, Garth T. Frost, Eugene Glick, Everett, Grandelius, Robert Krestel, Anthony Spennacchio, James Blenkhorn, Richard E. Carless, Van H. Williams, LeRoy R. Crane, Bud C. Crane, John N. Polonchek, Jesse L. Thomas, Frank Waters, George T. Guerre, Richard A. Berger, Albert R. Dorow, James E. Creamer, David H. Lumsden, Robert B. McCurry, Donald J. Hondorp, Harold Gasser, Sidney Stein, Donald L. Mason, Robert E. Swett, Howard Adams, Edward Schacki, Mark S. Blackman, Edward Bagdon, John Tobin, Carl Nestor, Gabriel Marek, J.C. Williams, George Markharn, Albert D. Yuhas, Harold L. Vogler, James Zito, Franklin E. Saylor, Carl W. Cappaert, Kent Esbaugh, Peter Fusi Jr., John P. Wheeler, Mike A. LaMagna, Henry J. Minarik, Rex J. Parsell, Dorne E., Dibble, John L. Gilman, Warren B. Huey, Phillip J. McCabe, James M. King, Robert J. McManus, Herbert Speerstra, Cornelius Corrigan, Lynn V. Conway, Eugene Estacion, George E. Hilla, William C. James, Willliam E. Miron, Fred D. Schenck, Edward F. Sobczak, Dewey D. Stevens, Emil J. Suarez, Stanley Swayman, George M. Wallace, Ralph D. Wenger, John Yocca William S. Spiegel, Martin J. Kelly, Lynn E. Chandnois, Daniel Pobojewski, Horace Smith.

1949

1st row (l to r): G.B. Smith, F. Waters, L. Chandnois, H. Smith, D. Mason, H. Vogler (capt), E. Bagdon, P. Fusi, J. Gilman, E. Glick, K. Esbaugh. 2nd row: D. Lumsden, C. Nystie, R. Parsell, C. Cappaert, H. Gasser, B. Crane, R. Wenger, D. Dibble, E. Grandelius, L. Crane. 3rd row: J. Blenkhorn, H. Minarik, J. Thomas, J. Williams, J. Tobin, R. Carey, R. Ciolek, W. Carey, C. Austin. 4th row: D. Coleman, A. Dorow, W. Horrell, J. Klein, J. Polonchek, C. Munn, J. Kobs, E. Edwards, and R. Kapp.

1950

Richard Abraham, Francis Agnew, Robert Benson, Wayne Benson, Douglas Bobo, Gale Bolthouse, Leo Boyd, Thomas Brogan, Robert Carey, William Carey,

Ross Case, Robert Ciolek, Don Coleman, Elwood Converse, LeRoy Crane, James Creamer, Paul Dekker, Dorne Dibble, Albert Dorrow, James Ellis, Dean Garner, Ray Gordon, Everett Grandelius, Robert Graves, William Horrell, William Hughes, Allen Jones, Lowell Kage, Frank Kapral, James King, Renaldo Kozikowski, Richard Kih, Frank Kush, Edwin Luke, Edward Manne, Gabriel Marek, Orlando Mazza, Don McAulliffe, Marvin McFadden, Henry Minarik, Jack Morgan, Richard Panin, Vincent Pisano, Roderick Place, Donald Quayle, John Rhodes, Gordon Serr, Donald Smith, Louis Smith, Sidney Stein, Dewey Stevens, Richard Tamburo, Deane Thomas, Willie Thrower, Jesse Thomas, Edward Timmerman, John Tobin, Richard Usher, Raymond Vogt, Douglas Weaver, Van H. Williams J.C. Williams, Robert Wheeler, John Wilson, John Yocca, Eugene Stroia, Robert Nagel.

1951

Thomas Baer, Harlan Benjamin, Wayne Benson, Douglas Bobo, LeRoy Bolden, Leo Boyd, Robert Breniff, Thomas Brogan, Robert Carey, William Carey, Ivan Cindrich, Robart Ciolek, Donald Coleman, Rex Corlesa, James Creamer, Paul Dekker, Donald Dohoney, Albert Dorow, Ellis Duckett, James Ellis, William Fate, Larry Fowler, Albert Fracassa, Charles Franks, Dean Garner, Robert Graham, Roy Gustafson, Ferris Hallmark, Terrence Henderson, William Horrell, William Hughes, Arthur Ingram, James Jebb, Allen Jones, Frank Kapral, Joseph Klein, Peter Knezevich, Dale Knight, Richard Kab, Donald Kuick, Frank Kush, Eugene Lekenta, Edwin Lake, Orlando Mazza, Donald McAulliffe, Marvin McFadden, Robert McMacken, Jack Morgan, Edward Murphy, James Neal, Richard Panin, Vincent Pisano, William Postula, Donald Quayle, William Reid, Fred Rody, Thomas Saldock, Donald Schiesswohl, Gordon Serr, Evan Slonac, Louis Smith, Ken Sparks, John Swett, Harry Tamburo, Richard Tamburo, Willie Thrower, Edward Timmerman, Raymond Vogt, Douglas Weaver, William Wells, John Wilson, Thomas Yewcic

1952

Howard J. Adams, Thomas Baer, Wayne Benson, Alex Bleahu, Douglas Bobo, LeRoy Bolden, Leo Boyd, Robert Breniff, Henry C. Bullough, Dan Carroll, Rex Corless, Donald E. Cutler, Paul Dekker, Donald Dohoney, Roland D. Dotsch, Ellis Duckett, Robert Edmiston, Jack E. Edwards, James Ellis, Charles L. Fairbanks, Dale E. Foltz, Larry Fowler, Albert Fracassa, Charles Frank, Charles S. Gelal, Ferris Hallmark, James Jebb, Donald F. Kauth, Joseph Klein, LaVerne A. Kline, Dale Knight, Frank Kush, Eugene Lakenta, Edwin Luke, Gerald B. Luzader, John J. Matsock, Donald McAulliffe, Donald Meyers, Eugene Molak, Jack Morgan, Robert J. Munson, Morley, Murphy, Gerald Musetti, James Neal, John J. Paior, Richard Panin, Norman Pearce, Vincent Pisano, William Postula, Victor A. Postula, William D. Quinlin, Bernard J. Raterink, Fred Rody, William L. Ross, Thomas Saidock, Donald Schiesswohl, R.P. Schrecengost, Gordon Serr, Evan Slonac, Warren J. Spragg, Harry Tamburo, Richard Tamburo, Willie Thrower, Edward Vogt, Douglas Weaver, William Wells, John Wilson, Thomas Yewcic, Bert A. Zagers.

1953

First Row, l-R: Bob Breniff, Don Schiesswohl, Jim Jebb, Fred Rody, Dale Knight, Head Coach Clarence "Biggie" Munn, Capt. Don Dohoney, Evan Slonac, Tom Yewcic, Chuck Frank, Jim Neal. Second Row, L-R: Ted Kepple, Henry Bullough, Jerry Luzader,

Charles Fairbanks, Dale Foltz, Don Kauth, Embry Robinson, Bill Postula, Billy Wells, Larry Fowler, Jim Ellis. Third Row, L-R: Gerald Musetti, LeRoy Bolden, John Matsock, Al Fracassa, Ellis Duckett, Ferris Hallmark, Carl Diener, John Lewis, Jim Hinesly, Alvin Lee, Morley Murphy, Bert Zagers. Fourth Row; l-R: Carl Nystrom, Dave Goodell, Leo Haidys, Tom Taylor, Norm Masters, Charles Alden, Randy Schrecengost, Roland Dotsch, Warren Spragg, Steve Foreman, Bill Quinlan, Alex Bleahu, Bill Lucy, Line Coach Hugh Daugherty. Fifth Row, L-R: Ray Eggleston, Ed Zalar, Travis Buggs, Jerry Volek, Dick Davidson, Bruce Tweddale, Noel Bufe, Gary Lowe, Earl Morrall, Gene Lekenta, Bill Smiley, Wayne Langevin, Assistant Coach Don Mason, End Coach Earle Edwards. Sixth Row, L-R: Frosh Mgr. Steve Morrissey, Ass't Trainger Gayle Robinson, Ass't Coach Bob Devaney, Backfield Coach Steve Sevo, Frosh Coach Dan Devine, Gerald Planutis, Vic Postula, John Paior, Joe Badaczewski, Bill Ross, Dale Hollern, Donald Mason, Ass't Coach John Kobs, Ass't Coach DeWayne King, Trainer Jack Heppinstall, Varsity Mgr. Keith Darby.

1954

Front row l to r: Morley Murphy, Ferris Hallmark, Fred Rody, Randy Schrecengost, Co-Capt. Don Kauth, Head coach Hugh Daugherty, Co-Capt. LeRoy Bolden, Bill Ross, Henry Bullough, Charles Fairbanks, Dale Foltz. Second row, l to r: Ellis Duckett, John Paior, John Matsock, Roland Dotsch, Ted Kepple, Norm Masters, Gerry Planutis, Gary Lowe, Al Fracassa, Alex Bleahu, Bert Zagers, Vic Postula. Third row, l to r: Ray Eggleston, Travis Buggs, Carl Nystrom, Earl Morrall, Embry Robinson, Jim Hinesly, Bill Lucy, Steve Foreman, Rod Hartwick, Charles Alden, Ed Zalar, Gerry Musetti, Clarence Peaks, John Lewis. Fourth row, l to r: Carl Diener, Jerry Volek, Dale Hollern, Julius McCoy, Noel Bufe, Lacey Bernard, Wayne Langevin, Bill Smiley, Joe Carruthers, Ron Latronica, Rudy Gaddini, Don Berger, Dave Goodell, Al Lee, Ross Case. Fifth row, l to r: James Blauvelt, Bob Jewett, Dennis Mendyk, Frank Nauyokas, Leo Haidys, Joe Badaczewsi, George Pepoy, John Matsko, Les Rutledge, Pat Wilson, Dave Trippett, Loren Wall, Louis Costanzo, Pete Sagan, Hal Pendley, Jim Bigelow, Dick Spitler. Rear row, l to r: Asst. manager, Don Meyers, Asst. trainer Millard Kelly, Asst. trainer Gayle Robinson, Asst. coach John Kobs, Asst. coach Burt Smith, Asst. coach Bill Yeoman, Line coach Don Mason, Freshman coach Everett Grandelius, End coach Bob Devaney, Backfield coach Dan Devine, Trainer ack Heppinstall, Varsity Manager Rudy Petzold.

1955

Front Row, left to right: Embry Robinson, Alvin Lee, Gerald Musetti, Gary Lowe, Capt. Carl Nystrom, Head Coach Hugh Duffy Daugherty, Gerald Planutis, Earl Morrall, Leo Haidys, Ed Zalar, Noel Bufe. Second Row, left to right: John Lewis, Jim Hinesly, Robert Jewett, John Matsko. Joe Badaczewskik, Dale Hollern, Charles Alden, Norm Masters, Rudy Gaddini, Don Berger, George Eyde.Third Row, left to right: Les Rutledge, George Pepoy, Harold Dukes, Lou Costanzo, Jim Bigelo, William Kaae, Walt Kowalczyk, Tony Kolodziej, Tom Anderson, Frank Nauyokas, Lacey Bernard, Lou Postula, Tom Saidock. Fourth Row, left to right: Joe Carruthers, Pat Wilson, Joseph Fomenko, Dennis Mendyk, Clarence Peaks, Howard Neely, Joel Jones, Mike Panitch, James Chidester, Don Gillbert, Arch Matsos, Dick Barker, Dave Jeter, Ed Roberts. Fifth Row, left to right: Gene Hecker, Dave Kaiser, John Soave, Don Zysk, Glenn

Burgett, Ron Rickens, Glen Briggs, Wallace Cleaver, Karl Perryman, Pat Burke, Andrew Aljian, John Capes, Cliff LaRose, Larry Harding, Robert Handloser, James Wulff. Sixth Row, left to right: Ken Early, equipment manager; Tow Diehm, assistant trainer; Gayle Robinson, assistant trainer; Robert Devaney, ends coach; Lou Agase, defensive line coach; Robert Popp, Dan Currie, Pete Sagan, Bernie Wierbowski, Darwyn Hepler, Jim Ninowski, Marcus Cisco, Adam Sieminski, Everett Grandelius, backfield coach; Burt Smith, offensive line coach; Bill Yeoman, assistant coach; John Wilson, assistant coach.

1956

Front Row, left to right: Noel Bufe, Vic Zucco, Dennis Mendyk, Clarence Peaks, George Pepoy, John Matsko, Head Coach Hugh Duffy Daugherty, Lacey Bernard, Tom Saidock, Rudy Gaddini, Pat Wilson Jim Hinesly. Second Row, left to right: Robert Jewitt, James Ninowski, Arch Matsos, Pat Burke, James Wulff, Mike Panitch, Howard Neely, Walter Kowalczyk, William Kaae, Tony Kolodziej, Dave Kaiser, Don Zysk, Don Gilbert, Don Berger, Jim Chidester. Third Row, left to right: Joel Jones, Bernie Wierbowski, Dave Jeter, Marcus Cisco, Harold Dukes, Richard Barker, Tom Anderson, Cliff LaRose, Robert Handloser, Ron Rickens, Adam Sieminski, Les Rutledge, Andy Aljian, Robert Popp, Dan Currie, Joe Carruthers, Robert Fitzgerald. Fourth Row, left to right: Russell Steele, Art Johnson, John Middleton, Robert Sanders, Don Arend, Greg Montgomery, Harry Guydan, Larry Cundiff, Tom Vershinski, Francis O'Brien, Larry Harding, Darwyn Hepler, Joseph Fomenko, Gene Hecker, John Soave, William Drew, Gerald McDonald, Dan Delgrosso, Ellison Kelly, Jerry McFarland, William Mazanec. Fifth Row, left to right: Blanche Martin, Richard Schmitt, Oarie Lemanski, Howard Guill, Robert Sieminski, James McDonald, Thomas Vukovich, Louis Slivensky, George Stevenson, Mark Tate, Ed Sutilla, Henry Young, Russell Kelly, Tom Husband, Robert Bercich, Palmer Pyle, Gerald Dake, Sam Williams, Don Wright, John Wilks. Sixth Row, left to right: Norm Sedelbauer, student manager; Bill Burt, assistant equipment manager; Ken Early, equipment manager; Tom Diehm, assistant trainer; Gayle Robinson, assistant trainer; John Polonchek, assistant coach; Bill Yeoman, assistant coach; Robert Devaney, ends coach; Doug Weaver, freshman coach; Everett Grandelius, backfield coach; Lou Agase, defensive line coach; Burt Smith, offensive line coach; Jack Heppinstall, trainer.

1957

First Row. left to right: Don Berger, Tony Kolodziej, Don Gilbert, Dan Currie, Capt. Pat Burke, Head Coach Hugh Duffy Daugherty, Walt Kowalczyk, Dave Kaiser, Jim Ninowski, Joe Carruthers. Second Row, left to right: Gene Hecker, Larry Harding, Adam Sieminski, Bob Jewett, Don Zysk, Don Arend, Jim Wulff, Harold Dukes, John Soave, Joe Fomenko, Les Rutledge, Ellison Kelly. Third Row, left to right: Bob Bercich, Dick Barker, Sam Williams, Bob Sanders, Fran O'Brien, Jerry McFarland, Blanche Martin, Ron Rickens, Bob Popp, Mike Panitch, Art Johnson, John Middleton, Cliff LaRose, John Baum, Bob Ricucci. Fourth Row, left to right: Norm Gerl, Barry Zindel, Bob Slezak, John Trueman, Larry Cundiff, Jerry Dake, Dan Delgrosso, Harry Guydan, Russell Kelly, Greg Montgomery, Palmer Pyle, Mark Tate, Don Wright, Henry Young, Bob Handloser, Andy Aljian, Park Baker, Pat Howell. Fifth Row, left to right: Jack Thur, Bruce Gnatkowski, Bill Draddy, Huebert Fisher, Tom Vershinski, Roger Donnahoo, Jack Davidson, Jim Chesney, Jim Chastain, Russ Cahill, Willie Boykin, Ted Bison, Bob Bisacre, Larry Bielat, John

Wilks. Sixth Row, left to right: Bob Sieminski, Paul Rochester, Art Liepold, Richard Peterson, David Northcross, Bill Rossi, Ken Miller, Tom McNeeley, Brian McNeeley, Jon Marx, Ray Lincolnhol, Dean Look, Harold Leigeb, Dan Follis. Seventh Row, left to right: Ken Earley and Bill Burt, equipment staff; trainers Gayle Robinson and Jack Heppinstall, assistant coaches Doug Weaver, Gordon Serr, Lou Agase, John Polonchek, Burt Smith, Evertt Grandelius and Bill Yoeman, student manager Bill Boutell.

1958

First row, left to right: Dick Barker, Ellison Kelly, John Middleton, Fran O'Brien, Arch Matsos, Head Coach Duffy Daugherty, Capt. Sam Williams, Mike Panitch, Don Arend, Art Johnson, Ron Rickens. Second Row, left to right: Jim Chastain, Ed Sutilla, Park Baker, Tom Vershinski, Jerry McFarland, Cliff LaRose, Bob Handloser, Jim Wulff, Paul Rochester, Harold Leigeb, Roger Donnahoo, Larry Bielat, Dean Look. Third Row, left to right: Bob Bercich, Greg Montgomery, Bill Rossi, Dan Follis, Larry Cundiff, Jack Thur, Ken Miller, George Perles, John Truman, Dave Northcross, Harry Guydan, Bob Sieminski, Dan Delgrosso, Henny Young, Bob Ricucci. Fourth Row, left to right: Allan Hill, Jim Jakubowski, Ed McLucas, Bob Hren, Barry Zindel, Pat Howell, John Wilks, Don Wright, Palmer Pyle, Jack Davidson, Mark Tate, Jim Chesney, Jon Marx, Rich Peterson, Tom Wilson, Ed Perpich. Fifth Row, left to right: Oscar Hahn, Tom Drahnak, Herb Adderley, Bill Wyatt, John Sharp, Jim French, Don Schultz, Pat Chirdon, Wayne Fontes, Ike Grimsley, Jason Harness, Art Liepold, Bob Guenther, Bob Tuttle, Fred Boylen, Mickey Walker, Fred Arbanas, Mike Nordstrom. Sixth Row, left to right: Ken Earley, equipment staff; trainers Jack Heppinstall and Gayle Robinson; assistant coaches Gordon Serr, Buck Nystrom, Lou Agase and Joh Polonchek; Bill Ferrier, Mike Hart, Don Kurcz, Santo Pasqualucci, Paul Hrisko; assistant coaches Bill Yeoman, Everett Grandelius and Burt Smith; assistant trainer Duke La Rue; Bull Burt equipment starr; Bob Mitchell, student manager.

1959

First row, left to right: Blanche Martin, Park Baker, Bob Bercich, Paul Rochester, Jim Chastain, Capt. Don Wright, Head Coach Hugh Duffy Daugherty, Dean Look, John Wilks, Palmer Pyle, Larry Cundiff. Second Row, left to right: Oscar Hahn, Fred Boylen, John Trueman, Jason Harness, Jon Marx, Larry Bielat, Dave Northcross, Barry Zindel, Tom Vershinski, Ike Grimsley, Fred Arbanas, Herb Adderley. Thirt Row, left to right: Paul Hrisko, Tony Kumiega, Bob Suci, Wayne Fontes, Jack Davidson, Willie Boykin, Bob Ricucci, Ed McLucas, Mickey Walker, Jim Chesneyk, Tom Wilson, Allan Hill, Don Schultz, Roy Parrott. Fourth Row, left to right: Ed Ryan, Fred MacEachron, Ben Bethel, Don Durcz, Carl Charon, Mike Biondo, Gary Ballman, Leroy Loudermilk, Jim Corgiat, Jim Bridges, George Hugus, John Luplow, Gerald Ohngren, John Sharp, Randy Mack. Fifth Row, left to right: Eddie James, Ken King, Don Stewart, Dave Manders, Bill Timm, Dick Wending, Don Kopach, Tom Winiecki, Danny Eakin, Bob Szwast, Larry Hudas, Art Brandstatter, Jake Lewandowski, Mitch Newman, Art Acosta, Pete Kakela. Sixth Row, left to right: Bill Burt, equipment staff; Ken Earley, equipment manager; Ted Robinson, student manager; Dan Boisture, Henry Bullough, Lou Agase and Calvin Stoll, assistant coaches; Mike Hart, Leo Hughts; Bill Yeoman and Burt Smith, assistant coaches; Gayle Robinson, head trainer; Duke LaRue and Dick Barker, assistant trainers.

1960

First Row, left to right: Oscar Hahn, Mickey Walker, Ike Grimsley, Co-Capt. Fred Boylen, Head Coach Hugh Duffy Daugherty, Co-Capt. Fred Arbanas, Jason Harness, Tom Wilson, Jim Chesney. Second Row, left to right: Paul Hrisko, Jim Bridges, Wayne Fontes, Dick Oxendine, Jim Gorgiat, Larry Hudas, Carl Charon, Santo Pasqualucci, Bob Suci, Tony Kumiega, Mike Biondo, Dave Manders. Third Row, left to right: Art Brandstatter, Dan Eakin, John Sharp, Pete Kakela, Don Stewart, Bob Szwast, Ron Hatcher, Tom Winiecki, Ed Ryan, Roy Parrott, Mitchell Newman, Gary Ballman, LeRoy Loudermilk, Bill Edwards. Fourth Row, left to right: Fred MacEachron, Bill Wendorf, Dave Herman, Ron Ross, Jim Hoffa, Clifton Roaf, Gary Oade, George Azar, Curt Langdon, George Stevenson, Bernie Palmateer, Ron Watkins, Don Richmond, Ed Youngs, John Daibas, Ken May. Fifth Row, left to right: Gerald Jellis, Roy Geisler, Tom Jordan, Jeff Abrecht, Herb Paterra, Jim Eaton, Mike Ward, Dick Schmenk, Ken Jones, Nelson Schrader, Art Valdez, Ted Guthard, Don Kawal, Ernie Clark, Alex Valcanorr, Eddie James, Jim Bobbitt. Sixth Row, Left To Right: Assistant Coaches Gordon Serr, Cal Stoll, Henry Bullough; Jim Kanicki, Ed Budde, Joe Balk,Barry Madill, Dave Behrman, Jim Roe, Pete Smith, Bill Zorn, Howard Mudd, Lonnie Sanders, George Saimes, Assistant Coaches Dan Boisture, Vince Carillot, Sid Stein. Seventh Row, Left To Right: Jim Arbury, Student Manager; Dick Barker Assistant Trainer; Gayle Robinson, Head Trainer; Assistant Coaches Burt Smith And Bill Yeoman; Ken Earley, Equipment Manager; Duke LaRue, Assistant Trainer; Bill Burt, Assistant Equipment Manager.

1961

First Row, Left To Right: Jim Bridges, Gary Ballman, Roy Parrott, Tony Kumiega, Mike Biondo, Head Coach Duffy Daugherty, Capt. Ed Ryan, Tom Winiecki, Pete Kakela, Bob Suci, Carl Charon. Second Row, Left To Right: Larry Hudas, Art Brandstatter, Dave Manders, Dick Oxendine, Bob Szwast, Don Stewart, Mitch Newman, Jom Corgiat, Ron Hatcher, Wayne Fontes, John Sharp, George Stevenson. Third Row,Left To Right: Lonnie Sanders, Tom Jordan, Ron Ross, Bill Zorn, Jim Kanicki, Ed Budde, George Azar, Jeff Abrecht, Pete Smith, Dave Behrman, Ron Watkins, Clifton Roaf, George Saimes. Fourth Row, Left To Right: Mike Currie, Bob Roop, Steve Mellinger, Hubert Benson, Ed Youngs, Dave Herman, Roger Lopes, Doug Miller, Gary Oade, Jim Bobbitt, Herman Johnson, Sherman Lewis, Dewey Lincoln. Fifth Row, Left To Right: Fred Maceachron, Ken Bankey, Charlie Migyanka, Dean Underwood, Dick Proebstle, Matt Snorton, Ed Lothamer, Fred Mushinskik, Charlie Brown, Mike Crow, Mike Marciniak, Ron Rubick. Sixth Row, Left To Right: Bill Burt, Assistant Equipment Manager; Ken Earley, Equipment Managers; Dick Barker, Duke Larue, Assistant Trainers; Henry Bullough, Dan Boisture, Vince Carillot, Bill Yeoman, Gordon Serr, Cal Stoll, Burt Smith, Assistant Coaches; Gayle Robinson, Head Trainer; Jim Arbury, Student Manager

1962

Front Row, Left To Right: Jim Kanicki, Ron Ross, Ed Budde, Jim Bobbitt, Head Coach Duffy Daugherty, Captain George Saimes, Ted Guthard, Bill Zorn, George Azar, Dave Behrman. Second Row, Left To Right: Lonnie Sanders, Gary Oade, Jeff Abrecht, Ernie Clark, Ron Watkins, Clifton Roaf, Tom Jordan, Pete Smith, Bernie Palmateer, Ed Youngs, Dave

Herman. Third Row Left To Right: Earl Lattimer, Mike Currie, Mike Marciniak, Mike Crow, Ed Lothamer, Fred Mushinski, Sherman Lewis, Dan Underwood, Steve Mellinger, Rahn Bentley, Bill Benson, Ron Rubick, Herman Johnson, Dewey Lincoln. Fourth Row, Left To Right: Bill Roth, Bill Holland, Roger Hailey, Larry Bringard, Matt Snorton, Herb Paterra, Dick Proebstle, Joe Begeny, Doug Miller, Charlie Brown, Charlie Migyanka, Rich Anderson, Bob Moreland, Dick Gordon, Ted Harris. Fifth Row, Left To Right: Dan Grimes, Tom Krzemienski, Ted Rohrer, Jerry McGowan, Doug Roberts, Lou Bobich, Mike Mcginn, Harry Ammon, Don Ross, George Haislipk, Mike Walsh, Ron Yonker, Ken Bankey, Ed Macuga, Dick Flynn, Jim Copeland. Sixth Row, Left To Right: Gordon Serr, John McVay, Henry Bullough, Vince Carillot, Dan Boisture, Cal Stoll, Assistant Coaches; John Tinnick, Bill Gordon, Wilfred Henry, Jerry Rush, Duke La Rue, Assistant Trainer; Burt Smith Freshman Coach; Gayle Robinson, Head Trainer; Mike Harris, Senior Manager; Ken Earley, Equipment Manager; Bill Burt, Assistant Equipment Manager.

1963

Front Row, Left To Right: Bill Benson, Ed Youngs, Dave Herman, Charlie Brown, Dewey Lincoln, Co-Capt. Dan Underwood, Head Coach Duffy Daughterty, Co-Capt. Sherman Lewis, Ed Lothamer, Fred Mushinski, Mike Currie, Steve Mellinger, Ron Rubick. Second Row, Left To Right: Ted Harris, Ken Bankey, Rahn Bentley, Charlie Migyanka, Matt Snorton, Earl Lattimer, Larry Paulik, Mike Marciniak, Roger Lopes, Joe Begeney, Jim Copeland, Ed Macuga, Dick Proebstle, Doug Roberts, Bob Moreland. Third Row, Left To Right: Jerry Rush, George Haislip, Harry Ammon, John Walsh, Ted Rohrer, Mike McGinn, Larry Bringard, Lou Bobich, Roger Hailey, Don Ross, Dick Anderson, Jack Schinderle, Dick Gordon, Boris Dimitroff, Randy Heine, Zack Benford, Jim Garrett. Fourth Row, Left To Right: Leon Burrell, Tony Angel, Don Weatherspoon, Mark Wittgartner, Ed Cotton, Harold Lucas, Dick Flynn, Bill Gordon, John Tinnick, Tom Krzemienski, Dan Phillips, Mike Whyte, Don Bierowicz, Bob Nanna, Bob Viney, Buddy Owens, Dave McCormick, Don Japinga. Fifth Row, Left To Right: Bill Burt, Assistant Equipment Manager; Ken Earley, Equipment Manager; Dan Boisture, Assistant Coach; Gordon Serr, Assistant Coach; Gayle Robinson, Trainer; Burt Smith, Freshman Coach and Administrative Assistant; Larry Mackey, Ron Goovert, Jim Proebstle, Steve Juday, Harlan Dodge, Lowell Burgess, John Karpinski, Bruce Look, Leland McGonigal, John McVay, Assistant Coach; Henry Bullough, Assistant Coach; Cal Stoll, Assistant Coach; Vince Carillot, Assistant Coach; John Clupper, Student Manager.

1964

Front Row, Left To Right: Dick Gordon, Rick Anderson, Dick Proebstle, Steve Mellinger, Lou Bobich, Capt. Charlie Migyanka, Head Coach Hugh Duffy Daugherty, Don Ross, Rahn Bentley, Mike McGinn, John Walsh, Ed Macuga. Second Row, Left To Right: Jack Schinderle, Harry Ammon, Herman Johnson, Roger Hailey, George Haislip, Jerry Rush, Randall Heine, Jim Copeland, Ted Rohrer, Tom Krzemienski, Dick Flynn, John Tinnick, Doug Roberts. Third Row, Left To Right: Harlan Dodge, Leland McGonigal, Dave McCormick, Ron Goovert, Steve Juday, Don Japinga, John Karpinski, Boris Dimitroff, Buddy Owens, Bob Viney, Tony Angel, Larry Mackey, Jim Garrett, Don Bierowicz. Fourth Row, Left To Right: Pat Gallinagh, Jim Stoppert, Frank Altimore, Jeff Richardson, Gene Washington, Mike Whyte, Jim Proebstle, Harold

Lucas, Eddie Cotton, Don Weatherspoon, Cedric Sweet, Steve Troychak, Jim Summers, John Grogan, Charles Thornhill. Fifth Row, Left To Right: Clinton Jones, Roger Stewart, Walt Forman, Ernie Pasteur, Jim Hoye, Charles Smith, Gary Rugg, Steve Yarian, Chuck Lowther, Phil Hoag, Richard Reahm, George Webster, Maurice Haynes, John Whitworth, Solomon Townsend, Keith Redd, Jerald Jones. Sixth Row, Left To Right: Burt Smith, Freshman Coach and Administrative Assistant; Dan Boisture, Offensive Backfield Coach; Vince Carillot, Defensive Backfield Coach; Cal Stoll, Ends Coach; Pete Dotlich, Richard Kenney, John Dennison, Robert Mahan, John Gorman, Larry Lukasik, John Mullen, Robart Brawley, Mike Dissinger, John Kettunen, Jerry West, John McVay, Assistant Backfield Coach; Henry Bullough, Defensive Line Coach; Gordon Serr, Offensive Line Coach. Seventh Row, Left To Right: Bill Burt, Assistant Equipment Manager; Ken Earley, Equipment Manager; Clyde Stretch, Assistant Trainer; Clinton Thompson, Assistant Trainer; Gayle Robinson, Head Trainer; Tom Debrine, Manager; Con Demos, Manager.

1965

Front Row, Left To Right: Jim Garrett, Buddy Owens, Don Bierowicz, John Karpinski, Boris Dimitroff, Co-Capt. Steve Juday, Head Coach Duffy Daugherty, Co-Capt. Don Japinga, Ed Macuga, Jack Schinderle, Bob Viney, Don Weatherspoon, Ron Goovert. Second Row, Left To Right: Pat Gallingagh, Jim Hoye, Pete Dotlich, Clinton Jones, Gene Washington, Larry Lukasik, Jim Proebstle, Tony Angel, Harold Lucas, Eddie Cotton, George Webster, Frank Altimore, Phil Hoag, Keith Redd, Jerry West. Third Row, Left To Right: Larry Smith Eric Marshall, Roger Stewart, Dick Kenney, Walt Forman, Chuck Lowther, Jim Summers, Charles Smith, Bob Brawley, John Grogan, Charley Thornhill, Jeff Richardson, Ernie Pasteur, Jerry Jones, John Kettunen, Tom Skidmore, Maurice Haynes, Emil Demko. Fourth Row, Left To Right: Tony Rutherford, Nick Jordan, Ed McLoud, Dwight Lee, Bob Lange, Dave Techlin, Rusty Malone, Fred Convertini, Tom Ammirato, John Mullen, Solomon Townsend, Mike Dissinger, Phil Brittain, William Grimes, Marty Hain Joe Pryzbycki, Bob Apisa, Ron Ranieri, Drake Garrett. Fifth Row, Left To Right: Jim Raye, John MacGillivray, Jim Juday, Clinton Meadows, Sterling Armstrong, John Whalen, Dennis Miller, Tony Conti, George Chatlos, Mike Woodward, Norm Jenkins, Ken Heft, Bill Bruce, Wade Payne, Mitch Pruiett, Jess Phillips. Sixth Row, Left To Right: Ken Earley, Equipment Manager; Martin Daly, Assistant Equipment Manager; Al Dorow, Assistant Backfield Coach; Ed Rutherford, Freshman Coach; Vince Carillot, Defensive Backfield Coach; Hank Bullough, Defensive Line Coach; Cal Stoll, Ends Coach; Dan Boisture, Offensive Backfield Coach; Clyde Stretch, Assistant Trainer; Clinton Thompson, Assistant Trainer, Dugald Tryon, Head Manager.

1966

Front Row, Left To Right: Dick Kenney, Bob Brawley, Larry Lukasik, John Mullen, Chuck Lowther, Co-Capt. Clinton Jones, Head Coach Duffy Daugherty, Co-Capt. George Webster, Charles Thornhill, Phil Hoag, Jeff Richardson, Jerry West, Gene Washington. Second Row, Left To Right: Wade Payne, Sterling Armstrong, Dwight Lee, Drake Garrett, Jim Kettunen, Jerry Jones, Pat Gallinagh, Charles Smith, Tom Skidmore, Dick Reahm, Jim Summers, Ron Ranieri, Larry Smith, Maurice Haynes. Third Row, Left to right: Jess Phillips, Eddy McLoud, Jim Juday, Nick Jordan, Tony Conti, Joe Pryzbycki, Dave Techlin, George Chatlos, Bob Lange, Mike Bradley, Mitch Pruiett, Clinton Meadows, Bob Apisa, Ken Heft,

Jimmy Raye. Fourth Row, Left To Right: Jack Zindel, Clinton Harris, Don Baird, Roger Ruminski, Gary McGaughey, Regis Cavender, Bill Ware, Al Brenner, Neal Peterson, Mike Mahady, Charles Bailey, Duane Mc Iver, Charles Wedemeyer, Jim Ruschak, Bill Refaco, Frank Waters. Fifth Row, Left To Right: Martin Daly, Assistant Equipment Manager; Ken Earley, Equipment Manager; Henry Bullough, Dan Boisture, Vince Carillot, Al Dorow, Assistant Coaches; Dwight Romagnoli, Ted Bohn, Bob Super, Mike Young, Mike Garofalo, Don Warnke, Dick Berlilnski, Paul Lawson; Cal Stoll, Ed Rutherford, Gordon Serr, Assistant Coaches; Gayle Robinson, Head Trainer; Clyde Stretch, Clinton Thompson, Assistant Trainers; Jim Orr, Manager.

1967

Front Row, Left To Right; Robert Apisa, Eddy McLoud, Mitch Pruiett, George Chatlos, Co-Capt. Tony Conti, Head Coach Duffy Daugherty, Co-Capt. Drake Garrett, Jo Przybycki, Ron Ranieri, Dave Techlin, Maurice Haynes. Second Row, Left To Right: Jimmy Raye, Sterling Armstrong, Clinton Meadows, William Grimes, Wade Payne, Robert Super, Dwight Lee, Ken Heft, Robert Lange, Larry Smith, Jess Phillips, Mike Bradley. Third Row, Left To Right: Don Warnke, Ted Bohn, Robert Jackson, Regis Cavender, Richie Jordan, Gary McGaughey, Charles Wedemeyer, Richard Berlinski, William Feraco, Roger Ruminski, Frank Waters, Allen Brenner, Nick Jordan. Fourth Row, Left To Right: Dave Thomas, Donald Law, Dan Champagne, Robert Miltenberger, Clifton Hardy, Michael Young, Neal Peterson, Jim Ruschak, William Ware, Michael Mahady, Paul Lawson, Don Baird, Charles Bailey, Tom Kutschinski. Fifth Row, Left To Right: Lawrence (Tody) Smith, John Lindquist, Calvin Fox, Ken Little, Helmut Goral, Bruce Kulesza, Dave Van Elst, Dave Schweinfurth, Steve Garvey, Gordon Bowdell, Ron Saul, Rich Saul, Chris Ripmaster, Ralph Skinner, Jack Pitts. Sixth row, Left To Right: Frank Foreman, Don Highsmith, Mike Dodd, La Marr Thomas, Craig Wycinsky, Ken Hines, Frank Traylor, Sam Sethman, Michael Turnbull, Kermit Smith, Richard Benedict. Seventh Row, Left To Right; Robert Bouma, Bryce Adolph, Managers; Marty Daly, Assistant Equipment Manager; Ken Earley, Equipment Manager; Vince Carillot, Ed Rutherford, Dave Smith, Henry Bullough, George Perles, Al Dorow, Cal Stoll, Gordon Serr, Assistant Coaches; Gayle Robinson, Head Trainer; Clyde Stretch, Clint Thompson, Assistant Trainers.

1968

Front Row, Left To Right: Mike Mahady, Regis Cavender, Bill Feraco, Ken Heft, Frank Waters, Head Coach Duffy Daugherty, Capt. Allen Brenner, Don Baird, Eddy McLoud, Dick Berlinski, Wade Payne, Neal Peterson. Second Row: Cliftin Hardy, Dave Van Elst, John Lindquist, Bob Super, Roger Ruminski, Mike Young, Nick Jordan, Charlie, Wedemeyer, Charles Bailey, Jack Zindel, Rick Benedict, Bruce Kulesza, Helmut Goral. Third Row: Ken Hines, Ken Little, La Marr Thomas, Kermit Smith, Frank Traylor, Don Highsmith, Ron Saul, Rich Saul, Lawrence Smith, Don Law, Frank Foreman, Tom Kutschinski, Gordon Bowdell, Chris Ripmaster. Fourth Row: Ron Curl, Gordon Longmire, Gary Parmentier, Joe Willing, Ron Slank, Mike Tobin, Gary Boyce, Craig Wycinsky, Calvin Fox, Mike Hogan, Tom Barnum, Vic Mittelberg, Richard Shultz, Joe Valerine, Doug Krause. Fifth Row: Gary Nowak, Wilt Martin, Robert Black, Bill Triplett, Tom O'Hearn, Vincent Cesarz, Bill Dawson, Art Berry, Harold Phillips, Frank Butler, Earl Anderson, Tom Beard, John Chikos, Ralph

Wieleba, Jay Breslin, Steve Kough. Sixth Row: Marty Daly, Equipment; Ken Earley, Equipment Manager; Cal Stoll, George Perles, Dave Smith, Vince Carillot, Al Dorow, Assistant Coaches; Dave Thomas, Errol Roy, Tom Love, Ron Joseph; Ed Rutherford, Gordon Serr, Don Coleman, Henry Bullough, Assistant Coaches; Gayle Robinson, Head Trainer; Clyde Stretch, Clinton Thompson, Assistant Trainers. Top Row: Robert Beery, Manager; Steven Clupper, Head Manager; Gerald Sternberg, Manager.

1969

Front Row, Left To Right: Rick Benedict, Craig Wycinsky, Don Highsmith, Ron Saul, Co-Capt. Frank Foreman, Head Coach Duffy Daugherty, Co-Capt. Rich Saul, Don Law, Don Baird, Dave Van Elst, Bruce Kulesza. Second Row, Left To Right: Ron Slank, Mike Tobin, Gordon Bowdell, Mike Mahady, Ten Bohn, Cal Fox, Ken Hines, Kermit Smith, Fred Convertini, Mike Howard, Ken Little, Dave Thomas. Third Row, Left To Right: Ken Milstead, Tom Beard, Joe Valerine, Tom O'Hearn, Ron Curl, Tom Barnum, Joe Willing, Mike Hogan, Tom Kutschinski, Vic Mittelberg, Bob Black, Gary Parmentier, Gary Nowak. Fourth Row, Left To Right: Ron Joseph, Errol Roy, Tommy Love, Harold Phillips, Wilt Martin, Art Berry, Bill Triplett, Clifton Hardy, Steve Kough, Bill Dawson, Mike Mc Cauley, Bob Gomez, Ralph Wieleba, Frank Butler. Fifth Row, Left To Right: Dan Werner, Hans Sudar, Bob Walerowicz, Tom Looby, Dan Kulikowski, Morgan Justice, Dave Beverlin, Tim Jones, Gary Halliday, Steve Piro, Doug Barr, Mark Stoll, Gary Van Elst, Robert Callard, Mike Morrissey. Sixth Row, Left To Right: Assistant Trainer Clinton Thompson, Henry Matthews, Herb Washington, Cliff Roberts, Jim Nicholson, Doug Halliday, Gene Pankner, Duane McLaughlin, Paul Lukovich, Scott Miltenberger, Steve Wagers, Brad Mc Lee, Eric Allen, Daryl Smith, Assistant Trainer Clyde Stretch. Seventh Row, Left To Right: Equipment Manager Ken Earley, Head Trainer Gayle Robinson, Assistant Coaches Gordon Serr, Henry Bullough, Dave Smith, George Perles, Ed Rutherford, Joe Carruthers; Billy Joe Du Pree, Cleothar Turner, Assistant Coaches Al Dorow, George Paterno, Sherman Lewis; Assistant Trainer Jerry Kimbrough, Assistant Manager Tom Burke, Head Manager Bob Beery, Assistant Equipment Manager Marty Daly.

1970

Front Row, Left To Right: Ron Curl, Art Berry, Clifton Hardy, Vic Mittelberg, Harold Phillips, Head Coach Duffy Daugherty, Earl Anderson, Wilt Martin, Tommy Love, Errol Roy, Tom Barnum. Second Row, Left To Right: Mike Tobin, Bob Black, Bill Dawson, Gary Parmentier, Ron Slank, Gordon Bowdell, Tom Kutschinski, Mike Hogan, Steve Kough, Bill Triplett, Frank Butler, Ralph Wieleba, Dave Thomas. Third Row, Left To Right: Dan Bruerd, Gary Halliday, Bob Walerowicz, Doug Halliday, Jay Breslin, Gary Nowak, Tom Beard, Calvin Fox, Duane McLaughlin, Gary Van Elst, David Beverlin, Dan Kulikowski, Morgan Justice. Fourth Row, Left To Right: Billy Joe Du Pree, Borys Shlapak, Doug Barr, Jim Nicholson, Eric Allen, Henry Matthews, Daryl Smith, Randy Davis, Brad McLee, Cliff Roberts, Mark Stoll, Mike Rasmussen, Dick Kluge, Dan Werner. Fifth Row, Left To Right; Marvin Roberts, Jerome Martin, Leland Wegener, Richard Hulkow, Dennis Macholz, Mark Loper, Mark Grua, Jim Bond, Ken Alderson, Greg Ward, Richard Salani, Darnelle Dickerson, Frank Timmons, Archie Mac Gillivray. Sixth Row, Left To Right: Ernest Hamilton, John Ruzich, Brad Van Pelt, Chris King, Doug Root, Willim Des Jardins, Mark Sokoll, Bryce Bowron, Mike Danielewicz, Joe De Lamielleure, Mark

315

Wojcik, John Crowell, George Mihaiu. Seventh Row, Left To Right: Head Manager Rick Drobot, Assistant Managers Chris Corwin, Harvey Schloss, Bob Roehl, Chuck Applegate; James Lear, Brian McConnell, Gail Clark, John Shinsky, Bob McClowry, Mark Charette, Bob Saley, Bill Valasco. Eighth Row, Left To Right: Assistant Coaches Tony Versaci, Gordon Serr, Sherman Lewis, Dave Smith, George Paterno, George Perles, Ed Rutherford, Joe Carruthers, Al Dorow; Team Physician Dr. Lawrence Jarrett, Head Trainer Gayle Robinson, Assistant Trainers Jerry Kimbrough, Dan Kinsey; Assistant Equipment Manager Martin Daly, Equipment Manager Ken Earley.

1971

Front Row, Left To Right: Daryl Smith, Eric Allen, Steve Kough, Doug Barr, Bill Dawson, Ron Joseph, Head Coach Duffy Daugherty, Henry Matthews, Frank Butler, Ron Curl, Errol Roy, Tom Barnum. Second Row: Ralph Wieleba, Dan Kulikowski, John Martin, Doug Halliday, Gary Van Elst, Duane McLaughlin, Gary Halliday, Scott, Miltenberger, Billy Joe Du Pree, Mike Rasmussen, Brad Van Pelt, David Beverlin, Mike Danielewicz, Dennis Macholz. Third Row: Mark Stoll, John Schalter, Mark Loper, Richard Hulkow, John Ruzich, Ken Alderson, Mark Grua, Jim Bond, Mark Charette, Frank Kolch, Chris King, Joe De Lamielleure, Bob McClowry, Bob Saley, Dan Werner, Frank Timmons. Fourth Row: Jim Luxton, Archie Mac Gillivray, Brian McConnell, Mark Sokoll, Marvin Roberts, Bill Valasco, Richard Salani, Richard Kluge, George Mihaiu, Ernie Hamilton, Gail Clark, Jim Walainis, Bruce Anderson, Tom Brown, Jim Higgins. Fifth Row: Dan Walker, John Lorente, Ray Kurpe, Bob Mills, Craig Omerod, Bob Theuerkauf, Charles Collins, Ray Nester, Paul Hayner, Jeff Wotring, Bruce Harms, Gary Hughes, Paul Manderino, James Taubert, Richard Pawlak, Lowell Wade. Sixth Row: Steve Miltenberger, Borys Shlapak, Jesse Williams, Mike Hurd, Mike Holt, Tony Ransom, Bill Simpson, Mark Niesen, Ron Kumiega, Tom Brown, Bill Chada, Bill Peters, Tom Kronner, Rex Wolfe, Tom Hoese. Seventh Row: Equipment Manager Ken Earley, Assistant Coach Gordon Serr, Assistant Equipment Managers Andy Taylor and Martin Daly, Assistant Team Physician Dr. Larry Jarrett, Head Trainer Gayle Robinson, Assistant Trainers Don Kiger and Jerry Kimbrough, Assistant Coaches Ed Rutherford, Sherman Lewis, Joe Carruthers, Dennis Stolz, George Perles, Ed Youngs, Assistant Managers Dan Kovacs and Steve Repko, Head Manager Rick Drobot, Assistant Managers Chris Corwin and Chuck Applegate.

1972

Front Row, Left To Right: George Mihaiu, Robert Saleh, Chris King, Brian McConnell, Co-Capt. Brad Van Pelt, Head Coach Duffy Daugherty, Co-Capt. Billy Joe Du Pree, Gary Van Elst, James Nicholson, Richard Hulkow, Duane McLaughlin. Second Row: Gail Clark, Kenith Alderson, Frank Timmons, John Martin, Marvin Roberts, John Shinsky, Joseph DeLamielleure, William Valasco, Mark Grua, James Bond, Richard Salani, Scott Miltenberger, Mark Charette. Third Row: Craid Omerod, Michael Holt, Michael Hurd, Damond Mays, Richard Pawlak, Raymond Nester, Michael Danielewicz, Dennis Macholz, Archie MacGillivray, Rex Wolfe, Robert Brown, Craig Dahlke, Paul Hayner, Ronald Kumiega, Tony Ransom. Fourth Row: Brian McKay, Clayton Montgomery, Jesse Williams, Jesse Williams, Ray Smith, Steven Miltenberger, Thomas Kronner, Charles Collins, Gary Hughes, Chris Boyd, Thomas Brown, Mark Niesen, Robert Mills, William Simpson, Paul Manderino. Fifth Row: Robert Parise, Steven Moerdyk, Steve Burton, Clarence Bullock, Michael

Jones, Marshall Dill, David E. Brown. Charles Wilson, William Klotz, Cheadrick Harriatte, David M. Brown, Ben Twichell, Max Myers, James Taubert, Charles Gordon, Ray Kurpe. Sixth Row: Dennis Voltattorni, William Varvari, Shawn Lazier, John Mihaiu, Thomas Cole, Brendon Barber, Tyrone Willingham, Mark Dalrymple, Dane Fortney, Greg Schaum, Tyrone Wilson, Arnold Morgado, Charlie Ane, Kellie Dean, Doug Won, Michael Smith, Michael Duda, Bradley Bishop. Seventh Row: Richard Lilly, Head Manager; Dan Kovacs, Manager, Troy Hickman, Assistant Equipment Manager; Marty Daly, Equipment Manager; Joseph Arnold, Mark De Coster, Greg Rimoldi, Greg Croxton, Anthony Hewitt, James Cordery, Patrick Loridas, Thomas Krier, John Wallisch, Mark Marchegiani, Otto Smith, Steve Repko, Craig Murray, Rob Lerner. Eight Row: Coaches Gordon Serr, Dennis Stolz, Joseph Carruthers, Ed Rutherford, Sherman Lewis, Ed Youngs, Herb Paterra, Jimmy Raye.

1973

Front Row: Paul Manderino, Rich Hulkow, Paul Hayner, Bob Mills, Dirk Kryt, Mike Danielewicz, John Shinsky, Head Coach Denny Stolz, Mike Holt, Bill Simpson, Mike Hurd, Damond Mays, Ray Nester, Tom Kronner, Rick Pawlak. Second Row: Chris Mushett, Tom Hoese, Bruce Harms, Steve Miltenberger, John Ruzich, Craig Dahlke, Ron Kumiega, Rex Rolve, Jim Taubert, Clayton Montgomery, Mark Niesen, Craig Omerod, Tony Ransom, Terry McClowy, Pat Mc Clowry, Steve Moerdyk, Brad Bishop. Third Row: Mike Smith, Brian McKay, David Brown, Larry Jackson, Charlie Baggett, Clarence Bullock, Charlie Wilson, Wendell Moore, Chead Hariatte, Mike Jones, Bob Love, Kellie Dean, Bob Parise, Steve Burton, Mike Duda, Doug Won, Jim Grannell, Charlie Ane, Arnold Morgado. Fourth Row: Dan Allison, Dane Fortney, Tom Standal, Ron Ninowski, Scott Evans, Pat Loridas, Julius Askew, Jim Cordery, Greg Croxton, Tyrone Willingham, Tyrone Wilson, Richard Washington, Greg Schaum, Otto Smith, Brendon Barger, Mark Marchegiani, Tom Krier, Dennis Voltattorni, Phil Smolinski, Jim Oliver, Mark DeCoster, Greg Hagbom. Fifth Row: Dave Duda, Greg Young, Mike Combest, Jon Ray, Bill Smith, Jim Sciarini, Tony Abler, Ray Spencer, Jim Epolito, Levi Jackson, Brad Smith, Mike Cobb, Ken Jones, Joe Hunt, Tony Marek, Dan Evans, Marc Stortini, Kim Rowekamp, Ron Lundquist, Tom Cole, Bill Varvarik, Dalrymple. Sixth Row: Student Trainer Mike Soloman, Student Managers Paul Weller, Craig Murphy, Steve Repko, Head Student Manager Rick Lilly, Joe Arnold, Richard Baes, John Breslin, Tom Hannon, Tony Bruggentheis, Marshall Lawson, Ron Brown, John Malinosky, Gary Hall, Greg Terry, Homer Barker, Anthony Porter, Harv Feinauer, Assistant Equipment Manager Troy Hickman, Student Equipment Assistant Mark Vollrath, Equipment Manager Marty Daly, Coordinator Of Training Clinton Thompson, Student Trainer Tim Kirschner. Seventh Row: Student Trainer Dan Murphy, Trainer Gayle Robinson, Student Trainer Dick Redfearn, Graduate Assistant Coaches Ernie Hamilton, Mike Rasmussen; Varsity Assistant Coaches Andy Mac Donald, Ed Youngs, Howard Weyers, Charles Butler, Dan Underwood, Sherman Lewis; Administrative Assistant Ed Rutherford, Graduate Assistant Coaches Doug Barr and Dino Paparella; Student Trainers Sue Schneider, Mike Mascaro, Sean Ovington; Trainer Jerry Kimbrough.

1974

Front Row Left to Right: Mike Hurd, Charles Baggett, Bob Parise, Steve Moerdyk, Paul Manderino, Co Capt.

Jim Taubert, Head Coach Denny Stolz, Co-Capt. Clarence Bullock, Terry McClowry, Mike Duda, Charles Ane, Jim Grannell. Second Row, Left to Right: Otto Smith, Wendell Moore, Greg Brewton, Chris Mushett, Brad Bishop, Joe Arnold, Mike Jones, Cheadrick Harriatte, Charles Wilson, Larry Jackson, Dane Fortney, Dennis Voltattorni, Jim Oliver, Greg Schaum. Third Row, Left To Right: Dave Duda, Jim Epolito, Greg Croxton, Rich Washington, Brendon Barber, Tyrone Wilson, Mark Dalrymple, Mark Fragel, Mark DeCoster, Greg Hagbom, Tyrone Willingham, Dan Allison, Tom Standal, Tom Hannon, Ken Jones. Fourth Row, Left to Right: John Breslin, Rich Baes, Jim Sciarini, John Malinosky, Harvey Finauer, Dan Evans, Nick Rollick, Craig Norwood, Jon Ray, Greg Young, Tony Marek, Gary Hall, Tony Bruggenthies, Greg Terry, Joe Hunt, Marshall Lawson, Bill Smith. Fifth Row, Left to Right: Jim Thomas, Al Pitts, Steve Abraham, Marty Kennedy, Alan Hamilton, Kim Rowekamp, Mike Cobb, Anthony Porter, Ken Ramsey, Ray Spencer, Levi Jackson, Larry Bethea, Marc Allen, Ed Smith, Craig Fedore, Bob Sammartino, Mike Imhoff, Charles Shafer, Hans Nielsen, Jim Earley. Sixth Row Left to Right: Tom Graves, Tom Birney, Leon Williams, Matt Sweet, John Daubenmeyer, Mel Land, Rod Hunsanger, Paul Rudzinski, Terry Williams, Claude Geiger, William Brown, Ted Bell, Tim Ruff, Frank Angelo, Ralph Plummer, Mike Dean, Read May. Seventh Row, Left to Right: Tim Kirschner, Sue Schneider, Ray Saltzman, Don Kaverman, Student trainers; Gayle Robinson, trainer; Dan Underwood, Ron Chismar, Andy MacDonald, assistant coaches; Troy Hickman, asst. equipment mgr.; Marty Daly, equipment mgr.; Jim Rankin, Peggy Pettit, Sean Ovington, student trainers; Clinton Thompson, coordinator of training. Eighth Row, Left to Right: Harold Farris, Jeff Arthurs, Jerry Goresch, John Wood, Paul Weller, student managers; Craig Murray, head mgr.; Bump Lardie, Mick Brzezinskik, Dino Paparella, Ernie Hamilton, graduate assistant coaches.

1975

First Row, Left To Right: Greg Brewton, Tyrone Wilson, Dane Fortney, Otto Smith, Charlie Baggett, Head Coach Denny Stolz, Greg Schaum, Pat McClowry, Tom Standal, John Powers, Tom Cole. Second Row: Leon Williams, Ken Ramsey, Brendon Barber, Rich Washington, Tyrone, Willingham, Greg Croxton, Dennis Voltattorni, Mark Dalrymple, Grag Hagbom, Jim Buckley, John Breslin, Rich Baes, Jim Earley. Third Row: Tom Graves, Tom Hannon, Joe Hunt, Mike Cobb, Ken Jones, Marshall Lawson, Ray Spencer, Levi Jackson, Anthony Porter, Tony Bruggenthies, Jon Ray, Greg Young, Dan De Rose, Mike Imhoss. Fourth Row: Charlie Shafer, Hans Nielsen, Terry Williams, Craig Fedore, John Malinosky, Greg Terry, Nick Rollick, Joe Malinowski, Dave Duda, Willie Smith, Tony Marek, Jim Sciarini, Kim Rowekamp, Paul Rudzinski, Dave Radelet, Ed Smith. Fifth Row: Larry Savage, Chris Bunbury, Larry Bethea, Ted Bell, Mel Land, Al Pitts, Steve Abraham, Bob Sammartino, Jim Thomas, Tom Birney, Frank Angelo, Tim Ruff, Chris Thomas, Dennis Kelly, Eugene Harris, Marty Kennedy, Ralph Plummer, Rod Hunsanger, John Vielhaber. Sixth Row: Jerome Stanton, Cleveland Jackson, Eugene Byrd, Doug Lantz, Regis Mc Quaide, Kirk Gibson, Bob Kenny, Tom Peterson, Pat Burke, John O'Leary, Bob Brand, Jim Johnson, Tony Borzi, John Daubenmeyer, Mike Dean, Eric Jones, Mike Decker, Rick Underman, Mike Hans. Seventh Row: Robert Washington, Bill Broadway, Ken Robinson, Terry Tindol, Ed Stanton, John Pokojski, Jim Hinesly, Ten Grabenhorst, Joe DiLeornardo, Mark Tapling, Dave Steenland, Curtis Griffin, James

McCullogh, Calvin Reed, Jess Moore, Craig Lonce. Eighth Row: Deb Koning, Bill Armstrong, Brian Dunckel, Jan Howell, Jeff Rowe, Student Trainers; Bob Lardie, Jim Szuch, Graduate Assistant Coaches; Dan Underwood, Bill Davis, Howard Weyers, Sherm Lewis, Andy MacDonald, Ed Youngs, Charlie Butler, Jimmy Raye, Ron Chismar, Assistant Coaches; Mike Duda, Bob Rankin, Graduate Assistant Coaches; Joann Reiter, Student Trainer; Sue Schneider, Trainer; Ray Saltzmann, Student Trainer; Don Kaverman, Graduate Student Trainer; Tim Kirschner, Trainer. Ninth Row: Doug Smith, Kevin McCarthy, Maria Della Corte, Harold Farris, Jeff Arthurs, Bob Sommer, Student Managers; Paul Weller, Head Student Manager; Troy Hickman Assistant Equipment Manager; Marty Daly, Equipment Manager; Clinton Thompson, Coordinator of Training; Gayle Robinson, Trainger, Jim Rankin, David Barringer, Student Trainers.

1976

First Row, Left To Right: Rich Washington, Brendon Barber, Tyrone Willingham, John Malinosky, Tony Bruggenthies, Head Coach Darryl Rogers, Tom Cole, Ray Spencer, Dave Duda, Dan De Rose, John Powers. Second Row: Tom Hannon, Leon Williams, John Breslin, Ken Ramsey, Joe Hunt, Mike Cobb, Levi Jackson, Jon Ray, Greg Young, Nick Rollick, Ken Jones, Otto Smith, Marshall Lawson, Rich Baes. Third Row: Jim Thomas, Mark Tapling, Mike Hans, Paul Rudzinski, Jim Earley, Ralph Plummer, Tony Marek, Jim Sciarini, Jim Epolito, Hans Nielsen, Mike Imhoff, Tom Peterson, Mike Dean, Dave Radelet, Tony Borzi. Fourth Row: Joe Di Leonardo, Jody Mc Culloh, Mike Densmore, Larry Savage, Mike Decker, Tom Graves, Bob Kenny, Craig Fedore, Charlie Shafer, Tom Birney, Larry Bethea, Ed Smith, Al Pitts, Terry Williams, Ted Bell, Mel Land, Anthony Porter. Fifth Row: Alan Davis, Mark Jones, Mark Marana, Dan Bass, Jim Prendergast, Scott Carver, Ted Grabenhorst, Curtis Griffin, Gene Byrd, Jerome Stanton, Calvin Reed, Eric Jones, Doug Lantz, Craig Lonce, Rick Underman, Dick Ott, Jim Hinesly, Regis McQuaide. Sixth Row: Angelo Fields, Matt Foster, Ed Abbott, Jeff Hewit, Terry Anderson, Clarence Williams, Mike Marshall, Mark Anderson, Rob Campion, Mark Brammer, Kirk Gibson, Ed Stanton, John Prokojski, Ed Wedley, Ken Robinson, Harry Hagstrom, Rick Audas, David Finkelstein, Steve Otis, Rod Strata, Alonzo Middleton. Seventh Row: Dr. Larry Jarrett, Team Physician; Clinton Thompson, Coordinator of Training and Staff Members Kathy Higgins, Gayle Robinson, Dave Barringer, John Van Zandt And Bill Armstrong; Assistant Coaches Ray Greene, C.T. Hewgley, Dave Krischke, Ray Sherman, Sherman Lewis, Mary Braden, Bump Lardie, Leon Burtnett, Dan Underwood, Ron Chismar and Bob Padilla; Training Staffers Don Kaverman, Ann Charback, Irene Medwid, Bob Caruso, Jan Howell, Sue Schneider, Jim Rankin, Tim Kirschner and Jim Madeleno. Eighth Row: Student Equipment Staffers Rich Moscarello, Thor Kolemainen, Jon Scott, Tom Magee, Marty Masterson and Brian Holland; Assistant Equipment Manager Troy Hickman; Student Managers Craig Morford, Bob Sommer (Head), Kevin Mc Carthy, Jeff Arthurs, Bart Estola, Jeff Minahan and Maria Dela Corte, and Medical Staffer Dort Rietzier.

1977

First Row, Left To Right: Tom Graves, Mike Imhoff, Paul Rudzinski, Dave Radelet, Tom Birney, Jim Thomas, Head Coach Darryl Rogers, Al Pitts, Jim Sciarini, John Malinosky, William Smith, Nick Rollick, Mike Dean. Second Row: Regis McQuaide, Larry Bethea, Hans Nielsen, Tom Peterson, Jim Earley, Chris Bunbury, Craig Fedore, Edgar Wilson, Ed

Smith, Kirk Gibson, Bob Kennyk, Jim Epolito, Mel Land, Marshall Lawson, Kim Rowekamp, Terry Williams. Third Row: Mike Densmore, Jim Hinesly, Mike Hans, Ed Stanton, Larry Savage, Mark Tapling, Craig Lonce, John Vielhaber, Curt Griffin, Eugene Byrd, Jerome Stanton, Mike Decker, Ted Grabenhorst, Eric Jones, Craig Raye, Walt Hoye, Charles Shafer. Fourth Row: Craig Simms, Joe Kolodziej, Don Wagberg, Eric Ross, Dick Ott, Jody McCulloh, Ken Robinson, Rob Campion, Steve Otis, Jim Prendergast, Matt Foster, Leroy Mc Gee, Barry Harris, Mark Brammer, Alan Davis, Mark Jones, Angelo Fields. Fifth Row: Jim Burroughs, Bruce Reeves, Samson Howard, Greg Brown, Clarence Williams, Terry Anderson, Mark Anderson, Rod Strata, Alonzo Middleton, Rick Audas, Craig Converse, Dan Bass, Mark Marana, Ray Stachowicz, Ike Griffin, Andy Schramm. Sixth Row: Bernard Hay, Gil Houston, Johnny Lee Haynes, Jeff Wiska, John McCormick, Brett Sheeran, Al Kimichik, Jim Kaiser, Terry McDowell, Rick Milhizer, Bert Vaughn, Joe Jacquemain, Mike Sciarini, Van Williams, Steve Smith. Seventh Row: Equipment Manager Troy Hickman; Student Equipment Staffers Mike Chismar, Marty Masterson, Tom Magee, Brian Holland; Assistant Coaches Bob Baker, Matt Means, Dan Underwood, Bob Padilla, Tyrone Willingham, Ron Chismar, Ray Sherman, C.T. Hewgley, George Dyer, Ray Greene, Sherman Lewis; Trainers Gayle Robinson, Sue Schneider; Coordinator of Training Clint Thompason. Eighth Row: Coordinator of Equipment Jon Phillips; Student Equipment Staffers Jon Scott, Thor Kolemainen, Mike Schoonover; Student Training Staffers Diane Beach, Mary Mc Elwain; Student Equipment Managers Kevin McCarthy, Jeff Arthurs (Head), Paul Schiele, Joe McGiness, Keith Schaffer, Mark Ruth, Jeff Minahen; Student Training Staffers Dort Rietzler, Wes Emmett, Brian Brown, Jim Madaleno, Kathy Higgins, Irene Medwid, Paul Beachier, Russ McNamer.

1978

First Row, Left To Right: Terry Williams, Mel Land, Barry Harris, Craig Raye, Craig Lonce, Jim Hinesly, Head Coach Darryl Rogers, Kirk Gibson, Tom Graves, Leroy Mc Gee, Charles Shafer, Mike Hans, Ed Smith. Second Row: Calvin Perkins, Regis McQuaide, Dick Ott, Ed Stanton, Larry Savage, Jody McCulloh, John Vielhaber, Mark Tapling, Curt Griffin, Ted Grabenhorst, Mike Decker, Eric Jones, Brett Sheeran, Ed Wedley. Third Row: Ben Baca, Van Williams, Steve Smith, Mike Densmore, Ken Robinson, Eugene Byrd, Jerome Stanton, Lonnie Middleton, Mark Brammer, Alan Davis, Rod Strata, Mark Anderson, Steve Otis, Matt Foster, Bert Vaughn. Fourth Row. Steve Blank, Tony Townsend, Joe Kolodziej, Jim Kaiser, Craig Converse, Ray Stachowicz, Bob Stachowicz, Terry McDowell, Dan Bass, Rick Augas, Tanya Webb, Mark Jones, Dave Whittle, Jeff Wiska, Andy Shramm. Fifth Row: Ron Mitchem, Derek Hughes, Darrin McClelland, George Cooper, Bruce Reeves, Johnny Lee Haynes, Rick Milhizer, Dan Danielak, Al Kimichik, John McCormick Joe Jacquemain, Mike Sciarini, Ike Griffin, Bernard Hay, Angelo Fields. Sixth Row: Jack Kirkling, Pat Mitten, Lance Petross, Joe Harewicz, Craig Saunders, Scot Mazur, Mike Muster, Rich Schario, Mike Marshall, Samson Howard, Jim Burroughs, Steve Maidlow, Jim Williams, Todd Scarlett, Bruce Williams, Bryan Boak. Seventh Row: Gayle Robinson, Ronnie Barnes, Kathy Hack, Trainers; Dr. David Hough, Team Physician; Clint Thompson, Coordinator Or Training; Rickey Greene, Jeff Fehlan, Darryl Brown, Tony Harris, Tom Piette, Bryan Clark, Mike Jones, Jack Hexum, Marv Mantos; Brian Holland, Jon Scott,Mike Schoonover, Mike Chismar, Student Equipment Assistants. Eighth Row: Sherm

Lewis, Bob Baker, Mo Forte, Ron Fondrich, Walt Harris, Kurt Schottenheimer, George Dyer, Dan Underwood, Ron Chismar, Matt Means, C.T. Hewgley, Assistant Coaches; David Henry, Strength Coach; Troy Hickman, Equipment Manager; Marty Masterson, Student Equipment Assistant; Jon Phillips, Coordinator Of Equipment. Ninth Row: John Mc Giness, Paul Schiele, Student Managers; Jeff Minahan, Head Student Manager; George Salvaterra, Mary McElwain, Paul Beachler, Becky Stormes, Keith Luxton, Marla Rufe, Wes Emmert, Jane Steinberg, Diane Beach, Brian Brown, Russ McNamer, Student Training Staffers; Charles Amori, Joe McGiness, Kam Hunter, Student Managers.

1979

Row 1 (L-R) Angelo Fields, Regis McQuaide, Eric Jones, Ted Grabenhorst, Mike Densmore, John Vielhaber, Larry Savage, Head Coach Darryl Rogers, Eugene Byrd, Lonnie Middleton, Dan Bass, Mark Anderson, Matt Foster, Steve Otis, Mark Tapling. Row 2 - Tanya Webb, Pat Baker, Jack Kirkling, Craig Converse, Rod Strata, Mark Brammer, Mike Decker, Curt Griffin, Ed Stanton, Alan Davis, Rick Audas, John McCormick, Dave Whittle, Jim Williams, Andy Schramm, Bob Stachowicz. Row 3 - Steve Maidlow, Rich Schario, Joe Harewicz, Mark Jones, Terry Bailey, Bruce Reeves, Mike Marshall, Steve Smith, Ike Griffin, Bernard Hay, Jeff Wiska, Jim Sciarini, Al Kimichik, Joe Jacquemain, Rick Milhizer, Tony Townsend, Johnny Lee Haynes. Row 4 - Jeff Fehlan, Bruce Williams, Todd Scarlet, Bryan Boak, Scott Mazur, Steve Blank, Mike Jones, Mike Muster, Tom Piette, Van Williams, Samson Howard, Jim Burroughs, Bryan Clark, Pat Mitten, Bert Vaughn, Ray Stachowicz, Morten Andersen. Row 5 - Wilfred Billingsley, Randy Lark, Gregg Lauble, Todd Langerveld, Terry Tanker, Howard McAdoo, James Neely, Chris Van Pelt, Marv Mantos, Lance Petross, Derek Hughes, George Cooper, Darrin McClelland, Darryl Brown, Ron Mitchem, Joe Kolodziej, Calvin Perkins. Row 6 - Scott Rich, Chris Landry, Jim Smith, Carl Williams, Denis Lavelle, Otis Grant, James Hodo, Joe Stevens, Walt Schramm, Smiley Creswell, Jon English, Marcus Toney, Ted Jones, Bob Mouch, Tony Ellis, Tony Woods, John Leister. Row 7 - Mo Forte, C.T. Hewgley, Matt Means, Walt Harris, Ron Marciel, George Dyer, Sherman Lewis, Dan Underwood, Bob Baker, Ron Chismar (Assistant Coach), Kam Hunter (Manager), Becky Stormes, Bob Ogar, Tom Lee (Training Assistants), Kathy Heck, Ron Barnes (Trainers), Charles Amori (Manager), Jim Madeleno (Training Assistant), Clinton Thompson (Coordinator or Training). Row 8 - Tom Magee, Brian Holland, Jon Scott (Equipment Assistants) Dr. David Hough (Team Physician), Tom Mackowiak, Jane Steinberg, Carolyn Vandell, Beth Harris, Diane Beach, Paul Adams, Carole Bovard, George Salvaterra, Dave Milford, Ryan Dling (Training Assistants), Mike Chismar (Equipment Assistant), Kevin McCarthy, John Mc Giness, Joe Mc Giness, Arv Pettit, Mark Ruth (Managers), John Anderson (Equipment Assistant), Troy Hickman (Assistant Equipment Manager) Jon Phillips (Coordinator Of Equipment).

1980

Row 1 (L-R) - Steve Smith Tony Townsend, Mark Jones, Joe Jacquemain, Dave Whittle, Mike Densmore, Head Coach Muddy Waters,Jim Williams, Rod Strata, Ray Stachowicz, Andy Schramm, Joe Kolodziej, Mike Marshall. Row 2 - Bernard Hay, Van Williams, John Kouri, Joe Stevens, Mike Penny, Mike Jones, Joe Harewicz, Terry Bailey, Smiley Creswell, Pat Mitten, Bruce Williams, Bruce Reeves, John

McCormick, Jeff Wiska, Mike Sciarini, Calvin Perkins. Row 3 - Al Kimichik, Johnny Lee Haynes, Bert Vaughn, George Cooper, Thomas Morris, Rich Ludwig, Tony Gilbert, Scott Rich, Chris Landry, Terry Tanker, Todd Scarlett, Mike Muster, Walt Schramm, Todd Langerveld, Marv Mantos, Jeff Fehlan, Ted Jones. Row 4 - Jim Smith, Otis Grant, Rick Milhizer, John Leister, Denis Lavelle, James Neely, James Hodo, Jim Scheib, Mike Bossory, Kirk Jacob, Brad Bache, Bob Brammer, Don Muhammad, David Moore, Milton Chaney, Carl Williams, Chris Van Pelt, Marcus Toney. Row 5 - Tony Ellis, Ron Mitchem, Bryan Boak, Greg Lauble, Everett Hall, Mark Kaczmarek, Mike Hoffman, Scott Auer, Brett Schlosser, Tom Robinson, Carter Kamana, Jim McTaggert, Chris Hayner, Tom Allan, Rich Babich, James Pippins, Howard Mc Adoo, Darrin McClelland. Row 6 - Jack Kirkling, Ike Griffin, Randy Lark, Tom Piette, Carl Banks, Daryl Turner, Derek Bunch, Warren Wells, Darryl Dixon, Tim Cunningham, Joel Waller, Nate Hannah, Ed Trubich, Rob Holland, Addie Gaddis, Steve Blank, Bryan Clark, Tony Woods. Row 7 - Dick Comar, Steve Schottel, Dave Driscoll, Ed Rutherford, Dave Arnold, Bryan Ford (Assistant Coaches), Dave Henry (Strength And Conditioning Coach); Mike Imhoff, Joe Pendry (Assistnat Coaches); Morten Andersen, Rich Scharlo, Steve Maidlow, Derek Hughes, Bob Mouch, Matt Means, Kurt Schottneyheimer, Tyrone Willingham, Ron Marciel, Sherman Lewis, Ted Guthard (Assistant Coaches); Mike Zimmer, Jerry Eisner, Kam Hunter (Managers). Row 8 - Troy Hickman (Assistant Equipment Manager); Jon Phillips (Coordinator Of Equipment); Tom Magee, Mike Garvey (Equipment Assistants); Bob Ogar, Jim Pratt, Ryan Kling (Training Assistants); Clint Thompson (Coordinator of Training); Bill Hyncik, Kathy Heck, Gayle Robinson (Trainers); Julie Hoopes, Tasha Bolton, Bob Marley, Paul Adams, Helen Laskaris, Gail Agbromitis, Al Bellamy, Brent Monroe, Trevor Jacques, Tom Mackowiak, Holly Letsche, Doug Locy (Training Assistants); Arv Pettit, Bill Featherstone, Charlie Amori, Mike Raczkowski.

1981

First Row, Left To Right: Calvin Perkins, Ike Griffin, Johnny Lee Haynes, Samson Howard, Jeff Wiska, Morten Andersen, George Cooper, Coach Frank "Muddy" Waters, John Leister, Terry Bailey, Jack Kirkling, Steve Maidlow, Al Kimichik, Bryan Clark, Bryan Boak. Second Row: Joe Harewicz, James Burroughs, Derek Hughes, Ron Mitchem, Darrin McClelland, John Kouri, Rich Scharlo, Tom Piette, Mary Mantos, Chris Landry, Mike Muster, Mike Jones, Tom Morris, James Neely, Tony Ellis, Marcus Toney. Third Row: Chris Van Pelt, James Pippens, Carl Williams, Steve Blank, Milton Chaney, Ken Stockwell, Rick Kolb, Denis Lavelle, Jim Smith, Todd Scarlett, Terry Tanker, Joe Stevens, Smiley Creswell, Todd Langerveld, James Hodo, Darryl Troxell, Aaron Roberts. Fourth Row: Tony Woods, Carter Kamana, Scott Auer, Tom Robinson, Jeff Spaulding, Jim Bob Jamb, Mike Bossory, Rich Babich, Tim Cunningham, Erik Kehrer, Gregg Lauble, Ted Jones, Otis Grant, Leroy Shepard, Lonnie Young, Alex Clark, Kelly Quinn, Al Ross. Fifth Row: Ed Pobur, Terry Lewis, Chris Hayner, Bob Mouch, Phil Parker, Brett Schloser, Walt Schramm, Mike Hoffman, Howard McAdoo, Chris Bell, Lance Hawkins, Jeff Fehlan, Tom Allan, Randy Lark, Allen Moore, John Perles, Warren Lester, Brian Lewandowski, Ralf Mojsiejenko. Sixth Row: John Hurt, Frank Bobak, Mike Greenslait, Derek Bunch, Carl Banks, Daryl Turner, Nate Hannah, Kirk Jacob, Mark Kaczmarek, Bill Covey, Joel Waller, Darryl Dixon, Jim Morrissey, Jeff Boorsma, Joe Curran,

Dennis Childs, Kevin Molcak, Dan Askey, Pete Uzzalino, John Wojciechowski. Seventh Row: Jon Phillips (Equipment), Troy Hickman (Equipment), Mike Raczkowski (Equipment), J.D. Anderson (Equipment), Mark Zimmer (manager), Bill Featherstone(Manager), Arv Pettit (Head Manager), Dave Henry (Strength Coach), Dave Driscoll (Coach), Matt Means (Coach), Steve Schottel (Coach, Ted Guthard (Coach), Kurt Schottenheimer (Coach), Ty Willingham (Coach), Sherman Lewis (Coach), Mike Zimmer (Manager), Kam Hunter (Manager), Jerry Eisner (Manager), Mike Garvey (Equipment), Tom Magee (Equipment), Brian Dawson (equipment), Ed Rutherford (Administrative Assistant).

1982

First Row, Left To Right: Rich Schario, John Kouri, Denis Lavelle, Calvin Perkins, Darrin McClelland, Tom Piette, Co-Captain John Leister, Head Coach Frank (Muddy) Waters, Co-Captain Carl Banks, Marv Mantos, Jack Kirkling, Steve Maidlow, Smiley Creswell, Otis Grant, Joe Stevens. Second Row: Howard McAdoo, Terry Tanker, Walt Schramm, Jim Smith, Lance Hawkins, Chris Bell, Marcus Toney, Carl Williams, James Neely, Chris Van Pelt, Tony Ellis, James Hodo, Ted Jones, Lonnie Young. Third Row: Mark Beaudoin, Mike Nelson, Keith Gates, Aaron Roberts, Bob Mouch, Ken Stockwell, Gregg Lauble, Randy Lark, Rick Kolb, Allen Moore, Tony Woods, Tim Cunningham, Leroy Shepherd, Nate Hannah, Tom Allan. Fourth Row: Dave Yarema, Mark Fincher, Jeff Marron, John Hurt, John Jones, Tom Robinson, Jim Bob Lamb, Jeff Spaulding, Scott Auer, Chuck Stoltys, Wankeith Akin, Derek Bunch, Daryl Turner, Mike Balasis, Bob O'Neill, Darryl Dixon. Fifth Row: Butch Rolle, Bill George, George Walker, Ed Pobur, Joe Curran, John Perles, Mike Greenslait, Mike Hoffman, Brett Schlosser, Dennis Childs, Mark Ckaczmarek, Greg Thornton, Tony Andrews, Brian Phelps, Mike Riba, Frank Bobak. Sixth Row: Jim Morrissey, Pat Williams, Donavon Taylor, Preston Gray, Rich Zerkel, Al Ross, Bill Covey, Joel Waller, Warren Lester, John Oleksik, Rick Babich, Greg Bolte, Dan Askey, John Wojciechowski, Darryl Troxell, Kelly Quinn, Steve Bogdalek. Seventh Row: Tom Tyree, Clark Brown, Vandelynn Jenkins, Carter Kamana, Terry Lewis, Anthony Bell, Jim Hidge, Veno Belk, Paul Bobbitt, Jim Rinella, Phil Parker, Ralf Mojsiejenko, Mark Napolitan, Joe Harris, Jeff Boorsma, John Roth, Jim Lewis, Mitch Wachman, John McDowell. Eight Row: Trainer Kelly Porterfield, Trainer Cathy Tuttle, Trainer Al Bellamy, Trainer Dave Foster, Trainer Julie Hoopes, Equipment Manager Peter Kindel, Manager John Tobin, Manager Clay Spragg, Co-Head Manager Mike Zimmer, Co-Head Manager Bill Featherstone, Manager Kam Hunter, Manager Mark Zimmer, Equipment Manager Troy Hickman, Head Equipment Manager Jon Phillips, Equipment Manager Mike Raczkowski, Equipment Manager Brian Dawson, Equipment Manager John Pappas, Equipment Manager Steve Sonoga, Trainer Sue Welch. Ninth Row: Trainer Paula Sammarone, Trainer Bob Broxterman, Coach Dick Comar, Assistant Brian Wood, Coach Al Kimichik, Assistant Arv Pettit, Coach Dave Driscoll, Ed Rutherford, Steve Beckholt, Coach Ty Willingham, Coach Grag Croxton, Dave Henry, Coach Mike Vite, Coach Kurt Schottenheimer, Coach Sherm Lewis, Coach Ted Guthard, Coach Turf Kauffman, Coach Matt Means, Coach Steve Schottel, Trainer Cathy Dolan, Trainer Doug Locy, Head Trainer Clint Thompson, Trainer Kathy Keck, Trainer Sharon Lenon.

1983

First Row, Left To Right: Tom Allan, Scott Auer, Rick Babich, Captain Carl Banks, Derek Bunch, Tim Cunningham, Darryl Dixon, Head Coach George Perles, Nate Hannah, Carter Kamana, Randy Lark, Tom Robinson, Terry Tanker, Daryl Turner, Tony Woods. Second Row; Dennis Childs, Joe Curran, John Hurt, Wankeith Akin, Greg Bolte, Bill Covey, Rick Kolb, Jim Bob Lamb, Allen Moore, Brian Phelps, Leroy Shepherd, Chuck Soltys, Ken Stockwell, John Jones, Warren Lester, Terry Lewis. Third Row: Ralf Mojsiejenko, Jim Morrissey, Phil Parker, Ed Pobur, Kelly Quinn, Aaron Roberts, Grag Thornton, John Wojciechowski, Lonnie Young, Ron Roseboro, Mark Napolitan, Carl Butler, Larry Jackson, Tony Manley, John Perles, Veno Belk. Fourth Row: Anthony Bell, Paul Bobbitt, Steve Bogdalek, Clark Brown, Mark Fincher, Keith Gates, John Mc Dowell, Bob O'neill, Jim Rinella, Butch Rolle, Donavon Taylor, Thomas Tyree, Mitch Wachman, Dave Yarema, Steve Adams, Dean Altobelli, Mark Beaudoin. Fifth row: Shane Bullough, Kevin Butts, Brian Cochran, Mike Hotrum, Toby Fairbanks, Dave Houle, Pete Hrisko, Mark Ingram, Ken Jackson, Mike Kirkling, Tim Landrum, Bruce Lowe, Mike Messenger, Brian Mitchell, Tim Moore, Bobby Morse, Mark Nichols, Jeff Paterra, Kevin Bozeman. Sixth Row: Chip Bowman, Mike Balasis, Mike Silverstone, Glennard Smith, Curtis Johnson, Jimmy Popp, Tyrone Rhodes, Doug Rogers, Pat Shurmur, Rob Stradley, Jeff Stump, Dave Wolff, Adam Grudzien, Joel Waller, Jordan Beck, Mike Brogan, Randy Genord, Al Ross, Rodney Parker. Seventh Row: Manager Clay Spragg, Manager John Tobin, Andy Spragg, Tom Hauck, Dick Hastings, Tony Andrews, Pat Williams, Bill Papp, Dave Bergeron, Rob Hatherly, Jeff Wieland, John December, Jeff Boorsma, Mike Mulholland, Pat Perles, Dave Weatherspoon, Vernon Shaw, Neil Kazmierzak, Manager Al De Graw, Manager Mark Zimmer. Eighth Row: Mgr. Scott Bielat, Mgr. Dan Mesaros, Mgr. Scott Seelig, Mgr. Vince Thompson, Trainer Al Bellamy, Trainer Bob Broxterman, Trainer Julie Felix, Trainer Kathy Tuttle, Trainer Susie Harkema, Trainer Phil Horton, Trainer Bernie Lattmer, Trainer Jerry Murphy, Trainer Joe Rawls, Trainer Kevin Schroeder, Head Trainer Clint Thompson, Head Eqpt. Mgr. Bob Knickerbocker, Eqpt. Mgr. Troy Hickman, Eqpt. Mgr. Peter Kindal, Eqpt. Mgr. Kyle Nystrom, Eqpt. Mgr. Mike Raczkowski, Eqpt. Mgr. Eddie Rivet. Eqpt. Mgr. John Pappas, Strength Coach Dave Henry. Ninth Row; Coach Greg Croxton, Coach Rick Kazmarek, Coach Charlie Baggett, Coach Steve Beckholt, Coach Larry Bielat, Coach Steve Furness, Coach Ted Guthard, Coach Buck Nystrom, Coach Norm Parker, Coach Bill Rademacher, Coach Nick Saban, Admin. Asst. Ed Rutherford, Coach Chuck King, Coach Randy Zimmerman.

1984

First Row, Left To Right: Tom Allan, Lonnie Young, Derek Bunch, Terry Lewis, Captain Jim Morrissey, Head Coach George Perles, Ralf Mojsiejenko, Aaron Roberts, John Hurt, Greg Thornton, Carter Kamana. Second Row: Kelly Quinn, Steve Bogdalek, Mark Beaudoin, Rick Babich, Bill Covey, Allen Moore, Carl Butler, Mark Napolitan, Larry Jackson, Veno Belk, Anthony Bell, Joe Curran, Phil Parker. Third Row: Dave Yarema, Ron Roseboro, Butch Rolle, Jim Potter, John Perles, Dennis Childs, Trent Annicharico, Alan Akana, John Jones, Warren Lester, Tony Manley, Jordan Beck, Ron Rowe, Jim Rinella, John Wojciechowski. Fourth Row: Thomas Tyree, Pat Shurmur, Tyrone Rhodes, Bobby Morse, Keith Gates, Shane Bullough, Dave Wolff, Dean Altobelli, Paul Bobbitt, Clark Brown, Mark Fincher, Mark Ingram,

318

John McDowell, Pat Perles, Doug Rogers, Donavon Taylor, Mitch Wachman. Fifth Row: Rob Stradley, Jimmy Popp, Mark Nichols, Tim Landrum, Toby Fairbanks, Kevin Butts, Steve Adams, Mike Malasis, Mike Brogan, Adam Grudzien, Pat Williams, Kevin Bozeman, Brian Cochran, Dave Houle, Pete Hrisko, Tim Moore, Jeff Paterra, Glennard Smith, Jeff Stump. Sixth Row: Dempsey Norman, Dave Martin, Joe Lucente, Todd Krumm, Tom Holba, Maurice Chamberlain, Willie Bouyer, Mike Anderson, Tom Hauck, Brian Mitchell, Curt Johnson, Neil Kazmierczak, Brandon Born, John Budde, Keith Fisher, Ken Hall, Dave Kiel, Kurt Larson, Tony Mandarich, Bobby McAllister, Jason Ridgeway. Seventh Row: Roger Mojsiejenko, Paul Martinelli, Jerry Langley, Chris Caudell, Craig Johnson, Bob Wasczenski, Vince Tata, Tom Scholle, Mike Sargent, Bernard Wilson, Greg Smith, Craig Walker, Lorenzo White, John Wilson, Mike Wilson, Scott Bowen, Rich Gicewicz, Craig Kulaszewski, Jeff Marron. Eight Row: Bob Knickerbocker, Coordinator Of Equipment; Troy Hickman, Equpt. Mgr.; John Pappas, Equpt Mgr.; Kyle Nystrom, Equpt. Mgr. Paul Edwards, Eqpt. , Craig Stockwell, Equpt. Mgr.; Eddie Rivet, Eqpt. Mgr.; Dan Mesaros, Mgr.; Scott Bielat, Mgr.; Tim Brogan; Steve Stagg; Royal Alexander; Kevin Foster; Gary Voss; Ken Toth; Brad Harrison; Dave Pruder, Mgr.; Jim Tobin, Mgr.; Jim Farrell. Mgr.; Scott Seelig, Mgr.; Al De Graw, Mgr.; Clay Spragg, Mgr. Ninth Row: Dr. Herb Ross, Kelly Porterfield, Trainer; Julie Felix, Trainer; Sally Nogle, Trainer; Joe Clark, Trainer; Paul Bragenzer, Trainer; Tim Roe, Trainer; Phil Horton, Trainer; Kathy Tuttle, Trainer; David Wilson, Trainer; Clint Thompson, Coordinator Of Training; Dave Henry, Strength Coach. Tenth Row: Coach Buck Nystrom, Coach Norm Parker, Coach Larry Bielat, Coach Rick Kaczmarek, Coach Greg Croxton, Coach Ted Guthard, Coach Steve Furness, Coach Randy Zimmerman, Coach Bill Rademacher, Coach Charlie Baggett, Coach Steve Beckholt, Coach Dave Kaple, Coach Nick Saban, Adm. Asst. Ed Rutherford, Vol. Asst. Brian Wood.

1985

FIRST ROW: Jim Potter, John Jones, Mark Beaudoin, Steve Bogdalek, Veno Belk, Joe Curran, Co-captain Anthony Bell, Head Coach George Perles, Phil Parker, Kelly Quinn, Butch Rolle, Jim Rinella, Co-captain John Wojciechowski, Warren Lester, Alan Akana. SECOND ROW: Bobby Morse, Shane Bullough, Dean Altobelli, Pat Williams, Ken Toth, Paul Bobbitt, Jordan Beck, Mark Fincher, John McDowell, Donavon Taylor, Keith Gates, Mitch Wachman, Dave Yarema, Mike Brogan, Mark Ingram, Tyrone Rhodes, Mike Balasis, Kevin Bozeman. THIRD ROW: Tim Moore, Brian Mitchell, Ron Rowe, Toby Fairbanks, Pete Hrisko, Tom Hauck, Brian Cochran, Kevin Butts, Steve Adams, Dave Wolff, Chris Caudell, Joe Bergin, Doug Rogers, Dave Houle, Neil Kazmierczak, Greg Montgomery, Mark Nichols. FOURTH ROW: Willie Bouyer, Brandon Born, Royal Alexander, Lorenzo White, Rob Stradley, Pat Shurmur, Jeff Paterra, Jimmy Popp, Glennard Smith, Jeff Stump, Curt Johnson, Dempsey Norman, Mike Sargent, Todd Krumm, Keith Fisher, Greg Smith, Bob Wasczenski, Mike Anderson, John Budde. FIFTH ROW: John Wilson, Mark Walker, Vince Tata, Roger Mojsiejenko, Tony Mandarich, Kurt Larson, Craig Johnson, Ken Hall, Tim Brogan, Maurice Chamberlain, Kevin Foster, Rich Gicewicz, Tom Holba, Dave Kiel, Joe Lucente, Dave Martin, Bobby McAllister, Jason Ridgeway, Gary Voss, Bernard Wilson. SIXTH ROW: Harlon Barnett, Travis Davis, Blake Ezor, John Keenoy, Rob Love, Chuck McSwigan, John Miller, James Moore, Kevin O'Keefe, Jeff Palmer, Freddie

Parker, Greg Pryjomski, Joe Pugh, Tim Ridinger, Andre Rison, Dave Simpson, Jim Szyman ski, Matt Vanderbeek, Maurice Ware, Chris Willertz. SEVENTH ROW: Jeremy Langley, Melvin Richendollar, Al Mc Clendan, Linwood Wright, Scott Everett, Otis Crosby, Lionel White, Chet Grzibowski, Greg Randall, Ron Ciszek, Pat Landry, Eric Wooten, Bruce Smith, David Giltner, Steve Montgomery, James Dickinson, Lynn Rogien, Sean Clouse, Conrad Calvano, Jim Sherocci, Tom Landreth. EIGHT ROW: Bob Knickerbocker, Co-ordinator of Equipment; Troy Hickman, Asst. Coordinator of Equipment; Craig Stockwell, Eqpt. Mgr.; Joe Rivet, Eqpt. Mgr.; Jim Parker, Eqpt. Mgr.; Paul Edwards, Eqpt. Mgr.; Kyle Nystrom, Eqpt. Mgr.; Scott Bielat, Head Mgr.; Chris Haas, Mgr.; Dave Pruder, Mgr.; Mary Mark, Trainer; Tom Moyer, Trainer; Mike Smela, Trainer; Rob Macek, Trainer; Mike Johnson, Trainer; Rick Tiller, Trainer; Cathy Dolan, Trainer; Julie Felix, Trainer; Pat Beckman, Trainer; Sally Nogle, Asst. Trainer; Dave Carrier, Asst. Trainer; Jeff Monroe, Coordinator of Training; James Farrell, Mgr.; Scott Seelig, Mgr., All DeGraw, Mgr.; Dave Henry, Strength Coach. NINTH ROW: Brian Wood, Statistician; Ed Rutherford, Adm. Asst.; Coach Norm Parker, Coach Buck Nystrom, Coach Nick Saban, Coach Steve Beckholt, Coach Bill Rademacher, Coach Larry Bielat, Coach Charlie Baggett, Coach Dave Kaple, Coach Clark Brown, Coach Ted Guthard, Coach Steve Furness, Coach Randy Zimmerman, Coach Ed Warriner, Coach Rick Browning.

1986

First Row: Andre Rison, Jerome Perrin, Kurt Larson, Dan Enos, Tom Holba, John Langeloh, Chris Caudell, Head Coach George Perles, Bobby Mc Allister, Jeff Paterra, Scott Everett, Mark Ingram, Brian Smolinski, Dean Altobelli, Dave Yarema. Second Row: Mike Iaquaniello, John Harris, Pete Hrisko, Willie Bouyer, Glen Mc Caldless, Ron Rowe, Odis Crosby, Fred Wilson, Tony Mitchell, Bobby Morse, Rob Stradley, Greg Montgomery, Troy Woody, Troy Carlson, Lenier Payton, Ken Wandzel. Third Row: Tyrone Rhodes, Lance Lamm, Rob Roy, Craig Johnson, John Kiple, John Miller, Tom Hauck, Mike Narduzzi, Maurice Chamberlain, Brian Jones, James Moore, Lorenzo White, Todd Krumm, Harlon Barnett, Mike Balasis, Monte Byers, Freddie Parker, Joe Pugh. Fourth Row: Paul Bobbitt, Tim Ridinger, Shane Bullough, Tim Moore, Kenny Kurtz, John Miller, Joe Bergin, Chuck McSwigan, Percy Snow, Bill Grace, Mike Sargent, Tim Brogan, Mike Gonzalez, Carlos Jenkins, Matt Bennett, David Sage, Mark Hill, John Rasico. Fifth Row: Ken Hall, Jason Ridgeway, Mike Anderson, Tim Currie, Dave Wolff, Dixon Edwards, Dave Martin, Kevin O'Keefe, Pat Shurmur, Vince Tata, Cliff Confer, Chet Grzibowski, Bob Kula, Chris Soehnlen, Tom Landreth, Mel Richendollar, Matt Vanderbeek, Boyd Meyers, Kendall Kowalski. Sixth Row: Dave Simpson, Jeff Cooper, Brian Mitchell, Doug Rogers, Mark Fincher, Jerry Helstowski, Dave Houle, Travis Davis, Dave Kiel, Eric Moten, Jim Cherocci, Tony Mandarich, Steve Montgomery, Bernard Wilson, Chris Willertz, Gary Voss, Lynn Rogien, John Keenoy. Seventh Row: Sean Clouse, Bob Fata, Mark Nichols, Bruce Smith, Rob Love, Doug Grzibowski, Brandon Born, Rich Gicewicz, Pat Landry, John Budde, Jeff Jones, Duane Young, Jim Dickinson, Jim Szymanski, Jeff Palmer, Matt Keller, Greg Soehnlen, Bob Martz, Greg Pryjomski. Eighth Row: Bob Knickerbocker, Troy Hickman, Joe Rivet, Craig Stockwell, Kyle Nystrom, Paul Edwards, Jimmy Parker, Mike Johnson, Jeff Monroe, Sally Nogle, Ron Gantner, David Pruder, Chris Haas, Erik Medina, Joe Shurmur, Scott Bielat, Dave Henry. Ninth Row: Gary Raff, Buck

Nystrom, Nick Saban, Morris Watts, Steve Beckholt, Greg Colby, Steve Furness, Charlie Baggett, Larry Bielat, Ed Rutherford, Bill Rademacher, Jeff Marron, Dave McLaughlin, Ed Warriner.

1987

First Row, Left To Right: Chris O'Neil, Andre Rison, Jerome Perrin, Adam Goldstein, Kurt Larson, Dan Enos, Kendall Dowalski, Tom Holba, Head Coach George Perles, Derrick Reed, Steve Sinclair, Mario Bongiorni, Bobby McAllister, Mike Iaquaniello, John Langeloh, David Singleton. Second Row: Darrin Eaton, Brian Smolinski, Jerry Todd, Chuck Sanders, Jeff Jacobs, Andre Harris, Tom Freeman, John Aerni, Willie Bouyer, Stacy Madden, Corey Pryor, Freddie Wilson, Tony Mitchell, Steve Piccanno, Scott Selzer, Rob Stradley, Bill Hare. Third Row: Greg Montgomery, Troy Woody, Lenier Payton, Ventson Donelson, Blake Ezor, Rob Roy, Craig Johnson, Cal Miller, Steve Black, Maurice Chamberlain, Darryl Burnett, Brian Jones, James Moore, Lorenzo White, Todd Krumm, Harlon Barnett, Freddie Parker. Fourth Row: Joe Pugh, John Kiple, Keith Boggus, Tim Ridinger, Chuck Bullough, Tim Moore, John Miller, Joe Bergin, John Dowels, Percy Snow, Mike Sargent, Tim Brogan, Lance Hostetler, Carlos Jenkins, David Sandler, Matt Keller, Chris Scott, Mark Hill, Chris Nickson. Fifth Row: Tony Briningstoll, John Skibo, Jason Ridgeway, Kerry Keyton, Chris Piwowarcyzk, Dixon Edwards, Greg Pryjomski, Dave Martin, Mike Jubenville, Kevin O'keefe, Pat Shurmur, Vince Tata, Cliff Confer, Chet Grzibowski, Bob Kula, Tom Landreth, Chris Soehnlen, Mike Anderson, Matt Vanderbeek, Boy Meyers. Sixth Row: Sean Clouse, Jeff Palmer, Eric Schulte, Dave Simpson, Jim Johnson, Duane Young, Kevin Robbins, John Repasky, Mike Staisil, Jerry Helstowski, Dave Houle, Travis Davis, Jeff Wittig, Dave Kiel, Brandon Born, Eric Moten, Tony Mandarich, Mike Rose, Doug Grzibowski, Steve Montgomery, Chris Willertz. Seventh Row: Bernard Wilson, Bob Fata, Mark Nichols, Bruce Smith, Rob Love, Clint Cerny, Rich Gicewicz, Pat Landreth, John Budde, Charles Kelly, Josh Butland, Jeff Case, Carlos Marino, Jim Dickinson, Jim Szymanski, Jeff Jones, Greg Soehnlen, Steve Voss, Bill Johnson, Flint Fulton, Ken Wandzel. Eighth Row: Bob Knickerbocker, Troy Hickman, Craig Stockwell, Kyle Nystrom Jim Parker, Mike Shandrick, Scott Maisel, Scott Bielat, Brad Alward, Joe Shurmur, Ron Gantner, Tory Lindlay, John Kible, Jeff Marmelstein, John Slade, Brian Knott, Kelly Depew, Mike Lawton, Leslie Grange, Dave Webster, Dave Fluker, Tom Mackowiak, Sally Nogle, Jeff Monroe, Dr. Ross, Dave Henry. Ninth Row: Gary Raff, Nick Saban, Morris Watts, Steve Beckholt, Greg Colby, Steve Furness, Pat Morris, Charlie Baggett, Larry Bielat, Ed Rutherford, Bill Rademacher, Norm Parker, Jeff Marron, Dave McLaughlin, Phil Parker, Dean Altobelli.

1988

FRONT ROW: Andre Rison, Brian Gilbert, Adam Goldsteirn, Jerome Perrin, Kurt Larson, Andy Kalakailo, Dan Enos, Head Coach George Perles, Courtney Hawkins, Kendall Kowalski, Derrick Reed, Steve Sinclair, Mario Bongiorni, Bobby McAllister, Mike Iaquaniello, Jack Gianpalmi. SECOND ROW: John Langeloh, Darrin Eaton, Brian Smolinski, Jerry Todd, Chuck Sanders, Tim Bryan, Tom Pasko, Randy Vanderbush, John Aerni, Andre Harris, Wlllie Bouyer, John Gieselman, Corey Pryor, Freddie Wilson, Brad Wylie. Tony Mitchell, Scott Selzer and BIll Hare. THIRD ROW: Tony Rollin, Troy Woody, Alan Haller, Lenier Peyton, Darrel Burnett, Ventson Donelson, Elvin Brown, Blake Ezor, Cory Williams, Rob Roy,

Steve Cowan, Craig Johnson, Mark Pickett, Duane Young, Hyland Hickson, Steve Black, Greg Halich, Brian Jones and James Moore. FOURTH ROW: Paul Knoerr, Tim Werkema, Tico Duckett, Thomas Sterling, Harlon Barnett, Jeff Iseler, George Alvarado, Freddie Parker, John Kiple, Paul Fruge, Mark McFarland, Keith Boggus, Tim Ridinger, Chuck Bullough, Mark Lacy, Ralph Apa, Steve Montgomery, John Miller, Willie Hill, Clint Cerny, John Dowels. FIFTH ROW: Percy Snow, Todd Murray, Tony Aguilo, Lance Hostetler, Carlos Jenkins, Chris Scott, Matt Keller, Mark Shapiro, Mike Maddis, Jon Skibo, Tony Briningstool, Kerry Keyton, Jason Ridgeway, Brian Hill, Chris Piwowarczyk, Rod Cole, Dixon Edwards, Dave Martin, Mike Jubenville, Greg Soehnlen, Dave St. Pierre. SIXTH ROW: Jeff Wittig, Brent Clark, Vince Tata, Ross Ivey, Cliff Confer, Pat Gillespie, Bob Kula, Chris Soehnlen, Thomas Landreth, Andy Roubos, Mike Anderson, Matt Vanderbeek, Boyd Meyers, Toby Heaton, Dave Simpson, Jim Johnson, Bob Henry, Kevin Robbins, Mitch Michura, Alex Lichacz, Mike Staisil. SEVENTH ROW: Bob Stoolmaker, Jeff Pearson, Bill Reese, Travis Davis, Geoffrey Cain, Matt Amacker, Peter Partchenko, Jon Campbell, Eric Moten, Tony Mandarich, Todd Grabowski, Bernard Wilson, Bob Fata, Jeff Graham, Rob Love, Mitch Lyons, Eric Rice, Rich Gicewicz, Steve Voss, John Budde and Josh Butland. EIGHTH ROW: Equip. Mgr. Bob Knickerbocker, Asst. Equip. Coordinator Troy Hickman, Student Equip. Mgrs. Jim Parker, Craig Stockwell, Dave Pruder, Jack Vainisi, and Mark Melkonian, Jeff Case, Carlos Marino, Jim Szymanski, Jeff Jones, Mike Edwards, Eric White, Kurt Prins, Bill Johnson, Roosevelt Wagner, Ernest Steward, Stamati Stathopoulous, Student Mngrs. Jeff Penix, Sean Lockhart, Bradley Alward, Erik Medina and Joe Shurmur, Student Athletic Trainer Jane Penet, Coordinator of Training Jeff Monroe and Strength Conditioning Coach Dave Henry. BACK ROW: Student Athletic Trainers Tory Lidley, Ed Lochre, Kim Benson, Vikki Stahl, and Mark Haynes, Assistant Coaches (standing) Greg Pscodna, Pat Shurmur, Keith Gilmore, Mike Denbrock, Gary VanDam, Gary Raff, Morris Watts, Steve Beckholt, Ed Rutherford, Steve Furness, Pat Morris, Anthony Folino, Norm Parker, Charlie Baggett, Bill Rademacher, and Larry Bielat, Student Athletic Trainers Sherrie Rice, Karen Thompson, Mike Lawton, Leslie Grange, Asst. Trainer Tom Machowiak, Asst. Trainer Dave Carrier and Dr. Doug McKeag. Not pictured: Mike Vanderjagt, Chris Willertz.

1989

First Row: Craig Thomas, Brian Gilbert, Corey Keyes, Kevin Collins, James Bradley, Dan Enos, Andy Kalakailo, Head Coach George Perles, Courtney Hawkins, Kendall Kowalski, Jody Dickerson, Jason Reinbold, Mario Bongiorni, Myron Bell, Kendall Van Horne, Matt Eyde, Ted Martin, John Langeloh. Second Row: Corey Williams, Darrin Eaton, Brian Smolinski, Jerry Todd, John Gieselman, Mike Shepard, Tim Bryan, Bob Guiney, Randy Vanderbush, Jim Miller, Cooper Green, Mike Vanderjagt, Corey Pryer, Joe DeBrincat, Freddie Wilson, Mark Mac Farland, Todd Murray, Jim Hepler. Third Row: Scott Selzer, Adam Abaron, Jeff Vogel, Tony Rollin, Alan Haller, Eddie Brown, Darryl Burnett, Ventson Donelson, Blake Ezor, Lance Harding, Rob Roy, Tom Bodell, Ty Hallock, Duane Young, Chad Daggy, Hyland Hickson, Steve Black, Steve Cowan, Brian Jones. Fourth Row: Brian Vooletich, James Rollins, Tico Duckett, La Shon Miller, Harlon Barnett, Todd Murray, Steve Wasylk,

John Kiple, Mike Krumm, Sean Louwers, Tim Riddinger, Chuck Bullough, Mark Lacy, Steve Montgomery, Mike Iaquaniello, Willie Hill, Chris Wease, Tim Currie, Percy Snow. Fifth Row: John McCougall, Scott Pitts, Roosevelt Wagner, Carlos Jenkins, Matt Keller, Chris Scott, Mike Maddie, Mark Shapiro, Tony Bringingstool, Rich Glover, Kerry Keyton, Chris Piwowarczyk, Brian Hill, Dixon Edwards, Mike Jubenville, George Haidamous, Brent Clark, Jeff Wittig, Brett Lorius. Sixth Row: Cliff Confer, Bob Kula, Scott LaLain, Chris Soehnlen, Eric Kelly, Matt Vanderbeek, Toby Heaton, Jeff Pearson, Jim Johnson, Bob Henry, Tom Spoelhof, Jeff Graham, Carrie Mitchell, Peter Partchenko, Bill Reese, Travis Davis, Matt Amacker, Eric Moten, Jon Campbell, Todd Grabowski. Seventh Row: Brice Adams, Bob Fata, Rob Fredrickson, John MacNeill, Mitch Lyons, Mike Oswald, John Dignan, Ed O'Bradovich, Josh Butland, Carlos Marino, Jim Szymanski, Jeff Jones, Mike Edwards, Eric White, Kurt Prins, Bill Johnson, Bobby Wilson, Ernest Steward, Chris Willertz, Bill Stoyanovich. Eighth Row: Equpment Managers: Bob Knickerbocker, Troy Hickman, Mark Melkonian, Jack Vainisi, Jim Parker, Dave Bourrie, Vince Nystrom; Athletic Trainers: Sally Nogle, Jeff Monroe, Tom Mackowiak, Dave Carrier, Ed Lochre, Mary Stanbra, Mike Post, Alice Barron, Ronit Hoffman, Jill Williamson, Paul Plummer, Jeff Gebhart, Brian Downie, Stephanie Anderson, Dave Yip; Team Physicians: Dr. Herb Ross, Dr. David Hough, Dr. Douglas McKeag, Dr. Dave Petron; Strength And Conditioning Coach David Henry. Ninth Row: Student Manages: Bayley Davis, Scott Klott, Gary Van Dam, Steve Beckholt, Charlie Baggett, Greg Pscodna, Larry Bielat, Mike Denbrock, Steve Furness, Pat Morris, Jim Nudera, Bill Rademacher, Chris Besanceney, Brad Alward, Joe Shurmur.

1990

First Row: Brian Howard, Kendall Van Horne, Corey Keyes, Mill Coleman, Jim Hepler, James Bradley, Dan Enos, Andy Kalakailo, Head Coach George Perles, Courtney Hawkins, Dave Nemer, Jody Dickerson, Mario Bongiorni, Chad McCarney, Eddie Brown, Jim DelVerne, Darrin Eaton. Second Row: Brian Smolinski, Sean Louwers, John Gieselman, Eric Hamilton, Tim Bryan, Bob Guiney, Randy Vanderbush, Jim Miller, Mark MacFarland, Chris Wease, Corey Pryor, Cortez Paige, Freddie Wilson, Jason Henry, Todd Murray, Steve Helfrich, Scott Seltzer, Tony Rollin, Alan Haller. Third Row: Opu Amachree, Myron Bell, Ed Davidson, Craig Thomas, Ricardo Jackson, Curtis Daniel, Rob Roy, Ty Hallock, Todd Drusback, John Shaply, Duane Young, Hyland Hickson, Jeff Isler, Steve Cowan, Steve Black, Brian Jones, T.J. Reterstroff, Brian Vooletich, James Rollins, Marcell Richardson. Fourth Row: Tico Duckett, Tim Hughes, Shannon Laynes, Steve Wasylk, Dale Feldpausch, Kevin Stansbery, Jay Greene, Eric Williams, Tom Bodell, Chuck Bullough, Mark Lacy, LaShon Miller, Tony Briningstool, Mike Iaquaniello, Sebastian Small, Willie Hill, John Campbell, Lance Harding. Fifth Row: Corey Baker, Karl Taylor, John Burke, Roosevelt Wagner, Carlos Jenkins, Matt Keller, Chris Scott, Mike Maddie, Ross Ivie, Rich Glover, Kerry Keyton, Chris Piwowarczyk, Scott Brown, Dixon Edwards, Robert Bielecki, Zeb Jones, Kerry Mitchell, Brice Abrams, Jeff Wittig. Sixth Row: Brett Lorius, Cliff Confer, Charles Cainstraight, Shane Hannah, Jason Eslinger, Paul Yarbrough, Dave Magnotta, Colin Cronin, Toby Heaton, Jeff Pearson, James Johnson, Bob Henry, Tom Spoelhof, Jeff Graham, Pete Partchenko, Bill Reese, Aaron Jackson, Matt Amacker, John Saxton. Seventh Row: Eric Moten, Jason Kamp, Brian DeMarco, Todd

Grabowski, Jerel McPherson, George Haidamous, Brian Winters, Rob Fredrickson, John McNeill, Mitch Lyons, Mark Birchmeier, John Dignan, Josh Butland, Ed O'Bradovich, Carlos Marino, Scott Lalain, Kevin Boron, David Riker, Jeff Jones. Eighth Row: Troy Hickman, Vince Nystrom, Scott Klott, Mark Melkonian, Chuck Hart, Jeff Gebhart, Ronita Hoffman, Mary Stanbra, Mike Strauss, Mike Edwards, Eric White, Kurt Prins, Corey Harris, Bill Johnson, Bobby Wilson, Ernest Steward, Mike Oswald, Bill Stoyanovich, Paul Plummer, Melissa Wuester, Cheri Swarthout, Heidi Stettler, Mary Davis, Chris Besanceney, Greg Haas, Baley Davis. Ninth Row: Dave Bourrie, Jack Vainisi, Pete Forsythe, Bob Knickerbocker, Walt Bazylewicz, Norm Parker, Gary Van Dam, Larry Williams, Morris Watts, Charlie Baggett, Pat Shurmur, Pat Morris, Steve Furness, Larry Bielat, Kip Wadell, Jim Nudera, Bill Rademacher, Billy Davis, Larry Smith, Gary Raff, Dino Folino, Tom Mackowiak, Sally Nogel, Jeff Monroe, Dr. Douglas McKeag, Dave Henry.

1991

First Row: Brian Vooletich, Ed O'Bradovich, John MacNeill, Bob Henry, Tony Briningstool, Josh Butland, Chuck Bullough, Bill Johnson, Head Coach George Perles, Jim Johnson, Courtney Hawkins, Alan Haller, Darrin Eaton, Andy Kalakailo, Chris Piwowarczyk, Tico Duckett, Roosevelt Wagner. Second Row: Matt Amacker, Tim Bryan, John Dignan, Toby Heaton, Willie Hill, Bret Johnson, Mitch Lyons, Mark MacFarland, Jim Miller, Kerry Mitchell, Todd Murray, Rob Fredrickson, Kurt Prins, William Reese, Tony Rollin, Ernest Steward, Todd Grabowski, Steve Wasylk, Jeff Graham. Third Row: Brice Abrams, Myron Bell, Mill Coleman, Peter Partchenko, Mike Maddie, Randy Vanderbush, Ty Hallock, Jon Gieselman, Sebastian Small, Brian DeMarco, Eric White, Corey Baker, Mark Birchmeier, Tom Bodell, Kevin Boron, Shane Hannah, Brian Howard, Aaron Jackson, Zeb Jones. Fourth Row: Ron Armstrong, Brett Lorius, Jason Eslinger, Stan Callender, Matt Christensen, Britton Crates, Colin Cronin, Curtis Daniel, Bill Stoyanovich, Bob Denton, Mike Edwards, Greg Duggins, Duane Goulbourne, Orion Hayes, Corey Keyes, Scott LaLain, Damian Manson, Frank Mobley, Muhsin Muhammad. Fifth Row: Greg Anderson, Brian Winters, Scott Brown, Jim DelVerne, Richard Glover, Jay Greene, Scott Greene, Juan Hammonds, Lance Harding, Corey Harris, Jim Hepler, Ross Ivey, Mark Lacy, David Magnotta, Napolion Outlaw, Bob Organ, Kevin Stansbery, Craig Thomas, Howard Triplett, Dave Aben, Opu Amachree. Sixth Row: Dennis Branson, Chris Bridgeman, Chuck Canestraight, Mike Cowen, Anthony Folino, Eric Hamilton, Ricardo Jackson, Kyle Kauffman, Jeff LaFave, Rob Lalain, Demetrice Martin, Dave Organek, Cortaz Paige, Robert Ribby, Marcel Richardson, T.J. Reterstroff, Steve Saxton, Mike Vorkapich, Bob Guiney, Ron Stokes, Ryan Martin. Seventh Row: Kendall Van Horne, Robert McBride, LaShon Miller, Eric Williams, Tai Apisa, Pat Brown, Craig Butler, Dan Cantrell, Mike Cowan, Hassen Dagher, Scott Drever, Al Fernandez, Bill Goodell, Geoff Gutowski, Brian Hanton, Rob Harden, Matt Heil, Chip James, Marqwn Williams, John Revels, Bret Karawsek. Eighth Row: Mark Melkonian, Jack Vainisi, Jay Nordstrom, Thom Watchorn, Dave Bourri, Vince Nystrom, Tony Popovski, Jason Scott, Mark Morgan, Roger Vell, Dan Terryberry, Brian Tenshaw, Mike Sislo, Eben Smith, Peter Forsythe, Brian Ransom, Kevin Lartigue, Greg Haas, Scott Klott, Chris Besanceney. Ninth Row: Bob Knickerbocker, Troy Hickman, Pete Morano, Margaret Bothe, Christine Roggenbuck, Lori Moore, Joe

Moulden, Scott Yurcisin, Jennifer Nitz, Jami Stanton, Mike Morand, Dave Schlaff, Chuck Hart, Dave Kindy, Sally Nogle, Dave Carrier, Tom Mackowiak, Jeff Monroe, Dr. Herbert Ross, Dr. David Hough, Dr. Douglas McKeag. Tenth Row: Dan Enos, Dan O'Brien, Tim Johns, Walt Bazylewicz, Norm Parker, Bobby Williams, Pat Shurmur, Ed Zaunbrecher, Larry Bielat, Charlie Baggett, Pat Morris, Dino Folino, Bill Rademacher, Kip Waddell, Billy Davis, Gary Raff, Gary Van Dam, Dave Henry.

1992

First Row: Ernest Steward, Jeff Graham, Ty Hallock, Todd Grabowski, Matt Amacker, Tony Rollin, Jim Miller, Mitch Lyons, Toby Heaton, Coach George Perles, Tico Duckett, William Reese, Mike Edwards, Todd Murray, Mark McFarland, Jim DelVerne, Tim Bryan, John Gieselman, Kurt Prins. Second Row: Mill Coleman, Matt Christensen, Stan Callender, Brian Winters, Craig Thomas, Peter Partchenko, Brian Howard, Juan Hammonds, John Dignan, Brice Abrams, Myron Bell, Robert Fredrickson, Brett Johnson, Brett Lorius, Kerry Mitchell, Steve Wasylk, Sebastian Small, Corey Harris, Bill Stoyanovich, Richard Glover. Third Row: Greg Anderson, Hickey Thompson, Dale Person, Pat Humphrey, Monty Brown, Eric Williams, Bob Organ, Damian Manson, Zeb Jones, Aaron Jackson, Shane Hannah, Jay Green, Jason Eslinger, Brian DeMarco, Colin Cronin, Corey Baker, Ross Ivey, Lance Harding, Kevin Boron, Mark Birchmeier. Fourth Row: Jim Hepler, Jamaal Crawford, Kendrick Cameron, Matt Beard, Steve Barnhill, Lester Anderson, Opuene Amachree, Yakini Allen, Howard Triplett, Napolean Outlaw, Muhsin Muhammad, Frank Mobley, Robert Mc Bride, Demetrice Martin, Orion Hayes, Scott Greene, Duane Goulbourne, Bob Denton, Brittan Crates, Luke Bencie, Ron Armstrong. Fifth Row: Anthony Folino, Todd Drusback, Dan Cantrell, Craig Butler, Chris Bridgeman, Chris Smith, Joel Sinclair, Delrico Simons, Robert Shurelds, Chris Salani, Todd Pearson, Brett Organe, Brian Mosallam, Gary Kuhn, Dave Kehr, Steve Holman, Terry Harvey, Todd Feeney, Kevin Stansberry. Sixth Row: Brian Baker, Mike Vorkapich, Tony Tunney, Dan Terryberry, Brian Tenshaw, Mike Sislo, Jeff Schram, Robert Ribby, John Revels, Tony Popovski, Vince Mastrometteo, Brian Kelley, Kyle Kauffman, Vince Gentile, Rob Harden, Brian Hanton, Eric Hamilton, Reggie Green, Ricardo Jackson, Robert Gardner. Seventh Row: James Wilson, Mike Whelan, Matt Waldis, Marlando Wade, Edwin Victory, Thurman Tucker, David Reese, Jason Moses, Willy Morgan, Robert McCrea, Aaron Lungaard, Jchaun Johnson, Micah Jennings, Greg Horvath, Pete Drzal, Robert Dozer, Mike Baser, Phil Baron. Eighth Row: Bob Knickerbocker, Troy Hickman, Marc Melkonian, Dave Bourri, Steve Culp, Pete Forsythe, Troy Henning, Chris Kingsley, Kevin Lartigue, Vince Nystrom, Brian Ransom, Jeff Sewick, Tom Watchorn, Dr. Steve Niergarth, Dr. Doug McKeag, Dr. Herb Ross. Ninth Row: Dave Carrier, Tom Mackowiak, Holly Kasavana, Toby Blosser, Lissa Cantu, Brian Farr, Kim Hurst, Dave Kindy, Stephen Kramer, Nicole Locke, Tricia Mazetti, Jill Moore, Art Samora, John Singerling, Carrie Smith. Tenth Row: Larry Ballew, Dan Enos, Gary VanDam, Bill Rademacher, Norm Parker, Morris Watts, Bobby Williams, Dino Folino, Charlie Baggett, Kip Waddell, Pat Morris, Ed Zaunbrecher, Pat Shurmur, David Henry, Walt Bazylewicz, Tim Johns.

1993

First Row: Mark Birchmeier, Bill Stoyanovich, Brian DeMarco, Brett Lorius, Bob Denton, Brice Abrams,

Mill Coleman, Craig Thomas, Jim Miller, Head Coach George Perles, Rob Fredrickson, Steve Wasylk, Matt Christensen, Juan Hammonds, Aaron Jackson, Rich Glover, Myron Bell, Stan Callender, Damian Manson. Second Row: Brian Howard, Scott Greene, Hickey Thompson, Duane Goulbourne, Steve Holman, Bob Organ, Monty Brown, Muhsin Muhammad, Luke Bencie, Robert Shurelds, Demetrice Martin, John Dignan, Dale Person, Robert McBride, Greg Anderson, Sebastian Small, Zeb Jones, Chris Salani, Yakini Allen. Third Row: Howard Triplett, Kendrick Cameron, Jamaal Crawford, Orion Hayes, Jay Greene, Chris Bridgeman, Matt Beard, Dave Kehr, Napoleon Outlaw, Aldi Henry, Pete Drzal, Kerry Mitchell, Brian Mosallam, Terry Harvey, Ricardo Jackson, Corey Harris, Corey Baker, Tony Popovski, Todd Pearson. Fourth Row: Robert Dozier, Britton Crates, Todd Feeney, Brett Organek, Joel Sinclair, Delrico Simons, Dan Cantrell, Craig Butler, Chris Smith, Kevin Stansbery, Anthony Folino, Robert Gardner, Brian Hanton, Rob Harden, Micah Jennings, Mike Vorkapich, Tony Tunney, Robert Ribby, Gary Kuhn, Steve Barnhill. Fifth Row: Shon Hart, Joshua Freeman, Dave Mudge, Brad Costello, Mitch McKinney, Ike Reese, Don Walker, Scott Shaw, Trey Sartin, Reggie Garnett, Tyrone Garland, Flozell Adams, Mark Renaud, Sheldon Thomas, Antwain Patrick, Brian Echols, Dan Hackenbracht, Cedric Saffold, Derrick Mason. Sixth Row: Marlando Wade, Vince Mastrometteo, Mike Sislo, Willy Morgan, Jason Moses, Mike Whelan, Actavis Long, Nigea Carter, Jason Glick, Todd Schultz, Damien Hiram, Marvin Wright, Greg Horvath, Tom Baird, Jason Krueger, Raleigh Pioch, Greg Olsen, Alim Butler, Floyd Bell. Seventh Row: Bob Knickerbocker, Troy Hickman, Brina Ransom, Kevin Lartigue, Dave Bourri, Thom Watchorn, Mike Cabana, Brandon Catto, Lee Beebe, Curtis Drake, Stan Hannah, Jonathan Thompson, Franklin Weaver, Troy Henning, Chris Kingsley, Steve Culp, Brian Carnaghi, Nick Pettit, Ryan Ledlow. Eighth Row: Doug McKeag, David Hough, Herb Ross, Toby Blosser, Karen Leonard, Bethany Ward, Norm Schielf, Amy Worthing, Fred Burnett, Terry Huntley, Arthur Samora, Pat Hoxsey, Joe Moulden, Roxanne Dahl, Tom Mackowiak, Holly Kasavana, Dave Carrier, Sally Nogle, Jeff Monroe, Chris Kovacs, Dean Olsen, Tom Shepard. Ninth Row: Larry Ballew, Bill Rademacher, Gary VanDam, Norm Parker, Morris Watts, Pat Shurmur, Ed Zaunbrecher, Bobby Williams, Skip Peete, Dino Folino, Kip Waddell, Steve Beckholt, Dan Enos, Pat Perles.

1994

Front Row: Muhsin Muhammad, Mill Coleman, Tony Banks, Shane Hannah, Brian DeMarco, Colin Cronin, Mark Birchmeier, Head Coach George Perles, Juan Hammonds, Duane Goubourne, Dale Person, Stan Callender, Damian Manson, Matt Christensen, Robert Shurelds. Second Row: Mike Vorkapich, Mike Sislo, Chris Salani, Aldi Henry, Nigea Carter, Corey Baker, Robert Denton, Napoleon Outlaw, Demetrice Martin, Reggie Garnett, Greg Anderson, Yakini Allen, Jay Greene, Orion Hayes, Ricardo Jackson, Sheldon Thomas. Third Row: Jeff Soskin, Frank Mobley, Brian Mosallam, Garykuhn, Dave Kehr, Todd Feeney, Luke Bencie, Tony Popovski, Anthony Folio, Pete Drzal, Todd Pearson, Stan Hannah, Carl Reaves, Terry Harvey, Delrico Simons. Fourth Row: Steve Barnhill, Matt Beard, Brad Costello, Octavis Long, Flozell Adams, Robert Gardner, Damien Hiram, Todd Schultz, Josh Freeman, Brian Echols, Tyrone Garland, Shon Hart, Don Walker, Marvin Wright, Dan Hackenbracht, Todd Vasicek. Fifth Row: Levon Porter, Greg Stewart, Craig Butler, Dan Cantrell, Rob

Harden, Dave Mudge, Jason Krueger, Scott Shaw, Chris Smith, Antwain Patrick, Derrick Mason, Marc Renaud, Alim Butler, Rober Dozier, Vince Mastromatteo. Sixth Row: Reid Ritter, John Hutchinson, Doug Donieczny, Scott Emsberger, Greg Reid, Josh Keur, Devon Georgia, Chris Gardner, Elroy Reese, Ike Reese, Dante Hardy, Tyrone Crenshaw, Amp Campbell, Nick Kallas, Jason Strayhorn, Travis Reece. Seventh Row: Dr. Doug McKeag, Dr. David Hough, Dr. Herb Ross, Dr. Randy Pearson, Dr. Steve Niergarth, Jeff Snipes, Ken Ordiway, Harold Major, Rob Dallaire, Sarah Strong, Shelly Smith, Lynn Aula, Nick Pettit, Pete Randall, Matt Harper, Kirk, Baldwin, Kevin McGinnis. Eighth Row: Jeff Monroe, Sally Nogle, Tom Mackowiak, Holly Kasavana, Dave Carrier, Tom Mallet, Vince Romano, Camilia, Joubert, Danielle Henry, Ryan Chorpenning, Jeff Robbins, Scott Shoemake, Ross Blackport, Thom Watchorn, Troy Henning, Mike Chowaniec, Don Mc Gaw, Steve Culp, Chris Kingsley, Pete Forsythe, Kevin Lartigue. Ninth Row: Troy Hickman, Bob Knickerbocker, Brad Salem, Mark Rhea, Kip Waddell, Dino Folino, Norm Parker, Henry Bullough, Morris Watts, Pat Shurmur, Bobby Williams, Pat Morris, Skip Peete, Gary Van Dam, Steve Beckholt, Bill Rademacher, Tom Shepard, Dean Olsen.

1995

Front Row: Robert Gardner, Dan Cantrell, Orion Hayes, Robert Shurelds, Tony Popovski, Demitrice Martin, Duane Goulbourne, Robert Denton, Tony Banks, Head Coach Nick Saban, Robert McBride, Yakini Allen, Scott Greene, Muhsin Muhammad, Napoleon Outlaw, Chris Salani, Luke Bencie, Vince Mastrometteo, Terry Harvey. Second Row: Don Walker, Jabbar Threats, Gary Kuhn, Marvin Wright, Carl Reaves, Aldi Henry, Brian Echols, Delrico Simons, Dave Kehr, Matt Beard, Todd Feeney, Chris Smith, Nigea Carter, Reggie Garnett, Derrick Mason, Elroy Reese, Brian Mossalam, Octavis Long, Scott Shaw. Third Row: Sam Eyde, Chris Gardner, Josh Keur, Travis Reece, Devon Georgia, Josh Freeman, Tyrone Garland, Dave Mudge, Ike Reese, Flozell Adams, Damien Hiram, Shon Hart, Todd Schultz, Mike Barry, Ray Hill, Amp Campbell, Charles Clark, Luke Todryk, Jason Grades. Fourth Row: Courtney Ledyard, Sorie Kanu, Bill Greene, Davarrio Carter, Bill Burke, Melvin Thomas, Jermain Stafford, Scott Ernsberger, Doug Konieczny, Greg Reid, Gus Ornstein, Shane Adkins, Sean Banks, Marcus Chapman, Dwayne Hawkins, Casey Jensen, Lemar Marshall, Brian McNulty, John Muskett. Fifth Row: Jeff Mt. Joy, Keith Burkett, David Fortino, Greg Stewart, Brad Rainko, Dan Vaughn, Raheem Miller, Max Nixon, Dimitrius Underwood, Robert Newkirk, Matt Laurino, Rick Vernon, Nick Mascia, Franklin Weaver, Chris McIntyre, Jon Walker, Adam Barisich. Sixth Row: Dr. Herb Ross, Dr. Randy Pearson, Eric Seeber, Tom Dompier, Brian Jones, Chris Smith, Jessica Mora, Missy Monroe, Kim Cornelisse, Vince Romano, Cheri Sessions, Liz Gavin, Leann Lousier, Tom Mackowiak, Dave Carrier, Sally Nogle, Jeff Monroe. Seventh Row: Bob Knickerbocker, Kevin Lartigue, Troy Henning, T.J. Henning, Don Mc Graw, Josh Pahl, Nick Pettit, Kevin McGinnis, Nick Gregory, Gabe Boice, David Kowalewski, Mike Chowaniec, Pete Randall, Kirk Baldwin, Ken Burcaw, Dan Hude, Matt Harper. Eighth Row: Trent Clark, Dan Wilt, Jason Ridgeway, Brad Salem, Mark Rhea, Gary VanDam, Charlie Baggett, Greg Colby, Jim Bollman, Pat Shurmur, Bobby Williams, Dean Pees, Mark Dantonio, Glenn Pires, Gary Tranquill, Ken Mannie.